The Face of
Old Testament
Studies

David W. Baker is Professor of Old Testament and Semitic Languages at Ashland Theological Seminary. With many works to his credit, he is the editor of the ETS Studies series and the coauthor of *More Light on the Path: Daily Scripture Readings from Hebrew and Greek*. His Ph.D. degree is from the University of London.

Bill T. Arnold is Professor of Old Testament and Semitic Languages at Asbury Theological Seminary. He is the author of *Encountering the Book of Genesis* and numerous journal articles and the coauthor (with Bryan Beyer) of *Encountering the Old Testament: A Christian Survey*. His Ph.D. degree is from Hebrew Union College.

The Face of Old Testament Studies

A Survey of Contemporary Approaches

Edited by
David W. Baker
and Bill T. Arnold

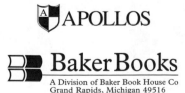

APOLLOS

Baker Books

A Division of Baker Book House Co
Grand Rapids, Michigan 49516

Published by Baker Books
a division of Baker Book House Company
P.O. Box 6287, Grand Rapids, MI 49516–6287

and

Apollos (an imprint of Inter-Varsity Press)
38 De Montfort Street, Leicester, LE1 7GP, England

Printed in the United States of America

Library of Congress Cataloging-in-Publication Data

The face of Old Testament studies : a survey of contemporary approaches / edited
    by David W. Baker and Bill T. Arnold.
        p.   cm.
    Includes bibliographical references and indexes.
    ISBN 0-8010-2215-0 (cloth)
    1. Bible. O.T.—Criticism, interpretation, etc.—History—20th century.
    2. Bible. O.T.—Study and teaching. I. Baker, David W. (David Weston), 1950–.
    II. Arnold, Bill T.
    BS1193.F33   1999
    221.6′09′045—dc21   99-37516

British Library Cataloguing-in-Publication Data

A catalogue record for this book is available from the British Library.
ISBN 0-85111-774-0

For information about academic books, resources for Christian leaders, and all new releases available from Baker Book House, visit our web site:
                        http://www.bakerbooks.com

Contents

        Sciences to Hebrew Scripture   *421*
        Charles E. Carter
16. Theology of the Old Testament   *452*
        R. W. L. Moberly

      Subject Index   *479*
      Author Index   *490*
      Scripture Index   *507*

Contributors

Murray R. Adamthwaite holds a Ph.D. from the University of Melbourne and is Lecturer at the Centre for Ancient and Classical Languages at the University of Melbourne, Melbourne, Australia.

Bill T. Arnold holds a Ph.D. from Hebrew Union College and is Professor of Old Testament and Semitic Languages at Asbury Theological Seminary, Wilmore, Kentucky.

David W. Baker holds a Ph.D. from the University of London and is Professor of Old Testament and Semitic Languages at Ashland Theological Seminary, Ashland, Ohio.

Charles E. Carter holds a Ph.D. from Duke University and is Associate Professor of Religious Studies at Seton Hall University, South Orange, New Jersey.

Mark W. Chavalas holds a Ph.D. from the University of California–Los Angeles and is Professor of History at the University of Wisconsin, La Crosse, Wisconsin.

David Diewert holds a Ph.D. from the University of Toronto and is Associate Professor of Biblical Languages at Regent College, Vancouver, British Columbia.

Edwin C. Hostetter holds a Ph.D. from Johns Hopkins University and is Professor of Biblical Studies at the Ecumenical Institute of Theology, Baltimore, Maryland.

David M. Howard Jr. holds a Ph.D. from the University of Michigan and is Professor of Old Testament and Hebrew at New Orleans Baptist Theological Seminary, New Orleans, Louisiana.

Gary N. Knoppers holds a Ph.D. from Harvard University and is Professor and Head of the Department of Classics and Ancient Mediterranean Studies at Pennsylvania State University, University Park, Pennsylvania.

V. Philips Long holds a Ph.D. from the University of Cambridge and is Professor of Old Testament at Covenant Theological Seminary, St. Louis, Missouri.

Tremper Longman III holds a Ph.D. from Yale University and is Robert H. Gundry Chair of Religious Studies at Westmont College, Santa Barbara, California.

7

Walter Moberly holds a Ph.D. from the University of Cambridge and is Lecturer in Theology at the University of Durham, Durham, England.

John N. Oswalt holds a Ph.D. from Brandeis University and is Research Professor of Old Testament at Wesley Biblical Seminary, Jackson, Mississippi.

Bruce K. Waltke holds a Th.D. from Dallas Theological Seminary and a Ph.D. from Harvard University and is Professor Emeritus of Biblical Studies at Regent College, Vancouver, British Columbia, and Professor of Old Testament at Reformed Theological Seminary, Orlando, Florida.

Gordon J. Wenham holds a Ph.D. from King's College, University of London, and is Professor of Old Testament at the Cheltenham and Gloucester College of Higher Education, Cheltenham, England.

H. G. M. Williamson holds a Ph.D. from the University of Cambridge and is Regius Professor of Hebrew at the University of Oxford, Oxford, England.

Al Wolters holds a Ph.D. from the Free University of Amsterdam and is Professor of Religion and Theology and Classical Studies at Redeemer College, Ancaster, Ontario.

K. Lawson Younger Jr. holds a Ph.D. from the University of Sheffield and is Professor of Old Testament, Semitic Languages, and Ancient Near Eastern History at Trinity International University, Deerfield, Illinois.

Preface

In the 1981 film *Chariots of Fire,* the track coach Sam Mussabini watches the runner Harold Abrahams practice and then approaches him to offer assistance. He tells him, "I can't make you win, but I think I can get you a couple of more yards." This same idea lies behind academic study of any discipline, not least that of the Old Testament. Scholars analyze the text using many and varied techniques, some ancient and some postmodern, some borrowed from other disciplines and others developed from within. All of these are designed not to reach complete understanding, but rather to move that understanding a small step forward. This volume seeks to chart some of these steps toward understanding within the multifaceted field of Old Testament studies.

Over seventy years ago, the Society for Old Testament Study started a series of volumes that set out "to give a general account of the present position in the various branches of Old Testament study."[1] More recently, the series "Sources for Biblical and Theological Studies" has sought to do the same through reprinting seminal articles and extracts that have moved forward various elements of the discipline of Old Testament studies, as well as tracing the history of the development of each element.[2]

---

1. G. W. Anderson, "Preface," in *Tradition and Interpretation: Essays by Members of the Society for Old Testament Study,* ed. G. W. Anderson (Oxford: Clarendon, 1979), v. Previous volumes were *The People and the Book: Essays on the Old Testament,* ed. A. S. Peake (Oxford: Clarendon, 1925); *Record and Revelation: Essays on the Old Testament by Members of the Society for Old Testament Study,* ed. H. W. Robinson (Oxford: Clarendon, 1938); and *The Old Testament and Modern Study: A Generation of Discovery and Research: Essays by Members of the Society,* ed. H. H. Rowley (Oxford: Clarendon, 1951).

2. The series, edited by D. W. Baker and published in Winona Lake, Indiana, by Eisenbrauns, has produced volumes on OT theology (*The Flowering of Old Testament Theology: A Reader in Twentieth-Century Old Testament Theology, 1930–1990,* ed. B. C. Ollenburger, E. A. Martens, and G. F. Hasel [1992]), literary criticism (*Beyond Form Criticism: Essays in Old Testament Literary Criticism,* ed. P. R. House [1992]), Deuteronomy (*A Song of Power and the Power of Song: Essays on the Book of Deuteronomy,* ed. D. L. Christensen [1993]), Genesis 1–11 (*"I Studied Inscriptions from before the Flood": Ancient Near Eastern, Literary, and Linguistic Approaches to Genesis 1–11,* ed. R. S. Hess and D. T. Tsumura [1994]), prophecy (*"The Place Is Too Small for Us": The Israelite Prophets in Recent Scholarship,* ed. R. P. Gordon [1995]), and social scientific approaches to OT study (*Community, Identity, and Ideology: Social Scientific Approaches to the Hebrew Bible,* ed. C. E. Carter and C. L. Meyers [1996]).

Other individual volumes have also discussed elements of the history of Old Testament study.[3]

One aspect of the development of the discipline that becomes clear when surveying developments during the twentieth century is the rise, and fall, of various methodologies. Some arise from comparative anthropological study (e.g., the concept of the amphictyony), but, when presumed parallels are found to be lacking, drop out of favor. This is not a condemnation of the broader area of socio-anthropological study, however, which continues to burgeon and provide cross-disciplinary insight, as reflected in its discussion here not only in its own chapter but also in the discussions of archaeology and prophecy. Others arise from literary analysis, where new means of interpretation are constantly applied from other literatures to that of the Bible. Some of these also are short-lived, since they prove unproductive or inappropriate to the biblical literature, though literary analysis itself is not thereby vitiated by these unproductive forays.

Some approaches arising over the last decades do appear, however, to be presuppositionally wrongheaded. In particular are some that approach nihilism, deriving from a postmodern abhorrence of absolutes, not only in ethics, which is beyond the purview of this volume, but also in interpretation. Some literary schools see the individual reader as sole and final arbiter of meaning, but an approach that allows equal validity to all interpretations ends up denying any value to any interpretation. Historical approaches that deny any usefulness to the only existing evidence, as the Old Testament often is to some of the events that it records, are implying that history can be written without evidence, an interesting espousal of "ahistorical history."

The present volume follows the model of the one-volume summaries of the discipline of Old Testament studies, particularly as it has developed during the closing decades of the twentieth century. One of its distinctives is that it notes contributions of conservative scholars whose significance has been recognized beyond their own camp. While some contributors have highlighted these in various ways, others have simply included them within the general discussion. This latter approach has special value since contributions should be judged by their acumen and insight, their ability to add distance in the race toward understanding,

---

3. See, e.g., H.-J. Kraus, *Geschichte der historisch-kritischen Erforschung des Alten Testaments,* 2d ed. (Neukirchen-Vluyn: Neukirchener Verlag, 1969), for the most exhaustive treatment; D. A. Knight and G. M. Tucker, eds., *The Hebrew Bible and Its Modern Interpreters* (Philadelphia: Fortress; Chico, Calif.: Scholars Press, 1985); and J. L. Mays, D. L. Petersen, and K. H. Richards, eds., *Old Testament Interpretation: Past, Present, and Future: Essays in Honor of Gene M. Tucker* (Nashville: Abingdon, 1995), for more recent collections.

rather than by the colors under which their authors race. The branding as "liberal" or "conservative" has too often been mistaken for engagement with the arguments put forward, and has hobbled those from across the theological spectrum who take such an exclusionary position. We hope that readers will value and evaluate the integrity and functionality of the arguments and positions based on merit rather than presupposition.

Although these chapters focus on developments from 1970 to the present, previous research is sometimes presented to provide needed context. Most of the articles in this volume were completed by 1997, with minor updates allowed through April 1999. Hence, even the terminal point for each essay is rather fluid, reflecting the dynamism and constant changes in the state of Old Testament research generally. Our attempt to sketch the contours of our ever-changing discipline must be supplemented by the reader's own willingness to follow the trajectories set by these essays.

Abbreviations

AAAS	*Annales archéologiques arabes, syriennes*
AASOR	Annual of the American Schools of Oriental Research
AB	Anchor Bible
ABD	*Anchor Bible Dictionary,* ed. D. N. Freedman et al., 6 vols. (New York: Doubleday, 1992)
ABR	*Australian Biblical Review*
ABRL	Anchor Bible Reference Library
AfO	*Archiv für Orientforschung*
AGJU	Arbeiten zur Geschichte des antiken Judentums und des Urchristentums
AJA	*American Journal of Archaeology*
AJBA	*Australian Journal of Biblical Archaeology*
AJSL	*American Journal of Semitic Languages and Literature*
ALUOS	Annual of Leeds University Oriental Society
AnBib	Analecta biblica
ANEP	*Ancient Near East in Pictures Relating to the Old Testament,* ed. J. B. Pritchard, 2d ed. with supplement (Princeton: Princeton University Press, 1969)
ANET	*Ancient Near Eastern Texts Relating to the Old Testament,* ed. J. B. Pritchard, 3d ed. with supplement (Princeton: Princeton University Press, 1969)
ANETS	Ancient Near Eastern Texts and Studies
AnOr	Analecta orientalia
AOAT	Alter Orient und Altes Testament
AOS	American Oriental Series
ARAB	D. D. Luckenbill, *Ancient Records of Assyria and Babylonia,* 2 vols. (Chicago: University of Chicago Press, 1926–27)
ARM	Archives royales de Mari
ASORDS	American Schools of Oriental Research Dissertation Series
ASTI	*Annual of the Swedish Theological Institute*
ATD	Das Alte Testament Deutsch
ATJ	*Ashland Theological Journal*
ATLA	American Theological Library Association
AUSS	*Andrews University Seminary Studies*
BA	*Biblical Archaeologist*
BaM	*Baghdader Mitteilungen*
BAR	*Biblical Archaeology Review*
BASOR	*Bulletin of the American Schools of Oriental Research*

BBB	Bonner biblische Beiträge
BBR	*Bulletin for Biblical Research*
BBVO	Berliner Beiträge zum Vorderen Orient
BEATAJ	Beiträge zur Erforschung des Alten Testaments und des antiken Judentums
BETL	Bibliotheca ephemeridum theologicarum lovaniensium
BFC	*Beyond Form Criticism: Essays in Old Testament Literary Criticism*, ed. P. R. House, SBTS 2 (Winona Lake, Ind.: Eisenbrauns, 1992)
BHT	Beiträge zur historischen Theologie
Bib	*Biblica*
BibInt	*Biblical Interpretation*
BibOr	Biblica et orientalia
BibRev	*Bible Review*
BJS	Brown Judaic Studies
BKAT	Biblischer Kommentar: Altes Testament
BLS	Bible and Literature Series
BN	*Biblische Notizen*
BSac	*Bibliotheca Sacra*
BT	*Bible Translator*
BTB	*Biblical Theology Bulletin*
BWANT	Beiträge zur Wissenschaft vom Alten und Neuen Testament
BZ	*Biblische Zeitschrift*
BZAW	Beihefte zur Zeitschrift für die alttestamentliche Wissenschaft
CAH	*Cambridge Ancient History*
CBQ	*Catholic Biblical Quarterly*
CBQMS	Catholic Biblical Quarterly—Monograph Series
CHJ	*Cambridge History of Judaism*
ConBOT	Coniectanea biblica, Old Testament
CRAIBL	*Comptes rendus de l'Académie des inscriptions et belles-lettres*
CR:BS	*Currents in Research: Biblical Studies*
CRINT	Compendia rerum iudaicarum ad novum testamentum
CThM	Calwer theologische Monographien
CTJ	*Calvin Theological Journal*
CTM	*Concordia Theological Monthly*
DBSup	*Dictionnaire de la Bible, Supplément*
DJD	Discoveries in the Judaean Desert
DSB—OT	Daily Study Bible—Old Testament
DSD	*Dead Sea Discoveries*
EA	El Amarna Tablets
EBC	*Expositor's Bible Commentary*, ed. F. E. Gabelein, 12 vols. (Grand Rapids: Zondervan, 1979–88)
EBib	Études bibliques
EI	*Eretz Israel*
ETL	*Ephemerides theologicae lovanienses*
EvQ	*Evangelical Quarterly*
EvT	*Evangelische Theologie*

ExpTim	*Expository Times*
FAT	Forschungen zum Alten Testament
FB	Forschung zur Bibel
FOTL	Forms of the Old Testament Literature
FRLANT	Forschungen zur Religion und Literatur des Alten und Neuen Testaments
HAR	*Hebrew Annual Review*
HAT	Handbuch zum Alten Testament
HBT	*Horizons in Biblical Theology*
HeyJ	*Heythrop Journal*
HS	*Hebrew Studies*
HSM	Harvard Semitic Monographs
HSS	Harvard Semitic Studies
HTR	*Harvard Theological Review*
HUCA	*Hebrew Union College Annual*
ICC	International Critical Commentary
IDBSup	*Interpreter's Dictionary of the Bible*, supplementary volume, ed. K. Crim (Nashville: Abingdon, 1976)
IEJ	*Israel Exploration Journal*
ILBS	Indiana Literary Biblical Series
Imm	*Immanuel*
INJ	*Israel Numismatic Journal*
Int	*Interpretation*
IRT	Issues in Religion and Theology
ISBE	*International Standard Bible Encyclopedia*, ed. G. W. Bromiley, rev. ed., 4 vols. (Grand Rapids: Eerdmans, 1979–88)
ITC	International Theological Commentary
JAAR	*Journal of the American Academy of Religion*
JANES	*Journal of the Ancient Near Eastern Society of Columbia University*
JAOS	*Journal of the American Oriental Society*
JARCE	*Journal of the American Research Center in Egypt*
JBL	*Journal of Biblical Literature*
JBS	Jerusalem Biblical Studies
JCBRF	*Journal of the Christian Brethren Research Fellowship*
JCS	*Journal of Cuneiform Studies*
JEA	*Journal of Egyptian Archaeology*
JETS	*Journal of the Evangelical Theological Society*
JHNES	Johns Hopkins Near Eastern Studies
JITC	*Journal of the Interdenominational Theological Center*
JJS	*Journal of Jewish Studies*
JNES	*Journal of Near Eastern Studies*
JNSL	*Journal of Northwest Semitic Languages*
JQR	*Jewish Quarterly Review*
JQRSup	Jewish Quarterly Review Supplement
JSem	*Journal for Semitics*
JSJ	*Journal for the Study of Judaism in the Persian, Hellenistic and Roman Period*

JSOT	*Journal for the Study of the Old Testament*
JSOTSup	Journal for the Study of the Old Testament—Supplement Series
JSS	*Journal of Semitic Studies*
JTC	*Journal for Theology and the Church*
JTS	*Journal of Theological Studies*
JTT	*Journal of Translation and Textlinguistics*
KAI	*Kanaanäische und aramäische Inschriften,* ed. H. Donner and W. Röllig, 2d ed., 3 vols. (Wiesbaden: Harrossowitz, 1966–69)
KAT	Kommentar zum Alten Testament
KHCAT	Kurzer Hand-Commentar zum Alten Testament
KTU	*Die Keilalphabetischen Texte aus Ugarit,* ed. M. Dietrich, O. Loretz, and J. Sanmartín, AOAT 24 (Neukirchen-Vluyn: Neukirchener Verlag, 1976)
LB	*Linguistica Biblica*
LCL	Loeb Classical Library
LUÅ	Lunds universitets årsskrift
LXX	Septuagint
MARI	*Mari, Annales de Recherches Interdisciplinaires*
MDOG	*Mitteilungen der deutschen Orient-Gesellschaft*
MSU	Mitteilungen des Septuaginta-Unternehmens, Abhandlungen der Akademie der Wissenschaften in Göttingen, Philologisch-historische Klasse
MT	Masoretic Text
NABU	*Nouvelles assyriologiques brèves et utilitaires*
NAC	New American Commentary
NBD	*New Bible Dictionary,* ed. D. R. W. Wood, 3d ed. (Leicester and Downers Grove, Ill.: InterVarsity, 1996)
NCB	New Century Bible
NEAEHL	*New Encyclopedia of Archaeological Excavations in the Holy Land,* ed. E. Stern, 4 vols. (Jerusalem: Israel Exploration Society; New York: Simon & Schuster, 1993)
NICOT	New International Commentary on the Old Testament
NIDBA	*New International Dictionary of Biblical Archaeology,* ed. E. M. Blaiklock and R. K. Harrison (Grand Rapids: Zondervan, 1983)
NIDOTTE	*New International Dictionary of Old Testament Theology and Exegesis,* ed. Willem A. VanGemeren, 5 vols. (Grand Rapids: Zondervan, 1997)
NT	New Testament
NTCS	*Newsletter for Targumic and Cognate Studies*
NVBS	New Voices in Biblical Studies
OBO	Orbis biblicus et orientalis
OBT	Overtures to Biblical Theology
OG	Old Greek
OIP	Oriental Institute Publications
OLA	Orientalia Lovaniensia analecta
OLP	*Orientalia lovaniensia periodica*
Or	*Orientalia* (Rome)

OrAnt	*Oriens antiquus*
OT	Old Testament
OTE	*Old Testament Essays*
OTL	Old Testament Library
OTS	*Oudtestamentische Studiën*
PEQ	*Palestine Exploration Quarterly*
PIBA	*Proceedings of the Irish Biblical Association*
PTMS	Pittsburgh Theological Monograph Series
RAI	Rencontre assyriologique internationale
RB	*Revue biblique*
RelSRev	*Religious Studies Review*
ResQ	*Restoration Quarterly*
RevB	*Revista bíblica*
RevExp	*Review and Expositor*
RevQ	*Revue de Qumran*
RSO	*Rivista degli studi orientali*
RTL	*Revue théologique de Louvain*
RTR	*Reformed Theological Review*
SAIW	J. L. Crenshaw, *Studies in Ancient Israelite Wisdom: Selected, with a Prolegomenon,* Library of Biblical Studies (New York: Ktav, 1976)
SANT	Studien zum Alten und Neuen Testament
SAOC	Studies in Ancient Oriental Civilization
SBFLA	*Studii biblici franciscani liber annuus*
SBLDS	Society of Biblical Literature Dissertation Series
SBLMS	Society of Biblical Literature Monograph Series
SBLSBS	Society of Biblical Literature Sources for Biblical Study
SBLSCS	Society of Biblical Literature Septuagint and Cognate Studies
SBLSP	*Society of Biblical Literature Seminar Papers*
SBLWAW	Society of Biblical Literature Writings from the Ancient World
SBT	Studies in Biblical Theology
SBTS	Sources for Biblical and Theological Study
ScrHier	Scripta hierosolymitana
SEÅ	*Svensk exegetisk årsbok*
SemSup	Semeia Supplements
SHANE	Studies in the History of the Ancient Near East
SJOT	*Scandinavian Journal of the Old Testament*
SOTS	Society for Old Testament Study
SR	*Studies in Religion*
SSN	Studia semitica neerlandica
ST	*Studia Theologica*
STDJ	Studies on the Texts of the Desert of Judah
StPohl	Studia Pohl
SWBAS	Social World of Biblical Antiquity Series
SWJT	*Southwestern Journal of Theology*
TBT	*The Bible Today*

TBü	Theologische Bücherei
TDOT	*Theological Dictionary of the Old Testament*, ed. G. J. Botterweck, H. Ringgren, and H.-J. Fabry (Grand Rapids: Eerdmans, 1974–)
ThStud	Theologische Studiën
TJ	*Trinity Journal*
TLZ	*Theologische Literaturzeitung*
TOTC	Tyndale Old Testament Commentaries
Trans	*Transeuphratène*
TRu	*Theologische Rundschau*
TS	*Theological Studies*
TUMSR	Trinity University Monograph Series in Religion
TynBul	*Tyndale Bulletin*
TZ	*Theologische Zeitschrift*
UF	*Ugarit-Forschungen*
USQR	*Union Seminary Quarterly Review*
VT	*Vetus Testamentum*
VTSup	*Vetus Testamentum*, Supplements
WBC	Word Biblical Commentary
WIAI	*Wisdom in Ancient Israel: Essays in Honour of J. A. Emerton*, ed. J. Day, R. P. Gordon, and H. G. M. Williamson (Cambridge: Cambridge University Press, 1995)
WMANT	Wissenschaftliche Monographien zum Alten und Neuen Testament
WTJ	*Westminster Theological Journal*
ZA	*Zeitschrift für Assyriologie*
ZAH	*Zeitschrift für Althebräistik*
ZAW	*Zeitschrift für die alttestamentliche Wissenschaft*
ZDPV	*Zeitschrift des deutschen Palästina-Vereins*
ZPEB	*Zondervan Pictorial Encyclopedia of the Bible*, ed. M. C. Tenney, 5 vols. (Grand Rapids: Zondervan, 1975)
ZTK	*Zeitschrift für Theologie und Kirche*

1

The Text of the Old Testament

Al Wolters

The field of Old Testament textual criticism deals with the history of the transmission of the text of the Hebrew Bible and the recovery of an authoritative starting point for its translation and interpretation. It does so largely on the basis of the surviving Hebrew manuscripts and the extant ancient versions, notably the Septuagint (Greek), Targums (Aramaic), Peshitta (Syriac), and Vulgate (Latin). In the period covered by the present volume (roughly 1970 to 1996) there has been intense scholarly activity in this subdiscipline of biblical studies, including the publication of many new Hebrew texts, the gradual completion of new critical editions of the ancient versions, and the development of major new theories about the history of the Old Testament text and the goals of its textual criticism. Alongside these major developments, there have been innumerable detailed investigations bearing on subordinate points of textual transmission and reconstruction. The following survey seeks to highlight the major trends and pays almost no attention to specific examples of more detailed work that has been done in the period under consideration.[1]

1. Among the many significant encyclopedia articles, chapters, and monographs surveying the field of Old Testament textual criticism since 1970, the following are especially noteworthy: S. Talmon, "The Old Testament Text," in *The Cambridge History of the Bible*, vol. 1, *From the Beginnings to Jerome*, ed. P. R. Ackroyd and C. F. Evans (Cambridge: Cambridge University Press, 1970), 159–99; reprinted in *Qumran and the History of the Biblical Text*, ed. F. M. Cross Jr. and S. Talmon (Cambridge, Mass.: Harvard University Press, 1975), 1–41; R. W. Klein, *Textual Criticism of the Old Testament: From the Septuagint to Qumran* (Philadelphia: Fortress, 1974); D. Barthélemy, "Text, Hebrew, History of," *IDBSup*, 874–84; E. Würthwein, *The Text of the Old Testament: An Introduction to the Biblia Hebraica*, trans. E. F. Rhodes (Grand Rapids: Eerdmans, 1979); B. K. Waltke, "The

The Dead Sea Scrolls

Without question the discovery and gradual publication of the biblical manuscripts among the Dead Sea Scrolls has had by far the greatest impact on the study of the Old Testament text in the twentieth century. It is not too much to say that the entire discipline has been revolutionized by these finds, since they have given scholars access to scores of manuscripts (or the fragmentary remains thereof) that are more than a thousand years older than any that had been available before. Unfortunately, although a number of the biblical scrolls were published soon after their discovery, many others were not. The delay in publication became the occasion of a great deal of controversy in the 1980s and early 1990s, but by the mid-1990s virtually all the biblical material had been published in one form or another, most of it in the series Discoveries in the Judaean Desert.[2]

The overall effect of these discoveries has been the recognition of considerable textual diversity in the three centuries preceding the de-

---

Textual Criticism of the Old Testament," *EBC*, 1:211–28; P. K. McCarter Jr., *Textual Criticism: Recovering the Text of the Hebrew Bible* (Philadelphia: Fortress, 1986); A. R. Millard, "The Text of the Old Testament," in *International Bible Commentary*, ed. F. F. Bruce (London: Marshall Pickering; Grand Rapids: Zondervan, 1986), 11–13; F. E. Deist, *Witnesses to the Old Testament* (Pretoria: NG Kerkboekhandel, 1988); M. J. Mulder, "The Transmission of the Biblical Text," in *Mikra: Text, Translation, Reading, and Interpretation of the Hebrew Bible in Ancient Judaism and Early Christianity*, ed. M. J. Mulder and H. Sysling, CRINT 2/1 (Assen: Van Gorcum; Minneapolis: Fortress, 1990), 87–135; E. Tov, "Textual Criticism, Old Testament," *ABD*, 6:393–412; idem, *Textual Criticism of the Hebrew Bible* (Minneapolis: Fortress; Assen/Maastricht: Van Gorcum, 1992); B. K. Waltke, "Old Testament Textual Criticism," in *Foundations for Biblical Interpretation*, ed. D. S. Dockery et al. (Nashville: Broadman & Holman, 1994), 156–86; E. R. Brotzman, *Old Testament Textual Criticism: A Practical Introduction* (Grand Rapids: Baker, 1994); J. E. Sanderson, "Ancient Texts and Versions of the Old Testament," in *New Interpreter's Bible* (Nashville: Abingdon, 1994), 1:292–304. The volume by Tov is now the standard scholarly treatment; the best brief discussion for nonspecialists is the article by Sanderson. Waltke is the best representative of a conservative theological perspective (see also Millard and Brotzman).

2. For a comprehensive listing of all the relevant manuscripts and bibliographic details on their publication up to 1992, see H. Scanlin, *The Dead Sea Scrolls and Modern Translations of the Bible: How the Dead Sea Scroll Discoveries Have Influenced Modern English Translations* (Wheaton: Tyndale, 1993), esp. pp. 41–103. Since 1992, the following volumes in the DJD series containing biblical texts have appeared: *Qumran Cave 4, IV: Palaeo-Hebrew and Greek Biblical Manuscripts*, ed. P. W. Skehan, E. Ulrich, and J. E. Sanderson, DJD 9 (Oxford: Clarendon, 1992); *Qumran Cave 4, VII: Genesis to Numbers*, ed. E. Ulrich et al., DJD 12 (Oxford: Clarendon, 1994); *Qumran Cave 4, IX: Deuteronomy, Joshua, Judges, Kings*, ed. E. Ulrich et al., DJD 14 (Oxford: Clarendon, 1995); *Qumran Cave 4, X: The Prophets*, ed. E. Ulrich et al., DJD 15 (Oxford: Clarendon, 1997). See also E. Ulrich, "An Index of Passages in the Biblical Manuscripts from the Judaean Desert (Genesis–Kings)," *DSD* 1 (1994): 113–29; and idem, "An Index of Passages in the Biblical Manuscripts from the Judaean Desert (Part 2: Isaiah–Chronicles)," *DSD* 2 (1995): 86–107.

struction of the second temple in A.D. 70. Specifically, it has now been confirmed by actual Hebrew manuscripts that not only the Masoretic Text (MT) but also the text of the Samaritan Pentateuch and the *Vorlage* or parent text of the Septuagint (LXX) had predecessors well before the turn of the era. It was not until about the end of the first century A.D. that the proto-Masoretic text-type (the consonantal framework of what was later elaborated by the medieval Masoretes into the MT) emerged as the sole witness to the text of the Hebrew Bible within Judaism. Consequently, it is now clear that in late second temple times, including the time of Jesus and the apostles, the text of the Old Testament was considerably more diverse than previously suspected.

A few examples can serve to illustrate this diversity. It has long been known that the Samaritan Pentateuch differed from the MT in a number of significant ways, some having to do with specifically Samaritan theology, and some having to do with harmonizing expansions. A text-type that includes these harmonizing expansions, but does not yet have the specifically Samaritan theological modifications, is represented by eight of the biblical scrolls among the Dead Sea Scrolls. The inference seems clear that the Samaritan Pentateuch represents a later stage of this same text-type, with the addition of the sectarian modifications.

A similar situation obtains with respect to the parent text of the LXX. One of the most dramatic differences between the LXX and the MT is found in the Book of Jeremiah: the LXX is roughly one-seventh shorter than the MT. It is therefore of exceptional interest that two fragmentary Hebrew manuscripts that reflect the shorter text of the LXX have turned up among the Dead Sea Scrolls (4QJer[b, d]). Less dramatic but still significant are the other Qumran biblical manuscripts that in many textual details seem to represent the same text-type as that on which the LXX is based.

It is also true, however, that the majority of biblical manuscripts discovered in the Judean desert are of the proto-Masoretic text-type. The large Isaiah scroll, for example (1QIsa[a]), offers a text of Isaiah that is clearly a forerunner of the MT, even though it occasionally allows us to correct the latter.

Theories to Account for the Textual Diversity

Given this textual evidence from the Dead Sea Scrolls, how does one account for the variety of textual forms in which the Bible was undeniably extant in the late second temple period? Scholars have developed a number of theories to account for this diversity. The first of these is the so-called local texts theory, first proposed by William F. Albright, and subsequently elaborated by his student Frank M. Cross Jr. In Cross's view, the textual diversity found in the manuscripts can be correlated with the three major text-types that underlie the LXX, the Samaritan Pentateuch, and the MT. Furthermore, these three textual traditions can also be roughly correlated with three geographical areas, Egypt, Palestine, and Babylon, respectively.[3]

A different theory has been advocated by Shemaryahu Talmon, who looks upon Cross's three main text-types not as traditions that developed in different geographical locales but as the remnants of a much greater textual diversity that is now lost to view. Talmon stresses the fact that text-types are created and preserved by religiously cohesive sociological groups: it was the Christian church that preserved the textual tradition represented by the LXX, the Samaritan sect that preserved the Samaritan text-type, and rabbinic Judaism that preserved the MT. It is probable that other textual traditions were preserved by other religious groups within Judaism, but these traditions have perished along with their historical bearers. The three that have survived are the leftovers of a textual diversity that was likely as varied as the religious landscape of Judaism and its offshoots. Another feature of Talmon's view is his concern not to isolate textual criticism from the broader questions of traditional historical criticism.[4]

Emanuel Tov challenges a key assumption in the theories of both Cross and Talmon: the view that the textual diversity of the Qumran finds can be reduced to basically three text-types. On the basis of a careful analysis of the biblical Dead Sea Scrolls, he concludes that they can be more profitably classified into five categories, not three. Alongside the three recognized by Cross and Talmon, he discerns one written in the distinctive "Qumran orthography," and another that is "unaligned," that is, not clearly associated with any of the other four. In Tov's analysis, the statistical distribution of these five kinds of texts is as follows: "proto-Masoretic" manuscripts: 60 percent; those written in the "Qumran practice": 20 percent; "pre-Samaritan" manuscripts and those approximating the LXX: together 5 percent; leaving about 15 percent for the unaligned biblical texts.[5]

---

3. F. M. Cross Jr., "The Evolution of a Theory of Local Texts," in *Qumran and the History of the Biblical Text*, ed. F. M. Cross and S. Talmon (Cambridge, Mass.: Harvard University Press, 1975), 306–20. The original version of the local texts theory, as proposed by Albright in 1955, is also reprinted in this volume ("New Light on Early Recensions of the Hebrew Bible," 140–46). It is of interest to note that a similar view was already put forward well before the Qumran discoveries by the evangelical scholar H. M. Wiener, "The Pentateuchal Text—A Reply to Dr. Skinner," *BSac* 71 (1914): 218–68, esp. 221; see Tov, *Textual Criticism*, 185 n. 44.

4. S. Talmon, "The Textual Study of the Bible—A New Outlook," in *Qumran and the History of the Biblical Text*, 321–400.

5. Tov, *Textual Criticism*, 114–17.

Finally, we may consider the views of Eugene Ulrich, a student of Cross, who has recently put forward his own theory of the textual diversity exemplified by the Qumran biblical manuscripts. Against Tov, he argues that neither the "Qumran practice" nor the "unaligned" status of certain manuscripts can be said to define distinctively *textual* groupings. In a manner reminiscent of Talmon (but without the latter's emphasis on religious groups), he stresses that a simple threefold or fivefold scheme cannot do justice to the great diversity of the biblical text in late second temple times. Instead, he sees a succession of "literary editions" of individual books (or parts of books) as temporary stages of the overall evolution of the biblical text toward its canonical form. Each literary edition was produced by a creative editor who was responding to a new religious situation, and each such edition could be called the "base text" with respect to subsequent scribal modifications. Again like Talmon, Ulrich seeks to integrate the concerns of "lower" and "higher" criticism into a single view of the long-term development of the biblical text.[6]

The Ancient Versions and the Samaritan Pentateuch

Although a substantial majority of the biblical texts discovered in the Judean desert can be classified as proto-Masoretic, it is nevertheless true that the Qumran finds have served to draw the attention of scholars to the variety of text forms current around the turn of the era. Paradoxically, the opposite is true of recent scholarship on the ancient versions. Whereas the versions had previously provided the chief evidence for readings that diverge from the MT, it is now becoming increasingly clear that the proto-Masoretic textual tradition underlies a good deal of the ancient versions, at least in certain phases of their textual transmission.

Septuagint

Recent Septuagint studies are a case in point. Since 1970 a number of volumes have appeared in the Göttingen edition of the LXX, accompanied by an impressive series of auxiliary studies.[7] As this hitherto most

6. E. Ulrich, "Pluriformity in the Biblical Text, Text Groups, and Questions of Canon," in *The Madrid Qumran Conference: Proceedings of the International Congress on the Dead Sea Scrolls, Madrid, 18–21 March 1991*, ed. J. T. Barrera and L. V. Montaner (Leiden: Brill, 1992), 37–40; idem, "Multiple Literary Editions: Reflections toward a Theory of the History of the Biblical Text," in *Current Research and Technological Developments on the Dead Sea Scrolls: Conference on the Texts from the Judaean Desert, Jerusalem, 30 April 1995*, ed. D. W. Parry and S. D. Ricks, STDJ 20 (Leiden: Brill, 1996), 78–105.

7. *Septuaginta, Vetus Testamentum Graecum Auctoritate Societatis Litterarum Gottingensis Editum* (Göttingen: Vandenhoeck & Ruprecht, 1931–). Of the twenty volumes that have been published to date, the following have appeared since 1970: *Esdrae liber I* (ed.

comprehensive and reliable edition of the LXX nears completion, scholars have begun to realize that its textual base shows much greater affinity to the MT than was previously assumed. For one thing, the study of the translation technique employed in many books of the LXX has made clear that Greek renderings that used to be taken as evidence of a non-Masoretic *Vorlage* can in many cases be explained as reflecting a Hebrew text that is identical with the MT. This is one of the most significant conclusions of the work, for example, of J. W. Wevers on the LXX text of the Pentateuch.[8] In other words, although it is clear that the parent text of the LXX does often represent a text-type that differs from the proto-Masoretic textual tradition, the degree of difference is often much smaller than previously thought. We find a particularly striking instance of this in Exodus 25–31 (God's instructions for building the tabernacle) and Exodus 35–40 (the carrying out of these instructions), where the LXX rendering of these two parallel passages differs quite significantly, both in vocabulary and sequence. Although this difference was previously taken as evidence for a *Vorlage* of Exodus 35–40 that was significantly different from the MT, Wevers argues that such an assumption is unnecessary. The Greek translation can be understood as the free rendering, by another translator, of a Hebrew text that is substantially the same as the MT.[9]

A second result of recent studies of the LXX is that it is now clear that the original Greek text (the so-called Old Greek) has undergone a series of revisions or recensions that have brought it into greater conformity with the proto-Masoretic text-type. The first of these is the so-called *kaige* recension (or "proto-Theodotion"), which had come to light, already before the period under review, through the work of D. Barthélemy.[10] This recension, which can be dated to the mid–first century B.C., is reflected in certain passages of LXX Samuel–Kings and in the fifth Greek version (Quinta) of Origen's Hexapla,[11] but most notably in

R. Hanhart, 1974); *Deuteronomium* (ed. J. W. Wevers, 1977); *Iudith* (ed. R. Hanhart, 1979); *Iob* (ed. J. Ziegler, 1982); *Numeri* (ed. J. W. Wevers, 1982); *Tobit* (ed. R. Hanhart, 1983); *Leviticus* (ed. J. W. Wevers, 1986); *Exodus* (ed. J. W. Wevers, 1991). For auxiliary studies see the series Mitteilungen des Septuaginta-Unternehmens (MSU), Abhandlungen der Akademie der Wissenschaften in Göttingen, Philologisch-historische Klasse (Göttingen: Vandenhoeck & Ruprecht).

8. See R. Hanhart, "Zum gegenwärtigen Stand der Septuagintforschung," in *De Septuaginta: Studies in Honour of John William Wevers on His Sixty-fifth Birthday,* ed. A. Pietersma and C. Cox (Mississauga, Ont.: Benben, 1984), 3–18, esp. 8–9.

9. J. W. Wevers, "The Building of the Tabernacle," *JNSL* 19 (1993): 123–31. This article is a popular summary of the detailed study found in idem, *Textual History of the Greek Exodus,* MSU 21 (Göttingen: Vandenhoeck & Ruprecht, 1991).

10. D. Barthélemy, *Les devanciers d'Aquila,* VTSup 10 (Leiden: Brill, 1963).

11. Tov, *Textual Criticism,* 145.

the Greek scroll of the Minor Prophets, discovered among the Dead Sea Scrolls. This scroll was published in 1990 by Tov.[12] From a textual point of view, it clearly represents a revision of the Old Greek toward the textual tradition of the MT. Similarly, a recent study by P. J. Gentry demonstrates that the asterisked materials in LXX Job represent a revision, to be dated to the early first century A.D., toward a proto-Masoretic Hebrew text.[13] Another revision of the Old Greek toward the proto-Masoretic text is the fifth column of Origen's Hexapla (third century A.D.), which would prove to be a particularly influential form of the LXX textual tradition.[14] The minor Greek versions (see below) can also be regarded as revisions of the LXX in the direction of the MT.[15]

A final point needs to be made in connection with the LXX. Although on the one hand the manuscript discoveries in the Judean desert provide concrete manuscript evidence of a distinct text-type like that underlying the LXX, on the other hand they serve to relativize distinctive Hebrew readings inferred from the Greek. Before the Qumran discoveries, it was easy to assume that the Hebrew *Vorlage* of the LXX, where it clearly differed from the MT, represented an older and therefore more original text. Such an assumption is no longer warranted, since we now know that the proto-Masoretic textual tradition can be traced as far back as the LXX and may in fact have been much more widely represented than the text-type underlying the latter. A distinctive LXX reading no longer has an automatic claim to greater antiquity.[16]

Minor Greek Versions

Traditionally, this designation refers to the Greek translations of Theodotion, Aquila, and Symmachus, which are often referred to as "the Three" in ancient sources. Since it has now become clear that the translation ascribed to Theodotion (who lived in second century A.D.) is actually the *kaige* recension of the first century B.C., this leaves only Aquila and Symmachus to be discussed in the present context. Aquila prepared his very literal translation about A.D. 125, while Symmachus produced his rather free and idiomatic rendering around A.D. 200. Both ver-

---

12. E. Tov, *The Greek Minor Prophets Scroll from Naḥal Ḥever*, DJD 8 (Oxford: Clarendon, 1990).

13. P. J. Gentry, *The Asterisked Materials in the Greek Job*, SBLSCS 38 (Atlanta: Scholars Press, 1995), 494–98. In Origen's edition of the LXX (the fifth column of his Hexapla) he marked with an asterisk material that was extant in his Hebrew text but not in the Old Greek.

14. See Deist, *Witnesses to the Old Testament*, 143–46; Tov, *Textual Criticism*, 25; Sanderson, "Ancient Texts and Versions," 301.

15. So Tov, *Textual Criticism*, 145–47.

16. See Würthwein, *Text of the Old Testament*, 64.

sions appear to be based on the *kaige* recension and continue its orientation to the proto-Masoretic textual tradition.[17] A number of recent studies have dealt with Aquila and Symmachus.[18]

Targums

Although the Targums are often not so much translations as paraphrases, there are stretches of text where they are sufficiently literal to allow a judgment as to the text-type of their Hebrew parent text. With the exception of the Job Targum from Qumran, the Hebrew text reflected in all the Targums is very close to the proto-Masoretic tradition.[19] The 1970s saw the completion of two major critical editions of the Targums: A. Sperber, *The Bible in Aramaic Based on Old Manuscripts and Printed Texts*,[20] and A. Díez Macho, *Neophyti I*.[21] The latter is a sumptuous edition of the copy of a Palestinian Targum discovered in the Vatican Library in 1956, which is variously dated to the first/second or fourth/fifth centuries A.D.[22] Mention should also be made of the English translation, with scholarly annotation, of the major Targums that Martin McNamara has undertaken.[23]

Peshitta

A new multivolume critical edition of the Peshitta of the Old Testament has been in the course of publication since 1966: *The Old Testament in Syriac according to the Peshitta Version: Edited on Behalf of the International Organization for the Study of the Old Testament by the Peshitta Institute, Leiden*.[24] It is being prepared by an international team of scholars and is now nearing completion. This monumental undertaking has

17. Tov, *Textual Criticism*, 146–47.

18. On Aquila, see K. Hyvärinen, *Die Übersetzung von Aquila*, ConBOT 10 (Lund: Liber Läromedel-Gleerup, 1977); and L. L. Grabbe, "Aquila's Translation and Rabbinic Exegesis," *JJS* 33 (1982): 527–36. On Symmachus, see J. G. Luis, *La versión de Símaco a los Profetas Mayores* (Madrid, 1981); and A. Salvesen, *Symmachus in the Pentateuch*, JSS Monograph 15 (Manchester: University of Manchester Press, 1991).

19. Tov, *Textual Criticism*, 149; Sanderson, "Ancient Texts and Versions," 303.

20. 4 vols. (Leiden: Brill, 1959–73).

21. 5 vols. (Madrid: Consejo Superior de Investigaciones Científicas, 1968–78).

22. Tov, *Textual Criticism*, 150.

23. M. McNamara et al., eds., *The Aramaic Bible: The Targums* (Wilmington, Del.: Glazier, 1987–). Nineteen volumes have appeared to date.

24. Leiden: Brill. After the sample edition of Song of Songs, Tobit, and 4 Ezra published in 1966, the following volumes have appeared: *Canticles or Odes, Prayer of Manasseh, Apocryphal Psalms, Psalms of Solomon, Tobit, 1 (3) Esdras* (1972); *Apocalypse of Baruch, 4 Esdras* (1973); *Kings* (1976); *Genesis, Exodus* (1977); *Judges, Samuel* (1978); *Proverbs, Wisdom of Solomon, Ecclesiastes, Song of Songs* (1979); *Dodekapropheton, Daniel-Bel-Draco* (1980); *Psalms* (1980); *Job* (1982); *Ezekiel* (1985); *Isaiah* (1987); *Leviticus, Numbers, Deuteronomy, Joshua* (1991); *Chronicles* (1998).

spawned a considerable number of monographs and articles on the transmission of the text of the Syriac Bible and is gradually replacing the badly outdated editions of the Peshitta published in the nineteenth century.[25]

The new studies associated with the Leiden Peshitta have led to a considerable clarification of the transmission history of the Syriac biblical text. It has become clear that this history can be divided into three stages: a first stage that ended with the sixth century A.D., a second corresponding roughly to the seventh and eighth centuries, and a third beginning in the ninth century. Most printed editions of the Peshitta reflect the third stage, which is farthest removed from the MT, while the printed text of the Leiden Peshitta generally reflects manuscripts of the second stage. But a small number of manuscripts preserve the text of the first stage (recorded in the second apparatus of the Leiden edition), which appears to have been quite a literal translation of a Hebrew text that was very close to the MT. It appears that the text of the Peshitta, through a process of inner-Syriac modifications, gradually moved away from a close approximation to an early stage of the MT. Consequently the divergences from the standard Hebrew text that are found in the third-stage textus receptus of the Peshitta are generally to be attributed not to a different Hebrew *Vorlage* but to developments within the Syriac tradition itself. In its earliest form the Peshitta attests to a Hebrew parent text that is already substantially that of the MT.[26]

Vulgate

Unlike any of the other ancient versions, the Latin Vulgate of the Old Testament has been available for some time in a complete and reliable critical edition. If we except the Apocrypha and the Book of Psalms, which are based on Greek originals, it is clear that the text of the Vulgate too is based on a Hebrew *Vorlage* that conforms closely to the MT.[27]

Samaritan Pentateuch

Although the Samaritan Pentateuch is not a translation, it may be conveniently treated together with the ancient versions.[28] A good deal of scholarly work continues to be done on this sectarian text-type, espe-

25. See P. B. Dirksen, "The Old Testament Peshitta," in *Mikra*, 255–97.
26. See M. D. Koster, "Peshitta Revisited: A Reassessment of Its Value as a Version," *JSS* 38 (1993): 235–68.
27. Tov, *Textual Criticism*, 153. See also B. Kedar, "The Latin Translations," in *Mikra*, 299–338, esp. 322.
28. So Brotzman, *Old Testament Textual Criticism*, 64–69.

cially since the discovery of pre-Samaritan texts at Qumran.[29] In the period under review, we have a new critical edition of the Samaritan Genesis by L.-F. Girón-Blanc, a three-volume study of the Samaritan Targum by A. Tal, and a monograph on the Arabic version by H. Shehadeh.[30] Especially noteworthy is the work of Judith Sanderson on one of the Qumran pre-Samaritan texts, 4QpaleoExod[m].[31] She concludes that the Hebrew textual traditions represented by the LXX, the MT, and the Samaritan Pentateuch were originally quite close, but that the first went its own way relatively early and developed an expansionist tendency, while the second and third stayed close together for some time. A century or so before the turn of the era, the pre-Samaritan tradition separated from the proto-Masoretic tradition and underwent some major expansions. Finally, the canonical form of the Samaritan Pentateuch was reached through a number of specifically sectarian expansions, especially relating to Mount Gerizim as cultic center rather than Jerusalem.[32] One consequence of this overall picture is that the proto-Masoretic tradition, being less subject to the expansionist tendencies of the other traditions, preserves an earlier stage of the text.[33] As Sanderson puts it in another context: "it is easy to recognize the relatively few harmonizing and clarifying expansions in the pre-Samaritan DSS [Dead Sea Scrolls] and the SP [Samaritan Pentateuch]. When those are discounted, the SP agrees substantially with the text behind the MT."[34] Paradoxically, as Waltke puts it (citing Cross), "the chief textual value of the Sam. Pent. is its indirect witness that MT is 'a superb, disciplined text.'"[35]

The Privileged Status of the Proto-Masoretic Tradition

Our survey of late-twentieth-century scholarship on the ancient versions and the Samaritan Pentateuch has revealed a paradoxical situation with respect to the MT and its antecedents. On the one hand its sta-

29. For a convenient recent summary of the history of scholarship on the Samaritan Pentateuch, see B. K. Waltke, "Samaritan Pentateuch," *ABD*, 5:932–40. See also idem, "The Samaritan Pentateuch and the Text of the Old Testament," in *New Perspectives on the Old Testament*, ed. J. B. Payne (Waco: Word, 1970), 212–39.

30. L.-F. Girón-Blanc, *Pentateuco hebreo-samaritano, Génesis* (Madrid: Consejo Superior de Investigaciones Científicas, 1976); A. Tal, *The Samaritan Targum of the Pentateuch*, 3 vols., Texts and Studies in the Hebrew Language 4 (Tel Aviv: Tel Aviv University Press, 1980–83); H. Shehadeh, "The Arabic Translation of the Samaritan Pentateuch: Prolegomena to a Critical Edition" (Ph.D. diss., Jerusalem, 1977).

31. J. E. Sanderson, *An Exodus Scroll from Qumran: 4QpaleoExod[m] and the Samaritan Tradition*, HSS 30 (Atlanta: Scholars Press, 1986).

32. Ibid., 311.

33. Ibid., 312.

34. Sanderson, "Ancient Texts and Versions," 299.

35. Waltke, "Samaritan Pentateuch," *ABD*, 5:938.

tus is that of only one of a number of textual traditions, and on the other it seems to have had a privileged position. Not only does it appear to preserve an older stage of the text than the Samaritan Pentateuch, but it seems to have been regarded, from the first century B.C. onward, as a standard against which the LXX should be corrected, and as the appropriate point of departure for new translations, notably the Targums, the Peshitta, and the Vulgate. There is certainly no dispute that after about A.D. 100 the proto-Masoretic text is regarded in Jewish circles as uniquely authoritative. It is telling that all the Hebrew biblical manuscripts found at Masada, Naḥal Ḥever, and Murabbaʿat (dated to the late first and the second centuries A.D.) belong to the proto-Masoretic text-type.[36] This raises the question: how did the privileged status of the proto-Masoretic tradition come about, and how far back in the history of textual transmission can it be discerned?

One answer to this question is that the textual tradition leading up to the MT was the result of a deliberate process of standardization undertaken by Jewish rabbis around the turn of the era. Thus, according to the influential theory of Cross, the proto-Masoretic text was the product of a deliberate recension, which drew on the various textual families available at the time.[37] As a result, "the promulgation of the new, standard recension evidently took place sometime near the mid-first century A.D."[38]

This view of the emergence of the proto-Masoretic text was severely criticized by Bertil Albrektson.[39] He pointed out that many of the reasons that had been given to support this view (the analogy of contemporary Greek textual critics in Alexandria; the requirements of Rabbi Aqiba's hermeneutical principles; the rabbinic story of the three scrolls in the temple; the Murabbaʿat scrolls as evidence of the new recension) could not withstand scrutiny. Furthermore, he argued persuasively that a text such as that of the Masoretic tradition, with its inconsistencies, haplographies and dittographies, erroneous word divisions, and other textual defects, could hardly be the result of a careful comparison of manuscripts and textual traditions.[40] Instead, Albrektson suggested that the survival of this particular text-type was probably simply a his-

---

36. E. Tov, "The History and Significance of a Standard Text of the Hebrew Bible," in *Hebrew Bible/Old Testament: The History of Its Interpretation,* vol. 1, ed. M. Saebø (Göttingen: Vandenhoeck & Ruprecht, 1996), 49–66, esp. 63.

37. See F. M. Cross Jr., "The Contribution of the Qumrân Discoveries to the Study of the Biblical Text," *IEJ* 16 (1966): 81–95, esp. 94–95; reprinted in *Qumran and the History of the Biblical Text,* 278–92, esp. 291–92.

38. Ibid., 95 (reprint, 292).

39. B. Albrektson, "Reflections on the Emergence of a Standard Text of the Hebrew Bible," *Congress Volume: Göttingen, 1977,* VTSup 29 (Leiden: Brill, 1978), 49–65.

40. Ibid., 59.

torical accident; it represented "what Pharisaic scribes happened to have left after the defeats imposed by the Romans."[41]

Albrektson also suggested, however, that the text-type favored by the Pharisees may already have enjoyed a special status before the Jewish revolts: "It had been handled in circles which devoted much care and attention to the word of Scripture, and so it is plausible that on the whole it should have an archaic and authentic character, lacking many of the defects of the so-called vulgar texts."[42] Others, too, have pointed out that the textual tradition lying back of the MT may have enjoyed a privileged status well before the end of the first century A.D. Not only was it already the dominant text-type among the Qumran finds (60 percent of all the biblical manuscripts, according to Tov),[43] and the standard toward which the *kaige* recension corrected the Old Greek in the first century B.C., but it may have been specially preserved by the religious leaders of the Jews.

We find this emphasis especially in Tov's standard work, *Textual Criticism of the Hebrew Bible.* In a section entitled "The Early Origins of the Consonantal Framework of 𝔐 [= MT]," he writes of the proto-Masoretic textual tradition:

> It may be surmised that it originated in the spiritual and authoritative center of Judaism (that of the Pharisees?), possibly even in the temple circles. It was probably the temple scribes who were entrusted with the copying and preserving of 𝔐. Though this assumption cannot be proven, it is supported by the fact that the temple employed correctors (מגיהים, *magihim*) who scrutinized certain scrolls on its behalf.[44]

Tov also suggests that the scribes who produced the biblical texts written in the Qumran practice "may have used proto-Masoretic texts,"[45] which again would indicate the antiquity and early authority of this textual tradition. In general, "the earliest Qumran finds dating from the third pre-Christian century bear evidence, among other things, of a tradition of the exact copying of texts belonging to the Masoretic family, that is, the proto-Masoretic texts."[46]

41. Ibid., 63.
42. Ibid.
43. In his 1996 article "Standard Text," Tov speaks of 40 percent (p. 60), but this appears to be a misprint. On p. 64 of the same article he again mentions 60 percent, as elsewhere.
44. Tov, *Textual Criticism,* 28 (cf. 190).
45. Ibid., 114. See also L. H. Schiffman, *Reclaiming the Dead Sea Scrolls* (Philadelphia: Jewish Publication Society, 1994), 172, who regards this possibility as a certainty: "Examining the Qumran text type [i.e., the biblical manuscripts written in the 'Qumran practice'—A. W.] we discover that it is originally based on proto-Masoretic texts."
46. Tov, "Standard Text," 57.

Tov's views on the antiquity and authority of the Masoretic textual tradition are closely akin to those of A. S. van der Woude, who goes even further in giving a privileged position to this strand of the textual history of the Old Testament.[47] He argues, for example, that revisions of the Old Greek toward this text-type can already be detected in the second century B.C.[48] He suggests a bold new hypothesis, saying

> that there was always a relative uniformity of textual tradition in the religious circles around the Temple of Jerusalem. This means that there was a basically uniform tradition *besides* a pluriform tradition in Palestine Judaism in the last centuries B.C., in the sense that only the proto-Masoretic textual tradition was passed on in Jerusalem, whereas elsewhere also biblical manuscripts circulated which bore close resemblance to the text of the Septuagint or the Samaritan Pentateuch or differed in other respects from the proto-Masoretic tradition.[49]

Tov has recently echoed these sentiments, and Lawrence H. Schiffman has come to similar conclusions.[50] If these scholars are right, the MT represents a textual tradition that can lay claim to a much higher degree of legitimacy than the other ancient witnesses to the Hebrew Bible.

Aims of Old Testament Textual Criticism

The heading of this section is also the title of a useful survey article by Waltke.[51] In it he identifies five different approaches to the task of the textual criticism of the Hebrew Bible that recent scholars have taken. These can be summarized as follows:

1. *Restore the original composition.* The goal here is to recover the author's *ipsissima verba,* "to establish the text as the author wished to have it presented to the public."
2. *Restore the final text.* Here the task is to recover the *ipsissima verba* not of the author but of the final redactor, assuming that

---

47. A. S. van der Woude, "Pluriformity and Uniformity: Reflections on the Transmission of the Text of the Old Testament," in *Sacred History and Sacred Texts in Early Judaism: A Symposium in Honour of A. S. van der Woude,* ed. J. N. Bremmer and F. García Martínez (Kampen: Kok Pharos, 1992), 151–69. A popular version of the same article is found in A. S. van der Woude, "Tracing the Evolution of the Hebrew Bible," *BibRev* 11 (1995): 42–45.

48. Van der Woude, "Pluriformity and Uniformity," 161.

49. Ibid., 163.

50. Tov, "Standard Text," 64: "Thus while a textual variety is clearly visible in the Qumran finds, beyond that variety one discerns the existence of a single textual family which probably reflected the standard text of the Pharisees"; and Schiffman, *Reclaiming the Dead Sea Scrolls,* 171–73.

51. B. K. Waltke, "Aims of OT Textual Criticism," *WTJ* 51 (1989): 93–108.

a particular literary unit of the Bible has gone through a process of evolution. Most modern textual criticism has operated with this goal.

3. *Restore the earliest attested text.* The aim here is not the redactor's final text, but the earliest form of the text for which there are actual textual witnesses. In this approach, which is that of the Hebrew University Bible Project and the UBS Hebrew Old Testament Text Project (see below), the text aimed at is usually that of the second century B.C., and conjectural emendations are disallowed, since these by definition have no manuscript support.

4. *Restore accepted texts (plural).* In this understanding of the text critic's task, the end in view is the text as it was accepted by a particular religious community, and texts may therefore differ according to the community in question. This is the tack taken by canonical critics like James A. Sanders and Brevard Childs, although the latter focuses on the text as accepted by the Jews, the MT.

5. *To reconstruct final texts (plural).* Here the text critic acknowledges that a particular book or pericope may have had two or more forms within the same canon, both or all of which have equal validity and need to be equally restored.

Waltke concludes his survey by suggesting that a different goal may be appropriate for different books of the Bible:

> The text critic's aim will vary according to the nature of the book. If a book had but one author, then the critic will aim to restore his original composition; if it be an edited text then he will seek to recover the final, canonical text. If he turns up more than one final text, he will turn his data over to the literary and canonical critic to determine whether the text is in process of developing into a final canonical text or whether it existed in more than one canonical form.[52]

With this rather eclectic approach, as defended by Waltke in 1989, we may contrast the views of Tov and Ulrich. Tov makes a basic distinction between the literary development and the textual transmission of the books of the Bible. In many cases, a given book of the Bible may have gone through a number of literary stages before reaching what he calls "the finished literary product," and this finished product, as received into the (proto-)Masoretic text, then stands at the begin-

52. Ibid., 107–8.

ning of the process of textual transmission. The goal of textual criticism is to recover that completed literary composition, which Tov calls "the original text."[53] By defining "original text" in this way, Tov means to exclude from the proper task of textual criticism both earlier stages of literary growth (e.g., the shorter version of Jeremiah found in the LXX and some Qumran biblical manuscripts) and later midrashic developments (such as the noncanonical additions to Esther and Daniel). Crucial to his description of the "original text" is its relationship to 𝔐 (= MT):

> The view that textual criticism should take into consideration only one textual entity from which all texts were derived is partly based on arguments that are socio-religious and historical rather than textual. The canonical concept that has been accepted in Judaism leads solely to the literary compositions that are reflected in 𝔐, and therefore it is these alone and not earlier or later stages that have to be considered.[54]

To highlight the fact that the text that must be restored is itself the end product of a literary development, Tov is at pains to emphasize that this text may be different from the wording of the original author:

> Even if the original formulations by the authors of the biblical books themselves, such as the words of the prophets, had been preserved, these, paradoxically, would be less important for the textual reconstruction than the last editions of the books. For example, if the very scroll which Jeremiah dictated to his scribe, Baruch (see Jeremiah 36), had been found, it would be less relevant to the issue under investigation than the final edition of the book containing the rewriting by the deuteronomistic editor.[55]

In short, it is Tov's view that "the biblical books in their final and canonical edition . . . are the objective of textual criticism."[56] This is a view with which Waltke now declares himself to agree substantially.[57]

Ulrich, on the other hand, does not want to restrict the goals of textual criticism to the original Masoretic shape of the canonical writings.[58] In his view, the textual critic should aim to restore all the various "literary editions" of the various writings that can be discerned in the overall evolution of the Hebrew Bible. This evolution is characterized

53. Tov, *Textual Criticism*, 171.
54. Ibid., 172.
55. Ibid., 178.
56. Ibid., 189.
57. Waltke, "Old Testament Textual Criticism," 175.
58. Ulrich, "Multiple Literary Editions."

by "faithful transmission occasionally punctuated by evolutionary leaps to a new, revised and expanded edition of biblical books."[59] The text-types represented by the LXX, the Samaritan Pentateuch, and the MT reflect such divergent literary editions, as do many of the other Qumran biblical manuscripts. The earliest recoverable edition can be called the "base text," although it too was probably based on an earlier edition that is now lost. This base text then becomes the point of departure of subsequent editions, usually through expansion.[60] Ulrich explicitly takes issue with Tov:

> Thus the target of "textual criticism of the Hebrew Bible" is not a single text. The purpose or function of textual criticism is to reconstruct the history of the texts that eventually become the biblical collection in both its literary growth and its scribal transmission; it is not just to judge individual variants in order to determine which were "superior" or "original." The "original text" is a distracting concept for the Hebrew Bible.[61]

For Ulrich, all stages of the development of the biblical text are equally authoritative and canonical. He therefore disagrees with Schiffman, for example, with respect to the status of 11QPs[a], which the latter (in agreement with Tov) considers to be a noncanonical compilation. Ulrich concludes his article by emphasizing the fully canonical status of this manuscript: "11QPs[a] and the other manuscripts described above should be viewed as variant forms of the multiple literary editions of the biblical books which had full claim to being authoritative scripture."[62]

Although Tov and Ulrich clearly disagree on the aims of Old Testament textual criticism, they probably do not have significantly different views on how the evolution of the biblical text actually took place. They disagree mainly on the normative status that is to be accorded to the MT.

Three Large-Scale Text-Critical Projects

It is against the background of the foregoing sketch of scholarly discussions of the Old Testament text that I should briefly mention the three major collaborative projects that are currently underway in this field of study.

The first is the Hebrew University Bible Project. This is a critical edition of the Hebrew Bible based on the Aleppo Codex (tenth century). So

59. Ibid., 90.
60. Ibid., 98.
61. Ibid., 98–99.
62. Ibid., 105.

far, only Isaiah and Jeremiah have been published.[63] This edition differs in a number of important ways from the standard scholarly edition of the Hebrew Bible, the *Biblia Hebraica Stuttgartensia*.[64] It has four apparatuses (for ancient versions, Hebrew texts from the second temple period, consonantal variants from medieval manuscripts, and differences in vocalization and accents from medieval manuscripts), it does not list conjectural emendations, and it does not evaluate the merits of competing readings. As a result, this edition, when completed, will offer the most reliable collection of textual variants for independent text-critical work available in any printed edition. Associated with this project is the publication, since 1960, of the journal *Textus*, which is exclusively devoted to the textual criticism of the Hebrew Bible.

A second project is the Hebrew Old Testament Text Project, with its Committee for Textual Analysis of the Hebrew Old Testament, which was sponsored by the United Bible Societies (UBS). Its purpose is to produce a competent text-critical commentary on the Old Testament for the many translations sponsored by the UBS. An initial fruit of the committee's labors was the *Preliminary and Interim Report on the Hebrew Old Testament Text Project*.[65] But a much more substantial publication is the final report of the committee, prepared by Dominique Barthélemy, of which three volumes have now appeared.[66] These massive volumes are a monument to careful text-critical scholarship and embody a wealth of information about the history of the biblical text and its interpretation. Although the body of the work is devoted to assessing the divergences from the MT that have been accepted in the major contemporary Bible versions, there are also extensive essays by Barthélemy on the history of Old Testament textual criticism and on the whole range of witnesses to the Old Testament text.[67] The committee divided the history of the text into four phases: (1) the prehistory of the text, which is the domain of literary analysis, (2) the earliest attested form of the text, (3) the standard text authorized by Jewish rabbis after the destruction of the temple, and (4) the MT of the ninth and tenth centuries

---

63. M. H. Goshen-Gottstein, ed., *The Hebrew University Bible: The Book of Isaiah*, 2 vols. (Jerusalem: Magnes, 1975–81); and C. Rabin, S. Talmon, and E. Tov, eds., *The Hebrew University Bible: The Book of Jeremiah* (Jerusalem: Magnes, 1997).

64. Stuttgart: Deutsche Bibelgesellschaft, 1967–77.

65. 5 vols. (New York: United Bible Societies, 1973–80).

66. D. Barthélemy, ed., *Critique textuelle de l'Ancien Testament*, vol. 1, *Josué, Juges, Ruth, Samuel, Rois, Chroniques, Esdras, Néhémie, Esther*; vol. 2, *Isaïe, Jérémie, Lamentations*; vol. 3, *Ezéchiel, Daniel et les Douze Prophètes*, OBO 50 (Fribourg: Éditions universitaires; Göttingen: Vandenhoeck & Ruprecht, 1982, 1986, 1992).

67. See, respectively, "L'histoire de la critique textuelle de l'Ancien Testament depuis ses origines jusqu'à J. D. Michaelis," in *Critique textuelle*, 1:*1–*65; "Introduction," in *Critique textuelle*, 3:i–ccxlii.

A.D. The committee took as its goal the recovery of phase 2, essentially the proto-Masoretic text.

With impressive erudition, Barthélemy discusses hundreds of emendations to the MT that have been proposed and accepted in modern commentaries and translations and finds most of them wanting. In volume 2, out of eight hundred emendations that were examined, only seventy-eight are found to be probable, and most of these do not materially affect the sense.[68] In short, these volumes constitute a massive vindication of the traditional Hebrew text.

Finally, a third collaborative project has been undertaken by the United Bible Societies as a spin-off of the work of the Hebrew Old Testament Text Project. This is a new edition of the *Biblia Hebraica*, with a selective listing of variants together with a textual commentary. This is being prepared by an international team of twenty-three scholars, who hope to complete their work by the year 2002.[69]

Theological Issues

One of the striking features of the scholarship surrounding the Old Testament text in the late twentieth century is the failure of biblical scholars to discuss the deeper theological issues that are raised by the new discoveries and theories. There are occasional exceptions, of course. Brotzman, for example, has a brief discussion of "Textual Criticism and Inspiration"—a discussion that Waltke calls a "unique contribution"—but this consists mainly of the argument that textual criticism allows us to recover the inspired autographs.[70] Elsewhere Waltke himself points out that the idea of "original autographs" may have to be modified to accommodate the possibility of two equally inspired editions of the same biblical book or pericope, but he does not elaborate on this theme.[71] Oddly enough, there seems to have been very little work done in this direction by evangelicals, whose theological identity is so closely bound up with the notion of inspired autographs.

It may be useful in this connection to take note of some of Barthélemy's recent work on the history of Old Testament criticism, especially with reference to the seventeenth-century discussions involving J. Morin, L. Cappel, and R. Simon.[72] At issue was the notion of inspired

68. P. Dion, review of *Critique textuelle*, vol. 2, in *JBL* 107 (1988): 738.

69. See A. Schenker, "Eine Neuausgabe der Biblia Hebraica," *ZAH* 9 (1996): 58–61.

70. Brotzman, *Old Testament Textual Criticism*, 22–24. See Waltke's foreword in Brotzman, *Old Testament Textual Criticism*, 10.

71. Waltke, "Aims of OT Textual Criticism," 107.

72. D. Barthélemy, *Critique textuelle*, 1:10–20; and idem, "L'enchevêtrement de l'histoire textuelle et de l'histoire littéraire dans les relations entre la Septante et le texte Massorétique," in *De Septuaginta*, 21–40.

autographs in their relation to the MT and the possibility that inspiration was not restricted to the work of the original author. Although the rise of modern historical criticism has altered the terms of the debate, as Barthélemy points out, the basic theological issues at stake have not changed. I would submit that it is to these issues, alongside the more precise tracing of the evolution of the biblical text, that the discipline of Old Testament textual criticism will have to give greater attention in the twenty-first century.

2

Epigraphic Light on the Old Testament

Mark W. Chavalas and *Edwin C. Hostetter*

Syro-Mesopotamia

The past generation has seen an explosion of epigraphic sources coming from Syria and Iraq (ancient Syro-Mesopotamia) that shed light on the larger framework of the Old Testament world. Because of their massive size, I will chronologically survey the most significant epigraphic finds and reevaluations and those that help to further an understanding of Old Testament material.

Uruk Period (ca. 4000–3000 B.C.)

The first evidence of writing (in the form of the archaic cuneiform script) in human history comes during the Uruk period, named after the southern Mesopotamian city of Uruk (biblical Erech). A new treatment of the texts from Uruk has caused a reevaluation of the origins and purpose of these early texts.[1] Over five thousand discarded archaic tablets and fragments dated to 3100 B.C. have been found at Uruk, most in a refuse area in the sacred precinct. These texts have now been enhanced by those of the Erlenmeyer collection, which have shed light on early accounting practices.[2] As a result of the aforemen-

---

The section on Syro-Mesopotamia was written by Mark W. Chavalas; that on Palestine and Egypt was written by Edwin C. Hostetter.

1. H. Nissen et al., eds., *Archaic Bookkeeping: Early Writing and Techniques of Economic Administration in the Ancient Near East* (Chicago: University of Chicago Press, 1993).

2. There are about eighty texts. They, along with objects, were the subject of a recent exhibit of early writing (as discussed in Nissen et al., eds., *Archaic Bookkeeping*, ix–xi).

tioned reappraisal, some have argued that writing originated not as a means of rendering language but as a system of recording information, developing as a consequence of the increasing demands of an expanded state and economy. There has also been a reassessment in the understanding of the evolution of writing. Many had expected to see earlier stages of pictographs (likely written on perishable materials) because of the uniformity in the use and shape of particular signs in the archaic script. A series of precursors to writing did exist in the Near East. Many Neolithic sites used counting symbols (normally called tokens) as early as the ninth millennium b.c.[3] By the early Uruk period, the tokens were for the most part discarded and impressed clay tablets were used, soon replaced with the pictographic texts. A number of the signs employed in the impressed texts were later graphically represented in the archaic cuneiform texts.[4] Some have therefore argued that the archaic script was the solution for an immediate problem;[5] thus writing was the next stage in the process of recording information.[6]

Early Bronze (ca. 3000–2100 b.c.)

Writing did not become a means of communication representing a spoken language until the third millennium b.c. in southern Mesopotamia. Moreover, it was not employed for literary purposes until midway in this period, as evidenced by discoveries at Abu Salabikh.[7] Literary texts concerning the military victories of Urnanshe of Lagash have been found at al Hiba,[8] now known to be the Sumerian city of Lagash, not Telloh, as had been previously thought.[9]

Although there is inscriptional evidence for the Akkadian period in southern Mesopotamia (ca. 2350–2150 b.c.) from Uruk, Ur, and Nippur, few texts have been found outside northern Mesopotamia in this period. Akkadian texts have been located in the Hamrin basin at Tell

3. See D. Schmandt-Besserat, *Before Writing*, 2 vols. (Austin: University of Texas Press, 1992). For an earlier critique of tokens as precursors of writing, see S. Lieberman, "Of Clay Pebbles, Hollow Clay Balls, and Writing: A Sumerian View," *AJA* 84 (1980): 339–58.

4. Schmandt-Besserat, *Before Writing*, 1:141–50.

5. Nissen et al., eds., *Archaic Bookkeeping*, 116–24.

6. Nissen, *The Early History of the Ancient Near East, 9000–2000 B.C.* (Chicago: University of Chicago Press, 1988), 214.

7. R. Biggs, *Inscriptions from Tell Abu Salabikh* (Chicago: University of Chicago Press, 1974); and R. Biggs and J. N. Postgate, "Inscriptions from Abu Salabikh, 1975," *Iraq* 40 (1978): 101–17.

8. V. Crawford, "Inscriptions from Lagash, Season Four, 1975–1976," *JCS* 29 (1977): 189–222.

9. Crawford, "Lagash," *Iraq* 36 (1974): 29–35.

Sleima, however, some of which indicate that the site's ancient name was Awal.[10] Forty more have recently been found as far away as Mari in Syria.[11]

The most spectacular epigraphic discoveries for this period are found in Syria, which until recently was thought to lack written sources (partly because of a dearth of references in antiquity), especially when compared to Mesopotamia proper. Thousands of cuneiform tablets have been uncovered predominantly from a major palatial archive at Tell Mardikh (ancient Ebla), written in a heretofore unknown Semitic language called Eblaite.[12] The major archival remains that have been discovered at Ebla show a wholesale adoption of the Sumerian cuneiform script at a very early date. The extent of Syria's cultural dependence (especially in regard to literature) on Mesopotamia is not a simple matter. Many of the religious texts at Ebla have their counterparts in the southeast; however, the incantations written predominantly in Eblaite have no attested parallel[13] and feature geographic and divine names pointing to a native Syrian context. Both Ebla and the aforementioned Mari (well known to Bible students for its archives) appear to have shared a common writing system, language, and calendar in this period.[14] Most likely the cultural borrowing was from Mari to Ebla and not the other way around.[15]

The first stratified epigraphic remains in the Khabur plains in Syria have recently been found at Tell Mozan (ca. 2300–2200 B.C.). Excavations have exposed two stratified cuneiform tablets dated to the late third millennium B.C. They appear to be administrative tablets written in Akkadian, but with Hurrian, Sumerian, and Akkadian proper names.[16] Moreover, the most recent season at Mozan has had great epigraphic significance, as the excavators have established that Mozan was indeed Urkish, a Hurrian capital in the third millennium

10. F. Rashid, "Akkadian Texts from Tell Sleima," *Sumer* 40 (1984): 55–56. More Sumerian literary texts have also been found at Tell Hadad; A. Cavigneaux and F. al-Rawi, "New Sumerian Literary Texts from Tell Hadad (Ancient Meturan): A First Survey," *Iraq* 55 (1993): 91–106.

11. J.-C. Margueron in H. Weiss, "Archaeology in Syria," *AJA* 95 (1991): 711.

12. The corpus of Ebla texts is being published in G. Pettinato et al., Materiali epigrafici di Ebla (Naples: Istituto Universitario Orientale di Napoli, 1979–); and A. Archi et al., Archivi reali di Ebla: Testi (Rome: Missione Archeologica Italiana in Siria, 1981–).

13. W. Hallo, "The Syrian Contribution to Cuneiform Literature," in *New Horizons in the Study of Ancient Syria*, ed. M. Chavalas and J. Hayes (Malibu: Undena, 1992), 72.

14. See I. Gelb, "Mari and the Kish Civilization," in *Mari in Retrospect*, ed. G. Young (Winona Lake, Ind.: Eisenbrauns, 1992), 197–200.

15. See Gelb, *Thoughts about Ibla: A Preliminary Evaluation*, Syro-Mesopotamian Studies 1.1 (Malibu: Undena, 1977), 15.

16. See L. Milano et al., *Mozan 2: The Epigraphic Finds of the Sixth Season* (Malibu: Undena, 1991), 1–34.

B.C.[17] Seal imprints with the name of "Tupkish, king of Urkish," have been found, along with the name of his queen and many retainers. Most of the seal impressions belonged to Queen Uqnitum and her staff. Some have even suggested that a Hurrian scribal tradition equivalent to Semitic Ebla may have existed in this region.[18]

Middle Bronze (ca. 2100–1600 B.C.)

A highly sophisticated private scribal tradition existed in southern Mesopotamia during the Ur III (2100–2000 B.C.) and Old Babylonian (2000–1600 B.C.) periods. Thus there was an increase in epigraphic remains found in domestic units at sites such as Larsa, Isin, and Mashkan-Shapir.[19] Those at Isin were in houses in which tablets were prepared and written and scribes were instructed. Furthermore, over twenty economic texts have been found from as far away as Bahrain in the Persian Gulf.[20] A yield of tablets from Tell al-Rimah (ancient Qattara) was discovered dated to the reign of Shamshi-Adad.[21] Most interesting is the archive of Iltani, wife of the ruler of Karana, which sheds light on feminine correspondence.[22]

Over fifty texts have been uncovered from Haradum (a small Babylonian border town on the Euphrates) from the 26th year of Samsuiluna (1723 B.C.) to the 18th or 19th year of Ammisaduqa (1627 B.C.).[23] They were found in private houses and in the mayoral residence, and included letters, judicial texts, administrative texts, cultic texts, and dis-

17. G. Buccellati and M. Kelly-Buccellati, "Urkesh: The Firt Hurrian Capital," *BA* 60 (1997): 77–96.

18. See G. Wilhelm, *The Hurrians* (Warminster: Aris & Phillips, 1989), 77–79, and Buccellati and Kelly-Buccellati, *Mozan I: The Soundings of the First Two Seasons* (Malibu: Undena, 1988), 31.

19. J.-L. Huot, *Larsa et 'Oueili: Travau de 1983* (Paris: Éditions recherche sur les civilisations, 1987); C. Walker and C. Wilcke, "Preliminary Report on the Inscriptions, Autumn 1975, Spring 1977, Autumn 1978," in *Isin-Išān Baḥrīyāt II*, ed. B. Hrouda et al. (Munich: Verlag der bayerischen Akademie der Wissenschaften, 1981), 91–102; E. C. Stone and P. Zimansky, "Mashkan-shapir and the Anatomy of an Old Babylonian City," *BA* 55 (1992): 212–18.

20. B. Andre-Salvini is preparing them for publication.

21. J. Eidem, "Some Remarks on the Iltani Archive from Tell al Rimah," *Iraq* 51 (1989): 67–78; J. Durand and D. Charpin, "Le nom antique de Tell al-Rimah," *RA* 81 (1987): 115ff.; S. Dalley et al., *The Old Babylonian Tablets from Tell al-Rimah* (London: British School of Archaeology in Iraq, 1976).

22. See Dalley, *Mari and Karana: Two Old Babylonian Cities* (London: Longman, 1984). Karana is now known to be the city of Qattara; see Eidem, "Some Remarks on the Iltani Archive from Tell al Rimah"; and Durand and Charpin, "Le nom antique de Tell al-Rimah."

23. F. Joannès, "Haradum et le pays de Suhum: d'après la documentation cunéiform à l'époque babylonienne ancienne," *Archéologia* 205 (1985): 56–59.

tribution lists. The image that they furnish of Haradum is a small enclosed village with an administration, elders, and a mayor. The letters attest to local commerce, riverboat traffic and the sale of wool, agricultural products, and slaves. The onomastic data show a mixed population, with a preponderance of West Semitic names. Haradum was destroyed after little more than a century, apparently either by nomads or by the inundation of the Euphrates.

There was also an increase in scribal activity in Syria, as evidenced from recent epigraphic remains from Terqa and Shubat Enlil. There is a body of epigraphic documentation at Terqa datable to the so-called dark age between the fall of Mari (ca. 1760 B.C.) and the fall of Babylon (ca. 1595 B.C.). At this time, Terqa was most likely the capital of the kingdom of Khana on the Middle Euphrates. Near the original summit of the mound, a large public building has been uncovered and found to contain, thus far, over thirty Khana period tablets, forcing a reevaluation of Khana chronology.[24] Terqa may have remained under Babylonian control during the reigns of Ammisaduqa and Samsuditana.[25] The kingdom appears to have been governed by several previously unknown kings bearing Hurrian names, showing that it passed under Mitanni control in the next period (after 1600 B.C.). Tell Leilan has revealed its name during the Old Babylonian period: Shubat-Enlil.[26] Associated cuneiform archives have been found within two large temples.[27] Lastly, over sixty economic texts have been found from the reign of Shamshi-Adad (1814–1781 B.C.) from Tell Biʾa. One of the texts mentions the city of Tuttul, establishing the site's name.[28]

Late Bronze (ca. 1600–1200 B.C.)

Recently discovered archives from Syria in the Late Bronze Age have shed light on how the Hittites, Mitanni, and Assyrians provided administrative rule in this area. These archives are especially important, since the primary Syrian centers in the Hittite period (e.g., Carchemish, Halab [Aleppo], and Wassukani) have not revealed such documents. An important Mitanni center along the Middle Euphra-

24. For the Terqa texts, see O. Rouault, *Terqa Final Reports 1: L'Archive de Puzurum* (Malibu: Undena, 1984). For Khana (Terqa) chronology, see A. Podany, "A Middle Babylonian Date for the Hana Kingdom," *JCS* 43–45 (1991–93): 53–62; and M. Chavalas, "Terqa and the Kingdom of Khana," *BA* 58 (1996): 90–103.

25. See, however, G. Buccellati, "The Kingdom and Period of Khana," *BASOR* 270 (1987): 46–49.

26. H. Weiss, "Tell Leilan and Shubat Enlil," *MARI* 4 (1984): 269–92.

27. Including a new fragment of the Sumerian King List; see C. Vincent, "Tell Leilan Recension of the Sumerian King List," *NABU* 11 (1990): 8–9.

28. E. Strommenger in H. Weiss, "Archaeology in Syria," 143–44.

tes was Tell Hadidi (ancient Azu), where a number of legal documents from this period were found.[29] Another of these influential Syrian cities was Ugarit, a town already well known for its archives that have revealed a great deal of comparative material for biblical studies. Most recently, over three hundred texts have been uncovered at Ugarit, some of which were found in the house of an official named Urtenu. The texts are primarily state documents, most written in Akkadian and a few in Ugaritic. Urtenu's house has not yet been fully excavated.[30]

Arguably, the most important recent finds coming from Syro-Mesopotamia in this period come from the Middle Euphrates sites of Emar, which have revealed nearly two thousand Late Bronze Age tablets and fragments.[31] The variety of cuneiform documentation at Emar includes Akkadian legal texts, letters, and ritual texts,[32] as well as some Hittite and Hurrian medical and divination texts. Over four hundred ritual texts were discovered in a scribal center in Temple M1 at Emar, nearly half of which describe apparently indigenous Emarite religious practices not attested in archives in Anatolia or Mesopotamia.[33] The most significant of the Emar ritual texts are the festivals, which expose local Middle Euphrates religious practice.[34] The literary corpus from Emar (omina, incantations, rituals, wisdom literature, etc.) appears to be as relevant for biblical studies as those of Ugarit.[35] Numerous sites in Syria have recently produced textual information concerning the reigns of many of the Middle Assyrian kings, especially Shalmaneser I (1273–1244 B.C.). Sources include findings at Tell Fray, over 600 texts and fragments from Tell Sheikh Hamad and Tell

29. R. Dornemann, "Tell Hadidi: A Millennium of Bronze Age City Occupation," in *Archeological Reports from the Tabqa Dam Project—Euphrates Valley, Syria,* ed. D. N. Freedman, 44 (Cambridge: ASOR, 1979), 144–49.

30. M. Yon in H. Weiss, "Archaeology in Syria," 139. P. Bordreuil and D. Pardee are presently preparing the most recent texts for publication.

31. For a recent study of Emar and its textual remains, see *Emar: The History, Religion, and Culture of a Bronze Age Town,* ed. M. Chavalas (Bethesda: CDL Press, 1996). Over eighty texts have been found at nearby Tell Munbaqa (ancient Ekalte). See W. Mayer, "Die Tontafelfunde von Tall Munbaqa/Ekalte 1989 and 1990," *MDOG* 125 (1993): 103–6, for the most recent discussion of the texts. See also D. Arnaud, *Recherches au pays d'Astata: Emar VI.1–4: Les textes sumériens et accadiens* (Paris: Éditions recherche sur les civilisations, 1985–87).

32. D. Arnaud, "La bibliothèque d'un devin Syrien à Meskéné-Emar (Syrie)," *CRAIBL* (1980): 375–87.

33. For Emarite religion, see D. Fleming, *The Installation of Baal's High Priestess at Emar: A Window on Ancient Syrian Religion,* HSS 42 (Atlanta: Scholars Press, 1992).

34. Fleming, "The Rituals from Emar: Evolution of an Indigenous Tradition in Second Millennium Syria," in *New Horizons,* ed. Chavalas and Hayes, 2–4.

35. Hallo, "Syrian Contribution to Cuneiform Literature," 82–87.

Amouda, and forty texts dating to the reign of Tukulti Ninurta I (1244–1208 B.C.) at Tell Chuera.[36] These all exhibit a complex Assyrian administrative presence in the area.

Early Iron (ca. 1200–600 B.C.)

The Early Iron Age in Syro-Mesopotamia was dominated primarily by Assyria. At the Assyrian capital of Nineveh, recent excavations have uncovered inscriptions of Sennacherib's construction of the north walls of the city.[37] A more spectacular discovery has been found in royal graves at Nimrud, one of the Assyrian capitals.[38] An underground brick tomb was found with inscriptions of Ashurnasirpal II (884–859 B.C.) and Shalmaneser III (858–824 B.C.). There was a rich assortment of jewelry, earrings, lapis, ivory, beads, and a ceramic coffin lid. A Late Babylonian period library has been found at Sippar (Abu Habba) containing mostly literary tablets, with duplicates from Nippur and elsewhere. Copies include a new historical inscription of the Akkadian king Manishtushu and an extension of the Weidner Chronicle.[39]

Syria has also recently revealed Early Iron Age textual material, the most spectacular of which is the discovery of a large life-size basalt statue at Tell Fakhariyah. It is unique because of a bilingual inscription on the statue, two-thirds of which is in Akkadian (Assyrian dialect), and one-third in ancient Aramaic, making it the oldest attested Aramaic inscription.[40]

Epigraphic material from Syro-Mesopotamia, although not always having a direct bearing on the Bible, continues to give evidence of a massive literary tradition in the ancient Near Eastern world to which the Israelite writers belonged.

36. A. Bounni and P. Matthiae, "Tell Fray, ville frontière entre hittites et assyriens au XIIIe siècle av. J. C.," *Archéologica* 140 (1980): 30–39; H. Kühne, "Tell seh Hamad/ Dur-katlimu: The Assyrian Provincial Capital in the Muhafazat Deir Az-Zor," *AAAS* 34 (1984): 160–79; for the tablets reputed to have come from Tell Amuda, see P. Machinist, "Provincial Governance in Middle Assyria and Some New Texts from Yale," *Assur* 3 (1982): 67–76; for Tell Chuera, see W. Orthmann in H. Weiss, "Archaeology in Syria," 120–22.

37. D. Stronach and S. Lumsden, "UC Berkeley's Excavations at Nineveh," *BA* 55 (1992): 227–33.

38. A. Fadhil, "Die in Nimrud/Kalhu aufgefundene Grabinschrift der Jaba," *BaM* 21 (1990): 461–70; idem, "Die Grabinschrift der Mullissu-Mukannisat-Ninua aus Nimrud/ Kalhu und andere in ihrem Grab gefundene Schriftträger," *BaM* 21 (1990): 471–82.

39. J. N. Postgate et al., "Excavations in Iraq," *Iraq* 49 (1987): 248–49; and F. al-Rawi and A. George, "Tablets from the Sippar Library II: Tablet II of the Babylonian Creation Epic," *Iraq* 52 (1990): 149ff.

40. A. Abou-Assaf et al., *La statue de Tell Fekherye et son inscription bilingue assyro-araméene* (Paris: Éditions recherche sur les civilisations, 1982).

Palestine and Egypt

This is a sampling of inscriptions that have significance for understanding the Bible and ancient Israel. The first group of epigraphs discussed was found in Palestine, while the second group was discovered in Egypt. Although the selection process for inclusion here was subjective, the results should enhance the reader's background knowledge of the Bible.

Palestinian Epigraphy

Arad Ostraca

Between 1962 and 1976 archaeologists at Arad unearthed Hebrew, Aramaic, Arabic, and Greek ostraca.[41] The Hebrew texts, preserved better than those in other languages, originated from the tenth through sixth centuries B.C., but especially during the later phases of the Judahite monarchical period. A particular group of eighteen Hebrew letters found together date from around 598 or 597, probably less than a decade before the comparable Lachish Letters (see below). This archive appears to have dealt mainly with the disbursement of rations to various people and places. One ostracon urged the dispatch to Ramath-negeb of troops rather than supplies in order to ward off a threat by the Edomites. Another mentions Yahweh's temple in Jerusalem. The reference is an extremely rare epigraphic survival from first temple times. Most of the collection was addressed to an Eliashib, perhaps quartermaster or even commandant at the Arad fortress.

Beth-shan Stelae

Both Pharaohs Seti I (1306–1290 B.C.) and Rameses II (1290–1224 B.C.) installed basalt stelae at Beth-shan to commemorate their expeditions

---

41. J. C. L. Gibson, *Textbook of Syrian Semitic Inscriptions*, 3 vols. (Oxford: Clarendon, 1971–82), 1:49–54; R. Hestrin, *Inscriptions Reveal*, 2d ed. (Jerusalem: Israel Museum, 1972), Eng. section, pp. 3–37, 75; R. B. Lawton, "Arad Ostraca," *ABD*, 1:336–37; A. Lemaire, *Inscriptions hébraïques*, Littératures anciennes du Proche-Orient 9 (Paris: Cerf, 1977–), 1:145–235; J. Lindenberger, *Ancient Aramaic and Hebrew Letters*, SBLWAW 4 (Atlanta: Scholars Press, 1994), 99–110; P. K. McCarter Jr., *Ancient Inscriptions: Voices from the Biblical World* (Washington, D.C.: Biblical Archaeology Society, 1996), 119–20; D. Pardee et al., *Handbook of Ancient Hebrew Letters: A Study Edition*, SBLSBS 15 (Chico, Calif.: Scholars Press, 1982), 24–67; J. Renz, *Handbuch der althebräischen Epigraphik* (Darmstadt: Wissenschaftliche Buchgesellschaft, 1995), 1:40–43, 347–53; K. A. D. Smelik, *Writings from Ancient Israel: A Handbook of Historical and Religious Documents*, trans. G. I. Davies (Edinburgh: Clark, 1991), 101–15; and J. A. Soggin, *Introduction to the Old Testament*, 3d ed., trans. J. Bowden, OTL (London: SCM; Louisville: Westminster/John Knox, 1989), 558–59.

thereabouts.[42] Shortly after his accession to the throne, Seti received word that a coalition based in a nearby town called Hammat had attacked Beth-shan. The text of one monument declares that three brigades defeated the alliance and reaffirmed Egyptian control throughout Canaan within a single day. According to his later stela, *'apiru* renegades stirred up trouble in Mount Yarmuta—probably the Jarmuth of Issachar in the high plateau approximately seven miles north of Beth-shan (Josh. 21:29).

Rameses' Beth-shan stela describes in conventional terms his victories over the Asiatics (or people from Canaan). In his fifth regnal year, revolts against his rule took place from Kadesh on the Orontes in the north to Ashkelon in the south. His campaigns were able, however, to repair most of the damage, and he had resecured the region of Palestine by the time he erected the stela during year nine of his reign.

Daliyeh Papyri

Dates recorded on the papyri range from 375 or 365 B.C. to 335, that is, within the reigns of Persian emperors Artaxerxes II and III and Darius III.[43] The documents include loans, deeds, contracts, and, most frequently, slave sales, conveyances, or manumissions. According to their own information, the papyri were drawn up in the city of Samaria. In the wilderness cave near Wadi ed-Daliyeh, directly associated with those private papers, were the skeletal remains of some two hundred men, women, and children, who seem to have all died at the same time. This suggests that a large group of patrician families from Samaria died together as refugees soon after Alexander the Great arrived in 332.

Attestation in the papyri of several public officials' names permits a correct presentation of the Samarian ruling families, notably the descendants of Nehemiah's fifth-century nemesis Sanballat (Neh. 2; 4; 6). Judging from names in the slave transactions, we can conclude that the main body of the population was Yahwistic. Nonetheless, even Jewish slaves were sold for life, without stipulations concerning release—a direct violation of such regulations as Exodus 21:2 and Deuteronomy 15:12.

Deir 'Alla Texts

An earthquake shattered the eighth-century B.C. sanctuary inscription

---

42. Y. Aharoni et al., *Macmillan Bible Atlas*, 3d ed. (New York: Macmillan, 1993), 38–41; and McCarter, *Ancient Inscriptions*, 45–46.

43. F. M. Cross, "Daliyeh, Wadi ed-," *ABD*, 2:3–4; D. M. Gropp, "Samaria (Papyri)," *ABD*, 5:931–32; McCarter, *Ancient Inscriptions*, 122–25; Soggin, *Introduction*, 567; and J. Zsengellér, "Personal Names in the Wadi ed-Daliyeh Papyri," *ZAH* 9 (1996): 182–89.

found at Deir ʿAlla in Transjordan.[44] From the fragments the excavators could assemble two large groups or combinations, in addition to smaller groups and single pieces. The first interlocking combination of lime-plaster fragments identifies itself as the book of the seer Balaam, Beor's son. Gods visited him one night in a dream. The next day, while fasting and weeping, Balaam related his vision of that divine council meeting. (Note Ps. 82:1 for the motif of a divine assembly—also viewed by a seer in 1 Kings 22:19.) The council had decreed a terrible catastrophe, apparently involving plunging the planet into darkness and destroying all life on it.

The coming of the gods at night with a message that the prophet then reported in the morning reminds us of Balaam's summons in Numbers 22. There too he is presented as a non-Israelite prophet, whom the Hebrews encountered when they encamped merely twenty-five miles south of Tell Deir ʿAlla. Both the biblical and extrabiblical stories employ the divine epithet "Shaddai," which English translations commonly render "Almighty" (see, e.g., Num. 24:4, 16). The title "Shaddai," possibly meaning "one of the mountain," applied to the chief decision-making gods, probably because these ruling gods gathered on a mountain in Canaanite tradition much like the Olympians in Greek mythology. The patriarchs knew the Abrahamic deity as Shaddai prior to learning the name Yahweh (Exod. 6:3).

Horvat Uza Ostraca

Seventeen ostraca—all except one in Hebrew—were recovered in 1983 during the second season of excavation at the Horvat Uza stronghold.[45] A restored letter, whose language and script are Edomite, contains six lines of text. They seem to concern the distribution of an amount of foodstuff or else the repayment of a loan of grain. The salutation inquired into the addressee's health and blessed him by Qaus, the chief god of Edom.

This, the only known Edomite text of connected narrative or discourse, dates to the early sixth century B.C. Since Judah controlled Horvat Uza in the seventh century, the ostracon suggests that Edomites captured the fort shortly ahead of its conquest by Babylonia. Here is important evidence for the early stages of the Edomite incursion into Judah, a process that eventually led to the establishment there of a province called Idumea (an appellation derived from the term *Edom*).

---

44. H. J. Franken et al., "Deir ʿAlla, Tell," *ABD*, 2:129–30; McCarter, *Ancient Inscriptions*, 96–98; Smelik, *Writings*, 80–88; and Soggin, *Introduction*, 559.

45. I. Beit-Arieh, "ʿUza, Horvat," *ABD*, 6:772–74; Lindenberger, *Ancient Aramaic*, 117–18; and McCarter, *Ancient Inscriptions*, 99–100.

Ketef Hinnom Scrolls

Inside the tomb chambers of a cave on a rocky knoll overlooking Jerusalem's Hinnom Valley to the east, two small scrolls made of silver leaf were discovered in 1979.[46] About twenty lines had been scratched into the surface of both scrolls. These fine engravings belong to the end of the seventh century B.C. or to the start of the sixth. The rolled-up foil cylinders had presumably been worn around the neck on cords passed through the center holes as amulets.

Part of the text on each plaque matches closely an abridged form of the so-called Aaronid benediction in Numbers 6:24–26. The Bible instructed Israel's priests to bless the people with those words (vv. 22–23, 27). The plaques seem to be the earliest quotation of a scriptural passage anywhere in the inscriptional record to date. Conversely, the epigraph could be regarded as a forerunner of what ultimately reached its definitive shape in Numbers. Either way, no earlier evidence of the complete divine name "Yahweh" appears at Jerusalem in any inscription.

Khirbet el-Qôm Inscriptions

At Khirbet el-Qôm is one of the longest Hebrew tomb inscriptions yet discovered from the Old Testament period.[47] The epitaph dates to the second half of the eighth century B.C. The burial chamber's owner, Uriah, was pronounced blessed apparently because he had been delivered from his enemies by Yahweh's Asherah. Scripture likewise mentions this important goddess, although the term *Asherah* there most often designates a sacred tree or pole used in worship. Probably the ritual object known as Asherah had something to do with the deity known as Asherah. A number of goddesses from the region around ancient Israel were personifications of the cultic presence of leading gods, whose consorts they frequently were. We may surmise that Yahweh's Asherah was his availability and accessibility—the visible marker or concrete form of which was the wooden object—at a worship location. The Asherah of Yahweh was then personified, apotheosized, and viewed as his consort.

Unknown to scholars until 1994 was the so-called stonecutter's inscription from el-Qôm: "Blessed be your stonecutter! May he lay old

46. McCarter, *Ancient Inscriptions*, 121–22; E. Puech, "Palestinian Funerary Inscriptions," *ABD*, 5:127; Renz, *Handbuch*, 1:447–56; and Smelik, *Writings*, 160–62.

47. R. Deutsch et al., *Forty New Ancient West Semitic Inscriptions* (Tel Aviv: Archaeological Center Publication, 1994), 27–30; J. S. Holladay Jr. et al., "Kom, Khirbet el-," *ABD*, 4:98; Hestrin, *Inscriptions*, Eng. section, 3; McCarter, *Ancient Inscriptions*, 110–11; Renz, *Handbuch*, 1:199–211; and Smelik, *Writings*, 152–55.

people to rest in this!"[48] The apparently traditional expression wished that the stonecutter, who prepared sepulchers for occupation, could lay people to rest in their old age—not in their childhood or prime.

Kuntillet ʿAjrud Fragments

Archaeological digs in 1975–76 at Kuntillet ʿAjrud, presumably a cultic center, though possibly a caravanserai, yielded a few Hebrew language inscriptions that originated from the end of the ninth or beginning of the eighth century B.C.[49]

A two-line ink epigraph, which has fallen off a plaster wall, invoked Yahweh of Teman (or Yahweh of the southland). So did the greeting on one of two big pithoi—pottery storage vessels—that were found broken. The jar's succeeding blessing, "May he bless you and may he keep you," exhibits a striking parallel to the priestly benediction in Numbers 6:24. The other pithos called on Yahweh of Samaria. Evidently the Hebrew God had various manifestations under which he could be worshiped. Yahweh of Teman was the form revered locally at Kuntillet ʿAjrud, whereas Yahweh of Samaria was the form revered at Israel's capital. That compares with how today we can distinguish between Mary of Lourdes and Mary of Fatima yet not imply that there is more than the one Mary. Furthermore, both pithoi refer to Yahweh's Asherah (see "Khirbet el-Qôm Inscriptions" above).

Lachish Letters

The language of these inscribed potsherds at Lachish reflected the popular Hebrew spoken in Judah during the early sixth century B.C.[50] They belong to the final period of the country's survival, before the destruction of such cities as Lachish, Jerusalem, and Azekah (cf. Jer. 34:7) by the Babylonian army in 586. Although scholars long supposed the writings to date from that year, they more reasonably date from 589. The ostraca reveal freedom of Judahite travel both within and outside the kingdom, so that the Babylonians would seem not yet to have invaded. The wartime correspondence was presumably penned between Zedekiah's refusal to pay tribute and Nebuchadnezzar's arrival to inflict retribution.

---

48. McCarter, *Ancient Inscriptions*, 111–12.

49. Ibid., 106–9; Z. Meshel, "Kuntillet ʿAjrud," *ABD*, 4:106–7; Renz, *Handbuch*, 1:47–64; and Smelik, *Writings*, 155–60. See also Arnold's discussion, chap. 14 of the present volume.

50. R. A. Di Vito, "Lachish Letters," *ABD*, 4:126–28; Gibson, *Textbook*, 1:32–49; Lemaire, *Inscriptions*, 1:83–143; Lindenberger, *Ancient Aramaic*, 99–103, 110–16; McCarter, *Ancient Inscriptions*, 116–19; Pardee, *Handbook*, 67–114; W. H. Propp, "Lachish," *The Oxford Companion to the Bible*, ed. B. M. Metzger and M. D. Coogan (New York: Oxford University Press, 1993), 418; Renz, *Handbuch*, 1:405–38; Smelik, *Writings*, 116–31; Soggin, *Introduction*, 558; and J. Woodhead et al., "Lachish," *NBD*, 660–61.

An inferior (named only once, Hoshaiah) addressed the letters to a superior (named thrice, Jaush). The latter probably commanded the Lachish garrison itself, while Hoshaiah was in charge of an outpost under the jurisdiction of Jaush. Ostracon no. 3 reported on the activities of an expedition that compelled a contingent of Hoshaiah's troops to accompany it to Egypt. Judah is known to have been seeking Egyptian assistance around that time (e.g., Ezek. 17:15).

Moabite Stone

Among the ancient ruins at Dhiban (scriptural Dibon) lay a toppled black basalt stela bearing a thirty-four line inscription that was written in the language of Moab around 840 or 830 B.C.[51] Moabite King Mesha commissioned the stone's erection to extol his achievements: he had freed his country from the control of neighboring Israel and had undertaken—in part with Israelite slave labor—various building projects. The Bible also reports the conflict between Moab and Israel at that time (2 Kings 3).

In Mesha's account we find a pair of intriguing parallels with the Old Testament generally. First, just as Yahweh becomes angry with the people of Israel, forsakes them, humbles them by turning them over to their adversaries, and finally, after a change in the deity's attitude, saves them, so too does Chemosh with the people of Moab. Second, on the apparent instruction of his national god, Mesha implemented the "ban" and ritually massacred the vanquished from several towns in honor of Chemosh—much like the Hebrew holy war practice in honor of Yahweh.

Plain of Sharon Bowls

Five bronze bowls have come to light at the site of Eliachin, a modern settlement just south of Hadera.[52] The engravings (in Aramaic except for one in Phoenician) date to either the sixth or fifth century B.C., within the early Persian period. The vessels were offerings dedicated at the shrine of an interesting group of gods called Ashtars, whose cult appears to have flourished in the Sharon plain. Two of the bowls were donated in gratitude to the Ashtars for saving or sparing the giver's life.

King Mesha's Moabite Stone incorporated an enigmatic reference to the West Semitic god Ashtar. Half a millennium earlier the deity's name had surfaced as Ashtar in the mythological literature of the Syrian

---

51. J. A. Dearman et al., "Mesha Stele," *ABD*, 4:708–9; Gibson, *Textbook*, 1:71–83; Hestrin, *Inscriptions*, Eng. section, pp. 30–32; McCarter, *Ancient Inscriptions*, 90–92; Smelik, *Writings*, 29–50; Soggin, *Introduction*, 553–54; and J. A. Thompson, "Moabite Stone," *NBD*, 777.

52. Deutsch, *Forty*, 69–89; and McCarter, *Ancient Inscriptions*, 100–102.

coastal city of Ugarit. The feminine form corresponding to Ashtar is Ashtart or Astarte (the scriptural Ashtoreth), a well-known Phoenician/ Canaanite goddess. Her Mesopotamian equivalent is the goddess Ishtar.

Samaria Ostraca

Several delivery receipts for jars of quality wine and fine oil shipped to the palace in Samaria have been found.[53] Most show dates of the ninth, tenth, or fifteenth year of the reign of an unspecified Israelite king. The numbers fit best with the 770s B.C. under Jeroboam II, unless the large corpus should be split—part belonging to the 790s under Jeroboam's father, Joash, and part to the 770s.

The ostraca noted the place of origin of the merchandise and thus point to geographical locations for clan districts within the Manassite tribal area. The places lie in a cluster around the capital city at distances of less than twelve miles. Personal names formed with a Baal element occur adjacent to others formed with a Yahweh element. This might or might not suggest a mixed religious population. Saul's naming of his sons Ishbaal and Jonathan illustrates how the Hebrews could incorporate either Baal or Yahweh components in their names (2 Sam. 4:1, 4). Moreover, Hosea 2:16 implies possibly that until the middle or late eighth century a believer could acceptably call Yahweh "Baal."

Siloam Tunnel Inscription

Six lines of writing were once carved on a wall near the mouth of a tunnel that emptied into a Jerusalem reservoir.[54] The language is classical Hebrew, strongly reminiscent of standard prose in the Old Testament. The tunnel brought water from ancient Jerusalem's principal water source, the Gihon spring in the Kidron Valley, to the Pool of Siloam at the lower end of the Tyropoeon Valley and inside the walled city. The inscription describes the dramatic final phases in the tunnel's construction and celebrates the success of an engineering feat. Starting at opposite ends, two gangs dug underground toward each other along a roughly north-south line and met at midpoint.

53. Gibson, *Textbook*, 1:15–13; Hestrin, *Inscriptions*, Eng. section, 7; I. T. Kaufman, "Samaria Ostraca," *ABD*, 5:921–26; Lemaire, *Inscriptions*, 1:21–81; McCarter, *Ancient Inscriptions*, 103–4; Renz, *Handbuch*, 1:79–109; Smelik, *Writings*, 51–62; and Soggin, *Introduction*, 554–55.

54. R. B. Coote, "Siloam Inscription," *ABD*, 6:23–24; Gibson, *Textbook*, 1:21–23; J. A. Hackett et al., "Defusing Pseudo-Scholarship: The Siloam Inscription Ain't Hasmonean," *BAR* 23.2 (1997): 41–50, 68; Hestrin, *Inscriptions*, Eng. section, 40–41; McCarter, *Ancient Inscriptions*, 113–15; Renz, *Handbuch*, 1:178–89; J. Rogerson et al., "Was the Siloam Tunnel Built by Hezekiah?" *BA* 59 (1996): 138–49; Smelik, *Writings*, 64–71; Soggin, *Introduction*, 555; and D. J. Wiseman, "Siloam," *NBD*, 1101–3.

There can be little doubt that the initiating authority for the project was Judah's King Hezekiah and that the inscription was written shortly before 701 B.C. A recent, vigorous challenge against this consensus has been carefully refuted by a host of scholars. Hezekiah undertook the excavation effort presumably in order to prepare for an anticipated siege by Assyria's King Sennacherib (see 2 Chron. 32:2–4, 30; 2 Kings 20:20). Centuries afterward, Ecclesiasticus 48:17 recalled the achievement: "Hezekiah fortified his city, and brought water into its midst; he tunneled the rock with iron tools, and built cisterns for the water" (NRSV).

Tel Dan Stela

In 1993 and 1994 were found three pieces of basalt that constitute the shattered remnants of an inscribed monument.[55] We cannot reconstruct a continuous translation of the Aramaic stela, but enough has survived to give a general idea of its content. This expert carving from the mid-ninth century B.C. describes an Israelite incursion into the land of the protagonist, who at that point became king. He then managed to repel the invasion with the help of his god Hadad. The text refers to the Israelite and Judahite monarchs Joram and Ahaziah, respectively—and most significantly calls the dynasty of Judah the "house of David." Some scholars have denied that the three fragments belong together or even that they mention the house of David. Despite these disputes, evidence in support of both affirmative propositions seems fairly clear.

The Aramean person who left the stela at Dan was in all likelihood the Damascene ruler Hazael. The monument presumably alludes to the events recorded in 2 Kings 8:28–29. After Joram had received wounds in a battle against Hazael's troops at the Israelite outpost Ramoth-gilead on the Transjordanian plateau, the king of Israel traveled for convalescence to the town Jezreel at the foot of Mount Gilboa. Judah's King Ahaziah, who had fought alongside him against the Arameans, joined him there.

Tell Siran Bottle

Students dug at a heavily eroded archaeological spot on the campus of the University of Jordan, six miles northwest of Amman, in 1972.[56] The unearthed Iron Age materials included an inscribed metallic bottle that had been cast from a mixture of copper, lead, and tin. The container

---

55. F. H. Cryer, "King Hadad," *SJOT* 9 (1995): 223–35; McCarter, *Ancient Inscriptions*, 86–90; W. M. Schniedewind, "Tel Dan Stela: New Light on Aramaic and Jehu's Revolt," *BASOR* 302 (1996): 75–90; and T. L. Thompson, "Dissonance and Disconnections: Notes on the *bytdwd* and *hmlk.hdd* Fragments from Tel Dan," *SJOT* 9 (1995): 236–40.

56. A. Lemaire, "Epigraphy, Transjordanian," *ABD*, 2:561–62; McCarter, *Ancient Inscriptions*, 98–99; and Smelik, *Writings*, 90–91.

held vegetable substances, primarily wheat and barley grains, that had been sealed inside with a metal cap secured by a pin running the length of the bottle. On the exterior this little bronze vessel bears a complete and quite legible inscription dating to approximately 600 B.C. The chief value of the text lies in the data it gives about the Ammonite language and history. Yet the historical information is obscure. We do not know for certain whether one Amminadab out of the pair cited was the ruler that the Neo-Assyrian emperor Ashurbanipal encountered in the first half of the seventh century or whether both Amminadabs cited on the bottle were the aforementioned's descendants and namesakes in the second half of the century.

Yavneh-Yam Ostracon

This legal petition was penned nine miles south of Joppa during the final decades of the seventh century B.C.[57] The fortress where it was found seems to have furnished an office for a possibly royal governor who ruled the surrounding area as well as administered justice. A farm-hand sent an appeal to that district governor for restitution. On the grounds of failing to meet his daily quota of harvested grain, the plaintiff's garment had been confiscated by a supervisor named Hoshaiah. The reaper claimed he really did meet the quota—something to which his colaborers could testify. Consequently, he pleaded with the governor to force a return of the unjustly appropriated cloak. The document may have alluded to Exodus 22:26–27 (22:25–26 MT) and Deuteronomy 24:12–13, where creditors were obligated to give back before dusk a garment taken in pledge. Although Hoshaiah's action did not match such a situation precisely, he clearly contravened the spirit of God's law.

Egyptian Epigraphy

Amarna Letters

Tell el-Amarna is the modern name for the ancient site Akhetaten.[58] Amenhotep IV (later called Akhenaten) established Akhetaten as the capital of Egypt under him and his immediate successors. During the

---

57. Gibson, *Textbook*, 1:126–30; Hestrin, *Inscriptions*, Eng. section, 26; Lemaire, *Inscriptions*, 1:259–68; Lindenberger, *Ancient Aramaic*, 96–98; McCarter, *Ancient Inscriptions*, 116; Pardee, *Handbook*, 15–24; Renz, *Handbuch*, 1:315–29; Smelik, *Writings*, 93–100; and Soggin, *Introduction*, 556–58.

58. W. Helck, "Amarna-Briefe," *Lexikon der Ägyptologie*, ed. W. Helck and E. Otto (Wiesbaden: Harrassowitz, 1972), 1:173–74; McCarter, *Ancient Inscriptions*, 16; N. Naʾaman, "Amarna Letters," *ABD*, 1:174–81; W. H. Propp, "Amarna Letters," *Oxford Companion to the Bible*, 22; G. Rachet, *Dictionnaire de la civilisation égyptienne*, 75; and M. J. Selman, "Amarna," *NBD*, 28.

second third of the fourteenth century B.C., Akhenaten, along with Amenhotep III before him and Tutankhamun after him, carried on an extensive international correspondence. Some of the Amarna Letters were sent by the rulers of other great powers—Assyria, Babylonia, Hatti, Mitanni—who wrote to the Egyptian kings as peers. Most of the clay tablets, however, came from Egypt's vassals in Canaan and Syria. A few letters are actually copies of those dispatched by the pharaohs to their vassal rulers or to the monarchs of the more distant states. Because peculiarities of language in the correspondence sent to the Egyptian court often reflected the local speech of the sender's region, the Amarna Letters hold special interest for linguists studying the period. The lapses of Canaanite scribes in particular have taught us about the prehistory of the later Hebrew language, which was closely related to their native dialects.

The messages between equal sovereigns largely concerned the exchange of ambassadors and expensive gifts, but occasionally concerned the marriage of a foreign princess to a pharaoh. The Syro-Palestinian letters describe the vicissitudes of cities such as Gezer, Shechem, Hazor, Ashkelon, Gaza, Lachish, Jerusalem, Rehob, Megiddo, Taanach, and Acco in the pre-Israelite era. These messages bespeak a time of unrest, intrigue, and intercity strife. For instance, Labayu of Shechem and his sons formed a strong coalition to expand their territory in the central hills. Biridiya of Megiddo, supported by Egyptian authorities, formed a countercoalition and brought the Shechemite offensive to an end. Meanwhile, Abdiheba of Jerusalem had "warned" the pharaoh that tribute being sent to Egypt would probably not arrive due to an ambush planned by Labayu and by Milkilu of Gezer. This complaint may have been a ruse, though, for in another letter Shuwardata of Hebron characterized Abdiheba as a rogue.

Book of the Dead

The Book of the Dead is an elaborate compilation of magical spells designed to bring about a dead person's resurrection and to provide safety from dangers in the afterlife.[59] The compilation reflects ritual acts performed during and following mummification and burial. Usually inscribed on papyrus scrolls, the written spells were buried with the de-

---

59. J. Assmann, "Survey of Egyptian Literature," *ABD*, 2:384–85; M. Heerma van Voss, "Totenbuch," in *Lexikon der Ägyptologie*, 6:641–43; C. Lalouette, *Textes sacrés et textes profanes de l'ancienne Égypte*, Connaissance de l'Orient 54, 63 ([Paris]: Gallimard, 1984), 1:270–76; M. Lichtheim, *Ancient Egyptian Literature: A Book of Readings*, 3 vols. (Berkeley: University of California Press, 1973–80), 2:117–32; McCarter, *Ancient Inscriptions*, 59–60; and G. Rachet, *Dictionnaire de la civilisation égyptienne*, References Larousse: Histoire (Paris: Larousse, 1992), 167.

ceased. Formulas abounded for the dead to receive gifts of drink, food, and fresh air, and to defend against crocodiles and monsters that populated the netherworld.

At the beginning of the New Kingdom, the Book of the Dead was still in process of formation. Drawing heavily at first on traditional materials, it was the direct successor of the Middle Kingdom's Coffin Texts, which in turn descended from the Old Kingdom's Pyramid Texts. The collection achieved its definitive, more strictly canonized shape in the Saite period (Twenty-sixth Dynasty, 664–525 B.C.), when all of its roughly two hundred spells were put into a set sequence of "chapters." Anybody could purchase a mass-produced copy, the prospective owner's name needing merely to be inserted into the ready-made scroll.

The majority of ancient Egyptians appear to have clung to the hope of a bodily afterlife and to a reliance on magic as the means to achieve it. Yet the Book of the Dead required the deceased person, upon reaching the Hall of the Two Truths, to declare innocence before Osiris and other assembled deities. In a so-called Negative Confession, the departed human being had to deliver a long and conventional recitation of sins not committed in order to pass the judgment of the gods.

Bubastite Portal

This hieroglyphic inscription primarily lists places Shoshenq I (945–924 B.C.) conquered in Palestine.[60] Most scholars believe the campaign concerns what 1 Kings 14:25–26 and 2 Chronicles 12:2–9 mention as an invasion by "Shishak." The Bible actually speaks about an invasion of only the fortified cities of Judah. Indeed, judging from the Bubastite Portal list, Jerusalem seems to have been Shoshenq's main initial target. On the way his army marched through Gaza to Gezer and then Aijalon and Gibeon—where presumably King Rehoboam of Judah paid the heavy tribute to Shishak. This act of submission evidently persuaded the pharaoh to spare the southern kingdom and turn northward. Many prominent cities of Jeroboam I's kingdom of Israel were enumerated on the doorway, while few principal towns of Judah were. We are left to wonder why Shoshenq so readily attacked his former protégé Jeroboam, who had once fled for Egypt subsequent to leading an abortive rebellion against Solomon.

Elephantine Papyri

During the fifth century B.C., the island of Elephantine in the Nile River housed a Jewish military colony in the service of the Persian occupation

60. Aharoni, *Macmillan Bible Atlas*, 91–92; and McCarter, *Ancient Inscriptions*, 56–57.

to guard against incursions from the south.[61] This colony's archives comprise for the most part Aramaic contracts and letters, which shed important light on its practices and customs.

The so-called Passover papyrus from a certain Hananiah instructed the colony's leader, Jedaniah, on the precise observance of Passover or Unleavened Bread. (Perhaps we should identify Hananiah with Hanani, brother of the scriptural Nehemiah.) But we can only guess whether the letter may have been sent, for instance, to establish a fixed date for Unleavened Bread or to bring Elephantine's Passover ceremonies into line with Jerusalem's. The reason cannot have been to introduce the Passover celebration to Elephantine, since several ostraca dating half a century earlier mentioned that festival.

At Elephantine, members of the colony had built a temple in honor of Yahu (an abbreviated form of Yahweh) under the Egyptian pharaohs, before the Persian conqueror Cambyses entered Egypt in 525. This temple was destroyed around 410. One of the papyrus letters addressed the governor of Judea (with a copy to the sons of the governor of Samaria) for permission to rebuild the temple and reinstitute sacrifice.

Execration Texts

The Egyptian state practiced the formal cursing of people who were deemed undesirable and who lay outside direct Egyptian control.[62] The rite involved either symbolizing the enemy in a clay, stone, or wood representation (whether inscribed or uninscribed) or else writing the enemy's name on a pottery vessel. A curse formula was then pronounced and the object deliberately smashed. A major collection of bowls dates from the middle or end of the Twelfth Dynasty (1991–1783 B.C.) under Senusert III or Amenemhet III and IV. A significant lot of figurines dates about a generation or two after the bowls, that is, to the end of the Twelfth Dynasty or the beginning of the Thirteenth (1783–ca. 1640).

Two or three personal names are often associated with the same place-name on the bowls. By contrast the figurines almost invariably record one chieftain per place. It has been argued that the bowls indicate a societal stage when each individual district was partitioned among a number of clan leaders in a nonsettled condition, while the figurines reveal a setting when each individual town was paired with a sin-

---

61. Lindenberger, *Ancient Aramaic*, 53–70; McCarter, *Ancient Inscriptions*, 125–27; B. Porten, "Elephantine Papyri," *ABD*, 2:445–55; and Soggin, *Introduction*, 564–67.

62. McCarter, *Ancient Inscriptions*, 42–43; and D. B. Redford, "Execration and Execration Texts," *ABD*, 2:681–82.

gle prince in a situation of increasing urbanization. This could reflect a Middle Bronze Age transition in Canaan and Syria from a population largely leading a nomadic existence or living in unwalled villages to a population beginning to cluster in well-defined cities.

Merenptah Stela

In 1220 B.C. an army of Libyans marched into the Delta of Egypt from the western desert.[63] The Egyptian pharaoh Merenptah attacked and defeated the foe and drove them out of his country. To commemorate this accomplishment he commissioned the composition of a victory poem. The hieroglyphic text's final pair of lines describe what appears to have been a separate battle against western Asian enemies, including Israel. The reference to Israel is the only occurrence of the name in Egyptian literature and is the earliest known mention from any ancient Near Eastern source. "Israel" here precedes a compound determinative that depicts a foreign people. (Determinatives were added to words to indicate the class or category to which they belonged.) Such a writing suggests that in the late thirteenth century Israel had developed a specific identity as a people but might not as yet have become a fixed political entity or state.

Sea Peoples Inscriptions

The group of persons designated "Sea Peoples" by modern historians seems to have come originally from the Aegean Islands as well as Anatolia.[64] Those of this group lived the life of pirates, raiding and plundering coastal towns, or of mercenaries, serving in the region's armed conflicts. Two separate records refer to an encounter between Rameses III and the Sea Peoples during the first quarter of the twelfth century B.C. The account of his eighth regnal year described the advance toward his realm of a Sea People alliance—a confederation of Philistines, Tjeker, Shekelesh, Denyen, and Weshesh. He boasted of halting and defeating the coalition and repelling it away from the Egyptian borders. The second record was found in a historical epilogue to a document that was composed shortly after Rameses' death to recount his benefactions and achievements. A portion of this papyrus recites his victory over the Sea Peoples: Denyen, Tjeker, Philistines, Sherden, and Weshesh.

63. Lichtheim, *Ancient Egyptian Literature*, 2:73–78; and McCarter, *Ancient Inscriptions*, 48–50.
64. McCarter, *Ancient Inscriptions*, 53–54; and R. Stadelmann, "Seevölker," *Lexikon der Ägyptologie*, 5:814–22.

Shabaka Stone

This stone was inscribed in approximately 710 B.C. at the behest of Egypt's King Shabaka from the Twenty-fifth or Kushite Dynasty.[65] An introductory passage alleges that Shabaka had the work copied from a much earlier manuscript, which was originally written on some perishable material like leather, papyrus, or wood, and which consequently was now "worm-eaten." Egyptologists divide over whether to date the composition as authentic to the Old Kingdom or to the Twenty-fifth Dynasty.

In either case, the text promotes the new or renewed status of Memphis as the Egyptian capital city and the supremacy of its patron deity Ptah as the cosmic creator. Ptah is given priority over the sun god Re, who created the world according to previous traditions. Although ancient Egypt usually described creation in physical terms—especially on the model of sexual procreation—Ptah here creates alone and through his thoughts and words. Scholars have compared the method with that ascribed to the God of Israel in Genesis 1.

Tale of Two Brothers

The papyrus containing this tale was written during the late Nineteenth Dynasty (1307–1196 B.C.), although at least the kernel of the story is older by a millennium.[66] It bears remarkable resemblance to the biblical episode of Joseph and Potiphar's wife in Genesis 39. The first half of the story finds Bata living within the household of his elder brother Anubis. One day the young Bata, a herder, helped Anubis, a farmer, to sow the latter's fields. When Anubis sent Bata back home to retrieve more seed, the former's wife tried in vain to seduce Bata. Feeling spurned, she slandered him that evening before her husband. Anubis became enraged and Bata was forced to flee. Very soon, however, the truth came out, and the brothers were reconciled. In the second part of the story the pharaoh made Bata crown prince of all Egypt.

---

65. Lalouette, *Textes*, 225–30; Lichtheim, *Ancient Egyptian Literature*, 1:51–57, 3:5; McCarter, *Ancient Inscriptions*, 58–59; and F. T. Miosi, "Memphite Theology," *ABD*, 4:691–92.

66. Assmann, *ABD*, 2:381; Lalouette, *Textes*, 2161–72; Lichtheim, *Ancient Egyptian Literature*, 2:203–11; and McCarter, *Ancient Inscriptions*, 48.

3

Archaeological Light
on the Old Testament

Mark W. Chavalas and Murray R. Adamthwaite

Syro-Mesopotamia

The past generation of archaeological research in Syria and Iraq (ancient Syro-Mesopotamia) has offered a great deal of background information for furthering our knowledge of Old Testament history, religion, and culture.

With the onset of the Gulf War, however, archaeological research in Iraq was interrupted: sites were bombed, museums looted, thousands of artifacts plundered, and clandestine digs abounded. Moreover, the social conditions in Iraq today do not allow for the resumption of work any time soon. This has caused scholars of ancient Iraq either to leave for more profitable areas to work (e.g., Turkey, Cyprus, or Syria) or to pause and reflect on the past years of archaeological research in Iraq. In the years immediately preceding the war, there had been a shift in research emphasis in Iraq. While many long-term projects continued, others were either begun or resumed at Warka, Abu Salabikh, Isin, Larsa, Nineveh, Nimrud, Kar Tukulti-Ninurta, Kish, Jemdet Nasr, and Nippur.[1] Because of the impending dam projects in Iraq, the State Antiquities Organization mounted a massive campaign of rescue opera-

---

The section on Syro-Mesopotamia was written by Mark W. Chavalas; that on Egypt and Palestine was written by Murray R. Adamthwaite.

1. For a general survey, see M.-T. Barrelet, ed., *L'Archéologie de l'Iraq du début de l'époque Néolithique à 333 avant notre ère: Perspectives et limites de l'interpretation anthropologique des documents* (Paris: Éditions du Centre National de la Recherche Scientifique, 1980).

tions in various regions of Iraq, including the Hamrin basin, the Haditha Dam project, and the Eski Mosul Dam region (now called the Saddam Dam Salvage Project).[2]

The situation in Syria has been vastly different. Compared to Iraq, Syria had not been the recipient of much archaeological investigation until the past generation. There are now, however, over sixty archaeological expeditions to Syria, most of which are concerned with periods that shed light on the Old Testament.[3]

Like Iraq, the last generation of research in Syria has witnessed numerous salvage projects in areas threatened by modern dam construction and other development projects, as well as numerous major projects that have revolutionized our understanding of the region. The Tishreen Dam project has probed many sites, collected environmental information, and has chosen some specific sites in which to do salvage operations. Since over two dozen sites in the Khabur basin in northern Syria are imperiled by dams, the Syrian government has assembled an international team to study the environmental setting of the Khabur plains.

Although they are separate because of modern political affiliations, I will henceforth combine the treatment of the archaeological research of Syria and Iraq. This survey is not exhaustive but emphasizes archaeological work of particular importance and relevance to developing a greater understanding of the background of the biblical world. Each chronological period will be treated separately, beginning with the Neolithic period and ending with the Iron Age.

Neolithic Period (ca. 8000–4000 B.C.)

Archaeological research in the past generation has shown that civilization in the early Neolithic period in the Near East (before the Halaf period, ca. 5200 B.C.) was far more widespread than previously thought. Not only did it flourish in the Levant, but from a series of chance discoveries and salvage operations there is now massive evidence of a widespread and uniform material culture (in terms of ceramics and lithics) from the Mediterranean coast to eastern Syria and northern Iraq. A Soviet team has investigated the Sinjar area (about 60 km. north of Mosul in northern Iraq), primarily at the site of Maghzaliyah, finding obsidian blades and other cultural material not similar to any else

2. See *Researches on the Antiquities of Saddam Dam Basin Project and Other Researches* (Baghdad: State Organization of Antiquities and Heritage, 1986); and M. Roaf, "A Report on the Work of the British Archaeological Expedition in the Eski Mosul Dam Salvage Project," *Sumer* 39 (1980): 68–87.

3. See H. Weiss, "Archaeology in Syria," *AJA* 95 (1991): 683–740; *AJA* 98 (1994): 101–58; and *AJA* 101 (1997): 97–149.

found in Iraq.[4] But this is not an isolated case, since there have been a large number of international teams in the Eski Mosul Dam Project region, finding material similar to that of the Natufian period in the southern Levant.[5] Many of the newly excavated sites in the Sinjar region in particular and in northern Iraq in general have shown new evidence for the beginning of agriculture and the transition to sedentary life. This has also been evidenced at the sites of Umm Dabagiyah and Tell es-Sawwan.[6] Syria likewise was a significant cultural force in the prehistoric Neolithic period with major centers of occupation in the Khabur and Balikh regions, both of which have been systematically surveyed, showing evidence of Neolithic levels at Tell Abu Hureyra, Tell Mureybit, and Tell Aswad, among others.[7] The Khabur basin project in particular has found innovations in agricultural technology, from the development of new cereals and livestock to the use of animal-drawn plows and new storage techniques.

The Halaf period (ca. 5200–4800 B.C.) has also been better understood because of the last generation of work in Syro-Mesopotamia. Because of the work at the mounds of Yarim Tepe, we can now perceive what appears to be a sudden spread of Halaf material culture into northern Syria, Iraq, and southern Turkey, much like that of the preceding periods.[8] A recent survey in the upper Balikh Valley in Syria has exposed a number of small Halaf period sites (but only a few larger permanent settlements, e.g., Tell Sabi Abyad), which have helped further our understanding of the origins of the Halaf culture.[9] Once thought to have originated in the later Ubaid period, seals—the earliest in Syria—have been

4. N. Bader, *Earliest Cultivators in Northern Mesoptamia: The Investigations of Soviet Archeological Expedition in Iraq at Settlements Tell Magzaliya, Tell Sotto, Kültepe* (Moscow: Nauka, 1989).

5. J. Huot et al., eds., *Préhistoire de la Mésopotamie: La Mésopotamie préhistorique et l'exploration recente du Djebel Hamrin* (Paris: Éditions recherche sur les civilisations, 1987); and J. Oates, "The Background and Development of Early Farming Communities in Mesopotamia and the Zagros," *Proceedings of the Prehistoric Society* 39 (1973): 147–81.

6. D. Kirkbride, "Umm Dabagiyah," in *Fifty Years of Mesopotamian Discovery,* ed. J. Curtis (London: British School of Archaeology in Iraq, 1982), 11–21. C. Breniquet, "Tell es-Sawwan 1988–1989: Comte rendu des fouilles menées par la DAFIQ," *Orient Express* 1.1 (1991): 7–8.

7. For a general description of the prehistoric period in Syria, see A. Moore, "The Prehistory of Syria," *BASOR* 270 (1988): 3–12.

8. N. Merpert and R. Munachev, "The Earliest Levels at Yarim Tepe I and Yarim Tepe II in Northern Iraq," *Iraq* 49 (1987): 1–37. Arpachiyah in northern Iraq was also excavated by I. Hijara; see idem et al., "Arpachiyah 1976," *Iraq* 42 (1980): 131–54. See also N. Yoffee and J. J. Clark, eds., *Early Stages in the Evolution of Mesopotamian Civilization: Soviet Excavations in Northern Iraq* (Tucson: University of Arizona Press, 1993).

9. P. Akkermans, *Excavations at Tell Sabi Abyad* (Oxford: British Archaeological Reports, 1989).

found at Sabi Abyad. A number of small sites (such as Khirbet Garsour) have also been studied in the north Jezira in Iraq.[10] The Halaf cultures must have employed methods of administration and agriculture that did not include many large settlements.[11] Theories now abound that the Halaf period was not an intrusion but an integral part of the Near East.

The southern portion of Iraq was until recently considered a latecomer to sedentary life, as no permanent settlements were known before the Ubaid period (ca. 5000 B.C.) at Eridu. But research on village sites such as Tell el-ʿOuelli (about 3 km. from Larsa) has pushed back the origins of permanent settlements in the south. According to the excavators, this small site exhibited an apparently egalitarian society and little foreign trade.[12] ʿOuelli displays fully developed agriculture and irrigation techniques without local antecedents. Furthermore, the water table at ʿOuelli did not allow the excavators to uncover the earliest levels of the site. The work at ʿOuelli shows that the succeeding Ubaid period did not exist without precedent but was a logical continuation of this earlier material culture. We now know that the Ubaid culture of southern Iraq was the first to expand into the north and into the Syrian Euphrates region.[13] Various Syrian sites such as Tell Brak, Tell Leilan, Tell Hammam al-Turkman, Zaidan, Carchemish, Samsat, a number of the mounds on the plain of Antioch, and Hama all have Ubaid material remains. In fact, an entire ceramic sequence from the Halaf to Ubaid periods can be seen in Syria from Halula.[14]

Uruk Period (ca. 4000–3000 B.C.)

Massive urbanization began in the Uruk period in southern Iraq. Recent archaeological excavations and surveys in Syria and northern Iraq (and as far away as Turkey) have given us a chance to explore a number of questions about the Uruk expansion and colonization into outlying areas.[15] Since lower Mesopotamia lacked the natural resources to sus-

10. T. Wilkinson, "The Development of Settlement in North Jezira between the Seventh and First Millennia B.C.," *Iraq* 52 (1990): 49–62.

11. S. Campbell, "The Halaf Period in Iraq: Old Sites and New," *BA* 55 (1992): 182–87.

12. J. Huot et al., "Ubadian Village of Lower Mesopotamia: Permanence and Evolution from Ubaid 0 to Ubaid 4 as Seen from Tell el Oueilli," in *Upon This Foundation: The Ubaid Reconsidered*, ed. E. Henrickson and I. Thuesen (Copenhagen: Museum Tusculanum Press, 1989), 19–42; and J. Huot, "The First Farmers at Oueilli," *BA* 55 (1992): 188–95.

13. J. Oates, "Ubaid Mesopotamia Reconsidered," in *The Hilly Flanks and Beyond: Essays in the Prehistory of Southwestern Asia Presented to Robert J. Braidwood*, ed. T. C. Young et al. (Chicago: University of Chicago Press, 1984), 251–81; and I. Thuesen, "Diffusion of Ubaid Pottery into Western Asia," in *Upon This Foundation*, 419–40.

14. M. Molist in H. Weiss, *AJA* 98 (1994): 105–6.

15. See G. Algaze, *The Uruk World System: The Dynamics of Expansion of Early Mesopotamian Civilization* (Chicago: University of Chicago Press, 1993).

tain its newly formed complex social system, it has been posited that the inhabitants had to import them from the periphery. Recent excavations show a loosely integrated supraregional interaction system using an informal mode of imperial domination. This was accomplished by the establishment of a network of strategically located enclaves and garrisons. The Uruk "states" appear to have had direct control of the Susiana plain and Upper Tigris, and intensified trade contacts in other areas. It has also been postulated that there may have been periodic military expeditions against areas resistant to trade.[16] In the north only a small number of urban-sized enclaves were found, surrounded by a cluster of dependent villages. The presence of urbanized sites with an Uruk assemblage represents not a break in the cultural sequence but a select infringement into the environment of the indigenous material cultures. The enclaves are found along the Euphrates (Tell Habuba Kabira, Jebel Aruda, Carchemish, and Samsat), the Khabur (Tell Brak), and Nineveh along the Tigris.[17] These settlements were large and heavily fortified. Their locations suggest that the Uruk polities desired to facilitate downstream commerce. Smaller stations also existed along the waterways and were links between large urban enclaves. Although many of the enclaves were fortified, there does not appear to be evidence of an attempt to control the hinterland. Rather, a take-over of strategic locations, tapping into preexisting trade networks, causes some to call this an informal empire.[18]

This trading relationship came to an abrupt halt in the succeeding Jemdet Nasr period (ca. 3000 B.C.) but had a profound impact on the sociopolitical and economic evolution of the indigenous cultures in Syria in particular. There was evidence of institutional change, with the copying of Uruk architecture, artifacts, ceramics, and sealing practices at many sites in the outlying areas. The Uruk expansion may have acted as a catalyst to foster growth to complexity and independent sociopolitical systems across northern Iraq and Syria.

Early Bronze (3000–2100 B.C.)

The Early Bronze Age represents the rise of city-states in the southern part of Iraq, or Sumer. Although there has been ongoing work at Abu Salabikh, and a reconsideration of work at Fara (ancient Shurrupak)

---

16. M. Larsen, "The Tradition of Empire in Mesopotamia," in *Power and Propaganda: A Symposium on Empires,* ed. M. Larsen (Copenhagen: Akademisk Forlag, 1979), 97.

17. See D. Sürenhagen, "The Dry Farming Belt: The Uruk Period and Subsequent Developments," in *The Origins of Cities in Dry-Farming Syria and Mesopotamia in the Third Millennium B.C.,* ed. H. Weiss (Guilford: Four Quarters, 1986), 7–44.

18. G. Algaze, "The Uruk Expansion: Cross-Cultural Expansion in Early Mesopotamian Civilization," *Current Anthropology* 30 (1989): 571–608.

and Kish,[19] the recent large-scale excavations at al-Hiba (ancient Lagash) have arguably helped the most to shed light on the Early Dynastic
(or Early Bronze) period of Mesopotamia (ca. 2900–2300 B.C.). One interesting feature there is the Ibgal temple, which has an oval exterior,
showing that the oval building type found at Khafaje was not as unusual as once thought.[20] The earliest brewery yet found was at Lagash,
dating to about 2500 B.C. Archaeological research has shown that much
of the city of Lagash was abandoned in the late Early Dynastic period,
only to be rebuilt by Gudea in the twenty-second century B.C.

In the Early Bronze Age, the indigenous cultures in northern Iraq
and Syria became more powerful, and southern Mesopotamian inter-
ference did not occur again for at least five hundred years. Whereas the
Uruk culture was able to penetrate the area relatively easily, the Sumerian and Sargonic kings were required to exercise force to control local
rulers and walled towns,[21] showing that the south was no longer unique
in its incipient urbanism.[22] A new type of settlement in dry-farming regions began to foster a new relationship with southern Mesopotamia.
Both the Khabur region (Tell Hamoukar, Tell Leilan, Tell Mozan, Tell
Brak, and Tell Chuera) and the plains of Aleppo in coastal Syria (Byb-
los, Homs, Ebla, and Qatna on the Euphrates) permitted the extensive
cultivation of wheat and barley without major irrigation, relying instead on dry farming and extensive raising of sheep and goat herds.[23]
Moreover, Akkadian period remains have been found in the Hamrin
basin in northern Iraq at several sites.[24] The political and economic organization of this region in the first half of the millennium is presently
unknown, but probably revolved around small towns, without any central control.[25]

It is not clear whether these newly created walled towns were initiated by the southerners or were autonomous.[26] One of these was Tell

19. J. N. Postgate, *Abu Salabikh Excavations*, vol. 1, *The West Mound Surface Clear-
ance* (London: British School of Archaeology in Iraq, 1983); H. P. Martin, *Fara: A Reconstruction of the Ancient City of Shuruppak* (Birmingham: Chris Martin, 1988); P. R. S.
Moorey, *Kish Excavations, 1923–1933* (Oxford: Clarendon, 1978).

20. D. Hansen, "Royal Building Activity at Sumerian Lagash in the Early Dynastic Period," *BA* 55 (1992): 206–12.

21. Algaze, "The Uruk Expansion," *Current Anthropology* 30 (1989): 601.

22. See I. Gelb, "Mari and the Kish Civilization," in *Mari in Retrospect*, ed. G. Young
(Winona Lake, Ind.: Eisenbrauns, 1992), 122.

23. H. Weiss, "Introduction: The Origins of Cities in Dry-Farming Syria and Mesopotamia in the Third Millennium B.C.," in *Origins of Cities*, 1–6.

24. D. Hansen, "A Reevaluation of the Akkad Period in the Diyala Region on the Basis
of Excavations from Nippur and in the Hamrin," *AJA* 86 (1982): 531–38.

25. H. Weiss, "Tell Leilan and Shubat Enlil," *MARI* 4 (1985): 269.

26. H. Weiss in *Origins of Cities*, 2.

Mardikh (ancient Ebla) in northwest Syria, the only site in that region that showed signs of sophistication in urbanization equal to any contemporary site in the south.[27] The city displayed cultural autonomy but historical continuity from earlier periods; it also had numerous similarities with Sumer, including the employment of the cuneiform script.

Like Ebla, Tell Hariri (ancient Mari) on the Euphrates exhibited notable cultural independence from the Sumerian south. Recent excavations have shown that the city may have been founded either at the end of the Early Dynastic I or at the beginning of the Early Dynastic II period.[28] The excavators may have located a dike in the hills south of the mound, a branching canal that traversed the city, and a number of canal feeders, facilitating the production of wheat. The city had a large wall, three rebuildings of the Ishtar temple, and a large Sargonic palace. Graves reminiscent of the Ur III period tombs have been uncovered in a small structure of the same period (ca. 2100 B.C.).

North of Mari on the Euphrates River is the site of Tell Ashara (ancient Terqa), which had a massive defensive system rivaling any other site of this period.[29] Further north in the Middle Euphrates region there is also evidence of occupation in the late third millennium B.C. at Selenkahiye and Tell Hadidi.[30] Still further north, the Tishreen Dam salvage project just south of Carchemish on the Euphrates near the Turkish border has revealed occupation in that area, showing an increase in the number of settlements in the second half of the third millennium B.C., notably Tell es-Sweyhat.[31]

Much has also been learned from investigations in the Syrian Khabur region about the Hurrians, a major ethnic group firmly rooted in the Mesopotamian tradition.[32] One of these Hurrian sites was Tell

27. General works concerning Ebla include P. Matthiae, *Ebla: An Empire Rediscovered*, trans. C. Holme (Garden City, N.Y.: Doubleday, 1981); G. Pettinato, *The Archives of Ebla: An Empire Rediscovered in Clay* (Garden City, N.Y.: Doubleday, 1981); idem, *Ebla: A New Look at History*, trans. C. F. Richardson (Baltimore: Johns Hopkins University Press, 1991).

28. The most recent excavation reports can be found in *MARI* 1–6 (1982–90), and J. Margueron in Weiss, *AJA* 98 (1994): 130–31.

29. G. Buccellati et al., *Terqa Preliminary Reports 10: Introduction and the Stratigraphic Record* (Malibu: Undena, 1979), 42–83.

30. M. van Loon, "1974 and 1975 Preliminary Reports of the Excavations at Selenkahiye near Meskene, Syria," in *Archeological Reports from the Tabqa Dam Project—Euphrates Valley, Syria*, ed. D. N. Freedman, 44 (Cambridge: ASOR, 1979), 97–113; R. Dornemann, "Tell Hadidi: A Millennium of Bronze Age City Occupation," in ibid., 113–51; idem, "Tell Hadidi: One Bronze Age Site among Many in the Tabqa Dam Salvage Area," *BASOR* 270 (1988): 13–42.

31. T. McClellan et al. in H. Weiss, *AJA* 95 (1991): 700–707; on Tell es-Sweyhat see T. McClellan and R. Zettler in H. Weiss, *AJA* 98 (1994): 139–42.

32. See G. Wilhelm, *The Hurrians*, trans. J. Barnes (Warminster: Aris & Phillips, 1989).

Chuera, which had similarities with the Sumerian south.[33] It showed evidence of the large stone architecture of this period, as well as a well-defined upper and lower citadel, typical of many of the northern Syrian centers. Another large site excavated in this region is Tell Mozan (ancient Urkesh),[34] which has a city wall and one of the largest bent-axis temple structures in this period, located on the high mound. The structure has walls 1.6 meters thick, in addition to a statue of a lion in a building interpreted as a cella. Tell Brak in this period had a number of large Akkadian period buildings and a unique ceramic sequence from the Uruk to Akkadian periods.[35] Lastly, the Middle Khabur Drainage Project has investigated the social and economic organization of small rural communities in this period, particularly the site of Raqaʾi.[36]

Near the border of Iraq on the Khabur plains of Syria is Tell Leilan.[37] There, the lower town shows evidence of third- and second-millennium B.C. settlements with a number of domestic units, drain-filled alleys, and planned streets.[38] The lower town appears to have been built about 2600–2400 B.C., and the excavators have speculated that a profound social transformation occurred soon after, changing Tell Leilan into a class-based society. The excavators have noticed that many walled cities of the type at Tell Leilan were constructed at this time.[39] It also has been speculated that these cities were not formed through intimate contact with the southern centralized states (i.e., Sargonic Akkad), but were the result of an indigenous and autonomous process. The urbanization in this area may have caused the southern states to move into the area during the Sargonic period.[40] Many of these walled towns were in fact larger than their southern counterparts.

33. W. Orthmann, "The Origin of Tell Chuera," in *The Origins of Cities*, 69.

34. G. Buccellati and M. Kelly-Buccellati, *Mozan 1: The Soundings of the First Two Seasons* (Malibu: Undena, 1988); idem, "Urkesh: The First Hurrian Capital," *BA* 60 (1997): 77–96.

35. D. Oates and J. Oates, "Akkadian Buildings at Tell Brak," *Iraq* 51 (1989): 193–211; idem, "Excavations at Tell Brak, 1990–1991," *Iraq* 53 (1991): 127–46.

36. H. Curvers and G. Schwartz, "Excavations at Tell al-Raqaʾi: A Small Rural Site of Early Northern Mesopotamia," *AJA* 94 (1990): 3–23.

37. H. Weiss, "Tell Leilan on the Habur Plains of Syria," *BA* 48 (1985): 5–35; and H. Weiss et al., "1985 Excavations at Tell Leilan, Syria," *AJA* 94 (1990): 529–82.

38. H. Weiss, "Tell Leilan 1989: New Data for Mid-Third Millennium Urbanization and State Formation," *MDOG* 122 (1990): 193–218.

39. H. Weiss, "The Origins of Tell Leilan and the Conquest of Space in Third Millennium Mesopotamia," in *Origins of Cities*, 83.

40. H. Weiss, "Third Millennium Urbanization: A Perspective from Tell Leilan," in *Tall al-Ḥamīdīya*, ed. S. Eichler et al., OBO Series Archaeologica 4.6 (Freiburg: Universitätsverlag, 1990), 2:163.

Middle Bronze (2100–1600 B.C.)

Although excavations continued at the sites of Isin, Larsa, and Tell ed-Der,[41] a number of moderately sized sites from the Middle Bronze Age (ca. 2100–1600 B.C.) in both Syria and Iraq have been excavated in the past generation, and have increased our overall understanding of the putative period of the biblical patriarchs. One of these is Mashkan-Shapir in the northernmost part of the confluence of the Tigris and Euphrates. The city was a major trade center and the residence of the last Larsa kings. Though its heyday was brief, whole building plans have been uncovered that have helped us to understand regional urbanism and town planning.[42]

Khirbit ed-Diniye (ancient Haradum, 90 km. southeast of Mari, situated on the Iraqi portion of the Middle Euphrates) was a new river town, apparently founded in the eighteenth century B.C. (after the fall of Mari) as a frontier province of Babylon and lasting for over a century. The Délégation Archéologique Française en Iraq performed a vast series of salvage projects at the site for six seasons in the 1980s.[43] Although the site of Haradum is very small, it had town wall fortifications. It was a planned urban center, exhibiting a very regular town layout, with straight streets connecting at right angles. The regularity of the city plan is a rare discovery in Syro-Mesopotamia, permitting the student a chance to view a very elaborate urban plan.

In this period (named the Old Syrian period in Syria) Syria continued to have close cultural relations with the Mesopotamian south. Excavations were made at a number of major political centers such as Shubat-Enlil (Tell Leilan),[44] a major Assyrian center at this time, ruled by Shamshi-Adad I (1814–1781 B.C.). It is evident that during his reign the upper Khabur triangle emerged for the first time as a dominant power. The area had not previously been integrated into a unified political system. Soon after his reign, however, the area reverted back to

---

41. E.g., B. Hrouda, ed., *Isin-Išān Baḥrīyāt*, vols. 1–2 (Munich: Verlag der Bayerischen Akademie der Wissenschaften, 1977–81); J. Huot, ed., *Larsa et 'Ouelli, travaux de 1978–1981* (Paris: Éditions recherche sur les civilisations, 1983); L. de Meyer, ed., *Tell ed-Der*, I–IV (Louvain: Peeters, 1977–84).

42. E. C. Stone and P. Zimansky, "Mashkan-shapir and the Anatomy of an Old Babylonian City," *BA* 55 (1992): 212–18.

43. C. Kepinski-LeComte et al., *Haradum I: Une ville nouvelle sur Le Moyen-Euphrate (XVIIIe–XVIIe siècles av. J.-C.)* (Paris: Éditions recherche sur les civilisations, 1992).

44. The identification of Tell Leilan as Shubat-Enlil is generally accepted; see D. Charpin, "Šubat-Enlil et le pays d'Apum," *MARI* 4 (1985): 129–40; H. Weiss, "Tell Leilan and Shubat Enlil," *MARI* 4 (1985): 269–92; and R. Whiting, "Tell Leilan/Šubat-Enlil: Chronological Problems and Perspectives," in *Tall al-Ḥamīdīya*, 2:167–218.

small, relatively independent and unintegrated city-states, much like the political polities of the third millennium B.C.[45]

About 50 km. north of Mari was Terqa, which gained importance later in this period.[46] There is a body of architectural documentation (a temple complex, an administrative complex, and private houses) coming from this site dated to the so-called dark age between the fall of Mari (ca. 1760 B.C.) and that of Babylon (ca. 1595 B.C.). At this time, Terqa was most likely the capital of the kingdom of Khana on the Middle Euphrates. Moreover, Terqa was a major Amorite center in this period and thus sheds light on the overall cultural environment of the patriarchs.

Late Bronze (1600–1200 B.C.)

New research has provided evidence that much of southern Mesopotamia was abandoned at the end of the eighteenth century for about four centuries. This was a long period of deurbanization, possibly resulting in part from a change in the course of the Euphrates.[47] Recent work at the site of Dilbat in central Iraq, however, has closed this intellectual gap in knowledge.

The situation in Syria in this period was quite different. The region suffered domination from both Egypt and Anatolia (Hittites), and endured a major Hurrian dynasty in the Khabur region (Mitanni), in addition to nomadic pressure and sedentarization, especially from the Arameans. Arising out of the ruins of Babylon, the Hurrians (kingdom of Mitanni) reasserted themselves in the Khabur region, uniting Syria for the first time since Shamshi-Adad I.

One of the most influential Syrian cities during this period was Ugarit, well known in the field of biblical studies. It was a major trading post on the Mediterranean coast that was tributary to Hatti. The art and architecture of this site have proved to differ from other earlier Syrian excavations, providing evidence of an independent cultural tradition. Current hydrographic surveys show that the town water at Ugarit evidently came from two small rivers encircling the mound.[48] Furthermore, remains of a stone mound have been discovered and have been interpreted as functioning as a river dam. This research enabled archaeologists to locate the main entrance to the town.[49]

---

45. For a survey of the sites in the Khabur region in this period, see D. Oates, "Walled Cities in Northern Mesopotamia in the Mari Period," *MARI* 4 (1985): 585–94.

46. For a general survey, see M. Chavalas, "Terqa on the Euphrates," *BA* 59 (1996): 90–103; G. Buccellati, "The Kingdom and Period of Khana," *BASOR* 270 (1988): 43–61.

47. J. Armstrong, "West of Edin: Tell al-Deylam and the Babylonian City of Dilbat," *BA* 55 (1992): 219–26.

48. Y. Calvert and B. Geyer, "L'eau dans l'habitat," *RSO* 3 (1987): 129–56.

49. M. Yon, "La ville d'Ougarit au XIIIe s. av. J.-C.," *CRAIBL* (1985): 705–21; idem, *The City of Ugarit at Tell Ras Shamra* (Winona Lake, Ind.: Eisenbrauns, 1998).

Although much of Syria was under political domination by Hatti in the latter part of this period, it had many thriving centers other than Ugarit with independent cultural traditions, such as Emar on the Euphrates. Although there is evidence of Hittite presence at Emar, especially in regard to architecture,[50] there was apparently no influx of Hittite population, and the culture was not deeply affected by their political and bureaucratic presence.

Early Iron (1200–600 B.C.)

Excavations have been renewed at Nineveh to understand its neighborhoods, dating to the first millennium B.C., that were overlooked in early excavations.[51] The overall design of the city has now been discerned. Sennacherib (ca. 705–681 B.C.) recast major components of the landscape for a sweeping urban design. The most spectacular portion was the work at the Halzi Gate, the southernmost port of entry. Here the last moments of active use were seen before the destruction of 612 B.C. It appears that the inhabitants took urgent steps to improve the quality of defense. In the vicinity of the gate were the remains of a number of people who died violently. Numerous bronze and iron arrowheads were found, overlapping the skeletons. One is able to speculate anew about why the allies were able to overcome the defenders in the north. Defenders were drawn to the north and south gates, while the Khosr River was flooded. The fall of Nineveh was clearly due to the effects of flooding.

Early on in the Iron Age Syria was subjected to destruction and fragmentation for at least four centuries until the rise of imperial Assyria. The site of Tell Afis north of Ebla, however, shows political and economic stability in this north central economic region when there was a "dark age" on the coast of Syria.[52] There was a dramatic increase in the size of sites in the later Iron Age (ninth century B.C. and onward), best exhibited by Tell Ahmar.[53]

It will doubtless take generations for biblical scholars to digest the relevant archaeological data from Syro-Mesopotamia that will shed light on the general geographical and cultural milieu of the Old Testament. The sheer wealth of information coming from this region affords many opportunities to better understand the biblical world.

50. G. Beckman, "Hittite Administration in Syria in Light of Texts from Hattusa, Ugarit, and Emar," in *New Horizons in the Study of Ancient Syria*, ed. M. Chavalas and J. Hayes (Malibu: Undena, 1992), 41–49.
51. D. Stronach and S. Lumsden, "UC Berkeley's Excavations at Nineveh," *BA* 55 (1992): 227–33.
52. S. Mazzoni in H. Weiss, *AJA* 95 (1991): 729–32.
53. G. Bunnens, *Tell Ahmar: 1988 Season* (Leiden: Brill, 1990).

Egypt and Palestine

The first biblical mention of Egypt occurs in the account of the patriarch Abraham when he went to Egypt to escape a famine and then became embroiled in a cover-up regarding his wife Sarai (Gen. 12:10–20). It would be hazardous to attempt to identify the king or pharaoh in this narrative with a king known from either Manetho or the Egyptian records.[54] For that very reason the incident exemplifies the emphasis adopted in this chapter: to highlight certain problems in the biblical text in regard to Egypt that as yet defy solution or at least leave some loose ends. These problems involve either historical correlations—for example, the perennial question of the pharaoh of the exodus—or identification of biblical sites once thought to be settled.

Another issue concerns the relation of the Bible to the archaeology of Palestine and Egypt, or more particularly the conclusions of certain archaeologists. For much of this century the Albright school has exercised considerable influence; some would say Albright has reigned supreme. In the years since his death in 1971, however, the scene has changed considerably. Many of his conclusions have either been overthrown or at least challenged. One example is the old chestnut regarding Abraham's camels. Albright's contention that the domestication of the camel did not take place until about 1100 B.C. was mainly based on the inscriptional evidence of the Broken Obelisk of Tiglath-pileser I (1115–1077 B.C.), now attributed to Ashur-bel-kala, which refers to the breeding of the Bactrian camel.[55] Unfortunately, observes Ripinsky, this school tended to ignore or explain away the now considerable archaeological evidence of early domestication.[56] In any case, the archaeological axiom remains that absence of evidence (in this case the inscriptional variety) is not equivalent to evidence of absence. In regard to the patriarchal narratives and early Israel, "historical minimalists" such as Redford, Van Seters, Thompson, Whitelam, and the like have argued against the older Albright consensus.[57] We indeed live in a post-Albright phase of

54. Manetho, an Egyptian priest of the third century B.C., arranged the history of Egypt into thirty dynasties. His history remains only in fragments preserved in other ancient authors. For a translation see *Manetho*, trans. and ed. W. G. Waddell, LCL (London: Heinemann; Cambridge, Mass.: Harvard University Press, 1940).

55. A. K. Grayson, *Assyrian Royal Inscriptions*, vol. 2 (Wiesbaden: Harrassowitz, 1976), no. 89; idem, *Assyrian Rulers of the Early First Millennium B.C. II (858–745 B.C.)*, Royal Inscriptions of Mesopotamia, Assyrian Periods 3 (Toronto: University of Toronto Press, 1996), 103–4.

56. M. Ripinsky, "Camel Ancestry and Domestication in Egypt and the Sahara," *Archaeology* 36.3 (1983): 26.

57. D. B. Redford, *A Study of the Biblical Story of Joseph (Genesis 37–50)*, VTSup 20 (Leiden: Brill, 1970); idem, *Egypt, Canaan, and Israel in Ancient Times* (Princeton: Prince-

biblical archaeology. I feel forced to accept many of the negative judgments of these scholars on the Albright consensus, but seek to solve these problems in a different way, in accord with a more positive approach to the biblical material, particularly in regard to early Israel.

Contrary to possible impressions, the approach to these and other issues is not primarily to engage in "Albright bashing," which, regrettably, seems in danger of becoming a fashion. Neither is it to adduce new evidence to buttress conventional theories having their origin with Albright, but rather to argue that in the light of new evidence conventional approaches have led to a dead end, and that a new approach is required. Some problems will have to remain unsolved until further evidence comes to hand. Other issues do have a solution, or at least the path to one, provided a different framework is adopted. Accordingly, in this chapter I concentrate on certain aspects of the Joseph story; the exodus-conquest problem, particularly in the light of the recent challenge by Redford to its historicity; and Egyptian-Israelite contacts during the first millennium B.C. Finally, I examine the location of Palestinian sites, with Gibeah as a case in point. As to literary matters, the old question of the relation of Proverbs and the Teaching of Amenemope has received thorough discussion over recent decades, and I refer the reader to those discussions.[58]

The Joseph Story: Aspects and Problems

As we introduce this set of narratives we immediately confront a historical minimalist such as Redford. While his discussion allows for some authenticity in matters of detail and local color, his main conclusion is that the narratives belong to and reflect the first millennium B.C. Although Kitchen has replied to him and made some worthwhile points on the linguistic and local color aspects, he has not addressed the matter of a precise historical location for Joseph.[59] First of all, however, some comments on the linguistic and local color aspects are in order.

The Episode of the Royal Cupbearer and Royal Baker

At the outset we should note a distinction between the royal butler (Egyp. *wbȝ nsw*), whose task it was to select wines, and the royal cup-

---

ton University Press, 1992); J. Van Seters, *Abraham in History and Tradition* (New Haven: Yale University Press, 1975); T. L. Thompson, *Early History of the Israelite People* (Leiden: Brill, 1992); K. Whitelam, "Recreating the History of Israel," *JSOT* 35 (1986): 45–70.

58. See, e.g., J. Ruffle, "The Teaching of Amenemope and Its Connection with the Book of Proverbs," *TynBul* 28 (1977): 29–68, and references.

59. K. A. Kitchen, "Review of Redford, *Study of the Biblical Story of Joseph*," *OrAnt* 12 (1973): 233–42.

bearer (Egyp. *wdpw nsw*), who presented the wine to the king after first tasting it in his presence.[60] Which office is to be understood by the Hebrew terms *mašqēh melek-miṣrayim* (Gen. 40:1) and *sár hammašqîm* (40:2) is difficult to specify. Vergote has proposed that the title of the first officer denotes the royal cupbearer (*wdpw*); however, Kitchen favors "butler" (*wbꜣ*) as the more precise equivalent.[61] The royal baker, by contrast, is an office as yet unidentified in Egyptian literature but that must have existed. In antiquity all were highly responsible roles. Both the butler and cupbearer had responsibility for the king's wine before the latter drank it. The royal baker's task would have been to ensure quality control in baked items, of which there was a wide variety. Certain Egyptian texts indicate a diverse fare of breads, pastries, fruit breads, cakes, and the like, particularly as funerary or temple offerings.[62] The Harris Papyrus, from the time of Rameses III, itemizes at least thirty different kinds of baked items in its list of temple offerings.[63]

From the royal food supply there was the constant danger of poisoning attempts resulting from palace intrigues. The imprisonment of the cupbearer and royal baker most likely reflects such an attempt on the king. Meanwhile, that these two landed in the same prison as Joseph indicates further that the prison was a detention center attached to "the captain of the (royal) guard" (*śar haṭṭabbāḥîm*, i.e., Potiphar) and also in proximity to the palace.[64] These conclusions appear safe and in turn reinforce the earlier proposal of a palace intrigue. When such intrigues occurred, Egyptian procedure was to round up all suspects, incarcerate them, interview each in turn, then charge and sentence (usually execution) the person(s) believed to be responsible, and reinstate the innocent. By way of illustration, one case is extant of a harem-inspired con-

60. The two are often confused in the literature. See, e.g., E. M. Blaiklock, "Cupbearer," *NIDBA*, 143. However, see relevant entries in R. O. Faulkner, *A Concise Dictionary of Middle Egyptian* (Oxford: Oxford University Press for the Griffith Institute, 1976), 58, 73.

61. J. Vergote, *Joseph en Égypte: Genèse chap. 37–50 à la lumière des études égyptologiques récentes* (Louvain: Publications universitaires, 1959), 33; K. A. Kitchen, "Review of Vergote, *Joseph en Égypte*," *JEA* 47 (1961): 159. Also G. J. Wenham, *Genesis 16–50*, WBC (Waco: Word, 1994), 381.

62. As noted in W. A. Ward, "Egyptian Titles in Genesis 39–50," *BSac* 114 (1957): 43–45.

63. The Harris Papyrus in J. H. Breasted, *Ancient Records of Egypt*, 5 vols. (Chicago: University of Chicago Press, 1906–7), 4: §§238, 291.

64. For information on Egyptian prisons, see W. C. Hayes, *A Papyrus of the Late Middle Kingdom in the Brooklyn Museum* (Brooklyn: Brooklyn Museum, 1955; reprinted 1972), 37–42. C. F. Aling (*Egypt and Bible History* [Grand Rapids: Baker, 1981], 37) draws attention to the Great Prison at Thebes, prominent during the Middle Kingdom. He speculates that this may have been the actual prison where Joseph was held, but the Twelfth Dynasty royal residence was at Itjtawy, in the Faiyum region. See J. Baines and J. Málek, *Atlas of Ancient Egypt* (Oxford: Phaidon; New York: Facts on File, 1984), 40.

spiracy to usurp Rameses III in favor of one of his sons.[65] In the investigation, a series of suspects is brought one by one to the "Place of Examination," and in turn each is convicted and sentenced or, in the case of the highborn, invited to commit suicide. Interestingly, several of the conspirators were palace butlers, and one of the examiners proved in the end to be a co-conspirator, again a palace butler, Pai-Bes.

The Land of Goshen

The name "Goshen" for the residential region of Jacob's extended family occurs in eleven texts beginning at Genesis 45:10, when Joseph makes the initial promise to his father of a settlement area, and ending in the context of the great hailstorm at the time of the exodus, Exodus 9:26. In the Hebrew text it is always referred to as the land or territory of Goshen, *'ereṣ gōšen*, giving the impression of a region. This impression is reinforced by the reference in Genesis 47:11, wherein the same region (or so it would appear) is designated as "the land of Rameses" *(bĕ'ereṣ ra'mĕsēs)*. In Egyptian records there is mention of *Gsmt*, but this could also be read as *Šsmt;* thus whether it is a reference to the biblical Goshen remains problematic, since it depends on the reading of the first biliteral sign.[66] Naville long ago argued (contra A. H. Gardiner) that *Gsmt* was the correct reading and that *m* and *n* can interchange in Semitic transcriptions.[67]

The Septuagint, however, gives a different impression. In both Genesis 45:10 and 46:34 it reads "in the land of Gesem of Arabia *(en gē Gesem Arabias)*. This reading is at least consistent with the *Gsmt* of the Egyptian monuments, if indeed that is the correct reading. Then in Genesis 46:28, 29 the reading is each time "at the city of Heroes" *(kath' Hērōōn polin)*. The latter reference places this city in the land of Rameses *(eis gēn Ramessē)*, the region mentioned in Genesis 47:11.

Suspicion that Goshen may have been a city that gave its name to the surrounding region comes from a fourth-century pilgrim, Egeria: "They arrived there at the place now known (from the fort there) as Clysma, and from Clysma we wanted to go on into Goshen to the so-called 'City

---

65. *ANET,* 214–16.

66. In *NBD* (483) Kitchen dismisses this reference as irrelevant, but in his entry in *ZPEB* (2:779) he is more open, citing Montet and Van Seters as supporting the possibility of this equation (see J. Van Seters, *The Hyksos: A New Investigation* [New Haven: Yale University Press, 1966], 146, 148). H. G. Stigers in *Theological Wordbook of the Old Testament,* ed. R. L. Harris, G. L. Archer, and B. K. Waltke, 2 vols. (Chicago: Moody, 1980), 1:174, is much more definite on the reading *Gsmt.* W. A. Ward, "Goshen," *ABD,* 2:1076, is more skeptical of the reading, but he does not appear to have studied the detailed arguments of E. Naville, "Geography of the Exodus," *JEA* 10 (1924): 28–32.

67. Naville, "Geography of the Exodus," 28–32.

of Arabia.' It gets its name from the region, which is called 'the land of Arabia, the land of Goshen.'"[68] While Egeria clearly echoes the LXX, just as surely she was recording local tradition, since she refers to her queries of the locals regarding biblical sites.[69] Another clue in the same vein that may confirm this is found in Josephus: "[Pharaoh] then permitted [Jacob] to live with his children in Heliopolis, for it was there that the king's own shepherds had their pasturage."[70] He seems to equate here the *Hērōōn polin* of the LXX, as above, with Heliopolis, Egyptian *Iunu*, the famous center of the worship of Reᶜ-Atum. This city, at the southern end of the Delta, is too far south of the region generally recognized as the biblical Goshen. A more likely candidate for the Septuagint's *Hērōōn* is Pithom (modern Tell er-Reteba), according to Thackeray.[71]

There is, however, another possibility for *Hērōōn*. The city Phacusa/Phakussa is mentioned by Ptolemy the Greek geographer-astronomer in his *Geographica*, in which he records that the nome of Arabia (the twentieth nome) had this city as its capital.[72] Phacusa is readily identifiable as modern Fakus, 7 km. south of modern Qantir.[73] The latter is now the accepted site of Pi-Rameses, the Nineteenth Dynasty Rameside palace, and prior to that the site of the Hyksos capital Avaris.[74] In turn, if we analyze the name Phacusa as Pa-Kes/Kus, an eastern Delta city in the immediate vicinity of Avaris, it is possible to see there a later version of the name Goshen, whereby the definite article *pʒ* attaches to the name Kus. The latter in turn may relate to the phonemes *g* and *s* of the LXX *Gesem*. If the Israelites were based here, then the cities of Pi-Rameses (Rameses) to the north and Pi-Tum (Pithom) to the east southeast are in the immediate general area. This concurs with the report of Egeria that "four miles from the city of Arabia [i.e., Goshen] is

---

68. *Egeria's Travels to the Holy Land*, trans. and ed. J. Wilkinson, rev. ed. (Jerusalem: Ariel; Warminster: Aris & Phillips, 1981), 100–101.

69. Ibid., 101.

70. *Jewish Antiquities* 2.7.6 §188.

71. H. St. J. Thackeray, *Josephus: Jewish Antiquities, Books I–IV*, Loeb Classical Library (London: Heinemann; Cambridge, Mass.: Harvard University Press, 1930), 243 n. z. Likewise Albright in *BASOR* 140 (1955): 31 n. 19. The connection suggested there with the much later Geshem the Arabian (Neh. 6:1, 6) is gratuitous. T. F. Wei, "Pithom," *ABD*, 5:377, sees the Pithom identification as at least a viable option; so also J. W. Wevers, *Notes on the Greek Text of Genesis* (Atlanta: Scholars Press, 1993), 787.

72. Ptolemy *Geographica* 1.4.5, 53.

73. Ward, "Goshen," 1076.

74. See the argument in Van Seters, *Hyksos*, 127–49; M. Bietak, *Avaris and Piramesse* (Oxford, 1986), 271–83; proposed by E. P. Uphill, "Pithom and Raamses: Their Location and Significance," *JNES* 27 (1968): 308–16; J. J. Bimson, *Redating the Exodus and Conquest*, 2d ed., JSOTSup 5 (Sheffield: Almond, 1981), 30–43, esp. 33–40; also Aling, *Egypt*, 65–69. In recent times Kitchen (*ZPEB*, 5:14) has also championed this site as that of Pi-Rameses.

Rameses."[75] Here then is a point where ancient versions and authors may well preserve traditions that provide important clues.

Chronological Setting of Joseph

The determination in more general terms of the time period for the Joseph story depends on the time period of the sojourn in Egypt. Here the 430 years of Exodus 12:40 is conventionally added to the 1275 of the late-date exodus to yield a time of about 1700 b.c. for Joseph, that is, the early Hyksos period. But certain texts would appear to militate against a Hyksos date. Consider, for example, Genesis 41:14: why would a Hyksos pharaoh require Joseph to shave? It is standard in Egyptian art that Egyptians are shown as clean shaven, whereas "Asiatics" always have beards.[76] Two chapters later, Genesis 43:32, it is clear that the court is filled with native Egyptians who wanted a clear demarcation from the Hebrews, since they abhorred the Asiatic shepherds. This is not consistent with a Hyksos court. Finally, if the pharaoh was a Hyksos monarch, why in Genesis 46:34 would Jacob have to de-emphasize his shepherd role to a king who had a similar background, if indeed the "shepherd-king" tradition is at all accurate? However, all these texts are consistent with a native Egyptian on the throne; thus Joseph lies outside the Hyksos period. Significantly, C. F. Pfeiffer, a late-date exodus advocate, expresses his discomfort with a Hyksos setting.[77]

A much more likely setting is in the Twelfth Dynasty, probably in the reign of Senusert (Sesostris) III or his successor, Amenemhet III. This will become apparent in the following section. For the present it can be noted that the el-Khataʾna or Goshen region, as above, abounds in ruins from the Twelfth Dynasty.[78] Meanwhile, it is interesting that Kitchen, an otherwise late-date advocate, argues that many of the names in the narrative (e.g., Zaphenath-paneah, Asenath, Potiphera, Gen. 41:45), belong to the Middle Kingdom and for the most part not later.[79]

Joseph's Land-Reform Initiatives

The account in Genesis 47:13–26 records the progressive acquisition by the palace of first the lands, then the livestock, and finally the very persons

75. *Egeria's Travels*, 102 n. 15.

76. Cf. the scene from the tomb of User-het depicting Egyptian barbers at work, *ANEP*, no. 80.

77. C. F. Pfeiffer, *Old Testament History* (Grand Rapids: Baker, 1973), 52.

78. *Atlas of Ancient Egypt*, 177–78.

79. K. A. Kitchen, "Genesis 12–50 in the Near Eastern World," in *He Swore an Oath: Biblical Themes from Genesis 12–50*, ed. R. S. Hess, G. J. Wenham, and P. E. Satterthwaite (Cambridge: Tyndale, 1993), 80–86.

of the Egyptian peasantry. An operative clause regarding this final phase of the process is found in Genesis 47:25, where the people admitted to Joseph, "You have saved our lives. . . . We shall be Pharaoh's slaves." Thus they sold themselves to the palace in return for the sustenance of life.

Though we do not otherwise know of such a practice in Egypt, it is known elsewhere in the ancient Near East. Certain Amarna texts refer to it in Syria-Palestine of the later Eighteenth Dynasty period, the Nippur texts of the Late Assyrian period likewise attest it, and it is implied in the Middle Assyrian laws.[80] By far the largest number of texts that attest this practice, however, come from the late Hittite–Middle Assyrian period, from Emar on the Middle Euphrates. No less than seventeen texts of this type are extant, some of which involve personal surrender in time of famine ("year of distress," *i-na MU KALA.GA* and variants), while others involve the sale of family members. One example of the latter category has already achieved some fame: foot impressions of four children were made and recorded in the contract, three of which have been recovered.[81]

All of these Emar famine texts are personal contracts, but as Hurowitz has observed, the technical term *bulluṭu*, "to keep alive," occurs in many of these documents.[82] In others the term used is *palāḫu*, "to take care of." This compares with the expression in Genesis 47:25, *heḥĕyitānû*, denoting the Egyptians' acknowledgment that since the palace administration has supplied essential provisions to maintain life during the famine, they are by recognized custom the slaves of the palace. Thus here is a wholesale entry into servitude along with movable and immovable property, whereby the palace stands in the place of the slave owner/dealer of the Emar texts.

At Emar many of the famine texts also reveal purchase of land "in a time of distress." Perhaps significantly, several of these transactions involve the local royal family of Emar acquiring property, though not, contrary to what one would expect, at bargain prices.[83] Many of the

80. See, respectively, EA 75:13–14; 81:39–40; 85:13–14; 90:36–9; W. L. Moran, *The Amarna Letters* (Baltimore: Johns Hopkins University Press, 1992), in loc., for translations; A. L. Oppenheim, "Siege Documents from Nippur," *Iraq* 17 (1955): 69–89. *ANET*, 183 §39, discussed in Oppenheim, "Siege Documents," 75.

81. See my thesis, "Late Hittite Emar," part B, chap. 4, to be published by Peeters. Initial discussion of the foot impressions is in E. Leichty, "Feet of Clay," in *DUMU-E2-DUB-BA: Studies in Honor of Åke W. Sjöberg*, ed. H. Behrens, D. Loding, and M. T. Roth (Philadelphia: Samuel Noah Kramer Fund, University Museum, 1989), 349–56; and my "Emar's Window on the Old Testament: A Preliminary View," *Buried History* 29 (1993): 82–86.

82. V. A. Hurowitz, "Joseph's Enslavement of the Egyptians (Genesis 47:13–26) in the Light of Famine Texts from Mesopotamia," *RB* 101 (1994): 355–62.

83. If anything, the price increases during a "time of distress," though more examples are needed to confirm this. See my "Late Hittite Emar," part B, chap. 5; E. Leichty, "Feet of Clay"; and my "Emar's Window on the Old Testament."

other transactions in this category, however, are acquisitions by private persons.

What these texts show is that entry into slavery during famine was a recognized procedure, and that in such a circumstance the obligation of the purchaser was "to maintain life" *(bulluṭu)*. In the texts, both this term and *palāḫu* have the status of legal *termini technici*. Since this procedure is now well attested from the Late Bronze Age texts, there is every reason to suppose that this in turn reflects a standard legal procedure from earlier times and is based on acknowledged legal precedent. This evidence, admittedly circumstantial, is therefore suggestive of a time setting for Genesis 47 in second-millennium Egypt, likely early rather than mid-millennium. Thus the narrative of Genesis 47 as it stands reflects a real procedure and indicates that it should be taken as a unitary narrative from somewhere near the time of the events described and not as a later redaction of disparate fragments that bears little relationship to what allegedly happened in the time of Joseph.

As to when this land reform probably took place it is worthwhile to note Battenfield's argument that the well-known administrative reforms of Senusert III constitute the chronological location for Joseph.[84] Under his rule the nomarchs lost their traditional power in favor of the vizier, who then directed the administration of the entire country. Battenfield argues that this centralization of power is precisely that of Joseph according to Genesis 47. A footnote to this is that under the feudal type rule of the Hyksos, borrowed from Syria-Palestine, power was dispersed back to the nomarchs, first in the Delta, then to all of Egypt; but this was a later development.[85]

However, this placement involves another problem. If, as will be argued below, the exodus is to be placed earlier than even the date postulated by the conventional "early date" model (i.e., prior to Thutmose III), yet Joseph is still to be placed in the Twelfth Dynasty (conventionally 1878–1843 B.C., but possibly lowered to 1836–1801 B.C.), the time span is much shorter than the 430 years of Exodus 12:40.[86] Here the testimony of the Septuagint should be assessed. In regard to the time of the sojourn, the LXX in Exodus 12:40 adds, after the words "in the land of Egypt," *kai en gē Chanaan* ("and in the land of Canaan"). This reading, also supported by the Samaritan Pentateuch, treats the 430 years as cov-

84. J. R. Battenfield, "A Consideration of the Identity of the Pharaoh of Genesis 47," *JETS* 15 (1972): 77–85.

85. Ibid., 84 nn. 44, 45.

86. K. A. Kitchen, "The Basics of Egyptian Chronology in Relation to the Bronze Age," in *High, Middle, or Low? Acts of an International Colloquium on Absolute Chronology Held at the University of Gothenburg, 20th–22nd August 1987*, ed. P. Åström (Gothenburg: Åströms, 1987–89), 1:44–45.

ering both the sojourn of the patriarchs in Canaan and that of the Israelites in Egypt. Scholars have often been ambivalent about this LXX reading, but it would appear to harmonize with Paul's observation in Galatians 3:17 that the law came 430 years after Abraham, a time frame that is difficult to harmonize with the traditional Masoretic Text.[87] However, the Dead Sea Exodus fragment from cave 2 seems to support the Masoretic reading, though the restoration is to some extent doubtful.[88] While a 215-year sojourn (half of 430 years) would be too short (possibly the Hyksos period could be reduced), nevertheless the shorter period, in accord with the LXX reading, remains within the bounds of plausibility.

Exodus and Conquest: Historicity and Date

Since an enormous amount of ink has been spilled on the vexed but as yet unsolved problem of the date of the exodus, the approach here, rather than arguing a specific case, is the more conservative one of laying down some parameters and guidelines for a way forward. Equally, some clear indication must be given concerning paths that have proved, in my view, to be dead ends. Meanwhile, in the light of evidence now apparent after excavations over many sites during the course of this century, and particularly in recent years, many critical scholars have now altogether abandoned the quest to harmonize the exodus with Egyptian history and have adopted instead quite radical approaches. Thus after nearly a century of discussion of this issue without a solution, it is time for all assumptions, "settled conclusions" (as believed), "historical benchmarks," literary analyses of sources, and speculative theories to be either seriously questioned or at least reinvestigated. This may be a painful process, but evangelicals must face the challenge of historical minimalists who insist on the pattern of evidence. For example, Redford argues strongly that the biblical account is so out of kilter with the known facts of Egyptian history, or of other civilizations for that matter, that the Bible must be jettisoned.[89] In the process he issues a challenge to conservative Jews, Christians, and even Muslims, whom he regards as obscurantist, to face the evidence. This is a challenge we must accept, but at the same time we must be prepared to depart radically from existing paradigms in order to find a harmony.

---

87. A good presentation of the arguments for and against is found in L. J. Wood, *A Survey of Israel's History*, rev. ed., revised by D. O'Brien (Grand Rapids: Zondervan, 1986), 65–69.

88. M. Baillet, J. T. Milik, and R. de Vaux, eds., *Les "Petites Grottes" de Qumrân: Exploration de la falaise, les grottes 2Q, 3Q, 5Q, 6Q, 7Q à 10Q, le rouleau de cuivre*, DJD 3 (Oxford: Clarendon, 1962), 51.

89. See Redford, *Egypt, Canaan, and Israel in Ancient Times*, 257–63.

Hence, at the outset, it is well to survey both the biblical and the archaeological sides of the debate, which in turn can serve as parameters for discussion. As to the former, the following points should, I believe, be accepted as firm.

The Exodus in Biblical Tradition

The exodus-conquest theme outside the Pentateuch is so pervasive and consistent that it cannot be arbitrarily dismissed. Whether one looks at the historical psalms, which celebrate God's great acts of deliverance at the exodus (cf. Ps. 74:12–15; 77:15–20; 78:12–53; 103:7; 105:25–42; 114:1–4; 136:10–16), prophecy (cf. Hos. 2:14–15; Jer. 2:1–6; Ezek. 16:8–13), or the "second exodus" theme (cf. Isa. 43:1–7; Jer. 23:7–8), the exodus is at the heart of Israel's historically based faith.

In all these (and many other) references, there is not a hint of a separate tradition such as might have come from tribes of a separate origin, still less of no exodus tradition at all. Thus if a separate "Sinai" tribal group merged with other tribes of a "non-Sinai" background in the land, as split-exodus theories maintain, this has taken place without leaving any trace of the latter "tradition."[90] Likewise, theories that discount the exodus and conquest traditions altogether encounter the same difficulty on an even greater scale. They must aver that the tradition somehow either crept into or even popped into Israel's consciousness, ultimately out of thin air. Yet, based on recent archaeological work, historical minimalists allege that successive local conquests in a drawn-out series of regional wars slowly coalesced into a tradition of a single conquest. With its almost complete discounting of the exodus tradition, this approach seems like theorizing without any real textual or transmissional warrant. We must first make sense of the text, then face the archaeological issues, and to these we now turn.

Archaeological Considerations

Turning from the exegetical to the archaeological, certain conclusions arising from recent excavations in Palestine are unavoidable, and any identification of the chronological locus of the exodus must satisfy the following incontestable facts.

The Archaeology of Palestine

At a series of sites all over Palestine the clear picture is that Egyptian occupation continued until the end of the Late Bronze Age (ca. 1150 B.C.). Sometimes the evidence of that Egyptian occupation occurs in the

90. K. A. Kitchen in particular makes this point; see his *Ancient Orient and Old Testament* (London: Tyndale, 1966), 71. See also the same point in idem, "Exodus," *ABD*, 2:701.

stratum immediately below that dated to the divided monarchy.[91] To begin with, from Lachish there occur several indications of Egyptian occupation in the Late Bronze period: sherds inscribed in hieratic with a fair degree of certainty belong to the late Rameside period and appear to indicate the operation of an Egyptian taxation system.[92] A bronze plaque bearing the prenomen of Rameses III provides the terminus post quem of the Lachish gatehouse where it was found, while a temple in Area P, though having manifestly Canaanite features, is just as clearly Egyptian in many of its other features.[93]

Megiddo reveals a similar picture. One of the subterranean chambers attached to the Canaanite palace yielded the famous Megiddo ivories, but one of these also bears the name of Rameses III.[94] At Beth-shan there was revealed a building in Egyptian style and a secondarily used statue of Rameses III.[95] The best interpretation of the building is that Beth-shan was an Egyptian stronghold at this time. In the south Hebron was uninhabited during the entire Late Bronze era.[96] In short, this is one striking fact that, among others, has driven such historical minimalists as P. Davies and T. L. Thompson to abandon the biblical accounts altogether.

All the above indicates that the Late Bronze era was one of Egyptian presence and occupation. Furthermore, this picture is so pervasive that on present historical-chronological schemes an Israelite presence much before 1150 B.C. is hard to reconcile with it. Therefore to harmonize this with a coherent conquest à la Joshua 1–11 is well-nigh impossible. Some scholars do indeed attempt such a harmony, but the evidence makes it appear as an exercise in special pleading. Other scholars such as A. Mazar, T. L. Thompson, and N. Gottwald have given up any such approach, and for them it is the biblical narrative that must be set aside.[97]

91. This became evident, for example, in the 1987 season at Lachish that I attended. To date, however, I am not aware that the report on this season has been published.

92. O. Goldwasser, "An Egyptian Scribe from Lachish and the Hieratic Tradition of the Hebrew Kingdoms," *Tel Aviv* 18 (1991): 248–52.

93. On the former see D. Ussishkin, *Excavations at Tel Lachish 1978–1983* (Tel Aviv: Tel Aviv University, Institute of Archaeology, 1983), 176. On the latter see idem, *Excavations at Tel Lachish 1973–1977* (Tel Aviv: Tel Aviv University, Institute of Archaeology, 1978), 10–25.

94. A. Mazar, *Archaeology of the Land of the Bible 10,000–586 B.C.E.*, ABRL (New York: Doubleday, 1990), 299.

95. Ibid., 297–98.

96. Ibid., 332. Bimson, *Redating*, 189, makes the same point.

97. See N. Gottwald, "Were the Israelites Pastoral Nomads?" *BAR* 4 (June 1978), 2–7; idem, "Response to William Dever," in *The Rise of Ancient Israel*, ed. H. Shanks (Washington, D.C.: Biblical Archaeology Society, 1992), 70–75. Also the conversation, "Face to Face: Biblical Minimalists Meet Their Challengers," *BAR* 23.4 (1997): 26–42, where N. P. Lemche, T. L. Thompson, W. Dever, and P. Kyle McCarter Jr. expound their minimalist views.

Alternatively, D. Ussishkin and others, following this evidence, favor a conquest, of sorts, after 1150 B.C.[98]

Another fact to emerge from excavation is that there is no pattern of Palestinian walled and fortified cities in the Late Bronze period. Indeed, archaeological investigation of many of the cities mentioned in the conquest narratives indicates a lack of any occupation at all in the Late Bronze era.[99] If Bimson and his school of chronological revisionists, for all their detractors, have contributed to the exodus-conquest problem at all, this is one solid conclusion.[100] According to the biblical account these heavily fortified cities provoked the fear of the Israelites (see Num. 13:28; Deut. 1:28). Hence if we are to take at all seriously not merely the walls of Jericho but the system of walled and fortified cities across the entire countryside, we must either rule out the Late Bronze period as a chronological context for the conquest or else discount the biblical record in this regard. The latter is not easy to do, however, since walled cities are linked with the "unbelief" theme of Israel's cultic memory (Ps. 106:24–26; Neh. 9:15–17; and possibly in mind in Ps. 95:9–11).

Amarna Age Palestine

Although the Amarna Letters have been known for over a century, the picture they provide of Canaan during the reigns of Amenhotep III and Amenhotep IV (Akhenaten) has not often been properly faced by advocates of the early-date model.[101] On the latter scheme Israel is in the land, yet the Amarna picture is that of a set of petty Canaanite kinglets with their internecine squabbles and parleys with the Egyptian pharaoh.[102] This on the face of it seems strongly to support the alternative late-date scheme whereby Amarna Canaan precedes the conquest.

98. As implied in *Tel Lachish 1978–1983*, 170.

99. A point made forcefully by M. Kochavi, "The Israelite Settlement in Canaan in the Light of Archaeological Surveys," in *Biblical Archaeology Today: Proceedings of the International Congress on Biblical Archaeology, Jerusalem, April 1984*, ed. J. Aviram (Jerusalem: Israel Exploration Society; Israel Academy of Sciences and Humanities in cooperation with the American Schools of Oriental Research, 1985), 54–60. Likewise J. M. Miller, "Archaeology and the Israelite Conquest of Canaan: Some Methodological Observations," *PEQ* 109 (1977): 87–93.

100. Bimson, *Redating*, chap. 7; J. J. Bimson and D. Livingston, "Redating the Exodus," *BAR* 13.5 (1987): 45.

101. Several early-date advocates still cling to the now untenable theory that the Habiru are the advancing Israelites under Joshua. See Wood, *Survey*, 82–84; G. L. Archer, *A Survey of Old Testament Introduction* (Chicago: Moody, 1974), 265–71. Aling, *Egypt*, 109–10, finally rejects such an identification but is obscure as to how to account for the Amarna phenomenon.

102. See R. K. Harrison, *Introduction to the Old Testament* (London: Tyndale; Grand Rapids: Eerdmans, 1969), 319.

Merenptah: A Terminus ad Quem

The reconstruction by Yurco of the Canaanite campaign reliefs of Merenptah at Karnak has seriously altered the picture of Israel from the Egyptian perspective in the Nineteenth Dynasty.[103] No longer can the famous "Israel Stela" be examined in isolation, nor can its historical testimony be dismissed. Merenptah must now be reckoned as a victorious pharaoh who subdued several Canaanite cities and defeated an Israelite army in the field. This immediately raises two significant problems: (1) if the late-date scheme is true, how could an Israelite army engage a pharaoh of Egypt so soon after its arrival in Canaan? and (2) in the "Israel register" on the Karnak wall, the relief depicts the Israelite army with chariots having six-spoked wheels long before chariotry is attested biblically as part of Israel's military technology.[104]

The Negev

The sites in the Negev and Transjordan connected with the wilderness wanderings and the initial conquest likewise reveal nothing of Bronze Age settlement corresponding to the biblical narratives of the conquest of Arad (Num. 21:1) and Hormah (Num. 21:2–3), or of the camp at Kadesh-barnea. This last site, identified with Ain el-Qudeirat, has revealed nothing from either the Late Bronze or Early Iron I, but during the united monarchy a royal fortress was erected.[105] At Tell Arad, usually but not unanimously identified with Canaanite Arad, there is a similar occupational gap between Early Bronze and the united monarchy period.[106] However, Aharoni identifies Canaanite Arad with Tel Malhata (Tell el-Milh), where Middle Bronze II remains evidenced a sedentary population in that period.[107]

Tell Hesban and Transjordan

A further problem arises in respect of Transjordan. In summary, with regard to identifying Tell Hesban with biblical Heshbon, we must face the fact that no remains exist prior to Iron I, and hence this site as the capital of an "Amorite state" is either a historical anachronism or

103. F. J. Yurco, "Merenptah's Canaanite Campaign," *JARCE* 23 (1986): 189–215. See also idem, "3,200-Year-Old Picture of Israelites Found in Egypt," *BAR* 16.5 (1990): 20-38; and the challenge by A. F. Rainey, with reply by Yurco, *BAR* 17.6 (1991): 56–61.

104. Note the problem that this poses for both Rainey and Yurco (ibid., 59, 61, respectively), who each explains it in his own (implausible) way.

105. Mazar, *Archaeology*, 330, 444; R. K. Harrison, "Kadesh Barnea," *NIDBA*, 275.

106. Mazar, *Archaeology*, 330.

107. Ibid., 330; Y. Aharoni, *The Land of the Bible: A Historical Geography*, trans. and ed. A. G. Rainey, 2d ed. (London: Burns & Oates; Philadelphia: Westminster, 1979), 215–16. See also Bimson, *Redating*, 190–91.

the site has been misidentified.[108] The same can be said of Moab generally: Late Bronze remains are in the main lacking.[109] There are, however, certain notable exceptions to this picture.

In regard to Tell Hesban particularly, this site was excavated by the Andrews University expedition over six seasons during the 1970s. In all, twenty-four strata were identified covering Iron Age I (1200 B.C.) to the Ottoman Empire period (A.D. 1870).[110] This leaves a problem for the Transjordan conquest as recorded in Numbers 21:21–31 and Deuteronomy 2:30–35, especially as Deuteronomy 3:5 notes that the cities of the Bashan area were heavily fortified, and it is highly likely that this description applies to the Heshbon region as well. Even the Iron Age evidence at Hesban was scanty, and probably represents an unfortified pastoral village.

The question arises, then, as to whether Tell Hesban is the correct site, despite what is essentially the same name. Since in antiquity names had a way of shifting around with the relocation of a sedentary population, the case for an alternative site should be investigated. Tell Jalul, 9 km. southeast of Hesban, would appear to be a good candidate, or possibly Tell el-ʿUmeiri, 10 km. northeast of Hesban. From surface surveys each one of these sites is a city with firm attestation of Middle and Late Bronze occupation.[111] It is perhaps significant that in the Late Iron Age and more particularly in the Persian period the evidence of occupation is slim but well attested at Hesban.[112] This admittedly circumstantial evidence could indicate a population shift at that time. If Tell Jalul is indeed the Heshbon of Numbers 21:26, it would fit with a late Middle Bronze era conquest as proposed by Bimson.

In summary, most sites in these regions mentioned in Numbers and in later Psalms reflecting on the incidents recorded in Numbers were, according to the archaeological picture, uninhabited in the Late Bronze period, either early or late. While some adjustments can be made to the picture because of possibly mistaken identifications, this conclusion in general still stands.

The only conclusion to draw from all the above considerations is that the Late Bronze era should be ruled out as a chronological setting for the exodus-conquest. This in turn entails that "burn levels" in a number

---

108. Mazar, *Archaeology*, 330; B. C. Chapman, "Heshbon," *NIDBA*, 236.

109. R. Ibach Jr., "Expanded Archaeological Survey of the Hesban Region," *AUSS* 16 (1978): 209–10, 213.

110. R. S. Boraas and L. T. Geraty, "1976 Heshbon Expedition," *AUSS* 16 (1978): 16, chart.

111. R. Ibach Jr., "An Intensive Surface Survey at Jalul," *AUSS* 16 (1978): 215–22; on Tell el-ʿUmeiri, see idem, "Expanded Archaeological Survey," 210.

112. Cf. the results for the Iron Age as reported in Ibach, "Expanded Archaeological Survey," 206–9.

of Palestinian sites, so frequently cited in this connection, are irrelevant to the issue.[113] Furthermore, if the exodus tradition is to be harmonized with archaeology and history, we must look elsewhere, in another archaeological period. Thus some are now advocating the Early Iron Age (Rendsburg), or, on other schemes, looking back to the Middle Bronze period (Bimson, Livingston).[114] I favor the latter approach.

Guidelines for a Solution

The above factors seem on the surface to present an impenetrable puzzle, and there are basically three alternatives, particularly in the light of the Yurco reconstruction of the Karnak wall. To draw these and other threads together, I set forth the following propositions.

The Late-Date Chronology Must Be Rejected

Before the archaeological discussion, some exegetical points are in order. The approach to Exodus 1 in much late-date-exodus literature proceeds on the assumption that the chapter covers a fairly short period that can be subsumed under one reign, which is usually then identified with that of either Seti I or more particularly his son and successor Rameses II.[115] On this view the assigning of the name "Ra'amses" to the city for Seti's time is proleptic, since Seti built only the palace. But this misconstrues the narrative of Exodus 1:8–22. What is recorded there is a series of increasingly repressive measures to counter the prodigious growth of the Hebrew people: first, the enslavement with the consequent construction of the two "store cities" (*'ārê miskĕnôt*); then, on the perceived failure of that policy, the intensification and extension of the slavery to all manner of projects, including field work (Exod. 1:14). Finally, the repressive policy climaxes in, first, enforced infanticide on the part of Hebrew midwives and then deliberate genocide by the native Egyptians.[116] Only at this last stage does Moses appear on the scene.

---

113. Argued exegetically quite cogently by E. H. Merrill, "Palestinian Archaeology and the Date of the Conquest: Do Tells Tell Tales?" *Grace Theological Journal* 3.1 (1982): 107–21. Merrill points out that the Book of Joshua records the implementation of the Mosaic conquest policy, that the Israelites merely captured (*lākad*) cities but did not burn (*śārap*) them. The simple fact is that the Israelites wanted to live in them, as stated in Josh. 24:13.

114. G. A. Rendsburg, "The Date of the Exodus and the Conquest/Settlement: The Case for the 1100s," *VT* 42 (1992): 510–27; Bimson and Livingston, "Redating the Exodus," 40–68. See also B. Wood, "Did the Israelites Conquer Jericho? A New Look at the Archaeological Evidence," *BAR* 16.2 (1990): 44–59.

115. See, e.g., Kitchen, *Ancient Orient*, 57 n. 3; also implied in the discussion by J. A. Thompson, *The Bible and Archaeology* (Exeter: Paternoster, 1962), 57–58.

116. Cf. the discussion in W. H. Gispen, *Exodus*, Bible Student's Commentary (Grand Rapids: Zondervan, 1982), 32–38 (a trans. of *Korte Verklaring der Heilige Schrift*). U. Cassuto adopts essentially the same exegesis; see his *A Commentary on the Book of Exodus*,

Clearly a lengthy period of time, possibly a century or more, is covered by this series of experiments in "population control" and "social engineering," since time would be necessary to implement and then assess the impact of each succeeding measure. Moreover, a natural reading of the narrative indicates that the construction of the cities belongs to the *beginning* of the oppression, not to the end as Kitchen contends.[117] Bimson, for example, envisages an Egyptian bondage from about 1700 B.C. to the exodus, which he places at 1470 B.C.[118] One suspects that in this late-date approach to the narrative, archaeological considerations control the exegesis.

A similar observation should be made about dating notices regarding the exodus. It is common in much of the literature on the exodus issue to regard the 430 years of Exodus 12:40 in a straightforward sense but the 480 years of 1 Kings 6:1 as artificial. This is despite the fact that the latter is matched with the fourth year of Solomon and that in the same chapter the completion of the temple is matched to the eleventh year of Solomon in a later month.[119] This sounds like normal arithmetic procedure rather than a treating of the figure as symbolic or representative. Again one suspects that the conventional explanation of the 480 years, that it represents twelve generations of the biblical "forty years" (in reality twenty-five), owes more to considerations of harmony with Egyptian history than to the demands of exegesis of the text.[120] The exodus was to Israel as the Norman Conquest is to England or the American Revolution to the United States: a pivotal event that serves as a historical watershed and dating point.

A final observation is that Judges 11:26, indicating an interval of 300 years between the conquest of Transjordan and the time of Jephthah, supports a straightforward interpretation of the 480-year figure. All too often late-date advocates either ignore the Judges text or give it passing mention in exodus discussions. Insofar as scholars regard its testimony

---

trans. from the Hebrew by I. Abrahams (Jerusalem: Magnes, Hebrew University, 1967), 11–16; also B. S. Childs, *Exodus* (London: SCM, 1974), 14, albeit in outline form and without historical comment.

117. Bimson, *Redating*, 39, makes this same point contra Kitchen, *Ancient Orient*, 57 n. 3.

118. Bimson, *Redating*, 222.

119. Cf. Kitchen, *ABD*, 2:702, who stigmatizes the acceptance of the 480 years as "the 'lazy man's solution,'" yet in *Ancient Orient*, 53, accepts the 430 years of Exod. 12:40 with little question, while the 480 years is for him "a total of selected figures" (*Ancient Orient*, 74). Redford, *Egypt*, 260, says the conventional treatment of the 480 years (i.e., 12 x 40 generations of 25 years each) "smacks of prestidigitation and numerology."

120. Thus Kitchen, *ABD*, 2:702, cites what for him is the real problem, i.e., the mention of Ra'amses in Exod. 1:11, whereby the exodus "could not precede the accession of [Rameses II] at the earliest"; he also cites other archaeological evidence.

at all, they usually seem more interested in explaining away the reference than in giving it due weight.[121]

The first proposal is a negative one, but nevertheless important: the conventional late-date scheme whereby either Seti I or even Rameses II is the pharaoh of the oppression, and the latter the pharaoh of the exodus, is untenable. This is so for the following reasons:

1. There is simply not enough time for Israel to depart from Egypt, spend forty years in the wilderness, conquer the land, and then, either during or just after the conquest, engage a well-equipped Egyptian army under Merenptah in his fifth year. Without engaging in a debate about precise chronology, we may date the 67 years of Rameses II's reign from 1279 to 1213 B.C. and the 10 years of his son Merenptah from 1213 to 1203 B.C.[122] The early years of Rameses' reign were occupied with a war against the Hittites and concluded with a treaty in year 21. Also in this period the new royal city of Pi-Rameses, the biblical Rameses, was constructed (almost certainly at the modern Qantir),[123] which would have occupied the same length of time, probably until about 1258 or 1255. An exodus before then, on this scheme, is highly unlikely. The assumption here is that Pi-Rameses was constructed just prior to the exodus, but this conflicts with the exegesis of Exodus 1:7–14 as a whole, which envisages a series of increasingly severe stages in the oppression, of which the building of the cities is merely the first.[124] Furthermore, this means that by the time Israel arrives Rameses has either died or is very close to death.

   Then we must consider the early reign of Merenptah: on any reckoning Israel has hardly arrived in the land when they face a battle with Egypt, about 1208. Add to this Yurco's reconstruction of the Ashkelon wall at Karnak: it depicts the Israelites with a chariot force (!) and many wearing long tunics. This implies for Yurco that the Israelites coalesced with and emerged from Canaanite society, and in turn implies for him that the conquest tradition must in large measure be discounted.[125]

---

121. As M. Woudstra observes in *The Book of Joshua*, NICOT (Grand Rapids: Eerdmans, 1981), 23. Kitchen, *Ancient Orient*, 74, treats this text in much the same way as he treats 1 Kings 6:1, as a computation. The analogies he draws may be interesting but are in no way demonstrative.

122. Kitchen, "The Basics of Egyptian Chronology," 1:38–40.

123. See the discussion in Bimson, *Redating*, 33–40. Kitchen (*ZPEB*, 5:14) has championed this site as that of Pi-Rameses.

124. See Bimson, *Redating*, 39. Aling, *Egypt*, 65–66, 69, makes the similar point.

125. Yurco, *BAR* 17.6 (1991): 61.

2. Death of a pharaoh during Moses' Midianite sojourn rules out Rameses II (or any other pharaoh) as the pharaoh of *both* the oppression and exodus. As is well known, there is no evidence of building activity at Qantir prior to the reign of Rameses II, until we go back to the Hyksos period and thence to the Middle Kingdom.[126] Because of the mention of Rameses in Exodus 1:11, and the known fact that Rameses II built Pi-Rameses in the Delta, the conventional conclusion is that this is the terminus a quo for the oppression and exodus. This entails also that Rameses is the pharaoh of both the oppression and the exodus. This conflicts, however, with Exodus 2:23, that there was a change of king during Moses' Midianite sojourn, apparently toward the end.[127] One scholar to note the problem is J. P. Hyatt. He thinks we must either opt for a Rameside exodus and discount Exodus 2:23, or adopt Merenptah as the exodus pharaoh and discount the wilderness wandering because of the "Israel stela" attestation.[128]

3. The radical compression of the judges period consequent to a late-date chronology constitutes a serious problem. While all admit some contemporaneity of judgeships, particularly in the latter stages, the text shows at least 250 years up to the time of Abimelech's abortive kingship. Each oppression is introduced by the formula, "the people of Israel again did evil" (Judg. 3:7, 12; 4:1; 6:1; 8:33; 10:6; 13:1). This certainly sounds like a sequential narrative. If this at all represents the real course of events, then much more is required than the approximately 150 years for the entire period, as on the late-date scheme. Even Harrison, a late-date advocate, is not entirely comfortable with this.[129]

4. Finally, the sequence of nineteen generations from Korah to Heman in David's time in 1 Chronicles 6:32–39 represents a period of at least 450 years, too long for any late-date chronology.[130] While Christine Tetley has tried to undermine the force of this consideration, she has to admit that at least some of her

---

126. Bietak, *Avaris*, 271–73.

127. The conventional conclusion, without due consideration of Exod. 2:23, can be found in E. M. Yamauchi, *The Stones and the Scriptures* (London: Inter-Varsity, 1972), 44; Kitchen, *ABD*, 2:702; M. Noth, *The History of Israel* (London: Black, 1960), 120; J. Bright, *A History of Israel*, 3d ed. (London: SCM, 1981), 123; E. W. Nicholson, *Exodus and Sinai in History and Tradition* (Oxford: Blackwell, 1973), 54.

128. J. P. Hyatt, *Exodus*, NCB (London: Oliphants, 1971), 43–44.

129. Note his discussion in *Introduction*, 330–31.

130. A point argued by Bimson, *Redating*, 88.

assumptions and identifications in the genealogical lists are speculative.[131]

The Conventional Early-Date Model Also Is Untenable

Another negative conclusion is that an Eighteenth Dynasty exodus is likewise impossible. More conservative scholars such as Aling, Davis, Wood, and Merrill adopt the 480 years of 1 Kings 6:1 as a straightforward figure that yields about 1447 B.C. as the date of the exodus, archaeologically Late Bronze I.[132] This makes Thutmose III the pharaoh of the oppression and Amenhotep II the pharaoh of the exodus. Yet there are some decisive objections to this view.

1. The location of the capital during the early Eighteenth Dynasty was Thebes in the south, and while Thutmose and his son Amenhotep II did maintain an alternative palace at Memphis, actual residence there seems to have been occasional.[133] Moreover, Memphis is still several days' journey from Goshen. This standard objection therefore remains.

2. Building activity by Thutmose III was conducted mainly in the south (at Karnak), and while there is evidence of building work in the Delta, it was neither at Qantir (the accepted site of Pi-Rameses) nor at Tell er-Reteba (Pithom).[134] In all, his building there was neither extensive nor protracted.

3. Chronology poses a problem, whichever scheme is adopted. If one opts for the short chronology (Kitchen) that gives Thutmose III the regnal dates of 1479–1425 and Amenhotep II as 1427–1400, the neat scheme would be upset in that the exodus would have to be redated to about 1420 B.C.[135] On the other hand, some historians adopt a long chronology for Thutmose, 1504–1450, which would be too early, though perhaps tolerable.[136]

131. M. C. Tetley, "The Genealogy of Samuel the Levite," *Buried History* 33 (1997): 20–30, 39–51.

132. Aling, *Egypt*, 53–96; J. J. Davis, *Moses and the Gods of Egypt* (Grand Rapids: Baker, 1971), 16–33; Wood, *Survey*, 65–86; E. H. Merrill, "Palestinian Archaeology," 107–21.

133. A. Gardiner, *Egypt of the Pharaohs* (Oxford and New York: Oxford University Press, 1961).

134. Ibid., 188. The clear evidence is that Pi-Rameses/Qantir was unoccupied during the Eighteenth Dynasty. See Bietak, *Avaris*, 273; Baines and Málek, *Atlas*, 176; W. H. Shea, "Exodus, Date of the," *ISBE*, 2:231, reporting the work of M. Bietak at Tell el-Dabᶜa. In regard to Pithom, the oldest building so far found at Tell er-Reteba is a Rameside temple to Atum. See Kitchen, *ABD*, 2:703.

135. Kitchen, "Egyptian Chronology," 52.

136. As in *CAH*, 2.1:818–19, after W. C. Hayes. Gardiner, *Egypt*, 443, proposes middle dates for Thutmose III, 1490–1436.

4. If the plague narratives are to be taken seriously, the combined effect of these, plus the loss of Egypt's slave labor force, would have been economically, agriculturally, and militarily devastating. To deny this point is ultimately to explain away the whole import and purpose of the plagues. But this period was precisely the period of Egyptian prowess, prosperity, and military expansion. To place the exodus here entails the conclusion that the event left hardly a scratch on Egypt or at most was for Egypt a temporary setback from which it quickly recovered. For that matter, a Rameside exodus faces the same objection.

5. We know of several Egyptian military expeditions through Palestine subsequent to Thutmose III: Amenhotep II (years 7, 9), Horemheb (probably), Seti I (year 1), Rameses II (year 5), Merenptah (year 5), none of which finds mention in the books of Judges or 1 Samuel. Omission of some is perhaps explicable, but omission of all is not. Again, the same objection applies to a Rameside exodus, as noted above in part, though perhaps not to the same degree.

Pathway to a Solution

As observed above, placing the exodus-conquest anywhere into the Late Bronze era is an exercise in fitting the proverbial square peg into the round hole. But radical rejection of the biblical narrative is ultimately a dead end also: it is simply too cavalier an approach to commend itself. The only path remaining is to seek a chronological locus elsewhere. Thus J. Bimson, B. Wood, and D. Livingston have sought such a locus at the end of the Middle Bronze, with a consequent extension of the Middle Bronze IIC terminus somewhere near 1400 B.C.[137]

There remains the problem of the Amarna letters and the picture of Palestine that emerges from them. This *can* be harmonized with an early-date perspective. While I will not rehearse here what I have written elsewhere, I will summarize the main points:

1. Labayu was *not* king of Shechem, and the only text that in any way links the two (EA 289) cannot be read so as to make him such. He is much more plausibly king of Pella *(Pí-hi-lì)* in Transjordan. Moreover, we cannot even be sure that *KUR Ša-ak-mi* in

---

137. See the diagram in Bimson and Livingston, "Redating," 46–47. A similar approach, though without relocating the Middle Bronze termination, is in B. Wood, "Did the Israelites Conquer Jericho?" 44–58; idem, "Dating Jericho's Destruction" (reply to P. Bienkowski), *BAR* 16.5 (1990): 47–49, 68–69.

EA 289:23 refers to Shechem.[138] With Labayu, and an alleged Labayan empire, removed from the central hill country, the scene is open to accommodate early Israel.

2. As has been shown in the various studies of the SA.GAZ denotation, *ḫapiru* or *ḫabiru* is most likely an inclusive term of opprobrium for social outcasts, but it can tolerably refer to the Israelites in the Canaanite context, even if not elsewhere.[139] No attempt is hereby made to equate *ʿibrî* and *ḫapiru/ḫabiru* phonetically, nor does there need to be.

With these two points in mind, the picture of Amarna Canaan that emerges is that of kinglets ruling precisely those cities that the Israelites are recorded as *not* having conquered under Joshua. Meanwhile, the Hapiru, whom the other kinglets regard as a common enemy, can in this context be identified with the Israelites. While certain exceptions remain, such as Lachish *(La-ki-su)*, we need to note that with the various oppressions and occupations during the judges period some territory and cities were lost to enemies. First Samuel 7:14 states that the Israelites recovered territory they had lost earlier to the Philistines. What was true in regard to the Philistines was likely true in regard to earlier conquerors.

Egypt and Palestine in the First Millennium B.C.

Before discussing first-millennium synchronisms, one point must be kept in mind when identifying the pharaoh of the exodus. Any such scheme must also consistently and plausibly identify the biblically attested kings of Egypt of later centuries (i.e., in the first millennium B.C.). Exegetical considerations are important in this regard. Two problems remain for the conventional scheme: the identities of "Zerah the Ethiopian" (2 Chron. 14:9) and "So, king of Egypt" (2 Kings 17:4) have proved to be scholarly enigmas, despite Kitchen's confident equation of So with Osorkon IV.[140] We examine each in turn.

138. See my "Labʾayaʾs Connection with Shechem Reassessed," *Abr-Nahrain* 30 (1992): 1–19, esp. 8–12. Partial support for the thesis has now come from a recently discovered cuneiform inscribed cylinder from Beth-shan. See W. Horowitz, "The Amarna Age Inscribed Clay Cylinder from Beth-Shean," *BA* 60 (1997): 97–102.

139. The literature on this theme is considerable, but see in particular the study by M. Greenberg, *The Hab/piru*, American Oriental Series 39 (New Haven: American Oriental Society, 1955); M. G. Kline, "The Ḫa-BI-ru—Kin or Foe of Israel?" *WTJ* 19 (1956): 1–24; *WTJ* 19 (1956): 170–84; *WTJ* 20 (1957): 46–70. Of more recent vintage see M. B. Rowton, "Dimorphic Structure and the Problem of the *ʿapirû-ʿibrîm*," *JNES* 35 (1976): 13–20; N. Naʾaman, "Habiru and Hebrews: The Transfer of a Social Term to the Literary Sphere," *JNES* 45 (1986): 271–88; N. P. Lemche, "Habiru," *ABD*, 3:6–10.

140. K. A. Kitchen, *The Third Intermediate Period in Egypt, 1100–650 B.C.*, 2d ed. with supplement (Warminster: Aris & Phillips, 1986), 372–75. On other contributions see below.

Zerah the Ethiopian

This admittedly untitled individual bearing the epithet "Cushite" (*zerah hakkûšî*, 2 Chron. 14:9 [14:8 MT]) is often either ignored or regarded as a mere military commander under an unmentioned Egyptian king (sometimes identified with Osorkon I).[141] This view ignores the parallel between the militia attributed to Zerah in 2 Chronicles 14:9 and that to Shishak in 2 Chronicles 12:2–3, both of whom are said to have "come out/up against Judah/Jerusalem with chariots and troops." How can one be admitted to have been a pharaoh (Shishak) but the other (Zerah) not? It is regular in the Old Testament for military forces to be ascribed to the king, not to a general (cf. Exod. 14:7, 9, Pharaoh; Num. 21:21–23, Sihon; 2 Kings 25:1, Nebuchadnezzar). Thus for exegetical reasons the explanation is unconvincing.

As to the historical question, this individual belongs to the divided monarchy period—according to the biblical text, in the reign of Asa and probably late in his fourteenth or early in his fifteenth year (2 Chron. 15:10). Following Thiele's chronology, this would place the event at about 894 b.c.[142] No pharaoh of Zerah's prowess seems to have existed in this period, based on either the conventional chronology or any radical revision. The only suggestion with any plausibility is that of Kitchen, that Zerah was a general of Nubian extraction acting for the aging Osorkon I.[143] Apart from the exegetical problem mentioned above, there is the problem of a lack of any historical evidence for a venture into Canaan by this pharaoh, either personally or by proxy. While we would not expect a defeat to be recorded, such a major incursion with a force of three hundred chariots plus a host of infantry would surely have had some successes deserving of record other than the encounter with Asa. But there is no indication of such at all. Thus the identity of Zerah remains a mystery.

The Identity of "So"

The mention of this king of Egypt in 2 Kings 17:4 has caused considerable fuss among historians, and there is no agreed solution as to his identity. Christensen opts for the suggestion that Tefnakht (I) is intended.[144] Meanwhile, there is the proposal that "So" is really the city

141. Ibid., 309.
142. E. R. Thiele, *The Mysterious Numbers of the Hebrew Kings*, rev. ed. (Grand Rapids: Zondervan, 1983), 82. Kitchen, *Third Intermediate Period*, 309, sets the date at 897, which does not affect the point made here.
143. Kitchen, *Third Intermediate Period*, 309.
144. See also the summary of the various other candidates in D. L. Christensen, "The Identity of 'King So' in Egypt (2 Kings XVII:4)," *VT* 39 (1989): 140–53. The older suggestion of "Sibʾe, turtan of Egypt," has now been abandoned.

of Sais and thus not an Egyptian king at all. This still has its advo-cates,[145] but it has not commended itself to others because it involves an arbitrary emendation of the text. Thus by the insertion of an addi-tional *ʾel* before *melek miṣrayim* to read "to So (= Sais), to the king of Egypt," the actual king is left unnamed. Kitchen has objected to such a procedure, pointing out that Israel had no dealings with Sais or the western Delta region. By contrast, as noted above, he alleges an abbre-viation of the name by which he confidently identifies him with (O)so(rkon) IV.[146] But what help Hoshea of Israel imagined he could obtain from this weak, shadow monarch, who ruled only part of the eastern Delta, Kitchen does not satisfactorily explain.[147] His appeal to a longstanding alliance with the Twenty-second Dynasty does not really answer the point, and besides, the "alliance" that Kitchen alleges is not well established from his evidence.[148] The adage of diplomacy, "your enemy's enemy is your friend," the common enemy in this case being Assyria, is a shaky basis for an alliance at the best of times, as history well shows. In summary, there is no real agreement, since all the pro-posed candidates have serious problems.

The Balaam Texts

The story of Balaam and his talking ass is familiar to Bible readers, and apart from the exegetical issues of the biblical text there is a consider-able amount of archaeological material to shed light on the Balaam ep-isode. In particular there is now extant a remarkable text from Deir ʿAlla in Transjordan that not only mentions Balaam but also attributes a prophecy to him.

Balaam's Home

According to the textual information Balaam's home is said to be (1) Pethor on the River in the land of "the sons of ʿmw" (*bĕnê ʿammô*, Num. 22:5), and (2) Pethor of Aram-Naharaim ("Aram of the Two Riv-ers," Deut. 23:4). The biblical Aram-Naharaim is not the Mesopotamia of classical sources and modern designation—the whole region be-tween the Euphrates and Tigris—but the northern part of that area from the Orontes to the Khabur. In particular, the term denotes the re-

---

145. Most recently, J. Day, "The Problem of 'So, King of Egypt' in 2 Kings XVII 4," *VT* 42 (1992): 289–301, esp. 293–94 nn. 25–30. See also W. H. Barnes, *Studies in the Chronol-ogy of the Divided Monarchy of Israel* (Atlanta: Scholars Press, 1991), 131–35.

146. Kitchen, *Third Intermediate Period*, 372–75.

147. Note Kitchen's own introduction to his account of this ephemeral king, ibid., 372.

148. Ibid., 375. Christensen concurs on this point; see "The Identity of 'King So.'"

gion around the bend of the Euphrates, south of Carchemish, past the ancient city of Emar, and downstream to Tuttul at the confluence of the Balikh and Euphrates.[149] The name can be identified with the Naharin of Egyptian campaign lists from the New Kingdom,[150] since the latter clearly corresponds to the region of the Euphrates bend. This much is straightforward. Likewise, Pethor is generally equated with the Pitru of the Kurkh Monolith Inscription of Shalmaneser III, which states that it is on the river Sagur (modern Sâjûr), the western tributary of the Euphrates that enters just south of the Carchemish.[151]

The only problem in this apparently neat scheme concerns *běnê ʿammô*. Following Albright, modern translations have given full consonantal status to the final radical of *ʿmw* to read *ʿAmaw*, which in turn seems to equate to the Amae of the Idrimi inscription. *ʿAmaw* appears in an inscription in the tomb of Qen-Amun, an official of Amenhotep II.[152] While Oller defends this identification against the criticism that the region is not named in Amenhotep II's own campaign lists, he does find a difficulty in the lack of mention in Hittite, Amarna, or Ugaritic archives.[153] Apart from this consideration, however, the Albright identification fits the data quite neatly, despite Oller's skepticism concerning the location of Amae/u.[154]

The Balaam Texts from Deir ʿAlla

In 1967 a remarkable set of Aramaic fragments turned up in the Transjordanian site of Deir ʿAlla.[155] Since they are discussed in chapter 2 of the present volume, only one aspect of them will be treated here.

Of considerable interest are the deities whom Balaam invokes: the *šdyn* and *šgr*. While André Lemaire alters Hoftijzer's restoration *lš[gr--]*

149. Cf. A. Malamat, "The Aramaeans," in *Peoples of Old Testament Times*, ed. D. J. Wiseman (Oxford: Clarendon, 1973), 140.

150. See Gardiner, *Egypt*, 178, 190, 194.

151. As argued by Albright in a comment on the Idrimi inscription. See W. F. Albright, "Some Important Recent Discoveries: Alphabetic Origins and the Idrimi Statue," *BASOR* 118 (1950): 15 and n. 13; also Malamat, "Aramaeans," 141.

152. As cited in Albright, "Some Important Recent Discoveries," 15–16 n. 13.

153. G. H. Oller, "The Autobiography of Idrimi: A New Text with Philological and Historical Commentary" (Ph.D. diss., University of Pennsylvania, 1977), 182–85. A possible mention of Amaʾu in an Emar text may supply this lack: *ni-ši MEŠ ša A-me-e*, in text 9:3, which Arnaud translates as "les gens d'Ameu." See D. Arnaud, *Les textes syriens de l'âge du bronze récent*, Aula Orientalis Supplementa 1 (Barcelona: Sabadell, 1991), 33–34. But problems of orthography and interpretation forbid any definite statement.

154. Layton has reinterpreted the biblical data to conclude that Balaam came from Deir ʿAlla in Ammon. See S. C. Layton, "Whence Comes Balaam? Num. 22,5 Revisited," *Bib* 73 (1992): 32–61.

155. For the editio princeps of the texts, see J. Hoftijzer and G. van der Kooij, *Aramaic Texts from Deir ʿAlla* (Leiden: Brill, 1976), 173–78 (transcription), 179–82 (translation).

to read *lš[m]š:* Sha[ma]sh, the sun deity, in line 6 (Hoftijzer, line 8),[156] there is no question of the reading in line 14 (Hoftijzer, line 16), *šgr w ʿštr:* "Šaggar and ʿAštar." The observation of Dalley and Teissier that Šaggar in North Syrian and Mari texts is a male deity would thereby in this text yield a standard coordinate pair of male-female deities.[157] Hence a good case can be made for asserting that *šgr* is in fact a deity, as appears to be the case in Ugaritic, Mari, and Old Babylonian texts. The component $^d30$ in Emarite names also could well be Šaggar, according to hieroglyphic seals (e.g., ^{d}30-a-bu is Šaggar-abu).[158]

The real interest, however, lies in the undoubted attestation of the *šdyn*-deities, since they seem to have clear links with the *šēdîm* of Deuteronomy 32:17 and Psalm 106:37. The more traditional translation of this term is "demons," cognate with Akkadian *šēdu* (same meaning); however, the Deir ʿAlla text gives a new aspect to the word. Here the *šdyn* are deities who take their place in a divine assembly *(wnṣbw . . . mwʿd)*, and who together with the other gods *(ʾlhn)* resolve to send catastrophe to the earth. But the *ʾlhn* gods reveal the plan to Balaam in a dream or vision. This certainly has its parallel with Numbers 22:8–9, 12, 19–20. Hence we can conclude that the *šdyn* are a group of gods, worshiped in Transjordan and possibly even in Canaan proper, and are most likely the same as the *šēdîm* of the two biblical texts above.[159] Indeed, they could well be the deities of the Baal-peor incident (Num. 25:3; Ps. 106:28). According to Numbers 31:16 it was Balaam who enticed Israel to sacrifice to strange gods at Baal-peor. Hence the mention of *šdym* in this general context of Psalm 106 is significant, in that according to the Aramaic texts these are the gods whom Balaam served.

Two Palestinian Sites

Two sites are significant in different ways: one for newly discovered cuneiform documents, the other a case in point regarding the uncertainty of site identification.

Hazor

In 1991 renewed excavations at Hazor brought to light a partly pre-

156. A. Lemaire, "Fragments from the Book of Balaam Found at Deir Alla," *BAR* 11.5 (1985): 34.

157. S. Dalley and B. Teissier, "Tablets from the Vicinity of Emar and Elsewhere," *Iraq* 54 (1992): 90–91.

158. Ibid., 90 nn. 43–53a.

159. Cf. the insightful discussion by J. Hackett, *The Balaam Text from Deir ʿAlla*, HSM 31 (Chico, Calif.: Scholars Press, 1980), 85–89.

served cuneiform tablet whose original locus was not apparent.[160] But the fragment could have some significance for pre-Israelite, or even early Israelite, history. The tablet is a portion of a letter to Ib-ni-[x] regarding the transfer of a young woman, and Ben-Tor suggests that the name might be restored as Ib-ni-[ᵈIM], that is, Ibni-Addu, a king of Hazor (*ᵁᴿᵁḪa-ṣu-ra*) attested also in the Mari documents.[161]

The biblical name Jabin *(yābîn)* occurs as the name of two kings of Hazor, one at the time of the conquest (Josh. 11:1, 10), the other in the time of the judges (Judg. 4:2). As Yadin, Malamat, and more recently Bimson have pointed out, an argument can be constructed to equate the Hebrew Jabin with the Ibni prefix, allowing for a missing theophoric component.[162] Since Ibni-prefix names are fairly common in the Amorite onomasticon, especially from Mari, it is readily understandable that there would have been several "Jabins" of Hazor, whatever the theophoric component in the names. The correspondence of this name with the biblical Jabin would make us understand the latter as a proper name rather than a dynastic title, as some have contended.[163]

Gibeah

While there is no dispute regarding the identity of Tell el-Qedah with Hazor, the site of Saul's palace at Gibeah, long thought to have been settled, is now disputed again. After Albright's excavations in 1922–23 and 1933 of an Iron Age citadel just north of Jerusalem, the site of Gibeah had been confidently identified with Tell el-Ful, as contrasted with an earlier identification with the modern village of Jeba. More recently, however, the original identification has been reasserted. Arnold in particular has argued that the Tell el-Ful–Gibeah equation is untenable on both literary-topographical and archaeological grounds, and has instead resurrected the older identification with Geba (modern Jeba).[164] The principal difficulties with Tell el-Ful are as follows:

160. W. Horowitz and A. Shaffer, "A Fragment of a Letter from Hazor," *IEJ* 42 (1992): 165–67.

161. For references to Ḫaṣura/Hazor in the Mari texts see ARM 16.1.1, 14; for Mari references to Ibni-Addu see ARM 16.1.2, 113.

162. Y. Yadin, *Hazor: With a Chapter on Israelite Megiddo*, Schweich Lectures, 1970 (London and New York: Oxford University Press for the British Academy, 1972), 5; idem, *Hazor: The Rediscovery of a Great Citadel* (New York: Random House, 1975), 16; A. Malamat, "Hazor: 'The Head of All Those Kingdoms,'" *JBL* 79 (1960): 17; Bimson, *Redating*, 181.

163. Note that Kitchen, *Ancient Orient*, 68, argues for this position.

164. P. M. Arnold, *Gibeah: The Search for a Biblical City*, JSOTSup 79 (Sheffield: JSOT Press, 1990).

1. According to 1 Samuel 14:16 Saul's watchmen at Gibeah could look on the Philistine disarray at Michmash. Tell el-Ful, however, is 7 km. away from the modern Mukhmas (Michmash), and even a watchtower would not afford a view from such a distance. From Geba, by contrast, such a view is clear and close.
2. The textual references indicate an association with sites north of Jerusalem, not with Jerusalem itself. Tell el-Ful is a mere 4 km. from the Old City, while the other sites such as Gibeon, Ramah, Mizpah, and Michmash are all to the north of Tell el-Ful.
3. According to 1 Samuel 14:2 Saul and his six hundred men lodged under the pomegranate *(hārimmôn)*, on the outskirts of Gibeah. This is surely the Rock of the Pomegranate/Rimmon *(selaʿ hārimmôn)* of Judges 20:45–47; 21:13—not a tree, but a rock formation. This can be identified with a formation 2 km. southeast of the Geba Pass, a cave named el-Jaia that looks like a split pomegranate and that could well accommodate the six hundred men of either Benjamin's (Judg. 20:47) or Saul's army (1 Sam. 14:2).[165]

Whether we accept Arnold's argument at every point or not, he has presented a good case, and it illustrates the more general point that identification of ancient sites in Palestine is far from settled.

While discussion of the above topics has been far from exhaustive, it is submitted in the hope that further research will shed more light on the unsolved problems that remain.

---

165. See ibid., chap. 2, for these points in more detail.

4

Literary Approaches to Old Testament Study

Tremper Longman III

Summarizing and evaluating the literary study of the Old Testament over the past quarter century is a daunting task. During that period of time, more books and articles that focus on the literary method and its application have appeared than in the previous century and a half.[1]

Indeed, the literary approach has been revitalized within the time period specifically covered by this survey. I begin at the moment of the method's rebirth, then acknowledge its earlier history, while exploring the reasons for its temporary demise. After this, I trace the associations between Old Testament studies and different permutations of literary studies beyond the formalism with which its modern phase began. After describing the current state of the field in the last half of the 1990s, I outline an agenda for the future.

(Re)birth of the Literary Approach to the Old Testament

From the perspective of biblical scholarship, the watershed was the publication of Robert Alter's *Art of Biblical Narrative* in 1981.[2] The liter-

---

1. A look at M. Minor, *Literary-Critical Approaches to the Bible: An Annotated Bibliography* (West Cornwall, Conn.: Locust Hill, 1992), confirms this impression. Of its 2,254 entries, the vast majority date after 1980 and very few were written before 1970. See also idem, *Literary-Critical Approaches to the Bible: A Bibliographical Supplement* (West Cornwall, Conn.: Locust Hill, 1996); and P. R. House, "The Rise and Current Status of Literary Criticism of the Old Testament," in *Beyond Form Criticism: Essays in Old Testament Literary Criticism*, ed. P. R. House, SBTS 2 (Winona Lake, Ind.: Eisenbrauns, 1992), 3–22; hereafter abbreviated as *BFC*.

2. R. Alter, *The Art of Biblical Narrative* (New York: Basic Books, 1981), though many would also point to the earlier significant study by E. Auerbach, *Mimesis: The Representation of Reality in Western Literature*, trans. W. Trask (Garden City, N.Y.: Doubleday, 1957), particularly chap. 1, entitled "Odysseus' Scar."

ary study of the Old Testament had been advocated by some before this time,[3] but Alter's study attracted the attention of the field in an unprecedented way and led to a renewed interest in the literary form of the biblical text. Whereas in the years before his work there were sporadic attempts at literary studies of the Old Testament,[4] afterward a movement was born.

At the time of the publication of *The Art of Biblical Narrative*, Alter was an established literary critic with a specialty in comparative literature. This book was his first major statement about the Old Testament. To describe why Alter's book captivated the imagination of countless biblical scholars requires some speculation. One might suggest that the regnant historical-critical methods were yielding fewer and fewer new insights. They also tended to obscure rather than illuminate the meaning of the final form of the text, which was of interest to many readers of the Bible. Source and form criticism of the Old Testament focused on small units of the text for the most part and were concerned with their prehistory. The literary approach advocated by Alter did not reject these diachronic methods[5] but reordered priorities so that biblical texts were examined in their final context as a literary whole.

Evangelical scholars, whose presence in the guild of Old Testament scholarship has been on the increase since 1980, were attracted to the literary approach because of its interest in the final form of the text and its tendency to treat biblical books as whole compositions rather than a collection of different sources. The literary approach allowed evangelical scholars to bracket the question of the historicity of narrative and carry on a conversation with their colleagues who did not share their views on

3. Most notably J. Muilenburg, "Form Criticism and Beyond," *JBL* 88 (1969): 1–18, reprinted in *BFC*, 49–69. In this publication of his SBL presidential address, Muilenburg calls on his fellow biblical scholars to go beyond an analysis of the small units of biblical text and their prehistory to attend to the rhetorical structure of the final form of the text. His challenge to supplement form-critical study of the Bible was heard by a few scholars in the next twelve years; see n. 4 below.

4. Besides Muilenburg, notable among these initial explorations are L. Alonso Schökel, *Estudios de Poetica Hebraea* (Barcelona: Juan Flors, 1963); D. J. A. Clines, *I, He, We, and They: A Literary Approach to Isaiah 53*, JSOTSup 1 (Sheffield: JSOT Press, 1976); idem, "Story and Poem: The Old Testament as Literature and Scripture," *Int* 34 (1980): 115–27, reprinted in *BFC*, 25–38; D. M. Gunn, *The Story of King David: Genre and Interpretation*, JSOTSup 16 (Sheffield: JSOT Press, 1980); D. Patte and J. F. Parker, "A Structural Exegesis of Genesis 2 and 3," *Genesis 2 and 3: Kaleidoscopic Structural Readings*, ed. D. Patte, *Semeia* 18 (1980): 55–75, reprinted in *BFC*, 143–61; S. Bar-Efrat, "Some Observations on the Analysis of Structure in Biblical Narrative," *VT* 30 (1980): 154–73, reprinted in *BFC*, 186–205.

5. Alter, *Art of Biblical Narrative*, 131–54, after all, argued that the Genesis narratives were the end result of "composite artistry."

the origin of the Bible.[6] It also provided arguments in favor of the unity of the biblical text whereas other scholars saw seams and breaks.[7]

Other developments in biblical studies had prepared the way for a ready acceptance of the literary approach, most notably canon criticism as developed by Brevard Childs, which was an important development in Old Testament studies since 1970.[8] Canon criticism also focuses on the final form of the biblical text and treats biblical books as literary wholes. Indeed, though Childs vigorously denies any influence, John Barton has persuasively demonstrated a formal similarity between canon criticism and the literary strategy called formalism (or New Criticism; see below).[9]

Finally, we must also acknowledge the persuasive power of Alter's readings of the biblical text. He did not lecture to biblical scholars; he

6. For examples of evangelical scholars using the literary approach in various ways, see D. Tsumura, "Literary Insertion (A x B Pattern) in Biblical Hebrew," *VT* 33 (1983): 468–82; idem, "Literary Insertion, A x B Pattern, in Hebrew and Ugaritic," *UF* 18 (1986): 351–61; L. Ryken, *How to Read the Bible as Literature* (Grand Rapids: Zondervan, 1984); R. B. Chisholm Jr., "Structure, Style, and the Prophetic Message: An Analysis of Isaiah 5:8–30," *BSac* 143 (1986): 46–60; K. J. Vanhoozer, "A Lamp in the Labyrinth: The Hermeneutics of 'Aesthetic' Theology," *TJ* 8 (1987): 25–56; idem, "The Semantics of Biblical Literature: Truth and Scripture's Diverse Literary Forms," in *Hermeneutics, Authority, and Canon*, ed. D. A. Carson and J. Woodbridge (Grand Rapids: Zondervan, 1986), 53–104; idem, *Biblical Narrative in the Philosophy of Paul Ricoeur: A Study in Hermeneutics and Theology* (New York and Cambridge: Cambridge University Press, 1990); T. Longman III, *Literary Approaches to Biblical Interpretation* (Grand Rapids: Zondervan, 1987); B. G. Webb, *The Book of the Judges: An Integrated Reading*, JSOTSup 46 (Sheffield: JSOT Press, 1987); L. C. Allen, "Ezekiel 24:3–14: A Rhetorical Perspective," *CBQ* 49 (1987): 404–14; R. P. Gordon, *I and II Samuel: A Commentary* (Grand Rapids: Zondervan; Exeter: Paternoster, 1989); V. P. Long, *The Reign and Rejection of King Saul: A Case for Literary and Theological Coherence*, SBLDS 118 (Atlanta: Scholars Press, 1989); K. L. Younger Jr., *Ancient Conquest Accounts: A Study in Ancient Near Eastern and Biblical History Writing*, JSOTSup 98 (Sheffield: JSOT Press, 1990); P. R. House, *The Unity of the Twelve*, JSOTSup 97 (Sheffield: Almond, 1990). These are just a few of many literary studies by evangelicals. Literary studies have also heavily influenced commentaries, introductions (see R. B. Dillard and T. Longman III, *An Introduction to the Old Testament* [Grand Rapids: Zondervan, 1994]), and other reference works by evangelical scholars.

7. A notable instance of this is G. J. Wenham, "The Coherence of the Flood Narrative," *VT* 28 (1978): 336–48, reprinted in *"I Studied Inscriptions from before the Flood": Ancient Near Eastern, Literary, and Linguistic Approaches to the Old Testament*, ed. R. S. Hess and D. T. Tsumura, SBTS 4 (Winona Lake, Ind.: Eisenbrauns, 1994), 436–47. Evangelicals were not the only ones to use the literary approach as an argument in favor of the unity of a biblical text; see also R. N. Whybray, *The Making of the Pentateuch: A Methodological Study*, JSOTSup 53 (Sheffield: JSOT Press, 1987); and I. M. Kikawada and A. Quinn, *Before Abraham Was: The Unity of Genesis 1–11* (Nashville: Abingdon, 1985).

8. See his *Introduction to the Old Testament as Scripture* (Philadelphia: Fortress, 1979).

9. J. Barton, *Reading the Old Testament: Method in Biblical Study* (Philadelphia: Westminster; London: Darton, Longman & Todd, 1984).

showed them how it was done, with striking results. His treatment of the biblical stories in *The Art of Biblical Narrative*, particularly those from Genesis, makes sense of and illuminates the biblical text. His work is also interesting to a broader audience, something that could not be said of many previous form-critical readings of the text.

Alter does not situate his approach to literary analysis within the panoply of different schools of thought, but his approach may generally be described as a kind of formalism or New Criticism. That is, Alter focuses on the text, not on the author or the reader; specifically he desires to describe the function of the ancient Hebrew literary conventions. While there are similarities between the literatures of different cultures and different time periods, each people, ancient Israelites included, tell their stories and write their poems in different ways:

> Every culture, even every era in a particular culture, develops distinctive and sometimes intricate codes for telling its stories, involving everything from narrative point of view, procedures of descriptions and characterization, the management of dialogue, to the ordering of time and the organization of plot.[10]

The purpose of Alter's analysis is to explore and understand the literary conventions of Hebrew stories and poems in order to understand their meaning.

Alter's work inspired many to attempt literary readings of biblical narrative. A number of biblical scholars followed his method in general outline.[11]

Ancient Precursors

I have already mentioned the work of Muilenburg and others who produced literary studies sporadically in the years before the blossoming of the method.[12] Further study reveals ancient roots to the practice of

---

10. R. Alter, "How Convention Helps Us to Read: The Case of the Bible's Annunciation Type Scene," *Prooftexts* 3 (1983): 115.

11. J. P. Fokkelman, *Narrative Art in Genesis*, SSN 17 (Amsterdam: Van Gorcum, 1975), 11–45, was a precursor. Others include A. Berlin, *Poetics and Interpretation of Biblical Narrative*, BLS 9 (Sheffield: Almond, 1983); M. Weiss, *The Bible from Within: The Method of Total Interpretation* (Jerusalem: Magnes, 1984); J. Licht, *Storytelling in the Bible* (Jerusalem: Magnes, 1986); S. Bar-Efrat, *Narrative Art in the Bible*, BLS 17 (Sheffield: Almond, 1989). M. Sternberg, *The Poetics of Biblical Narrative: Ideological Literature and the Drama of Reading*, ILBS (Bloomington: Indiana University Press, 1985), also comes from this general school of thought, though a major point of his book is that Alter wrongly reduces the biblical text to a literary function, thus neglecting its ideological purpose.

12. See nn. 3 and 4.

applying literary methods, concepts, and insights to biblical narrative and poetry.

Indeed, Stephen Prickett has persuasively argued that the application of literary studies to biblical studies is not a totally new phenomenon but rather is the reintegration of an age-old union.[13] He attributes the separation of biblical studies from literary analysis to the forces of the Enlightenment. Specifically, he cites the founding of the University of Berlin in 1809 as the moment, symbolic at least, when literary studies and biblical studies parted paths. He believes that when the biblical department was removed from the humanities and placed with a separate theology department a "glacial moraine" was erected between the Bible and its literary perception.

Previous to this time it was a matter of course for the Bible to be understood in literary terms. One need only appeal to the early church fathers to illustrate this claim. Augustine and Jerome were trained in classical rhetoric and poetics. As a result, they frequently applied the principles of literature that they learned in school to the study of the Bible. They often compared biblical stories and poems with ones familiar to them in classical literature. The result was, from a modern perspective, a distortion of understanding and evaluation of the biblical texts. Jerome, for example, scanned Hebrew poems and described their poetic form in labels developed for Greek and Latin poetry.[14] James Kugel quotes Jerome as saying:

> What is more musical than the Psalter? which in the manner of our Flaccus or of the Greek Pindar, now flows in iambs, now rings with Alcaics, swells to a Sapphic measure or moves along with a half-foot? What is fairer than the hymns of Deuteronomy or Isaiah? What is more solemn than Solomon, what more polished than Job? All of which books, as Josephus and Origen write, flow in the original in hexameter and pentameter verses.[15]

Jerome is just one example that can be multiplied throughout the history of the Christian and Jewish interpretation of the Bible. The literary study of the Bible in the latter part of the twentieth century is a reunion of a split that took place due to an unwarranted and unhealthy obsession with historical criticism of the Old Testament.[16]

---

13. S. Prickett, *Words and the Word: Language Poetics and Biblical Interpretation* (New York and Cambridge: Cambridge University Press, 1986).

14. See J. Kugel, *The Idea of Biblical Poetry: Parallelism and Its History* (New Haven: Yale University Press, 1981), 149–56.

15. Quoted in ibid., 159–60.

16. In Prickett's words, "To discuss biblical hermeneutics in the light of poetic theory is not to apply an alien concept, but to restore a wholeness of approach that has been disastrously fragmented over the past hundred and fifty years" (*Words and the Word*, 197).

The reemergence of the literary study of the Bible, however, was not a monolithic phenomenon. Biblical scholars observed very quickly that formalism was not the only literary game in town. Some competing literary reading strategies began to dot the landscape of the guild. These different approaches are not always easy to understand or to relate to one another. With this in mind, I offer the following description.

Conceptual Map of Literary Approaches to the Old Testament

While formalism continues as a viable literary approach within biblical studies, other methods have made their impact as well. Indeed, biblical studies reflects the situation in the field of literary theory. Literary theory, like most academic studies, is a rather fractious discipline. Different schools of thought compete with each other for dominance. New approaches to literature have appeared with increasing frequency, and after a lag of time biblical scholars assimilate the new method and apply it to the text that is the object of their attention.

In surveying the different schools of literary study that biblical scholars have employed over the past few decades, I describe them in the order that they made their entrance into the field. This is not to say that when a new approach was introduced into biblical studies the old approach disappeared. The new approach becomes a kind of avant-garde, while the older approaches continued to be practiced in books and articles.

At this point, I am merely descriptive and illustrative. Having already described the "close reading" of Alter and others, I now define four schools of thought: structuralism and semiotics, deconstruction, reader-response, and ideological readings (particularly Marxist and feminist approaches, as well as New Historicism). At the conclusion of this brief survey, I describe the situation as it is at the present moment before moving to a concluding evaluation of the literary approach.

Structuralism and Semiotics

Structuralism and semiotics are two labels that are sometimes used interchangeably and at other times slightly differently. In their manifestation in literary theory,[17] however, both focus on the nature of the literary text as sign.

17. I am concentrating on the use of these terms in literary theory and their application to biblical studies. As V. P. Poythress has pointed out, "structuralism is more a diverse collection of methods, paradigm and personal preferences than it is a 'system,' a theory or a well-formulated thesis" ("Structuralism and Biblical Studies," *JETS* 21 [1978]: 221). Most important, perhaps, structuralism is broad in that it claims to be "not a method of inquiry, but a general theory about human culture" (Barton, *Reading the Old Testament*, 77–88).

Most studies of the history of the idea of structuralism begin with the pioneering work of the Swiss linguist Ferdinand de Saussure.[18] Others appeal to the work of the American philosopher Charles Sanders Peirce for a richer conception of the nature of the sign.[19] Such neat distinctions are interesting and important, but not for our purpose, which is to give a general description of this movement and its application to the literary study of the Bible.

At the heart of structuralism is the sign, whether linguistic, literary, or cultural. The sign is understood as having two parts, the signifier and the signified. The signifier is the word, the text, the custom. The signified is that to which these refer, the concept.[20]

As we focus on the nature of the literary text as sign, we see that the text is made up of a number of linguistic signs or words. Structuralism's initial insight is that the literary work is an arbitrary system of signs. That is, the signs that constitute a literary work have an arbitrary or conventional, not an inherent or necessary, relationship to that which they signify. The arbitrary nature of language is illustrated by the fact that different languages have each adopted different names for the same object, state, or action. If there were a necessary connection between a dog and the word *dog,* then French would not use the term *chien* nor would German use the term *Hund.*

Two further observations made by structuralist thought become increasingly important later. First, Saussure argued that language is made up of differences: "In the language itself, there are only differences. Even more important than that is the fact that, although in general a difference holds, in a language there are only differences, and no positive terms."[21] The difference between the words *hat, cat,* and *bat* is a single letter, and language is built on such differences.

One of the important insights that structuralism made concerning literature is that it, like language itself, operates by certain "conventions." Like syntax, grammar, and lexicon of a linguistic system, the literary conventions are underlying structures that may be discerned across literature as a whole. To be competent in a language does not

18. See his posthumously published *Course in General Linguistics,* ed. C. Bally and A. Sechehaye, trans. W. Baskin (London: Owen, 1959; reprinted, New York: McGraw-Hill, 1966).

19. See M. Shapiro, *The Sense of Grammar: Language as Semiotic* (Bloomington: Indiana University Press, 1983), 25–102, for a cogent description of a Peircean semiotic as applied to language and literature.

20. For helpful general discussions of structuralism, see J. Culler, *Structuralist Poetics: Structuralism, Linguistics, and the Study of Literature* (Ithaca: Cornell University Press; London: Routledge & Kegan Paul, 1975); T. Hawkes, *Structuralism and Semiotics,* New Accents (Berkeley: University of California Press; London: Methuen, 1977).

21. Saussure, *Course,* 118.

mean learning every word or every possible syntactical arrangement, but it does mean learning the basic rules of the language. The same is true of literature. To be literarily competent does not mean knowing the literature exhaustively, but being aware of the major conventions, or literary devices, genres, and so forth. After all, according to structuralist thought, the meaning of a text is found not in the author's intention but in the text's conventional code. Reading is a "rule-governed process."[22]

When understood as simply describing the native literary conventions of a particular culture or time, this type of analysis is not much different from the formalism practiced by Alter. But some structuralist analysis of narrative in the Bible is quite esoteric in a way that obscures rather than illumines the meaning of a text.

Perhaps this tendency toward an obscure and esoteric analysis of the text is in part due to the scientific pretension of the approach. Structuralists desire to give literary studies a method of approaching texts that can be demonstrated and repeated. R. C. Culley summarized it by saying that structuralists "are seeking a method which is scientific in the sense that they are striving for a rigorous statement and an exacting analytical model."[23] This desire sometimes leads to treating a literary text like a problem to be solved by a mathematical formula.[24]

This quasi-scientific impulse with its resulting esotericism may also have to do with structuralism's obsession with binary opposition. Structuralists' study of the sign leads them to believe that signs (including linguistic and literary signs) derive their meaning by opposition with other signs.

A recent example of a structuralist/semiotic approach to biblical literature is E. J. van Wolde's analysis of Genesis 2–3.[25] In this study, she combines the insights of the folklorist A. J. Greimas and the American philosopher C. S. Peirce to produce a very sophisticated form of analysis of these chapters in Genesis, beginning with the forms of expression, which are the various phonological, prosodic, and semantic wordplays,

22. Culler, *Structuralist Poetics*, 241. According to R. Scholes, *Semiotics and Interpretation* (New Haven: Yale University Press, 1982), 14, both readers and authors are "divided psyches traversed by codes."

23. R. C. Culley, "Exploring New Directions," in *The Hebrew Bible and Its Modern Interpreters*, ed. D. A. Knight and G. M. Tucker (Philadelphia: Fortress; Chico, Calif.: Scholars Press, 1985), 174.

24. R. M. Polzin reduces the Book of Job to the following mathlike formula: $F_x (a) : F_y (b) = F_x (b) : F_a r (y)$. See his *Biblical Structuralism: Method and Subjectivity in the Study of Ancient Texts*, SemSup (Philadelphia: Fortress, 1977), 75. See comments on E. J. van Wolde below.

25. E. J. van Wolde, *A Semiotic Analysis of Genesis 2–3: A Semiotic Theory and Method of Analysis Applied to the Story of the Garden of Eden*, SSN 25 (Assen: Van Gorcum, 1989).

to the discursive form, which is the final interpretation resulting from the interaction between reader and text.[26]

In her general description of semiotics in the first part of the book, van Wolde represents well the essential insight of this approach into the sign nature of language, literature, and reality. But she also illustrates well the quasi-scientific and obscurantist nature of the approach as she reduces Genesis 2 and 3 to a series of formulas that only the initiated can understand. Reading her comments on these formulas and their exegetical implications leads one to question the need for such a convoluted approach to the text, considering that her interesting ideas about the meaning of the text could be discovered simply through the normal rules of close reading. It is for these reasons that few scholars would consider themselves structuralists today.[27]

Reader-Response Approach

New Criticism (formalism) wrests the focus of literary attention from the author and his intention to the text itself. Positing the "intentional fallacy,"[28] it makes attempts to understand a literary work via the biography or psychology of an author appear misguided. Structuralism and semiotics took on a quasi-scientific cast, but by focusing solely on the text, they ignored the author.

Even with a common focus of study—the text—it is not at all unusual to have as many interpretations as there are readers of a text. This observation illustrates the role of the reader in the interpretive process. Readers come to the same text from different gender, racial, and economic perspectives, all influencing their understanding of a text.

In general, and at its simplest, reader-response theory can be described as those literary approaches that recognize that the reader has

26. It is in Peirce, rather than Greimas, that van Wolde finds her methodological justification for including the perspective of the reader; cf. *Semiotic Analysis*, 23.

27. Other examples of structuralist studies of the Old Testament include R. Barthes, "The Struggle with the Angel: Textual Analysis of Genesis 32:23–33," in R. Barthes et al., *Structural Analysis and Biblical Exegesis: Interpretational Essays*, trans. A. M. Johnson Jr., PTMS 3 (Pittsburgh: Pickwick, 1974), 21–33; R. Detweiler, *Story, Sign, and Self: Phenomenology and Structuralism as Literary Critical Methods*, SemSup (Philadelphia: Fortress; Chico, Calif.: Scholars Press, 1978); E. V. McKnight, *The Bible and the Reader: An Introduction to Literary Criticism* (Philadelphia: Fortress, 1985); D. Jobling, *The Sense of Biblical Narrative: Three Structural Analyses in the Old Testament (1 Samuel 13–31, Numbers 11–12, 1 Kings 17–18)*, JSOTSup 7 (Sheffield: JSOT Press, 1978).

28. The intentional fallacy, first proposed by W. K. Wimsatt and M. C. Beardsley in 1946, "identifies what is held to be the error of interpreting or evaluating a work by reference to the intention, the conscious design or aim, of the author who wrote the work" (cf. M. H. Abrams, *A Glossary of Literary Terms*, 4th ed. [New York: Holt, Rinehart, Winston, 1981], 83).

a share in the act of literary communication.[29] A more specific description of that share, however, uncovers the difference of opinion among different advocates of this approach. Readers do more than recognize and describe the meaning of a text as if it is totally external to them. But do readers shape the meaning of a text to their situation or do they actually construct the meaning?

W. Iser articulates a moderate reader-response approach that acknowledges that the text is external to the reader and serves as a restraint on the interpreter's understanding.[30] That is, different interpreters can shape the text to their situation, but they have to justify their reading by means of the text.[31] By contrast, Stanley Fish believes that the interpretive community actually constructs the meaning of a text.[32] The text has no inherent or determinate meaning.

Before passing on to the next stage of literary approach, I would like to describe what might be called ideological criticism here, as a subset of reader-response criticism. Ideological criticism is the practice of interpreting texts from a decidedly ideological viewpoint. The most common such interpretations are feminist and Marxist.[33] One might also

29. See W. S. Vorster, "Readings, Readers and the Succession Narrative: An Essay on Reception," *ZAW* 98 (1986): 351–62, reprinted in *BFC,* 395–407.

30. His works include *The Act of Reading: A Theory of Aesthetic Response* (Baltimore: Johns Hopkins University Press, 1978).

31. A similar sentiment is expressed by the biblical scholar E. V. McKnight: "The relationship between reader as subject (acting upon the text) and the reader as object (being acted upon by the text), however, is not seen as an opposition but as two sides of the same coin. It is only as the reader is subject of text and language that the reader becomes object. It is as the reader becomes object that the fullness of the reader's needs and desires as subject are met" (*The Bible and the Reader,* 128).

32. See his *Is There a Text in This Class? The Authority of Interpretive Communities* (Cambridge, Mass.: Harvard University Press, 1980).

33. Besides the work of Alice Bach, described below, a representative list of important feminist works includes P. Trible, *God and the Rhetoric of Sexuality,* OBT (Philadelphia: Fortress, 1978); C. V. Camp, *Wisdom and the Feminine in the Book of Proverbs,* BLS 11 (Decatur and Sheffield: Almond, 1885); J. C. Exum, "Murder They Wrote: Ideology and the Manipulation of Female Presence in Biblical Narrative," *USQR* 43 (1989): 19–39; A. L. Laffey, *An Introduction to the Old Testament: A Feminist Perspective* (Philadelphia: Fortress, 1988; reprinted as *Wives, Harlots, and Concubines: The Old Testament in Feminist Perspective* [London: SPCK, 1990]); M. Bal, *Lethal Love: Feminist Literary Readings of Biblical Love Stories,* Indiana Studies in Biblical Literature (Bloomington: Indiana University Press, 1987). See also *The Bible and Feminist Hermeneutics,* ed. M. A. Tolbert, *Semeia* 28 (1983).

In the field of literary studies in general, for Marxist interpretation see F. Jameson, *The Political Unconscious: Narrative as a Socially Symbolic Act* (Ithaca: Cornell University Press, 1981). See also N. K. Gottwald, "Literary Criticism of the Hebrew Bible: Retrospect and Prospect," in *Mappings of the Biblical Terrain: The Bible as Text,* ed. V. L. Tollers and J. Maier (Lewisburg, Pa.: Bucknell University Press; London and Toronto: Associated University Presses, 1990), 27–44; F. O. García-Treto, "A Reader-Response Approach to

place New Historicism in this category, though I am unaware of any biblical study that takes this viewpoint as a conscious starting point.[34]

Feminist interpretation approaches the text from a definite ideological point of view, beginning with the view that women have been subjugated through most if not all of human history. This subjugation is often embedded in literary works. It is the function of feminist interpretation first of all to expose the patriarchy of literary and biblical texts and then either to reject the text completely or to reclaim it by subverting it.

Alice Bach, for instance, in her provocative but, in the final analysis, failed reading of the *Sotah* in Numbers 5, offers a clear example.[35] Her failure arises from her unwillingness to enter the world of the text where the ancient promise of descendants makes childbearing a critical theological enterprise. She also refuses to enter the world of the text that expects God to work through material means (the potion that the woman drinks) as the text expresses he would. The result is that she sees women being treated callously by being forced to drink a suspicious liquid because of the mere jealousy of their husbands. Since God is not behind the rite, the woman may be put through a horrible ordeal unjustly, and in any case the root of the jealousy is the result of a double standard and male sexual anxiety.

Such readings are extremely important in jarring us out of our own interpretive fantasy worlds. We all read the text from a restricted presuppositional stance, and we need the readings of others outside our own "faith stance" to alert us to our misconceptions. But they are misconceptions about the *text*. The text, in the tradition of Iser and others, is the final arbiter of meaning. We must justify our interpretation in its light.

Deconstruction

Formalism (New Criticism) moved the field away from authorial intention and toward the text. Structuralism and semiotics also looked to the text for the meaning of a literary work. Reader-response criticism

---

Prophetic Conflict," in *The New Literary Criticism and the Hebrew Bible*, ed. J. C. Exum and D. J. A. Clines, JSOTSup 143 (Sheffield: Sheffield Academic Press, 1993), 114–24; T. K. Beal, "Ideology and Intertextuality: Surplus of Meaning and Controlling the Means of Production," in *Reading between Texts: Intertextuality and the Hebrew Bible*, ed. D. N. Fewell (Louisville: Westminster/John Knox, 1992), 27–40. See also *Ideological Criticism of Biblical Texts*, eds. D. Jobling and T. Pippin, *Semeia* 59 (1992).

34. See H. A. Veeser, *The New Historicism* (New York and London: Routledge, 1989), though *Semeia* 51 (1990), titled *Poststructural Criticism and the Bible: Text/History/Discourse*, ed. G. A. Phillips, comes close with influence from Michel Foucault and Hayden White, an important contemporary philosopher of history.

35. A. Bach, "Good to the Last Drop: Viewing the Sotah (Numbers 5:11–31) as the Glass Half Empty and Wondering How to View It Half Full," in *New Literary Criticism*, 26–54.

casts doubt on this enterprise by highlighting the role of the reader in the shaping or even creation of the meaning. One might predict the next move on the basis of the direction of previous thought. Since the locus of meaning has proved so elusive, perhaps we should entertain the possibility that there is no determinate meaning in the text to begin with.[36]

Deconstruction attacks the heart of structuralism by questioning the relationship between a sign and that which it signifies.[37] That is, there is slippage between the two with the result that literary communication is on unstable ground. Deconstruction questions structuralism's objective and scientific pretensions.

But first, I must comment on an important presupposition of deconstruction that will be relevant to my later evaluation. Deconstruction denies the presence of an absolute signifier.[38] That is, nothing and no one exists outside and above the literary process that insures the viability of communication. Advocates of deconstruction regard any assertions of an absolute signifier as maintaining a false logocentrism. Nothing and no one, whether author, speaker, or God, is present out there to ground the meaning of a text. Literary texts have no determinate meaning, and one common feature of a deconstructive analysis is to undermine any attempts to provide a stable meaning for a text.

Deconstruction is most often associated with the work of the French philosopher Jacques Derrida, who had a major influence on Western literary theory from the late 1960s through the 1980s. In literary theory, Derrida's influence was mediated through Geoffrey Hartman and the Yale school of deconstruction;[39] but today, while still practiced, it no longer has the force and power it once enjoyed in philosophical and literary circles.

36. As we will see below, certain forms of reader-response approach also deny the presence of any determinate meaning in the text, and that provides the rationale for the reader to create it.

37. S. Moore, *Poststructuralism and the New Testament* (Minneapolis: Fortress, 1994), 13, describes deconstruction as a "strategic recasting" of structural linguistics. For insightful introduction to deconstruction as a literary method, see J. Culler, *The Pursuit of Signs: Semiotics, Literature, Deconstruction* (Ithaca: Cornell University Press, 1981); idem, *On Deconstruction: Theory and Criticism after Structuralism* (London: Routledge and Kegan Paul, 1982); C. Norris, *Deconstruction: Theory and Practice* (London: Methuen, 1982); V. B. Leitch, *Deconstructive Criticism: An Advanced Introduction* (New York: Columbia University Press, 1983).

38. Abrams, *Glossary of Literary Terms*, 38, describes the absolute signifier as "an absolute foundation, outside the play of language itself, which is adequate to 'center' (that is, to anchor and organize) the linguistic system in such a way as to fix the particular meaning of a spoken or written discourse within that system."

39. See Leitch, *Deconstructive Criticism*, 88, 116–21, and more popularly, C. Campbell, "The Tyranny of the Yale Critics," *New York Times Magazine*, Feb. 9, 1986.

Derrida attacks the Western philosophical tradition that subordinates writing to speaking. Since at least Plato, speech has been thought to bear a closer relationship to pure thought than does writing. Writing removes communication a step further from authorial presence. Derrida contends that this attitude, which underlies Western philosophy, demonstrates a stubborn belief in presence that must be undermined. He argues instead for the priority of writing over speech. He believes that writing is a clearer illustration of what characterizes all language acts: the slippage between sign and referent, signifier and signified. Derrida's extreme language skepticism calls into question the act of literary communication.

The fundamental force behind Derrida's writing is his heightening the distance between signifier and signified. Here he threatens the possibility of literary communication. He begins with Saussure's premise that a sign has no inherent meaning but finds meaning only in distinction from other elements in the semiotic system. Meaning is thus a function not of presence but of absence. Derrida's concept of "differance" is helpful here. (The *a* in "differance" shows that the word is a neologism, constructed from two different French words, one meaning "to differ," the other "to defer.") The meaning of a linguistic or literary sign is based on its difference in comparison with other signs and as such is always deferred, or delayed. With deconstruction one enters the "endless labyrinth."[40] Meaning is never established; the pun becomes the favored interpretive device.

This interpretive strategy reads a text looking for the inevitable aporia that a literary text will produce due to the slippage between a sign and that which it signifies. The aporia, or "undecidables," will show that the text produces no certain meaning. The only option is to play with the text.[41]

As we will see later, deconstruction is still a lively option in biblical studies. Often, however, it is one of a number of interpretive strategies adopted by a contemporary critic. To illustrate a deconstructive analy-

40. F. Lentricchia, *After the New Criticism* (Chicago: University of Chicago Press; London: Methuen, 1980), 166.
41. Characteristic of Derrida is an analysis of pivotal philosophers such as Plato, Rousseau, Saussure, Lévi-Strauss, and Austin. He exposes their logocentrism (belief in a "metaphysics of presence"), which is implied in their fundamental phonocentrism (priority of speech over writing). He probes the text of these philosophers until he uncovers an aporia (a basic contradiction), which usually involves the philosopher's use of metaphor or some other rhetorical device. Metaphor is key in this regard because it displays the slippage between sign and referent. Its use by the philosopher demonstrates, contra the philosophers, that the truth claims of philosophy are no different from those of fiction.

sis of a biblical text I go back to an early example, Peter Miscall's analysis of the David and Goliath story.[42]

The traditional interpretation of David's confrontation with Goliath is guided by the narrator of the story. David is a young man who is visiting his brothers on the front line as the Israelites encounter the Philistines who encroach on their land. The Philistines have suggested individual combat as the way in which the conflict can be resolved. They have no fears; after all, their champion is Goliath, a seemingly unbeatable professional soldier. He is huge and armed to the teeth.

David, on the other hand, is inexperienced, not even a part of the army of Israel. Nonetheless, Goliath's arrogance affronts him and he takes up the cause of Yahweh. He refuses armor and weapons like the sword or shield in favor of facing Goliath only with a slingshot and his faith in Yahweh. With Yahweh's aid (1 Sam. 17:45–47) he defeats the giant and Israel wins the day.

Miscall, however, suggests a subversive reading of the text. David is not so much faithful as he is cunning, not so much naive as scheming. After all, without armor, David can run circles around Goliath. With a simple slingshot he can dispatch Goliath without getting close enough to be struck by his weapons.

The result of this analysis is a demonstration that there is no stable meaning of the text. Deconstructive analyses result in a basic skepticism in the light of the indeterminacy of the meaning of the text.[43] This suspicion continues in the poststructuralist era.

Contemporary Poststructuralist Approaches

Since the 1940s, the field of literary studies has passed through successive stages of new approaches to literary texts. Once the connection with authorial intention was severed, the search was on for a new locus of meaning. Starting with the text (formalism/New Criticism/structuralism), attention moved to the reader (reader-response and ideological readings) and then finally to a denial of any meaning at all.

Deconstruction appeared to many to be as far as one could go.[44]

---

42. See P. D. Miscall, *The Workings of Old Testament Narrative*, Semeia Studies (Philadelphia: Fortress; Chico, Calif.: Scholars Press, 1983), 57–83.

43. While deconstruction is a leading part of the poststructuralist approach, described in the next section, Miscall is the best example of a predominantly deconstructive approach to the text. His other studies include: "Jacques Derrida in the Garden of Eden," *USQR* 44 (1990): 1–9; and *1 Samuel: A Literary Reading*, Indiana Studies in Biblical Literature (Bloomington: Indiana University Press, 1986). See also *Derrida and Biblical Studies*, ed. R. Detweiler, *Semeia* 23 (1982).

44. But we should note the efforts of N. Royle, *After Derrida* (New York and Manchester: Manchester University Press, 1995), to read Derrida in the light of New Historicism.

Where could one turn after denying meaning? Indeed, many have gone no further. While suffering serious setbacks in the late 1980s and early 1990s, deconstruction lives on. It is premature to pronounce Derrida's thought passé, but it is no longer ruling the literary roost.

Some have taken a turn back to history. New Historicism scorns the idea that literature is totally nonreferential.[45] It advocates the historical setting of texts; it also insists on the textual setting of history.

But, at least in biblical studies, the best adjectives for describing current literary practice are "varied" and "eclectic." On the one hand, all the above-mentioned methods are still used by scholars. Though the avant-garde has moved far beyond formalism, some scholars still find it productive.[46] Deconstruction has been rapidly declining in literary theory since the revelation of Paul de Man's early involvement in fascism, but it too is still practiced by biblical scholars.

The cutting edge of the field, however, is not only varied in its approach to the literary study of the Bible but is also eclectic. That is, it utilizes not one but a variety of approaches at the same time. This trend in biblical studies may be illustrated by two recent collections of writings produced by some of the most active members of the guild: *The New Literary Criticism and the Hebrew Bible*[47] and *Reading between Texts: Intertextuality and the Hebrew Bible*.[48]

These two works contain the writings of twenty-six scholars, who may not agree in details but who share a broad consensus on what a literary approach to the text means. Foundational to their approach is the assertion that the text has no determinate meaning. This belief, of course, shapes the goal of the interpretive task. If there is no meaning to be discovered in the text, then the interpreter's job is to construct a meaning. In a postmodern world, it seems wrong, even ridiculous, to believe that we can recover some hypothetical author's meaning or even believe that the text itself contains the clues to its meaning.[49] If anything,

---

45. See Veeser, *New Historicism*, and *Semeia* 51.

46. Many of the essays in L. Ryken and T. Longman III, *A Complete Literary Guide to the Bible* (Grand Rapids: Zondervan, 1993), may be called formalist, describing native literary conventions to understand the meaning of the biblical book under study.

47. Ed. J. C. Exum and D. J. A. Clines, JSOTSup 143 (Sheffield: Sheffield Academic Press, 1993).

48. Ed. D. N. Fewell (Louisville: Westminster/John Knox, 1992).

49. Of course, postmodernism's skepticism flows out of its denial of God. One would think that this would immediately invalidate it as a Christian worldview. But T. J. Keegan, "Biblical Criticism and the Challenge of Postmodernism," *BibInt* 3 (1995): 1–14, argues, unsuccessfully in my opinion, that Christian scholars can still profitably use postmodern approaches. However, this judgment does not imply that Christian reading of the Bible cannot benefit from a postmodern critique of modernism; see my "Reading the Bible Postmodernly," *Mars Hill Review* 12 (1998): 23–30.

the reader is the one who endows the text with meaning,[50] and since readers represent diverse cultures, religions, genders, sexual preferences, and sociological and economic backgrounds, how can any right-minded person insist on something so naive as a determinate meaning?

An additional trait of contemporary literary approaches to biblical interpretation rests awkwardly with its denial of the determinate meaning of a biblical text. Clines and Exum assert, and the essays in their volume illustrate, a desire to move beyond interpretation of the text to critique of the text. They call for a method of interpretation that challenges the worldviews of our literature.[51] While such a challenge seems to contradict the claim that the text has no meaning, one gets the impression that most of the authors of these two volumes feel it is their task to undermine the message of the text in the interests of their own pressing concerns.[52]

Alice Bach's essay on the *Sotah* (Numbers 5), mentioned above in regard to feminist reader-response criticism, illustrates these principles well.[53] In the first place, she practices diverse literary methods in her study including feminist, deconstructive, and psychoanalytic approaches. Second, she constructs, supposedly from the perspective of her gender, the underlying ideology of the text. In this regard, she argues that the text, a description of a ritual to be undertaken in the case of a wife suspected of adultery, is really masking male anxieties concerning their own sexuality and is exerting a divinely sanctioned control on woman's sexuality. She then moves beyond interpretation, or the construction of the text's meaning, to critique, basically pointing out how bad and unjust and ridiculous the text is.

In the light of her denial of determinate meaning, it is unlikely that Bach would be shaken to hear that her interpretation has little to do with the clear message of the text. The *Sotah* is not about sexual anxieties as such but about the importance of paternity in the fulfillment of the promise of offspring in Genesis 12:1–3. The text also does not reflect

---

50. "A text means whatever it means to its readers, no matter how strange or unacceptable some meanings may seem to other readers"; so Clines and Exum, *New Literary Criticism*, 19.

51. Ibid., 14.

52. See D. J. A. Clines, *Interested Parties: The Ideology of Writers and Readers of the Hebrew Bible*, Gender, Culture, Theory 1 (Sheffield: Sheffield Academic Press, 1995). In this book of collected essays, Clines proposes that we read the Hebrew Bible from left to right (unlike English, Hebrew is correctly read from right to left). This seems to be his version of a hackneyed idiom of contemporary critics of the Bible who read "against the grain" of the biblical text. That is, they do not like what they read so they argue with the text from the standpoint of their modern prejudices. See specifically Clines's essay "The Ten Commandments, Reading from Left to Right," chap. 2 in *Interested Parties*.

53. Bach, "Good to the Last Drop," 26–54.

a willful disregard for women's rights. In other words, innocent women are not being harmed as a result of male pettiness. Rather, God super-intended the ritual, and innocent women would be exonerated, while duplicitous women would be implicated.[54]

While Bach's essay illustrates the general trends in contemporary lit-erary studies, the most telling essay in these two books is one written by Clines himself, "A World Established on Water (Psalm 24): Reader-Response, Deconstruction, and Bespoke Criticism."[55] In this essay, he focuses his attention on Psalm 24 by subjecting it to the three reading strategies listed in the subtitle to his chapter. What he does with Psalm 24 is not as important or as interesting as what he seems to be advocat-ing methodologically, especially under the name "bespoke criticism." On the basis of the lack of meaning of biblical texts and the importance of community acceptance of interpretation, he presents himself as the "bespoke interpreter," based on the analogy with the "bespoke tailor." The "bespoke tailor," he reminds us, cuts the cloth according to the cus-tomer's specifications. So, he argues, since there is no determinate meaning, we should tailor our interpretation to meet the needs of the group we are addressing, those who are paying us for our wares.[56]

Perhaps this is the logical route to go once one loses faith in any kind of authority of the text, any kind of determinate meaning. It is almost too easy to poke fun at such a view of interpretation, suggesting other more colorful but less respectable analogies to someone who manipu-lates his or her product to bring the best price. But there are other al-ternatives to Clines. The first is to refuse to base one's presuppositions on the work of the "masters of suspicion," Marx, Nietzsche, and Freud, and instead to consider building them on the authoritative text itself.[57] The other is to acknowledge, as Clines does, the absence of meaning in the text, and then to resign oneself to silence. Perhaps I am being nos-talgic for the 1960s, but I find much more noble and honest existential-ism's avowal of meaninglessness, followed by despair, than postmod-ernism's embrace of meaninglessness, followed by play and ideological manipulations of the text.

---

54. Further, it is wrong to charge the Bible with a double standard. David too is held responsible for his adultery with Bathsheba.

55. In *New Literary Criticism*, 79–90.

56. Ibid., 87.

57. A wonderful first step toward the construction of a distinctively Christian under-standing of literature, which also takes into account the helpful insights of deconstruc-tion, is the work of M. Edwards, *Towards a Christian Poetics* (London: Macmillan; Grand Rapids: Eerdmans, 1984). See also K. J. Vanhoozer, *Is There a Meaning in This Text? The Bible, the Reader, and the Morality of Literary Knowledge* (Grand Rapids: Zondervan, 1998).

Into the Future with Literary Studies

Once again, we have been able only to take a glimpse at the activity in literary studies and the Bible over the past quarter of a century. To attempt more would require at least a monograph. It is not the usual academic hyperbole to say that interest in the literary approach to the Bible has been unprecedented during this time period.

Indeed, the interest has been so great that at one time it was possible to believe that we were in the midst of a paradigm shift in biblical studies, that is, a shift away from obsession with issues of history and diachrony to a concern with the text "as it stands."[58] Few today would go so far, however, and indeed in literary studies there is presently a healthy swing back to matters of history from both an evangelical as well as a historical-critical perspective.[59] Nonetheless, to the detriment of our understanding of the text, many contemporary literary scholars continue to "bracket" historical (as well as theological/ideological) questions as they study the Bible.

The popularity of the literary approach has not gone unchallenged,[60] but most students of the Bible are not so much put off by it as they are overwhelmed by the different varieties of literary approaches as well as by the technical and philosophical sophistication needed to understand and apply these approaches. While many of the most recent literary studies of the Bible are eclectic, a host of different approaches are advocated, with considerable competition among them.

Moore and Carr have helpfully pointed out that there are three basic stances one can take toward biblical narrative with its gaps, doublets, and tensions.[61] One might explain the narrative as the result of the convergence of different textual traditions (source criticism). This would be a more traditional historical approach. A second stance would be to understand the gaps, repetitions, and tensions as a function of all literature. All literature is "undecidable." All literature ultimately subverts

---

58. D. Robertson, "Literature, the Bible as," *IDBSup*, 548; and J. D. Crossan, "'Ruth amid the Alien Corn': Perspectives and Methods in Contemporary Biblical Criticism," in *The Biblical Mosaic*, ed. R. Polzin and E. Rothman, Semeia Studies (Philadelphia: Fortress; Chico, Calif.: Scholars Press, 1982), 199.

59. For the former, see in particular V. P. Long, *The Art of Biblical History* (Grand Rapids: Zondervan, 1994). For the latter, a good recent example of a book that is sensitive to history and literary issues in the study of the composition of the Pentateuch is D. Carr, *Reading the Fractures of Genesis: Historical and Literary Approaches* (Louisville: Westminster/John Knox, 1996).

60. Most notably by J. Kugel, "On the Bible and Literary Criticism," *Prooftexts* 1 (1981): 99–104.

61. Moore, *Poststructuralism and the New Testament*, 66–71; Carr, *Reading the Fractures*, 10–11.

itself. This is the starting point of deconstruction and poststructuralism.[62] The third stance is that of narrative criticism. The text appears to have gaps, unwarranted repetitions, and tensions. We simply need to recover the ancient literary conventions that will help us elucidate the text. There are no ultimate contradictions here.

It is this third view that I advocate. While the other approaches throw some light on the nature of the biblical text, the most fruitful avenue to pursue is the one with which this essay began, namely formalism.[63] But I acknowledge that any exploration of the literary nature of the text is just one aspect of the interpretive task, and it must be complemented by other approaches, including those that focus on history and theology.

62. Poststructuralism not only asserts that the text is divided against itself (prohibiting any determinative meaning) but adds that the same is true of the reading subject.

63. For a fuller, more descriptive presentation of my views, see my *Literary Approaches to Biblical Interpretation;* and L. Ryken and T. Longman III, eds., *A Complete Literary Guide to the Bible,* with bibliographies.

5

Pondering the Pentateuch:
The Search for a New Paradigm

Gordon J. Wenham

Three decades ago pentateuchal studies seemed to have arrived at a comfortable consensus.[1] The documentary hypothesis popularized by J. Wellhausen in his *Prolegomena to the History of Israel* (Germ. 1878) and by S. R. Driver in his *Introduction to the Literature of the Old Testament* (1891) and in his numerous commentaries had come to be almost universally accepted among the academic community. Since it was first advocated, there had been some powerful challenges to the documentary hypothesis, but by 1970 these had been forgotten, and everyone who wanted to be thought a serious Old Testament scholar had to believe in J, E, D, and P and in the dates assigned to them by the consensus.

The nineteenth-century version of the documentary hypothesis had been made more comfortable for the twentieth century by updating the model in a few respects. A. Alt, for example, had argued in "The God of the Fathers" (Germ. 1929) that the religion of the patriarchs as portrayed in Genesis is typical of seminomads and that at least some of the promises made to them by God may go back to patriarchal times.[2] Thus although the earliest pentateuchal sources J and E may have been committed to writing some thousand years after the period in which the pa-

1. G. J. Wenham, "Trends in Pentateuchal Criticism since 1950," *The Churchman* 84 (1970): 210–20.
2. Reprinted in A. Alt, *Kleine Schriften zur Geschichte des Volkes Israel*, vol. 1 (Munich: Beck, 1953), 1–78; in English translation as *Essays on Old Testament History and Religion*, trans. R. A. Wilson (Garden City, N.Y.: Doubleday; Oxford: Blackwell, 1968), 1–100.

triarchs lived, they still preserve a kernel of authentic historical tradition. In his study on "The Origins of Israelite Law" (Germ. 1934) he likewise argued that the casuistic ("if a man does . . .") laws of the Pentateuch reflect standard Near Eastern legal formulation and were probably borrowed from the Canaanites soon after the settlement, while the apodictic ("thou shalt not . . .") laws were uniquely Israelite and probably derive from covenantal settings such as Sinai.[3] Neither type of law, then, goes back quite to the time of Moses, but its origin may have been much closer to his time than the documentary hypothesis would have led one to suppose.

Alt's disciples continued the process of arguing for an essential continuity between the biblical accounts of the patriarchal and Mosaic ages and historical reality. G. von Rad in "The Form-Critical Problem of the Hexateuch" (Germ. 1938) argued that the present form of the Hexateuch had grown out of a very ancient creed enshrined in Deuteronomy 26:5–9, which sums up Israelite history from the time of Jacob to the conquest.[4] The same pattern of thought controls the present shape of the Hexateuch. Thus the essential kerygma of the Hexateuch has not changed over many centuries; later retellers of the story have filled it out and enriched it. Similarly, his great commentary on Genesis (Germ. 1949), while working within the framework of the documentary hypothesis, gives a theological interpretation in which the Christian themes of sin, grace, and promise are prominent.[5]

If von Rad tended to emphasize theological continuity between the earliest and latest theologies in the Pentateuch, Alt's other great disciple, M. Noth, did the same for the history and sociology of early Israel. In *The System of the Twelve Tribes of Israel* (Germ. 1930) he argued that the twelve-tribe league of Israel, its covenantal organization, and worship at the central sanctuary go back to the earliest days of the judges.[6] Then in *A History of Pentateuchal Traditions* Noth argued that behind both the literary sources J and E lay a common, probably oral tradition, G *(Grundlage)*, which originated in the judges period.[7] G contained five major themes: guidance out of Egypt, guidance into the land, promise

3. *Kleine Schriften*, 1:278–332; *Essays*, 101–71.

4. G. von Rad, *Das formgeschichtliche Problem des Hexateuchs* (Stuttgart: Kohlhammer, 1938); English translation in *The Problem of the Hexateuch and Other Essays*, trans. E. W. Trueman Dicken (New York: McGraw Hill; Edinburgh: Oliver & Boyd, 1966), 1–78.

5. G. von Rad, *Genesis*, ATD (Göttingen: Vandenhoek & Ruprecht, 1949); in English, *Genesis*, trans. J. H. Marks, 2d ed., OTL (Philadelphia: Westminster; London: SCM, 1972).

6. M. Noth, *Das System der zwölf Stämme Israels* (Stuttgart: Kohlhammer, 1930).

7. Trans. B. W. Anderson (Englewood Cliffs, N.J.: Prentice-Hall, 1972); original German edition: *Überlieferungsgeschichte des Pentateuch* (Stuttgart: Kohlhammer, 1948).

to the patriarchs, guidance in the wilderness, and revelation at Sinai. Once again the drift of Noth's work was to suggest that the pentateuchal sources gave us a more accurate picture of earliest Israel than their late date would imply.

Across the Atlantic, W. F. Albright, his disciples, and fellow travelers such as E. A. Speiser and C. H. Gordon had been piling up parallels between the patriarchal stories and second-millennium laws and social customs that seemed to demonstrate the essential historicity of the biblical tradition. Furthermore, they identified many of the poems within the Pentateuch as very early (e.g., Gen. 49, Exod. 15, Num. 23–24, Deut. 33) and appealed to them in support of the later prose narratives. On the basis of such evidence R. de Vaux affirmed "that these traditions have a firm historical basis," while J. Bright claimed: "We can assert with full confidence that Abraham, Isaac, and Jacob were actual historical individuals."[8] Thus the general conclusion from all these studies was that, although the Pentateuch was composed from sources written many centuries after the events it describes, it was a fairly valid account of both the history and the theology of earliest Israel.

Admittedly, students new to the academic study of the Old Testament might have been struck by the discrepancies between, for example, the biblical account of Moses and the critical accounts, but those brought up on the skepticism of Wellhausen found the mid-century critical stance reassuring. Wellhausen had written: "We attain to no historical knowledge of the patriarchs, but only of the time when the stories about them arose in the Israelite people; this later age is here unconsciously projected . . . into hoar antiquity, and is reflected there like a glorified mirage."[9] The traditio-historical approach of the Alt school on the one hand and the archaeological approach of the Albright school on the other had laid to rest scholarly unease about the implications of the documentary hypothesis, and by 1960 it was well-nigh universally agreed to be one of the "assured results of modern criticism."

But since the 1970s the comfortable consensus has begun to break up. There have been challenges to the principle of source analysis; there is uncertainty about the dating of the sources themselves and doubt about the validity of the alleged archaeological parallels. In the 1980s the debate intensified, and as we approach the end of the millennium there is no sign of it being resolved. On the one hand there are those

---

8. R. de Vaux, *The Early History of Israel*, vol. 1, trans. D. Smith (Philadelphia: Westminster; London: Darton, Longman & Todd, 1978), 200; original French edition: *Histoire ancienne d'Israel* (Paris: Gabalda, 1971); J. Bright, *A History of Israel*, 2d ed. (Philadelphia: Westminster; London: SCM, 1972), 91.

9. J. Wellhausen, *Prolegomena to the History of Ancient Israel*, trans. J. S. Black and A. Menzies (1885; reprinted Cleveland: World, 1965), 318–19.

who argue that the J source, traditionally regarded as the earliest major source, is both post-Deuteronomic and postexilic. On the other there are those who deny the existence of J and E altogether, proposing instead a pervasive Deuteronomic layer through Genesis to Deuteronomy, whereas Noth had denied that any Deuteronomic hand could be discerned in Genesis–Numbers. By and large, those who adopt these approaches are also quite skeptical about the value of archaeological parallels to the Bible and tend to maintain that the Pentateuch is fictional. Going in a totally different direction, other scholars have argued that the Priestly source, traditionally supposed to be the latest source, may come from the early monarchy period with elements from the judges period. Others have suggested that both the J source and Deuteronomy may be earlier than conventional criticism suggests. No longer is it just different versions of the documentary hypothesis that find their advocates, but as at the beginning of the nineteenth century, both fragmentary and supplementary hypotheses enjoy support. Others prefer to give up trying to establish how the text originated and concentrate instead on its final form and meaning.

Among those writing most prolifically about the Pentateuch today there is thus no consensus. "Every man does what is right in his own eyes." Doubtless there is still a strong and silent majority of those who grew up with the traditional documentary hypothesis and feel no inclination to jettison it, and given the lack of an agreed alternative hypothesis there is a certain justification in a wait-and-see policy. The academic community is looking for a fresh and convincing paradigm for the study of the Pentateuch, but so far none of the new proposals seems to have captured the scholarly imagination.

A diversity of methods has led to the variety of conclusions that now characterizes the world of pentateuchal studies. This makes it very difficult to review adequately the scholarly approaches that have emerged in the last few decades; hence this essay attempts to highlight some of the key developments in the discussion, evaluate their strengths and weaknesses, and finally make suggestions for future research.

The first trend apparent in this period is the tendency toward a unitary reading of the text as opposed to the dissection practiced by traditional source criticism. For some, this is a methodological principle prompted by New Criticism in literary theory or by canonical criticism; for others, the motivation seems more pragmatic and arises out of a feeling of dissatisfaction with source-critical exegesis. Pragmatism seems to have been a major factor prompting the abandonment of the J/E analysis of the Joseph story. In 1968 R. N. Whybray wrote a short article suggesting that the usual source analysis of Genesis 37–50 was inappropriate and that the Joseph story was much more of a unity than usually held.[10] Then in 1970 D. B. Redford wrote a full-length study of the Joseph story that argued not for the interweaving of two originally independent sources J and E, but for a Judah source (J) being subsequently expanded by a Reuben (E) source. Commenting on these new ideas, von Rad noted that they did show that the Joseph story could be understood as a substantial unity, but that still left the duplication of J and E in the rest of the Pentateuch to be explained. This, he said, "must come from a comprehensive new analysis of the Pentateuchal narrative material, which we urgently need."[11] These must be almost the last words von Rad wrote, as he died in 1971. The next decade saw a variety of answers to his call. But before looking at the comprehensive new analyses that have been offered, we should note some of the integrative readings of the Joseph story that have been put forward.

In two books and several articles, G. W. Coats argued for the unity of much of Genesis 37–50, as did H. Donner, W. L. Humphreys, R. E. Longacre, H. Schweizer, and H. C. White.[12] C. Westermann also supported a more unified reading in the third volume of his Genesis commentary.[13] Among these writers there is broad agreement that chapters 37 and 39–45 constitute a story from a single source, but there is less unanimity about chapter 38 (the Judah and Tamar episode) and chapters 46–50 with its P-like list (46:8–27), the account of Joseph's famine relief (47:13–26), Jacob's blessing (chap. 49), the various interlinkages with the Jacob cycle (chaps. 25–35), and the renewed fraternal reconciliation (50:15–21). Do these apparently unrelated episodes not suggest that we are dealing with material from a variety of sources?

Although it is easy to affirm diversity of sources on the basis of genre and content, it is also apparent that at some time some editor or author

10. R. N. Whybray, "The Joseph Story and Pentateuchal Criticism," *VT* 18 (1968): 522–28.

11. Von Rad, *Genesis,* 440.

12. G. W. Coats, *From Canaan to Egypt: Structural and Theological Context for the Joseph Story,* CBQMS 4 (Washington, D.C.: Catholic Biblical Association, 1976); idem, *Genesis, with an Introduction to Narrative Literature,* FOTL (Grand Rapids: Eerdmans, 1983); idem, "The Joseph Story and Ancient Wisdom: A Reappraisal," *CBQ* 35 (1973): 285–97; idem, "Redactional Unity in Genesis 37–50," *JBL* 93 (1974): 15–21; H. Donner, *Die literarische Gestalt der alttestamentlichen Josephsgeschichte* (Heidelberg: Winter, 1976); W. L. Humphreys, *Joseph and His Family: A Literary Study* (Columbia: University of South Carolina Press, 1988); R. E. Longacre, *Joseph: A Story of Divine Providence* (Winona Lake, Ind.: Eisenbrauns, 1989); H. Schweizer, *Die Josefgeschichte* (Tübingen: Francke, 1991); H. C. White, *Narration and Discourse in the Book of Genesis* (Cambridge: Cambridge University Press, 1991); idem, "The Joseph Story: A Narrative Which 'Consumes' Its Content," in *Reader Response Approaches to Biblical and Secular Texts,* ed. R. Detweiler, *Semeia* 31 (1985): 49–69.

13. C. Westermann, *Genesis 37–50,* BKAT 1.3 (Neukirchen-Vluyn: Neukirchener Verlag, 1982); English translation by J. J. Scullion (Minneapolis: Augsburg; London: SPCK, 1986).

thought these materials were interconnected. Could the modern tendency to posit multiple sources reflect modern readers' failure to perceive the connections that were self-evident to the author? Along these lines Humphreys and Alter, for example, have drawn attention to the numerous verbal and thematic linkages between Genesis 38 and the surrounding chapters, so that far from it being a foreign body in its context, it "provides a counterpointing commentary on what we have witnessed of this family and a proleptic look at what is yet to come."[14]

The issues in chapters 46–50 are more complex and cannot be dealt with here. It must suffice to say that Coats has made a good case for seeing the Joseph story continuing to 47:26. Then Longacre argues that in chapters 48–50 the blessing of Jacob, "in that it is poetry, seems to be intended to be a high point of the *toledot ya'qob* (i.e., chs. 37–50), if not the whole book of Genesis. . . . In this chapter . . . we have a glimpse of the embryonic nation—with the Judah and Joseph tribes destined to have preeminence in the south and north respectively."[15] Similarly, Schweizer has underlined the significance of the renewed plea for mercy by Jacob's brothers in 50:14–26. "Whoever eliminates this scene really eliminates the climax of Gen. 50 if not . . . that of the whole original Joseph story."[16] Furthermore, in my commentary I have attempted to show how the arrangement of the conclusions of the Abraham and Jacob cycles in 22:1–25:10 and 35:1–29 parallels the close of the Joseph story in 48:2–50:14.[17] While this does not show that a variety of sources may not have been used in compiling these chapters, it does suggest a more coherent redactional or authorial policy than has been recognized hitherto.

These attempts to read the Joseph story as a unity involve only minor modifications to the old model of the documentary hypothesis. With J. Van Seters, *Abraham in History and Tradition*,[18] the outline of a completely fresh paradigm of the Pentateuch began to emerge. He has developed his proposals in numerous articles and in two further books, *Prologue to History: The Yahwist as Historian in Genesis* and *The Life of Moses: The Yahwist as Historian in Exodus–Numbers*.[19] These books are

---

14. Humphreys, *Joseph and His Family*, 37; R. Alter, *The Art of Biblical Narrative* (New York: Basic Books, 1981), 3–12.

15. Longacre, *Joseph*, 23, 54.

16. H. Schweizer, "Fragen zur Literaturkritik von Gen 50," *BN* 36 (1987): 68.

17. *Genesis 16–50*, WBC (Dallas: Word, 1994), 461–62.

18. J. Van Seters, *Abraham in History and Tradition* (New Haven: Yale University Press, 1975).

19. *Prologue to History: The Yahwist as Historian in Genesis* (Louisville: Westminster/John Knox, 1992); *The Life of Moses: The Yahwist as Historian in Exodus–Numbers* (Louisville: Westminster/John Knox, 1994).

radical in abandoning many of the traditional criteria for source analysis, offering a totally fresh view of the contents of the sources, their dating and interrelationships, and finally arguing that these books of the Pentateuch contain very little historical tradition; they should rather be understood as ideological fiction. I shall look at these books in order of publication, spending most time on the first, for it has had the most impact on other scholars.

Abraham in History and Tradition, as its title suggests, divides into two parts. The first part attacks the position of Albright, Speiser, Gordon, and others who had argued that parallels between Genesis and second-millennium Mesopotamia demonstrated the historicity of the Genesis accounts. On the contrary, Van Seters argues that the nomadic lifestyle of the patriarchs fits better into the late Neo-Assyrian or even the Neo-Babylonian period, that is, the seventh and sixth centuries B.C.[20] Similarly he finds parallels between the lists of the children of Abraham and Ishmael and the names of Arabian tribes found in Neo-Assyrian and Neo-Babylonian texts.[21] Next Van Seters turns to the alleged parallels between the social and legal customs associated with marriage, adoption, sale, and covenant making in Genesis and the ancient Near East.[22] He argues that it is wrong to compare the biblical accounts just with early second-millennium texts, for in fact some customs changed very little between the second and the first millennium, and indeed some biblical practices correspond more closely with oriental customs of the first millennium than with those of the second millennium. Finally he looks at the sites that Genesis says the patriarchs visited and asserts that the archaeological evidence does not show that these places were inhabited in the early second millennium in the way that one would expect if the traditions originated then.[23] In particular, the story of Abraham's battles with the kings in Genesis 14 appears to have been written by a Judean in the Babylonian exile.

Van Seters's arguments against the historicity of Genesis were supported by T. L. Thompson in his misleadingly titled *The Historicity of the Patriarchal Narratives.*[24] Thompson's work is much more thorough and judicious than that of Van Seters. He draws attention to some of the fallacies that have characterized the archaeological defense of Genesis, but he is not so dogmatic as Van Seters in propounding an alternative, very late setting for the traditions in Genesis. Since the publication of

20. *Abraham,* 13–38.
21. Ibid., 39–64.
22. Ibid., 65–103.
23. Ibid., 104–22.
24. T. L. Thompson, *The Historicity of the Patriarchal Narratives: The Quest for the Historical Abraham,* BZAW 133 (Berlin and New York: de Gruyter, 1974).

these two books, scholars have generally admitted that the arguments for the antiquity and authenticity of the Genesis accounts are not so cogent as Speiser and others alleged, but that is not to say the balance of probability may not still lie in that direction.[25]

Here it is sufficient to note that Van Seters uses his historical argument as a springboard for a fresh approach to the source criticism of Genesis. After a review of earlier critical approaches, he outlines his own methodology, which holds loosely to many of the criteria employed by traditional source critics. Only duplication of episodes is a clear marker of different sources (e.g., 12:10–20 and chap. 20, or chaps. 15 and 17). Repetition within a story may not indicate different sources since it may be merely stylistic. Nor does variation in vocabulary or divine names suffice to separate sources, though material analyzed into sources on other grounds may be identified through distinctive vocabulary.[26] Finally he suggests that Olrik's epic laws, first used by Gunkel in his Genesis commentary, provide a good guide to distinguishing originally oral material in the tradition.[27]

He then proceeds to examine the duplicate narratives in Genesis 12–26. From the three stories of a patriarch passing off his wife as his sister, he believes he can see three stages in the tradition. Closest to oral tradition and the earliest is 12:10–20. Then comes 20:1–18, which presupposes knowledge of the first story and must therefore have been written after it. Finally, 26:1–11 alludes to both chapters 12 and 20, and must have been written last of all. According to classical source criticism both chapters 12 and 26 come from the same hand (J), while chapter 20 comes from E. But Van Seters argues that only chapter 26 should be ascribed to J. Genesis 12:10–20 is part of an early tradition that included only three episodes in the life of Abraham. This was subsequently expanded by some material now found in chapters 20–21, traditionally ascribed to E. Then at last came the real Yahwist, responsible for nearly all the non-Priestly material in Genesis 12–26, including 26:1–11. Throughout his literary discussion, Van Seters tends to argue for the substantial unity of material usually ascribed to J and to suggest that it comes later in biblical history than traditionally supposed. Discussing Genesis 15, for example, he notes its kinship with Deuteronomic ideas and Deutero-Isaiah, and suggests that the boundaries of the land (15:18–21) suit the exilic era better than any other period.[28] He

25. For further discussion see A. R. Millard and D. J. Wiseman, eds., *Essays on the Patriarchal Narratives* (Winona Lake, Ind.: Eisenbrauns; Leicester: InterVarsity, 1980); and for a brief assessment of the debate, Wenham, *Genesis 16–50*, xx–xxviii.
26. Van Seters, *Abraham*, 155–57.
27. Ibid., 159–61.
28. Ibid., 263–78.

regards the P material essentially as a supplement to J and dates it to the postexilic period. He holds that chapter 14 is later still: the kings of the East are a coy way of referring to the Persians, while vv. 18–20 (Melchizedek and Abraham) attempt to justify syncretism that may have occurred in the late fourth century. Thus, according to Van Seters, Genesis reached its present form about 300 B.C.[29]

In his later works Van Seters tries to show that his critical conclusions hold for other parts of the Pentateuch. In *Prologue to History,* Van Seters deals with the parts of Genesis not considered in his first book about Abraham. Most of it is concerned with the primeval history, Genesis 1–11, which Van Seters compares with both Near Eastern and Greek mythology. He thinks it has an affinity with Greek antiquarian writers active in the late first millennium as well as with Mesopotamian sources. He suggests that this is explained if the Yahwist lived in the Babylonian exile, where he could have encountered these ideas. Van Seters also looks at the Jacob and Joseph stories, again drawing comparisons with other promise texts, especially Second Isaiah, which he believes confirms a late date for J.

In *The Life of Moses,* Van Seters completes his case for a complete reordering of the documentary hypothesis. As in his earlier works, he tends to view the JE material as a unity emanating from the Yahwist, and argues for its late date. Basically, the Yahwist was writing an introduction to the Deuteronomistic History (Deuteronomy to Kings) and borrowed freely and creatively from these earlier works in writing his own. Thus Deuteronomy's brief allusions to conquests in Transjordan or to the golden calf are turned into full-scale accounts. Joshua's encounter with the captain of the host of Israel becomes the model for the burning bush. Moses' reluctance to be a prophet is modeled on the calls of Isaiah and Jeremiah, and the idea of an exodus from a land of oppression derives from Second Isaiah.

> The call of Moses reflects very well the nature of the Yahwistic composition of the Pentateuch. As a writer of the exilic period, the Yahwist made extensive use of both the DtrH [Deuteronomistic History] and a corpus of prophetic traditions to shape his presentation of Moses and the exodus. The call narrative is not the beginning of the prophetic call tradition but the end of the process by which Moses becomes the greatest of all the prophets. He experiences a theophany like that of Isaiah and of Ezekiel, but in a way that epitomizes the divine presence forever afterward, as the menorah. He becomes the reluctant prophet who struggles with the people's unbelief, like Jeremiah. He is given the dual task of proclaiming both salvation to his people and judgment on the rulers, in this case the hea-

29. Ibid., 304–8.

then. As in Second Isaiah, the God of the patriarchs becomes revealed as the God of the exodus deliverance.[30]

Van Seters's approach is a tour de force. It might be described as the ultimate application of Wellhausen's view that the law came after the prophets. Wellhausen meant that the laws within the Pentateuch were post-prophetic: for Van Seters the whole Torah, laws plus narrative, was written after and modeled on the prophets. If Van Seters's view is right, it has even more serious consequences for the historicity of the Pentateuch than the traditional documentary hypothesis. Though some may see this as the reductio ad absurdum of the documentary hypothesis, his view that the J(E) redaction is no earlier than the exile has found a number of adherents, most notably E. Blum and C. Levin (see below). My evaluation of this approach must therefore wait until I have reviewed some other modern views. At this point it is sufficient to say that while I do not find Van Seters's views persuasive, it is difficult to find decisive and cogent counterarguments. This highlights one of the chief problems in current debate: the lack of agreed scholarly criteria and starting points.

If Van Seters is the leading North American dissident in the field of pentateuchal criticism, in Germany this title must go to Rolf Rendtorff, whose *Problem of the Process of Transmission in the Pentateuch* (Germ. 1977) represented not a modification of the documentary hypothesis and its conclusions but an outright challenge to its methods.[31] According to Rendtorff, the methods of source criticism as exemplified in Wellhausen's work and the methods of form criticism first practiced by Gunkel are fundamentally incompatible. Yet Gunkel and his successors, including Noth and von Rad, tried to combine the two methods. On the one hand they used form criticism to explain the development of pentateuchal traditions in the oral stage of transmission. On the other hand they affirmed that these oral traditions somehow coagulated into the literary sources, J, E, P, and so on.

Rendtorff believes that the form-critical approach is the right starting point and that its approach should be carried through into the explanation of the larger units.

The Pentateuch as a whole as it lies before us is no longer the point of departure, but rather the concrete individual text, the "smallest literary unit." The work begins as it were at the opposite end. The contexts in

30. Van Seters, *Life of Moses*, 63.
31. R. Rendtorff, *Das überlieferungsgeschichtliche Problem des Pentateuch*, BZAW 147 (Berlin: de Gruyter, 1977); translated as *The Problem of the Process of Transmission in the Pentateuch*, trans. J. J. Scullion, JSOTSup 89 (Sheffield: JSOT Press, 1990).

which each individual text now stands, however large, are not yet a matter of attention in this approach, nor must they be the primary concern of the interpreter.[32]

He illustrates his approach by a discussion of the patriarchal narratives. He begins with the Joseph story, which most people agree is a distinct entity that stands on its own. He follows Gunkel's proposal that the Jacob stories are a combination of two cycles, one dealing with Jacob and Esau and the other with Jacob and Laban. But the Abraham and Isaac stories do not form such tightly knit cycles: each episode seems rather independent, and this suggests what they were like in the earliest stage of oral tradition. They have subsequently been linked up by adding the divine promises of descendants, land, and blessing. The different formulations of the promises (e.g., sometimes "land," sometimes "descendants," sometimes "to you," sometimes "to your descendants") give a clue to the different stages in the process of amalgamation. These divine promises in their simplest form glued together the Abraham stories. Meanwhile, other stories about other themes were developing (e.g., the primeval history, the Joseph story, the exodus, Sinai). But at this stage one should not talk about a documentary source running from creation to conquest. Linking all the blocks of stories up into a lengthy narrative akin to our Pentateuch did not occur till a Deuteronomist or someone like him did this, often developing the land promise to connect the previously separate blocks together.

Rendtorff thus argues that it is quite misleading to talk about a Yahwist or Elohist, for there never was a stage in the growth of the Pentateuch when the J or E traditions existed as connected documents covering all the earliest history of Israel. Nor is it valid to speak of a P source. The criteria for assigning material to the P source are often circular and are just special pleading. On chapter 23 he says: "When all is said and done, I see no valid reasons for accepting that Genesis 23 is a part of a P-narrative, but numerous reasons against."[33] According to Rendtorff, there is less P material in Genesis than often supposed, and it merely represents a supplementary layer helping to link together the originally independent blocks of narrative in the same way as the Deuteronomic layer does.

His work contains many other sharp jibes at the methods of literary criticism and at the dating criteria that are often invoked.[34]

32. Ibid., 23.
33. Ibid., 156.
34. E.g., on linguistic criteria for source division, ibid., 113, 118.

It must be conceded that we really do not possess reliable criteria for dating of the pentateuchal literature. Each dating of the pentateuchal "sources" relies on purely hypothetical assumptions which in the long run have their continued existence because of the consensus of scholars. Hence, a study of the Pentateuch which is both critical and aware of method must be prepared to discuss thoroughly once more the accepted datings.[35]

Despite his belief that the dating of the Yahwist in the time of the united monarchy is an example of consensus dating rather than proof, he is not advocating a late dating of the Pentateuch. He explicitly criticizes those who would date J late. Indeed, he argues that the Deuteronomic editor responsible for producing the overall shape of the Pentateuch may have operated two centuries earlier than often surmised.[36] He also notes that "the common dating of the 'priestly' sections, be they narrative or legal, to the exilic or the post-exilic period, likewise rests on conjecture and the consensus of scholars, but not on unambiguous criteria."[37]

In this book, Rendtorff does not pretend to offer a comprehensive refutation of the documentary hypothesis; rather he intends to open up the subject to debate about methods.[38] In that regard, his book must be viewed as a success, and his pupil Erhard Blum has, in two long works, put Rendtorff's method into practice throughout the Pentateuch. To Blum's work I now turn.

In *Die Komposition der Vätergeschichte*, Blum traces the multiple stages of growth through which the patriarchal stories have passed.[39] The earliest elements are found in the stories of struggle between Jacob and Esau and between Jacob and Laban in Genesis 25, 27, and 31. "Obviously this text cannot be dated before David's subjugation of Edom."[40] This was next expanded by the addition of other stories in Genesis 27–33. The interest in Israel, northern sanctuaries such as Bethel, and the special place of Joseph among the sons of Jacob date this material between the period of the united monarchy and Josiah's destruction of the Bethel sanctuary.

The next stage in the development of the tradition involved filling out the story of Jacob and his sons that begins in chapter 25 and ends in chapter 50. That these stories concern the northern tribes (e.g., Joseph)

35. Ibid., 201–2.
36. Ibid., 203.
37. Ibid.
38. Ibid., 181.
39. E. Blum, *Die Komposition der Vätergeschichte*, WMANT 57 (Neukirchen-Vluyn: Neukirchener Verlag, 1984).
40. Ibid., 202–3.

and yet look to the leadership of Judah points to a period when Judah was asserting its supremacy over the north. This, Blum suggests, points to the reign of Josiah, who attempted to control that area.

Meanwhile, stories about Judah and its neighbors, Moab and Ammon, circulated in the southern kingdom. These relationships are reflected in the narrative about Abraham and Lot (Gen. 13, 18–19). These were tacked on to the Jacob narrative to form the first patriarchal history (*Vätergeschichte* 1). According to Blum, this must have been done at the earliest sometime between the fall of Samaria and the fall of Jerusalem.[41]

During the exile a second form of the patriarchal history (*Vätergeschichte* 2) was produced. This involved filling out the Abraham stories (e.g., parts of chaps. 12, 16, 21, 22, 26) and connecting that material with the promise of descendants, the gift of the land, and blessing.

In the postexilic period, perhaps between 530 and 500, the patriarchal history was first linked to the rest of the Pentateuch through the editorial work of D, the Deuteronomist.[42] In Genesis his hand is evident in chapters 15, 18, 22:16ff., 24, and some other places; he may be responsible for inserting chapters 20 and 21 dealing with Abimelech. This editor stresses God's response to the faith and obedience of Abraham (e.g., 15:6; 22:16–18; 26:2–5) and is concerned about marrying outside the community (chap. 24), a preoccupation of the postexilic community.

Like the Deuteronomistic layer, the Priestly layer is the only other layer that is found throughout the Pentateuch. Blum's second volume, *Studien zur Komposition des Pentateuch*, deals first with the Deuteronomistic redaction of the Pentateuch and then second with the Priestly texts.[43] J and E are never mentioned, though in some respects Blum's D-layer is like Van Seters's late and expanded J. But in his definition and dating of P, Blum comes closest to traditional pentateuchal criticism. He regards it as a layer rather than a source, but it does include passages like chapter 23, which Rendtorff was dubious about, as well as the *tôlĕdōt* formulas and chapter 17.

C. Levin's *Der Jahwist* is a response to the Rendtorff-Blum approach.[44] Levin accepts that, as far as the Yahwistic material is concerned, it is right to think in terms of a supplementary hypothesis, whereby successive editions of J were produced, each expanding J. He

41. Ibid., 297.
42. Ibid., 392.
43. E. Blum, *Studien zur Komposition des Pentateuch*, BZAW 189 (Berlin and New York: de Gruyter, 1990).
44. C. Levin, *Der Jahwist* (Göttingen: Vandenhoeck & Ruprecht, 1993), 34.

also concurs with Rendtorff and Blum that there was no full E source. Only Genesis 20–22, a Genesis midrash, can be termed E. But whereas Rendtorff and Blum stress the oral origin of the material later assigned to J, Levin argues that J used sources. He thinks his J is roughly equivalent to Van Seters's late J and Blum's *Vätergeschichte* 2, but he thinks J wrote an account of Israel's history that runs from Genesis 2 to Numbers 24.[45] Contrary to Rendtorff and Blum, who think the first panpentateuchal redactor was a Deuteronomist, Levin holds that J was consciously refuting Deuteronomy's demand for a central sanctuary.[46] J does this by portraying Abraham and the other patriarchs worshiping at a variety of sites (e.g., 12:7, 8; 13:18; 28:16), and prefacing the laws in Exodus 21–23 by an altar law (Exod. 20:24–26) that allows worship anywhere. Levin therefore suggests that J was written by one of the royal deportees trying to offer hope of a return to the land and a practical program of worship in exile. J was aimed at the early exiles, such as those in the colony of Elephantine. J then follows the Deuteronomic law, but it precedes both the Deuteronomistic History and Second Isaiah, both of whom seem to be familiar with its contents.

After J had edited the earlier sources into a coherent, national origin story, it was supplemented at various places (J^s), and then P was added. Since P was an independent source before it was combined with J, Levin admits that at this point he follows a documentary hypothesis. Eventually there were yet further additions (R^s) to the material. Thus, according to Levin, the Tetrateuch grew like this: J + P + D + other additions, not J + E + D + P as the normal documentary theory maintained.

R. N. Whybray, well known for his studies of wisdom literature, returned to a discussion of the Pentateuch with *The Making of the Pentateuch: A Methodological Study.*[47] Its subtitle indicates its focus, a discussion of the methods used by pentateuchal critics. Chapter 1 explains and evaluates the methods of criticism used to formulate the documentary hypothesis. Chapter 2 looks at the traditio-historical method, and chapter 3 explains his own proposal.

Whybray begins by observing that the documentary hypothesis, the fragmentary hypothesis, and the supplementary hypothesis are not mutually exclusive. Indeed, at many points the classic defenders of the documentary hypothesis invoked fragmentary or supplementary explanations where something did not seem to fit the profile of one of the main

45. Ibid., 34.
46. Ibid., 430.
47. JSOTSup 53 (Sheffield: JSOT Press, 1987). For his earlier discussion of the Joseph story see "The Joseph Story and Pentateuchal Criticism," *VT* 18 (1968): 522–28.

documents—J, E, or P. Indeed, of all the types of explanation for the growth of the Pentateuch,

> the least plausible of them is the Documentary Hypothesis. For whereas the Fragment and Supplement Hypotheses envisage relatively simple, and it would seem, logical processes and at the same time appear to account for the unevennesses of the completed Pentateuch, the Documentary Hypothesis is not only much more complicated but also very specific in its assumptions about the historical development of Israel's understanding of its origins.[48]

Whybray has two fundamental objections to the documentary hypothesis. First, it is illogical and self-contradictory and fails to explain what it professes to explain. The Pentateuch is split up into sources, because it is held that the present text contains redundant repetition and contradiction. The original sources, it is held, were noncontradictory and not repetitious, and the documentary hypothesis labors to reconstruct them on this assumption. But when the sources were linked together, a repetitious and contradictory account was produced. Why, asks Whybray, should we suppose that the methods of Hebrew writers changed so drastically? If early writers did not tolerate contradiction or repetition, why did later writers revel in it? But if later writers did not mind such features, why should we suppose that the earlier sources did not contain contradiction and repetition? But if they did, how can we separate out the sources? "Thus the hypothesis can only be maintained on the assumption that, while consistency was the hallmark of the various documents, *in*consistency was the hallmark of the redactors."[49]

Second, Whybray maintains that the phenomena of repetition and stylistic variation found in the Pentateuch, which the documentary hypothesis is alleged to explain, may be understood quite differently, as they usually are in other literatures. For example, since other religious texts use a variety of names for God, why should a change of divine name in Genesis signal a change of source? Sometimes there could be a theological reason why one name is preferred to another; at others the writer may just unconsciously want a change. Repetition is often done for stylistic reasons or to emphasize something (e.g., for rhetorical effect and in poetic parallelism). It is now recognized that the study of repetition may give important insights into the meaning of the text and the skill of the author. Furthermore, Whybray holds that the attempts to describe the theology of J or E rest on too narrow a base to be convincing. But if this applies to these relatively lengthy texts, how much

48. Ibid., 18.
49. Ibid., 49.

less plausible are the attempts of Rendtorff and Blum to define editorial layers on the basis of alleged editorial passages.

Having argued that the documentary style of analysis is both too complicated and implausible, Whybray proceeds in chapter 2 to criticize the traditio-historical approach of Gunkel and Noth more trenchantly still. He argues that the task of tradition critics is even more difficult than that of source critics. At least the latter deal with partially extant texts, but the former deal with hypothetical reconstructions for which we have no tangible evidence.

> The Documentary Hypothesis is simply an attempt to unravel the extant text: to show that the material is composite and to explain how it came to be arranged in its present form. As has been stated, the documentary critics did not think it possible to penetrate back beyond the extant words of the Pentateuch and to discover and identify earlier forms of the material which no longer exist and for which there is no direct evidence. This can only be done on the basis of some even more fundamental assumptions.[50]

These assumptions include the oral origin of these traditions, their faithful transmission over many centuries, and that Israelite patterns of transmission were like those in other cultures. Whybray argues that there is little to support these suppositions and few good extrabiblical parallels to unravel the process of oral transmission in Israel. It is one vast speculation. "Much of Noth's detailed reconstruction of the Pentateuchal traditions was obtained by *piling one speculation upon another*."[51] He illustrates his point by outlining how Noth believed the Lot stories grew out of a place-name, Beth-haran, in Numbers 32:36. He remarks justly, "There is not a single feature of this series of speculations which is supported by concrete evidence, from the mysterious rise and fall of a 'Haran tradition' to the supposition of an otherwise unattested—and surely quite unnecessary—deity Haran. But each supposition is made to serve as the basis for another."[52] Noth's method is characterized by "an undue propensity to pile hypothesis upon hypothesis and so to construct a whole 'tradition-history' out of the flimsiest of 'clues.'"[53]

Rendtorff and Blum profess to be tradition critics, but Whybray says this is true only in the sense that they see the process of growth that characterized the oral phase continuing in the literary phase, for their methods of analysis of the text are much closer to classic source criti-

50. Ibid., 138–39.
51. Ibid., 194.
52. Ibid., 196.
53. Ibid., 198.

cism. He finds their conclusions less than convincing. "Rendtorff has merely replaced the comparatively simple Documentary Hypothesis which postulated only a small number of written sources and redactors with a bewildering multiplicity of sources and redactors."[54] As for Blum, Whybray thinks his approach is if anything more complex and more dogmatic, yet less demonstrable, than Rendtorff's.

So what does Whybray himself believe? His agnosticism about most of the complex reconstructions of the documentary and tradition critics is manifest. He considers most of their hypotheses at best unverifiable and at worst illogical speculation. Let us admit that we just do not know much about the growth of the Pentateuch. Modern literary criticism (cf. Alter and Clines) has shown that the Pentateuch is a well-constructed work, which indicates that it is the work of an author, not the end product of haphazard growth like the Midrash. So let us suppose it is the work of one writer from the late sixth century as Van Seters argued. Whybray thinks the parallels Van Seters noted with the Greek historians are quite valid; they were writing the history of their people from earliest times to their own day. Though they claim to be using written sources from time to time, they evidently rewrite them in their own words and even more so when they retell oral information. Greek writers do not mind repeating themselves or varying their style, so why should these features in Hebrew literature be ascribed to different sources or layers? Van Seters and Rendtorff have been going in the right direction in seeing the Pentateuch as an essentially single literary work by either the late Yahwist or a Deuteronomist, but they have failed to take them to their logical conclusion. "There appears to be no reason why (allowing for the possibility of a few additions) the *first* edition of the Pentateuch as a comprehensive work should not also have been the *final* edition, a work composed by a single historian."[55] Van Seters, Rendtorff, and Blum regard the P material as post-J, but Whybray notes that M. Haran and A. Hurvitz (discussed below) have argued that P is preexilic. Hence the P material could be just one of the sources used by the author of the Pentateuch. Most of the narratives were based on folktales or made up by the author. This means that most of the story should be regarded as fiction, including "the whole presentation of Moses . . . in its present form."[56]

On the one hand, Whybray's work on the Pentateuch could be viewed as the logical conclusion of the direction in which much pentateuchal criticism has been moving in the last three decades. More and more

54. Ibid., 210.
55. Ibid., 232–33.
56. Ibid., 240.

studies have been insisting on the sixth century as the time in which the whole work started to take shape, and there has been an ever stronger trend to unitary readings and a reaction against minute dissection. On the other hand, he could be viewed as the embodiment of the English commonsense tradition as opposed to the Continental love of complex theorizing. His book is a powerful and valid critique of the methods that have been taken for granted in pentateuchal criticism for nearly two centuries. Nonetheless, though I think his model for the composition of the Pentateuch is essentially correct (one major author using a variety of sources),[57] he has not demonstrated this by giving detailed attention to the texts, nor has he shown that it was composed so late or should be regarded as fiction.

Though in recent study of the Pentateuch the pace has been set by those rejecting traditional critical views, many studies take these views for granted. One of the few attempts to refute the radical arguments is K. Berge, *Die Zeit des Jahwisten,* which tries to turn the critical clock back in various ways.[58] Its chief thrust is to argue that J was indeed composed in the tenth century B.C., in the time of David and Solomon. Berge argues that the promises of nationhood (Gen. 12:2) and victory over other nations (27:27–29) fit the period of the Davidic-Solomonic empire. The promise that God would be with the patriarchs shows that memories of the patriarchs and the wilderness wanderings were still alive. He thinks the alleged parallels with Deuteronomic literature and Deutero-Isaiah are weak; and even if they were valid, similarity of ideas does not mean a similar date of composition. The weight of the points under discussion is that they together all indicate one and the same period as the likeliest time of origin: the early period of the empire.[59]

Another significant contribution from a more traditional critical position is S. Boorer, *The Promise of the Land as Oath.*[60] Boorer examines those passages in Genesis to Deuteronomy that mention within a Deuteronomistic context that God is giving the land to Israel because of his oath to the patriarchs. She compares each passage to Deuteronomy and concludes that they were written in the following order: Exodus 32:13 and 33:1; Numbers 14:23a; Deuteronomy 10:11; Deuteronomy 1:35; Numbers 32:11. Boorer argues that her findings rule out the views of Van Seters, who would date the Yahwistic redaction post-Deuteronomy,

---

57. I argued the same independently of Whybray in my commentary, *Genesis 1–15,* WBC 1 (Waco: Word, 1987). See further my "The Priority of P," *VT* 49 (1999): 240–58.

58. K. Berge, *Die Zeit des Jahwisten,* BZAW 186 (Berlin: de Gruyter, 1990). He also believes in E as a separate source.

59. Ibid., 313.

60. S. Boorer, *The Promise of the Land as Oath: A Key to the Formation of the Pentateuch,* BZAW 205 (Berlin: de Gruyter, 1992).

and of Rendtorff, who believes that several of these texts come from the same Deuteronomistic layer. "Our results support most closely Wellhausen's overall conception of the formation of the Pentateuch, and also lend some support to aspects of the second paradigm initiated by Noth."[61] Though the evidence for her conclusion is presented at great length, it rests on too narrow a basis to be compelling.

In Europe and the United States pentateuchal critics have concentrated their attention on the narratives, particularly those of Genesis. Very little attention has been given to the laws and instructions usually identified as Priestly, even though they constitute more than half of Genesis through Numbers. Israeli and American Jewish scholars, however, often prefer another paradigm of pentateuchal criticism. Following Y. Kaufmann, scholars like A. Hurvitz, M. Haran, J. Milgrom, and M. Weinfeld have argued that P precedes D, indeed may be contemporary with J.[62]

Now I. Knohl has produced an important study of this material that profoundly challenges many accepted views.[63] According to the traditional documentary hypothesis, the Priestly material has several components. One of the earlier sections is the Holiness Code (H; Lev. 17–26), which is often dated in the early exile, whereas the bulk of the Priestly code (P) may be up to a century later. Furthermore it is usually held that there are P insertions or editorial changes to H.

Knohl challenges all these points. Employing methods used in the critical analysis of the Talmud, he argues that the Holiness School edited the P material, not vice versa. By comparing the P version of the festivals in Numbers 28–29 with the H version in Leviticus 23, he shows that the latter is an H expansion of a P text. For example, Leviticus 23:39–43 looks like a supplement to the P text 23:33–38. In 23:21 the first and last parts of the verse appear to be glosses on the middle part of the verse. His criterion for detecting glosses is "that they may be removed without disturbing the logical order of the original sentence."[64]

61. Ibid., 437.

62. Y. Kaufmann, *The Religion of Israel: From Its Beginnings to the Babylonian Exile*, trans. and abridged by M. Greenberg (Chicago: University of Chicago Press, 1960); A. Hurvitz, *A Linguistic Study of the Relationship between the Priestly Source and the Book of Ezekiel* (Paris: Gabalda, 1982); M. Haran, *Temples and Priestly Service in Ancient Israel* (Oxford: Clarendon, 1978; reprinted, Winona Lake, Ind.: Eisenbrauns, 1995); J. Milgrom, *Leviticus 1–16: A New Translation with Introduction and Commentary*, AB 3 (New York: Doubleday, 1991); M. Weinfeld, "Social and Cultic Institutions in the Priestly Source against Their Ancient Near Eastern Background," in *Proceedings of the Eighth World Congress of Jewish Studies*, vol. 5 (Jerusalem: World Union of Jewish Studies, 1983), 95–129.

63. I. Knohl, *The Sanctuary of Silence: The Priestly Torah and the Holiness School* (Minneapolis: Fortress, 1995).

64. Ibid., 12.

The double title of 23:2, 4 makes it appear likely that vv. 2–3 are both additions. This close analysis of Leviticus 23 allows Knohl to determine the characteristics of P and H. For example, in P God speaks in the third person, whereas in H he speaks in the first. P is concerned purely with cultic matters (e.g., sabbath sacrifices), whereas H is concerned with moral matters (e.g., not working on the sabbath). Using a mixture of linguistic, theological, and content-related criteria, Knohl goes on to argue that wide stretches of P material have been edited by H. These come from Exodus, Leviticus, and Numbers. He argues that "there are many indications of HS editing of PT material but . . . no evidence at all for influence in the opposite direction."[65] Not only did HS edit PT and not vice versa, but "HS is responsible for the great enterprise of editing the Torah, which included editing and rewriting the legal scrolls of the PT and blending them with the non-Priestly sources."[66] In other words, Knohl sees HS not simply as a pentateuchal source but as the last redactor of the Pentateuch. In his schema HS has a similar nature and role to P in the classical documentary hypothesis.

Having delineated the content of HS and PT, Knohl proceeds to analyze their leading religious ideas. PT differentiates sharply between the Genesis era and the Mosaic era. In the Genesis era, God is known as Elohim or El Shaddai; from the time of Moses, as Yahweh. The early period was characterized by unmediated revelation, God's direct care for humankind, and his intervention to punish. In the Mosaic era he spoke only to Moses, and both punishment and atonement are impersonal; indeed, few acts are ascribed to God. PT shuns anthropomorphisms in the Mosaic era. It wants to emphasize the loftiness of God. "The impersonal, nonanthropomorphic language of the period of Moses expresses the majesty of the holy and its awesomeness."[67] Indeed, Knohl believes that PT did not envisage any prayer, song, or praise in the cult. He admits that songs and prayers were used in other places and in much Israelite worship. But "the PT description is an idealized approach, which apparently was never put into practice outside

65. Ibid., 204. Because Knohl believes that H and P have not always been correctly distinguished, his definitions of H and P do not always coincide with the traditional ones. For this reason he speaks of HS = Holiness School and PT = Priestly Torah.

66. Ibid., 6. Cf. 101: "HS is responsible for the final form of the books of Exodus, Leviticus and Numbers. In places that contain Priestly traditions alongside those of JE, the editorial stamp of HS is evident. The characteristics of this editing project are transition passages, skillfully constructed to create frameworks for the various traditions; the blending of Priestly and non-Priestly language; and marked affinities to the language of Ezekiel. Even passages belonging primarily to PT bear signs of HS's editing; this indicates that PT came into the possession of HS in the form of individual scrolls, and it was HS that edited and combined them."

67. Ibid., 146–47.

the limited area in which the Priestly cult was performed."[68] PT was not interested in the land, agriculture, kingship, and administrative procedures—only the cult. Furthermore it does not know of any moral code given to Moses: all the laws he received had to do with the cult. Finally it sees the God-Israel relationship sealed at Sinai not as a bilateral conditional covenant *(běrît)* but as a one-sided divinely imposed pact *(ʿēdût)*. This relationship is "independent of the relation of reward and punishment—humans recognize their true status and are transformed into people who 'worship through love,' without expecting any recompense for their deeds."[69] This level of theological abstraction and lofty conception of God remained unequaled in Judaism until the Jews of the Middle Ages interacted with philosophy.

In HS, however, we have a development of Priestly theology that incorporates both the ideas of PT about holiness and the centrality of the cult with more popular notions of a God who is concerned with everyday life outside the cult; who wants all Israel, not just the priests, to be holy; and who regards the whole land, not just the sanctuary, as holy. "According to PT, holiness, which results from God's presence, is restricted to the cultic enclosure. . . . HS, on the other hand, believes that the holiness of God expands beyond the Sanctuary to encompass the settlements of the entire congregation, in whose midst God dwells."[70] What is more, HS understands that holiness involves morality and social justice, as shown by all the laws in Leviticus 19. "Through absorbing morality and social justice into the concept of holiness, and through extending the demand to live a life of holiness to the entire community, it [HS] combines the many streams of faith and cult present in the Israelite nation. For HS, the primary mission of the entire nation is the attainment of holiness; it is this that separates Israel from the nations."[71]

Having analyzed the different theological stances of HS and PT, Knohl finally tries to locate them historically. He thinks that Leviticus 17 suggests that HS was written in a period when the cult was being centralized, because it forbids the offering of sacrifice anywhere but at the tabernacle. This could connect it with Hezekiah's or Josiah's reforms. He thinks the former more likely as Molech worship was a problem in the eighth century. Also, the eighth century was a time of social polarization, which HS tries to counter with the jubilee provisions of Leviticus 25. The eighth-century prophets like Amos and Isaiah savagely attacked priestly rituals and demanded moral purity. HS counters

68. Ibid., 149.
69. Ibid., 158.
70. Ibid., 185.
71. Ibid., 198.

this prophetic onslaught by insisting that holiness does involve morality, but also that the cult has its proper place. "We thus find a moral refinement of the purely cultic conception, stemming from Priestly circles themselves, under the influence of the prophetic critique."[72] The prophetic preaching about social and moral issues led to the priests emerging from their introverted world, solely preoccupied with cultic holiness, and interacting with popular concerns. Thus Knohl dates the emergence of HS somewhere in the late eighth century. These writing priests continued their work over a period of time, however, finally compiling the whole Pentateuch in the spirit of HS in the late exile or shortly after the return to Zion.

PT was written before HS. Indeed, it probably originated in the period when Solomon's temple was being built in the mid-tenth century. "We may safely assume that the establishment of the 'King's Temple' of Jerusalem and the creation of a closed, elitist Priestly class dependent on the royal court are all part of the background leading to the development of PT."[73] The loftiness and abstraction of PT by no means require a late date. PT and J probably came into existence about the same time. "If we add the flourishing of poetry, psalmody and wisdom literature, we may generalize by saying that this was the peak period of all Israelite literature—in every genre."[74]

Knohl's work marks such a break with the consensus view of pentateuchal criticism that it is quite exhilarating. His analysis of the redaction of P texts by HS is at many points convincing. He has made a good case for holding that many P texts have been edited by HS. His methods and conclusions seem more sober and empirical than most attempts at source and redaction criticism. His exposition of the theological stance of HS is masterly. But his view of P and his dating arguments seem less well-grounded. These depend too much on arguments from silence: PT does not mention something, therefore it did not believe in it. It does not include moral commands, therefore its concept of holiness is purely cultic. We do not have the original PT, however, only the version edited by HS. We therefore cannot be sure what PT once contained, only what parts HS chose to retain. In fact, PT does begin with several moral passages, about the duty of procreation (Gen. 1:28), keeping the sabbath (Gen. 2:1–3), murder (Gen. 9:6), and food laws. And it insists that Abraham, father of the nation, be perfect (Gen. 17:2). Knohl acknowledges these points but thinks these apply to all people, not just Israel. It is in the Sinai revelation that moral commands are missing.

72. Ibid., 215.
73. Ibid., 221–22.
74. Ibid., 222 n. 78.

Again we do not know what PT may have said here: are we to imagine an account of Sinai that did not include or assume the Decalogue? But certainly putting the accounts of Genesis 1, 9, and 17 before the Sinai law-giving gives them special force and underlines PT's concern with moral issues.

Similarly, one might argue that we do not know what was said or sung during worship, but we assume that something was said because this was standard throughout the ancient Near East and also accords with other Old Testament texts. Knohl makes the opposite assumption: that the absence of reference to singing or prayer with the sacrifices means nothing was said. But as archaeologists say, "Absence of evidence is not evidence of absence." It would seem extraordinary, if PT were written to describe temple worship in Solomon's time, a time when Knohl says psalmists were also active, that the text would envisage a sanctuary of silence. Knohl notes two texts (Lev. 16:21 and Num. 5:19) that do mention prayer.

Similarly, it is odd that other legal texts in the Old Testament deal with ethical issues and envisage them as part of holiness, but only PT does not. Could it be that the original, putative PT dealt with such issues but such passages were replaced or rewritten by HS?

Knohl's view that PT antedates HS has been accepted by J. Joosten in an excellent exegetical study of the Holiness Code, but he questions whether the Holiness School was active for as long as Knohl suggests.[75] He contends that Hurvitz has put forward the strongest arguments in favor of the preexilic date of P and H based on their archaic vocabulary and that this dating is confirmed by the implied audience of H.[76] They are understood to be living in the land of Canaan but are invited to imagine themselves as receiving the laws at Sinai as a way of impressing on them the relevance of these events to their situation. The text pictures the people of Israel enjoying real autonomy: they are not beholden to foreign powers as they were in the exilic and postexilic eras. This is most evident in the description of the *gēr* (resident alien), who is a real foreigner, not a convert to Judaism, who is bound to observe the most important religious and moral laws (e.g., on idolatry, blasphemy, and sex) but is not compelled to participate in Israelite worship.[77] The idea that God really dwells with his people in the land is also fundamental in H, and this too is incompatible with the loss of the temple in the exile. The failure to mention the king leads Joosten to suggest that H was not produced by

75. J. Joosten, *People and Land in the Holiness Code: An Exegetical Study of the Ideational Framework of the Law in Leviticus 17–26*, VTSup 67 (Leiden: Brill, 1996), 16 n. 82.
76. See Hurvitz, *Linguistic Study*.
77. Joosten, *People and Land*, 63–70.

those living in the capital but by country people, perhaps rural priests.[78] Joosten admits that all these arguments are rather tenuous, but he concludes: "No convincing arguments contradicting a date in the monarchical period are known to me, however. To the contrary, the most convincing approach to the problem of dating, the linguistic method developed by A. Hurvitz, strongly favours the pre-exilic period."[79]

Within all this turmoil about the existence of E and the dating of J, H, and P, one fixed point remains in the broad consensus: the date of Deuteronomy and the Deuteronomistic history. Ever since de Wette argued in 1805 that Deuteronomy's laws were aimed at limiting all worship to the one sanctuary in Jerusalem,[80] scholars have widely accepted that the composition of the Deuteronomic code must be connected either as program or product of Josiah's reforms in 622 B.C. And since M. Noth first proposed that the present Book of Deuteronomy is the initial volume of a unified history of Israel whose other volumes are the Former Prophets, his views have been widely accepted. But most recently C. Westermann has pointed out that the different books are distinctive in their presentation of history and do not constitute a unified history.[81]

In *Law and Theology in Deuteronomy* J. G. McConville has indirectly offered the most serious challenge to the linkage between Deuteronomy and Josiah's reform. He argues that Deuteronomy subordinates legal precision to theological rhetoric in order to encourage the people to obey the law. Thus the differences between its code and other OT collections represent not historical development but theological motivation. Second, he endorses the Israeli/Jewish stance that Deuteronomy comes after P, not before it. Third, he holds that the attempt to link the laws on the place of the altar, profane slaughter, feasts, and priestly dues with Josiah's reform has actually led to their misinterpretation. Nowhere do these laws show evidence of the revolution in cultic practice that is usually said to have marked the Josianic reform. "On the contrary there were signs of continuity in cultic practice, and indications that Deuteronomy generally legislated for conditions which characterized a considerably earlier period than Josiah."[82] McConville finds it difficult to be more dogmatic than this about the dating of Deuteron-

78. Ibid., 163.

79. Ibid., 9, quotation on 207.

80. W. M. L. de Wette, *Dissertatio critica-exegetica qua Deuteronomium a prioribus pentateuchi libris diversum* (Jena, 1805).

81. C. Westermann, *Die Geschichtsbücher des Alten Testaments: Gab es ein deuteronomistisches Geschichtswork?* (Gütersloh: Chr. Kaiser, 1994).

82. J. G. McConville, *Law and Theology in Deuteronomy*, JSOTSup 33 (Sheffield: JSOT Press, 1984), 155.

omy, though he does say "the laws are consistently compatible with Deuteronomy's self-presentation as speeches on the verge of the promised land."[83] With most pentateuchal critics' attention focused on the source criticism of Genesis, McConville's work has not been widely noticed, but if a new critical paradigm is to emerge, it will have to reckon with McConville's arguments.

So far I have discussed only diachronic approaches to pentateuchal criticism, that is, attempts to trace how the Pentateuch evolved over time. But such studies involve much speculation and reconstruction of texts, which, as Whybray said, involves piling hypothesis upon hypothesis. But within the last few decades, synchronic methods have come into prominence. These look at the shape of the text at a particular point in time and discuss its shape, literary form, and meaning without reference to its earlier stages. These synchronic readings have had an impact on diachronic studies to a greater or lesser extent. The studies of Van Seters, Rendtorff, Blum, and Whybray all adopt some of the insights of the New Criticism. But some purely synchronic studies, while not always denying the validity of diachronic study, deliberately eschew it or introduce it only as an afterthought.

D. J. A. Clines heralds this new wave of study.[84] He laments the vast attention given to the unprovable speculations of source criticism and the neglect of the present shape of the Pentateuch. He stresses that he does not deny the validity of diachronic study, but he thinks it occupies too much scholarly attention.

> It is ironic, is it not, that the soundest historical-critical scholar, who will find talk of themes and structures "subjective" in the extreme, will have no hesitation in expounding the significance of a (sometimes conjectural) document from a conjectural period for a hypothetical audience of which he has, even if he has defined the period correctly, only the most meagre knowledge, without any control over the all-important questions of how representative of and how acceptable to the community the given document was.[85]

Clines goes on to distinguish theme from plot, subject, intention, narrative pattern, and so on. The theme of a work is its "central or dominating idea," and he argues that "the theme of the Pentateuch is the partial fulfillment . . . of the promise to or blessing of the patriarchs."[86]

---

83. Ibid. McConville has refined his views in J. G. McConville and J. G. Millar, *Time and Place in Deuteronomy*, JSOTSup 179 (Sheffield: JSOT Press, 1994), 89–141.

84. D. J. A. Clines, *The Theme of the Pentateuch*, JSOTSup 10 (Sheffield: JSOT Press, 1978).

85. Ibid., 14.

86. Ibid., 18, 29.

The promises focus on descendants, the divine-human relationship, and land. Most of the rest of his book is taken up with showing how these are developed in different parts of the Pentateuch, and that recognition of the theme allows us to see the coherence of sections of the Pentateuch, such as the Book of Numbers, often regarded as confused and illogical. In the penultimate chapter he shows how this understanding of the Pentateuch's theme fits in with the needs of the exilic community who could have read the story of Israel's wanderings outside the land as prefiguring their own life in exile. According to Clines, this shows that attention to the major literary issues such as theme may clarify historical issues, so that synchronic and diachronic study need not be in opposition to each other.

Other studies emphasizing the final form of the text have tended to look at shorter sections. In *The Redaction of Genesis*, G. A. Rendsburg deals with the whole of Genesis, while J. P. Fokkelman and M. Fishbane each look at parts of Genesis, including the Jacob cycle (chaps. 25–35).[87] More recent works on the narratives of Genesis include L. A. Turner and R. Syrén.[88] Many other studies of parts of Genesis have appeared in journals and in books such as those by J. Licht, R. Alter, and M. Sternberg.[89] Studies on other parts of the Pentateuch have been fewer, but a final form reading of Exodus 32–34 has been offered by R. W. L. Moberly, of Numbers by D. T. Olson, and of Deuteronomy by R. Polzin.[90] In various books and articles R. Westbrook has been offering synchronic readings of biblical law, especially Exodus 21–22.[91] This brief list gives only a hint of the range of new work now devoted to interpreting the final form of the text. Much of it is exciting and fresh, but as with all studies, conclusions need to be weighed against the text itself to establish their validity.

Though most final-form studies pay lip service to the continuing place of diachronic study, few have really attempted to create a new syn-

87. G. A. Rendsburg, *The Redaction of Genesis* (Winona Lake, Ind.: Eisenbrauns, 1986); J. P. Fokkelman, *Narrative Art in Genesis*, SSN 17 (Amsterdam: Van Gorcum, 1975); M. Fishbane, *Text and Texture* (New York: Schocken, 1979).

88. L. A. Turner, *Announcements of Plot in Genesis*, JSOTSup 96 (Sheffield: JSOT Press, 1990); R. Syrén, *The Forsaken First-Born*, JSOTSup 133 (Sheffield: JSOT Press, 1993).

89. J. Licht, *Storytelling in the Bible* (Jerusalem: Magnes, 1978); R. Alter, *The Art of Biblical Narrative*, ILOS (New York: Basic Books, 1981); M. Sternberg, *The Poetics of Biblical Narrative* (Bloomington: Indiana University Press, 1985).

90. R. W. L. Moberly, *At the Mountain of God*, JSOTSup 22 (Sheffield: JSOT Press, 1983); D. T. Olson, *The Death of the Old and the Birth of the New: The Framework of the Book of Numbers and the Pentateuch*, BJS 71 (Chico, Calif.: Scholars Press, 1985); R. Polzin, *Moses and the Deuteronomist* (New York: Seabury, 1980).

91. E.g., R. Westbrook, *Studies in Biblical and Cuneiform Law* (Paris: Gabalda, 1988). See also J. M. Sprinkle, *"The Book of the Covenant": A Literary Approach*, JSOTSup 174 (Sheffield: JSOT Press, 1994).

thesis bringing together the two ends of the discipline. An exception is R. W. L. Moberly, *The Old Testament of the Old Testament.*[92] He begins by looking at two passages in Exodus 3 and 6, which tell of the revelation of the name of Yahweh to Moses. In the first, Moses standing before the burning bush asks God what his name is. He is told "I am that I am" (i.e., Yahweh). In the second passage, God simply introduces himself: "I am Yahweh. I appeared to Abraham, to Isaac, and to Jacob, as God Almighty, but by my name Yahweh I did not make myself known to them" (Exod. 6:2–3). Standard documentary criticism sees these texts as justifying the analysis of pentateuchal narratives into the main sources, E in Exodus 3:14–15 and P in Exodus 6:2–3, because they could be held to be repeats. They also enable a contrast to be made with the J source, which uses the name Yahweh frequently in the patriarchal stories, whereas E and P say it was an innovation from the time of Moses.

Moberly, however, shows that Exodus 6 is not simply repeating Exodus 3. Indeed, the plot of the narrative demands that something like chapter 6 follow chapter 3. Thus, if it is right to distinguish sources here, which Moberly doubts, both the old E source and late P source agree that there is a distinction to make between the religious experience of Moses and that of the patriarchs. Why then is God so often referred to as "Yahweh" in Genesis? Moberly argues that this does not represent a historical perspective peculiar to the J source; rather it is a way of insisting that the God who spoke to the patriarchs was the same God who spoke to Moses. The patriarchs may have known God as El Shaddai or El or Elohim, but that does not mean he was a different deity from Moses' Yahweh. The use of the name Yahweh in Genesis is a reminder of the continuity between patriarchal and Mosaic religion, and also that patriarchal history is told from the perspective of Mosaic Yahwism. Thus, all the putative sources in the Pentateuch see both continuity and difference between the ages.

Moberly goes on to explore other points of similarity and difference between the patriarchal and Mosaic periods as the texts portray them. While the patriarchs worship one God, there is not the exclusivism that characterizes Mosaic monotheism. The patriarchs generally live peaceably with the Canaanites, without trying to exterminate them or drive them out as the Mosaic law requires. God reveals himself directly to the patriarchs, and they themselves build altars and offer sacrifices without the mediation of Moses or the priests. The patriarchs practice circumcision, but it is not clear that they observed the sabbath or food laws that figure so largely in later books of the Pentateuch. Finally, "the no-

92. R. W. L. Moberly, *The Old Testament of the Old Testament,* OBT (Minneapolis: Fortress, 1992).

tion of holiness, which from Exodus onward is a basic characteristic of God and a major requirement for Israel, is entirely lacking in the patriarchal traditions."[93]

Moberly argues that the relationship between the patriarchal stories and the rest of the Pentateuch is like that between the Old and New Testaments. The same God revealed himself in both Testaments, but the coming of Christ revealed a radical new perspective on his nature. Similarly the revelation at Sinai represented a new theological dispensation in his dealings with Israel. That is not to invalidate the old revelation given to the patriarchs or to say that their experience of the life of faith is not most illuminating to later ages, but it is to insist that the revelation to Moses, like the coming of Christ, brought new insights into God's character and purposes unknown before.

Thus, penetrating the mind of the writers of Genesis and Exodus is for Moberly the prerequisite for a new approach to pentateuchal criticism. He questions whether it is useful to speak of a Yahwist anymore, when this title reflects the erroneous view that J held that the name Yahweh was known prior to Moses, whereas E and P did not hold that. "If our thesis is correct, this distinguishing characteristic is unwarranted, for we have argued that all the pentateuchal writers shared a common and undisputed tradition that the name YHWH was first revealed to Moses, but they all felt free nonetheless to use the name YHWH in the patriarchal context."[94]

Moberly suggests that the whole project of naming the sources J, E, and P is flawed, because so much rests on postulating religious distinctions between the sources, which really represent differences between the patriarchal era and the Mosaic dispensation. He would prefer a different approach. "It would be most helpful to adopt categories that are descriptive of the content of the text: patriarchal traditions (subdivided into Abraham, Jacob, and Joseph cycles . . .); similarly Mosaic traditions" (again subdivided).[95] Then one can proceed to find the linking vocabulary and theological themes that spanned these different sections of text and build up a new critical theory. This may sound a little like the program of Rendtorff and Blum, but Moberly emphasizes that he thinks tradition criticism tends to be far too speculative.[96] He also thinks much historical criticism tends to read against the grain of the text instead of trying to appreciate the text's own theological perspective. For example, John Ha has argued that the purpose of Genesis 15 is to encourage the exiles by replacing the bilateral Sinai covenant with a

---

93. Ibid., 99.
94. Ibid., 177.
95. Ibid., 181.
96. Ibid., 180.

one-sided divine promise.[97] But this is to misread Genesis completely: it is looking back on the patriarchs from the standpoint of Mosaic Yahwism, so it cannot be denying the fundamentals of the Sinai covenant. "Ha's way of reading the text turns the logic and dynamic of the pentateuchal story upside down."[98] But there are of course many examples of pentateuchal critics misreading the text in this way.

Finally, Moberly's approach to the distinctiveness of the patriarchal era, which he holds is recognized by the writers themselves, makes the skepticism of Van Seters and others about the historicity of these traditions unwarranted. The pentateuchal writers cannot be simply projecting back into the patriarchal past contemporary popular religious practice with which they disagree. The writers believed in Mosaic Yahwism, yet they have described different beliefs and practices that they are supposed to have wanted to abolish without condemnation. Indeed, they have gone further:

> They have given traditions depicting non-Yahwistic ethos and practices the considerable luster of inseparable association with the ancestor of Israel's faith, Abraham, and the eponymous ancestor of the whole nation, Jacob/Israel. They have refrained from all adverse comment. And they have gone to considerable lengths to relate such material to Mosaic Yahwism in the way we have shown above. One would have thought that straightforward suppression would not only have been easier but also more in keeping with the generally exclusive and polemical nature of Yahwism in Exodus–Deuteronomy.[99]

Thus the debate about the Pentateuch continues. In the present situation of scholarly polarization, sometimes the polemic is becoming so strident that the different sides in the debate are in danger of neglecting valid criticism of their own positions.[100] There is certainly as yet no consensus on a new paradigm for understanding the growth of the Pentateuch. Many feel that the claims of the old source criticism are exaggerated and that more attention should be given to the final form of the text. But while the New Critical methods have greatly enhanced the appreciation of the biblical narratives, they will need to be combined with sober historical criticism (cf. Moberly and Knohl) if a satisfactory new model of pentateuchal origins is to emerge.

---

97. J. Ha, *Genesis 15: A Theological Compendium of Pentateuchal History*, BZAW 181 (Berlin: de Gruyter, 1989).

98. Moberly, *Old Testament*, 188.

99. Ibid., 195.

100. Cf. G. J. Wenham, "Method in Pentateuchal Source Criticism," *VT* 41 (1991): 84–109.

6

Historiography of the Old Testament

V. Philips Long

Among the various features on the face of Old Testament studies, the historiography of the Old Testament is one of the most widely discussed but least well defined. Not only do the differing personalities and perspectives of various scholars prompt them to trace the contours of this feature in sometimes radically different ways, but there is ambiguity even as to what constitutes the proper object of study. Consider, for instance, the assigned title of this essay. Is the phrase "of the Old Testament" to be understood as a subjective genitive or an objective genitive? Is our concern in this essay to be with the oft-noted historical consciousness of ancient Israel, evident in the purportedly historiographic writings of the Old Testament (subjective genitive), or with the various recent attempts to write a history of ancient Israel (objective genitive)? In other words, is our focus to be on "biblical history, i.e., the history as told in the Bible," or on "Israelite history, i.e., the history of ancient Israel as modern research presents it"?[1] In short, are we to concern ourselves with *Israel's history writing* or with *writing Israel's history?*

Since the intent of the present volume is to survey the state of Old Testament *studies*, the emphasis of this essay naturally falls on the latter. But perhaps I may take the ambiguity in the title as an encouragement to give some attention to both these matters in the pages that follow. Until recently the two have been viewed as interrelated issues, and even today the distance between biblical Israel and historical Israel remains a disputed matter. Some scholars regard the two as rather closely

---

1. M. Tsevat, "Israelite History and the Historical Books of the Old Testament," in *The Meaning of the Book of Job and Other Biblical Essays* (New York: Ktav, 1980), 177–87 (citation is from 177).

tied—"biblical history" being an essentially reliable literary representation of selected aspects of "Israelite history"—while others view the two as virtually unrelated—"biblical history" being little more than a literary fiction with minimal bearing on the reconstruction of ancient Israelite history.[2]

Whether one's concern is with ancient Israel's history writing or with writing ancient Israel's history, one cannot read far into contemporary scholarly discussion without becoming aware that the study of the "historiography of the Old Testament" is in a state of flux.[3] No longer does Troeltschian-style historical criticism enjoy the hegemony that it held in mainline scholarship in the nineteenth century and for much of the twentieth (though in some scholarly circles the method continues to dominate). In the last several decades, modern literary approaches have arisen to offer alternatives to traditional historical-critical practice and in some instances to challenge earlier conclusions. Yet literary readers themselves are far from unified. Robert Morgan describes "the recent [i.e., post-1960] history of secular literary criticism [as] a hurricane of conflicting tendencies."[4] Literary critics often seem unable to agree on what constitutes a properly literary approach to the Old Testament. Some are convinced that a competent literary reading of texts is a necessary condition for discovering the texts' truth claims, be they historical, theological, or whatever; others assume that the biblical texts should be read as "pure" literature, largely devoid of historiographical intent and thus useless for purposes of historical reconstruction.

While traditional historical criticism (diachronic) and modern literary criticism (synchronic) debate how the biblical texts are to be read (or processed), other contemporary approaches show little interest in texts at all. Among socio-archaeological circles today, one sometimes hears a call to abandon the biblical texts, or at least to set them aside, so that a genuine history of Israel, or Syria-Palestine, can be reconstructed on the basis of the more "objective" data unearthed by archaeological investigation. But of course artifactual evidence does not emerge from the ground with museum labels already affixed, and so

2. A recent, extreme example of the latter viewpoint is that of P. R. Davies, who insists on distinguishing "three Israels: one is literary (the biblical), one is historical (the inhabitants of the northern Palestinian highlands during part of the Iron Age) and the third, 'ancient Israel,' is what scholars have constructed out of an amalgam of the two others" (Davies, *In Search of "Ancient Israel,"* JSOTSup 48 [Sheffield: Sheffield Academic Press, 1992], 11). In principle, the basic tripartite distinction is useful, but few scholars are likely to be happy with the size of the wedge that Davies drives between the three.

3. R. Rendtorff, "The Paradigm Is Changing: Hopes—and Fears," *BibInt* 1 (1993): 34–53.

4. R. Morgan, with J. Barton, *Biblical Interpretation*, Oxford Bible Series (Oxford: Oxford University Press, 1988), 217; see also 218.

even archaeologists must bring to bear an explanatory model of some sort to achieve any meaningful synthesis of the data. Here the social sciences are ready and willing to step forward. The biblical texts—so the argument goes—are not to be trusted (at least not for purposes of historical reconstruction), because they, like most ancient texts, stem from elitist (i.e., educated) male circles.[5] Instead, many contemporary scholars look to the quantifying and generalizing methods of the social sciences as a means of reconstructing "history from below."

We shall return to these matters presently, but for now I mention them simply to indicate that the last quarter century or so may have seen more upheaval in the study of the "historiography of the Old Testament" than was apparent for many decades prior. In short, the discipline is in a state of flux, or, to put it more positively, in a state of ferment. This is perhaps not a bad thing. For when a discipline is in flux, it has the opportunity to rethink its foundations and, if need be, to rebuild itself on a surer footing.

Before rebuilding can begin, however, it is necessary to examine how the present foundations of the discipline were laid. Thus the next section offers a brief sketch of trends in the scholarly study of the historiography of the Old Testament that have led up to the current state of affairs. A further section then surveys prevalent contemporary approaches and seeks to discover why there is such wide disagreement among scholars as to how Israel's history is to be reconstructed and such wide divergence in the results achieved. A final section seeks to discover some way out of the impasse in which contemporary discussion of the historiography of the Old Testament finds itself.

How Did We Get Where We Are? A Brief History of the Study of the Historiography of the Old Testament

The history of scholarship pertaining to ancient Israelite historiography and to the reconstruction of ancient Israel's history is well surveyed in a number of places, and I need not fully rehearse it here.[6] Particularly

---

5. See W. G. Dever, "'Will the Real Israel Please Stand Up?' Part II: Archaeology and the Religions of Ancient Israel," *BASOR* 298 (1995): 45 (hereafter, "Archaeology and the Religions"). Dever notes that the charge of male bias is leveled not only against the biblical texts but against traditional biblical and even archaeological scholarship. For a description, though not necessarily an endorsement, of the bias charge, see also J. M. Miller, "Reading the Bible Historically: The Historian's Approach," in *To Each Its Own Meaning: An Introduction to Biblical Criticisms and Their Application*, ed. S. R. Haynes and S. L. McKenzie (Louisville: Westminster/John Knox, 1993), 25.

6. The following are but a sampling of the many works that might be mentioned: R. de Vaux, "Method in the Study of Early Hebrew History," in *The Bible in Modern Scholarship*, ed. J. P. Hyatt (Nashville: Abingdon, 1965), 15–29; J. H. Hayes, "The History of the

worthy of note, both for its wide scope and the conciseness of its coverage, is the survey provided by John Hayes in *Israelite and Judaean History*. Hayes's survey begins with the first treatments of Israelite and Judean history in the Hellenistic period, moves through the medieval period, then on to a discussion of developments from the Renaissance to the Enlightenment. He then considers developments in the nineteenth century, before finally concluding with a brief look at current approaches. Hayes's last section requires updating, as the volume was published in 1977, but his survey retains its value for the reasons given and for the extensive bibliographies that accompany each section.

Pertinent to our concern in this essay is Hayes's observation that "the foundations of modern historiography were laid in the Renaissance," a period noted for its "militant humanism" as well as its "intellectual and technological accomplishments."[7] It was in this period that "'middle-range explanations'—what we today would call sociological, economical, geographical, climatic considerations—" began to be used.[8] Following the Renaissance period, but still breathing its air, the seventeenth century witnessed, in the writings of thinkers such as Grotius, Hobbes, and Spinoza, the emergence of assumptions that many modern biblical critics still hold—for example, that the Bible is to be treated like any other book and that literary inconsistencies, repetitions, and the like discredit traditional notions such as the Mosaic authorship of the Pentateuch. It is important to note, as Hayes points out, that these thinkers "had moved away from the typical Jewish and Protestant view of religious authority and revelation and that their criticism was probably the result rather than the cause of such a move."[9] In other words, for thinkers such as Grotius, Hobbes, and Spinoza, it was not so much the development of new critical methods that forced the abandonment of the older model of reality as it was the abandonment of the traditional, bib-

---

Study of Israelite and Judaean History," in *Israelite and Judaean History*, ed. J. H. Hayes and J. M. Miller, OTL (London: SCM; Philadelphia: Westminster, 1977), 1–69; J. M. Miller, "Israelite History," in *The Hebrew Bible and Its Modern Interpreters*, ed. D. A. Knight and G. M. Tucker (Philadelphia: Fortress; Chico, Calif.: Scholars Press, 1985), 1–30; J. R. Porter, "Old Testament Historiography," in *Tradition and Interpretation: Essays by Members of the Society for Old Testament Study*, ed. G. W. Anderson (Oxford: Clarendon, 1979), 125–62; H. G. Reventlow, "The Problem of History," in *Problems of Old Testament Theology in the Twentieth Century*, trans. J. Bowden (Philadelphia: Fortress, 1985), 59–124; J. A. Soggin, "Probleme einer Vor- und Frühgeschichte Israels," *ZAW* 100 Supplement (1988): 255–67; E. Yamauchi, "The Current State of Old Testament Historiography," in *Faith, Tradition, and History: Old Testament Historiography in Its Near Eastern Context*, ed. A. R. Millard, J. K. Hoffmeier, and D. W. Baker (Winona Lake, Ind.: Eisenbrauns, 1994), 1–36.

   7. Hayes, "History of the Study of Israelite and Judaean History," 34.
   8. Ibid., 39.
   9. Ibid., 46.

lically derived model of reality, or worldview, that prompted the development of new methods.

Moving to the eighteenth century, we see the Bible and Christianity subjected to "an unprecedented and trenchant examination and critique" at the hands of the deists.[10] While the deists were by no means uniform in their approach to the Bible, "as a rule, they sought to distil the biblical traditions, to siphon off the supernatural, the miraculous, and the unbelievable, and to leave behind the pure essence of a reasonable faith"[11]—reasonable, that is, in terms of the fundamental assumptions of the Enlightenment. Robert Morgan cites Reimarus as a typical, if exceptionally influential, deist of the eighteenth century. Reimarus "believed in God, but not in revelation, miracles, or other supernatural interventions."[12] Reimarus sought in his writings "to destroy a traditional Christianity based on biblical revelation and miracle, and replace it with the rational, natural religion popular among intellectuals of the Enlightenment or 'age of reason.'"[13] Again, what is to be noted here is that it was a commitment to a particular (in this case, rationalistic and naturalistic) model of reality that encouraged the development and application of rationalistic critical methods, and not the emergence of new methods that forced acceptance of a new model of reality.[14]

Building on trends begun in the preceding two centuries, the nineteenth century saw a number of major developments relevant to the historiography of the Old Testament. Among these, if I may draw together Hayes's remarks, are the following:

1. an increase in religious liberalism that was "less dogmatic in its theological orientation, more progressive in its relationship to contemporary culture and thought, and more humanistic in its perspectives than previous generations";
2. advances in "general historiography," including the development of "a positivistic approach to history, which not only at-

---

10. Ibid., 47.
11. Ibid., 48.
12. Morgan, *Biblical Interpretation*, 53.
13. Ibid., 53–54.
14. For more on the impact of Enlightenment rationalism on the historical study of the Bible, see ibid., esp. chap. 2, "Criticism and the Death of Scripture," and chap. 3, "History and the Growth of Knowledge"; see also V. P. Long, *The Art of Biblical History*, Foundations of Contemporary Interpretation 5 (Grand Rapids: Zondervan, 1994), 99–116; C. Westermann, "The Old Testament's Understanding of History in Relation to That of the Enlightenment," in *Understanding the Word: Essays in Honour of Bernhard W. Anderson*, ed. J. Butler, E. Conrad, and B. Ollenburger, JSOTSup 37 (Sheffield: JSOT Press, 1985), 207–19.

tempted but also believed it was possible to reconstruct past history 'as it had actually happened'";
3. the decipherment of the languages of Israel's ancient Near Eastern neighbors in Egypt and Mesopotamia;
4. a new level of activity and competence in the historical geography of the Near East; and
5. the gradual rise to dominance of the pentateuchal documentary hypothesis, along with the belief that the "character, content, and date of the individual documents were . . . of great significance in understanding the religious development of Israelite and Judaean life and in evaluating the historical reliability of the documentary materials."[15]

   Each of these nineteenth-century developments has made itself felt in twentieth-century biblical scholarship, but none has escaped challenge or failed to precipitate new debate:

1. nineteenth-century-style liberalism has been challenged by neoorthodoxy and neoevangelicalism: these movements, while not wishing to ignore the concerns of contemporary culture, have stressed the primacy of a theocentric over a merely humanistic perspective on life's ultimate issues;
2. positivistic history has come under considerable strain through advances in general hermeneutics and a greater awareness of the distinction between "brute facts" of the past, which are of course no longer subject to observation, and "historical facts" as they are perceived in the present by means of probability judgments based on the available evidence;
3. the decipherment of, for example, Egyptian hieroglyphics and Akkadian cuneiform has opened up a whole new world of comparative literary studies and with this advance has raised significant questions as to the proper uses and potential abuses of comparative material in the study of the Bible;
4. the greatly increased archaeological and geographical exploration of the "lands of the Bible" has raised as many questions as it has answered, not least as regards the interrelationship of textual and artifactual evidence in the reconstruction of Israel's history; and finally,
5. the documentary hypothesis, promoted most effectively in the nineteenth century by J. Wellhausen, has been rigorously challenged in the twentieth, as have other literary theories

---

15. Hayes, "History," 54–55.

and, indeed, the whole general approach of Wellhausen and his followers.[16]

That Wellhausen-style literary criticism has been seriously challenged and, in the minds of many, undermined has far-reaching implications for the historical study of the Old Testament, since, as Hayes maintains, "the primary influence on Wellhausen's reconstruction of Israelite *history* was . . . the results and consequences of his *literary* study of the Old Testament" (italics mine).[17]

Where Are We Now? Contemporary Approaches to the Historiography of the Old Testament

As suggested above, the seventeenth to nineteenth centuries introduced sweeping changes in the way many people viewed the world. These shifts in worldview in turn gave rise to the development of new methods of research and to significant changes in already existing methods. Not surprisingly, the radical disjunction between the Enlightenment model of reality, which left no place for divine activity in the realm of human history, and the pervasive biblical model of reality, in which the creator God is the "Lord of history" and the controlling actor on its stage,[18]

16. See, e.g., R. Rendtorff, who believes that "the traditional Documentary Hypothesis has come to an end" ("The Paradigm Is Changing," 44). For a survey of the current state of scholarship on the Pentateuch, see D. A. Knight, "The Pentateuch," in *The Hebrew Bible and Its Modern Interpreters,* ed. D. A. Knight and G. M. Tucker (Chico, Calif.: Scholars Press, 1985), 263–96.

17. Hayes, "History," 63.

18. So, e.g., D. N. Freedman, "The Biblical Idea of History," *Int* 21 (1967): 43: "The fixed points in the biblical view of history are at the beginning and at the end. The point of departure is the confident assertion that God is the lord of history and that nothing of importance happens without his decision, whether active or permissive"; G. B. Caird, *The Language and Imagery of the Bible* (London: Duckworth; Philadelphia: Westminster, 1980), 217–18: "the most important item in the framework within which the people of biblical times interpreted their history was the conviction that God was lord of history. He uttered his voice and events followed (Isa. 55:11–12). Thus the course of events was itself a quasi-linguistic system, in which God was disclosing his character and purpose. . . . The interpretation of God's history-language required the exercise of moral judgment (Jer. 15:19; cf. Heb. 5:14), and it was the task of the prophet to be the qualified interpreter. . . . The prophet thus discharged for his people the kind of responsibility which in this chapter we have been ascribing to the historian"; M. Delcor, "Storia e profezia nel mondo ebraico," *Fondamenti* 13 (1989): 33: "Di fatto, più che dei testimoni i profeti sono degli interpreti della storia, che non è altro che l'opera delle nazioni, ma diretta in ultima instanza da Dio che è il vero padrone degli eventi" [In fact, more than witnesses, the prophets are the interpreters of the (his)story, which is none other than the affairs of nations, but is ultimately directed by God, who is the true lord of the events] (my translation); J. M. Miller, "Reading the Bible Historically," 12: "the Bible presupposes a dynamic natural world into which God intrudes overtly upon human affairs from time to time"; cf.

posed a challenge to believing Jewish and Christian scholars who wished to remain true both to "the faith" and to their scholarly calling.[19] Naturally, all reputable scholars wished to make use of "scientific" methods in their research, but the purely naturalistic premises of the Enlightenment inevitably introduced a point of tension for theists.

Today perhaps more scholars than ever before are beginning to question the adequacy of Enlightenment assumptions for dealing with the biblical literature, but it is probably still the case that the majority take them for granted. Thus our present task of exploring and attempting to explain current trends in the historical study of the Old Testament cannot be accomplished without some further attention to the roots out of which contemporary branches of learning have grown. Among the more obvious outgrowths of the Enlightenment is the historical-critical method, to which we now turn.

The Historical-Critical Method

The historical-critical method no longer enjoys the dominance it once had; social science methods and modern literary approaches (discussed below) are each providing alternative paradigms for today's scholars. Still, the continued influence of the historical-critical method should not be underestimated. Thus it is both wise and necessary to gain some understanding of its philosophical underpinnings.

The following words, penned by D. F. Strauss in his groundbreaking *Life of Jesus*, are typical of the Enlightenment reasoning that gave rise to the historical-critical approach to the Bible. (While Strauss's focus was on the historicity, or rather lack thereof, of the NT Gospels, the same kind of philosophical framework made itself felt in studies of OT historiography.) Seeking to articulate criteria whereby one could assess the historical value of an account, Strauss contended that an account is to be deemed unhistorical when

> the narration is irreconcilable with the known and the universal laws which govern the course of events. Now according to these laws, agreeing with all just philosophical conceptions and all credible experience, the absolute cause never disturbs the chain of secondary causes by single arbitrary acts of interposition, but rather manifests itself in the produc-

---

also H. W. Wolff, "The Understanding of History in the Old Testament Prophets" (trans. K. Crim), in *Essays on Old Testament Interpretation*, ed. C. Westermann (London: SCM, 1963 [original German edition, 1960]), 353–54; U.S. edition titled *Essays on Old Testament Hermeneutics* (Richmond: John Knox, 1963).

19. Cf. W. Brueggemann, "The Prophetic Word of God and History," *Int* 48 (1994): 239–51; Westermann, "The Old Testament's Understanding of History."

tion of the aggregate of finite causalities, and of their reciprocal action. When therefore we meet an account of certain phenomena or events of which it is either expressly stated or implied that they were produced immediately by God himself (divine apparitions—voices from heaven and the like), or by human beings possessed of supernatural powers (miracles, prophecies), such an account is in so far to be considered as not historical.[20]

As I have noted elsewhere,[21] Strauss's argument can be reduced to the following syllogism:

1. Every account irreconcilable with the known and universal laws that govern events is unhistorical.
2. Every account in which God disturbs the natural course of events is irreconcilable with the known and universal laws that govern events.
3. Therefore, every account in which God disturbs the natural course of events is unhistorical.

While the above syllogism qualifies as *logically valid,* it merits acceptance as *ontologically true* only if each of its premises is true. This raises significant questions. Whence comes knowledge of "the universal laws that govern events"? By what authority does Strauss believe himself in a position to pronounce on "all just philosophical conceptions and all credible experience"? On what grounds does one assume that "God never disturbs the natural course of events"? Strauss's premises are hardly the results of the application of new methods to the available data; rather, they can only be regarded as *metaphysical* assumptions about the nature of reality. That is, the premises themselves constitute "statements of faith," nothing more and nothing less.

That this Enlightenment faith continues today to influence scholarly debate about Old Testament historiography can hardly be disputed. That it creates a tension for religiously oriented scholars wishing to "keep the faith" both with their religious convictions/communities and with their scholarly guilds is equally indisputable. As Robert Morgan observes, for example, the problem for religious persons doing biblical studies is "how to speak meaningfully of 'God whom we worship' in a culture whose rational methods do not use such religious language."[22]

20. D. F. Strauss, *The Life of Jesus Critically Examined,* trans. G. Eliot, ed. P. C. Hodgson (Philadelphia: Fortress; London: SCM, 1972), 88.
21. *Art of Biblical History,* 110.
22. *Biblical Interpretation,* 275.

As for the application of rational methods to historical study, probably no one has been more influential than Ernst Troeltsch (1865–1923).[23] Troeltsch is credited with the establishment of the three well-known principles of the historical-critical method—criticism, analogy, and correlation—although there are foreshadowings already in Strauss's *Life of Jesus*.[24] While the precise construal of each of the three principles is open to debate (as we shall see in the next section), traditional historical criticism of the Old Testament has tended to understand "criticism" in terms of a presupposed skepticism toward one's sources,[25] "analogy" in a more or less narrow sense whereby present human experience limits what can qualify as "historical" in the past,[26] and "correlation" as limiting potential historical causation to either natural forces or human agency.[27] The application of Troeltsch's three principles to the Old Testament has, not surprisingly, raised grave difficulties.

According to J. M. Miller, the historical-critical method has difficulty with the "frequent references in the ancient texts to divine involvement

23. On the recent revival of interest in the work of Troeltsch, see, e.g., R. Morgan, "Troeltsch and Christian Theology," in *Ernst Troeltsch: Writings on Theology and Religion*, trans. and ed. R. Morgan and M. Pye (Louisville: Westminster/John Knox, 1990), 208–33. For Troeltsch's own articulation of his historical method, see "Ueber historische und dogmatische Methode in der Theologie," in E. Troeltsch, *Gesammelte Schriften*, vol. 2, *Zur religiösen Lage, Religionsphilosophie und Ethik* (Aalen: Scientia Verlag, 1962), 729–53; English readers may also consult his article "Historiography," *Encyclopaedia of Religion and Ethics*, ed. J. Hastings, 13 vols. (Edinburgh: Clark, 1914), 4:716–23. For these and further titles, see C. Brown, *History and Faith: A Personal Exploration* (Grand Rapids: Zondervan, 1987), 44 n. 22.

24. E.g., in addition to his primary negative criterion for establishing the nonhistoricity of a document (i.e., direct involvement of the "absolute cause"), Strauss (*Life of Jesus*, 88) mentions two secondary criteria: (1) the so-called "law of succession, in accordance with which all occurrences, not excepting the most violent convulsions and the most rapid changes, follow in a certain order of sequence of increase and decrease" (this anticipates Troeltsch's principle of correlation); and (2) "all those psychological laws, which render it improbable that a human being should feel, think, and act in a manner directly opposed to his own habitual mode and that of men in general" (cf. Troeltsch's principle of analogy).

25. E.g., V. A. Harvey, *The Historian and the Believer: A Confrontation between the Modern Historian's Principles of Judgment and the Christian's Will-to-Believe* (New York: Macmillan, 1966), 111: "The beginning of wisdom in history is doubt"; G. W. Ramsey, *The Quest for the Historical Israel: Reconstructing Israel's Early History* (Atlanta: John Knox, 1981; London: SCM, 1982), 7: "the first requirement of a good historian is a healthy streak of skepticism"; Davies, *In Search*, 13: "Credulity does not become an historian. Scepticism, rather, is the proper stance"; cf. also J. Barr, *The Scope and Authority of the Bible* (Philadelphia: Westminster; London: SCM, 1980), 30–31.

26. In Troeltsch's own words (as rendered in W. J. Abraham, *Divine Revelation and the Limits of Historical Criticism* [Oxford: Oxford University Press, 1982], 100): "Harmony with the normal, familiar or at least repeatedly witnessed events and conditions as we know them is the distinguishing mark of reality for the events which criticism can recognise as really having happened or leave aside."

27. On this third principle, see ibid., 105–8.

in human affairs . . . , especially when the involvement is depicted as direct and overt." Even among those historians who "may not specifically deny the supernatural or miraculous," it would appear from the history books they write that they disregard "overt supernatural activity as a significant cause" in history and are "skeptical of claims regarding supposedly unique historical occurrences which defy normal explanation—i.e., the miraculous."[28]

Thus, Enlightenment-style historical criticism of the Old Testament finds itself fundamentally at odds with its source. It can hardly accept the Old Testament story as *history,* because that *story* contains too many elements that by (Straussian or Troeltschian) definition are "unhistorical." At best one may use the Old Testament as a body of data from which one can extract "historical" information (if at all) only by most rigorously applying the canons of historical criticism as outlined above. But again, the very center of Old Testament historiography—the notion that God is the Lord of history—is denied a priori by the fundamental assumptions of the historical method as typically practiced.[29]

In short, there is a distinctly atheological, or even anti-theological, tendency in the historical-critical method that casts doubt on the value—for historical purposes at least—of much of the biblical text, since the Bible is pervaded by a divine presence that is anything but inactive in human affairs. As G. von Rad observed more than three decades ago,

> [Israel] could only understand her history as a road along which she travelled under Jahweh's protection. For Israel, history consisted only of Jahweh's self-revelation by word and action. And on this point conflict with the modern view of history was sooner or later inevitable, for the latter finds it perfectly possible to construct a picture of history without God. It finds it very hard to assume that there is divine action in history. God has no natural place in its *schema.*[30]

Von Rad rightly noted that this fundamental distinction between Israel's own conception of history and "the modern view" brings "the historical interpretation of the Old Testament" into "a kind of crisis"—indeed, it places the two conceptions on a collision course. He also rightly anticipated "a question" that would "occupy theologians for a long time

28. *The Old Testament and the Historian* (Philadelphia: Fortress, 1976), 17.

29. Cf. J. Goldingay, *Approaches to Old Testament Interpretation,* updated edition (Leicester: Apollos; Downers Grove, Ill.: InterVarsity, 1990), 72–73.

30. Von Rad's original essay, "Offene Fragen im Umkreis einer Theologie des Alten Testaments," *TLZ* 88 (1963): 402ff., appears in English translation as a postscript in his *Old Testament Theology,* 2 vols., trans. D. M. G. Stalker (New York: Harper & Row; Edinburgh: Oliver & Boyd, 1962–65), 2:410–29 (citation from 418).

to come"—"whether it is still possible to say that each view is of equal value in considering the phenomenon of Israel's history in its various conceptions, or whether nowadays we must choose between them."[31]

Developments in scholarship since von Rad first posed this question suggest that, more often than not, a choice is indeed felt to be necessary.[32] For those who continue today to practice Troeltschian-style historical criticism, the historiography of the Old Testament (i.e., Israel's history writing) is seldom allowed to speak for itself but is consistently "reconceptualized." For example, after noting that "our modern historical-critical methodologies presuppose a quite different understanding of historical reality than does the Bible," Miller submits that "historical-critical methodology would collapse altogether if the traditional Judeo-Christian understanding of God's dynamic involvement in human history were even taken as a possibility." "What this means," Miller continues, "is that we modern critical historians, while depending on the Bible for almost all of our direct information about ancient Israel, constantly reconceptualise what the Bible reports so as to bring its historical claims into line with our own late twentieth century notions of historical reality."[33]

We shall return to the issue of "late-twentieth-century notions of historical reality" below, but first we must consider two other approaches that attract much attention today. Perhaps in part as a consequence of historical criticism's metaphysically driven "methodological disqualification" of the Old Testament as a viable repository of historical information, scholars interested in reconstructing the history of ancient Israel have increasingly turned to other types of investigation. Prominent among these are what might broadly be described as the social science methods.

Social Science Methods

The publication in 1986 of J. M. Miller and John Hayes's *A History of Ancient Israel and Judah*[34] was met with great interest among biblical

---

31. Ibid., 417–18.

32. In his influential book *In Search of History: Historiography in the Ancient World and the Origins of Biblical History* (New Haven: Yale University Press, 1983; reprinted, Winona Lake, Ind.: Eisenbrauns, 1997), J. Van Seters articulates the standard approach as follows: "the historian tells 'how it actually was' and therefore excludes wonders and direct appearances and 'physical' intervention by the deity."

33. "New Directions in the Study of Israelite History," *Nederduitse Gereformeerde Teologiese Tydskrif* 30 (1989): 152–53; cf. idem, "Reading the Bible Historically," 15: "[there is an] obvious tension between the dynamic and theocentric view of nature and history presupposed by the biblical writers and the more 'scientific' or positivistic approach to reality that characterizes modern Western thought."

34. London: SCM; Philadelphia: Westminster, 1986.

scholars who concerned themselves with historical method and with the reconstruction of Israel's history. A particularly burning question, it seemed, was what part the biblical literature should play in historical reconstructions of ancient Israel. The Annual Meeting of the Society of Biblical Literature in that same year saw lively discussion of Miller and Hayes's approach, and, in the following year, an issue of the *Journal for the Study of the Old Testament* put into print some of the highlights of that discussion.[35]

In his introduction to that *JSOT* issue, P. R. Davies characterized the Miller-Hayes volume as belonging to the genre of "'biblical history' in that it accepts the priority of the literary testimony of the Bible."[36] It was not the case, of course, that the Miller-Hayes volume accepted the biblical depiction of Israel's history as basically reliable; I have just noted Miller's view about reconceptualizing what the Bible reports to bring it into line with late-twentieth-century notions of historical reality. But still, like their historical-critical predecessors, Miller and Hayes continued to hold to the importance of the biblical literature for reconstructing a history of ancient Israel. They held this view, as Davies noted, "not for theological or religious reasons but, as the authors see it, for pragmatic ones."[37]

For his part, Davies expressed hope that the Miller-Hayes volume might mark the "end of the road for the genre 'biblical history,'" for it was his conviction that "the way forward—if it exists—would seem to lie with the (combined) methods of the social sciences: sociology, anthropology and archaeology."[38] Since Davies penned these words, many others have expressed similarly negative sentiments regarding the viability of *biblical* histories of Israel and have sought to find new ways to proceed using social science methods.[39]

35. *JSOT* 39 (1987).
36. Ibid., 3.
37. Ibid.
38. Ibid., 4.
39. The literature is vast and growing rapidly; the following are but a sampling: N. P. Lemche, "On the Problem of Studying Israelite History: Apropos Abraham Malamat's View of Historical Research," *BN* 24 (1984): 94–124; idem, "Is It Still Possible to Write a History of Ancient Israel?" *SJOT* 8.2 (1994): 165–90; M. Weippert and H. Weippert, "Die vorgeschichte Israels in neuem Licht," *TRu* 56 (1991): 341–90; K. W. Whitelam, "Recreating the History of Israel," *JSOT* 35 (1986): 45–70; idem, "Between History and Literature: The Social Production of Israel's Traditions of Origin," *SJOT* 2 (1991): 60–74; idem, "Sociology or History: Towards a (Human) History of Ancient Palestine?" in *Words Remembered, Texts Renewed: Essays in Honour of John F. A. Sawyer*, ed. J. Davies, G. Harvey, and W. G. E. Watson, JSOTSup 195 (Sheffield: Sheffield Academic Press, 1995), 149–66. For criticism of the antitextual stance adopted by many social science approaches today, see W. W. Hallo, "Biblical History in Its Near Eastern Setting: The Contextual Approach," in *Scripture in Context: Essays on the Comparative Method*, ed. C. D. Evans, W. W. Hallo,

Contemporary socio-archaeological or socio-anthropological approaches are not without ancestry, of course, which stretches back to Max Weber and beyond.[40] But it is fair to say that, beginning with Mendenhall and Gottwald in the 1960s and 1970s, there has been a revival of interest in social science approaches that is "now gaining strength in the work of younger American biblical scholars such as Frick, Flanagan, Coote, Halpern, and Thompson, complemented in Europe by de Geus, Lemche, and others."[41]

What the various social science approaches have in common is a desire to move away from an emphasis on *idiographic* concerns—a focus on "great individuals" as primarily responsible for historical change—and to emphasize *nomothetic* concerns—"laws" of historical change that can be linked with social, economic, geographic, climatic concerns, and the like (what I earlier referred to as "middle-range explanations").[42] Many have looked to the field of Syro-Palestinian archaeology as holding the best promise of yielding an "objective," or "scientific," history of Israel. Others have gravitated toward the quantifying methods of sociology or anthropology in an effort to bring historical study more into line with the methods of the natural sciences. The most promising social science approaches seek to employ a "highly multidisciplinary approach," which is of course commendable. Unfortunately, however, as Miller notes, "it can hardly be said that this multidisciplinary approach has produced any notable breakthroughs or compelling clarifications—at least none that does not depend as much on the researcher's methodological presuppositions and working models as upon the various data compiled."[43]

In view of the chiefly nomothetic concerns of the social science approaches, it comes as no surprise that Old Testament narratives (whose idiographic orientation tends to focus on significant, specific events in the lives of individuals and nations) are often regarded as of little value—if not downright hindrances—to the reconstruction of the his-

and J. B. White, PTMS 34 (Pittsburgh: Pickwick, 1980), 1–26; idem, "The Limits of Skepticism," *JAOS* 110 (1990): 187–99; S. Herrmann, "Observations on Some Recent Hypotheses Pertaining to Early Israelite History" (trans. F. Cryer), in *Justice and Righteousness: Biblical Themes and Their Influence,* ed. H. Reventlow and Y. Hoffman, JSOTSup 137 (Sheffield: Sheffield Academic Press, 1992), 105–16; Rendtorff, "Paradigm Is Changing," 34–53; Yamauchi, "Current State of Old Testament Historiography," 1–36. For a useful anthology of seminal essays, see C. E. Carter and C. L. Meyers, eds., *Community, Identity, and Ideology: Social Science Approaches to the Hebrew Bible,* SBTS 6 (Winona Lake, Ind.: Eisenbrauns, 1996).

40. On early sociological studies, see Dever, "Archaeology and the Religions," 37–38; C. Osiek, "The New Handmaid: The Bible and the Social Sciences," *TS* 50 (1989): 260–78.

41. Dever, "Archaeology and the Religions," 40.

42. Following Hayes, "History," 39. For more on the idiographic/nomothetic distinction, see Long, *Art of Biblical History,* 135–44.

43. "Reading the Bible Historically," 25.

tory of Israel. In a recent essay, S. Herrmann traces the gradual decline of the Old Testament as a significant factor in the reconstruction of Israel's history.[44] Beginning with the work of Astruc in the eighteenth century, Herrmann surveys briefly the contributions of Wellhausen, Gunkel, Alt, Weber, Noth, Albright, Mendenhall, de Geus, Gottwald, Lemche, Thompson, and so on. Herrmann observes that scholars up to Albright, whatever differences existed among them, at least agreed that the Bible was central to any attempt to reconstruct the history of ancient Israel.[45] Not so any longer.

In the 1960s the work of George Mendenhall began to undercut previous consensus positions, such as the notions that the twelve tribes of Israel entered Canaan from the outside at the time of or shortly before the "conquest," that they were nomads or seminomads prior to their settlement in the land, and that they were ethnically related and thus distinct from the Canaanites. As scholars swayed by Mendenhall began to lose confidence in these former areas of agreement, so too they began to lose confidence in the biblical testimony on which the earlier areas of consensus were based.[46] Unlike their predecessors who had assumed at least some significant relationship between the Old Testament and the history of ancient Israel, many scholars today either ignore the Old Testament as a historical source or reject it outright.[47]

As noted above, the setting aside of the biblical text as an important historical source has not led to significant new breakthroughs. Apart from a few very general points of agreement, there is little unanimity. Mendenhall is sharply critical of Gottwald;[48] Thompson of Ahlström;[49] Dever of Thompson, Ahlström, and Davies;[50] and Halpern of "minimalists" of all sorts.[51]

44. "Die Abwertung des Alten Testaments als Geschichtsquelle: Bemerkungen zu einem geistesgeschichtliches Problem," in *Sola Scriptura: VII Europäischer Theologen-Kongreß, Dresden 1990*, ed. H. H. Schmid and J. Mehlhausen (Gütersloh: Mohn, 1993), 156–65.

45. Ibid., 159.

46. Ibid., 159–60.

47. So ibid., 160–61.

48. Mendenhall, "Ancient Israel's Hyphenated History," in *Palestine in Transition: The Emergence of Ancient Israel*, ed. D. N. Freedman and D. F. Graf, SWBAS 2 (Sheffield: Almond, 1983), 91–102: "Gottwald's attempt to present us with a historical account of the beginnings of biblical history is truly a tragic comedy of errors" (102).

49. Thompson, "Gösta Ahlström's History of Palestine," in *The Pitcher Is Broken: Memorial Essays for Gösta W. Ahlström*, ed. S. W. Holloway and L. K. Handy, JSOTSup 190 (Sheffield: Sheffield Academic Press, 1995), 420–34.

50. Dever, "'Will the Real Israel Please Stand Up?' Part I: Archaeology and Israelite Historiography," *BASOR* 297 (1995): 62–69 (hereafter "Archaeology and Israelite Historiography").

51. B. Halpern, "Erasing History: The Minimalist Assault on Ancient Israel," *BibRev* 11.6 (1995): 26–35, 47. By minimalists, Halpern has in mind those writers who "late date"

One of the few dominant threads, then, in the rather variegated fabric of contemporary social science approaches is the general diminishment of the importance of the biblical text as a historical source. Thompson contends, for example, that exegesis and historical reconstruction are best pursued independently of one another.[52] But setting aside the biblical text has done little to resolve the crisis in biblical scholarship, contrary to Thompson's apparent hope and expectation. It has merely freed scholars from the constraints of the biblical story line to write monographs and textbooks that tell stories of their own construction.[53] There is little agreement as to what a "scientific," socioeconomic history of Israel should look like. And even if today's social scientists should achieve a consensus, a large number of scholars would continue to agree with R. Smend that "we can still learn more about ancient Israel, including her history, from reading the historical books of the Old Testament than from reading the best textbook today on this subject matter; and a textbook is perhaps at its best when its author knows that."[54]

Does this mean that social science methods have little to offer? Not at all! There is certainly a place for writing "history from below." But it must be understood that histories written on the basis of social science researches alone do not present the whole picture, nor are they the only kinds of histories that are worth writing. That the Old Testament itself

---

virtually all biblical material to the Persian period and thus conclude that the Bible can tell us little about earlier periods in Israel's history. With characteristic forthrightness, and not a little irony, Halpern writes: "The views of these critics [he has specifically in mind Thompson, Davies, and Van Seters] would seem to be an expression of despair over the supposed impossibility of recovering the past from works written in a more recent present—except, of course, that they [the critics] pretend to provide access to a 'real' past in their own works written in the contemporary present" (p. 31). Furthermore, contends Halpern, in order to free themselves to write their own stories, minimalist scholars must simply sweep aside much archaeological and inscriptional evidence that would lend support to the picture painted, e.g., by the books of Kings. As to what motivates the minimalists, Halpern again has a theory and the boldness to state it: "In one the motivation may be a hatred of the Catholic Church, in another of Christianity, in another of the Jews, in another of all religion, in another of authority" (p. 47). While it is always hazardous to speculate on someone else's motives, Halpern's comment does rightly highlight that one's historical reconstructions invariably to some extent reflect one's worldview and fundamental belief system. I would only add that those who recognize this fact are in a better position to minimize distorting influences than those who do not.

52. For bibliography and critique, see Herrmann, "Abwertung," 162.

53. E.g., of Lemche's reconstruction of ancient Israel independent of the OT, F. H. Cryer writes: "He proffers a model based on modern sociological studies of nomadism, ethnicity, and the like. In so doing, Lemche is in reality composing a new 'source,' . . . that is, he proposes for our consideration a narrative of his own devising" (cited by Herrmann, ibid.).

54. "Tradition and History: A Complex Relation" (trans. D. Knight), in *Tradition and Theology in the Old Testament*, ed. D. Knight (Philadelphia: Fortress, 1977), 66–67.

does not present the kind of history in which social scientists are most interested does not justify simply dismissing the Old Testament's more idiographic historiography as fiction. Even Lemche admits that "the Old Testament [would be] a most obvious starting point for the study of Israelite history and even prehistory," were it not that "the Old Testament model—or account—of early Israelite history is . . . disproved by the archaeological sources to such a degree that I consider it better to leave it out of consideration."[55] But is Lemche's confidence in the "assured results" of archaeological investigation warranted? Is his dismissal of the Old Testament model on the basis of archaeological sources justified? Today's assured results may well be tomorrow's discarded theories, and if there is any lesson to be learned from the "biblical archaeology" debates of the past, it is that we should go slowly in declaring just what archaeology has "proved" or "disproved."

In the end, the issue comes down to reading and interpretation. On the one hand, how are the material evidences to be "read," or interpreted?[56] On the other hand, how are the texts, biblical and others, to be read and interpreted? I noted already the fact that Wellhausen's historical conclusions rested squarely on his literary judgments. Similarly, it comes as no surprise that whenever the fit between socio-archaeological theories and biblical texts is debated, much depends on how the evidences—both material and textual—have been interpreted. This brings us to another prevalent contemporary approach to the Old Testament that has a (sometimes overlooked) bearing on Old Testament historiography: modern literary approaches.[57]

Modern Literary Methods

Perhaps a good place to begin in discussing these methods is with some definitions. What do we mean by "literary" methods, and why do we prefix the adjective "modern"? While the appropriateness of labeling the Old Testament as "literature" continues to be debated,[58] most contemporary approaches assume a broad definition of literature, such as "an interpretive presentation of experience in artistic form" characterized by "artful verbal expression and compelling ideas."[59] On these

---

55. "On the Problem of Studying Israelite History," 121–22.

56. Cf. F. Brandfon, "The Limits of Evidence: Archaeology and Objectivity," *Maarav* 4 (1987): 5–43.

57. For a fuller treatment of the social scientific study of the Old Testament, see chap. 15 of the present volume.

58. For a recent, insightful discussion, see M. Z. Brettler, *The Creation of History in Ancient Israel* (London and New York: Routledge, 1995), 14–19.

59. For the first definition see L. Ryken, *The Literature of the Bible* (Grand Rapids: Zondervan, 1974), 13. For the second, A. Berlin, "On the Bible as Literature," *Prooftexts* 2 (1982): 324. For further discussion, see Long, *Art of Biblical History*, 149–54.

terms the Old Testament's library of literary genres would certainly qualify for a literary approach. The purpose of the adjective "modern" is to distinguish newer literary critical approaches (which tend to be synchronic, or text-immanent) from old-style literary criticism (which tends to be diachronic, or excavative). The older tended to dissect texts into putative sources in the hope of distinguishing earlier material from later accretions and redactions. It was believed that by detecting earlier source material, one could draw closer to historical reality. The more recent trend is to take more seriously the text in its final form. The effect has been to restore to the text its "voice."

But what do modern literary studies have to do with historical questions? Confronted by biblical texts that are no longer silenced by dissection and fragmentation but are again able to speak, some scholars see an opportunity to hear more clearly what the texts have to say, including what they may have to say about the historical past; others, however, take the literary turn as an opportunity to call into question whether what the biblical texts say has any relevance to historical reconstruction in the first place.[60] To some the older, diachronic historical criticism and the newer, synchronic "literary" approaches seem quite different in aim and orientation (even diametrically opposed). But as Barton has pointed out, there is considerable common ground between them:

> If we take the most obviously fragmentative branch of historical criticism, source analysis, still flourishing all over the world despite the supposed paradigm-shift away from it: there can be no doubt that the underlying perceptions that make such criticisms possible are essentially literary ones, related to the attempt to appropriate a text as a living whole, cohering in all its parts. Its German name, *Literarkritik*, is not the misnomer people sometimes think it. The difference between the different sorts of critic is a matter of how soon they give up this attempt in the face of a perception that they are dealing with recalcitrant material. Literary critics today, like other kinds of "final form" interpreters, generally see themselves as having a duty to persist with a holistic approach until the whole text is in focus as a unified entity, even if this involves suppressing intuitive suspicions that the text was not originally designed by anyone to have exactly its present form. Source critics on the other hand allow such suspicions to have full rein, and are content when they have divided the text into sections each of which in itself has a coherent shape. But in both cases the mental processes involved are literary. Both are concerned with the *Gestalt* of the text, with the attempt to grasp it as a comprehensible whole. Historical critics are much readier than modern literary interpret-

60. Such sentiments can be found in the works of, e.g., Barr, Davies, Lemche, Thompson, Whitelam, and others.

ers to accept the possibility that the text is not such a whole. But the question ought to be discussable between them, not regarded as just a matter of incomprehensible expectations.[61]

Barton makes an important point. For too long, scholars have failed to see, or perhaps to admit, that the results of newer literary approaches have a bearing on the results of older literary criticism.[62] But as D. R. Hall insists, "We should not only ask what new insights the literary perspective gives us today, but also ask how far the absence of that perspective in the past invalidated the methods, and therefore the conclusions, of the scholars concerned."[63] In his 1983 presidential address to the International Organization for the Study of the Old Testament, L. Alonso Schökel articulates four options for how the newer (synchronic) and the older (diachronic) methods might interact: through mutual condemnation, courteous noncommunication, division of labor, or dialogue. For his part, he prefers dialogue, "even if it should lead to open controversy."[64] The plea of Alonso Schökel, Barton, and others that the older and the newer brands of literary criticism should engage in dialogue is welcome, for it should be obvious that a given textual feature— repetition, for example—cannot logically be cited both as a mark of authorial disunity and as a mark of authorial ingenuity, both as evidence of composite authorship and as evidence of authorial competence.

While improved literary readings of biblical texts should yield a clearer grasp of the texts' truth claims, be they theological, historical, or whatever, one must admit that some modern literary approaches undercut interest in the historiographical import of the Bible. Sometimes a focus on literary categories (such as characterization, plot, point of view, pacing) leads to a genre mistake, whereby what was written as utilitarian literature (history, legislation, liturgy, preaching, etc.) is read as pure literature (simply art for art's sake).[65] The danger of this form of reductionism has been recognized as long as talk of the "Bible

61. J. Barton, "Historical Criticism and Literary Interpretation: Is There Any Common Ground?" in *Crossing the Boundaries: Essays in Biblical Interpretation in Honour of Michael D. Goulder*, ed. S. E. Porter, P. M. Joyce, and D. E. Orton, Biblical Interpretation 8 (Leiden: Brill, 1994), 7.

62. See, e.g., R. W. L. Moberly's insightful discussion of "The Relationship between the Study of the Final Text and the Study of Its Prehistory," in *At the Mountain of God: Story and Theology in Exodus 32–34*, JSOTSup 22 (Sheffield: JSOT Press, 1983), 22–27; cf. V. P. Long, *The Reign and Rejection of King Saul: A Case for Literary and Theological Coherence*, SBLDS 118 (Atlanta: Scholars Press, 1989), esp. 7–20.

63. *The Seven Pillories of Wisdom* (Macon, Ga.: Mercer University Press, 1990), 110.

64. L. Alonso Schökel, "Of Methods and Models," *Congress Volume: Salamanca, 1983*, ed. J. A. Emerton, VTSup 36 (Leiden: Brill, 1985), 7–8. See also Long, *Reign and Rejection*, 10–14.

65. See Long, *Reign and Rejection*, 13, for a critique of this error.

as literature" has been around. Commenting on the literary enjoyment of the Bible, T. S. Eliot once wrote:

> While I acknowledge the legitimacy of this enjoyment, I am more acutely aware of its abuse. The persons who enjoy these writings *solely* because of their literary merit are essentially parasites; and we know that para- sites, when they become too numerous, are pests. I could fulminate against the men of letters who have gone into ecstasies over "the Bible as literature," the Bible as "the noblest monument of English prose." Those who talk of the Bible as a "monument of English prose" are merely admir- ing it as a monument over the grave of Christianity. I must try to avoid the by-paths of my discourse: it is enough to suggest that just as the work of Clarendon, or Gibbon, or Buffon, or Bradley would be of inferior liter- ary value if it were insignificant as history, science and philosophy respectively, so the Bible has had a *literary* influence upon English litera- ture *not* because it has been considered as literature, but because it has been considered as the report of the Word of God. And the fact that men of letters now discuss it as "literature" probably indicates the *end* of its "literary" influence.[66]

Precisely the above error is sometimes made in contemporary dis- cussion of the place of the Old Testament in the reconstruction of Is- rael's history. As H. H. Klement warns in a discussion of the relevance of literary interpretation for historical study, literary approaches to the Bible are always in danger of slipping into a reductionism whereby the Bible is viewed merely as literary art, while historical questions are sim- ply *ausgeblendet* (shaded out).[67] In other words, inherent in the literary approach is the danger of losing sight of and interest in the historical truth claims of the text.

Conclusion

In view of the different purposes, perspectives, and potential pitfalls of each of the three approaches discussed above, it is not surprising that

66. *Selected Essays: New Edition* (New York: Harcourt, Brace, 1950), 244–45; cited by J. A. Fitzmyer, "Historical Criticism: Its Role in Biblical Interpretation and Church Life," *TS* 50 (1989): 250 n. 17. For more on the potentials and pitfalls of literary approaches to the Bible, see T. Longman III, *Literary Approaches to Biblical Interpretation*, Foundations of Contemporary Interpretation 3 (Grand Rapids: Zondervan, 1987), 47–62; M. Sternberg, *The Poetics of Biblical Narrative: Ideological Literature and the Drama of Reading*, ILBS (Bloomington, Ind.: Indiana University Press, 1985), chap. 1; A. C. Thiselton, *New Hori- zons in Hermeneutics: The Theory and Practice of Transforming Biblical Reading* (Grand Rapids: Zondervan; London: Marshall Pickering, 1992), chap. 13, esp. 475–79, 502.

67. "Die neueren literaturwissenschaftlichen Methoden und die Historizität des Alten Testaments," in *Israel in Geschichte und Gegenwart*, ed. G. Maier (Wuppertal: Brockhaus; Giessen and Basel: Brunnen, 1996), 88.

scholars today often hold widely divergent views about both the history of ancient Israel and the character of ancient Israel's history writing. As we have seen, and as I have argued in more detail elsewhere,[68] the standard historical-critical approach leaves little or no room for God in history, social science approaches often have little room for the Old Testament texts themselves, and modern literary approaches sometimes show little interest in historical concerns at all. No wonder the discipline is in flux.

Whether it be the diminishment of the theological, historical, or literary impulse of the Old Testament, each is unfortunate if, as Sternberg has forcefully argued, biblical narrative is "a complex, because multifunctional, discourse . . . regulated by a set of three principles: ideological, historiographic, and aesthetic."[69] Any method that neglects or denies one or more of these impulses is a deficient method. Indeed, Herrmann rightly contends that "the crisis in which the study of the early history of Israel now finds itself has largely been brought about by rather one-sided theories."[70]

So where do we go from here? Will progress require entirely new approaches? Probably not. But progress will require that some modifications be made to the manner in which each method is conceived and appropriated. The next section seeks to offer suggestions as to what the way forward might look like.

Where Do We Go from Here? Is There a Way Forward in the Study of the Historiography of the Old Testament?

In concluding his very useful 1985 survey of the state of mainline scholarship on Old Testament historiography, J. M. Miller wrote: "Probably there is no other area of biblical studies so obviously in need at the moment of some fresh ideas based on solid research."[71] Writing ten years later, M. Z. Brettler observed simply: "The old consensus is gone, and there is no indication that a new one is developing to replace it."[72]

To be sure, new ideas with respect to method have not been lacking. Indeed, if there is anything that characterizes contemporary biblical scholarship generally, it is the rapid turnover of methodological approaches. It seems to me, however, that whatever fresh ideas may emerge on the level of method, real progress in understanding will be

68. *Art of Biblical History*, chap. 4.
69. *Poetics*, 41.
70. "Observations," 115.
71. "Israelite History," 1–30.
72. *Creation of History in Ancient Israel*, 6.

made only as scholarly discussion is taken to a deeper consideration of the models, or worldviews, that scholars themselves (consciously or unconsciously) embrace and that underlie the diverse methods that today's scholars employ. The state of flux (some use the term *crisis*) in which the study of the history and historiography of ancient Israel now finds itself may provide just the opportunity to wrestle with the all-important foundational questions. After all, as V. A. Harvey has observed,

> all of our judgments and inferences [including historical ones] take place
> . . . against a background of beliefs. We bring to our perceptions and
> interpretations a world of existing knowledge, categories, and judgments.
> Our inferences are but the visible part of an iceberg lying deep below the
> surface.[73]

My contention is that the way forward in the study of Israel's history and historiography must involve greater attention to the subsurface portion of the iceberg. What B. A. Scharfstein says of philosophy seems equally applicable to the issue before us: "we will be able to be more objective only if we learn to conceal our subjectivity less."[74]

Thus Harvey is right to stress the vital role played by background beliefs (models of reality, worldviews, or whatever term we choose) in arriving at historical judgments. Harvey is also right to warn against "sweeping appeals to the modern world-view,"[75] though, ironically, he comes close to just such an appeal in his own discussion. There is much truth in his assertion that "we are in history as fish are in water, and our ideas of possibility and actuality are relative to our time." There is also a measure of truth in F. H. Bradley's "ethical imperative" for historical study (cited approvingly by Harvey) that "one ought to make his interpretation of the past consistent with his interpretation of the present."[76] But these very observations should at least raise the question of whether there is such a thing as *the* modern worldview. Do all moderns share a monolithic "interpretation of the present"? Harvey's unqualified use of "we" in various statements betrays an assumption on his part that there is but one modern view of things. He writes, for instance, "we *cannot* see the world as the first century saw it. . . . Our memories are indelibly stamped with the new vision of reality. . . . We have a new consciousness."[77]

73. *The Historian and the Believer,* 115.
74. Quoted in M. Broshi, "Religion, Ideology, and Politics and Their Impact on Palestinian Archaeology," *Israel Museum Journal* 6 (1987): 32.
75. *The Historian and the Believer,* 115.
76. Ibid., 114.
77. Ibid., 115.

In this apparent assumption of a monolithic "modern" worldview, Harvey is not alone. Lemche, for example, first describes "the so-called 'primitive' idea of causality" whereby "everybody considered his fate an expression of the will of God, the outcome of his God's approval or rejection of his behaviour," and then contrasts this ancient view with *the* modern view: "there exists an almost absolute contrast between our idea of history and of the world and the one common among ancient peoples. Therefore, from the beginning the endeavour to reconstruct the historical course of events on the basis of a single documentary source from the ancient Near East is really without prospect of success."[78] Clearly, Lemche's dismissal of the Bible as a viable source of historical information does not result so much from the application of particular methods to the biblical text but rather from the conflict between Lemche's and the Bible's "idea of history and of the world."[79]

Again, this simply raises the question of whether it is appropriate to generalize about *the* modern worldview, as if there were but one. For Harvey, Lemche, Davies, and many others, the answer would seem to be yes. After all, has not R. Bultmann taught us that "it is impossible to use electric light and the wireless and to avail ourselves of modern medical and surgical discoveries, and at the same time to believe in the New Testament world of spirits and miracles"?[80] But surely not all modern people find this bit of Bultmannian logic compelling. Are we to understand that scientific advances in the understanding of the material world and of secondary causes eventually destroy the viability of belief in the spirit world and the Absolute Cause? Secular materialists may be attracted to such a notion, but theistic believers will not be. Surely moderns may come to understand and believe many things unknown to the ancients and yet, like the ancients, remain theists. And if theists, then their belief in God will be one of the most, if not the single most, important of the "background beliefs" that come into play in making historical judgments.

Thus I would argue that a way forward in discussions of the historiography of the Old Testament might begin by framing the discussion not in terms of a "primitive" versus a "modern" worldview but rather in terms of a "theistic" versus an "a-" or "nontheistic" worldview. And since, as M. Stanford puts it, "the final colour and shape of a historian's construction is bestowed by his or her own *Weltanschauung* ['world-

78. "On the Problem of Studying Israelite History," 119–20.
79. Cf. also Davies's insistence that "our modern understanding of what constitutes historiography, and indeed what constitutes the past, is different" from the Bible's ("Method and Madness: Some Remarks on Doing History with the Bible," *JBL* 114 [1995]: 703).
80. Cited approvingly by Harvey, *The Historian and the Believer,* 114.

view'],"[81] I would also stress the importance of scholars' offering some indication in their writings of their core beliefs about Reality. I understand that this is not standard practice in scholarly discussion, where some continue to propagate the myth of personal objectivity.[82] But until greater care is taken to determine where points of disagreement between scholars actually lie, we are destined to talk past each other. As E. L. Greenstein stresses, "I can get somewhere when I challenge the deductions you make from your fundamental assumptions. But I can get nowhere if I think I am challenging your deductions when in fact I am differing from your assumptions, your presuppositions, your premises, your beliefs."[83]

Finally, I would contend that scholars should take some care to insure that harmony exists between the worldview that they themselves embrace and the worldview underlying the methods they employ. Where incompatibility is discovered (e.g., when theistic scholars find themselves using methods that are by definition atheistic), they should either adjust their own core beliefs, reject the incompatible method in favor of a method more in keeping with what they believe to be the truth about "God, the universe, and everything," or make whatever modifications are necessary to bring the method into line with Reality as they understand it.

In what follows I suggest how the three major approaches discussed in the preceding section might be adjusted to bring them into line with a theistic set of background beliefs.[84]

Refining the Canons of the Historical-Critical Method

In his highly instructive discussion of *Divine Revelation and the Limits of Historical Criticism,* W. J. Abraham asks whether the believer may

---

81. *The Nature of Historical Knowledge* (Oxford: Blackwell, 1986), 96.

82. To be sure, most hermeneutically aware interpreters will readily admit their *personal* subjectivity. But there can still be a tendency to attribute a kind of objectivity to their chosen *method.* Davies, for instance, insists that "it is precisely because I am no more free from subjectivity than any human being that I insist on working to a methodology that will enable me and my fellow historians to agree on what counts as historical knowledge and how we aim to secure it" ("Method and Madness," 704). But Davies's stance raises several questions. Does not the "methodology" itself rest on certain assumptions? Are not other assumptions possible, even contrary assumptions (such as those which some moderns might share with the ancient historians)? And might not these other assumptions call for significant methodological modifications?

83. "The Role of Theory in Biblical Criticism," in *Proceedings of the Ninth World Congress of Jewish Studies: Jerusalem, August 4–12, 1985* (Jerusalem: World Union of Jewish Studies, 1986), 167.

84. Due to space considerations, my comments must be brief; for more, see my *Art of Biblical History,* chap. 4.

not continue to believe and yet still lay claim to the title of historian. Abraham argues that an affirmative answer is possible, provided that the three chief principles of the historical method are appropriately defined. The principle of criticism, for instance, must be defined not in terms of systematic doubt but in terms of a thoughtful appraisal of the evidence in keeping with its source. For those who regard the Bible as either not at all interested in history or as hopelessly incapable of conveying historical information, skepticism toward the possibility of drawing historically valuable information from the Bible will indeed be the appropriate "critical" attitude. But for those who do not share these views, "systematic doubt" may be "the most inappropriate procedure imaginable for dealing with the Bible."[85] As regards the principle of analogy, Abraham argues for a broad, rather than a narrow, definition, whereby plausibility is not judged solely by analogy to the historian's own personal experiences or those of contemporaries, but where reasonable arguments can be made for belief in occurrences with which the historian may have no personal acquaintance and where not only may the present serve as a key to the past, but the past may also serve as a key to the present.[86] Finally, as regards the principle of correlation, Abraham argues for a formal rather than a material definition. According to the latter, historical change can be brought about only by natural causes or human agency. According to the former, agency is defined as *personal* agency, not merely human agency, and thus God is allowed back into the picture.[87]

Now, to be sure, some might object to such a procedure. Davies, for instance, states authoritatively: "I don't allow divine activity or any unqualifiable or undemonstrable cause as an arguable factor in historical reconstruction, and, even if I were to accept privately the possibility of such factors, I do not see how I could integrate such explanations into anything recognizable as a historical method."[88] What must not be overlooked, however, is that this statement is itself a statement of faith, that is, a metaphysical statement.[89] As Abraham observes: "If the historian discounts theological considerations as irrelevant, he does not en-

85. G. Maier, *Biblical Hermeneutics*, trans. R. W. Yarbrough (Wheaton, Ill.: Crossway, 1994), 24.

86. For full discussion, see Abraham, *Divine Revelation*, chap. 5. He uses the example of a remote people group being convinced through reasonable discussion to believe in a moon landing, even though such an event is completely foreign to anything they personally have known.

87. Ibid., 108.

88. "Method and Madness," 700.

89. See I. W. Provan, "Ideologies, Literary and Critical: Reflections on Recent Writing on the History of Israel," *JBL* 114 (1995): 586–606.

tirely cease to be theological. He is simply assuming the truth of certain
negative theological statements. . . . It were odd if the historian could
only rely on theological assertions when they are negative rather than
positive."[90] In short, then, if the canons of the historical-critical method
are refined along the lines suggested by Abraham, "there is nothing unhistorical in relying on theology."[91] In pursuing the task of the historian, the theist need suppress his metaphysical convictions no more
than the atheist.

But one might object: if God, for whom all things are possible, is allowed a role in history, does this not render probability judgments
(upon which historical science depends) impossible? Do not those who
embrace the biblical view of God as a worker of wonders lose their capacity to judge the probability of miraculous accounts they hear? What
about Harvey's contention that while "very few historians . . . would
hesitate to apply the category 'legend' to the story of the saint who, after
being beheaded, walked a few hundred yards to a cathedral with his
head under his arm, entered the sanctuary and there sang the *Te
Deum*," "traditional belief" simply cannot account for the fact that modern people immediately tend to reject such stories as impossible?[92]

In response, one must ask whether Harvey's contention is true. Most
"traditional" believers, although reticent simply to dismiss miracle stories a priori, do have a conscious or subconscious set of criteria by
which they judge whether an unusual story deserves credence. To begin
with, most would agree with the assumption that God does not need-
lessly multiply miracles. Thus, while believing that with God all things
are *possible*, traditional believers are far from credulously accepting all
strange stories as *probable*. Further, just as some people are regarded as
more reliable witnesses than others (on the basis of their known character and the consistency of what they say), traditional believers usually
regard some sources of information as more deserving of credence than
other sources (e.g., texts of known and tested character that tell a coherent story involving apparently historical truth claims will be trusted
over texts of unknown character whose story seems confused or inco-
herent). Finally, thoughtful believers innately apply a formal principle
of correlation that asks of miracle reports, "Just why would God choose
to do that? How does this putative miracle fit within the larger scheme
of God's working?" If satisfactory answers are not forthcoming, the report is not believed (or, if it nevertheless appears that something para-
normal has occurred, an explanation may be sought along the lines sug-

---

90. Abraham, *Divine Revelation,* 158.
91. Ibid.
92. *The Historian and the Believer,* 115–16.

gested by, e.g., Matt. 24:24). Thoughtful believers do not understand miracles as "bolts out of the blue" but as special divine actions interconnected with the larger matrix of the divine governance of the world.

In this section I have argued that the historical-critical method, though atheistic in its customary formulation, can be brought into line with a theistic worldview, provided that the canons of the method are refined as described above. As we turn now to the social scientific methods (e.g., anthropology, archaeology, sociology), we may again acknowledge their usefulness, provided that the claims of the methods are restricted in a manner consistent with their essentially nomothetic, as distinct from idiographic, character.

Restricting the Claims of the Social Sciences in Historical Reconstruction

Briefly stated, the social sciences are well suited to deal with general features of societies and cultures, but they are usually ill suited to pronounce on specific events and individuals. Their rightful function, then, is to provide background information against which the specific actions of individuals and groups can be better understood. As B. Halpern puts it, the chief function of the social sciences is to describe "the abiding institutions and patterns of culture, against which the quicker movements that catch the scholarly eye are visible."[93]

So long as practitioners recognize the proper role of the social sciences in addressing background concerns, their studies provide a valuable service. It is only when they begin to make pronouncements on the likelihood of specific events that they exceed the limitations of their chosen method—and may wittingly or unwittingly find themselves writing histories that bear a greater resemblance to their present concerns than to past realities. I have written at some length elsewhere on this potential danger, and I will not belabor the point here.[94]

I noted above that an especially unfortunate aspect of some social scientific studies of ancient Israel is their tendency to downplay literary evidence, which is often our best (or only) evidence of specific individuals, actions, and events. Here I would simply stress that the antiliterary tendency is not a necessary component of the methods themselves. In an essay on social science approaches to the early history of Israel, Dever emphasizes the relevance of, for example, archaeological investigation for reconstructing a history of early Israel.[95] Not surprisingly,

---

93. *The First Historians: The Hebrew Bible and History* (San Francisco: Harper & Row, 1988), 122.

94. See *Art of Biblical History*, 135–49.

95. "Archaeology and Israelite Historiography," 61–80.

Dever is quick to remind us that "archaeology cannot be used to 'prove the Bible.'" But he is just as insistent that "there are a number of points at which datable Iron Age archaeological evidence and literary references in the Bible do 'converge' in such a way as to suggest contemporaneity." According to Dever, this is "a fact that responsible historians cannot deny."[96] With this much, at least, I may heartily agree.

Less certain is Dever's contention that "archaeological data will take precedence, will constitute much of the 'primary' data in future, especially for the pre-Monarchical period," since "any new 'hard data' in ancient Israel will come, by definition, out of the ground—artifacts or texts—not out of the Hebrew Bible, which is a closed corpus."[97] While there is some force in Dever's assertion, we should at least note that, although the Old Testament is a closed corpus, the task of understanding that closed corpus is far from completed. Indeed, much suggests that at numerous points the biblical texts have heretofore been misunderstood. Sometimes an archaeological discovery, an anthropological insight, or a sociological observation may prompt a reconsideration of a text, which may in turn lead to an improved interpretation of that text. At other times, the improved literary competence arising from the numerous studies in biblical poetics, narrative criticism, and so on may have a similar effect. The point is simply that, if we would attempt a correlation of texts and artifacts, we must first take care that both text and artifact have been rightly interpreted. As de Vaux observed more than a quarter century ago: "If the results of archaeology seem to be opposed to the conclusions of text criticism, the reason may perhaps be that not enough archaeological facts are known or that they have not been firmly established; the reason also may be that the text has been wrongly interpreted."[98] This brings us again to the literary task required of those who would deal responsibly with the historiography of the OT.

Rethinking the Consequences of Modern Literary Criticism for Historical Reconstruction

In my earlier discussion of modern literary approaches to the Old Testament and their import with respect to the historiography of the Old Testament, I noted the tendency of some literary critics to slip into a reductionism in which they view the Old Testament as "pure" literature—simply art for art's sake. This slippage is unfortunate and unnecessary.

96. Ibid., 72.
97. Ibid., 71.
98. R. de Vaux, "On Right and Wrong Uses of Archaeology," in *Near Eastern Archaeology in the Twentieth Century: Essays in Honor of Nelson Glueck*, ed. J. A. Sanders (Garden City, N.Y.: Doubleday, 1970), 78.

A truly literary approach will want to "do justice" to the literature by acknowledging whatever kinds of truth claims it makes, whether they be purely literary or, as is often the case in the Bible, historical and theological as well. Much of the Bible appears to have been written as utilitarian literature intent on communicating information, commanding obedience, calling to repentance, and so on, and it is perverse to ignore or deny these intentionalities and to reduce the biblical texts to the level of pure (autotelic) literature.

Reasons for ignoring the apparent historical truth claims of much Old Testament narrative vary from scholar to scholar. For some, the failure may stem from a kind of primal rebellion that insists on asking, "Did God really say . . . ?" (Gen. 3:1); for others it may stem from a methodological straitjacket that insists that texts describing divine action are historically suspect; and for still others it may stem simply from the naive assumption that literature and history are mutually exclusive categories. The corrective for the first type of failure comes only with a radical change of heart and mind (what the Bible calls "repentance"). The corrective for the second involves making adjustments to the method so as to bring it into line with theistic reality. The corrective for the third involves simply recognizing that literature and history are not mutually exclusive concepts. As regards this last point, an analogy from the visual arts may help.

A portrait is both art and history; that is, it is an artistic creation serving a referential end. On the one hand, in appreciating a portrait, one may admire its artistry (the consummate brushwork, the well-conceived composition, the judicious selection of detail), but if one fails to recognize that all of this artistry is marshaled to serve a historical purpose (to capture a true and telling likeness of a historical person), then one has simply missed the main point. This I would liken to the ahistorical literary approaches that one sometimes encounters in biblical studies today. On the other hand, one may approach a portrait fully aware of its referential/historical intent but with little understanding of the artistic medium in which it is rendered. The danger in such cases is that lack of awareness of *how* the medium communicates may lead to misunderstandings of just *what* the medium communicates. This I would liken to some historical-critical approaches that seek to mine the biblical texts for historical information but do not approach them with sufficient literary sensitivity to do them justice.

Just as the best way to "read" a portrait and to grasp its significance is to combine historical interest with competent appreciation of the artistic medium employed, so the best way to "read" the historiography of the Old Testament is to combine historical interest with competent appreciation of the literary medium employed. In short, the better one understands the artistic workings of portrait or biblical text, the better one grasps the (historical) subject depicted.

It is just in this regard that modern literary approaches to biblical texts may have much to offer, provided they can avoid the ahistorical fallacy. The last couple of decades have witnessed an impressive increase in fresh literary readings of individual Old Testament texts, and some of these readings call into question historical judgments based on earlier, inferior literary readings. More importantly still, there has been an explosion of interest in the workings, or poetics, of Old Testament literary genres (especially narrative and poetry). These studies are providing a generally improved sense of the rhetoric of biblical texts, and historians interested in Old Testament historiography may have much to gain from them. As D. Levin observed more than three decades ago in a different context, "One of the first contributions that the critic of history can make is to serve as an intelligent reader who is willing to understand and discuss the rhetoric in which history is written."[99]

Conclusion

If the crisis in the study of Old Testament historiography/history of Israel is in some measure due to "rather one-sided theories," as I noted earlier, citing Herrmann, then the best hope for the future of the historical study of the Old Testament will lie in more integrative approaches that make use of a variety of methods. A multifaceted methodological approach has the advantage of containing within itself a system of checks and balances, whereby the results achieved by one method can be checked against the results achieved by the others. In this essay I have focused on three methodological approaches that have a bearing on the historiography of the Old Testament, and I have made suggestions as to how each can most appropriately be conceived and employed by theistic scholars. Specifically, I suggested refining the canons of the historical-critical method, restricting the claims of the social science methods, and rethinking the consequences of modern literary methods. Provided that the necessary methodological adjustments are made, an integrative approach that attends to each of the Old Testament's chief impulses—theological, historical, and literary—will stand the best chance of doing justice both to ancient Israel's history writing and to the writing of ancient Israel's history.

In addition to discussing methods, I tried to underscore the importance of attending more closely to the reality models embraced (con-

99. *In Defense of Historical Literature: Essays on American History, Autobiography, Drama, and Fiction* (New York: Hill and Wang, 1967), 23.

sciously or unconsciously) by interpreters and implicit in texts. Attention to worldview issues, to metaphysical core convictions, is essential because it is often at this level, rather than at the level of specific observations and results, that tensions and disagreements among interpreters and texts lie. I recognize, of course, that a call to be more self-reflective and open about one's own fundamental beliefs will be challenged by some who might like to contrast faith with "objective" science. But, as J. Degenaar insists, "Theoretical self-reflection raises historiography to a higher level, for the historian can now take into account his (hidden) assumptions."[100]

---

100. "Historical Discourse as Fact-Bound Fiction," in *Facts and Values: Philosophical Reflections from Western and Non-Western Perspectives*, ed. M. C. Doeser and J. N. Kraay, Martinus Nijhoff Philosophy Library 19 (Dordrecht and Boston: Martinus Nijhoff, 1986), 76.

7

Early Israel in Recent Biblical Scholarship

K. Lawson Younger Jr.

Over the last twenty years, biblical studies has witnessed tremendous changes in the study of early Israel. During this period a number of scholars have surveyed or reviewed the state of scholarship.[1] An examination of these surveys reveals an exponential increase in both the quantity of literature devoted to the subject and the number of new theoretical models being applied to the data.

Despite N. P. Lemche's recent proclamation that "the debate in this area is almost at an end,"[2] it is becoming more and more unlikely that a consensus will develop among biblical scholars concerning the early history of Israel any time in the near future. If anything, there is a heightened rhetoric that in some instances obscures the real issues.[3]

---

1. To name just a few, listed chronologically: B. S. J. Isserlin, "The Israelite Conquest of Canaan: A Comparative Review of the Arguments Applicable," *PEQ* 115 (1983): 85–94; J. J. Bimson, "The Origins of Israel in Canaan: An Examination of Recent Theories," *Themelios* 15.1 (1989): 4–15; R. Gnuse, "BTB Review of Current Scholarship: Israelite Settlement of Canaan: A Peaceful Internal Process—Part 2," *BTB* 21 (1991): 109–17; R. S. Hess, "Early Israel in Canaan: A Survey of Some Recent Evidence and Interpretations," *PEQ* 125 (1993): 125–42; N. K. Gottwald, "Recent Studies of the Social World of Premonarchic Israel," *CR:BS* 1 (1993): 163–89; E. H. Merrill, "The Late Bronze/Early Iron Age Transition and the Emergence of Israel," *BSac* 152 (1995): 145–62; N. P. Lemche, "Early Israel Revisited," *CR:BS* 4 (1996): 9–34; D. Merling Sr., *The Book of Joshua: Its Theme and Role in Archaeological Discussions*, Andrews University Seminary Doctoral Dissertation Series 23 (Berrien Springs, Mich.: Andrews University Press, 1997), 1–105.

2. Lemche, "Early Israel Revisited," 9–34.

3. Both W. G. Dever and K. W. Whitelam resort to a high degree of rhetoric in their exchange in *JSOT*: W. G. Dever, "The Identity of Early Israel: A Rejoinder to Keith W. Whitelam," *JSOT* 72 (1996): 3–24; K. W. Whitelam, "Prophetic Conflict in Israelite History: Taking Sides with William G. Dever," *JSOT* 72 (1996): 25–44. This is also true of Dever and Lemche in *CR:BS*: W. G. Dever, "Revisionist Israel Revisited: A Rejoinder to

This lack of consensus regarding premonarchic Israel can be seen in the very diverse reconstructions that employ the same basic data.[4] As the field of biblical studies enters a new millennium, the only apparent consensus is that the Albrightian "conquest model" is invalidated.

In the last two decades, archaeological interest has expanded from simply excavating urban sites to regional surveys that are yielding important data concerning small village culture where early Israel finds its setting. But as Norman Gottwald correctly observes, in the midst of all the new evidence and fresh hypothesizing, there have arisen radical doubts about the historical value of the biblical origin traditions that greatly complicate the inquiry. In short, the knowledge gained along the archaeological and sociological fronts is offset by an attrition along the literary front that had been the foundation for previous reconstructions of Israel's origins.[5]

After brief summaries of the different models, I offer a short presentation of some important factors. This is followed by a discussion concerning the role of the Book of Joshua and some suggestions for the development of a more comprehensive model that considers all the data.

Niels Peter Lemche," *CR:BS* 4 (1996): 35–50; N. P. Lemche, "Response to William G. Dever, 'Revisionist Israel Revisited,'" *CR:BS* 5 (1997): 9–14; and of I. W. Provan, T. L. Thompson, and P. R. Davies in *JBL*: I. W. Provan, "Ideologies, Literary and Critical: Reflections on Recent Writing on the History of Israel," *JBL* 114 (1995): 585–606; T. L. Thompson, "A Neo-Albrightean School in History and Biblical Scholarship?" *JBL* 114 (1995): 683–98; and P. R. Davies, "Method and Madness: Some Remarks on Doing History with the Bible," *JBL* 114 (1995): 699–705. In this regard, the suggestions of N. K. Gottwald are positive steps forward ("Triumphalist versus Anti-Triumphalist Versions of Early Israel: A Response to Articles by Lemche and Dever in Volume 4 [1996]," *CR:BS* 5 [1997]: 15–42).

4. E.g., W. G. Dever, "The Late Bronze–Early Iron I Horizon in Syria-Palestine: Egyptians, Canaanites, 'Sea Peoples,' and 'Proto-Israelites,'" in *The Crisis Years: The Twelfth Century B.C. from beyond the Danube to the Tigris*, ed. W. A. Ward and M. S. Joukowsky (Dubuque: Kendall/Hunt, 1992), 99–110; I. Finkelstein, *The Archaeology of the Israelite Settlement* (Jerusalem: Israel Exploration Society, 1988); but cf. I. Finkelstein, "The Emergence of Israel: A Phase in the Cyclic History of Canaan in the Third and Second Millennia B.C.E.," in *From Nomadism to Monarchy: Archaeological and Historical Aspects of Early Israel*, ed. I. Finkelstein and N. Naʾaman (Jerusalem: Israel Exploration Society, 1994), 150–78; Gnuse, *BTB* 21 (1991): 109–17; N. K. Gottwald, *The Tribes of Yahweh: A Sociology of the Religion of Liberated Israel, 1250–1050 B.C.E.* (Maryknoll, N.Y.: Orbis, 1979); B. Halpern, *The Emergence of Israel in Canaan*, SBLMS 29 (Chico, Calif.: Scholars Press, 1983); N. P. Lemche, *Ancient Israel: A New History of Israelite Society*, trans. F. H. Cryer, Biblical Seminar 5 (Sheffield: JSOT Press, 1988); idem, *Die Vorgeschichte Israels: Von den Anfängen bis zum Ausgang des 13. Jahrhunderts v. Chr.*, Biblische Enzyklopädie 1 (Stuttgart: Kohlhammer, 1996); W. H. Stiebing Jr., *Out of the Desert? Archaeology and the Exodus/Conquest Narratives* (Buffalo, N.Y.: Prometheus, 1989); and K. W. Whitelam, *The Invention of Ancient Israel: The Silencing of Palestinian History* (London and New York: Routledge, 1996).

5. Gottwald, "Recent Studies," 163. An important volume dealing with some of the essential issues is *The Origins of the Ancient Israelite States*, ed. V. Fritz and P. R. Davies, JSOTSup 228 (Sheffield: Sheffield Academic Press, 1996).

Summary of the Models

Theories in Which Israel Originates from outside Canaan

The Conquest Model

While the settlement process may have been complex, this view argues that archaeology has vindicated the essential historicity of the biblical narratives of Joshua.[6] This archaeological evidence consists of a number of sudden and violent destructions in the thirteenth century of many sites (e.g., Hazor, Lachish).[7] The Book of Joshua was understood to narrate a straightforward threefold campaign (central, southern, northern) that was a blitzkrieg of the land—an understanding undergirded by archaeology.

There are, however, significant problems with the theory. William Dever argues that only two sites out of nineteen with possible identifications with sites in Joshua demonstrate evidence of destruction in the thirteenth century.[8] Thus archaeology shows the Albrightian conquest model to be mistaken because its claim that the Israelites destroyed numerous Canaanite sites conflicts with the material evidence.

---

6. W. F. Albright, "Archaeology and the Hebrew Conquest of Palestine," *BASOR* 58 (1935): 10–18; idem, "The Israelite Conquest of Canaan in the Light of Archaeology," *BASOR* 74 (1939): 11–23; idem, "The Role of the Canaanites in the History of Civilization," in *The Bible and the Ancient Near East: Essays in Honor of William Foxwell Albright*, ed. G. E. Wright (1961; reprinted, Winona Lake, Ind.: Eisenbrauns, 1979), 328–62. See also Y. Yadin, "Is the Biblical Account of the Israelite Conquest of Canaan Historically Reliable?" *BAR* 8 (1982): 16–28; idem, "Biblical Archaeology Today: The Archaeological Aspect," in *Biblical Archaeology Today: Proceedings of the International Congress on Biblical Archaeology, Jerusalem, April 1984* (Jerusalem: Israel Exploration Society, Israel Academy of Sciences and Humanities in cooperation with the American Schools of Oriental Research, 1985), 21–27; J. Bright, *A History of Israel*, 3d ed. (Philadelphia: Westminster, 1981), 132. While Malamat follows the basic conquest model, his understanding is much more sophisticated; see A. Malamat, "Israelite Conduct of War in the Conquest of Canaan," in *Symposia Celebrating the Seventy-Fifth Anniversary of the Founding of the American Schools of Oriental Research (1900–1975)*, ed. F. M. Cross (Cambridge, Mass.: American Schools of Oriental Research, 1979), 35–55; idem, "How Inferior Israelite Forces Conquered Fortified Canaanite Cities," *BAR* 8 (1982): 24–35; idem, "Die Frühgeschichte Israels: Eine methodologische Studie," *TZ* 39 (1983): 1–16; idem, "Die Eroberung Kanaans: Die israelite Kriegsführung nach der biblischen Religion," in *Das Land Israel in biblischer Zeit*, ed. G. Strecker (Göttingen: Vandenhoeck & Ruprecht, 1983), 7–32.

7. P. Lapp put it this way: "the stratigraphic evidence . . . outside the coastal cities and the Plain of Jezreel, points . . . strongly to the thoroughgoing destruction of nearly all important cities in the last half of the 13th century" (Lapp, *Biblical Archaeology and History* [New York: World, 1969], 295; see also idem, "The Conquest of Palestine in the Light of Archaeology," *CTM* 38 [1967]: 283–300).

8. Dever, "Israel, History of (Archaeology and 'the Conquest')," *ABD*, 3:545–58, esp. 548; see also Lemche, "Early Israel Revisited," 13–15.

But the model was doomed from the beginning because of its literal, simplistic reading of Joshua. The Book of Joshua itself does not claim such a sweeping widespread destruction by the Israelites. It specifically states otherwise (e.g., Josh. 11:13). Moreover, the conquest account in Joshua is a highly selective, stylized narrative. It is not intended to convey the complete story of Israel's emergence in the land; nor is it to be read in a simple, literal fashion. For example, the narration of the conquest of the cities of the south (Josh. 10:28–42) should not be read as implying a total destruction of the physical structures of these sites, as it so frequently is.[9] Its repetitive, stereotypical presentation marked with hyperbole demands a much deeper reading. Hence, the archaeological record would have inevitably contradicted the model as Albright expressed it, since the biblical reading supporting the theory was too simplistic.

The Peaceful Infiltration Model

This model posits that the Israelites were nomadic and semi-nomadic clans who over a period of centuries, and from several different directions, gradually and peacefully settled the unoccupied hill country. Gradual sedentarization took place and eventually the land became dominated by Israel.[10] A loose political association developed around the worship of Yahweh and having the shape of a "twelve-tribe" amphictyony.[11] Thus, with a military conflict essentially excluded, this model in its original form postulated that the tension between Canaanites and Israelites was essentially the same as that between farmers and nomads.

Adam Zertal has argued that the distribution of ceramic types in the settlement pattern in the region of Manasseh demonstrate a slow east-to-west settlement of pastoral nomads entering from Transjordan.[12]

9. K. L. Younger Jr., "The 'Conquest' of the South (Joshua 10:28–39)," *BZ* 17.2 (1995): 255–64.

10. A. Alt, "The Settlement of the Israelites in Palestine," in *Essays on Old Testament History and Religion*, trans. R. A. Wilson (Oxford: Oxford University Press, 1953), 135–69; M. Noth, *The History of Israel*, trans. P. R. Ackroyd, 2d ed. (New York: Harper & Row, 1960), 66–84; M. Weippert, *The Settlement of the Israelite Tribes in Palestine: A Critical Survey of Recent Scholarly Debate*, trans. J. D. Martin, SBT 2/21 (London: SCM, 1971), 1–146; J. M. Miller, "Archaeology and the Israelite Conquest of Canaan: Some Methodological Observations," *PEQ* 109 (1977): 87–93; J. Strange, "The Transition from the Bronze Age to the Iron Age in the Eastern Mediterranean and the Emergence of the Israelite State," *SJOT* 1 (1987): 1–19, esp. 18–19; A. Lemaire, "Aux origines d'Israël: La montagne d'Éphraïm et le territoire de Manassé (XIII–XIe siècle av. J.-C.)," in *La protohistoire d'Israël de l'exode à la monarchie*, ed. J. Briend et al. (Paris: Cerf, 1990), 183–292.

11. An amphictyony is a league of tribes or cities, usually with six or twelve members, bound by common allegiance to a deity and to the god's shrine.

12. A. Zertal, "Israel Enters Canaan—Following the Pottery Trail," *BAR* 17.5 (1991): 28–47, esp. 36–41; idem, "The Trek of the Tribes As They Settled in Canaan," *BAR* 17.5 (1991): 48–49, 75.

This has not gone unchallenged,[13] and is in all likelihood insufficient to bolster the infiltration model.

In Baruch Halpern's estimation, since Rameses II was the pharaoh of the oppression (Exod. 1:11), then Merenptah was the pharaoh of the exodus of Israel from Egypt.[14] Thus the Israel mentioned on the Merenptah Stela was a displaced group of "homesteaders" who migrated south from Syria through northern Transjordan. Later, a group of escaped slaves from Egypt arrived and transformed Israel's beliefs with the "myth" of the exodus, of the conquest, and of the deity Yahweh.

The model has been criticized on a number of fronts.[15] It has been especially criticized for the importation of the amphictyony concept from classical Greece.[16] The anthropological assumptions underlying the theory's original assertion have also been shown to be inaccurate.[17] But recent proponents of the theory have emphasized the continuous presence of nomadic groups living in symbiotic relationship with the settled inhabitants throughout the Near East.[18] These groups could easily move into the hill country of Canaan and occupy it.[19] Whether these groups were internal or external to Canaan is the area

13. W. Dever, "How to Tell a Canaanite from an Israelite," in *The Rise of Ancient Israel: Symposium at the Smithsonian Institution, October 26, 1991*, ed. H. Shanks et al. (Washington, D.C.: Biblical Archaeology Society, 1992), 26–60, esp. 49–51.

14. B. Halpern, "The Exodus from Egypt: Myth or Reality?" in *The Rise of Ancient Israel*, ed. Shanks et al., 87–113, esp. 102–8. See also Halpern, *Emergence of Israel in Canaan*, 117, 216.

15. See the critique of Lemche, "Early Israel Revisited," 11–13.

16. See, e.g., Gottwald, *Tribes of Yahweh*, 347–57.

17. See, e.g., M. Chaney's evaluation, "Ancient Palestinian Peasant Movements and the Formation of Premonarchic Israel," in *Palestine in Transition: The Emergence of Ancient Israel*, ed. D. N. Freedman and D. F. Graf, SWBAS 2 (Sheffield: Almond, 1983), 39–90, esp. 43. The infiltration model as Alt proposed it seems to rest on a late-nineteenth/early-twentieth-century nostalgic anthropology about the Bedouin that was unaware of how pastoralism really operates (see Lemche, *Ancient Israel*, 19–21).

18. V. Fritz even proposes the name "symbiosis hypothesis" for the theory. See "Conquest or Settlement?" *BA* 50.2 (1987): 84–100; idem, "The Israelite 'Conquest' in the Light of Recent Excavations at Khirbet el-Mehash," *BASOR* 241 (1981): 71–88. Whereas Noth favored the thirteenth century B.C. as the time when Israel's ancestors entered the land, Fritz pushes their arrival back to the fourteenth or fifteenth century B.C. This longer period of sedentarization allows for Israel to become archaeologically "visible," since semi-nomads leave few traces of their existence. Their penetration was from the south into Judah, and their sedentarization was a response to changed economic conditions that affected the whole of Canaanite society at the end of the Late Bronze Age.

19. Some scholars have suggested connecting these nomads with the ʿapiru, Shasu, or exodus Israelites. M. Weippert identifies them with the Shasu, known primarily from Egyptian texts and reliefs (ca. 1500–1150 B.C.). See "The Israelite 'Conquest' and the Evidence from Transjordan," in *Symposia*, ed. Cross, 15–34; idem, "Canaan, Conquest and Settlement of," *IDBSup*, 125–30. See also D. B. Redford, *Egypt, Canaan, and Israel in Ancient Times* (Princeton: Princeton University Press, 1992), 275–80.

of current debate, which naturally centers on the issue of ethnicity (see below).

Theories in Which Israel Originates from within Canaan

The Revolt Models

Mendenhall. In George Mendenhall's reconstruction, Israel originates in the alliance of extensive rural Canaanite groups with a small but vital group of slaves who brought with them the myth of deliverance from bondage by the god Yahweh and a political structure that centered in covenant allegiance to this deity.[20]

Through their control of the surrounding agricultural land and villages, the semi-independent city-states of Canaan created sharp social stratification between, on the one hand, the king and his urban population and, on the other hand, the rural farmers and herdsmen. The result was that the urban population oppressed the rural people. The emergence in Canaan of an alienated group identified in the contemporary inscriptions as *Ḫabiru/Ḫapiru* (= the Hebrews) was the catalyst that incited revolt among the peasant farmers.

Thus there was no real conquest of Canaan at all but rather a peasants' revolt against the network of interlocking Canaanite city-states. According to Mendenhall, however, this "revolt" was more of a "cultural and ideological revolution than a political one."[21]

Gottwald. Likewise, Gottwald understands the origins of ancient Israel in terms of a "revolt" as opposed to a "conquest" or an "infiltration."[22] He differs greatly from Mendenhall in that he sees the origins in primarily a political revolution along the lines of Marxist ideology. For him, the key to understanding (and appropriating) the origins of Israel is the Marxist interpretive matrix. Thus one is to understand the "revolt" as the overthrow of the power of the "feudal" city-states by "a cohesive and effective revolutionary" peasant proletariat.[23] The origin of the people of Israel lay in their socioeconomic and religious revolution.

Anthropologically, there are significant problems with the theory (as pointed out especially by Lemche).[24] First, nomads do not need to have

---

20. G. E. Mendenhall, "The Hebrew Conquest of Palestine," *BA* 25 (1962): 66–87; idem, *The Tenth Generation: The Origins of the Biblical Tradition* (Baltimore and London: Johns Hopkins University Press, 1973); idem, "Biblical History in Transition," in *The Bible and the Ancient Near East*, ed. Wright, 32–53; idem, "Ancient Israel's Hyphenated History," in *Palestine in Transition*, ed. Freedman and Graf, 91–103.

21. Mendenhall, "Ancient Israel's Hyphenated History," 92.

22. See Gottwald, *Tribes of Yahweh*, 192–209.

23. Ibid., 586.

24. N. P. Lemche, *Early Israel: Anthropological and Historical Studies on the Israelite Society before the Monarchy*, VTSup 37 (Leiden: Brill, 1985).

an egalitarian system of rulership. Second, rather than farmers and urban dwellers being opposed to one another, they are often interdependent on one another.[25] Third, sedentarization is not necessarily an advance on nomadism.

Extrabiblically, it is clear that in the vast majority of cases the term *Ḥapiru* cannot to be equated with the biblical Hebrews.[26] There are too many philological, ethnic-social, and historical problems to equate the two. This assessment is reinforced by the recently discovered "Hapiru" Prism.[27]

Biblically, there are also problems. Since the ideology that lies behind the text of Joshua is one like that underlying other ancient Near Eastern conquest accounts—namely, imperialistic—then "egalitarian, peasant" Israel is employing a transmission code that is self-contradictory.[28]

Other Theories in Which Israel Is Indigenous

In the last decade the scholarly trend has been to understand the Israelites as indigenous to Canaan.[29] There are various nuances, but the basic underlying assumption is that Israel did not originate outside Canaan. This has been augmented by the general trend to date the pen-

25. Lemche emphasizes a polymorphic view of traditional oriental society as opposed to the dimorphic view of Gottwald.

26. A. F. Rainey, "Who Is a Canaanite? A Review of the Textual Evidence," *BASOR* 304 (1996): 1–15; idem, "Unruly Elements in Late Bronze Canaanite Society," in *Pomegranates and Golden Bells: Studies in Biblical, Jewish, and Near Eastern Ritual, Law, and Literature in Honor of Jacob Milgrom*, ed. D. P. Wright, D. N. Freedman, and A. Hurvitz (Winona Lake, Ind.: Eisenbrauns, 1995), 481–96.

27. See M. Salvini, *The Ḥabiru Prism of King Tunip-Teššep of Tikunani* (Rome: Istituti Editoriali e Poligrafici Internazionali, 1996). On this prism, 438 men are named and identified as *Ḥapiru*. Some of these men have Hurrian names, and others Semitic names; all appear to be dependents (either soldiers or servants) of the Hurrian king Tunip-Teššup (ca. 1500 B.C.). Obviously, here *Ḥapiru* is not an ethnic designation.

28. See K. L. Younger Jr., *Ancient Conquest Accounts: A Study of Ancient Near Eastern and Biblical History Writing*, JSOTSup 98 (Sheffield: Sheffield Academic Press, 1990), 255. For further rebuttal of the "peasant revolt" theory, see A. J. Hauser, "Israel's Conquest of Palestine: Peasants' Rebellion?" *JSOT* 7 (1978): 2–19; idem, "The Revolutionary Origins of Ancient Israel: A Response to Gottwald," *JSOT* 8 (1978): 46–69; and B. Halpern, "Sociological Comparativism and the Theological Imagination: The Case of the Conquest," in *"Sha'arei Talmon": Studies in the Bible, Qumran, and the Ancient Near East Presented to Shemaryahu Talmon*, ed. M. Fishbane and E. Tov, with W. W. Fields (Winona Lake, Ind.: Eisenbrauns, 1992), 53–67.

29. Some scholars are difficult to assess. Thus H. Ringgren concludes: "I assume that social changes in the Canaanite community led to (or were caused by?) the formation of a group called Israel. Whether or not this group had anything to do with the habiru is uncertain, but not unlikely. An element coming from Edom/Egypt may have joined this group bringing with them their god Yahweh" ("Early Israel," in *Storia e tradizioni di Israele: Scritti in onore di J. Alberto Soggin*, ed. D. Garrone and F. Israel [Brescia: Paideia, 1991], 217–20, esp. 219–20).

tateuchal and Deuteronomistic sources as much later than once thought so that these sources are now understood as simply the ideological product of the restored, postexilic Jewish community and therefore in the vast majority of cases convey only late and fictitious traditions. There is, of course, a wide range within this trend with particular, individual exceptions (e.g., Dever, Finkelstein, Ahlström, Coote). A number of these scholars feel that archaeology alone or for the most part can explain the origins of the Israelite states. While there are some major differences in the various interpretations of the archaeological data, the differences among most of these scholars revolve around the issue of the ethnicity of the Iron I central hill country inhabitants. Hence the questions center on: Are these central hill country people "Israel" or not? Where did they come from? Did they derive from the lowland Canaanite city-states or from pastoralists in the eastern areas? What caused them to settle in the highlands? Was there any cultural difference between Canaanites and Israelites?

Dever. Dever has written a plethora of articles addressing the issues surrounding an understanding of Israelite origins.[30] While his own view has evolved, it is possible to describe it in the following way. He stresses that both the continuity and discontinuity between the Late Bronze Age and Iron Age cultures are important to a study of the emergence of the "proto-Israelites." There is a clear continuity in the material culture, especially in the pottery repertoire, between the Late Bronze Age sites in the *lowlands* and the Iron I sites in the *highlands*.[31]

---

30. Besides the articles already mentioned, see W. G. Dever, "Archaeology, Ideology, and the Quest for an 'Ancient' or 'Biblical' Israel," *Near Eastern Archaeology* 61 (1998): 39–52; idem, "Ceramics, Ethnicity, and the Question of Israel's Origins," *BA* 58 (1995): 200–213; idem, "The Tell: Microcosm of the Cultural Process," in *Retrieving the Past: Essays on Archaeological Research and Methodology in Honor of Gus W. Van Beek*, ed. J. D. Seger (Starkville, Miss.: Cobb Institute of Archaeology, 1996), 37–45; idem, "'Will the Real Israel Please Stand Up?' Archaeology and Israelite Historiography: Part I," *BASOR* 297 (1995): 61–80; idem, "Archaeology, Texts, and History: Toward an Epistemology," in *Uncovering Ancient Stones: Essays in Memory of H. Neil Richardson*, ed. L. M. Hopf (Winona Lake, Ind.: Eisenbrauns, 1994), 105–17; and idem, "The Collapse of the Early Bronze Age in Palestine: Toward a Systemic Analysis," in *L'urbanisation de la Palestine à l'âge du Bronze ancien*, ed. P. de Miroschedji (Oxford: BAR International Series, 1989), 235–46.

31. See also along similar lines, Gottwald, "Recent Studies," 175–76. Callaway argued against any semi-nomadic origins for the Iron I settlers, preferring to view them as Canaanite villagers displaced from the coastal plain and the Shephelah. To him the cause of these refugees' movement was pressure and conflict as the result of the arrival of the Philistines and other "Sea Peoples." These highland settlers eventually emerged as Israel, so that Israel's origins must ultimately be sought in the Canaanite villages of the plains and lowlands. See J. A. Callaway, "A New Perspective on the Hill Country Settlement of Canaan in Iron Age I," in *Palestine in the Bronze and Iron Ages: Papers in Honour of Olga Tufnell*, ed. J. N. Tubb (London: Institute of Archaeology, 1985), 31–49. A few years later, however, Callaway sees the origins in a myriad of different peoples: "In short, Israel

In his estimation, this indicates that the inhabitants of the Iron I sites originated from the sedentary (especially rural) population of the Late Bronze Age sites.[32] The residents of the Iron I sites were "pioneer farmers settling the hill-country frontier of central Palestine, which had been sparsely occupied before Iron I."[33] They were "displaced Canaanite agriculturalists from the fringe of Canaanite society, creating brand new, small, isolated sites without a city wall."[34] Dever employs a collapse model to explain the process of the wave of hill country population.[35] These settlers utilized technological advances best related to subsistence agriculture and small-scale stockbreeding, including the intensive terracing of hillsides, the hewing of water cisterns, stone silos and large "collar-rim" jars for storage, and the introduction of iron implements. The high degree of usage of these technological advances combined with "the stereotyped 'agglutinative' plan with clusters of homogeneous four-room or courtyard houses" argues for the unique ethnicity of this group.[36] Since "the basic Israelite material culture of Iron I prevails until the fall of Judah in the early sixth century B.C.E.," this group is best designated "proto-Israelite" (in order to stress the continuity with the later Israelite states).[37] Dever argues adamantly that

---

seems to have emerged from a 'melting pot' of peoples in the land of Canaan at the beginning of Iron Age I, peoples whose origins can be traced only rather generally and in many different directions" ("The Settlement in Canaan," in *Ancient Israel: A Short History from Abraham to the Roman Destruction of the Temple*, ed. H. Shanks [Washington, D.C.: Biblical Archaeology Society, 1988], 53–84, 243–45, esp. 78). See further D. Hopkins, *The Highlands of Canaan: Agricultural Life in the Early Iron Age*, SWBAS 3 (Sheffield: Almond, 1985).

32. Cf. also G. Ahlström, *Who Were the Israelites?* (Winona Lake, Ind.: Eisenbrauns, 1986), 26–36.

33. Dever, "How to Tell a Canaanite from an Israelite," 52.

34. Dever, "Late Bronze–Early Iron I Horizon in Syria-Palestine," 105.

35. Ibid., 105–7. The factors included the decline of the Egyptian empire in Palestine, the exhaustion of natural resources, the cessation of international trade, both the decline and innovation in technology, and ethnic movements such as the Sea Peoples. These set in motion a downward spiral that fed on itself, increasing in momentum until the disintegration of the Bronze Age culture in Syria-Palestine was inevitable. "Collapse, in general, ensues when the center is no longer able to secure resources from the periphery, usually having lost the 'legitimacy' through which it could 'disembed' goods and services of traditionally organized groups. . . . Economic disaster, political overthrow, and social disintegration are the likely products of collapse" (*The Collapse of Ancient States and Civilizations*, ed. N. Yoffee and G. L. Cowgill [Tucson: University of Arizona Press, 1988], 13). See also M. Liverani, "The Collapse of the Near Eastern Regional System at the End of the Bronze Age: The Case of Syria," in *Center and Periphery in the Ancient World*, ed. M. Rowlands, M. Y. Larsen, and K. Kristiansen (Cambridge: Cambridge University Press, 1987), 66–73. Similarly, I. Sharon, "Demographic Aspects of the Problem of the Israelite Settlement," in *Uncovering Ancient Stones*, ed. Hopfe, 119–34.

36. Dever, "Ceramics, Ethnicity, and the Question of Israel's Origins," 200–213.

37. Dever, "How to Tell a Canaanite from an Israelite," 46.

these Iron I people were not pastoral nomads settling down in the hill country.[38]

Finkelstein. Like Dever, Israel Finkelstein has written numerous articles and a book concerned with Israelite origins. And like Dever, his view has evolved over the last decade. In 1988 Finkelstein suggested a pastoral nomadic model as an explanation of Israelite origins.[39] Although nomadic groups are difficult to detect archaeologically, he argued that sanctuaries and cemeteries attest to the existence of such groups during the Late Bronze Age, who may tentatively be identified with the *shasu* referred to in ancient (mostly Egyptian) texts. The three evidences for these "sedentarizing pastoralists" are:

1. Pillared four-room houses,[40] which were a successful adaptation to the environment from the Bedouin tent. But since architectural forms are generally linked with their environments, the origins of this house might better be sought in developments within rural village life rather than from Bedouin/pastoralist antecedents.[41]

2. Proliferating use of silos for grain storage, which "generally characterizes groups in the process of sedentarization or societies organized in local rural frameworks."[42] But Douglas Esse rebuts this, claiming that the presence of such silos need not imply a group of pastoralists in the process of "sedentarization."[43]

3. Ḥāṣēr-style elliptical settlement compounds, which reflect the intermediate stage between pastoralism and rural village life, that is, the process of settling down. But these compounds might also reflect simply functional requirements rather than a process. They may illustrate specialized architecture for the pastoralist end of the continuum, contemporary with the four-room house construction of the village end of the continuum.[44] Finkelstein understood these architectural items to be attributable to a distinct ethnic group, the Israelites. He subsequently

---

38. Dever, "Ceramics, Ethnicity, and the Question of Israel's Origins," 200–213.

39. Finkelstein, *Archaeology of the Israelite Settlement.* See D. Esse, review of *The Archaeology of the Israelite Settlement,* by I. Finkelstein, *BAR* 14.5 (1988): 8–10.

40. See Y. Shiloh, "The Four Room House: Its Situation and Function in the Israelite City," *IEJ* 20 (1970): 180–90; and A. Mazar, *Archaeology of the Land of the Bible (10,000–586 B.C.E.),* ABRL (New York: Doubleday, 1990), 340–45, 485–89.

41. So argues Esse, review of Finkelstein, 10.

42. Finkelstein, *Archaeology of the Israelite Settlement,* 266.

43. Esse, review of Finkelstein, 10.

44. Ibid.

revised the ethnic part of his argument (1991 and all subsequent references).[45]

Finkelstein has recently suggested a more sophisticated theory based on regional survey data from the Early Bronze I through Iron I periods and combined with Braudel's *la longue durée*. Thus he argues for distinct demographic developments between the lowlands and the highlands throughout history.[46] He asserts that there were cyclic rhythms in the occupational history of all three zones of the southern Levant in the fourth to first millennia B.C.: in the lowlands, rise and collapse of urban civilizations; in the steppelands, settlement oscillations with rise and collapse of desert polities (in particular, alternating periods of sedentarization and nomadization in the southern and eastern steppes); and in the highlands, waves of settlement with intervals of decline.[47]

In the central hill country in the third and second millennia B.C., there were three waves of settlement (the Chalcolithic period and Early Bronze; Middle Bronze II–III; and Iron I) with two intervals of decline (Intermediate Bronze, including the Middle Bronze I; and Late Bronze).[48] The three waves of settlement demonstrate certain parallels in material culture and political developments. All three led to the rise of complex political formations; but while the first two degenerated, the third resulted in full-scale statehood.[49] Pastoralism is especially evident in the two intervals of settlement decline.

Thus, to Finkelstein, the best way to explain these settlement fluctuations is in terms of socioeconomic change. The shifts toward sedentary or pastoral society were made for socioeconomic reasons, and not as the result of migrations of new groups or demographic fluctuations from the lowlands. Early Israel was "the latest phase in the long-term, cyclic processes of settlement oscillations and rise and fall of territorial entities in the highlands."[50] It was the third stage in the process of movement from indigenous pastoral nomadism to sedentarization in the central hill country.[51]

45. Finkelstein, "The Emergence of Israel in Canaan: Consensus, Mainstream and Dispute," *SJOT* 5.2 (1991): 47–59; idem, "Ethnicity and Origin of the Iron I Settlers in the Highlands of Canaan: Can the Real Israel Stand Up?" *BA* 59 (1996): 198–212, esp. 206.

46. Finkelstein, "Emergence of Israel," in *From Nomadism to Monarchy*, ed. Finkelstein and Naʾaman, 150–78.

47. Ibid.; idem, "Ethnicity and Origin of the Iron I Settlers," 207.

48. Finkelstein, "Ethnicity and Origin of the Iron I Settlers," 207.

49. Finkelstein, "Emergence of Israel," in *From Nomadism to Monarchy*, ed. Finkelstein and Naʾaman, 171–77.

50. Finkelstein, "Ethnicity and Origin of the Iron I Settlers," 207. Note the similarities to Coote and Whitelam (see discussion below).

51. Finkelstein, "Emergence of Israel," in *From Nomadism to Monarchy*, ed. Finkelstein and Naʾaman, 163–69.

Finkelstein recognizes some broader, short-term, local, political, economic, and social events such as foreign interventions and migration of local and alien groups. These noncyclic phenomena explain the dissimilarities between the phases of the cyclic processes. Thus the emergence of Israel and the other "national" entities in the southern Levant was determined by a combination of long-term history and short-term historical circumstances.[52]

While Finkelstein's insights are helpful, it is important to remember that the lack of data for the history of the ancient Near East limits the historian's ability to elucidate cyclic patterns. The elucidation of such patterns even in modern settings is not without problems. How much more so in the very ancient settings of the third and second millennia B.C.? Furthermore, there is always the danger, inherent in Braudelian time scales, to reduce the historical explanation to environmental determinism—a criticism that has been leveled on that generation of French *Annales* scholarship (see below).

Lemche. Lemche considers the traditions of Israel's early history to be so late as to be useless for historical reconstruction: "I propose that we decline to be led by the biblical account and instead regard it, like other legendary materials, as essentially ahistorical, that is, as a source which only exceptionally can be verified by other information."[53] His alternative reconstruction is based entirely on what can be deduced from archaeological materials of the social, economic, cultural and political developments in Palestine towards the close of the second millennium. He feels that all of this indicates that there was a very gradual (re)tribalization process from the fourteenth century B.C. on and that Israel is the product of this evolutionary process.[54] Thus Israel is in part a continuation and intensification of the social marginalization of the Amarna age city-state populace.[55]

Perhaps most controversial is Lemche's view of the Canaanites.[56] For him, the biblical tradition of the Canaanites is not a historically accurate reflection of the ethnic situation of the Iron Age I period (ca. 1200–1000 B.C.). The term *Canaan* in the second-millennium sources was imprecise and ambiguous and may have designated a vast area of

52. Finkelstein, "Ethnicity and Origin of the Iron I Settlers," 209.

53. Lemche, *Early Israel*, 411–35 (quotation on 411); idem, *Ancient Israel*, 85–90, 100–102.

54. Lemche, *Early Israel*, 411–32.

55. Lemche, *Ancient Israel*, 85–91.

56. N. P. Lemche, *The Canaanites and Their Land: The Tradition of the Canaanites*, JSOTSup 110 (Sheffield: Sheffield Academic Press, 1991), 48–51; idem, *Prelude to Israel's Past: Background and Beginnings of Israelite History and Identity*, trans. E. F. Maniscalco (Peabody, Mass.: Hendrickson, 1998), 104–5.

territory from southeastern Anatolia to the Egyptian border or a smaller area within it. "Canaanite" was a name used by scribes to designate a person who did not belong to the local society or kingdom, while "Canaan" was considered to be a country different from one's own. The biblical Canaanites, as other pre-Israelite nations of the Old Testament, are to be seen "as literary and ideological figures, playing the villain's part in a literary plot about dominance in Palestine."[57] The biblical writers applied the term *Canaanite* to describe the former inhabitants of the land whom their own ancestors had defeated and dispossessed.

As Rainey has recently explicated, however, the second-millennium textual evidence demonstrates that there was a geographical entity known at this time as "Canaan."[58] Furthermore, the people were known and recognized themselves as "Canaanites." While there may have been some theological overlay by the biblical writers, the idea that the Canaanites were the former inhabitants of Palestine is not a literary construction; nor is the description of their land a late scribal invention. "Their memory," as Naʾaman has shown, "was rooted in the people's consciousness, and their image was invoked by Israelite scribes to convey a message according to their own historiographical objectives and didactic-theological aims."[59]

Coote and Whitelam. Coote and Whitelam explicitly reject the biblical narratives as a source for the reconstruction of Israel's early history.[60] Rather, the historian's task is "to explain the archaeological record in the context of comparative history and anthropology." Two of the first among biblical scholars to approach their study from the perspective of the French school of *les Annales,* Coote and Whitelam seek to view the origin of Israel as part of Palestine's history, following a pattern well known from the territory itself, instead of tracing this origin on the basis of what they considered to be late and secondary sources found in the Bible. The origin of Israel is to be found in the context of an economic decline that occurred at the end of the Late Bronze Age, resulting from a breakdown of the inter-regional trade on which Canaan's urban economy ultimately depended, and spurred a combination of other processes. Thus Israel's early history is simply part of a repeating and nor-

57. Lemche, *Canaanites and Their Land,* 51.
58. Rainey, "Who Is a Canaanite?" 1–15.
59. N. Naʾaman, "The Canaanites and Their Land," *UF* 26 (1994): 397–418, esp. 415. Lemche's dismissal of this article as "simplistic and hardly adequate" is not an answer at all to Naʾaman's substantial scholarly criticisms. See now also N. Naʾaman, "Four Notes on the Size of Late Bronze Age Canaan," *BASOR* 313 (1999): 31–37.
60. R. B. Coote and K. W. Whitelam, *The Emergence of Early Israel in Historical Perspective,* SWBAS 5 (Sheffield: Almond, 1987), 117–38.

mal process of fluctuation between two extremes: a flourishing system of small states engaged in rich trade and this same system dissolving into a series of other independent, self-contained units. At the time of the Late Bronze–Early Iron transition, the settlement of various groups such as peasants, bandits, and pastoral nomads into villages in the hill country "was given political and incipient ethnic form in the loosely federated people calling themselves Israel."[61]

One major criticism of this study, however, is that Coote and Whitelam "have employed a historical theory about long-term developments without reference to another part of the historian's craft, the close scrutiny of historical sources pertinent to the period under investigation. Coote and Whitelam have bypassed the evidence of the Amarna letters from Palestine!"[62]

Thompson. T. L. Thompson argues that evidence of a period of drought in the eastern Mediterranean during the last part of the second millennium B.C. was a major factor in the origin of early Israel.[63] In his estimation, the transition in Palestine from the Late Bronze Age to the Early Iron Age was caused by increasing drought and the effects of shortages within the land. He does not find in the hill country settlements of Iron I any evidence of migrations from outside, certainly no evidence of an entity such as Israel. Instead, he surmises that this is a continuation of a process already begun in the Late Bronze Age and reflecting subsistence strategies among native Palestinians. He feels that the settlers of the Iron I hill country were not re-sedentarized nomads (contra Finkelstein 1988), but instead should be linked to the lowland inhabitants who were dispersed eastward.[64] Thompson expends a great amount of ink arguing that the biblical texts are of no value in the historical reconstruction of the history of Palestine. In his estimation, all of the biblical texts are the product of the Persian period, "when Israel itself is a theologoumenon and a new creation out of tradition."[65]

61. Ibid., 136.
62. Lemche, "Early Israel Revisited," 22. See the discussion of the Amarna Letters below.
63. T. L. Thompson, *Early History of the Israelite People from the Written and Archaeological Sources*, SHANE 4 (Leiden: Brill, 1992), 216–19, 304–5. Note here the similarity to Dever above.
64. Ibid., 10–12 (see esp. n. 48).
65. Ibid., 423. Thompson observes that "many of the fictive and folkloric qualities of the stories of Genesis–Kings can legitimately be described as manifest and explicit. Their referential and historical qualities, on the other hand, are substantially less so, and are rather to be described as possible and, at best, implicit" (T. L. Thompson, "Gösta Ahlström's History of Palestine," in *The Pitcher Is Broken*, ed. S. W. Holloway and L. K. Handy, JSOTSup 190 [Sheffield: Sheffield Academic Press, 1995], 422).

Ahlström. Ahlström argues that although around 1200 B.C. something called Israel certainly existed in Palestine, this was hardly the Israelite nation of the Old Testament.[66] In the highlands of Palestine at the transition from the Late Bronze Age to the Early Iron Age, there was a very mixed demographic situation.[67] The population included: (1) Canaanites who had withdrawn from the cities of the coastal plain or the Galilee; (2) Indo-Europeans of Aegean origin (like the biblical Danites, whom Ahlström identifies with the descendants of one group among the Sea Peoples, the Danuna, probably Homer's *Danaioi*);[68] (3) people of Anatolian origin; (4) individuals of Hurrian background; and (5) other ethnic groups and subgroups.

At this time (according to Ahlström), "Israel" was not an ethnic name but the name of a territory (based on his understanding of the Merenptah Stela; see below).[69] Only at a much later date was it taken up by King Saul as the name of his territorial state of central Palestine. It was the selection of the exilic Jews many centuries later that changed the name into an ideological concept, the "Israel" of the Bible.

Davies. Davies brings together much that is in Thompson, Ahlström, and Lemche.[70] In an attempt to add clarity to the discussion, Davies argues that there are three "Israels": *historic* Israel, *biblical* Israel, and *ancient* Israel. "*Historic* Israel" would be the Israel referred to in ancient Near Eastern inscriptions from its first occurrence in the Merenptah Stela down to the Assyrian sources of the first millennium. Most references speak of a tiny state in north and central Palestine roughly between 900 and 700 B.C. "*Biblical* Israel" is the Israel of the Old Testament, an ideological concept produced by the late Persian-Hellenistic Hasmonean Judaism in an attempt to justify its self-identity (i.e., to vindicate its continued existence after the disastrous fall of Jerusalem and the exile). "*Ancient* Israel" is the scholarly construction of an Israel on the basis of both *historic* and *biblical* Israel.[71] For Davies there is no archaeological reason to identify the Iron I population of the central hill country with *historic* Israel. Indeed, the Israel of the Hebrew Bible is a late literary construct, without any archaeological or historical setting.

---

66. Most recently, G. Ahlström, *The History of Ancient Palestine from the Palaeolithic Period to Alexander's Conquest*, JSOTSup 146 (Sheffield: Sheffield Academic Press, 1993).

67. Ahlström, *Who Were the Israelites?* 11–24; idem, "The Origin of Israel in Palestine," *SJOT* 5 (1991): 19–34.

68. But note Rainey's cogent objections ("Who Is a Canaanite?" 11).

69. Ahlström, "Where Did the Israelites Live?" *JNES* 41 (1982): 133–38; G. W. Ahlström and D. Edelman, "Merneptah's Israel," *JNES* 44 (1985): 59–61.

70. P. R. Davies, *In Search of "Ancient Israel,"* JSOTSup 148 (Sheffield: Sheffield Academic Press, 1992).

71. Ibid., 11–25.

Whitelam. Whitelam contends that a substitution of terminology is needed.[72] Instead of a history of Israel, it is the task of the historian to write a history of Palestine, and instead of speaking exclusively about "Israelites," thereby indicating members of the biblical nation of Israel, historians should speak about Palestinians, the ancient inhabitants of the landscape of Palestine, who were as distinctive or nondistinctive as the mountain dwellers of Lebanon in the second and first millennia B.C.

During the history of Palestine, the brief period of the history of the kingdoms of Israel and Judah was part of the fluctuation between flourishing small states and periods of dissolution. The rise of these states was not an event—hence no collapse theory like Dever's is invoked—but rather a lengthy process involving many economic and social factors. Archaeology cannot determine the ethnicity of the early Iron I settlers since they were simply a small segment of this process.

Factors

Philosophy of History

There can be little doubt about the recent popularity of the *Annales* school. Or perhaps more correctly the interest is in Braudelian time scales, if the recent penchant for the quotation of the phrase *"la longue durée"* by biblical and archaeological scholars is any indication. However, it is clear from the usage of this phrase that not all of these scholars have read the *Annales* philosophers. For one thing, the *Annaliste* movement is not monolithic. Braudel is a voice, but certainly not the only voice. The movement is united not so much by a coherent method or theory or singular viewpoint as by a common reaction against narrative, politically based history. But even this has changed so that "fourth-generation" *Annalistes*[73] are returning to narrative political history.[74]

---

72. K. W. Whitelam, *The Invention of Ancient Israel: The Silencing of Palestinian History* (London and New York: Routledge, 1996). See the review of Lemche, "Clio Is Also among the Muses! Keith W. Whitelam and the History of Palestine: A Review and a Commentary," *SJOT* 10 (1996): 88–114.

73. It is difficult to assess what the impact of "New Historicism" will be on historiographic issues in the Hebrew Bible. For examples of New Historicist readings, see L. Rowlett, "Inclusion, Exclusion, and Marginality in the Book of Joshua," *JSOT* 55 (1992): 15–23; and esp. idem, *Joshua and the Rhetoric of Violence: A New Historicist Analysis*, JSOTSup 226 (Sheffield: Sheffield Academic Press, 1997). For an introduction to New Historicist methodology, see P. Barry, *Beginning Theory: An Introduction to Literary and Cultural Theory* (Manchester: Manchester University Press, 1995), 172–90. See also the essays devoted to New Historicism in *BibInt* 5.4 (1997).

74. For political narrative, see the signal by J. Le Goff, "After Annales: The Life as History," *Times Literary Supplement* (14–20 April 1989), 394, 405. For overviews of the *Annales* school, see P. Burke, "Overture: The New History, Its Past and Its Future," in *New Perspectives on Historical Writing*, ed. P. Burke (University Park, Pa.: Pennsylvania State

While it is good to see biblical and archaeological scholars beginning to pay some attention to the philosophy of history as the theoretical undergirding of their inquiries, there are certainly more contributions in the arena of the philosophy of history than simply the *Annales* movement![75] I have wrestled with some of these issues in the first chapter of my monograph.[76] More recently, and perhaps more cogently, Marc Brettler has investigated some of these issues that are important to any investigation and reconstruction of Israelite history.[77] But there is much more that can and should be done in this area by biblical scholars. While speaking directly concerning the revolt model, Hauser aptly sums up a caution that should be remembered in every respect: "The forces of history in general, and the psyche of man in particular, are a vast labyrinth of interacting impulses, and to attempt to reduce these to essentially *one* element is unrealistic."[78]

Archaeology

Rural Studies

Regional demographic surveys and nomadic studies have greatly increased in the last fifteen years. As a result our knowledge of the history

---

University Press, 1992), 1–23. This contains the best straightforward, concise outline of the *Annaliste* movement. See also J. Bintliff, "The Contribution of an *Annaliste*/Structural History Approach to Archaeology," in *The Annales School and Archaeology*, ed. J. Bintliff (Leicester: Leicester University Press, 1991), 1–33; P. Burke, *The French Historical Revolution: The Annales School, 1929–89* (Stanford: Stanford University Press, 1990); S. Clark, "The *Annales* Historians," in *The Return of Grand Theory in the Human Sciences*, ed. Q. Skinner (Cambridge: Cambridge University Press, 1985), 177–98; T. Stoianovich, *French Historical Method: The Annales Paradigm* (Ithaca and London: Cornell University Press, 1976); and A. B. Knapp, "Archaeology and *Annales*: Time, Space, and Change," in *Archaeology, Annales, and Ethnohistory*, ed. A. B. Knapp (Cambridge: Cambridge University Press, 1992), 1–21. For some recent evaluation with reference to archaeology, see R. W. Bulliet, "*Annales* and Archaeology," in *Archaeology, Annales, and Ethnohistory*, 131–34; and A. Sherratt, "What Can Archaeologists Learn from Annalistes?" in *Archaeology, Annales, and Ethnohistory*, 135–42. See also P. Carrard, "Theory of a Practice: Historical Enunciation and the *Annales* School," in *A New Philosophy of History*, ed. F. Ankersmit and H. Kellner (Chicago: University of Chicago Press, 1995), 108–26.

75. For example, a very important essay on historicity has recently been written by N. F. Partner, "Historicity in an Age of Reality-Fictions," in *A New Philosophy of History*, ed. F. Ankersmit and H. Kellner (Chicago: University of Chicago Press, 1995), 21–39. Also see C. Lorenz, "Can Histories Be True? Narrativism, Positivism, and the 'Metaphorical Turn,'" *History and Theory* 37.3 (1998): 309–29.

76. Younger, *Ancient Conquest Accounts*, 25–58, 267–79.

77. M. Z. Brettler, *The Creation of History in Ancient Israel* (London and New York: Routledge, 1995). Cf. also M. Ottosson, "Ideology, History, and Archaeology in the Old Testament," *SJOT* 8 (1994): 207–23; R. Sollamo, "Ideology, Archaeology, and History in the Old Testament: A Brief Response to Magnus Ottosson's Paper," *SJOT* 8 (1994): 224–27.

78. Hauser, "Israel's Conquest of Palestine," 7.

of the land of Palestine has greatly increased, especially in the earlier periods.

Nonetheless, Anthony Frendo's recent article is an important reminder of the capabilities and limitations in ancient Near Eastern nomadic archaeology.[79] For instance, there are various types of pastoralism, of which pastoral nomadism is but one. Moreover, these different types of pastoralism may not be adequately reflected in archaeological materials, making their reconstruction much more difficult and often arbitrary.[80] Thus, no matter how refined one's field techniques are, there are times when the material remains of nomads are no longer recoverable by the archaeologist. Yet it would be incorrect to conclude that no pastoral nomads had been around in a particular area at a particular time in the ancient Near East simply because archaeologists have not uncovered their remains.[81]

It is also essential to remember the limitations and subjectivity inherent in regional surveys. All of this information is helpful and useful so long as caution is employed,[82] since the accuracy of such surveys is not guaranteed. Miller notes correctly: "Having conducted one of the regional archaeological surveys, I must tell you that surveys are not entirely reliable either. The data collected represent a highly selective sampling at best and are usually open to a range of interpretation."[83] Christa Schäfer-Lichtenberger adeptly adds:

> Stones and walls do not speak for themselves and even their descriptions are not unambiguous. Data derived from archaeological artifacts exist only in linguistic form. Being elements of a linguistic structure, however, they are subject to an interpretation as well. The description of archaeological findings is already interpretation and it is subject, like any other literary form of expression, to the singular choice of the narrative proce-

---

79. A. J. Frendo, "The Capabilities and Limitations of Ancient Near Eastern Nomadic Archaeology," *Or* 65 (1996): 1–23.

80. O. Bar-Yosef and A. Khazanov, "Introduction," in *Pastoralism in the Levant: Archaeological Materials in Anthropological Perspectives*, ed. O. Bar-Yosef and A. Khazanov, Monographs in World Archaeology 10 (Madison, Wis.: Prehistory Press, 1992), 3.

81. Frendo, "Capabilities and Limitations," 18, 23.

82. For instance, I have recently employed Zvi Gal's survey of Iron II Galilee (*Lower Galilee during the Iron Age*, ASORDS 8 [Winona Lake, Ind.: Eisenbrauns, 1992]) in a study of the deportations of the Israelites in order to argue for a uni-directional policy of deportation by Tiglath-pileser III (as opposed to the more usual bi-directional policy of the Assyrians). But the regional survey information is only part of the evidence, and the thesis does not rest solely on it. See K. L. Younger Jr., "The Deportations of the Israelites," *JBL* 117 (1998): 201–27.

83. J. M. Miller, "Is It Possible to Write a History of Israel without Relying on the Hebrew Bible?" in *The Fabric of History: Text, Artifact, and Israel's Past*, ed. D. V. Edelman, JSOTSup 127 (Sheffield: Sheffield Academic Press, 1991), 93–102, esp. 100.

dure, to the concept of explanation, as well as to the value-orientation of the descriptive archaeologist. And—depending on the perspective of the describer or the observer—there are various interpretational levels which can be differentiated, ranging from the singular data to the immediate context, or from the immediate and the extended environment to a geographical region or even beyond.[84]

Ethnicity

The crux revolves around whether it is possible to identify the highland settlements of the Late Bronze–Iron Age transition as "Israelite."[85] Dever's answer is affirmative: these are proto-Israelites.[86] He argues on the basis of ceramic continuity that the inhabitants of the Late Bronze–Iron Age highland sites are indigenous.[87]

Finkelstein, however, feels that identifying ethnicity in the material culture is a "perplexing, complex, and treacherous task."[88]

> If material culture of the Iron I highlands sites did not depart from the Late Bronze traditions until ca. 1100–1050, how can one distinguish a distinct new *ethnos* in the late-thirteenth century, over a century before this point of departure? I refer to the methodological problem of identifying this supposed *ethnos*, not to the theoretical question whether it existed or not. Overnight creation of an ethnic entity is difficult to comprehend even in cases of discontinuity in the material culture; how much more in this case of continuity.[89]

84. C. Schäfer-Lichtenberger, "Sociological and Biblical Views of the Early State," in *Origins of the Ancient Israelite States*, ed. Davies and Fritz, 78–105, esp. 79–80.

85. See the discussion of H. G. M. Williamson, "The Concept of Israel in Transition," in *The World of Ancient Israel*, ed. R. E. Clements (Cambridge: Cambridge University Press, 1989), 141–61; W. E. Rast, *Through the Ages in Palestinian Archaeology: An Introductory Handbook* (Philadelphia: Trinity Press International, 1992), 110. The "low level of planning" is another characteristic of these sites. See Z. Herzog, "Settlement and Fortification Planning in the Iron Age," in *The Architecture of Ancient Israel: From the Prehistoric to the Persian Periods*, ed. A. Kempinski and R. Reich (Jerusalem: Israel Exploration Society, 1992), 231–74. Two recent important essays are found in *Ethnicity and the Bible*, ed. M. G. Brett, Biblical Interpretation 19 (Leiden: Brill, 1996): M. G. Brett, "Interpreting Ethnicity: Method, Hermeneutics, Ethics," 3–22; and D. V. Edelman, "Ethnicity and Early Israel," 25–55. A new monograph has now been devoted to the topic. See K. L. Sparks, *Ethnicity and Identity in Ancient Israel: Prolegomena to the Study of Ethnic Sentiments and Their Expression in the Hebrew Bible* (Winona Lake, Ind.: Eisenbrauns, 1998).

86. Dever, "Revisionist Israel Revisited," 35–50; idem, "Cultural Continuity, Ethnicity in the Archaeological Record, and the Question of Israelite Origins," in *Avraham Malamat Volume*, ed. S. Aḥituv and B. A. Levine, *EI* 24 (Jerusalem: Israel Exploration Society, 1993), 22–33, esp. 33 n. 22.

87. See Dever, "Identity of Early Israel," 3–24, esp. 13–18.

88. Finkelstein, "Ethnicity and Origin of the Iron I Settlers," 203.

89. Ibid., 198–99.

While Finkelstein's own arguments concerning the formation of ethnic identity can be used (as he does) to undermine Dever's position, they also undermine his own. The same "perplexing, complex, and treacherous task" in identifying ethnicity in the material culture that Finkelstein applies to the archaeological data to argue against Dever also appertains, so that Finkelstein has no real grounds for denying the existence of a distinctive Israelite ethnicity. Cutting through all the anthropological rhetoric, it is evident that archaeology is not really in a very good position to say all that much authoritatively about ethnicity (especially about the ethnicity of the latter part of the second millennium B.C.).[90]

Sometimes the data can be used in conflicting ways in the ethnicity debate. On the one hand, Dever argues that collared-rim jars are not indications of Israelite ethnicity. The rims were simply functional differences between the pottery of urban and rural sites. That they are found in earlier periods and in Transjordan in clearly non-Israelite contexts indicates that these receptacles "are not an Israelite-type vessel."[91] Yet he argues that these collared-rim jars are one of the "discontinuous and new" indications of "proto-Israelite" ethnicity.[92]

According to Dever, the common early Israelite pottery turns out to be nearly identical to that of the late thirteenth century B.C.; it comes right out of the Late Bronze Age urban Canaanite repertoire.[93] Moreover, the Israelite alphabetic script may simply be a development of the Canaanite alphabetic tradition.

One item that may prove promising in the ethnicity debate is that of pig husbandry.[94] In the Bronze Age this was practiced in both the lowlands and the highlands. In Iron I, pigs appear in great numbers in the Shephelah and the southern coastal plain (Tel Miqne/Ekron, Tel Batash, and Ashkelon). But they seem to disappear from the faunal assemblages of the central hill country. Pigs were apparently already taboo in the hill country of Iron I, while they were quite popular at a proto-Ammonite site and numerous Philistine sites.[95] Pig husbandry may be the most valuable area for the study of ethnicity of an Iron I

90. Edelman asserts: "Little positive can be said about the ethnicity of premonarchic Israel" ("Ethnicity and Early Israel," in *Ethnicity and the Bible*, 54).

91. Dever, "How to Tell a Canaanite from an Israelite," 26–60, esp. 43–44.

92. Dever, "Identity of Early Israel," 3–24, esp. 15.

93. Dever, "How to Tell a Canaanite from an Israelite," 40. But see cautions of Edelman, "Ethnicity and Early Israel," 44.

94. Perhaps archaeologically documented food systems can reflect ethnicity (or religious dietary distinctions?). See B. Hesse, "'Pig Lovers and Pig Haters': Patterns of Palestinian Pork Production," *Journal of Ethnobiology* 10 (1990): 105–205.

95. See B. Hesse, "Animal Use at Tel Miqne-Ekron in the Bronze Age and Iron Age," *BASOR* 264 (1986): 17–27; idem, "'Pig Lovers and Pig Haters.'"

site.[96] This type of ethnic indicator is ultimately ideological.[97] However, it is premature to draw any definite conclusions about dietary prohibitions at these highland sites since the data are so few and inadequate. Only a tiny fraction of the hundreds of sites that have been dated to the Iron I period have been excavated, and a very small part of these have been dug systematically.[98]

In my opinion, the fact that the early Israelites were in almost every case culturally indistinct from the Canaanites is not surprising.[99] The biblical traditions do not hide the fact that Israelite origins come out of the Semitic stock of the Levant. Such general Asiatic ethnic links are consistently maintained in the Hebrew Bible (from the earliest writings to the latest), although it was apparent that in some way the ancient Israelites *perceived* a difference between themselves and other Levantine groups.[100] Thus should we really expect to find "smoking gun" evidence of Israelite material culture distinctions? In fact, the biblical traditions evince an attitude of assimilation on the part of the Israelites, who were determined to make themselves indistinguishable from the other inhabitants of the hill country (cf. Judg. 3:5–6).[101] Certainly over a period of time and especially with the rise of the monarchy, distinctions may have developed, but even these de-

96. L. E. Stager, *Ashkelon Discovered* (Washington, D.C.: Biblical Archaeology Society, 1991), 9, 19, 31; and Finkelstein, "Ethnicity and Origin of the Iron I Settlers," 206. See also Hess, "Early Israel in Canaan," 125–42.

97. Ideology, especially as it is conveyed through textual materials, can also be a means of detecting ethnicity. For an example, see C. Zaccagnini, "The Enemy in the Neo-Assyrian Royal Inscriptions: The 'Ethnographic' Description," in *Mesopotamien und seine Nachbarn: Politische und kulturelle Wechselbeziehungen im Alten Vorderasien vom 4. bis 1. Jahrtausend v. Chr.*, ed. H.-J. Nissen and J. Renger, BBVO 1, RAI 25 (Berlin: Dietrich Reimer, 1982), 409–24.

98. See Edelman's cautious assessment ("Ethnicity and Early Israel," 47–49).

99. Burial practices are another area where ethnicity may be indicated. See, e.g., the results of the studies of R. Gonen, *Burial Patterns and Cultural Diversity in Late Bronze Age Canaan*, ASORDS 7 (Winona Lake, Ind.: Eisenbrauns, 1992); and E. Bloch-Smith, *Judahite Burial Practices and Beliefs about the Dead*, JSOTSup 123 (Sheffield: Sheffield Academic Press, 1992). The current data on Iron I burials is relatively scanty. See Edelman, "Ethnicity and Early Israel," 53–54.

100. This is not surprising since tribal or clan identity can also generate such feelings.

101. Archaeologically speaking, there appear to be few distinctions religiously between the ancient Israelites and Canaanites. An important qualification, however, should be remembered: religious beliefs and convictions are very difficult to trace, even when written sources exist. Therefore, what historic Israel believed or did not believe will always be to some extent uncertain or unprovable. See M. S. Smith, *The Early History of God: Yahweh and the Other Deities of Ancient Israel* (San Francisco: Harper & Row, 1990); J. C. de Moor, "Ugarit and Israelite Origins," in *Congress Volume: Paris, 1992*, ed. J. A. Emerton, VTSup 61 (Leiden: Brill, 1995), 205–38; and J.-M. van Cangh, "Les origines d'Israël et de la foi monothéiste: Apports de l'archéologie et de la critique littéraire," *RTL* 22 (1991): 305–26, 457–87.

velopments would not speak necessarily in every case to issues of ethnic origins.

Extrabiblical Texts

Merenptah Stela

The earliest extrabiblical mention of "Israel" is found in the Merenptah Stela (ca. 1207 B.C.): "Israel is wasted, his seed is not."[102] Two recent studies offer excellent summaries of the different problems and interpretations of the inscription.[103] Both Hasel and Hoffmeier rightly note that the inscription's mention of Israel provides historical information that should not be dismissed regarding the origins of ancient Israel. Moreover, the literary structure of the inscription reinforces that Israel was an entity within the region of Canaan, a people, possibly sedentary, and not a city-state or territory (contra Ahlström above). It was powerful enough to be included within a list of the other political powers in Canaan.

A number of interpreters identify the new ethnic group that was formed in the highlands in the Iron I with the "Israel" named on the Merenptah Stela. Thus, for example, Dever states concerning the Iron I inhabitants: "This ethnic group may be presumed to be roughly the same as that which had called itself 'Israelite' since the late 13th century B.C.E. and was thus well enough established to be listed as 'Israel' . . . in the well known 'Victory Stele' of Merneptah."[104] Finkelstein argues that since scholars do not agree on the size, socioeconomic nature (pastoral or sedentary people), or geographical location of Merenptah's Israel, "one cannot make an *instinctive* connection between Israel of 1207 B.C. and the area where the Israelite monarchy emerged two centuries later" (emphasis mine).[105] But since Israel must have been one of the peoples in Canaan according to the Merenptah Stela, it seems likely that at least some of the material culture from some of these hill country sites is Israelite. Dever's argument for continuity with the later Israelite monarchic material culture may prove significant as well in this connection.

---

102. See K. A. Kitchen, *Ramesside Inscriptions, Historical and Biographical*, 8 vols. (Oxford: Blackwell, 1975–90), 4:19.3–8.

103. M. G. Hasel, "*Israel* in the Merneptah Stela," *BASOR* 296 (1994): 45–61. He adeptly discusses a number of issues that cannot be entered into here (though I must disagree with his interpretation of *prt* in this context as "grain"). See also J. K. Hoffmeier, *Israel in Egypt: The Evidence for the Authenticity of the Exodus Tradition* (New York and Oxford: Oxford University Press, 1997), 27–31, 44–46; and F. J. Yurco, "Merneptah's Canaanite Campaign," *JARCE* 23 (1986): 189–215.

104. Dever, "Cultural Continuity," 24.

105. Finkelstein, "Ethnicity and Origin of the Iron I Settlers," 203.

To deny that there is any connection between the "Israel" *(ysr·r/l)* of the Merenptah Stela and early biblical Israel (as described in the earliest biblical texts) is tantamount to denying that "Israelite" (^kur^*sir·alāia*) in Shalmaneser III's Kurkh Monolith has any connection to biblical Israel (as described in the so-called Deuteronomistic History's account of the divided monarchy). The problem with accepting the Merenptah citation is that it is too early for some scholars' reconstructions of "historic" Israel.

Amarna Tablets

Any study of the origins of Israel must employ the study of the Amarna Letter corpus.[106] The corpus provides a glimpse at the historical background to the rise of ancient Israel. These letters enable us to reconstruct in some detail the territorial, political, social, and economic situation in the lowlands and highlands of Canaan in the fourteenth century B.C.[107] The corpus is an important source for understanding the identification of the *'apîrû*.[108] Their use can prevent incorrect conclusions concerning the archaeological data.[109]

Tribal Organization

An understanding of the societal components of early Israel, whether Israelite households, clans, or tribes, is hindered by the fragmentary biblical and archaeological evidence.[110] The household seems to have

---

106. An example in this regard can be seen in Rainey, "Who Is a Canaanite?" 1–15.

107. See N. Na²aman, *Borders and Districts in Biblical Historiography*, JBS 4 (Jerusalem: Simor, 1986); idem, "Historical-Geographical Aspects of the Amarna Tablets," in *Proceedings of the Ninth World Congress of Jewish Studies: Panel Sessions: Bible Studies and Ancient Near East*, ed. M. Goshen-Gottstein (Jerusalem: Magnes, 1988), 17–26.

108. Rainey, "Unruly Elements"; see also idem, "Who Is a Canaanite?"; and Salvini, *Ḥabiru Prism*, 12–55.

109. See N. Na²aman, "The Contribution of the Amarna Letters to the Debate on Jerusalem's Political Position in the Tenth Century B.C.E.," *BASOR* 304 (1996): 17–27; idem, "Cow Town or Royal Capital?" *BAR* 23.4 (1997): 43–47, 67.

110. See Gottwald, *Tribes of Yahweh*, 228–341; Lemche, *Early Israel*, 245–90; L. Stager, "The Archaeology of the Family in Ancient Israel," *BASOR* 260 (1985): 1–36; J. W. Rogerson, "Was Early Israel a Segmentary Society?" *JSOT* 36 (1986): 17–26; idem, *Anthropology and the Old Testament* (Oxford: Blackwell, 1978; reprinted, Sheffield: JSOT Press, 1984); A. G. Auld, "Tribal Terminology in Joshua and Judges," in J. A. Soggin et al., *Convegno sul Tema: Le Origini di Israele (Roma, 10–11 Febbraio 1986)* (Rome: Accademia Nazionale dei Lincei, 1987), 87–98; Halpern, "Sociological Comparativism," in *Shaʿarei Talmon*, 53–67; H. Cazelles, "Clans, état monarchique, et tribus," in *Understanding Poets and Prophets: Essays in Honour of George Wishart Anderson*, ed. A. G. Auld, JSOTSup 152 (Sheffield: Sheffield Academic Press, 1993), 77–92; F. Lambert, "Tribal Influences in Old Testament Tradition," *SEÅ* 59 (1994): 33–58; and S. Bendor, *The Social Structure of Ancient Israel: The Institution of the Family (Beit ²Ab) from the Settlement to the End of the Monarchy*, JBS 7 (Jerusalem: Simor, 1996).

been the fundamental unit of social structure, with the *mišpāḥâ*, "max-imal lineages" (i.e., a descent group that established ties of kinship be-tween families through a common ancestor who was no longer living), adding to a protective and social function. The tribe, however, is more difficult to define, since social groups can be bound together in many different ways: by descent, by residence, by common dialect, or by a common religion. In the Old Testament, tribes were certainly groups connected to one another by residence and descent as well as possibly dialect (cf. Judg. 12:6, where the Ephraimites could not pronounce the word *shibboleth*). Studies of modern tribal societies demonstrate that Old Testament tribal culture was not necessarily an evolutionary stage following that of the band and preceding the state, but could represent a social form in its own right.[111] The term *tribe* may be applied to any kind of organization that has unity at the center but freedom and vari-ation at the periphery. In the Old Testament, therefore, a tribe seems to be the largest social unit for mutual defense against foreigners or other Israelite social units.[112]

While the amphictyonic proposal was rightly rejected, in doing so biblical scholars often forgot that anthropology provides a range of confederate forms among pre-state peoples that may be used with heu-ristic caution to examine the ways in which the village communities of early Israel might have been able to join in a larger whole. These tribal confederations are leagues that facilitate important political, eco-nomic, social, and religious purposes.[113]

Zecharia Kallai has recently investigated once again the twelve-tribe systems of Israel.[114] He notes that four different systems for organiza-tion of the tribal lists exist in the biblical material. He concludes that the phenomenon of one basic assemblage of eponyms in all systems, and the points of contact between the geographical distribution of the tribes and the genealogical representation of the tribal interrelation-ships, support the suggestion that all schemes stem from one formal-ized structure, from which the other diverse modes of representation are extrapolated. The eminent place of the twelve-tribe systems among the fundamental historiographical concepts is unqualified. There are, therefore, no earlier or later historical situations that created the di-verse schemes or their variants. The different literary formulations are

111. Lambert, "Tribal Influences," 33–58.
112. See the discussion and bibliography in Gottwald, "Recent Studies," 178–80.
113. Gottwald observes: "While properly suspicious of the biblical traditions that show a tribal people solely formed and united by religious commitment, scholars are con-scious that some form of early Israelite unity involving religion is not to be excluded" (ibid., 181).
114. Z. Kallai, "The Twelve-Tribe Systems of Israel," *VT* 47 (1997): 53–90.

only modes of utilization and application of these systems, reflecting requirements of presentational emphasis.

The Role of the Book of Joshua

Besides the rejection of the Albrightian "conquest" model, the general consensus among OT scholars is that the Book of Joshua has no value in the historical reconstruction. They see the book as an ideological retrojection from a later period—either as early as the reign of Josiah or as late as the Hasmonean period.[115]

Many objections to the use of the Book of Joshua in the reconstructive process are based on supposed contradictions between Joshua and Judges. These are routinely expressed in the following way: Joshua presents a complete conquest by "all Israel," while Judges presents the conquest as tribal and incomplete. However, better narrative reading strategies that recognize the figurative aspects of both the Joshua account and that of Judges eliminate these supposed contradictions and demonstrate that these are instead the results of simplistic reading agendas.[116] Hence Judges 1 is no more historically accurate than Joshua 10–11. Both are complex, artistic impositions of form on the past and must be carefully read as such.

It is readily admitted that there are textual difficulties, corruptions, and apparent internal contradictions.[117] Moreover, this does not mean that we have a final authoritative interpretation of these passages. Quite to the contrary, much more work is needed. But literality has only obscured the interpretation.

---

115. For the former, see N. Naʾaman, "The 'Conquest of Canaan' in the Book of Joshua and in History," in *From Nomadism to Monarchy*, ed. Finkelstein and Naʾaman, 218–81. For the latter see J. Strange, "The Book of Joshua: A Hasmonaean Manifesto?" in *History and Traditions of Early Israel: Studies Presented to Eduard Nielsen, May 8th, 1993*, ed. A. Lemaire and B. Otzen, VTSup 50 (Leiden: Brill, 1993), 136–41. The evidence is certainly stronger for a Josianic date. How much is a retrojection of the ideology of this period or how much reflects certain historical events is difficult to determine simply based on the text's date. See T. C. Römer, "Transformations in Deuteronomistic and Biblical Historiography: On 'Book-Finding' and Other Literary Strategies," *ZAW* 109 (1997): 1–11.

116. For Joshua, see Younger, *Ancient Conquest Accounts*, 197–237, 310–21; idem, "The 'Conquest' of the South," 255–64; for Judges 1, see idem, "The Configuring of Judicial Preliminaries: Judges 1:1–2:5 and Its Dependence on the Book of Joshua," *JSOT* 68 (1995): 75–92. It is ironic that the phrase *běnê yiśrāʾēl* occurs sixty-one times in the Book of Judges (see D. Block, "'Israel'—'Sons of Israel': A Study in Hebrew Eponymic Usage," *SR* 13.3 [1984]: 301–26). The final editor/writer of the Book of Judges clearly presents the Israelites as perceiving themselves as a single family throughout the book.

117. Cf., e.g., Josh. 15:63 ≠ Judg. 1:8 ≠ 1:21. See Younger, "Configuring of Judicial Preliminaries," 84 n. 27.

Often the Book of Joshua is discredited because of supposed contradictions with the archaeological record. Indeed, there seem to be irreconcilable contradictions between the biblical account and the archaeological record (e.g., the issues surrounding Jericho, Ai, and Gibeon).[118] But this opinion concerning contradictions between Joshua and archaeology is usually based on two misconceptions.

First, it is based on a "literal," surface reading of Joshua (both Albrightians and "revisionists" have read and do read the text of Joshua this way). Thus the Book of Joshua is read to state that there were massive destructions by the Israelites as they "conquered" the land. When the archaeological record does not bear this out, it is the Book of Joshua that is wrong (when it is rather the interpretation that is wrong).

Second, it is based on strong or "hard" objectivism in archaeology (i.e., archaeology without the biblical text can supply all the answers).[119] By declaring that archaeology is more reliable than the Hebrew Bible for dealing with the origin and early history of Israel, many archaeologists ignore the extent to which Syro-Palestinian archaeology itself is infused with many subjective assumptions derived from various, and sometimes self-contradictory, philosophical perspectives (including in many instances assumptions based on the Bible itself).[120] This over-optimism in archaeology with which detailed results are used to construct global images may only deepen, rather then bridge, the gap between archaeology and texts.[121]

Different types of events are more or less likely to be displayed in the archaeological record. So, for example, Elizabeth Stone asserts: "Changes in government, since their effects on the general population is [sic] subtle, can rarely, if ever, be identified archaeologically, whereas social and economic changes which radically affected the entire population are more likely to leave their mark."[122] Hence, in the course of an

---

118. For a recent concise discussion of these, see R. S. Hess, *Joshua: An Introduction and Commentary*, TOTC (Downers Grove, Ill., and Leicester: InterVarsity, 1996). Merling has also addressed the role of the Book of Joshua in the archaeological discussions (*Book of Joshua*, 106–273). For Jericho in particular, see B. G. Wood, "Did the Israelites Conquer Jericho? A New Look at the Archaeological Evidence," *BAR* 16.2 (1990): 44–58; P. Bienkowski, "Jericho Was Destroyed in the Middle Bronze Age, Not the Late Bronze Age," *BAR* 16.5 (1990): 45–46, 69.

119. Dever's pronouncements that archaeologists will write "*the only competent histories* of ancient Palestine" (emphasis mine) is an example of this overconfidence in the discipline. See Dever, "Identity of Early Israel," 19. Note also Whitelam's response, "Prophetic Conflict in Israelite History," 35.

120. Miller, "Is It Possible to Write a History of Israel?" 101.

121. J. N. Postgate, "Archaeology and Texts—Bridging the Gap," *ZA* 80 (1990): 228–40, esp. 239.

122. E. C. Stone, *Nippur Neighborhoods*, SAOC 44 (Chicago: Oriental Institute, 1987), 32 n. 7.

excavation, the association of a destruction in the archaeological record is not necessarily an easy task for the archaeologist.

For a number of archaeologists there is only evidence of military activity or "conquest" when there is significant evidence of the site's destruction. This is problematic on at least three counts. First, many open-field battles have been the decisive grounds upon which conquests have been achieved in war from the beginning of history until the present. Second, complete or even partial destructions are not necessary for the subjugation of a city. Third, the present nature of site excavation cannot always reveal the particulars of a city's capture since manual destructions are virtually impossible to identify and are often not considered by archaeologists.[123]

While J. N. Postgate addresses the issues surrounding archaeology and texts in Mesopotamian contexts, his perceptive insights apply very much to the context of Palestinian/biblical archaeology.

> The correlation of observation in the course of an excavation with a known political event must involve a degree of assumption, and over-hasty identification of "political" events by excavators has led to some of the best known archaeological controversies—one need only think of the sack of Troy, or the argument surrounding the destruction of the Early Bronze palace at Tell Mardiḫ, to realize the dangers to be avoided. Identifying destructions is as risky as identifying races in the archaeological record, and this explains why many excavators have avoided making the attempt. On the other hand, situations exist, such as the fall of the Assyrian Empire, in which the relevance of the political event is too obvious to be ignored, and few would question the correlation of the destruction of the Nabu Temple at Nimrud and the smashing of the vassal treaties in its throne-room with an enemy attack at this time. It is, of course, where the archaeological evidence is less absolute and the event less all-embracing that uncertainties may creep in, and here the need for some paradigms is all too obvious. In each case, it is necessary to proceed carefully from both ends of the equation: to ask what the historical evidence for the event is, and then to look at the archaeological data equated with it.[124]

A further difficulty is that population migrations are not always easy to trace archaeologically, especially those of nomadic groups. The Hittite historical narratives, correspondences, and treaties often mention

---

123. It is clear that at least on some occasions the Assyrians practiced manual destructions exclusive of fire. See, e.g., the report on Sargon's conquest of the city of Ulhu in his "Letter to the God" (see *ARAB* 2:87–88, §161; and W. Mayer, "Sargons Feldzug gegen Urartu—714 v. Chr. Text und Übersetzung," *MDOG* 115 [1983]: 65–132, esp. 88–93).

124. Postgate, "Archaeology and Texts," 230–31.

peoples on the move and the need to prevent these movements. Yet little is known about any of these movements.[125]

In addition, it is also important to recognize the great significance of the migration process. The migration to the New World had a tremendous impact on the history of the world. The recent migration of Russian Jews to Israel has had notable repercussions on the politics of the Middle East. These events do not always find sufficient explanation in the context of the Braudelian *la longue durée*.

Suggestions for a More Comprehensive Model

1. Recognize the Complexity of the Picture That the Book of Joshua Paints

Two items are often overlooked in a reading of the Book of Joshua: the use of hyperbole and the use of ideology and propaganda. Hyperbole was a major feature of ancient Near Eastern history writing. A recognition of its use can help eliminate misunderstandings of the biblical accounts. The use of ideology and propaganda is also important (in this case the hyperbole underscores the ideology and should caution the reader not to be too literal in the interpretation of the text). A cognizance of these items will enable the interpreter to read through the text.

Another important component is the realization that the process of occupation was complex, not simply a quick military conquest but a long process of infiltration, fighting (including infighting), and transformation and realignment. The Book of Joshua itself advocates such an understanding of Israel's rise (e.g., Josh. 11:18; 13:1), as does the Book of Judges.

Finally, it is important to recognize the complexity of other biblical materials (e.g., Judges 1). There is a danger in emphasizing one piece of evidence over another. This has especially been done in the case of Joshua 10 and Judges 1. Neither of these is more historically accurate than the other. Both have impositional structures that require sophisticated reading strategies.[126]

---

125. G. Beckman, *Hittite Diplomatic Texts*, ed. H. A. Hoffner Jr., SBLWAW 7 (Atlanta: Scholars Press, 1996), 11–143.

126. Younger, "Configuring of Judicial Preliminaries," 86–87. This would also apply to Sara Japhet's understanding of the Chronicler's presentation in 1 Chron. 1–9 that Israel was indigenous to Canaan. See her "Conquest and Settlement in Chronicles," *JBL* 98 (1979): 205–18; idem, *The Ideology of the Book of Chronicles and Its Place in Biblical Thought*, Beiträge zur Erforschung des Alten Testaments und des antiken Judentums 9 (Frankfurt am Main: Lang, 1989).

2. Recognize the Complexity of the Picture
That the Archaeological Record Paints

It is important to remember the limitations of different archaeological methods. The fallacy of assuming that the material culture has a logical and necessary priority over the written evidence should be avoided. At the same time, the written evidence needs to be interpreted through the context of the archaeological evidence.[127] Each must be interpreted in its own context and allowed to inform the other. The particular weight given to the written sources depends on a variety of factors, always keeping in mind the ideological perspectives of the written materials. Postgate's suggestion to proceed carefully from both ends of the equation (i.e., to ask what the historical evidence for the event is, and then to look at the archaeological data equated with it) seems to be fundamental in this instance.

3. Use Comparative Literary Analysis of Synchronic
Types to Uncover the Ways in Which the Ancient
Near Eastern Peoples Wrote Their Accounts

In the case of ancient conquest accounts, a comparative literary methodology permits the historian to perceive that the conquest accounts in Joshua are very similar to those of other ancient Near Eastern peoples. This approach can help prevent improper generalizations about the biblical texts.[128] Such an approach is also helpful in the case of boundary descriptions and town lists,[129] or in understanding the biblical narrative concerning the building of the temple.[130]

---

127. The famous crux of the Siloam Tunnel inscription (i.e., the meaning of the term *zdh*) may be solved by interpreting the word through the matrix of the archaeological and geological evidence. See Younger, "The Siloam Tunnel Inscription—An Integrated Reading," *UF* 26 (1994): 543–56.

128. Younger, *Ancient Conquest Accounts*, 258–60.

129. R. S. Hess, "Late Bronze Age and Biblical Boundary Descriptions of the West Semitic World," in *Ugarit and the Bible: Proceedings of the International Symposium on Ugarit and the Bible, Manchester, September 1992*, ed. G. Brooke, A. Curtis, and J. Healey, Ugaritisch-biblische Literatur 11 (Münster: Ugarit-Verlag, 1994), 123–38; idem, "A Typology of West Semitic Place Name Lists with Special Reference to Joshua 13–21," *BA* 59 (1996): 160–70; idem, "Asking Historical Questions of Joshua 13–19: Recent Discussion concerning the Date of the Boundary Lists," in *Faith, Tradition, History: Old Testament Historiography in Its Near Eastern Context*, ed. A. R. Millard, J. K. Hoffmeier, and D. W. Baker (Winona Lake, Ind.: Eisenbrauns, 1994), 191–205.

130. V. Hurowitz, *I Have Built You an Exalted House: Temple Building in the Bible in Light of Mesopotamian and Northwest Semitic Writings*, JSOTSup 115, JSOT/ASOR Monographs 5 (Sheffield: Sheffield Academic Press, 1992).

Conclusion

In light of these concerns, we must recognize that the rise of ancient Israel was complex, not comprehensible in terms of simply one factor. While looking at the process through Braudelian time scales is helpful, one should not slight the important political and individualistic ingredients. It was a long process of infiltration, transformation, and realignment.

The biblical text indicates the inclusion of different groups (e.g., Josh. 9; Judg. 4:11). In addition, the lack of conquest accounts for the occupation of certain areas (what could be called "conquest lacunae") such as Shechem (Josh. 8:30–35; 24:1, 32) may attest to a peaceful infiltration of the area by the Israelites.

But Israel's rise certainly involved military conquests (also including infighting).[131] This complex process was the result (not in every instance separable) of political, economic, religious, and environmental circumstances.[132] The collapses of the Egyptian empire and the Canaanite city-state system and the Sea Peoples' migration were important factors. Drought may also have contributed. While Israel's rise contained some indigenous (both pastoral and sedentary) elements, there were undoubtedly some extraneous elements too.

Conclusion

We should reject the view that the biblical account has no value in the historical reconstruction of the period. We should also reject the view that the biblical account is all that is sufficient for the process of historical reconstruction. The biblical account is highly selective—and therefore *incomplete* as a source for historical reconstruction. Moreover, it requires much hard work at interpretation since it is highly structured in its narration.[133] This feature has sometimes been mistaken as an excuse to disqualify the biblical account from consideration. But to do this *limits* the reconstruction by not considering *all* the evidence (biased as it may be in its presentation).[134] This would be like ignoring the

---

131. A. Mazar's approach is helpful at this point. He suggests that "the conquest tradition must be understood as a telescoped reflection of a complex historical process in which some of the Canaanite city-states, weak and poor after three hundred years of Egyptian domination, were replaced during the Iron Age I by a new national entity, Israel" (Mazar, *Archaeology of the Land of the Bible*, 334).

132. On some of these factors see F. S. Frick, "Ecology, Agriculture, and Patterns of Settlement," in *World of Ancient Israel*, ed. Clements, 67–93.

133. This is why we should be open to various different readings of a text (and not disqualify them a priori). Different perspectives open new vistas, although some readings will be of greater value to the efforts of the historian than others.

134. Whybray has recently argued that the OT historical books do contain some reliable historical data and can be used as a source of facts upon which to build history. See

Annals of Sargon in a reconstruction of the fall of Samaria because of a perceived bias in his writings. All history writing (ancient or modern) requires a de-biasing process in our reading. How successful we are in that process may vary, but we are obligated to make the effort nonetheless. The biblical traditions—when read properly—do reveal a viable account, very much in the tradition of conquest accounts from the ancient Near East as a whole.

Archaeologically, the material cultural remains are highly partial and selective. This fact concerning the paucity of evidence means that the archaeological evidence too is *incomplete* as a source for historical reconstruction. The material cultural remains also require much hard work at interpretation. Pottery has been known to be misread and misinterpreted.

Therefore, a methodology that considers all the evidence and draws from all the data is a methodology that will inevitably produce better reconstructions.[135] And it is to this end that archaeological and historical scholars should proceed.[136]

R. N. Whybray, "What Do We Know about Ancient Israel?" *ExpTim* 108 (1996): 71–74. See also the remarks of J. G. McConville, "Faces of Exile in Old Testament Historiography," in *After the Exile: Essays in Honour of Rex Mason*, ed. J. Barton and D. J. Reimer (Macon, Ga.: Mercer University Press, 1996), 27–44.

135. G. A. Rendsburg's recent synthesis offers some positive insights along these lines: "The Early History of Israel," in *Crossing Boundaries and Linking Horizons: Studies in Honor of Michael C. Astour on His 80th Birthday*, ed. G. D. Young, M. W. Chavalas, and R. E. Averbeck (Bethesda, Md.: CDL Press, 1997), 433–53.

136. The following volume appeared too late for incorporation in this article: S. Aḥituv and E. D. Oren, eds., *The Origin of Early Israel: Current Debate: Biblical, Historical, and Archaeological Perspectives*, Iren Levi-Sala Annual Seminar 1997; Beer Sheva 12 (Beersheba: Ben-Gurion, 1998).

8

The Historical Study of the Monarchy: Developments and Detours

Gary N. Knoppers

Among the periods that constitute Israelite history, the united and divided monarchies have been the most intensively studied by modern scholars. This brief survey, necessarily selective, focuses on how scholarly treatments of certain issues have developed or changed over the past three decades. Where possible, the essay is also prospective, posing topics that deserve reexamination or further research. Special attention is given, first of all, to an important methodological shift in the study of the monarchy: the increasing popularity, if not dominance, of archaeology and epigraphy. Then follows a study of other, more specific issues: the existence of the united monarchy, the historical context of the early divided kingdom, the impact of the Assyrian campaigns, and new interpretations of the Babylonian exile.

The Question of Sources

Scrutiny of recent histories of the monarchy reveals a greater dependence on archaeology and epigraphy and concomitantly a lesser dependence on literary (biblical) texts as sources.[1] To be sure, the attempt to

1. There are, for instance, many methodological and theoretical differences between the recent treatments of T. L. Thompson (*Early History of the Israelite People: From the Written and Archaeological Sources*, SHANE 4 [Leiden: Brill, 1992], 306–7) and J. S. Holladay ("The Kingdoms of Israel and Judah: Political and Economic Centralization in the Iron IIA–B [ca. 1000–750 B.C.E.]," in *The Archaeology of Society in the Holy Land*, ed. T. E. Levy [London: Leicester University Press, 1995], 368–74), but they agree on one thing: the need to reconstruct the past only through recourse to the material remains.

relate archaeological and epigraphical finds to the history of Israel and Judah was also a constituent feature of older treatments.[2] But if the appeal to archaeology served to buttress histories of Israel, which were written basically according to a biblical chronology, there is now a trend to eschew recourse to biblical texts altogether. Since my own approach involves paying significant attention to the testimony of biblical texts, I examine this trend at some length and defend the use of literary materials to write history.

A number of factors have contributed to the growing dependence on archaeology and epigraphy. First, an unprecedented amount of archaeological activity has taken place in Israel and Jordan during the past quarter century. Hence, formulating a new history of the monarchy inevitably involves making sense of important archaeological and epigraphic data. Second, the application of new methodologies, such as the "new" archaeology, provides unprecedented insight into ancient Palestinian life—demography, ethnicity, housing, socioeconomic conditions, dietary habits, and so forth.[3] Since much ancient Israelite history was written with reference to the activities of YHWH and major human leaders, such as kings, priests, and prophets, new anthropological and archaeological approaches provide a fuller picture of the past than was previously available.

But the keen interest in archaeological evidence has been accompanied by a reassessment of biblical evidence. Ironically, this reassessment has involved the coalescence of two quite unrelated developments. The surge of growth in the study of the Bible as literature has called attention to the sophisticated compositional techniques employed by biblical authors.[4] This has been helpful in gaining a better

---

2. M. Noth, *The History of Israel,* trans. P. R. Ackroyd, 2d ed. (London: Black, 1960), 204–16; W. F. Albright, *The Archaeology of Palestine* (reprinted, Gloucester, Mass.: Smith, 1971), 118–28; J. Bright, *A History of Israel,* 3d ed. (Philadelphia: Westminster, 1981), 183–228; J. A. Soggin, "The Davidic-Solomonic Kingdom," in *Israelite and Judaean History,* ed. J. H. Hayes and J. M. Miller, OTL (Philadelphia: Westminster; London: SCM, 1977), 332–80; S. Herrmann, *A History of Israel in Old Testament Times,* trans. J. Bowden (Philadelphia: Fortress, 1981), 131–86; A. Lemaire, "The United Monarchy," in *Ancient Israel: A Short History from Abraham to the Roman Destruction of the Temple,* ed. H. Shanks (Washington, D.C.: Biblical Archaeology Society; Englewood Cliffs, N.J.: Prentice-Hall, 1988), 85–108; G. Ahlström, *The History of Ancient Palestine from the Palaeolithic Period to Alexander's Conquest,* JSOTSup 146 (Sheffield: JSOT Press, 1993), 501–42.

3. See S. L. Dyson, "From New to New Age Archaeology: Archaeological Theory and Classical Archaeology—A 1990s Perspective," *AJA* 97 (1993): 195–206; S. Bunimovitz, "How Mute Stones Speak: Interpreting What We Dig Up," *BAR* 21.2 (1995): 58–67, 97; and the essay by C. Carter in the present volume, chap. 15.

4. See the survey of V. P. Long, *The Art of Biblical History,* Foundations of Contemporary Interpretation 5 (Grand Rapids: Zondervan, 1993), and his essay in the present volume, chap. 6.

sense of what ancient Israelite writers were claiming or, just as importantly, not claiming in composing their works. But, in so doing, recent studies have underscored that history writing is a form of literature.[5] As examples of ancient history writing, Samuel–Kings and Chronicles are secondary witnesses to historical events. Many advocates of the new literary approach refrain from discussing the historical reliability of the biblical books they study. Indeed, some are very careful to distinguish their work from that of historical reconstruction.[6] Nevertheless, one effect of the focus on histories as works of art has been to distance these narratives from the external events to which they refer.[7]

A development largely unrelated to the rise of the new literary criticism has been the growing tendency in traditional historical-critical circles to date more books (or parts thereof) to the exilic and postexilic ages. Three decades ago many scholars interpreted the narrative units they isolated within Samuel—the ark narrative (1 Sam. 4:1b–7:1; 2 Sam. 6),[8] the history of David's rise (1 Sam. 16:14–2 Sam. 5),[9] and the succession narrative (2 Sam. 9–20; 1 Kings 1–2)[10]—as documents dating to the time of the united monarchy. The succession narrative, in particular, has been viewed as one of the world's first great works of history, an insightful and nuanced portrayal of court politics written soon after the events it depicts, perhaps during the reign of Solomon.[11] Other scholars have come to question this dominant interpretation, viewing

5. The importance of this development has also been recently emphasized by I. Provan, "Ideologies, Literary and Critical: Reflections on Recent Writing on the History of Israel," *JBL* 114 (1995): 585–606.

6. M. Sternberg, *The Poetics of Biblical Narrative*, ILBS (Bloomington: Indiana University Press, 1985), 24–26; D. M. Howard, *An Introduction to the Old Testament Historical Books* (Chicago: Moody, 1993), 23–58; Long, *Art of Biblical History*, 58–87.

7. Some literary studies do, of course, question the characterization of certain narratives as historical. Note, e.g., the nomenclature "prose fiction," used by R. Alter, *The Art of Biblical Narrative* (New York: Basic Books, 1981), 23–26.

8. E.g., P. D. Miller Jr. and J. J. M. Roberts, *The Hand of the Lord: A Reassessment of the "Ark Narrative" of 1 Samuel* (Baltimore: Johns Hopkins University Press, 1977); P. K. McCarter, *I Samuel*, AB 8 (Garden City, N.Y.: Doubleday, 1980), 23–26.

9. McCarter, *I Samuel*, 27–30, provides references.

10. Also called the court history of David; see L. Rost, *The Succession to the Throne of David*, trans. M. D. Rutler and D. M. Gunn (Sheffield: Almond, 1982), 65–114; Noth, *History*, 205; P. K. McCarter, "Plots, True or False: The Succession Narrative as Court Apologetic," *Int* 35 (1981): 355–67; T. Ishida, "'Solomon Who Is Greater Than David': Solomon's Succession in 1 Kings I–II in the Light of the Inscription of Kilamuwa, King of YʾDY-Śamʾal," in *Congress Volume: Salamanca, 1983*, ed. J. A. Emerton, VTSup 36 (Leiden: Brill, 1985), 145–53.

11. G. von Rad, "The Beginnings of Historical Writing in Ancient Israel," in *The Problem of the Hexateuch and Other Essays*, trans. E. W. Trueman Dicken (New York: McGraw-Hill, 1966), 205–21; B. Halpern, *The First Historians: The Hebrew Bible and History* (San Francisco: Harper & Row, 1988).

these narratives as products of the late preexilic age, the exile, or even the postexilic period.[12] Revisionist treatments have not gone unchallenged,[13] but the earlier consensus about the dating of materials in Samuel no longer exists.

To take a second example, many scholars have taken the history of the northern monarchy in 1 Kings 11 through 2 Kings 17 to contain a great deal of useful information about preexilic conditions, even though the final edition of Kings was acknowledged to stem from the exile (2 Kings 25:27–30).[14] Others have questioned this assessment and date the primary edition of the Deuteronomistic History to the postexilic age.[15] The shift in perspective is apparent in the recently published two-volume history of Israelite religion by Rainer Albertz, which devotes more space to the exile and the postexilic period than it does to the preexilic period.[16] Reflecting recent trends, Albertz dates much of the Pentateuch and the Former Prophets to the exilic and postexilic periods. The coverage given to later periods reflects, therefore, as much a shift in dates assigned to legal and historical materials in the Bible as it does a renewed appreciation of the literature traditionally attributed to the postexilic era.

The reevaluation and redating of the biblical evidence has consequences for historical reconstruction. The later the work, the greater the distance between the writer and the events she or he depicts. Chro-

---

12. The succession narrative can serve as an example; see E. Würthwein, *Die Erzählung von der Thronfolge Davids—theologische oder politische Geschichtsschreibung?* ThStud 115 (Zurich: Theologischer Verlag, 1974); F. Langlamet, "Pour ou contre Salomon? La rédaction prosalomonienne de I Rois, I–II," *RB* 83 (1976): 321–79, 481–528; J. Van Seters, *In Search of History* (New Haven: Yale University Press, 1983), 277–91; J. A. Soggin, "Prolegomena on the Approach to Historical Texts in the Hebrew Bible and the Ancient Near East," in *Avraham Malamat Volume*, ed. S. Aḥituv and B. A. Levine, *EI* 24 (Jerusalem: Israel Exploration Society, 1993), 212–15.

13. See the essays by R. P. Gordon, "In Search of David: The David Tradition in Recent Study," 285–98; and A. Millard, "Story, History, and Theology," 37–64, both of which appear in *Faith, Tradition, and History: Old Testament Historiography in Its Near Eastern Context*, ed. A. Millard, J. Hoffmeier, and D. W. Baker (Winona Lake, Ind.: Eisenbrauns, 1994). Also relevant is the study of B. Halpern, "The Construction of the Davidic State: An Exercise in Historiography," in *The Origins of the Ancient Israelite States*, ed. V. Fritz and P. R. Davies, JSOTSup 228 (Sheffield: Sheffield Academic Press, 1996), 44–75.

14. For references, see G. N. Knoppers, *Two Nations under God: The Deuteronomistic History of Solomon and the Dual Monarchies*, vol. 1, *The Reign of Solomon and the Rise of Jeroboam*, HSM 52 (Atlanta: Scholars Press, 1993), 17–56.

15. So, e.g., A. G. Auld, *Kings without Privilege: David and Moses in the Story of the Bible's Kings* (Edinburgh: Clark, 1993).

16. R. Albertz, *A History of Israelite Religion in the Old Testament Period*, vol. 1, *From the Beginnings to the End of the Monarchy;* vol. 2, *From the Exile to the Maccabees*, trans. J. Bowden, OTL (Louisville: Westminster/John Knox, 1994).

nological distance need not entail that a later writer will be less accurate than an earlier writer. Otherwise, all modern historiography dealing with the ancient past—separated by millennia from its subject matter—would be hopeless. The notion that an author close to the events inevitably writes a history superior to that of an author writing centuries later reflects some naive assumptions about the nature of history writing. Nevertheless, in biblical criticism chronological distance is commonly seen as an indication of unreliability.[17] Adopting the view that a literary work is late usually involves casting aspersions on its historical veracity.[18] Hence, even though new applications of historical-critical research are quite different from various incarnations of the new literary criticism, they have had a similar effect in casting doubt on whether biblical texts can be used as reliable sources for historical research.

After this survey of reasons for the present preoccupation with archaeology as well as recent developments in historical-critical study, it may be appropriate to offer some comments. The disciplines of archaeology and epigraphy have added an invaluable dimension to the study of the past that was barely available a century ago. Nevertheless, there are drawbacks in predicating history solely upon these disciplines, because these scholarly pursuits have their own problems and limitations.[19] Archaeology may provide context and a sense of process by illumining broad eras within Israelite and Judahite history, but excavations rarely confirm or discredit discrete events. Nor have archaeologists attained such technical sophistication that ceramic assemblages can be dated to a particular generation. In dealing with excavated sites, archaeologists can differ in their presuppositions, questions, methods, dating of strata, and understanding of material finds. Promoting an exclusively archaeological approach to guarantee an objective, "scientific" approach to the recovery of the past is misguided and belied by the profound divergence in assumptions, methods, and interpretations among the archaeologists themselves. My argument is not that archaeology should be defined by biblical studies but

---

17. In this respect, the position of G. Ahlström is unusual. He holds to a postexilic date for Samuel–Kings, yet draws heavily on these works to write extremely detailed accounts of the careers of Saul, David, and Solomon (*History*, 429–542).

18. Witness the way some scholars have treated Chronicles. The Chronicler's History presents many of its own historiographic challenges, but its testimony should not be summarily dismissed. See S. Japhet, "The Historical Reliability of Chronicles," *JSOT* 33 (1985): 83–107; G. N. Knoppers, "History and Historiography: The Royal Reforms," in *The Chronicler as Historian*, ed. M. P. Graham, K. G. Hoglund, and S. L. McKenzie, JSOT-Sup 238 (Sheffield: JSOT Press, 1997), 178–203.

19. A point emphasized by E. Yamauchi, "The Current State of Old Testament Historiography," in *Faith, Tradition, and History*, ed. Millard et al., 1–36.

that an active dialogue should exist between them.[20] Comparing biblical claims with material evidence is admittedly a complicated matter. Sophistication is needed in relating material remains to literary evidence, but the two should be compared.

If the exclusive preference for archaeology in some recent treatments of Israelite history is imbalanced, the dismissal of practically all the biblical evidence as both late and unreliable is equally unwarranted. To be sure, absolute certainty about the dates of composition for the various writings that make up the Hebrew Scriptures is impossible. Aside from the fragmentary pendant discovered a few years ago bearing a text similar to Numbers 6:24–26, our earliest copies of biblical texts are the Dead Sea Scrolls and the Septuagint.[21] Nevertheless, what is the likelihood that the diverse poems, traditions, literary complexes, and books that make up the Old Testament can all be attributed to the postexilic period, or for that matter, to any one period? Such a stance evinces a strange kind of positivism, an auspicious confidence that diverse, complex texts are all late and have no value for historical reconstruction. Aside from the formidable problem of language (the distinctive traits of Late Biblical Hebrew), it seems improbable that much of the Pentateuch, the Former Prophets, the Latter Prophets, the Psalms, the wisdom literature, and, of course, the rest of the Writings all stemmed from postexilic Jerusalem. As a scholar who works with Persian period materials, I am happy to see more attention given to the postexilic era, but this attention must be sustained, giving close study to the question of *Sitz im Leben*. One needs to demonstrate how Yehud (postexilic Judah) produced all of the Hebrew Scriptures.[22] The Persian period must function as more than a dumping ground for texts scholars do not think were written during the monarchy. In short, the various biblical writings may have achieved their final and definitive form in the postexilic period, but it seems implausible that the Persian age witnessed the very composition of all these books.[23]

Arguments for a diversity of preexilic, exilic, and postexilic dates for biblical historical writings best fit the complexity of the evidence. To

---

20. See also W. G. Dever, "Archaeology, Texts, and History-Writing: Toward an Epistemology," in *Uncovering Ancient Stones: Essays in Memory of H. Neil Richardson,* ed. L. M. Hopfe (Winona Lake, Ind.: Eisenbrauns, 1994), 105–17.

21. G. Barkay observes that the relationship between the text on the pendant and its biblical counterpart is complex: "The Priestly Benediction on Silver Plaques from Ketef Hinnom in Jerusalem," *Tel Aviv* 19 (1992): 139–92.

22. To my knowledge, only P. R. Davies has seriously attempted to do this: *In Search of "Ancient Israel,"* JSOTSup 148 (Sheffield: JSOT Press, 1992), 49–112.

23. Contra Thompson, *Early History,* 415–23. See further the essay by H. G. M. Williamson in the present volume, chap. 9.

begin with, there is a diachronic dimension to the relationship among certain biblical texts that belies the thesis that they were all written by different writers working in the same period. Space limitations do not permit a discussion of all the relevant historical writings, but returning to the texts mentioned above, I can give two examples. The copious consideration given to the ark and its role within Israelite society in 1 and 2 Samuel contrasts with the subordination of the ark to the temple in the Deuteronomistic presentation of the temple's dedication (1 Kings 8).[24] Comparison with an incontestably postexilic work, the Chronicler's History, also bears consideration. The Chronicler carefully draws from a variety of earlier biblical writings, including Samuel and Kings, to forge a highly stylized presentation of how the Jerusalem temple fulfills all previous Israelite cultic institutions.[25] Even more so for the Chronicler than for the Deuteronomist, the ark has become one of a number of cultic symbols that are only of penultimate interest to the primary interest in the temple.[26] Comparison of the three narratives dealing with the ark in Samuel, Kings, and Chronicles suggests significant chronological distance among them.

There are also positive arguments to be made for a preexilic dating of the Deuteronomistic coverage of the northern kingdom. As Baruch Halpern has observed with reference to the names and dates supplied by extrabiblical inscriptions, the Deuteronomistic History accurately records the names and relative dates of a variety of Israelite, Judahite, and foreign kings.[27] Hence, whatever dates one assigns to the material in Kings, its value for historical reconstruction should be clear. In addition to the external controls afforded by epigraphy, one can also appeal to internal evidence within the Deuteronomistic History. The extraordinary detail the Deuteronomist devotes to the emergence, history, and

---

24. S. E. Balentine, *Prayer in the Hebrew Bible: The Drama of Divine-Human Dialogue*, OBT (Minneapolis: Fortress, 1993), 80–88; G. N. Knoppers, "Prayer and Propaganda: The Dedication of Solomon's Temple and the Deuteronomist's Program," *CBQ* 57 (1995): 229–54.

25. R. L. Braun, "Solomon, the Chosen Temple Builder: The Significance of 1 Chronicles, 22, 28, and 29 for the Theology of Chronicles," *JBL* 95 (1976): 581–90; H. G. M. Williamson, "The Accession of Solomon in the Books of Chronicles," *VT* 26 (1976): 351–61; P. Welten, "Lade—Tempel—Jerusalem: Zur Theologie der Chronikbücher," in *Textgemäß: Aufsätze und Beiträge zur Hermeneutik des Alten Testaments: Festschrift für Ernst Würthwein*, ed. A. Gunneweg and O. Kaiser (Göttingen: Vandenhoeck & Ruprecht, 1979), 169–83.

26. J. W. Wright, "The Legacy of David in Chronicles: The Narrative Function of 1 Chronicles 23–27," *JBL* 110 (1991): 229–42.

27. B. Halpern, "Erasing History—The Minimalist Assault on Ancient Israel," *BibRev* 11.6 (1995): 26–35, 47. See also idem, "The State of Israelite History," in *Reconsidering Ancient Israel and Judah: Recent Studies in the Deuteronomistic History*, ed. G. N. Knoppers and J. G. McConville, SBTS 8 (Winona Lake, Ind.: Eisenbrauns, forthcoming).

decline of the northern monarchy seems to address predominately pre-exilic issues.[28] Conversely, the arguments that all of this material is postexilic polemic, written either against the Samarians or as an object lesson to Jews in Yehud, are not persuasive.[29] The anti-Samarian argument does not explain why the Deuteronomist blames a Judean (Solomon) for the division, commends the rise of a northerner (Jeroboam) to power, and champions the formation of an independent Israelite state.[30] Comparison with the work of a postexilic writer—the Chronicler—is again pertinent. The Chronicler views both Jeroboam's cult and kingdom as seditious from their inception.[31] The Chronicler's historiographic judgment is of considerable consequence, because it leads him to omit the independent history of the northern kingdom except when it affects Judah. The Chronicler's stance makes sense in a postexilic context but it contrasts with the concerns of the preexilic (Josianic) Deuteronomist, who likely writes when the impact of the Assyrian campaigns against Israel and Judah were still sharply felt.[32] As for the narratives about the northern realm in Kings functioning as a diatribe to postexilic Jews, one has to ask why a postexilic Deuteronomist would write so extensively about the northern kingdom and so little about the southern kingdom. An object lesson might warrant a few stories, but it seems implausible that a postexilic Judean writer would add an immense amount of material about the long-defunct northern monarchy—approximately three quarters of the coverage within 1 Kings 12–2 Kings 17—for such a purpose.

To summarize, there are both positive and negative arguments in favor of positing a variety of dates for the composition of the historical books within the Hebrew Scriptures. Moreover, even if one rejects an early date for the composition of the primary edition of the Deuteronomistic History in favor of an exilic or even postexilic date, the chro-

---

28. G. N. Knoppers, *Two Nations under God: The Deuteronomistic History of Solomon and the Dual Monarchies*, vol. 2, *The Reign of Jeroboam, the Fall of Israel, and the Reign of Josiah*, HSM 53 (Atlanta: Scholars Press, 1994), 229–54.

29. See, respectively, Davies, *In Search of "Ancient Israel"*; Auld, *Kings without Privilege*, 172.

30. See 1 Kings 11:1–14:20; LXX 3 Rgns. 12:24a–z; and Knoppers, *Two Nations*, 1:135–223; 2:13–120.

31. G. N. Knoppers, "Rehoboam in Chronicles: Villain or Victim?" *JBL* 109 (1990): 423–40; idem, "'Battling against Yahweh': Israel's War against Judah in 2 Chron. 13:2–20," *RB* 100 (1993): 511–32. For a different view, see H. G. M. Williamson, *Israel in the Books of Chronicles* (Cambridge: Cambridge University Press, 1977), 110–18.

32. B. Halpern, "Jerusalem and the Lineages in the Seventh Century B.C.E.: Kingship and the Rise of Individual Moral Liability," in *Law and Ideology in Monarchic Israel*, ed. B. Halpern and D. W. Hobson, JSOTSup 124 (Sheffield: JSOT Press, 1991), 11–107; Knoppers, *Two Nations*, 2:112–20.

nological distance between the composition of this work and the events it depicts does not constitute sufficient grounds to dismiss its value for history. Advances in archaeology and epigraphy are welcome. But the Deuteronomistic History remains indispensable for historical reconstruction.

The Debate about the United Monarchy

Three decades ago scholars viewed the united monarchy as one of the most secure periods for historical reconstruction. This rare scholarly consensus was remarkable. Even though there were keen debates about the ancestral age and the Mosaic age, virtually all modern historians wrote histories of ancient Israel that included, if not commenced with, the monarchy of David and Solomon.[33] But this near unanimity of opinion has disappeared. The issue is not simply a divergence of opinion between so-called maximalists, who gave considerable credence to biblical descriptions of the united monarchy, and so-called minimalists, who were much more hesitant to do so. There are now scholars who think that all traditional theories of the united kingdom are obsolete. According to revisionist thinkers, Saul, David, and Solomon are all fictional, not historical, characters.[34] Indeed, the united monarchy itself is allegedly a construct of scribes writing during the Persian or Hellenistic periods.[35] The reasons for the scholarly reevaluation are many, but three factors seem to stand out: new readings of the material evidence, the reinterpretation of pertinent literary evidence, and the effect of new socioeconomic studies.[36] To grasp the force of revisionist treatments, it will be useful to sketch the old consensus.

Past studies associated the kingdom of David, and especially that of Solomon, with a number of specific changes in the material culture of

33. In the earlier work of J. A. Soggin, the united monarchy represented the threshold from the past as fable to the past as history: "The Davidic-Solomonic Kingdom," in *Israelite and Judaean History*, ed. Miller and Hayes, 332–80; idem, *A History of Israel: From the Beginnings to the Bar Kochba Revolt, A.D. 135*, trans. J. Bowden (London: SCM, 1984), 41–85 (published in the U.S. as *A History of Ancient Israel* [Philadelphia: Westminster, 1984]).

34. Davies, *In Search of "Ancient Israel,"* 16–48, 69; M. M. Gelinas, "United Monarchy—Divided Monarchy: Fact or Fiction?" in *The Pitcher Is Broken: Memorial Essays for Gösta W. Ahlström*, ed. S. W. Holloway and L. Handy, JSOTSup 190 (Sheffield: Sheffield Academic Press, 1995), 227–37; Thompson, *Early History*, 306–7, 415–23; T. L. Bolin, "When the End Is the Beginning," *SJOT* 10 (1996): 3–15; N. P. Lemche, "From Patronage Society to Patronage Society," in *Origins of the Ancient Israelite States*, 106–20.

35. They do not fit the nomenclature "minimalist," because these scholars do not think there is anything to minimize.

36. What follows is only a summary. For further details and references, see G. N. Knoppers, "Vanishing Solomon: The Disappearance of the United Monarchy from Recent Histories of Ancient Israel," *JBL* 116 (1997): 19–44.

ancient Canaan. Historians also made a series of correlations between the account of Solomon's reign in Kings and international developments in the ancient Near East. I begin with the connections made between biblical and archaeological evidence. Scholars have associated Solomon's building activities, which take up no small part of his reign,[37] with the rise of monumental architecture in the tenth century B.C.[38] Excavations at three of the cities rebuilt by Solomon—Hazor, Megiddo, and Gezer (1 Kings 9:15–17)—revealed that the defense systems at these sites seemed to exhibit nearly identical fortification patterns. Yigael Yadin influentially claimed that each of these towns was surrounded by casemate walls and included a six-chambered gateway of similar measurements.[39] Scholars also pointed to a general pattern of urbanization in the Iron Age—the rebuilding and expansion of old towns and the establishment of new ones.[40] Indeed, the construction of numerous walled cities, public buildings, and fortifications is said to be a characteristic feature of Iron II.[41] The variety and layout of different types of towns—administrative-military centers, cities with both residential and administrative or military quarters, and capitals—has also been deemed significant, suggesting some degree of urban planning.[42] Scholars theorized that a state was responsible for both the (re)construction of the cities and the presence of a variety of public

37. 1 Kings 5:27–7:51; 9:15–19, 24; 11:27; cf. 2 Chron. 3:1–17; 4:1–5:1; 8:1, 4–6, 11. In 1 Chron. 22–29 David devotes much of the latter part of his reign to preparing for Solomon's construction of the temple.

38. E.g., W. G. Dever, "Monumental Architecture in Ancient Israel in the Period of the United Monarchy," in *Studies in the Period of David and Solomon*, ed. T. Ishida (Winona Lake, Ind.: Eisenbrauns, 1982), 269–306; idem, "Archaeology and 'the Age of Solomon': A Case Study in Archaeology and Historiography," in *The Age of Solomon: Scholarship at the Turn of the Millennium*, ed. L. K. Handy, SHANE 11 (Leiden: Brill, 1997), 217–51; V. Fritz, "Salomo," *MDOG* 117 (1985): 47–67; G. Barkay, "The Iron Age II–III," in *The Archaeology of Ancient Israel*, ed. A. Ben-Tor, trans. R. Greenberg (New Haven: Yale University Press, 1992), 305.

39. Y. Yadin, *Hazor: The Head of All Those Kingdoms (Joshua 11:10)*, Schweich Lectures, 1970 (London: Oxford University Press, 1972), 135–64.

40. J. M. Miller and J. H. Hayes, *A History of Ancient Israel and Judah* (Philadelphia: Westminster, 1986), 209–11; A. Mazar, *Archaeology of the Land of the Bible 10,000–586 B.C.E.*, ABRL (New York: Doubleday, 1990), 387–89; V. Fritz, *The City in Ancient Israel*, Biblical Seminar 29 (Sheffield: Sheffield Academic Press, 1995), 76–77; idem, "Monarchy and Re-urbanization: A New Look at Solomon's Kingdom," in *Origins of the Ancient Israelite States*, 187–95.

41. E.g., V. Fritz, *An Introduction to Biblical Archaeology*, JSOTSup 172 (Sheffield: JSOT Press, 1994), 148–49; R. Reich, "Palaces and Residencies in the Iron Age," in *The Architecture of Ancient Israel: From the Prehistoric to the Persian Periods*, ed. A. Kempinski and R. Reich (Jerusalem: Israel Exploration Society, 1992), 202–22.

42. Y. Shiloh, "Elements in the Development of Town Planning in the Israelite City," *IEJ* 28 (1978): 36–51; Z. Herzog, "Administrative Structures in the Iron Age," in *Architecture of Ancient Israel*, 223–30.

buildings within them.[43] Other evidence cited for the presence of a state included the establishment of new fortresses[44] and a marked increase in population.[45]

If the descriptions of Solomon's building activity in Kings seemed to correspond to the evidence provided by the material remains, the same can be said for descriptions of Solomon's diplomatic relations and epigraphic remains from this period. One such correlation was, of course, the possibility of a strong regional Davidic-Solomonic state itself. The decline of major states, such as Egypt, Assyria, and Hatti, made it possible for minor states to emerge or reassert themselves. Another correlation made by scholars involves Israelite-Egyptian relations.[46] For example, Kenneth Kitchen attempted to corroborate the description of Solomon's marriage to a daughter of the pharaoh, demonstrating that such diplomatic marriages between members of the Egyptian royal family and the royal families of other states were more common than scholars had previously recognized.[47] Kitchen argued that the Egyptian king (probably Siamun) arranged this diplomatic marriage to pursue common martial and commercial interests over against the Philistines.[48]

During the past decade the critical consensus about the united kingdom has come apart. This significant turnabout has been propelled by a reconsideration of the literary and the archaeological evidence as well as by the application of new social scientific methods. How similar the "Solomonic" six-chambered gates really are is now in dispute.[49] The discovery of six-chamber gates at Ashdod and Lachish, both of which date to the end of the tenth century, has given rise to doubts about the uniqueness of the state architecture found at Megiddo, Hazor, and Gezer.[50] Some scholars have come to question the tenth-century date of

43. Y. Aharoni, *The Archaeology of the Land of Israel*, ed. M. Aharoni, trans. A. F. Rainey (Philadelphia: Westminster, 1982), 210ff.; W. G. Dever, "Solomon and the Assyrian Period 'Palaces' at Gezer," *IEJ* 35 (1985): 217–30; Fritz, *City*, 117–20; Z. Herzog, "Settlement and Fortification," in *Architecture of Ancient Israel*, 250–61.

44. A. Mazar, "Iron Age Fortresses in the Judaean Hills," *PEQ* 114 (1982): 87–109; idem, *Archaeology*, 390–96; Ahlström, *History*, 524–26; Fritz, *City*, 77–93. These included a network of so-called fortresses in the Negev; see R. Cohen, "The Iron Age Fortresses in the Central Negev," *BASOR* 236 (1980): 61–79.

45. Bright, *History*, 217.

46. 1 Kings 3:1; 5:1, 10; 8:51, 53, 65; 9:16, 24; 10:26–29; 11:1, 17–22, 40.

47. 1 Kings 3:1; 7:8; 9:16, 24; 11:1. K. A. Kitchen, *The Third Intermediate Period in Egypt (1100–650 B.C.)* (Warminster: Aris & Phillips, 1973), 280–83; idem, "Egypt and East Africa," in *Age of Solomon*, 106–26.

48. Kitchen, *Third Intermediate Period*, 8, 280–82.

49. D. Milson, "The Design of the Royal Gates at Megiddo, Hazor, and Gezer," *ZDPV* 102 (1986): 87–92; Herzog, "Settlement and Fortification," 265–69.

50. Holladay, "Kingdoms of Israel and Judah," 384–85; Herzog, "Settlement and Fortification," 265–69.

relevant fortifications at Gezer, Hazor, and Megiddo.[51] This has led to a vigorous debate, because other scholars have challenged the pottery analysis upon which such redating is partially based.[52] The contemporary excavators of Gezer and Hazor have sought to confirm the earlier tenth-century dates.[53] Nevertheless, the debate continues.[54]

The debates about material evidence have included so-called fortresses in the Negev, the date, identity, and function of which have all been thrown into question. Israel Finkelstein thinks that the distribution and construction of these sites indicates a "sedentarization" of inland desert people caused by economic prosperity.[55] But Ze'ev Meshel posits a coexistence of external (royal) and local (nomadic) initiatives to explain the emergence of these sites.[56] The issue is unsettled. The disagreement is, however, itself telling. Scholars can agree on the importance of certain sites, but come to very different conclusions about what this means for Israelite history.

The third factor complicating the study of the united monarchy is the application of social scientific methodology. For example, recent archaeological surveys point to general population growth in the Iron Age, but depict the eighth century, not the tenth, as the apex of this

51. A. Kempinski, *Megiddo: A City-State and Royal Centre in North Israel*, Materilien zur allgemeinen und vergleichen Archäologie 40 (Munich: Beck, 1989), 98; G. J. Wightman, "The Myth of Solomon," *BASOR* 277–78 (1990): 5–22; D. Ussishkin, "Gate 1567 at Megiddo and the Seal of Shema, Servant of Jeroboam," in *Scripture and Other Artifacts: Essays on the Bible and Archaeology in Honor of Philip J. King*, ed. M. D. Coogan et al. (Louisville: Westminster/John Knox, 1994), 410–28; I. Finkelstein, "On Archaeological Methods and Historical Considerations: Iron Age II and Samaria," *BASOR* 277–78 (1990): 109–19; and the response by W. G. Dever, "On Myths and Methods," *BASOR* 277–78 (1990): 121–30.

52. L. E. Stager, "Shemer's Estate," *BASOR* 277–78 (1990): 93–107; R. Tappy, *The Archaeology of Israelite Samaria*, vol. 1, *Early Iron Age through the Ninth Century B.C.E.*, HSS 44 (Atlanta: Scholars Press, 1992).

53. R. W. Younker, "A Preliminary Report of the 1990 Season at Tel Gezer: Excavations at the Outer Wall and the Solomonic Gateway (July 2–August 10, 1990)," *AUSS* 29 (1991): 19–60; W. G. Dever, "Further Evidence on the Date of the Outer Wall at Gezer," *Near East Archaeology Society Bulletin* 38 (1993): 39–52. According to A. Ben-Tor, recent excavations at Hazor have verified that the casemate wall and gate in question date to the tenth century: "Tel Hazor, 1994," *IEJ* 45 (1995): 65–68; idem, "Tel Hazor, 1995," *IEJ* 46 (1996): 65–68.

54. I. Finkelstein contends that the renewed excavations at Tel Gezer actually support his case that the fortification system in question dates to a later period: "Penelope's Shroud Unravelled: Iron II Date of Gezer's Outer Wall Established," *Tel Aviv* 21 (1994): 276–82. See also his "Archaeology of the United Monarchy: An Alternative View," *Levant* 28 (1996): 177–87; and the response by A. Mazar, "Iron Age Chronology: A Reply to I. Finkelstein," *Levant* 29 (1997): 157–67.

55. I. Finkelstein, *Living on the Fringe: The Architecture and History of the Negev, Sinai and Neighbouring Regions in the Bronze and Iron Age*, Monographs in Mediterranean Archaeology 6 (Sheffield: Sheffield Academic Press, 1995), 104–29.

56. Z. Meshel, "The Architecture of the Israelite Fortresses in the Negev," in *Architecture of Ancient Israel*, 294–301.

growth.[57] M. Broshi and I. Finkelstein estimate the population of western Palestine to be about 150,000 in 1000 B.C., but around 400,000 in 750 B.C.[58] The revised demographics have led to revisionist reconstructions of tenth-century history. Based on what they consider to be the sparse population of the Judean highlands in the tenth and ninth centuries, T. L. Thompson, E. A. Knauf, and M. M. Gelinas have questioned whether Judah could have had a state prior to the eighth or seventh century B.C.[59] In Thompson's view, Jerusalem became a city-state for only limited periods in the late eighth and mid-seventh centuries, after competing for centuries against other regional towns, such as Hebron, Lachish, and Gezer.[60] D. W. Jamieson-Drake doubts whether a small Jerusalem could have sustained the scribal bureaucracy necessary to produce a variety of major (biblical) texts prior to the eighth and seventh centuries.[61]

Revisionist reactions to the established consensus about the united monarchy have themselves been subjected to critique. In his recent study, J. S. Holladay emphasizes not only similarities between the material culture at various sites, such as Hazor, Megiddo, Lachish, and Gezer, but also the distribution of these sites and their importance for trade.[62] He argues that the construction of fortifications and public buildings at these strategic sites can be explained only as a concerted political action. Holladay also calls attention to the continuity in monumental material culture from the tenth century to the ninth century, an era in which the existence of an Israelite (northern) kingdom is not denied. In his view, both the similarities and the continuity buttress the case for the existence of a territorial state in the tenth century.[63]

A case can also be made against Thompson's model of regional but competing towns. Material evidence from sites in which public structures take up a large part of the tel raises the question of whether these were independent, self-sustaining residential towns. Indeed, Holladay

---

57. D. W. Jamieson-Drake, *Scribes and Schools in Monarchic Judah*, SWBAS 9, JSOT-Sup 109 (Sheffield: Almond, 1991), 48–80; I. Finkelstein, "Environmental Archaeology and Social History: Demographic and Economic Aspects of the Monarchic Period," in *Biblical Archaeology Today, 1990*, ed. A. Biran and J. Aviram (Jerusalem: Israel Exploration Society, 1993), 60–64.

58. M. Broshi and I. Finkelstein, "The Population of Palestine in Iron Age II," *BASOR* 287 (1992): 50–53.

59. Thompson, *Early History*, 312; E. A. Knauf, "King Solomon's Copper Supply," in *Phoenicia and the Bible*, ed. E. Lipiński, Studia Phoenicia 11, OLA 44 (Louvain: Department Oriëntalistiesk, 1991), 180; Gelinas, "United Monarchy," 230.

60. *Early History*, 290–92, 331–34.

61. *Scribes and Schools*, 76–80, 138–39.

62. Holladay, "Kingdoms of Israel and Judah," 368–98.

63. Ibid., 371–72.

argues that the different types of urban sites evince a transformation from a segmented society to a nation state.[64] Finally, the evidence provided by the recently discovered Tel Dan inscription has some relevance for the early monarchy. If the reading of *bytdwd* (line 9) as "house of David" is well founded, as most scholars believe, this text points to the historical existence of David as the founder of a dynasty.[65] But even if one does not accept the reading "house of David," the stela, along with the earlier ninth-century Mesha Stela, attests that states in ancient Palestine could control territories far beyond the confines of their own capitals.

The results of archaeological surveys are worthy of further discussion, because they are capable of different explanations. The results of these surface surveys caution against overextended claims about Israel's status in the tenth century, but they do not exclude Israel and Judah from having states until the ninth and eighth-seventh centuries, respectively. One should not confuse impoverishment of archaeological remains with impoverishment of culture. Comparative analysis raises questions whether historical conclusions drawn from archaeological surveys by revisionists are too extreme. As the Amarna Letters attest, Jerusalem was fully capable of producing documents already in the Late Bronze Age. Assuming that the population of Jerusalem did not decrease substantially during the early Iron Age, there is no good reason to believe that scribes under David and Solomon could not have written texts as well. To take a second example, population estimates of ancient Nuzi attribute some two thousand people to this city. But archaeological excavations have revealed some 6,500 texts as being written at various locations within this town. If one assumes, along with archaeologists, that the population of Jerusalem tripled or quadrupled by the late eighth century, this need not entail that tenth-century Jerusalem lacked the requisite resources to produce texts.[66] If scribes in Nuzi produced such a volume of texts, it is clearly conceivable that scribes in Iron II

---

64. Ibid., 372–78.

65. Another possible translation of *bytdwd* is "house of (the god) Dod." See A. Biran and J. Naveh, "An Aramaic Stele Fragment from Tel Dan," *IEJ* 43 (1993): 81–98; idem, "The Tel Dan Inscription: A New Fragment," *IEJ* 45 (1995): 1–18; E. A. Knauf, A. de Pury, and T. Römer, "**BaytDawīd* ou **BaytDōd?*" *BN* 72 (1994): 60–69; B. Halpern, "The Stela from Dan: Epigraphic and Historical Considerations," *BASOR* 296 (1994): 63–80.

66. Population estimates of eighth-century Jerusalem vary considerably: 7,500 in mid-century (Finkelstein, "Environmental Archaeology," 58); 15,000 in the late eighth century (A. Ofer, "Judah," *The Encyclopedia of Near Eastern Archaeology*, ed. E. M. Meyers et al. [New York: Oxford University Press, 1997], 253–57); an unspecified higher figure (Barkay, "Iron Age," 364–68). On the link between the Amarna Letters and Jerusalem, see now N. Naʾaman, "The Contribution of the Amarna Letters to the Debate on Jerusalem's Political Position in the 10th Century B.C.E.," *BASOR* 304 (1996): 17–27.

Jerusalem could have authored literature as well. In short, the reasoning that Jerusalem was too small in the tenth and ninth centuries to harbor scribes and produce texts is unconvincing.

A third consideration bears on the matter of scribes, urban centers, and the production of texts. The same surface surveys that point to relatively low population estimates for the tenth century B.C. also point to low figures for Persian period Yehud.[67] Yet this is precisely the time in which revisionist studies locate the creation of virtually all biblical texts. If the united monarchy never existed and Judah could not have produced any texts before the eighth century, the same would have to hold for sparsely populated Yehud. Finally, it bears noting that Broshi and Finkelstein cite the same surface surveys employed by Jamieson-Drake and Thompson to make the opposite point. They point to the remarkable consistency of population growth from the tenth through the mid-eighth century to argue that the establishment of a centralized state was a critical condition for significant population increase.[68] Thus, whereas some scholars have cited surface surveys to deny the early existence of Israelite and Judahite states, others have employed the same evidence to argue that such states were necessary to induce and sustain population growth and economic development.

As the previous discussion makes clear, studies of the united monarchy are in a state of flux. The Davidic-Solomonic kingdom has itself become a site of conflicting opinions. In light of demographic considerations, material remains, epigraphic testimony, and the complexity of the biblical evidence, there is a need to reconsider a range of issues. Perhaps current excavations underway at Hazor, Jezreel, Megiddo, and other sites will clarify some of the disputes. In any case, the evidence currently available does not warrant the disappearance of the united kingdom from histories of ancient Israel. Revisionist treatments have succeeded better in questioning certain aspects of the older scholarly consensus than they have in substantiating their own proposals. In my judgment, the pertinent issues are neither the existence of David and Solomon nor the existence of their realm, but the nature, organization, size, and clout of the state over which they presided. These issues merit further study.[69]

---

67. A. Ofer, "Judean Hills Survey," *NEAEHL* 3 (1993): 814–16; C. E. Carter, "The Province of Yehud in the Post-Exilic Period: Soundings in Site Distribution and Demography," in *Second Temple Studies*, vol. 2, *Temple and Community in the Persian Period*, ed. T. C. Eskenazi and K. H. Richards, JSOTSup 175 (Sheffield: JSOT Press, 1994), 106–45.

68. "Population of Palestine," 55.

69. Note the range of opinions expressed by A. Millard, "Texts and Archaeology: Weighing the Evidence: The Case for King Solomon," *PEQ* 123 (1991): 19–27; idem, "Solomon: Text and Archaeology," *PEQ* 123 (1991): 117–18; idem, "King Solomon in His

The Early Dual Monarchies

Like the united monarchy, the period of the early divided monarchy has been the subject of renewed debate. Three questions dominated earlier discussions: (1) Why did the united kingdom fail? (2) Why did Solomon's successor, Rehoboam, take such a rigid negotiating position with the northern leadership at the Shechem council (1 Kings 12:1–20)? and (3) Why did the Egyptian pharaoh Shishak (Shoshenq) invade Canaan in the early divided monarchy, considering that relations between Israel and Egypt had been quite favorable during the united monarchy?

The most commonly cited reason for the sudden collapse of the united kingdom has involved the origin and development of the Davidic-Solomonic monarchy. The united kingdom was an aberration, a centralized polity artificially imposed on fractious southern and northern tribes either by the force of David's personality (a personal union) or by the weight of foreign policy considerations (*Realunion*).[70] Such an arrangement could survive, even thrive, in good conditions. But a fragile alliance, whether originally driven by a charismatic personality or by stark political realities, was bound to fray and rupture if conditions deteriorated considerably. As historians have often observed, Solomon's pattern of fortifying strategic sites enabled him to consolidate control over trade and commerce within Israel, but it also exacerbated social tensions by placing great demands on his people.[71] The claim of Pocock about Greek history being an exercise in political ironies may also hold true for Israel in the tenth century: "an intelligible story of how men's actions produce results other than those they intended."[72] The very policy designed to protect and enhance Israel's position in the

---

Ancient Context," in *Age of Solomon*, 30–53; J. M. Miller, "The Old Testament and Archaeology," *BA* 50.1 (1987): 55–63; idem, "Solomon: International Potentate or Local King?" *PEQ* 123 (1991): 28–31; idem, "Separating the Solomon of History from the Solomon of Legend," in *Age of Solomon*, 1–24; J. A. Dearman, *Religion and Culture in Ancient Israel* (Peabody, Mass.: Hendrikson, 1992), 51–69; Knauf, "King Solomon's Copper Supply," 180–84; idem, "Le roi est mort, vive le roi! A Biblical Argument for the Historicity of Solomon," in *Age of Solomon*, 81–95; H. M. Niemann, *Herrschaft, Königtum und Staat: Skizzen zur soziokulturellen Entwicklung im monarchischen Israel*, FAT 6 (Tübingen: Mohr, 1993), 273–82.

70. For the former, see A. Alt, "The Formation of the Israelite State in Palestine," in *Essays on Old Testament History and Religion*, trans. R. A. Wilson (Garden City, N.Y.: Doubleday, 1968), 171–237. For the latter, see A. Malamat, "A Political Look at the Kingdom of David and Solomon and Its Relations with Egypt," in *Studies in the Period of David and Solomon*, 194.

71. Alt, "Formation," 236–37; Herrmann, *History of Israel*, 190; Ahlström, *History*, 505–9, 543–48.

72. J. G. A. Pocock, *Politics, Language, and Time: Essays on Political Thought and History* (New York: Atheneum, 1971; London: Methuen, 1972).

Levant rendered the monarchy vulnerable to internal dissension and revolt.

If earlier scholars viewed the artificiality of the united monarchy as a major reason for its fall, they blamed the incompetence or insensitivity of Rehoboam, Solomon's hapless successor, as hastening its demise. The unyielding negotiating stance Rehoboam took with respect to taxes at the assembly of Shechem ensured that the disgruntled northern representatives would reject the Davidic monarchy they had come to despise. Whether Rehoboam's negotiating stance was determined by his father's ill-conceived social policies, his political naïveté, or his ineptitude in following bad advice varies according to different ancient and modern interpretations.[73] But Rehoboam's plight may have been more complicated than having merely to manage northern dissatisfaction with his father's policies. A change in Egyptian fortunes and policies, from the reign of Psusennes II (959–945 B.C.) to the ascent of Shishak (= Shoshenq I; 945–924 B.C.), led to the resurgence of Egyptian power. This may help to explain why Rehoboam was reluctant to give in to the northern representatives at Shechem.[74] He may have thought that such concessions would only weaken his own position.

Scholars have pointed to the change in Egyptian regimes as the catalyst for a critical reversal in Israelite-Egyptian relations. Shishak's rise to power, for example, has been cited to illumine the flight of Jeroboam.[75] Whereas Siamun saw a strategic interest in an alignment with Israel, Shishak wished to reassert Egyptian hegemony in Canaan. Providing asylum to one of Solomon's foes could have contributed to the destabilization of Solomon's regime (1 Kings 11:26–40).[76] The most famous indication of the change in Egyptian-Israelite relations is, of course, the invasion of Shishak itself (1 Kings 14:25–26; 2 Chron. 12:1–12). In this case, comparisons can be made with evidence supplied by both epigraphic sources and archaeological excavations. The fragmentary stela at Megiddo, the fragmentary temple inscription at Karnak, and the destruction of various sites near the end of the tenth century have all been cited by modern scholars as being essentially congruent with the notice of Shishak's invasion in 1 Kings

73. 1 Kings 12:1–20; LXX 3 Rgns. 12:24a–z; 2 Chron. 10:1–17; 13:4–12. See J. C. Trebolle Barrera, *Salomòn y Jeroboàn: Historia de la recensión y redacción de I Reyes 2–12, 14,* Institución San Jeronimo 10 (Valencia: Investigación Bíblica, 1980), 82–241.

74. B. Halpern, "Sectionalism and Schism," *JBL* 93 (1974): 519–32.

75. Kitchen, *Third Intermediate Period*, 293–94.

76. N. P. Lemche, *A New History of Israelite Society,* Biblical Seminar 5 (Sheffield: Sheffield Academic Press, 1988), 142; D. B. Redford, *Egypt, Canaan, and Israel in Ancient Times* (Princeton: Princeton University Press, 1992), 312–15.

14:25–26.[77] Here, it seemed, was an impressive convergence of archaeological, epigraphic, and literary evidence.

But in recent years this convergence of evidence has been questioned by two new interpretations of Solomon's relations to Egypt and the circumstances surrounding Shishak's invasion. First, Giovanni Garbini contends that Shishak invaded Canaan during the reign of Solomon and not during the reign of Rehoboam.[78] The biblical authors located the Shishak invasion in the early history of Judah to avoid disparaging Solomon's exalted reputation. Second, Thompson cites the fragmentary Karnak inscription to deny the existence of both Israel and Judah in the tenth century.[79] Because this text mentions only individual sites and neither Judah nor Israel, it purportedly constitutes evidence against the existence of these states.

One can discern complementary trends at work in the theories of Garbini and Thompson. The biblical evidence is treated with considerable historical suspicion, and the interpretation given to the remaining evidence turns an older theory on its head. In the case of the Shishak campaign, one is left with contradictory assessments of the same archaeological and epigraphic remains. Ironically, the Shishak material still constitutes crucial evidence for the reconstruction of tenth-century history. But in one theory the Karnak relief corroborates 1 Kings 14:25–26, while in another theory the Karnak relief undermines it.

Are the new interpretations compelling? It does not appear so. The new theories exhibit, in my judgment, some major flaws. To begin with, Garbini's thesis that the author of Kings misled his readers by locating the Shishak campaign in Rehoboam's reign assumes that he knew otherwise. Whatever one makes of the epigraphic evidence, this reading of Kings carries little force. In his periodization of Solomon's reign (1 Kings 1–11) the Deuteronomist expends no small amount of energy sullying Solomon's reputation himself. The author castigates Solomon for constructing numerous high places, worshiping at these

---

77. M. Noth, "Die Shoschenkliste," *ZDPV* 61 (1938): 277–304; B. Mazar, "The Campaign of Pharaoh Shishak to Palestine," in *Volume du Congrès: Strasbourg, 1956*, VTSup 4 (Leiden: Brill, 1957), 57–66; S. Herrmann, "Operationen Pharao Schoschenks I. am östlichen Ephraim," *ZDPV* 80 (1964): 55–79; Y. Aharoni, *The Land of the Bible*, trans. and ed. A. F. Rainey, rev. ed. (Philadelphia: Westminster, 1979), 323–30; Kitchen, *Third Intermediate Period*, 293–300, 432–41; N. Naʾaman, "Israel, Edom, and Moab in the Tenth Century," *Tel Aviv* 19 (1992): 71–93; A. Mazar, *Archaeology*, 397–98. For a somewhat different view, see Redford, *Egypt, Canaan, and Israel*, 312–15.

78. G. Garbini, *History and Ideology in Ancient Israel*, trans. J. Bowden (London: SCM; New York: Crossroad, 1988), 30–32.

79. *Early History*, 306–7. Thompson's reconstruction has been followed by Davies (*In Search of "Ancient Israel*,*"* 42–73) and Gelinas ("United Monarchy," 230–33).

illicit sanctuaries, and worshiping other gods (11:1–13).[80] The Deuteronomist's careful presentation of Solomon's decline associates these sins with YHWH's inciting of Solomon's enemies and a series of revolts that weaken his kingdom (11:14–40).[81] The Deuteronomist is so concerned to censure Solomon's conduct that he, in fact, blames Solomon for a catastrophe that occurs after his death—the division. Surely, if the author believed that Shishak's invasion occurred during Solomon's reign, it would have fit beautifully into his typology of Solomon's decline. Given the Deuteronomist's trenchant criticism of Solomon, the very fact that he locates this event in the context of Rehoboam's reign is important, but for the opposite reason Garbini supposes. It reveals some historiographical restraint on the part of the biblical writer.

Concerning the Shishak evidence, Thompson's theory has encountered criticism from Diana Edelman. She claims that Thompson has adopted an uncritical reading of the Karnak relief, confusing a traditionally phrased, propagandistic assertion of Egyptian hegemony over Canaan with a straightforward litany of conquered sites.[82] In this view, the list of Shishak's conquests obfuscates the political realities of the lands affected by his invasion. The point that the Shishak relief should be subjected to as much critical scrutiny as the biblical text is well taken. Nevertheless, Edelman's rejoinder allows for but does not prove the existence of a united monarchy. The difference between the readings of Thompson and Edelman suggests that the Karnak relief by itself does not constitute decisive evidence for either case.

Perhaps one of the strongest arguments that can be made for the older interpretation is its explanatory power in addressing different kinds of evidence. It accounts for both the (re)construction of many sites and the destruction of some of them (e.g., Megiddo). Similarly, the continuity from tenth-century to ninth-century material culture in Israel and Judah comports with a contentious but essentially peaceful split between the northern and southern tribes. Finally, that Judah,

---

80. In the context of the Deuteronomistic History, the indictment is quite severe; see Knoppers, *Two Nations*, 1:135–59. The Deuteronomist mentions the influence of Solomon's foreign wives, but he places primary blame for Solomon's decline on Solomon himself. See S. J. D. Cohen, "Solomon and the Daughter of Pharaoh: Intermarriage, Conversion, and the Impurity of Women," *JANES* 16–17 (1984–85): 23–37; G. N. Knoppers, "Sex, Religion, and Politics: The Deuteronomist on Intermarriage," *HAR* 14 (1994): 121–41.

81. Some of these, the Deuteronomist concedes, began earlier in Solomon's reign (1 Kings 11:15, 21, 23, 25). See further Knoppers, *Two Nations*, 1:162–68.

82. D. V. Edelman, "Solomon's Adversaries Hadad, Rezon, and Jeroboam: A Trio of 'Bad Guy' Characters Illustrating the Theology of Immediate Retribution," in *Pitcher Is Broken*, 188.

with the possible exception of a few sites (e.g., Gezer, Beth-horon, Gibeon, Aijalon), was spared widespread destruction in Shishak's campaign resonates with the claim that Rehoboam delivered heavy tribute to Shishak (1 Kings 14:25–26).[83] To be sure, the older view is not without difficulties. It does not explain, for example, why the Chronicler attributes more destruction to Judahite cities than the Deuteronomist does (2 Chron. 12:2–4).[84] In spite of such problems, the older view still represents the most compelling explanation of the literary (biblical), archaeological, and epigraphic evidence.

The Impact of the Assyrian Campaigns

Intensive study of biblical texts, Near Eastern inscriptions, and archaeology often leads to a better sense of what distinguishes different eras in Israelite and Judahite history. In some instances (e.g., the united monarchy), scholars from different disciplines may disagree about the interpretation of critical evidence. In other instances, historians, epigraphers, or archaeologists may recognize the importance of a specific era before biblical scholars do. An example of the latter is the eighth-century history of Israel and Judah. In coming to terms with tumultuous developments in the eighth century, biblical studies has some catching up to do with archaeology and epigraphy. Indeed, the evidence for growth in the early eighth century renders the evidence for subsequent devastation and deportation all the more striking.[85]

Surface surveys reveal that the northern kingdom reached its peak in population by the mid-eighth century.[86] Israel's king during most of this time, Jeroboam II (793–753 b.c.), seems to have been adept politically. Ruling while Syria was in decline and Assyria in temporary decline, he succeeded in expanding the frontiers of his state. Jeroboam II apparently regained territory from Syria and controlled at least part of

---

83. Aharoni, *Land,* 323–26.

84. T. Willi thinks that the Chronicler has rewritten the Kings account of Shishak's campaign according to the model supplied by Sennacherib's invasion of Judah (*Die Chronik als Auslegung,* FRLANT 106 [Göttingen: Vandenhoeck & Ruprecht, 1972], 175).

85. D. Ussishkin's dating of material remains at Lachish (stratum III) was critical, because he dated this destruction layer to the time of Sennacherib's invasion (*The Conquest of Lachish by Sennacherib* [Tel Aviv: Tel Aviv University Press, 1982]). Based on the pottery assemblages associated with stratum III (late eighth century) and stratum II (early sixth century), the remains from other sites were restudied and redated. Some of the destruction layers formerly associated with the Babylonian campaigns have now been associated with the earlier Assyrian campaigns. For an overview, see Barkay, "Iron Age," 328–29.

86. Broshi and Finkelstein, "Population of Palestine," 48–51.

Transjordan.[87] Some historians believe that the size of his kingdom rivaled that of the earlier Omrides.[88]

The eighth century also began as a period of growth for Judah. Archaeological excavations and surveys disclose a large increase in the number of towns and fortifications in the Judean hill country.[89] Public works projects included walls, water systems, and fortifications.[90] The most famous of these public works is the Siloam tunnel, which Kings and Chronicles ascribe in different terms to Hezekiah.[91] The discovery of *lmlk* jar impressions, forty-four of which stem from the Jewish Quarter alone, testifies to significant royal involvement in the administration of Jerusalem and Judah.[92] To be sure, there is ongoing debate about the precise purpose of these jars.[93] But the two-winged sun and four-winged scarab are most likely royal emblems. Hence, the existence and diffusion of these impressions in the late eighth century, continuing to some extent in the early seventh century, bear witness to the influence of a central administrative or military organization.[94]

The impressive increase in the settlement of Judah included Jerusalem itself.[95] There is some debate whether Jerusalem's population in-

87. 2 Kings 14:23–29; Amos 6:12–14; Miller and Hayes, *History*, 307–9.

88. E.g., S. Horn, "The Divided Monarchy," in *Ancient Israel*, ed. Shanks, 127. On Israel's comparative might during the dynasty of Omri, see Barkay, "Iron Age," 319–23.

89. Y. Shiloh, "Judah and Jerusalem in the Eighth–Sixth Centuries B.C.E.," in *Recent Excavations in Israel: Studies in Iron Age Archaeology*, ed. S. Gitin and W. G. Dever, AASOR 49 (Winona Lake, Ind.: Eisenbrauns, 1989), 97–103.

90. A. Mazar, "Iron Age Fortresses," 87–109; Y. Shiloh, "Underground Water Systems in Eretz-Israel in the Iron Age," in *Archaeology and Biblical Interpretation: Essays in Memory of D. Glenn Rose*, ed. L. G. Perdue, L. E. Toombs, and G. L. Johnson (Atlanta: John Knox, 1987), 203–45; Jamieson-Drake, *Scribes and Schools*, 81–106; Barkay, "Iron Age," 332–34, 369.

91. 2 Kings 20:20; 2 Chron. 32:30. For the inscription commemorating the completion of this conduit, see *KAI*, no. 189.

92. J. Rosenbaum, "Hezekiah's Reform and Deuteronomistic Tradition," *HTR* 72 (1979): 23–44; Ahlström, *History*, 697–701; S. Japhet, *I and II Chronicles*, OTL (Louisville: Westminster/John Knox, 1993), 977–83; B. Halpern, "Sybil, or the Two Nations? Archaism, Alienation, and the Elite Redefinition of Traditional Culture in Judah in the 8th–7th Centuries B.C.E.," in *The Study of the Near East in the Twenty-First Century*, ed. J. S. Cooper and G. M. Schwartz (Winona Lake, Ind.: Eisenbrauns, 1996), 291–338.

93. N. Naʾaman, "Hezekiah's Fortified Cities and the *LMLK* Stamps," *BASOR* 261 (1986): 5–21; N. Avigad, *Discovering Jerusalem* (Nashville: Nelson, 1983), 43–44; A. Mazar, *Archaeology*, 455–57; Halpern, "Jerusalem," 19–34.

94. The strongest biblical evidence for such administrative reorganization and consolidation of power comes from the Chronicler's presentation of Judahite kings, including Hezekiah (2 Chron. 29–32). Aside from the mention of Hezekiah's water works in Jerusalem, there is no indication in Kings of noncultic reforms among eighth-century Judahite monarchs. See Knoppers, "History and Historiography," 189–202.

95. A. Mazar, *Archaeology*, 438–62; Halpern, "Jerusalem," 19–34; Jamieson-Drake, *Scribes and Schools*, 48–73; Ofer, "Judean Hills Survey," 814–15.

crease began in the eighth century or somewhat earlier in the ninth century.[96] In any case, one of the archaeological discoveries pointing to Jerusalem's expansion is the remains of a city wall, seven meters thick, which Avigad dated to the late eighth century.[97] The discovery of both this so-called Broad Wall and a variety of other structures and artifacts gives new credence to the view that the settlement of Jerusalem expanded to the Western Hill in the preexilic period. Kathleen Kenyon's excavations suggest that the expansion of Jerusalem continued on its eastern slopes in the late monarchy.[98]

It is against this background of growth, prosperity, and expansion in the kingdoms of Israel and Judah that one can best understand the devastating impact of the Assyrian western campaigns. One of these, the invasion of Tiglath-pileser III (734 B.C.), resulted in the annexation of much of Galilee and Gilead and reduced Israel to the status of a client kingdom. Costly for both Israel and Judah was the Syro-Ephraimite War, which left Israel weakened and Judah a vassal kingdom of Assyria.[99] The invasion of Shalmaneser V (723–722 B.C.) ended the kingdom of Israel altogether and is said to have involved the deportation of 27,290 of its citizens.[100]

Most damaging for Judah was the invasion of Sennacherib in 701 B.C., which profoundly affected its material and social life.[101] Sennacherib's campaign inflicted ruin on many of Judah's cities.[102] On this issue, his assertion that he decimated "46 of his [Hezekiah's] strong-walled cities, as well as the small cities in the environs, which were without number,"[103]

96. M. Broshi, "The Expansion of Jerusalem in the Reign of Hezekiah and Manasseh," *IEJ* 24 (1974): 21–26; Broshi and Finkelstein, "Population of Palestine," 51–54; cf. Barkay, "Iron Age," 364–68.

97. Isa. 22:9–11; Avigad, *Discovering Jerusalem*, 45–60; Y. Shiloh, "Jerusalem," *NEAEHL*, 2:705–8.

98. K. M. Kenyon, *Digging up Jerusalem* (New York: Praeger, 1974), 129–65.

99. 2 Kings 16; Isa. 7:1–13; 2 Chron. 28. B. Oded discusses the costs involved of receiving Assyrian aid (*damiqtu*, favor), even to a loyal protégé ("Ahaz's Appeal to Tiglath-Pileser III in the Context of the Assyrian Policy of Expansion," in *Biblical Archaeology Today, 1990*, 63–71).

100. *ANET*, 284; 2 Kings 17; 18:9–12. The degree to which Sargon II (721–705) was also involved in the invasion or deportation need not detain us; see Soggin, *History of Israel and Judah*, 233–36; B. Oded, *Mass Deportations and Deportees in the Neo-Assyrian Empire* (Wiesbaden: Ludwig Reichert, 1979); B. Becking, *The Fall of Samaria: An Historical and Archaeological Study*, SHANE 2 (Leiden: Brill, 1992). On the introduction of Assyrian material culture, see Barkay, "Iron Age," 351–53.

101. F. J. Gonçalves, *L'expédition de Sennachérib en Palestine dans la littérature hébraïque ancienne*, EBib, n.s., 7 (Paris: Lecoffre, 1986), 102–36; Miller and Hayes, *History*, 353–63.

102. Halpern, "Jerusalem," 34–49; Ahlström, *History*, 665–707.

103. D. D. Luckenbill, *The Annals of Sennacherib*, OIP 2 (Chicago: University of Chicago Press, 1924), 32–34.

comports with the claim of 2 Kings 18:13 that "Sennacherib, king of Assyria, came up against all of the fortified cities of Judah and captured them." The archaeological evidence points both to marked depopulation, through either devastation or deportation, and to systematic destruction of many Judahite towns and border fortresses.[104] A. Ofer's recent surface surveys suggest, for example, that Sennacherib killed or exiled most of the inhabitants of the Shephelah and about 50–70 percent of the inland residents.[105] Because of the devastation and depopulation, S. Stohlmann speaks of a "Judaean exile after 701 B.C.E."[106]

The history of Judahite expansion is an important topic in its own right, demonstrating, for example, that one does not have to look simply to the seventh century for evidence of Judahite state expansion. But, for the purposes of this discussion, two other points need to be stressed. First, it is still a commonplace in biblical studies to date biblical references to exile to some point after the Babylonian exile. Such a stance ignores the threat of exile in ancient Near Eastern treaties and presumes that the demise and exile of the northern kingdom failed to have a major impact on those who lived in the southern kingdom.[107] Even if one conceded, for the sake of argument, that both of these considerations were irrelevant, one would still be left with explaining the devastation, death, and dislocation caused by Sennacherib's invasion. One does not have to wait until the Babylonian exile for an event that triggered tremendous suffering, anguish, and upheaval in Judah. Given the crisis caused by the Assyrian campaigns, one need not posit the Babylonian exile as the occasion for the rise of radical approaches to the practice of Israelite religion, such as centralization, monotheism, and the elimination of all rival cults to the Jerusalem temple. The appearance of these tenets in legal, historical, and prophetic texts is best understood as a preexilic phenomenon.[108] If such beliefs were simply an exilic creation, this would not explain why people adopted them. It

104. On depopulation see Aharoni, *Archaeology*, 253–66; A. Mazar, *Archaeology*, 544–47; Halpern, "Jerusalem," 30–34. Sennacherib's deportation figure is incredibly high: 200,150 (Luckenbill, *Annals*, 33). On destruction see Aharoni, *Archaeology*, 253–69; M. Cogan and H. Tadmor, *II Kings*, AB 11 (New York: Doubleday, 1988), 223–51; A. Mazar, *Archaeology*, 416–40; Ahlström, *History*, 707–16.

105. Broshi and Finkelstein, "Population of Palestine," 55–56; Ofer, "Judah."

106. S. Stohlmann, "The Judaean Exile after 701 B.C.," in *Scripture in Context II: More Essays on the Comparative Method*, ed. W. W. Hallo, J. C. Moyer, and L. G. Perdue, PTMS 34 (Winona Lake, Ind.: Eisenbrauns, 1983), 147–75.

107. M. Weinfeld, *Deuteronomy and the Deuteronomic School* (Oxford: Clarendon, 1972), 129–33.

108. Many scholars have at least recognized this to be so in the case of Deuteronomy; see the various entries in *Das Deuteronomium: Entstehung, Gestalt und Botschaft*, ed. N. Lohfink, BETL 68 (Louvain: Leuven University Press, 1985).

seems more likely that to many people who survived the Babylonian exile, the events of 586 B.C. confirmed that earlier principles, however radical they appeared at the time, were on the mark.[109]

I have maintained that the impact of the Assyrian campaigns deserves more attention from scholars in biblical studies. But this impact should not be construed as simply negative. Although Israel fell
and Judah suffered tremendous devastation, Jerusalem survived the
Assyrian crisis. The endurance of Jerusalem and its Davidic king is a
major cause for rejoicing in the Deuteronomistic presentation of
Hezekiah's reign, which concentrates on the crisis created by Sennacherib's foray into Judah.[110] The emphasis on Hezekiah's continuing trust in YHWH is apparent negatively in the Assyrian taunts
against Hezekiah and his God (e.g., 2 Kings 18:30–35) and positively
in Hezekiah's prayers, which recall the prayers of David and Solomon
at other critical moments in the history of Jerusalem.[111] Considering
that by 701 B.C. the Jerusalem temple and the Davidic dynasty had already existed for centuries, it is not surprising that Judahite authors
discerned in the survival of Jerusalem a confirmation of the divine
promises to David and Jerusalem (19:34; 20:6). Following the failure
of other gods to deliver their peoples from the Assyrian onslaught,
YHWH's deliverance of Jerusalem established a decisive difference
between YHWH and "no-gods," the "human handiwork of wood and
stone" (19:18). The larger implications of this experience for historical
reconstruction should be clear. One need not look to the Babylonian
exile for a historical context in which theologies of YHWH's perpetual
commitment to David and Zion might first arise.[112] The preexilic period provides other, more compelling possibilities. In short, the eighth
and seventh centuries should be viewed as a pivotal era and, as such,
the matrix in which at least some of the biblical literature took
shape.[113]

109. Obviously, this verdict was not unanimous (Jer. 45:15–19).

110. 2 Kings 18:13–19:37. Some of the remaining materials (e.g., Hezekiah's illness in
2 Kings 20:1–11) have been edited with a view to the Assyrian invasion. See G. N. Knoppers, "There Was None Like Him: Incomparability in the Books of Kings," *CBQ* 54 (1992):
418–25.

111. 2 Sam. 7:18–29; 1 Kings 8:22–53; 2 Kings 19:15–19; 20:2–3. See further R. L.
Pratt, "Royal Prayer and the Chronicler's Program" (diss., Harvard Divinity School,
1987).

112. Contra T. Veijola, *Die ewige Dynastie: David und die Entstehung seiner Dynastie
nach der deuteronomistischen Darstellung,* Annalae Academiae Scientiarum Fennicae B
193 (Helsinki: Suomalainen Tiedeakatemia, 1975), 71–90.

113. Some scholars would locate the composition of some wisdom literature in this
era as well; see most recently J. Blenkinsopp, *Sage, Priest, Prophet: Religious and Intellectual Leadership in Ancient Israel* (Louisville: Westminster/John Knox, 1995), 32–37.

Interpreting the Babylonian Exile

If modern scholars have only recently begun to appreciate the importance of the eighth century for coming to grips with a formative development in the history of Judah, they have generally been consistent in recognizing the importance of the Babylonian exiles of 598/597 and 586 B.C. Following a period of gradual but impressive recovery in the Judean hills, the Judean desert, and the Negev during the seventh century, the upheaval caused by the Babylonians created a new crisis in Judah: the end of the Davidic kingdom, the destruction of the temple, the loss of livelihood for the priesthood, the razing of Jerusalem, the deportation of many people, and the death of others.[114]

There has also been surprising agreement about the causes of Judah's demise. Historians have portrayed Judah's leadership in the last quarter century of its existence as overwhelmed by international developments, either unable or unwilling to make the difficult choices that would be best for the long-term prospects of their people. More specifically, scholars have referred to the geopolitical changes resulting from the disintegration of the Assyrian Empire, ill-timed foreign policy shifts, the negative effects of factionalism within Judah, how Judah's last kings were vulnerable to the whims of Egypt and Babylon or victims of failed alliances, and how the Davidic state was "sucked into the maelstrom of international affairs."[115]

Where one sees a strong divergence of opinion is over neither the fact of the exile nor its underlying reasons, but paradoxically over the nature of the exile itself. Scholars disagree about what the Babylonian destructions and deportations involved. Three decades ago there were basically three positions. C. C. Torrey saw the exile as "a small and relatively insignificant affair" involving a relatively small number of nobles.[116] Jerusalem recovered quickly and was soon rebuilt. In Torrey's view, the accounts of the Babylonian captivity in Kings, Ezra, and Ezekiel are exaggerated, if not historically spurious.

The views of W. F. Albright may be taken as representative of a second position. Responding to Torrey, Albright stressed the havoc and

114. Miller and Hayes, *History*, 377–436; Finkelstein, "Environmental Archaeology," 58–64; Ahlström, *History*, 733–803.

115. See, respectively, A. Malamat, "The Last Years of the Kingdom of Judah," in *Archaeology and Biblical Interpretation*, ed. Perdue, Toombs, and Johnson, 287; Horn, "Divided Monarchy," 143–49; B. Oded, "Judah and the Exile" (trans. Y. Gitay), in *Israelite and Judaean History*, 472–73; Ahlström, *History*, 788–89; Soggin, *History of Israel and Judah*, 264; Miller and Hayes, *History*, 377.

116. C. C. Torrey, *Ezra Studies* (Chicago: University of Chicago Press, 1910; reprinted, New York: Ktav, 1970), 285; idem, *The Chronicler's History of Israel* (New Haven: Yale University Press, 1954).

devastation caused by the Babylonians. Based on the archaeological evidence available to him, Albright depicted Jerusalem and Judah becoming a kind of territorial tabula rasa.[117] The despoliation, carnage, and banishment were so severe that the traditional culture of Judah ceased to exist, at least within the land. Albright recognized, however, that a relatively small number of people survived the traumatic events of the early sixth century.

The views of P. R. Ackroyd may be taken as representative of a third position.[118] Like Albright, Ackroyd stressed the gravity of the disaster. But Ackroyd also pointed to issues involving the use of terminology, such as "exile" and "restoration," citing evidence that not all Judahites were exiled and that some sacrifices continued at the temple altar (e.g., Jer. 41:4–5). More so than Albright, Ackroyd took an interest in those who remained in the land following the assassination of Gedaliah (2 Kings 25:22–26).

In recent years more radical views of the exile have appeared, drawing upon older theories. Although he agrees with Albright on virtually nothing else, Thompson has (unknowingly?) refashioned Albright's theory. Whereas Albright traced continuity between the exilic community and its former existence in Judah, Thompson avers that the dislocation and displacement caused by the Babylonian campaigns were so pervasive that the national ethnicity of Judah, if this region ever achieved such a thing, ceased to exist either in the land or among the exiles.[119] For Thompson, the notion of a postexilic restoration is a pious fiction designed to buttress immigrant claims to a new territory.

The concern of Torrey and Ackroyd to reconstruct the history of the remaining community in the land has been given a radical new twist by R. P. Carroll, who insists that "there was no serious change in social conditions during the sixth century."[120] Those biblical scholars who embrace Albright's position have allegedly adopted the biblical view of the Babylonian invasions, deeming those who remained in the land as insignificant and championing the elite who were cast out. In Carroll's view, the books of Leviticus, Kings, Isaiah, Jeremiah, Ezekiel, Chronicles, Ezra, and Nehemiah together constitute a "deportation literature," a production of the postexilic community designed to defend its exclusivistic policies.[121] Carroll's judgments are, therefore, both similar to

117. W. F. Albright, *The Biblical Period from Abraham to Ezra* (New York: Harper, 1963), 81–86, 110–11; idem, *Archaeology*, 140–42.

118. P. R. Ackroyd, *Israel under Babylon and Persia*, New Clarendon Bible (Oxford: Oxford University Press, 1970), 1–25.

119. Thompson, *Early History*, 334, 415.

120. R. P. Carroll, "The Myth of the Empty Land," *Semeia* 59 (1992): 79.

121. Ibid., 87–88. Carroll is, in fact, inclined to think that "much—in some sense perhaps *all*—of the literature of the Hebrew Bible must be regarded as the documentation of

and different from those of Thompson. Both view the relevant biblical literature as postexilic ideological constructs justifying the usurpation of territory from the indigenous population. But whereas Thompson posits complete discontinuity, Carroll, like Torrey, assumes a fundamental continuity between the preexilic, exilic, and postexilic communities in Judah.

From this brief synopsis of major scholarly positions, it is apparent that historians hold strikingly different assumptions about the Babylonian captivity. Recent discussions of the material remains are, however, of some help in evaluating the tenability of these theories. Archaeologists no longer think that the damage caused by the Babylonian invasions was as pervasive as Albright believed. The early-sixth-century destructions seem to have affected only Jerusalem and limited surroundings. Occupation gaps exist at Lachish, Tell Beit Mirsim, and Tel Batash, but there is continuity of occupation at Gibeon, Mizpah, and Bethel.[122] Iron Age culture survives in Transjordan, the coastal strip, the northern regions, and the Negev.[123] The territory of Benjamin was largely spared destruction.[124] Although Jerusalem seems to have suffered tremendous damage, even here the destruction was not total. Barkay's excavations in the Hinnom Valley have yielded some burial artifacts from the sixth century, perhaps as late as 500 B.C.[125] In summary, there is evidence for the destructive effect of the Babylonian invasions in Jerusalem and its surroundings and for continuity of occupation in a number of other areas. Any historical reconstruction should do justice to both.

What of the biblical evidence? Is it as monolithic as some suppose? It is certainly true that almost all of the relevant biblical books, with the notable exception of Lamentations, follow a story line that proceeds from the Babylonian destructions to the life of the exilic community in Babylon. As a result, we know relatively little of the community that remained behind after 582 B.C. But it does not follow from all of this that the biblical books unilaterally favor the returnees. The account in

---

their [the returnees'] claims to the land and as a reflection of their ideology" (p. 85). See also his commentary, *Jeremiah*, OTL (Philadelphia: Westminster/John Knox, 1986), 55–81.

122. The older overview by E. Stern is still useful: "Israel at the Close of the Monarchy: An Archaeological Survey," *BA* 38 (1975): 26–54.

123. The continuity has led Barkay to argue that not 586 B.C. but 530–520 B.C. marks the end of "Israelite" material culture, because only at this time does one see the emergence of some features of Achaemenid material culture ("The Redefining of Archaeological Periods: Does the Date 588/586 B.C.E. Indeed Mark the End of Iron Age Culture?" in *Biblical Archaeology Today, 1990*, 106–12).

124. A. Mazar, *Archaeology*, 548–49.

125. G. Barkay, *Ketef Hinnom: A Treasure Facing Jerusalem's Walls* (Jerusalem: Israel Museum, 1986).

2 Kings 24–25, for example, details the Babylonian exile of 598/597 B.C., the destruction associated with the Babylonian exile of 586, and the evacuation to Egypt (582), ending with the amnesty given to Jehoiachin in exile. Important theological motifs inform this presentation, for example, the exodus back to Egypt (25:22–26).[126] Such an emphasis on divine judgment upon *all* of Jerusalem and Judah can hardly be construed as a mark of favor on the returnees. There is simply no mention of a return in Kings.[127]

Nor do the various biblical presentations speak with one voice. The Chronicler draws on the Deuteronomistic presentation but offers his own distinctive presentation of Judah's demise. In S. Japhet's view, Chronicles mentions only one, apparently partial, exile (586 B.C.) and lacks any discussion of major devastation to Judah (2 Chron. 36:17–20).[128] Chronicles ends optimistically with the decree of Cyrus authorizing a return to the land and the rebuilding of the temple.[129] Whether the Chronicler also posits uninterrupted settlement in the land, as Japhet contends, is uncertain.[130] In my judgment, the Chronicler tries to strike a balance between the plight of those left in the land and the plight of those sent into exile. Whatever the case, Chronicles associates less disarray with the Babylonian exile(s) than does Kings.

Cursory study of Kings and Chronicles suggests that each of the major biblical writings dealing with exile needs to be studied on its own terms. When due attention is given to distinctive contexts and points of view, a more complex picture emerges. Such complication bears on the larger subject of Judahite history in the early sixth century. Avoiding grand generalizations about this era seems the better part of wisdom. Given the evidence provided by Lamentations concerning the piety of those who survived the Babylonian onslaught, stereotypes about pure (i.e., the exiles) and impure (i.e., the survivors in Judah) miss the mark. Moreover, it is quite unlikely that either the community left in Judah or

126. R. E. Friedman, "From Egypt to Egypt: Dtr[1] and Dtr[2]," in *Traditions in Transformation: Turning Points in Biblical Faith: Essays Presented to Frank Moore Cross, Jr.*, ed. B. Halpern and J. Levenson (Winona Lake, Ind.: Eisenbrauns, 1981), 167–92; N. Naʾaman, "The Deuteronomist and Voluntary Servitude to Foreign Powers," *JSOT* 65 (1995): 37–53.

127. That the book ends enigmatically has generated a variety of explanations. See the overview of Howard, *Introduction*, 169–229.

128. S. Japhet, *The Ideology of the Book of Chronicles and Its Place in Biblical Thought*, BEATAJ 9 (Frankfurt am Main: Lang, 1989), 364–73.

129. My reference is to the end of Chronicles in its present form. Some scholars dispute that 2 Chron. 36:23 was the original conclusion to the Chronicler's work. See, e.g., W. Rudolph, *Chronikbücher*, HAT 21 (Tübingen: Mohr, 1955), 338; F. M. Cross, "A Reconstruction of the Judean Restoration," *JBL* 94 (1974): 4–18; H. G. M. Williamson, *1 and 2 Chronicles*, NCB (Grand Rapids: Eerdmans, 1982), 412–19.

130. Japhet, *Ideology*, 373.

the community in exile stood still. There was undoubtedly development in both.[131] Precisely by recognizing both continuity and change in the communities of Judah and Babylon, one can begin to appreciate the tensions one finds in the books of Ezra and Nehemiah, when the two communities came into contact once again.

Conclusions

In many respects, recent historical studies of the monarchy mirror larger trends in the field of Old Testament studies. The last three decades have seen developments in traditional disciplines as well as the application of new, largely social scientific, disciplines. It would be misleading to suggest that this increasing diversity is simply a great step forward. The situation is more complex. If in earlier histories of the monarchy there was the danger of relying exclusively on one kind of methodology or one kind of evidence, there is now a danger of compartmentalization and fragmentation. Scholars trained in different humanistic and social scientific disciplines focus on certain kinds of evidence to the exclusion of others. More so than ever, there is a need for integration. Given the new methods and the different kinds of material and literary evidence, it would be a shame not to employ all available means to illumine the history of ancient Israel and Judah.

131. J. Janssen, *Juda in der Exilszeit*, FRLANT 69 (Göttingen: Vandenhoeck & Ruprecht, 1956), 39–54; Ackroyd, *Israel*, 34–161; Oded, "Judah and the Exile," in *Israelite and Judaean History*, ed. Miller and Hayes, 476–80; R. W. Klein, *Israel in Exile*, OBT (Philadelphia: Fortress, 1979), 1–22.

9

Exile and After: Historical Study

H. G. M. Williamson

During the middle decades of the twentieth century, the postexilic period of Israelite history and literature was relatively neglected. In the period here under review, however, this situation has been radically transformed so that now, as will shortly appear, this is one of the liveliest fields in the whole discipline of Old Testament study.[1] (For this reason, the bulk of the following survey concentrates on this period, though the exile receives some limited attention in a later section.) Before we consider the main historical topics that have received particular attention, it is worth noting some of the major factors that have led to this transformation and mentioning some of the principal publications (frequently collaborative) to which it has given rise.

Factors Leading to Renewal of Interest

First, at the level of the history of religion, with its inevitable influence on theology, there has been a marked reaction against the earlier view (a relic of nineteenth-century scholarship) that the postexilic period witnessed a sharp decline from the religious and ethical heights of the preexilic prophets into a priestly, ritually dominated legalism. While many factors have contributed to this reevaluation, its significance for

---

1. It is noteworthy, for instance, that the first two issues of a new journal devoted to surveying the current state of biblical research both contain articles of direct relevance to this field; see T. C. Eskenazi, "Current Perspectives on Ezra–Nehemiah and the Persian Period," *CR:BS* 1 (1993): 59–86; and E. M. Meyers, "Second Temple Studies in the Light of Recent Archaeology: Part 1: The Persian and Hellenistic Periods," *CR:BS* 2 (1994): 25–42. Note too J. W. Kleinig, "Recent Research in Chronicles," *CR:BS* 2 (1994): 43–76.

our purposes is that scholars have become more aware of the need to study this period in its own right, including its history.

Second, there has been a noteworthy tendency to take this period more seriously as the time when the Hebrew Scriptures were brought close to their definitive form. In some extreme cases this involves setting the very composition of much of the literature at this late date. Even where this is not the case, newer critical methods that focus on the value of the final form of the text rather than exclusively on what may be hypothetically reconstructed of its "original" form mean that far more attention than used to be the case is paid to the latest elements in the literature and to the shape that the final editors have given both to the individual books and to the more extensive collections that they make up. The desire to understand better the social setting of this activity has undoubtedly been a stimulus to historical study.

Third, the archaeological profile of this period, which, like its literary counterpart, had previously lain in the shadows, has achieved a sharper focus. Because of the intrusive nature of later Hellenistic building techniques on the one hand and the failure always to distinguish Iron Age II (preexilic) from Iron Age III (Persian period) levels on the other, there was a tendency for the material culture of the period to be squeezed out of the interpretation of archaeological remains generally, but this has now been largely corrected. At the same time, some few but significant epigraphic discoveries have again focused attention on the need for closer attention to their wider archaeological context.

Fourth, the Achaemenid period has come into greater prominence in the study of the history of the ancient Near East in general as study of Persian remains has allowed a more sympathetic appreciation of their "side of the story," which had previously been seen through the eyes of the Greek historians alone. As part of this wider interest, the history of Judah, which is better documented than that of many other regions, has attracted the interest of scholars with other than specifically biblical interests.

Finally, the impact of the social scientific approach to history in general has been brought to bear on this period with considerable vigor in recent years in the hope that it may shed fresh light on largely familiar data that have been repeatedly worked over in the past. Traditional historical methods have been thought largely to have reached an impasse: the same problems and range of possible solutions tend to be presented in the textbooks without any sense that real progress in understanding is being achieved and with an occasionally expressed frustration that, while more and more time is spent discussing such minutiae as the order of the high priests, we know practically nothing about the "real stuff" of history such as the economic and social conditions that determined the lives of the bulk of the population.[2] We have allowed our agenda to be set by the highly selective nature of the concerns of the biblical authors rather than by those of professional historians.

Principal Publications on This Period

These trends in research can all be illustrated by referring to some of the more significant publications in recent years.[3] The *Cambridge History* series, for instance, has no less than three separate projects that are all relevant to our topic. Most obvious, of course, is the first volume of *The Cambridge History of Judaism*, which is largely devoted to the Persian period, covering the history, archaeology, religion, and literature of Judaism both in Judah and in the Diaspora.[4] From the Persian side, *The Cambridge History of Iran*, vol. 2, *The Median and Achaemenian Periods*,[5] gives a massive survey of the Persian Empire as a whole, much of it directly relevant to Jewish affairs, while three separate volumes of the second edition of *The Cambridge Ancient History* each has a chapter or section covering the history of Judah in Persian times, as well as including other relevant background information.[6]

2. See, for instance, K. W. Whitelam, "Recreating the History of Israel," *JSOT* 35 (1986): 45–70.

3. Note that no evaluation is implied by the order in which they are listed here. Several recent single-authored histories of the Achaemenid Empire now replace the rather outdated work of A. T. Olmstead, *History of the Persian Empire* (Chicago: University of Chicago Press, 1948), namely, J. M. Cook, *The Persian Empire* (London: Dent; New York: Schocken, 1983); R. N. Frye, *The History of Ancient Iran* (Munich: Beck, 1984); M. A. Dandamaev, *A Political History of the Achaemenid Empire*, trans. W. J. Vogelsang (Leiden: Brill, 1989); A. Kuhrt, *The Ancient Near East c. 3000–330 BC*, 2 vols. (London and New York: Routledge, 1995), 2:647–701; P. Briant, *Histoire de l'empire perse: De Cyrus à Alexandre* (Paris: Fayard, 1996).

4. Ed. W. D. Davies and L. Finkelstein (Cambridge: Cambridge University Press, 1984). While I have expressed serious misgivings about the concept that lies behind this project as a whole and about the manner in which it has been carried out, many of the individual contributions are of great value; cf. my review, *VT* 35 (1985): 231–38.

5. Ed. I. Gershevitch (Cambridge: Cambridge University Press, 1985).

6. I. Eph'al, "Syria-Palestine under Achaemenid Rule," *CAH*, vol. 4, *Persia, Greece, and the Western Mediterranean, c. 525 to 479 B.C.*, ed. J. Boardman et al., 2d ed. (Cambridge: Cambridge University Press, 1988), 139–64; H. Tadmor, "Judah," *CAH*, vol. 6, *The Fourth Century B.C.*, ed. D. M. Lewis et al., 2d ed. (Cambridge: Cambridge University Press, 1994), 261–96. Tadmor explains the difference between the two contributions as follows: "That chapter looked at Judah as a part of the Achaemenid empire; here we try to consider its internal development during the period" (p. 261); see also T. C. Mitchell, "The Babylonian Exile and the Restoration of the Jews in Palestine (586–c. 500 B.C.)," *CAH*, vol. 3.2, *The Assyrian and Babylonian Empires and Other States of the Near East, from the Eighth to Sixth Centuries B.C.*, ed. J. Boardman et al., 2d ed. (Cambridge: Cambridge University Press, 1991), 410–60.

Another collaborative project was the Achaemenid History Workshop, which met between 1981 and 1990 and whose deliberations have now been published in eight volumes.[7] While its focus was broad, some of the specific topics treated directly affect the study of Persian period Judah and are suggestive from a comparative point of view of the Persian treatment of subject peoples in general.

Closer to the center of our topic is the Paris-based Association pour la recherche sur la Syrie-Palestine à l'époque perse, an international association with a new journal, *Transeuphratène* (first published in 1989), which publishes not only the conference proceedings of the association but also other research articles and bibliographical surveys. "Trans-Euphrates" was the name of the Persian satrapy that included Judah,[8] so that this is clearly of great relevance to our topic. Some of the methods and approaches of the association have been set out in J. Élayi and J. Sapin, *Nouveaux regards sur la Transeuphratène.*[9] They are extremely critical both of the "men and movements" approach to history and to the heavily textually based method that characterizes it, arguing instead for the value of an interdisciplinary approach that combines the expertise of a wide range of specialties. Biblical scholars will find that the concerns that have usually dominated their work are put firmly in their place! Despite this, many of the articles that have appeared in the new journal deal with familiar issues, and the importance of seeing the history of Judah within the context of its position alongside its neighboring provinces within the Persian Empire (for which the evidence has indeed frequently to be culled from a range of diverse and scattered sources) is made clear.

A last cooperative venture deserving mention is the ongoing work of the Society of Biblical Literature's Sociology of the Second Temple Consultation, part of whose deliberations has been published.[10] Readers will find here a stimulating mixture of new data, fresh hypotheses, and critical evaluation, with "sociology" interpreted broadly, the whole thus reflecting the consciously exploratory nature of this work in its early stages.

---

7. *Achaemenid History I–VIII*, ed. H. Sancisi-Weerdenburg et al., 8 vols. (Leiden: Nederlands Instituut voor het Nabije Oosten, 1987–94).

8. See M. Heltzer, "A Recently Published Babylonian Tablet and the Province of Judah after 516 B.C.E.," *Trans* 5 (1992): 57–61, with references to the principal earlier literature; but note especially in addition A. F. Rainey, "The Satrapy 'beyond the River,'" *AJBA* 1 (1969): 51–78.

9. Turnhout: Brepols, 1991.

10. *Second Temple Studies*, vol. 1, *Persian Period*, ed. P. R. Davies, JSOTSup 117 (Sheffield: JSOT Press, 1991); see too the publication of a separate SBL symposium, *Second Temple Studies*, vol. 2, *Temple and Community in the Persian Period*, ed. T. C. Eskenazi and K. H. Richards, JSOTSup 175 (Sheffield: JSOT Press, 1994).

Finally, the work of a few individual scholars deserves mention, for alongside the continuing enterprise of research, which comes to expression in articles, monographs, commentaries, and reference works, there have been some noteworthy attempts at overall synthesis. E. Stern's updated and translated dissertation on the archaeology of the period is widely recognized as a magisterial contribution, correcting many of the misconceptions of earlier writers, and establishing a firm framework into which newer discoveries can be fitted.[11] L. L. Grabbe has written an extremely valuable textbook on the history of the Jews in the second temple period that sets out and evaluates the major primary sources of whatever sort, discusses particular topics, and then presents a synthesis of the whole.[12] Data and interpretation are thus clearly distinguished (something that not all textbooks achieve), so that the work should be of service for students of whatever critical persuasion. Last, the second volume of R. Albertz's history of Israelite religion is devoted to the exilic and postexilic periods.[13] Taking full account of more recent sociological approaches to this subject, it marks a major advance on its predecessors while remaining very much the interpretation of an individual scholar.

Approach and Method

As this survey indicates, there is considerable uncertainty at the present time concerning what a historian of the exilic and Persian periods of Judah should be attempting to do. Some of the more recent approaches have bluntly rejected traditional concerns, which concentrate on a textually based reconstruction of the course of political events, focused on prominent people and movements of thought, with external evidence from archaeology and other sources used only for background, illustration, and correction. They have urged instead that more attention

11. *The Material Culture of the Land of the Bible in the Persian Period 538–332 B.C.* (Warminster: Aris & Phillips; Jerusalem: Israel Exploration Society, 1982); see too H. Weippert, *Palästina in vorhellenistischer Zeit* (Munich: Beck, 1988), 682–718.

12. *Judaism from Cyrus to Hadrian,* 2 vols. (London: SCM; Minneapolis: Fortress, 1992). The Persian period is treated in 1:27–145. Other important textbooks include J. M. Miller and J. H. Hayes, *A History of Ancient Israel and Judah* (London: SCM; Philadelphia: Westminster, 1986); and G. W. Ahlström, *The History of Ancient Palestine from the Palaeolithic Period to Alexander's Conquest,* with a contribution by G. O. Rollefson, ed. D. Edelman, JSOTSup 146 (Sheffield: JSOT Press, 1993). Note too E. M. Yamauchi, *Persia and the Bible* (Grand Rapids: Baker, 1990); and J. L. Berquist, *Judaism in Persia's Shadow: A Social and Historical Approach* (Minneapolis: Fortress, 1995).

13. *A History of Israelite Religion in the Old Testament Period,* vol. 2, *From the Exile to the Maccabees,* trans. J. Bowden, OTL (London: SCM; Louisville: Westminster/John Knox, 1994; German original, 1992).

should be paid to such issues as the economic base and organization of the province's life, the social structure of the population and its pattern of settlement, and the impact of wider imperial concerns on local affairs. There is a tendency, therefore, to read the texts with suspicion, believing that they hide these wider, and ultimately more significant, concerns beneath a veneer created by the desire to present the course of events within a familiar and locally acceptable pattern.

This dichotomy is unfortunate. First, since we are dealing with a period that by the standards of modern historical writing is poorly served with source material of any kind, it is churlish to ignore or undervalue any potential source of information. Second, it is methodologically mistaken to drive a wedge between individuals and society at large. On the one hand, particular individuals may serve as a catalyst for significant change in any sphere, while on the other hand those individuals are more often than not the product of their society; neither, therefore, can be satisfactorily understood without the other. Third, while one must recognize that there are more varieties of history than the political (which may include the religious), the latter remains a legitimate concern of the historian, for whom chronology and the critical evaluation of written sources remains the best hope of achieving progress. If this means careful examination of lists of high priests, for instance, then that task should not be shunned. Equally, however, one should acknowledge that that type of research inevitably allows its agenda to be set by the vagaries of what happens to have been preserved for us. It therefore remains a healthy exercise to ask questions that are not explicitly set by the written sources and to test whether models and hypotheses based on sometimes quite other societies and scenarios may not cast fresh light on what still remains opaque in familiar texts. In other words, there seems to be no room for the luxury of an ideological rejection of any single approach. What is needed is a sober eclecticism, which necessarily involves the historian in a measure of reliance on the work of specialists in related disciplines. As much recent work has shown, the historical enterprise in this as in many other periods cannot but be a collaborative venture. That this may lead to unsettling challenges from either party is only to be expected.[14]

At this point, therefore, and especially for those who are primarily students of the Bible, it is imperative to come to terms with the nature of the written source material at our disposal. For the exilic period, there is no narrative text of a historical nature whatever. Attention here

14. For an example that seeks to reflect on such challenges, see K. D. Tollefson and H. G. M. Williamson, "Nehemiah as Cultural Revitalization: An Anthropological Perspective," *JSOT* 56 (1992): 41–68.

must naturally focus, therefore, on the postexilic period as recorded in the books of Ezra and Nehemiah. Although other books,[15] and indeed material from outside the Bible altogether, furnish some scraps of information, no other source even begins to provide a consecutive narrative of events in Judah of the Persian period in the manner of Ezra and Nehemiah.

Closer examination soon shows, however, that even these primary sources are less straightforward in this regard than might at first appear. These two books cover a period of well over one hundred years[16] (even assuming an early date for Ezra), and yet the events that they describe relate to only a handful of years, scattered unevenly throughout the period. As I have sought to emphasize more than once elsewhere,[17] these few isolated events cannot be associated in the normal cause-and-effect continuum that is of the essence of historical writing. Quite legitimately from their point of view, the authors of this material see continuity in terms of God's direction of the course of the postexilic restoration, so that, for instance, "After these things" can serve to bridge a gap of more than fifty years at Ezra 7:1. In terms of the divine economy, that is fine: Ezra's mission was the next significant step in God's plan. To say the least, however, it leaves an awkward gap for anyone seeking to give a historical account of the period, whether political, social, economic, or other. If we do not have material with which to fill in this or other such gaps, then it is better to admit the fact and concede that we are simply not in a position to write a history of this period in any normal sense. As we shall see, we can make some progress toward that goal, but it is better to be honest about the limitations of what is available to us as historians and not to present an account as though it were a seamless narrative. A broader and more general account is perhaps more realistic and attainable, and it leaves the theologian and student of literature free to analyze these books more explicitly on their own terms.

The other, and more encouraging, side of this particular coin is that we have in these books what in my opinion are firsthand accounts of

15. Several biblical books were certainly written during this period, such as Isaiah 56–66, Joel, Haggai, Zechariah, Malachi, and Chronicles (probably also Ruth and Jonah), whereas many, if not most, of the remainder would have been edited and brought close to their final form at this time. There is thus much potential here for indirect historical information, particularly about religious and social beliefs and customs; cf. Berquist, *Judaism in Persia's Shadow*. To exploit this material requires a great deal of prior critical analysis, however, and even then much remains inevitably hypothetical. Constraints of space unfortunately preclude attention to these important matters here.

16. Two hundred, in fact, if the Jaddua of Neh. 12:11 is correctly identified as the high priest at the time of Alexander the Great.

17. See H. G. M. Williamson, *Ezra, Nehemiah*, WBC (Waco: Word, 1985), xlviii–xlix et passim; idem, *Ezra and Nehemiah*, OT Guides (Sheffield: JSOT Press, 1987), 79–81.

the greatest historical value for the few events that they do describe. If this is correct, then two important consequences follow. First, they give us certain fixed points to which any broader account must do full justice. Second, and equally important, they provide a minimum of secure data by which to test models and hypotheses that are applied to this period of history; it would not be adequate to appeal to what we do not know as a justification for giving historical speculation free reign. This opinion has remained controversial throughout the period under review, however, and so deserves fuller discussion. Since the material relating to Ezra and Nehemiah themselves is treated later on, I here concentrate on some of the sources apparently included in Ezra 1–6.

At the start of our period, the consensus of opinion (insofar as there was one) favored the authenticity of the various Aramaic letters in Ezra 4–6[18] and the inventory of returned temple vessels in Ezra 1:9–11. The list of those who returned from Babylon in Ezra 2 was also agreed to be archival, though its date and unity have always been debated. Greatest uncertainty surrounded the authenticity of the Hebrew form of the edict of Cyrus in Ezra 1:2–4, earlier general skepticism having been only partly deflected by E. Bickerman.[19]

Three new or strengthened arguments have been added to bolster this consensus about the Aramaic letters. First, during the 1970s a number of detailed studies of the form and style of Aramaic letters that have been preserved from elsewhere in the Persian Empire were under-

---

18. This followed especially the earlier studies of E. Meyer, *Die Entstehung des Judentums: Eine historische Untersuchung* (Halle: Niemeyer, 1896); H. H. Schaeder, *Esra der Schreiber*, BHT 5 (Tübingen: Mohr, 1930); and R. de Vaux, "Les décrets de Cyrus et de Darius sur la reconstruction du temple," *RB* 46 (1937): 29–57. The last-named work is available in English as, "The Decrees of Cyrus and Darius on the Rebuilding of the Temple," in *The Bible and the Ancient Near East*, trans. D. McHugh (Garden City, N.Y.: Doubleday, 1971; London: Darton, Longman & Todd, 1972), 63–96.

19. E. Bickerman, "The Edict of Cyrus in Ezra 1," in *Studies in Jewish and Christian History*, AGJU 9.1 (Leiden: Brill, 1976), 72–108. The important study of A. Kuhrt, "The Cyrus Cylinder and Achaemenid Imperial Policy," *JSOT* 25 (1983): 83–97, should be noted at this point. (See too P.-R. Berger, "Der Kyros-Zylinder mit dem Zusatzfragment BIN II Nr. 32 und die akkadischen Personennamen im Danielbuch," *ZA* 64 [1975]: 192–234.) In contrast with some exaggerated claims for the extent to which the Cyrus Cylinder authenticates the decrees of Cyrus and Darius in Ezra, she shows that it is composed in accordance with traditional Mesopotamian royal building texts, that it relates exclusively to the fortunes of Babylon and—by extension—to the Babylonian pantheon, and that it does not speak of the restoration of destroyed cult centers (the translation in *ANET*, 316, is misleading on this point). There is thus no reference to a general return of displaced people, so that the parallel with the biblical text, though valuable as far as it goes, is not as close as has sometimes been claimed, nor are Cyrus's policies as unprecedented as is often supposed. While the cylinder is thus compatible with a positive evaluation of the biblical evidence, the latter should be determined on other, primarily internal, grounds in the first instance.

taken.[20] With one qualification to be noted below, the forms of letters in Ezra conform well to these conventions, and L. V. Hensley has made the important point that Greek letter-writing practices were quite different, making the suggestion of later fabrication less likely.[21]

Second, I have myself tried to demonstrate in a detailed study that a number of peculiar features in these chapters can be most naturally explained on the assumption that a later editor was working on the basis of the actual letters themselves.[22] For instance, some of the information and awkward transitions in the text (e.g., at 4:6–11; 6:3–6) give evidence of the editor working into his account material from the subscript, summary, and address as well as from the body itself of the letters, implying that he had a copy of the document itself to hand. Again, much of the surrounding narrative (apart from what could be deduced from such obvious alternative sources as Haggai and Zech. 1–8) is written up directly out of the wording of the letters themselves, suggesting that they were indeed his primary source rather than a literary embellishment to an alternative account, whether fictitious or real. Finally, it is noteworthy that the course of the narrative is almost wholly determined by what is included in these documents and so does not include material that we might otherwise have expected him to describe, such as the return journey from Babylon or the course of the rebuilding of the second temple.[23] This gives the impression of a historian working responsibly with his sources and not fabricating an account that outstripped the evidence at his disposal.

20. See P. S. Alexander, "Remarks on Aramaic Epistolography in the Persian Period," *JSS* 23 (1978): 155–70; J. D. Whitehead, "Some Distinctive Features of the Language of the Aramaic Arsames Correspondence," *JNES* 37 (1978): 119–40; P.-E. Dion, "Les types épistolaires hébréo-araméens jusqu'au temps de Bar-Kokhbah," *RB* 96 (1979): 544–79; J. A. Fitzmyer, "Aramaic Epistolography," in *A Wandering Aramean: Collected Aramaic Essays*, SBLMS 25 (Missoula, Mont.: Scholars Press, 1979), 183–204. A new edition of the relevant texts has now appeared to supersede earlier collections: B. Porten and A. Yardeni, *Textbook of Aramaic Documents from Ancient Egypt*, vol. 1, *Letters* (Jerusalem: Hebrew University Department of the History of the Jewish People, 1986). There is also a handy collection available in J. M. Lindenberger, *Ancient Aramaic and Hebrew Letters*, SBLWAW 4 (Atlanta: Scholars Press, 1994).

21. Hensley, "The Official Persian Documents in the Book of Ezra" (diss., University of Liverpool, 1977).

22. "The Composition of Ezra i–vi," *JTS*, n.s., 34 (1983): 1–30; see also Williamson, *Ezra, Nehemiah*, ad loc. General support, but including much criticism of detail, comes from B. Halpern, "A Historiographic Commentary on Ezra 1–6: Achronological Narrative and Dual Chronology in Israelite Historiography," in *The Hebrew Bible and Its Interpreters*, ed. W. H. Propp, B. Halpern, and D. N. Freedman (Winona Lake, Ind.: Eisenbrauns, 1990), 81–142.

23. This may explain what R. P. Carroll finds to be a suspicious gap in our knowledge; cf. "So What Do We *Know* about the Temple? The Temple in the Prophets," in *Second Temple Studies*, 2:34–51.

Third, by means of a comprehensive survey, P. Frei has reinforced the older argument that often official Achaemenid edicts responded to requests from local officials and used the same technical language of the request in framing their response.[24] The use of "Jewish" phraseology in some of these documents is therefore no necessary objection to their authenticity.[25]

While most commentators on the biblical books have remained with the earlier consensus on the basis of such arguments, not all have been persuaded. Alongside some who in general terms simply cannot bring themselves to accept that anything is as it seems to be, a few have tried to argue that confidence in the authenticity of these documents is unwarranted. Grabbe, for instance, reports having had his mind changed on this matter by Gunneweg's commentary.[26] His chief complaint is that defenders of authenticity have generally contented themselves with replying to objections (i.e., the third argument mentioned above), which is a circular and unfalsifiable position. What is needed, he urges, is a fresh examination from first principles that does not start out with a positive presupposition. Furthermore, even if one accepts that the documents are basically authentic, they may have been reworked by Jewish scribes,[27] and since even small changes can completely alter the tone and tenor of a text, this means that they are of little historical value.

In reply, while one must concede that proof of the sort that Grabbe and others seem to require is unattainable (but then so too is the reverse), he has not, perhaps, taken adequately into account (and certainly has not attempted to answer) the various points made above that positively favor the view that an editor was working directly from original documents. The answering of objections to this view is not, of course, intended as a positive argument, as Grabbe rightly insists, but it retains its importance in showing that apparently Jewish elements are not an insuperable problem against a position that is initially sup-

24. P. Frei, "Zentralgewalt und Lokalautonomie im Achämenidenreich," in P. Frei and K. Koch, *Reichsidee und Reichsorganisation im Perserreich*, OBO 55 (Freiburg: Universitätsverlag; Göttingen: Vandenhoeck & Ruprecht, 1984), 8–43. Frei has repeated his argument, but also attracted several critical responses, in the first issue of the new journal *Zeitschrift für Altorientalische und Biblische Rechtsgeschichte* (1995).

25. I have attempted elsewhere to show in addition that some aspects of these letters to which exception has been taken on such grounds can be seen to fit well with what we know of Achaemenid policy generally from the Elamite texts from Persepolis; see "Ezra and Nehemiah in the Light of the Texts from Persepolis," *BBR* 1 (1991): 41–61.

26. L. L. Grabbe, "Reconstructing History from the Book of Ezra," in *Second Temple Studies*, 1:98–106; cf. idem, *Judaism*, 30–36; A. H. J. Gunneweg, *Esra*, KAT 19.1 (Gütersloh: Mohn, 1985).

27. Grabbe cites J. Blenkinsopp, *Ezra–Nehemiah*, OTL (London: SCM; Philadelphia: Westminster, 1988), 119–23, 126–27, as a representative of this mediating position.

ported on independent and positive grounds. In my opinion, therefore, the argument in favor of the authenticity of these documents remains overwhelmingly more probable.

The Constitutional Status of Judah

I turn next to what is, perhaps, the most fundamental historical topic confronting the student of the postexilic period: the constitutional status of the province of Judah and of the Jewish community within it. During the period under review, these two issues have become separated because of the suggestion that within the political province there was a separate entity that has come to be known as the *Bürger-Tempel-Gemeinde,* or "Citizen-Temple Community."

Throughout the middle decades of the twentieth century, understanding of the status of Judah within the Persian period was colored by an influential essay by A. Alt, in which he had argued that until Nehemiah's time Judah had been administered as part of the province of Samaria.[28] Only with Nehemiah was it constituted as a separate province, and it was this that provoked so much opposition from Sanballat and his allies. Already in 1971 M. Smith had written a vigorous refutation of this view, but several authors since have continued to defend it.[29]

During the past twenty years, new epigraphical data have come to light that have caused the majority of scholars to reconsider some of the literary evidence that Alt had sought to explain away and so to reject his view. Inevitably, the arguments are too detailed and complex to be presented here in full,[30] but the principal points may be listed. (1) A hoard of bullae and seals published by Avigad in 1976 most probably refers to a governor of the province of Yehud in the late sixth century B.C. (i.e.,

---

28. A. Alt, "Die Rolle Samarias bei der Entstehung des Judentums," in *Festschrift Otto Procksch zum 60. Geburtstag* (Leipzig: Deichert and Hinrichs, 1934), 5–28; reprinted in idem, *Kleine Schriften zur Geschichte des Volkes Israel,* vol. 2 (Munich: Beck, 1953), 316–37.

29. M. Smith, *Palestinian Parties and Politics That Shaped the Old Testament* (New York: Columbia University Press, 1971), 193–201; cf. esp. E. Stern, "Seal-Impressions in the Achaemenid Style in the Province of Judah," *BASOR* 202 (1971): 6–16; idem, *Material Culture,* 209–13, modified in "The Persian Empire and the Political and Social History of Palestine in the Persian Period," *CHJ,* 1:70–87 (esp. 72 and 82–83); F. C. Fensham, "Mĕdînâ in Ezra and Nehemiah," *VT* 25 (1975): 795–97; S. E. McEvenue, "The Political Structure in Judah from Cyrus to Nehemiah," *CBQ* 43 (1981): 353–64.

30. See, e.g., H. G. M. Williamson, "The Governors of Judah under the Persians," *TynBul* 39 (1988): 59–82; A. Lemaire, "Populations et territoires de la Palestine à l'époque perse," *Trans* 3 (1990): 31–74. For a full collection of all inscriptions from this region in the Persian period, see too Lemaire's extremely valuable surveys: "Les inscriptions palestiniennes d'époque perse: un bilan provisoire," *Trans* 1 (1989): 87–105, with an update in *Trans* 4 (1991): 113–18.

well before Nehemiah).[31] (2) The references to Sheshbazzar (Ezra 5:14) and Zerubbabel (Hag. 1:1, 14) as governor should therefore also be taken at face value. (3) Nehemiah's reference to "the governors who were before me" (Neh. 5:15) makes best sense in context if he is referring to those who held the same position as he did himself. (4) The correspondence in Ezra 4:7–23 clearly presupposes that Judah enjoyed a measure of autonomy; if Judah had been under Samarian rule, there would have been no need for officials from there to act in the manner here described. (Similarly, in Ezra 5 we should have expected Tattenai to approach the Samarian officials, not the Jews directly.) (5) There is a complete lack of direct evidence either for Judah's incorporation into Samaria after the fall of Jerusalem[32] or for a radical change in constitutional status at the time of Nehemiah.

The names of eight or nine governors of Judah are now known to us: Sheshbazzar, Zerubbabel, and Nehemiah from the biblical sources, Elnathan, Yehʿezer, and Ahzai from bullae and seals,[33] Bagohi from the Elephantine papyri, and Yehizqiyah from coins.[34] To these we should probably add "Yohanan the priest," mentioned on a coin of the fourth century B.C.[35] This coin raises interesting constitutional questions that cannot yet be definitively answered. Since it is of an identical type to that of Yehizqiyah, it seems probable that Yoha-

31. N. Avigad, *Bullae and Seals from a Post-Exilic Judean Archive*, Qedem 4 (Jerusalem: Institute of Archaeology, Hebrew University, 1976). The date is deduced from paleographical evidence and the likely identification of "Shelomith the *ʾmt* [wife/official?] of Elnathan the governor" with the Shelomith of 1 Chron. 3:19 (postexilic Davidic family; the rarity of women named either in genealogies or on seals, both of which could be explained if she held some official position, suggests this identification); cf. A. Lemaire's review of Avigad, *Bullae and Seals* in *Syria* 54 (1977): 129–31; E. M. Meyers, "The Shelomith Seal and the Judean Restoration: Some Additional Considerations," *EI* 18 (1985): 33*– 38*; idem, "The Persian Period and the Judean Restoration: From Zerubbabel to Nehemiah," in *Ancient Israelite Religion: Essays in Honor of Frank Moore Cross*, ed. P. D. Miller et al. (Philadelphia: Fortress, 1987), 509–21. Some other governors are named on seal impressions from Ramat Rahel, but it remains controversial whether any should be dated before Nehemiah.

32. See esp. K. G. Hoglund, *Achaemenid Imperial Administration in Syria-Palestine and the Missions of Ezra and Nehemiah*, SBLDS 125 (Atlanta: Scholars Press, 1992), 84–85.

33. Cf. Avigad, *Bullae and Seals*, 5–7, 11–13; Y. Aharoni, *Excavations at Ramat Rahel: Seasons 1959 and 1960* (Rome: University of Rome, Centro di Studi Semitici, 1962), 28; idem, *Excavations at Ramat Rahel: Seasons 1961 and 1962* (Rome: University of Rome, Centro di Studi Semitici, 1964), 19, 43.

34. See L. Y. Rahmani, "Silver Coins of the Fourth Century B.C. from Tel Gamma," *IEJ* 21 (1971): 158–60; L. Mildenberg, "*Yᵉhüd*-Münzen," in Weippert, *Palästina*, 719–28.

35. See D. Barag, "A Silver Coin of Yohanan the High Priest and the Coinage of Judea in the Fourth Century B.C.," *INJ* 9 (1986–87): 4–21. Less certainly, add too the "Jaddua" of another coin published by A. Spaer, "Jaddua the High Priest?" *INJ* 9 (1986–87): 1–3; but cf. n. 83 below.

nan held the same office, that is, governor *(peḥâ)*. But does "the priest" mean the high priest? Does this indicate that by this time the office of high priest and governor had merged? Was he simply given authority at some time of grave crisis or transition? All these speculations have been advanced (and see further below), but our ignorance of the true answer serves as a useful reminder that we know practically nothing about the history of Judah during the whole of the last century of Persian rule.

The other major topic relating to the constitution of Judah was outlined in a series of articles in the 1970s by the Latvian scholar J. P. Weinberg. Although these were at first rather overlooked by biblical scholars, the increasing interest in an approach to our topic by way of the social sciences has brought them to belated prominence, and this will doubtless be furthered by the recent publication of an English translation of a selection of the most important of these articles.[36] There are signs that a number of scholars are appealing to Weinberg's theory as a basis for their research in related areas, so that careful consideration is imperative.

The essence of Weinberg's theory is that a distinction should be drawn between the imperial province of Judah (initially Samaria) and the Jewish community that lived within it and that was granted a privileged status by the Persians as a citizen-temple community, a type of organization for which it is thought there were analogies elsewhere in the empire. In the first part of the period, this community, with the temple as its social and economic center, was a minority of only some 20 percent of the population of Judah, living in three isolated enclaves in the coastal area, Jerusalem and its environs, and the southern part of the Jordan Valley. Although this was only an emerging form of the citizen-temple community proper, it was already favored by Cyrus with

---

36. J. P. Weinberg, *The Citizen-Temple Community*, trans. D. L. Smith-Christopher, JSOTSup 151 (Sheffield: Sheffield Academic Press, 1992). This collection includes a new essay, "The Postexilic Citizen-Temple Community: Theory and Reality," 127–38, in which Weinberg summarizes and updates his position, as well as responding to some early criticisms. It may be noted that Smith provides a useful introduction, in which he locates Weinberg's research within the broader context of Soviet ancient historiography. For Smith's own use of Weinberg's work, see D. L. Smith, *The Religion of the Landless: The Social Context of the Babylonian Exile* (Bloomington, Ind.: Meyer-Stone, 1989), 106–26. Other early responses include H. Kreissig, "Eine beachtenswerte Theorie zur Organisation altvorderorientalischer Tempelgemeinden im Achämenidenreich: Zu J. P. Weinbergs 'Bürger-Tempel Gemeinde' in Juda," *Klio* 66 (1984): 35–39; and, more positively, P.-E. Dion, "The Civic-and-Temple Community of Persian Period Judaea: Neglected Insights from Eastern Europe," *JNES* 50 (1991): 281–87. More recently, see, e.g., J. Blenkinsopp, "Temple and Society in Achaemenid Judah," in *Second Temple Studies*, 1:22–53; P. R. Bedford, "On Models and Texts," in ibid., 154–62; and R. A. Horsley, "Empire, Temple and Community—but no Bourgeoisie!" in ibid., 163–74.

permission to return from Babylon and to rebuild the temple because of his desire to secure a loyal element in the population of the province as part of his strategic plans for the conquest of Egypt. However, after 458 B.C., Weinberg's date for Ezra's mission, the community increased to about 70 percent of the population, it was accorded substantial powers of internal administrative control, and its members were granted tax exemption by Artaxerxes I. Later on, as the community became an ever larger proportion of the population of Judah, the high priest came also to hold the role of civil governor. This was a personal union only, however, a full merger not coming about until the Hellenistic period.

An important element in this reconstruction is the social and economic structure of the community. Weinberg stresses the degree of disruption caused by the Babylonian exile, and he finds that by the time of the return the Jews had organized themselves into quasi-agnatic groups known as "the fathers' house" *(bêt ʾābôt)*. Linking back to the ideology of earlier Israel, these "fathers' houses" controlled the community's land as inalienable property, dividing it into smaller parcels for the use of the separate constituent families. This resulted in a noteworthy degree of social homogeneity.

An important consequence of the theory is that most of what we read in the biblical texts is the history of this community, not of the politically wider province of Judah. Its leaders, such as Zerubbabel and Nehemiah, were not governors as usually understood, but officially designated leaders of the citizen-temple community alone. It would therefore be a mistake to interpret their role and policies as though they affected the province as a whole within the satrapy of Trans-Euphrates. There are clearly far-reaching implications here for our understanding of the history of Judah throughout the Persian period.

Because of the complexity of the issues involved and the fact that they affect our interpretation of so many of the postexilic historical texts, I have examined them in a separate study,[37] of which only the chief points can be summarized here. First, Weinberg lays great emphasis on the results of his statistical analysis of the demographic profile of postexilic Judah, in which he finds that the Jews were only an increasing minority of the population. There are several problems here, however. Without any argument, he asserts that the list in Ezra 2/ Nehemiah 7 of those who returned "at the first" (Neh. 7:5) provides a profile of the emerging citizen-temple community in 458 B.C., the time of Ezra. While some scholars date this list to the time of Nehemiah,

---

37. "Judah and the Jews," in *Studies in Persian History: Essays in Memory of David M. Lewis,* ed. M. Brosius and A. Kuhrt (Leiden: Nederlands Instituut voor het Nabije Oosten, 1998), 145–63.

most continue to see it as a reflection of the composition of the community at the time of the rebuilding of the temple in 520–515 B.C.[38] Moreover, its apparent combination[39] of those who had returned from exile (grouped by family association) with those who had remained in the land (grouped by place of residence) suggests that the list gives a broader representation of the population of Judah at that time than Weinberg suggests.

This conclusion is supported by two further important considerations. On the one hand, Weinberg continues to follow Alt's proposal that Judah was not an independent province before Nehemiah, but only part of Samaria. If that were right, then it would be legitimate to ask about the constitutional status of a minority Jewish element, but we have seen that this theory should almost certainly be abandoned. On the other hand, Weinberg's statistics about the population of Judah should be radically revised in the light of recent research. His approach was in any case highly speculative: he arrived at a figure of more than 200,000 inhabitants of Judah by a process of comparison with his estimate of the preexilic population, the number of those deported, and so on. This was already contentious, since no account was taken of the severe reduction in the size of Judah[40] or of the possible impact of the Babylonian conquest even on those who remained. In consequence, figures as small as a mere 10 percent of Weinberg's figure had been proposed. Most recently, however, this whole issue has been put on a firmer scientific basis by the detailed research of C. E. Carter,[41] who has been able to make use of recent surface surveys of Judah and Benjamin as well as to benefit by the methodological advances of the so-called new archaeology in the process of population estimates. The results of his study are that "the population of Yehud ranges from a low of 11,000 in the late-sixth/early-fifth centuries B.C.E. to a high of 17,000 in the late-fifth/early-fourth centuries B.C.E."[42] Part of the explanation for this much lower figure is that Carter excludes the relatively fertile

---

38. With good reason, in my opinion; see Williamson, *Ezra, Nehemiah*, 28–32. Cf. K. Galling, "Die Liste der aus dem Exil Heimgekehrten," in *Studien zur Geschichte Israels im persischen Zeitalter* (Tübingen: Mohr, 1964), 89–108. The most recent to date it to Nehemiah's time is Blenkinsopp, *Ezra–Nehemiah*, 83.

39. Cf. S. Japhet, "People and Land in the Restoration Period," in *Das Land Israel in biblischer Zeit*, ed. G. Strecker (Göttingen: Vandenhoeck & Ruprecht, 1983), 103–25.

40. On the debate about the borders of postexilic Judah, see the summaries of research in Lemaire, "Populations et territoires," 36–45; and C. E. Carter, "The Province of Yehud in the Post-Exilic Period: Soundings in Site Distribution and Demography," in *Second Temple Studies*, 2:106–45, esp. 108–13.

41. Carter, "Province of Yehud." Part of this article is based on Carter's Ph.D. dissertation (Duke University, 1991), which I have not been able to consult.

42. Ibid., 108.

region of the Ono Valley in the Shephelah (Lod, Hadid, and Ono), which the literary sources suggest was part of the province at this time.[43] Even if we make allowances for this, it is clear that Weinberg's estimate is too high. When this is coupled with the other points made above, it becomes apparent that the total Jewish community comprised a far greater proportion of the population of Judah as a whole, so that it is questionable whether we should contemplate any separate constitutional arrangement for them.

Second, Weinberg draws what I regard as illegitimate consequences about the nature of Ezra's mission. His suggestion that the whole of the Jewish community was exempted from tax at this time seems to be flatly contradicted by Nehemiah 5:4, and is in any case based on an improbable exegesis of Ezra 7:24, a verse that is most naturally understood as granting exemption only to the cultic officials (not the laity), in line with Achaemenid practice in some other cases.[44] Furthermore, the suggestion that Nehemiah was not the civil provincial governor accords neither with the scope of his activities, nor with his dealings as an equal with the governors of neighboring provinces, such as Sanballat of Samaria, nor with the implication of Nehemiah 5:14–18 that Nehemiah's jurisdiction was the same as that of his predecessors whose activities are described in terms of civil authority. In view of Nehemiah's role, and the complete silence of our sources about some alternative authority, there seems to be no room left for a separate administrative level in the province at that time.

Finally, the temple in Jerusalem does not seem to have played the central economic role that it did in the societies with which Weinberg compares it. Indeed, the evidence of Haggai, and later of Malachi and of Nehemiah 10 and 13, is that the temple was constantly neglected. Of course, it was an important ideological symbol for the community, not only in Judah but increasingly in the Diaspora, but so far as we know it owned no land and did not exercise any form of control over title to property by way of membership of its community.[45]

We may conclude, therefore, that there was a considerably closer overlap between the Jewish community and the Persian province of Judah in terms of both population and administration than the citizen-

43. The matter has continued to be debated throughout the period of this survey; see most recently J. Sapin, "Sur le statut politique du secteur de Ono à l'époque perse," in *Lectio Difficilior Probabilior? Mélanges offerts à Françoise Smyth-Florentin*, ed. T. Römer (Heidelberg: Wissenschaftliche-theologische Seminar, 1991), 31–44 (not available to me).

44. Cf. Williamson, "Ezra and Nehemiah in the Light of the Texts from Persepolis," 50–54. I have discussed the exegesis of Ezra 7:24 more fully in "Judah and the Jews."

45. See Bedford, "On Models and Texts," 156–57.

temple community model suggests, and nowhere is there evidence that the Jewish community was treated differently from others who may have lived within the province. The special consideration given to the temple by the Achaemenid kings is to be differently explained, and it remained heavily circumscribed.

Particular Topics

The Exilic Period

So far, this survey has concentrated on broad historical topics that affect the very nature of the Judean community during most of the period under review. They set the framework, as it were, for the discussion of particular topics and events. In turning now to these, we shall find, somewhat disconcertingly, that frequently there is little progress to report. The problems addressed are familiar from earlier periods of research, and basically the same answers are reformulated. Where this is so, I make little more than passing reference to them, in order to be able to concentrate on areas where fresh proposals have been made.

As far as the period of the exile itself is concerned, the picture has changed little in recent years.[46] In the almost complete absence of textual sources, we have only archaeological evidence to guide us, and here the picture continues to be consolidated of widespread destruction of major towns in Judah to the south of Jerusalem (e.g., Lachish, Azekah, Ramat Rahel, Arad), but of greater continuity (or re-establishment) of habitation to the north, in the territory of Benjamin (Bethel, Gibeon, Tell el-Fûl, and Mizpah, the probable site of Babylonian administration).[47] The situation at Jerusalem itself is less clear. It was certainly destroyed following its capture, and it is not certain how soon after settle-

---

46. For a useful earlier survey, see, e.g., B. Oded, "Judah and the Exile," in *Israelite and Judaean History*, ed. J. H. Hayes and J. M. Miller, OTL (London: SCM; Philadelphia: Westminster, 1977), 435–88; and cf. H. M. Barstad, "On the History and Archaeology of Judah during the Exilic Period: A Reminder," *OLP* 19 (1988): 25–36, now expanded into a brief monograph, *The Myth of the Empty Law* (Oslo: Scandinavian University Press, 1996). Within the limits of the present chapter, it is not possible to deal with the history of the Jews in exile or in the Dispersion, for which see the valuable essays by M. Dandamayev, E. J. Bickerman, E. Bresciani, and B. Porten in *CHJ*, 1:326–400; see too the stimulating suggestions about the exiles' mechanisms for survival in Smith, *Religion of the Landless*. G. N. Knoppers also discusses the exile in chap. 8 of the present volume.

47. Cf. S. S. Weinberg, *Post-Exilic Palestine: An Archaeological Report* (Jerusalem: Israel Academy of Sciences and Humanities, 1969); A. Mazar, *Archaeology of the Land of the Bible, 10,000–586 B.C.E.* (New York: Doubleday, 1990), 458–60, 548; G. Barkay, "The Iron Age II–III," in *The Archaeology of Ancient Israel*, ed. A. Ben-Tor (New Haven and London: Yale University Press, 1992), 302–73, esp. 372–73.

ment resumed, though there is evidence that some sort of a cult was continued on the ruined temple site.[48]

Nor has there been much progress on determining the social structure and economic life of those who remained in the land. It is generally agreed that it was the urban elite who, by and large, were exiled to Babylon, but whether the land was radically redistributed among the remaining rural classes as part of the Babylonian imperial policy or whether they simply moved opportunistically into the vacated estates remains uncertain. Judging by the situation in the Persian period, at least, it would appear that the southern part of Judah was infiltrated and settled by Edomites, though even here it is possible to exaggerate.[49]

In contrast with the proposal of Alt that Judah was subsumed into the province of Samaria by the Babylonians, the possibility is now more widely canvassed that they followed their normal practice elsewhere of maintaining the geopolitical status quo, a possibility reinforced by the fact that, unlike the Assyrians, they did not introduce a new foreign elite into the land. This has allowed several recent writers to speculate that Judah continued to be ruled as a vassal kingdom, and that the Davidic monarchy did not come to as abrupt an end as has normally been supposed.[50] As is well known, the much earlier bilingual inscription from Tell Fekherye shows that someone titled "governor" by the imperial power could legitimately be styled "king" by the local population,[51] and a similar state of affairs characterized a number of the western states (e.g., the various Phoenician cities, Cypress, and Cilicia) during the Persian period itself. Might the same have applied to Gedaliah in Babylonian Judah[52] and perhaps even to Zerubbabel and Elnathan (the husband of the probably Davidic Shelomith) in the early

---

48. Cf. Jer. 41:5; Zech. 7:1–7. It is likely that some elements from this exilic liturgy have survived, for instance in the Book of Lamentations and in certain Psalms; I have suggested a similar setting for Nehemiah 9 and Isa. 63:7–64:12; cf. H. G. M. Williamson, "Structure and Historiography in Nehemiah 9," in *Proceedings of the Ninth World Congress of Jewish Studies: Panel Sessions: Bible Studies and Ancient Near East*, ed. D. Assaf (Jerusalem: Magnes, 1988), 117–31; and idem, "Isaiah 63,7–64,11: Exilic Lament or Post-Exilic Protest?" *ZAW* 102 (1990): 48–58.

49. Cf. J. R. Bartlett, *Edom and the Edomites*, JSOTSup 77 (Sheffield: Sheffield Academic Press, 1989), 147–61.

50. See P. Sacchi, "L'esilio e la fine della monarchia Davidica," *Henoch* 11 (1989): 131–48; F. Bianchi, "Le rôle de Zorobabel et de la dynastie davidique en Judée du VIe siècle au IIe siècle av. J.-C.," *Trans* 7 (1994): 153–65.

51. Cf. A. Abou-Assaf et al., *La statue de Tell Fekherye et son inscription bilingue assyro-araméenne* (Paris: Éditions recherche sur les civilisations, 1982), esp. 62 and 111–12.

52. Cf. P. R. Ackroyd, *The Chronicler in His Age*, JSOTSup 101 (Sheffield: Sheffield Academic Press, 1991), 91–92; Miller and Hayes, *History*, 421–24.

Persian period?[53] If so, did this situation persist throughout the exile? Does such a view help with the interpretation of the passages about Zerubbabel in Haggai and Zechariah? Unless further texts are discovered, such possibilities are likely to remain in the realm of tantalizing speculation.

The Persian Period

The early years of Persian rule in Judah also throw up a crop of particular issues that again can be said to have been only recycled in the period under review. The authenticity of the primary sources, on which there has been some progress, was discussed above, as was the issue of Judah's constitutional status. The identity of Sheshbazzar remains uncertain, though the view that he was the same as the Shenazzar of 1 Chronicles 3:18, so making him another Davidic descendant, now looks increasingly unlikely.[54] Some continue to think that the editor of Ezra identified him with Zerubbabel, a view at least as old as Josephus,[55] though again this is historically improbable, if Ezra 5:14 is to be believed. Similarly, the date of Zerubbabel's return to Jerusalem remains contentious. Ezra 3 seems to imply that he came during the reign of Cyrus, although his status alongside Sheshbazzar is then unexplained. As has long been noticed, however, his activities as there described seem to fit better the slightly later period of the first years of Darius, and most scholars therefore date his return then. In my commentary I suggested a compromise, based on a closer analysis of the nature of the composition in this chapter as a whole.[56] If 4:4–5 is understood as a "summary notation," which recapitulates the preceding unit rather than describes a new development, it suggests that the altar building in 3:1–6 should be separated chronologically from the start of the temple building in 3:7–4:3, so that the former could be assigned to Cyrus's reign and the latter to Darius's.

---

53. Cf. A. Lemaire, "Zorobabel et la Judée à la lumière de l'épigraphie (fin du VIᵉ S. av. J.-C.)," *RB* 103 (1996): 48–57. Lemaire also observes that one of Avigad's bullae reads *yhwd/ḥnnh*, and so wonders whether Zerubbabel was first succeeded by his son Hananiah (1 Chron. 3:19).

54. See P.-R. Berger, "Zu den Namen ששבצר und שנאצר," *ZAW* 83 (1971): 98–100; P.-E. Dion, "ששבצר and סנורי," *ZAW* 95 (1983): 111–12. In my view, his title "prince of Judah" in Ezra 1:8 is to be explained on the basis of the author's "second exodus" typology, so that it gives us no historical information as to his identity; cf. Williamson, *Ezra, Nehemiah*, 17–19.

55. E.g., M. Saebø, "The Relation of Sheshbazzar and Zerubbabel—Reconsidered," *SEÅ* 54 (1989): 168–77; J. Lust, "The Identification of Zerubbabel with Sheshbassar," *ETL* 63 (1987): 90–95.

56. *Ezra, Nehemiah*, 43–45.

This proposal has not found favor, however,[57] so that we seem to be little further forward.

In view of my earlier rejection of the citizen-temple community theory, it becomes necessary to reconsider the issue of the state of relations between those who returned from Babylon and those who remained in the land. Several factors have been considered of late to suggest that these were not perhaps as strained at first as has often been thought. Textual evidence includes the apparent association of both groups in the list of Ezra 2, which probably comes from the time of the building of the temple,[58] the incorporation of exilic liturgies into the religious heritage of the community at large, and the complete lack of any sign of such discord in such contemporary texts as Haggai and Zechariah 1–8.[59] To this may be added some reflections of K. Hoglund on the subject of land rights at this time, often thought to be the chief source of conflict between the two communities. Summarizing the results of archaeological surveys of the region, he has shown that, in contrast with the neighboring territories, Judah saw a marked increase in the number of settlements at the start of the Persian period and that some 65 percent of the total number of settlements had not been occupied during the Iron II period. He explains this as part of an imperial domain policy of ruralization, which would have affected the local population as much as those who returned, and concludes that "there would be no land claims by any group rooted in the notion of familial or tribal possession. *The presumption of a class struggle between exiles and 'remainees' over land rights does not fit the evidence of the pattern of these Persian period villages.*"[60]

How, then, does one explain the textual evidence for discord in Ezra 1–6? This is where the importance of a source- and redaction-critical study becomes apparent.[61] Ezra 4:1–3 is part of the later redactor's composition, but there is evidence that it is based on authentic source material.[62] The paragraph clearly speaks of inhabitants of the old northern

---

57. See, e.g., Halpern, "Historiographic Commentary on Ezra 1–6." Halpern's conclusions are comparable with those of the earlier valuable study of S. Japhet, "Sheshbazzar and Zerubbabel—against the Background of the Historical and Religious Tendencies of Ezra–Nehemiah," *ZAW* 94 (1982): 66–98.

58. See Japhet, "Temple and Land."

59. See H. G. M. Williamson, "Concept of Israel in Transition," in *The World of Ancient Israel: Sociological, Anthropological, and Political Perspectives,* ed. R. E. Clements (Cambridge: Cambridge University Press, 1989), 141–61; B. Schramm, *The Opponents of Third Isaiah: Reconstructing the Cultic History of the Restoration,* JSOTSup 193 (Sheffield: Sheffield Academic Press, 1995), 62–64.

60. K. Hoglund, "The Achaemenid Context," in *Second Temple Studies,* 1:54–72.

61. See Williamson, "Composition of Ezra i–vi," 1–30; see also idem, *Ezra, Nehemiah,* ad loc.; Halpern, "Historiographic Commentary on Ezra 1–6," 81–142.

62. See Williamson, *Ezra, Nehemiah,* 49–50.

kingdom of Israel, now the province of Samaria, approaching the temple builders and being rebuffed. Writing as much as two centuries later, and following a long history of disputes between the provincial officials, our redactor understandably labels this group "the enemies of Judah and Benjamin" (Ezra 4:1), and subsequently refers to them as *ʿam haʾāreṣ*, "the people of the land." (Note that, in contrast, the contemporary prophets Haggai and Zechariah still use this term for members of the Judean community, closer to preexilic usage [cf. Hag. 2:4; Zech. 7:5].)[63] This fact must determine our interpretation of his use of the same term in Ezra 3:3, which is equally certainly part of the redactor's composition and for which there is less evidence of an underlying source. The phrase is there used in the plural, "the peoples of the land" preventing the immediate building of the temple by intimidation. This, then, is part of a later rationale for the delay in temple building (external opposition; contrast the very different explanation in Haggai), and gives no evidence of a serious internal split within Judah at the time.

The next phase for which we have written evidence relates to the work of Ezra and Nehemiah. Here, of course, the most notorious historical problem concerns their chronological order. During the period under review there has been a greater tendency to favor the traditional order, as implied by the biblical text,[64] though a late date for Ezra (398 B.C., in the seventh year of Artaxerxes II) still has some support.[65] The intermediate date for Ezra (428 B.C.) has been dropped from consideration altogether. Here again, very little new evidence has been brought to bear in recent years, and as the arguments have frequently been rehearsed elsewhere there seems little point in traversing the same ground again.[66]

A major task for the historian to settle concerns the authenticity of the primary sources. So far as Nehemiah is concerned, scholars have

63. Cf. A. H. J. Gunneweg, "עם הארץ—A Semantic Revolution," *ZAW* 95 (1983): 437–40.

64. So, for instance, all the major commentaries from this period: e.g., Blenkinsopp, Clines, Fensham, Gunneweg, Kidner, Williamson, Yamauchi.

65. See Miller and Hayes, *History*, 468–69; Ahlström, *History*, 862–88; and, most recently, A. Lemaire, "La fin de la première période perse en Égypte et la chronologie judéenne vers 400 av. J.-C.," *Trans* 9 (1995): 51–61.

66. See, e.g., E. M. Yamauchi, "The Reverse Order of Ezra/Nehemiah Reconsidered," *Themelios* 5 (1980): 7–13; Grabbe, *Judaism*, 88–93, who makes the correct observation that if the Ezra material is largely unhistorical, then much of the debate loses its force. I have presented a similar survey with comments and conclusions in *Ezra and Nehemiah*, 55–69. The attempts to link Ezra's mission with the Achaemenid desire for a loyal Judah in the face of disturbances in the west, whether caused by Egypt, Greece, or general unrest, can be used to support either main date, and so cancel each other out. Contrast O. Margalith, "The Political Role of Ezra as Persian Governor," *ZAW* 98 (1986): 110–12 (but note that there is no evidence that Ezra was sent to Jerusalem as governor).

generally accepted that the first-person material in the Book of Nehemiah can be traced back to his own account of his activity, thus making it a source of the first importance.

This confidence has recently been slightly modified in two directions. First, D. J. A. Clines has underlined the extent to which a detailed literary analysis ("a narrative told by a narrator who is also the author") can lead to a radical questioning of many of the apparently historical details of the text.[67] This is an instructive and highly entertaining piece, which certainly serves at the least as a forceful reminder that Nehemiah had axes of his own to grind in writing, and that allowances must be made for this in interpretation. This does not, however, make the whole a work of historical fiction, nor does Clines claim that it does.[68] Indeed, as I have independently argued elsewhere, everything that Nehemiah claims to have accomplished finds in the Book of Nehemiah itself a parallel, third-person source in which the same accomplishments are achieved by the community as a whole, acting under priestly direction.[69] This observation serves both to support the general historical drift of the narrative and to underscore Nehemiah's own bias from a different direction. Second, and rather more radically, Hoglund has followed Eskenazi in an analysis of this same switch from first- to third-person narrative to suggest that this is "not an indication of the utilization of a distinct source," but rather "a deliberate literary device by the narrator to involve the reader in the unfolding drama of events." Hoglund does not think that the accounts were not based on sources, only that we cannot use the present text to reconstruct a first-person account by Nehemiah.[70] This conclusion seems improbable to me,[71] but even if it were justified it would still not remove Nehemiah from the realm of history.

In the case of Ezra, things are less straightforward, and opinions have continued to be sharply divided. G. Garbini has revived the theory

67. D. J. A. Clines, "The Nehemiah Memoir: The Perils of Autobiography," in *What Does Eve Do to Help? and Other Readerly Questions to the Old Testament*, JSOTSup 94 (Sheffield: Sheffield Academic Press, 1990), 124–64.

68. Indeed, he concludes his essay by maintaining that the intention of his analysis has been "to show that a strict regard to the literariness of the document and to the role of the reader in the processing of the document is inevitably profitable *for the historian*" (emphasis mine).

69. H. G. M. Williamson, "Post-Exilic Historiography," in *The Future of Biblical Studies: The Hebrew Scriptures*, ed. R. E. Friedman and H. G. M. Williamson, Semeia Studies (Atlanta: Scholars Press, 1987), 189–207, esp. 192–98; idem, *Ezra, Nehemiah*, xxxii–xxxiii.

70. Hoglund, *Achaemenid Imperial Administration*, 46; following T. C. Eskenazi, *In an Age of Prose: A Literary Approach to Ezra–Nehemiah*, SBLMS 36 (Atlanta: Scholars Press, 1988), 129–35. Recently, J. Becker has even gone so far as to suggest that the work is simply a fabrication by the Chronicler; cf. *Der Ich-Bericht des Nehemiabuches als chronistische Gestaltung*, FB 87 (Würzburg: Echter Verlag, 1998).

71. See Tollefson and Williamson, "Nehemiah as Cultural Revitalization," 41–68.

that Ezra never existed at all.[72] Grabbe believes that he did but that we can know effectively nothing about him or his work because of the lack of authentic source material.[73] Gunneweg thinks that the edict of Artaxerxes (Ezra 7:12–26, the most important source relating to Ezra) is not authentic but that it nevertheless reflects some reasonably well-established aspects of Persian policy toward local cults.[74] Many others continue to uphold to varying degrees the authenticity both of the edict and of the wider "Ezra Memoir" (Ezra 7–10; Neh. 8).

Since a full discussion of this topic would far outstrip the confines of the present chapter, I can here give only a summary of some points that seem to support a relatively conservative conclusion and that have not, apparently, been overturned by the recent more critical suggestions. (1) Older arguments from style (i.e., that the author of the Ezra material is indistinguishable from the Chronicler) do not stand up in the light of more recent research. Most of the similarities that have been observed are no more than characteristics of late biblical Hebrew generally, so that it is the differences that are more significant. (2) The relationship between the edict of Artaxerxes and the rest of the Ezra account is noteworthy. Some aspects of the edict, such as leading a return of volunteers from Babylon and the transportation of gifts, are recounted with studied care and with precise detail of procedure that could well be based on the incorporation of preexisting documents (e.g., 8:1–14, 24–30, 33–34). Others, however, receive not a hint of being carried out (esp. 7:25–26). It is thus difficult to believe that the report is a "midrash" on the edict;[75] if either the narrative had been based solely on the text of the edict, or indeed, if both had been written by the narrator from scratch, we should have expected a better fit. (3) Coupled with this are a number of points of detail, such as place-names (8:15, 17), an inventory (8:26–27), curious local color (10:9, 13), and an unexpected hitch in the preparations for the journey (8:15ff.), that are clearly not based on the edict but that also have no apparent origin other than historical memory. Furthermore, if those many scholars are right who believe that Nehemiah 8 originally be-

---

72. G. Garbini, *History and Ideology in Ancient Israel*, trans. J. Bowden (London: SCM; New York: Crossroad, 1988), 151–69.

73. L. L. Grabbe, "What Was Ezra's Mission?" in *Second Temple Studies*, 2:286–99 (this essay also includes a useful survey of proposals about the purpose of Ezra's mission); cf. idem, *Judaism*, 94–98.

74. *Esra*, 129–43.

75. So, e.g., W. T. in der Smitten, *Esra: Quellen, Überlieferung und Geschichte*, SSN 15 (Assen: Van Gorcum, 1973), ultimately following M. Noth, *Überlieferungsgeschichtliche Studien*, vol. 1 (Halle: Niemeyer, 1943), 145–48 (in English translation as: *The Chronicler's History*, trans. H. G. M. Williamson, JSOTSup 50 [Sheffield: Sheffield Academic Press, 1987], 62–65).

longed between Ezra 8 and 9, then clearly the editor must have been working with antecedent source material when he moved it for theological reasons to its present position. (4) The switches between third- and first-person narrative are most naturally explained as due to an editor partially rewriting an earlier first-person account. In particular, I have argued elsewhere that this has resulted in certain tensions in the present form of the introductory paragraph (7:1–10) that give evidence of this process, and that alternative explanations for this feature of the text are not convincing.[76]

Despite all that has been asserted to the contrary since, therefore, I remain of the opinion that the Ezra material is best understood as being based on a first-person report by Ezra on the first year of his work (once Nehemiah 8 is seen as having come originally from between Ezra 8 and 9, all the dates fit naturally in sequence into a twelve-month period), in which he sought to demonstrate that he had made a good (but not complete) start on carrying out the terms of his commission.[77] When due allowance is made for the editorial activity already referred to, it follows that this source can reasonably be used for historical purposes.

With regard to the historical interpretation of the missions of Ezra and Nehemiah, by far the most stimulating new proposal in recent years has come from Hoglund.[78] He seeks to set them in the wider context of Persian imperial policy in the mid–fifth century in a far more integrated manner than the usual approaches, which think only in terms of seeking to reward or to gain the loyalty of the province during or following the troubled period of the Megabyzos revolt. Indeed, his examination of Greek historical sources leads him (controversially) to deny that there ever was such a revolt. Instead, he argues that the real threat to the empire at this time came from Greek support for the Egyptian revolt, an intervention that meant that the incident developed effectively into a struggle for control of the whole of the eastern Mediterranean, including the Levantine coast. This severe challenge to Persian hegemony in the region led to a change in military and administrative policies, aimed at tightening imperial control. The primary archaeological evidence for this he finds in "the widely dispersed remains of a distinctive form of fortress, unique to the mid–fifth century," located at highly visible sites overlooking communication routes. Since they would have been manned by imperial garrisons, they may be seen as "the indelible

---

76. See Williamson, *Ezra, Nehemiah*, 89–91 and 145–49.

77. The terms of the edict itself are not as impossible as some have supposed; cf. Williamson, "Ezra and Nehemiah in the Light of the Texts from Persepolis"; and idem, *Ezra, Nehemiah*, 97–105.

78. *Achaemenid Imperial Administration*, and, more briefly, "Achaemenid Context."

fingerprint of the hand of the Achaemenid empire tightening its grip on local affairs in the Levant."[79]

Nehemiah's role fits neatly into this picture. The refortification of Jerusalem (not only walls, but also a fortress [2:8] with a commander [7:2]) is quite uncharacteristic of urban centers at this time, and so must indicate some radical shift in policy (contrast the situation in Ezra 4:7–23, earlier in Artaxerxes' reign), namely, that Jerusalem now became a defensive center as part of this policy of militarization. Nehemiah's economic reforms in chapter 5 also fit with this picture. Since imperial garrisons had to be supported by the local population, the new policy would have put a considerable strain on the fragile economy of the region. Nehemiah's reform was thus intended to alleviate the situation, so enabling the community as a whole to meet its increased obligations.

It is noteworthy that the problem of mixed marriages is treated by both Nehemiah and Ezra, which suggests to Hoglund that it too should be seen as an outworking of their role as imperial officials and not be related to independent or internal sectarian concerns, as is usually supposed. This leads him to a reconsideration of Ezra's mission as well. Here he advances two suggestions in particular. First, the evidence for a reorganization of the legal system is interpreted as a further device for tightening control between the imperial center and a subject territory at a time when that relationship was being developed; once again, the threat posed to the Levant by Greek intervention is seen as adequate motivation for this. Second, the issue of marriage is shown to have implications for land tenure. If the Judean community held their land as a dependent population (since all conquered territory was ultimately regarded as imperial domain), it would be intelligible that a redefinition of community membership might be necessary at a time when the degree of control over each section of the population was particularly sensitive.

In advancing his proposals, Hoglund is not unaware that the texts as we now have them are written for other, more overtly theological purposes; he does not suggest that these imperial motivations can be read off from the surface of the accounts. His point, however, is that to make historical sense of them demands that they be set in a context wider than was necessary for the biblical authors themselves. This in itself is reasonable, and his attempt to present a coherent interpretation that takes account of the often diverse activities of the reformers is laudable. Clearly, a full evaluation will take more time than has yet been available. How reliable, for instance, is his dating of the distinctive style of fortress to the short period to which he assigns them, bearing in mind

---

79. *Achaemenid Imperial Administration*, 243.

in particular the difficulties in dating the founding (rather than the abandonment) of single-period sites? To what extent does his understanding of Achaemenid treatment of subject peoples fit with what is known from elsewhere, such as Babylon? How will classical scholars respond to his dismissive treatment of Ctesias and his account of the Megabyzos revolt? And how convincing is his treatment of the issue of mixed marriages in particular? The attempt to see this as part of "an effort to compel loyalty to the imperial system by tying the community's self-interest to the goals of the empire" seems to require further support.[80] Clearly, therefore, Hoglund has opened up many avenues for further exploration both in regard to the texts at our disposal and in terms of wider imperial strategies, which are the subject of the accumulation of a mass of disparate detail. Meanwhile, whatever may be thought of Nehemiah's mission, we should note that there continue to be those who would favor a more traditional portrayal of Ezra's concerns as focused more parochially on the Jewish law and cult.[81]

As I have already indicated, our knowledge of the history of Judah in the fourth century B.C. is practically nonexistent. The main problem is that, in the absence of any continuous narrative, we have no framework into which to fit such pieces of isolated information as we currently possess. The result is that even so fundamental an issue as dating the material is disputed.

This may best be illustrated by one of the few written texts that relate to this period: the much later account of Josephus in his *Jewish Antiquities*. In particular, he includes a story of how the high priest Joannes murdered his brother Jesus in the temple and how in consequence a Persian official named Bagoses imposed a tax on the daily sacrifices (11.7.1 §§297–301). In 1977 I first sought to demonstrate that, on the basis of Josephus's established editorial procedures elsewhere that are also in evidence here, this story must have been based on an earlier source that was likely to be reliable. Second, Josephus's own dating was shown to be untrustworthy, because he was unaware of the true length of Achaemenid rule and so shortened it by as much as two generations: Artaxerxes II and III and Darius II and III were thus conflated. On the

---

80. Ibid., 244. It should be noted in passing that what is usually regarded as the very strict policy on mixed marriages pursued by Ezra and Nehemiah was not shared by all the members of the community, as the more open stance of the Chronicler in the following century indicates. Other books, such as Ruth and Jonah, may further show that, as is to be expected, the whole question of the relationship between the Jews and their neighbors was probably a lively topic of debate throughout the Persian period.

81. Cf. J. Blenkinsopp, "The Mission of Udjahorresnet and Those of Ezra and Nehemiah," *JBL* 106 (1987): 409–21; Williamson, "Concept of Israel in Transition"; idem, *Ezra and Nehemiah*, 69–76.

evidence from the source itself as isolated, I therefore suggested that, as many earlier scholars had thought, the story should be dated to the reign of Artaxerxes III, Bagoses being identified with the Bagoas, a Persian general known from classical sources.[82] Support for this conclusion has been thought to come from the coin of "Yohanan the priest," which D. Barag dates to the mid–fourth century, since it is said to demonstrate that there was a high priest of that name (= Greek Joannes) at that time.[83]

While the argument for Josephus's use of a source and for the fact that he was himself chronologically confused about the last century of Persian rule has been widely accepted, the specific dating proposed for this incident has not. On the basis of one of the Elephantine papyri, which shows that in 408 B.C. (during the reign of Artaxerxes II) there was a high priest Johanan and a governor named Bagohi in Jerusalem, several recent studies have sought to uphold a late-fifth-century date for the incident, which had established itself as the most popular date during the middle part of the twentieth century.[84]

It is not necessary to reopen the debate in the present context. The important point to appreciate is that, while we almost certainly have reliable information about a particular incident, there can be no certainty about when to date it. As all the scholars mentioned agree, both proposed dates are possible, and the difference in opinion is largely a matter of weighing probabilities. For the historian this is frustrating. If we could be sure of the date, we might be able to go on to speculate on a number of important issues, such as the political role of the high priest, the possible divisions of opinion in Jerusalem on contemporary

---

82. See H. G. M. Williamson, "The Historical Value of Josephus' *Jewish Antiquities* XI 297–301," *JTS*, n.s., 28 (1977): 49–66.

83. Barag, "Silver Coin"; see too idem, "Some Notes on a Silver Coin of Yohanan the High Priest," *BA* 48 (1985): 166–68; idem, "Bagoas and the Coinage of Judea," in *Proceedings of the XIth International Numismatic Congress*, vol. 1, ed. T. Hackens and G. Moucharte (Louvaine-la-Neuve: Association Professeur Marcel Hoc, 1993), 261–65. Barag associates the incident with the supposed Judean involvement in the Tennes rebellion, for which he had previously argued independently; cf. "The Effects of the Tennes Rebellion on Palestine," *BASOR* 183 (1966): 6–12. The evidence for this is questionable, however, and has not generally been followed. One should note too that Barag's dating of the coin is questioned by a few scholars, e.g., J. W. Betlyon, "The Provincial Government of Persian Period Judah and the Yehud Coins," *JBL* 105 (1986): 633–42.

84. The papyrus is no. 30 in A. Cowley, *Aramaic Papyri of the Fifth Century B.C.* (Oxford: Clarendon, 1923), 108–19. See D. R. Schwartz, "On Some Papyri and Josephus' Sources and Chronology for the Persian Period," *JSJ* 21 (1990): 175–99; J. C. VanderKam, "Jewish High Priests of the Persian Period: Is the List Complete?" in *Priesthood and Cult in Ancient Israel*, ed. G. A. Anderson and S. M. Olyan, JSOTSup 125 (Sheffield: Sheffield Academic Press, 1991), 67–91; L. L. Grabbe, "Who Was the Bagoses of Josephus (*Ant.* 11.7.1 §§297–301)?" *Trans* 5 (1992): 49–55.

policies, and so on. But in the absence of further evidence, this would be unwise.

The other major point of discussion during this period has been an assessment of the impact of the discovery of the Aramaic papyri from Wâdī ed-Dâliyeh in 1962. Already in the years immediately following their discovery, F. Cross, who was entrusted with their publication, had made known the basic historical facts that could be gathered from them and had used these to construct some further-ranging hypotheses that related to the history of Judah as well as Samaria, to which they primarily belong. Then at the start of the period here under review he offered an overall synthesis of the results.[85] The papyri attest the governorship of a Sanballat later than Nehemiah's rival and also of his two sons, *yšʿyhw* or *ydʿyhw*[86] and Hananiah. Already, of course, the Elephantine papyri had indicated that Sanballat I was succeeded by his son Delaiah. It therefore appears both that there was a "dynastic" element to the governorship of Samaria at this time, and that the family may have practiced papponymy (the naming of a child after his grandfather: the two Sanballats). In view of this, the previously otherwise unattested office of yet another Sanballat at the end of the Persian period, referred to by Josephus (*Ant.* 11.7.2 §§302–3), becomes plausible. Cross's reconstructed list may not be complete, however, as there are coins of a certain Jeroboam, who also could have been a governor.[87] From this basis, Cross went on to suggest that the list of Jerusalem high priests (cf. Neh. 12:10–11) might also be defective, for if papponymy was practiced here as well, some names could have been lost by haplography. Further, he suggested that another detail of Josephus's account could be authentic, namely, the stories of the expulsion from Jerusalem of Manasseh, brother of the high priest Jaddua, because of his marriage to a daughter of Sanballat, and Sanballat's subsequent building of a temple for him on Gerizim at about the time of Alexander the Great (*Ant.* 11.8.2 §§306– 12). This would therefore furnish us with important information about the founding of the Samaritan cult.

85. F. M. Cross, "A Reconstruction of the Judean Restoration," *JBL* 94 (1975): 4–18. While the official final publication of these papyri is still awaited, Cross has provided a preliminary publication of the two best preserved of them in "Samaria Papyrus 1: An Aramaic Slave Conveyance of 335 B.C.E. found in the Wâdī ed-Dâliyeh," *EI* 18 (1985): 7*– 17*; and "A Report of the Samaria Papyri," in *Congress Volume: Jerusalem, 1986*, ed. J. A. Emerton, VTSup 40 (Leiden: Brill, 1988), 17–26.

86. The name is damaged, and so the precise reconstruction is hypothetical; nevertheless, Lemaire ("Populations et territoires," 44–45 n. 67, and 66 n. 209) wonders whether the recently published Jaddua coin (Spaer, "Jaddua the High Priest?") might not refer to him rather than to a Jerusalem high priest.

87. See Y. Meshorer and S. Qedar, *The Coinage of Samaria in the Fourth Century B.C.* (Los Angeles: Numismatic Fine Arts International, 1991), coins 23–27; cf. pp. 14 and 49.

After gaining some initial favor, Cross's theory has come in for considerable criticism.[88] There is, as we have seen, some numismatic support for a high priest Johanan at about the period Cross postulates, but beyond that there are a number of inconsistencies in the detail of his proposals, and in particular there is still much to be said for the older view that the story in Josephus is a variant of the similar account in Nehemiah 13:28. Once again, we see how, in the absence of a firm chronological framework of events, it is all too easy to allow "floating" incidents to be misplaced and for our historical account to be skewed in consequence.

There is one further observation about this closing century of Persian rule that future discoveries may help to fill out. As the number of official seals, bullae, and coins has increased, it has become apparent that toward the end of the period there was shift away from the use of Aramaic script and language in favor of Hebrew.[89] It is tempting to see evidence here for a resurgence of religious and nationalist interest and to link this with the possible evidence we have seen for a greater involvement of the priestly class in the civil government of the province. Other data might be added to this, such as the probable radical reorganization of the priesthood as a whole at this time,[90] the general unrest in the western part of the empire, and so on. In view of the fate already noted of other speculative hypotheses concerning this period, however, prudence suggests that we would do better to await further hard evidence.

Conclusion

In sum, one may conclude that during the period here under review, very little progress on historical reconstruction has been made on the basis of study of the biblical texts themselves (this does not, of course, refer to textual, literary, or theological study, where a more positive tale could be told). Most of the options had all been canvassed long before, and they have merely been rearranged and re-presented. Such advances as have been made have been seen to come almost entirely either from new archaeological and epigraphical data, or from setting the biblical

---

88. See Schwartz, "On Some Papyri"; VanderKam, "Jewish High Priests"; Grabbe, "Who Was the Bagoses?"; G. Widengren, "The Persian Period," in *Israelite and Judaean History*, ed. Hayes and Miller, 489–538, esp. 506–9; H. G. M. Williamson, "Sanballat," *ABD*, 5:973–75; idem, *Ezra, Nehemiah*, 399–401; and L. L. Grabbe, "Josephus and the Reconstruction of the Judean Restoration," *JBL* 106 (1987): 231–46.

89. See Lemaire, "Inscriptions"; J. Naveh and J. C. Greenfield, "Hebrew and Aramaic in the Persian Period," *CHJ*, 1:115–29; Barag, "Silver Coin," 17–19.

90. Cf. H. G. M. Williamson, "The Origins of the Twenty-Four Priestly Courses," in *Studies in the Historical Books of the Old Testament*, ed. J. A. Emerton, VTSup 30 (Leiden: Brill, 1979), 251–68.

narratives more effectively into their wider background in the Achae-menid Empire, understanding of which has progressed rapidly. It may be doubted whether all the historical questions that the biblical texts raise will approach a solution on this basis in the future, but the hope may certainly be expressed that some will and, perhaps more impor-tantly, that our understanding of what we think we already know will be refined as developing historical light is shed on this familiar material.

10

Israelite Prophets and Prophecy

David W. Baker

Since knowledge in biblical studies is increasing exponentially, as it is in every field of knowledge, a survey of the discipline must follow some organizing principle in order to make sense. This encounter with the Israelite prophets and their world can do no less, so to bring some semblance of order to the vast amount of literature dealing with them that has appeared over the past three decades,[1] I use a variant of a model de-

---

1. Among several recent surveys, see W. McKane, "Prophecy and the Prophetic Literature," in *Tradition and Interpretation: Essays by Members of the Society for Old Testament Study,* ed. G. W. Anderson (Oxford: Clarendon, 1979), 163–88; R. P. Gordon, "A Story of Two Paradigm Shifts," in *The Place Is Too Small for Us: The Israelite Prophets in Recent Scholarship,* ed. R. P. Gordon, SBTS 5 (Winona Lake, Ind.: Eisenbrauns, 1995), 3–26; L. L. Grabbe, *Prophets, Priests, Diviners, and Sages in Ancient Israel: A Socio-Historical Study of Religious Specialists in Ancient Israel* (Valley Forge, Pa.: Trinity Press International, 1995), 66–118; and essays by P. D. Miller Jr., "The World and Message of the Prophets," 97–112; M. A. Sweeney, "Formation and Forms in Prophetic Literature," 113–26; and K. P. Darr, "Literary Perspectives on Prophetic Literature," 127–43, in *Old Testament Interpretation: Past, Present, and Future: Essays in Honor of Gene M. Tucker,* ed. J. L. Mays, D. L. Petersen, and K. H. Richards (Nashville: Abingdon, 1995). For extensive bibliographies, see H. O. Thompson, *The Book of Daniel: An Annotated Bibliography,* Books of the Bible 1 (New York: Garland, 1993); idem, *The Book of Jeremiah: An Annotated Bibliography,* ATLA Bibliography Series 41 (Lanham, Pa., and London: Scarecrow, 1996); idem, *The Book of Amos: An Annotated Bibliography,* ATLA Bibliography Series 42 (Lanham, Pa., and London: Scarecrow, 1997); the relevant sections in *Elenchus Bibliographicus Biblicus of Biblica* (Rome: Pontifical Biblical Institute), which finished with volume 65 covering 1984 and was replaced by *Elenchus of Biblica* (Rome: Pontifical Biblical Institute, 1988–) starting with 1985 publications; and W. G. Hupper, *An Index to English Periodical Literature on the Old Testament and Ancient Near Eastern Studies,* ATLA Bibliography Series 21 ([Philadelphia]: American Theological Library Association; Metuchen, N.J.: Scarecrow, 1987–).

veloped by David L. Petersen.[2] He divides the field of prophetic study into two, "Prophetic Identity," discussing models and general issues, and "Prophetic Literature," discussing methods of study.[3] I propose to organize this study under four main headings that follow a chronological progression. The first, "Precomposition," explores the person of the prophet and his background, including his definition and role in the historical and social setting. "Composition" and "Transmission" look at the prophets' formulation of their message and its subsequent use and development. Finally, "Application" briefly highlights a growing trend in exploring the use of Old Testament texts in contemporary preaching and teaching.

Scholars have looked at each of these issues, asking the following questions:

Precomposition
- Who were the prophets?
- Where did the prophets fit in their society?
- How did the prophets understand who they were?
- With whom do the prophets compare, both in their own time and in recent periods?
- Where do the prophets fit in time and place?

Composition
- How did the prophets speak?
- What kinds of messages did they give?

Transmission
- How did the prophetic messages move from speech to text?
- How did others use their words?
- Can we recover their words?

Application
- What are the theological interests of the prophets?
- What relevance do the prophets have for us today?

As can be readily seen, the boundaries between these elements are somewhat fluid, some areas crossing into more than one section. As long as the categories are not understood as exclusive, the model should serve a heuristic function.

---

2. D. L. Petersen, "Introduction: Ways of Thinking about Israel's Prophets," in *Prophecy in Israel*, ed. D. L. Petersen, IRT 10 (Philadelphia: Fortress, 1986), 1–21.
3. Ibid., 2.

Precomposition

Who Were the Prophets, and Where Did They Fit in Their Society?

The very definition of prophecy, and the identification of a prophet, have reached a new intensity of discussion in recent years.[4] Rather than simply looking at a biblical reading of what prophets were, as found, for example, in Deuteronomy 18 or 2 Kings 17:13, recent study has been informed by sociological readings of the text that have built on previous work by such thinkers as Max Weber.[5] Scholarship has sought to place the prophetic person and role within a wider social context.[6] This involves locating prophets by noting the role they played in society in relation to other institutions, such as the monarchy and the priesthood.

Biblically, the prophets saw their authority deriving from a call by God, being his messengers[7] or servants (Josh. 1:1–2; 2 Kings 14:25,

4. B. Vawter, "Were the Prophets *Nābî's?*" *Bib* 66 (1985): 206–20; Petersen, "Introduction"; M. Weippert, "Aspekte israelitischer Prophetie im Lichte verwandter Erscheinung des Alten Orients," in *Ad bene et fideliter seminandum, Festgabe für Karlheinz Deller zum 21. February 1987*, ed. G. Mauer and U. Magen, AOAT 220 (Kevelaer: Butzon & Bercker; Neukirchen-Vluyn: Neukirchener Verlag, 1988), 287–319; Gordon, "Story," 3–26; J. Blenkinsopp, *Sage, Priest, Prophet: Religious and Intellectual Leadership in Ancient Israel*, Library of Ancient Israel (Louisville: Westminster/John Knox, 1995), 115–19.

5. M. Weber, *Ancient Judaism*, trans. and ed. H. H. Gerth and D. Martindale (Glencoe, Ill.: Free Press, 1952); idem, *The Theory of Social and Economic Organization*, trans. A. M. Henderson and T. Parsons, ed. T. Parsons (New York: Free Press, 1964); idem, *On Charisma and Institution Building*, ed. S. Eisenstadt (Chicago and London: University of London Press, 1968); idem, *Economy and Society*, ed. G. Roth and C. Witlich, trans. E. Fischoff et al. (Berkeley: University of California Press, 1978). See D. L. Petersen, "Max Weber and the Sociological Study of Ancient Israel," in *Religious Change and Continuity*, ed. H. Johnson (San Francisco: Jossey-Bass, 1979), 117–49; B. Lang, "Max Weber und Israels Propheten," *Zeitschrift für Religions- und Geistesgeschichte* 36 (1984): 156–65. See the useful collection regarding this field, including an excerpt from Weber, in C. E. Carter and C. L. Meyers, eds., *Community, Identity, and Ideology: Social-Scientific Approaches to the Hebrew Bible*, SBTS 6 (Winona Lake, Ind.: Eisenbrauns, 1996).

6. R. R. Wilson, *Prophecy and Society in Ancient Israel* (Philadelphia: Fortress, 1980); idem, *Sociological Approaches to the Old Testament*, Guides to Biblical Scholarship, OT Series (Philadelphia: Fortress, 1984), partially reprinted in *Place Is Too Small*, ed. Gordon, 332–44; Gordon, "Story," 21–22; R. P. Carroll, "Prophecy and Society," in *The World of Ancient Israel: Sociological, Anthropological, and Political Perspectives*, ed. R. E. Clements (Cambridge: Cambridge University Press, 1989), 203; Grabbe, *Prophets, Priests*, 66–118.

7. For one who does see a prophet receiving authority through inspiration, see B. Uffenheimer, "Prophecy, Ecstasy and Sympathy," in *Congress Volume: Jerusalem, 1986*, ed. J. A. Emerton, VTSup 40 (Leiden: Brill, 1988), 257–69: "The living experience of divine grace was so compelling that man felt the obligation to become a messenger to the cultic congregation and to his fellow man in general." See also R. E. Clements, "Introduction: The Interpretation of Old Testament Prophecy, 1965–1995," in *Old Testament Prophecy: From Oracles to Canon* (Louisville: Westminster/John Knox, 1996), 1–19; P. D. Miller Jr., "The World and Message of the Prophets: Biblical Prophecy in Its Context," in *Old Testament Interpretation*, ed. Mays, Petersen, and Richards, 101.

etc.). From a sociological perspective, most of that authority derived from society itself as the audience of the message.[8] One could say that the prophets would be the servants of society. This newer, sociological approach highlights the importance of the recipients of the message in recognizing the messenger as a prophet, grounding his or her identity upon that recognition. It often does not take into account any concept, whether actual or self-delusional, of divine call, which, from a biblical perspective, is more foundational than societal recognition for establishing one as a prophet.[9]

Those in society could well have also recognized prophets as authoritative if they saw parallels with another authoritative figure from the past, Moses. He was recognized as both authoritative lawgiver and prototypical prophet (Deut. 18:15–22; 34:10–12). Scholars have noted linguistic, structural, and thematic links between Moses on the one hand and Isaiah, Jeremiah, and Ezekiel on the other.[10] Some scholars do see an early, preexilic existence of ones called, either at that period or later, "prophets,"[11] while others see the title, if not the function, as a post-

8. B. O. Long, "Prophetic Authority as Social Reality," in *Canon and Authority: Essays on Old Testament Religion and Theology,* ed. B. O. Long and G. W. Coats (Philadelphia: Fortress, 1977), 3–20; idem, "Social Dimensions of Prophetic Conflict," *Semeia* 21 (1982): 31–43; G. M. Tucker, "Prophecy and the Prophetic Literature," in *The Hebrew Bible and Its Modern Interpreters,* ed. D. A. Knight and G. M. Tucker (Chico, Calif.: Scholars Press, 1985), 325–68. Cf. T. W. Overholt, "The Ghost Dance of 1890 and the Nature of the Prophetic Process," *Ethnohistory* 21 (1974): 37–63; idem, "Jeremiah and the Nature of the Prophetic Process," in *Scripture in History and Theology: Essays in Honor of J. Coert Rylaardsam,* ed. A. L. Merrill and T. W. Overholt, PTMS 17 (Pittsburgh: Pickwick, 1977), 129–50; idem, "Commanding the Prophets: Amos and the Problem of Prophetic Authority," *CBQ* 41 (1979): 517–32.

9. Gordon points out that the prophets' self-awareness was more important to them than societal acceptance, since they carried out their calling even if not accepted by their audience ("Story," 22). There is a debate whether the prophets were aware of their identity (R. P. Gordon, "Where Have All the Prophets Gone? The 'Disappearing' Prophet against the Background of Ancient Near Eastern Prophecy," *BBR* 5 [1995]: 67–86) or not (A. G. Auld, "Prophets through the Looking Glass: Between the Writings and Moses," *JSOT* 27 [1983]: 3–23).

10. M. O'Kane, "Isaiah: A Prophet in the Footsteps of Moses," *JSOT* 69 (1996): 29–51; C. R. Seitz, "The Prophet Moses and the Canonical Shape of Jeremiah," *ZAW* 101 (1989): 3–27; J. D. Levenson, *Theology of the Program of Restoration of Ezekiel 40–48,* HSM 10 (Cambridge, Mass.: Scholars Press, 1976); H. McKeating, "Ezekiel the 'Prophet Like Moses,'" *JSOT* 61 (1994): 97–109.

11. V. W. Rabe, "Origin of Prophecy," *BASOR* 221 (1976): 125–28; Vawter, "Were the Prophets Nābîʾs?"; T. W. Overholt, "Prophecy in History: The Social Reality of Intermediation," *JSOT* 48 (1990): 3–29; H. M. Barstad, "No Prophets? Recent Developments in Biblical Prophetic Research and Ancient Near Eastern Prophecy," *JSOT* 57 (1993): 39–60; B. Peckham, *History and Prophecy: The Development of Late Judean Literary Traditions,* ABRL (New York: Doubleday, 1993), 554; Gordon, "Where Have All the Prophets Gone?" 57–86.

exilic innovation.[12] This prophetic association with Moses highlights one of the roles of the prophet as applying *tôrâ* to the life of the people, calling them to return to the covenant that forged them into a nation.[13]

This attempt to change the people's behavior is done by what would be termed "preaching" today,[14] persuading through the gamut of rhetorical devices (see below under "How Did the Prophets Speak?"). The necessity for constant repetitions of the prophetic cry for repentance and return to the covenant, at times by several messengers addressing a single generation, and at other times by prophets challenging subsequent generations, would indicate that these men and women[15] were not, on the whole, recognized by their audience as actual, authoritative messengers from God. Presumably, if society had so recognized them, their message would have been more efficacious. In other words, if prophets are defined by society's recognition of them and their function as noticeably affecting the life and behavior of that society, one would question whether prophets actually existed in ancient Israel, since practical impact was negligible as evidenced by the lack of meaningful, sustained response to their message. That most of those in Israelite society appear not to have recognized prophetic authority as having any practical effect on how they lived leads one to question the sociological emphasis on the role society played in recognizing and legitimizing prophetic authority. The prophets regarded their divine commissioning as providing their authority, an authority that was independent of the response of the people to whom they spoke.

Some have suggested that the authority of the prophet altered over time. In the earlier, classical period, they were deliverers of the inspired, oral word from God, while later they were somewhat replaced by inspired interpreters of a previously received word. As W. M. Schniedewind would have it, they changed from "interpreters of historical events" to "inspired text interpreter[s]."[16]

---

12. Auld, "Prophets through the Looking Glass"; R. P. Carroll, "Poets Not Prophets: A Response to 'Prophets through the Looking Glass,'" *JSOT* 27 (1983): 25–31; idem, "Inventing the Prophets," *Irish Biblical Studies* 10 (1988): 24–36.

13. R. E. Clements, *Prophecy and Tradition* (Oxford: Blackwell, 1975), 55–57, 85; Miller, "World and Message of the Prophets."

14. G. V. Smith, *An Introduction to the Hebrew Prophets: The Prophets as Preachers* (Nashville: Broadman & Holman, 1994).

15. While all the Israelite writing prophets were male, female prophets were also active in Israel. See, e.g., J. Jarick, "The Seven (?) Prophetesses of the Old Testament," *Lutheran Theological Journal* 28 (1994): 116–21.

16. W. M. Schniedewind, *The Word of God in Transition: From Prophet to Exegete in the Second Temple Period*, JSOTSup 197 (Sheffield: Sheffield Academic Press, 1995), specifically 236, 241. See a similar development of the role of the scribe in D. W. Baker, "Scribes as Transmitters of Tradition," in *Faith, Tradition, and History: Old Testament Historiography in Its Near Eastern Context*, ed. A. R. Millard, J. K. Hoffmeier, and D. W. Baker (Winona Lake, Ind.: Eisenbrauns, 1994), 65–78.

Prophets have long been felt to play a particular social function in relation to the religious cult in Israel.[17] A spectrum of opinion has been expressed. Some see a cultic tie with most of the prophets, their livelihood deriving from their service to the temple.[18] Others eschew any prophet-cult tie whatsoever, though R. P. Gordon sees the latter strict bifurcation as now being on the wane.[19] A close look at the biblical evidence would suggest that this strict polarization, like most such, cannot be taken to an extreme, since there is internal biblical evidence for differing relationships for each of the prophets with the official cult, ranging from participant to strong critic. There would also have been a mutual influence, with the prophets having their religious upbringing in the context of the official cult, but also needing at times to provide a cautionary voice against some of its practices.[20]

With Whom Do the Prophets Compare from Their Own Time Period and Geographical Region?

If, as Klaus Koch has suggested, Israelite prophecy is part of an "international movement,"[21] insight should be available from Israel's neighbors. Other ancient Near Eastern societies do show prophetic phenomena similar to those recorded in the Old Testament.[22] These societies include the Semitic-speaking societies in Mesopotamia that were temporally and spatially proximate to Israel.[23] Texts discovered to date

17. G. W. Ahlström, *Joel and the Temple Cult of Jerusalem*, VTSup 21 (Leiden: Brill, 1971); A. R. Johnson, *The Cultic Prophet and Israel's Psalmody* (Cardiff: University of Wales Press, 1979); W. H. Bellinger, *Psalmody and Prophecy*, JSOTSup 27 (Sheffield: JSOT Press, 1984), 78–82. See McKane, "Prophecy and the Prophetic Literature," 183; G. M. Tucker, "Prophecy and the Prophetic Literature," in *The Hebrew Bible and Its Modern Interpreters*, ed. Knight and Tucker, 325–68; and Gordon, "Story," 9–12.

18. See, e.g., S. Mowinckel, "Psalms and Wisdom," in *Wisdom in Israel and the Ancient Near East*, ed. M. Noth and D. W. Thomas, VTSup 3 (Leiden: Brill, 1960), 306; and discussion and references in Wilson, *Prophecy and Society*, 8–10.

19. Gordon, "Story," 12. See also Grabbe, *Prophets, Priests*, 112–13.

20. J. Jeremias, *Kultprophetie und Geschichtsverkündigung in der späten Königszeit Israels*, WMANT 35 (Neukirchen-Vluyn: Neukirchener Verlag, 1970).

21. K. Koch, *The Prophets*, vol. 1, *The Assyrian Period*, trans. M. Kohl (London: SCM, 1982; Philadelphia: Fortress, 1983), 12.

22. H. Ringgren, "Prophecy in the Ancient Near East," in *Israel's Prophetic Tradition: Essays in Honour of Peter R. Ackroyd*, ed. R. J. Coggins, A. Phillips, and M. A. Knibb (Cambridge: Cambridge University Press, 1982), 1–11.

23. Actual prophetic texts are discussed below. Divination was one of the common means of determining the will of the deity in Mesopotamia, as well as elsewhere in the ancient Near East, and in this way has some links with prophecy. See J. Vervant, *Divination et Rationalité* (Paris: Seuil, 1974); J. Lust, "On Wizards and Prophets," in *Studies on Prophecy: A Collection of Twelve Papers*, VTSup 26 (Leiden: Brill, 1974), 133–42; J. Wright, "Did Amos Inspect Livers?" *ABR* 23 (1975): 3–11; I. Starr, *The Ritual of the Diviner*, Bibliotheca Mesopotamica 12 (Malibu: Undena, 1983), dealing mainly with divination in

come mainly from two historical periods, the earlier, Old Babylonian (eighteenth century B.C.) texts from Mari[24] and those more recently discovered at Ischali,[25] and the later, Neo-Assyrian texts (seventh century B.C.).[26] Unlike the biblical texts themselves, which are fixed and few in

---

Mesopotamia; H. W. F. Saggs, *The Encounter with the Divine in Mesopotamia and Israel* (London: Athlone, 1978); M. Dietrich, *Deutungen der Zukunft in Briefen, Orakeln und Omina*, vol. 2.1 of *Texte aus der Umwelt des Alten Testaments*, ed. O. Kaiser et al. (Gütersloh: Mohn, 1986); M. D. Ellis, "Observations on Mesopotamian Oracles and Prophetic Texts: Literary and Historiographic Considerations," *JCS* 41 (1989): 127–86; I. Starr, *Queries to the Sun God: Divination and Politics in Sargonid Assyria*, State Archives of Assyria 4 (Helsinki: University of Helsinki Press, 1990); F. H. Cryer, *Divination in Ancient Israel and Its Near Eastern Environment: A Socio-Historical Investigation*, JSOTSup 142 (Sheffield: JSOT Press, 1994); V. A. Hurowitz, "Eli's Adjuration of Samuel (1 Samuel iii 17–18) in the Light of a 'Diviner's Protocol' from Mari (AEM I/1,1)," *VT* 44 (1994): 483–97; A. Jeffers, *Magic and Divination in Ancient Palestine and Syria*, Studies in the History and Culture of the Ancient Near East 8 (Leiden: Brill, 1996).

24. See F. Ellermeier, *Prophetie in Mari und Israel*, Theologische und orientalistische Arbeiten 1 (Herzberg: Jungfer, 1968); S. D. Walters, "Prophecy in Mari and Israel," *JBL* 89 (1970): 78–81; J. F. Ross, "Prophecy in Hamath, Israel, and Mari," *HTR* 63 (1970): 1–28; H. B. Huffmon, "The Origins of Prophecy," in *Magnalia Dei: The Mighty Acts of God: Essays on the Bible and Archaeology in Memory of G. Ernest Wright*, ed. F. M. Cross, W. E. Lemke, and P. D. Miller Jr. (Garden City, N.Y.: Doubleday, 1976), 171–86; E. Noort, *Untersuchungen zum Gottesbescheid in Mari: Die 'Mari-prophetie' in der alttestamentlichen Forschung*, AOAT 202 (Kevelaer: Butzon & Bercker; Neukirchen-Vluyn: Neukirchener Verlag, 1977); M. Weinfeld, "Ancient Near Eastern Patterns in Prophetic Literature," *VT* 27 (1977): 178–95; H. B. Schmökel, "Mesopotamian Texts, Introduction," in *Near Eastern Religious Texts Relating to the Old Testament*, ed. W. Beyerlin, trans. J. Bowden, OTL (Philadelphia: Westminster; London: SCM, 1978), 68–73; Wilson, *Prophecy and Society*, 98–110; J.-M. Durand, *Archives épistolaires de Mari*, I/1, ARM 26 (Paris: Éditions recherche sur les civilisations, 1988), esp. his introduction to this important collection of newly published texts, 377–412, 455–63; M. Weippert, "Aspekte israelitischer Prophetie im Lichte verwandter Erscheinung des Alten Orients," in *Ad bene et fideliter seminandum*, 287–319; A. Malamat, *Mari and the Early Israelite Experience* (Oxford and New York: Oxford University Press, 1989), 79–96 and 125–44 are excerpted in *Place Is Too Small*, ed. Gordon, 50–73; R. P. Gordon, "From Mari to Moses: Prophecy at Mari and in Ancient Israel," in *Of Prophets' Visions and the Wisdom of Sages: Essays in Honour of R. N. Whybray on His Seventieth Birthday*, ed. H. A. McKay and D. J. A. Clines, JSOTSup 162 (Sheffield: JSOT Press, 1993), 63–79; A. Schart, "Combining Prophetic Oracles in Mari Letters and Jeremiah 36," *JANES* 23 (1995): 75–93.

25. M. D. Ellis, "The Goddess Kititum Speaks to King Ibalpiel: Oracle Texts from Ischali," *MARI* 5 (1987): 235–56; cf. Grabbe, *Prophets, Priests*, 90–91.

26. A. K. Grayson, *Babylonian Historical-Literary Texts*, Toronto Semitic Texts and Studies 3 (Toronto and Buffalo: University of Toronto Press, 1975); S. Parpola, *Letters from Assyrian Scholars to the Kings Esarhaddon and Assurbanipal*, AOAT 5.2 (Kevelaer: Butzon & Bercker; Neukirchen-Vluyn: Neukirchener Verlag, 1983); M. Weippert, "Assyrische Prophetien der Zeit Asarhaddons und Assurbanipals," in *Assyrian Royal Inscriptions: New Horizons in Literary, Ideological, and Historical Analysis*, ed. F. M. Fales, Oriens Antiqui Collectio 17 (Rome: Istituto per l'Oriente, 1981), 71–104; Weippert, "Aspekte israelitischer Prophetie"; Ellis, "Observations"; S. Parpola and K. Watanabe, *Neo-Assyrian Treaties and Loyalty Oaths*, State Archives of Assyria 2 (Helsinki: Helsinki University Press, 1988); A. Livingstone, *Court Poetry and Literary Miscellanea*, State Archives of

number, these extrabiblical texts are increasing in discovery and publication all of the time, so the potential to shed increasing light on prophecy is great.

The Mari texts are in the form of letters that report revelations received and provide insight into the various personnel, both professional and lay, acting as divine intermediaries.[27] The Ischali texts are few and fragmentary but indicate that the practice of intermediation was not restricted to Mari in this period. The activities of intermediaries in this early period seem to be more marginal to the regular societal practices, since confirmation of the revelation is often sought by other means such as divination or a confirmatory oath.[28]

The Assyrian prophetic texts include collections of revelations, as well as individual texts. Intermediaries are at times, but not always, given titles, one of which (*maḥḥû*, ecstatic) was also found at Mari.[29] While similarities of practice have been found in these more distant areas, etymological cognates of the Israelite term *nābîʾ*, "prophet," have been found at Mari,[30] and much more recently at the geographically closer, thirteenth-century site of Emar (Meskene) in northern Syria.[31] These cognates with the biblical term indicate that prophecy as connected with the *nābîʾ* could have originated in the west.[32]

Assyria 3 (Helsinki: Helsinki University Press, 1989); M. Nissinen, "Die Relevanz der neuassyrischen Prophetie für die alttestamentliche Forschung," in *Mesopotamica, Ugaritica, Biblica: Festschrift für Kurt Bergerhof zur Vollendung seines 70. Lebensjahres am 7. Mai, 1992*, ed. M. Dietrich and O. Loretz, AOAT 232 (Kevelaer: Butzon & Bercker; Neukirchen-Vluyn: Neukirchener Verlag, 1993), 217–58. Summary also in H. B. Huffmon, "Prophecy, Ancient Near Eastern," *ABD*, 5:480–81.

27. See the helpful summaries in Huffmon, "Prophecy, Ancient Near Eastern," *ABD*, 5:478–79.

28. W. L. Moran, "New Evidence from Mari on the History of Prophecy," *Bib* 50 (1969): 15–56; S. Dalley, C. B. F. Walker, and J. D. Hawkins, *Old Babylonian Texts from Tel al-Rimmah* (London: British School of Archaeology in Iraq, 1976), 64–65 on text 65.

29. J. S. Holladay, "Assyrian Statecraft and the Prophets of Israel," *HTR* 63 (1970): 29–51 (reprinted in *Prophecy in Israel*, ed. Petersen, 122–43); Wilson, *Prophecy and Society*, 111–19; F. R. Magdalene, "Ancient Near Eastern Treaty-Curses and the Ultimate Texts of Terror: A Study of the Language of Divine Sexual Abuse in the Prophetic Corpus," in *A Feminist Companion to the Latter Prophets*, ed. A. Brenner, Feminist Companion to the Bible 8 (Sheffield: Sheffield Academic Press, 1995), 326–52; Grabbe, *Prophets, Priests*, 93–94.

30. Durand, *Archives épistolaires de Mari*, 444; see 377–79 for a discussion; D. E. Fleming, "The Etymological Origins of the Hebrew *nābîʾ*: The One Who Invokes God," *CBQ* 55 (1993): 217–24.

31. D. Arnaud, *Recherches au pays d'Aštata: Emar*, 3 vols. (Paris: Éditions recherche sur les civilisations, 1985–87), 353, 360, 375, 377, 385–86, 403; Fleming, "Etymological Origins," 220; idem, "*Nābû and Munabbiātu*: Two New Syrian Religious Personnel," *JAOS* 113 (1993): 175–83.

32. Gordon, "Story," 20.

Even closer to Israel geographically and linguistically is the seventh-century Aramaic Balaam document from Deir ʿAlla in Jordan.[33] Speaking of "Balaam, son of Beor," it indicates a knowledge of the biblical character of that name in the geographical area of his activities as recorded in the Old Testament text (Num. 22–24). This earliest extant Canaanite prophetic text does not exactly parallel the biblical accounts, but it is useful in studying the redactional transmission of prophetic material,[34] a matter to which we return below.

The Egyptian story of Wen-Amun describes the hero's encounter with ecstatic activity among the Phoenicians.[35] The biblical account also records ecstatic activity in this geographical area (1 Kings 18), but there have been no native texts to provide firsthand information.

As for Israel's non-Semitic neighbor, Egypt has not yielded close parallels to Israelite prophecy. Divination was widely practiced (see Gen. 44:1–5), but divine speech was not a source of revelation.[36] Asia Minor does have evidence of "divine speaking" in a list of sources of messages from the gods compiled by the Hittite king Mursilis II (fourteenth century B.C.).[37]

A suggested prophetic function as covenant mediator (cf. Deut. 18:15–19)[38] has been offered support by linking it with treaties from second-millennium Mesopotamia,[39] though the rise in interest in first-millennium prophecy has usurped some of the argument. While specifically covenantal references might not be found in some prophetic texts, scholars suggest that a literary form called the "covenant lawsuit" (e.g., Isa. 1; Amos 3:9–15) recalls a national covenant of which the prophets were aware and to which they were calling the people to return.[40] This

33. See chap. 2 of the present volume under "Deir ʿAlla Texts" and chap. 3 under "The Balaam Texts from Deir ʿAlla" for bibliography concerning this inscription.

34. Petersen, "Introduction," 6.

35. *ANET,* 26; A. Cody, "The Phoenician Ecstatic Wenamūn: A Professional Oracular Medium," *JEA* 65 (1979): 99–106.

36. Huffmon, "Prophecy, Ancient Near Eastern," *ABD,* 5:481; Grabbe, *Prophets, Priests,* 86–87.

37. C. Kühne, "C. Hittite Texts, II. Prayers, 6: The So-Called Second Plague Prayer of Mursilis II," in *Near Eastern Religious Texts,* ed. Beyerlin, 169–74; R. Lebrun, *Hymnes et Prières Hittites* (Louvain-la-Neuve: Centre de l'histoire des religions, 1980). See Weippert, "Aspekte israelitischer Prophetie," 287–319; and Huffmon, "Prophecy, Ancient Near Eastern," *ABD,* 5:477–78.

38. Wilson, *Prophecy and Society,* 158–59; D. L. Petersen, *The Roles of Israel's Prophets,* JSOTSup 17 (Sheffield: JSOT Press, 1981), 83–84.

39. See D. J. McCarthy, *Treaty and Covenant: A Study in Form in the Ancient Oriental Documents and in the Old Testament,* 2d ed., AnBib 21A (Rome: Biblical Institute Press, 1981).

40. E.g., M. O. Boyle, "The Covenant Lawsuit of the Prophet Amos III 1–IV 13," *VT* 21 (1971): 338–62; A. Schoors, *I Am God Your Saviour: A Form-Critical Study of the Main*

legal setting cannot be demonstrated in every case, so it must still be treated as tentative.[41]

With Whom Do the Prophets Compare from More Recent Times and More Geographically Distant Regions?

A recent innovation in attempting to determine the role of prophet is the use of cultural anthropology, particularly to find parallels between biblical prophets and those in more modern societies who perform somewhat the same functions.[42] Robert Wilson was a pioneer in this area, especially looking at African societies, with Thomas Overholt finding similarities with North American Indian "prophets."[43] Wilson paid particular attention to the claim that ecstasy or a trance state was characteristic of all prophecy, including that of Israel, a position held by some in the past.[44] He understands this purportedly stereotypical

---

Genres in Is. xl–lv, VTSup 24 (Leiden: Brill, 1973), 176–89; K. Nielsen, *Yahweh as Prosecutor and Judge: An Investigation of the Prophetic Lawsuit (Rîb-Pattern)*, JSOTSup 9 (Sheffield: JSOT Press, 1979); idem, "Das Bild des Gerichts (rib-Pattern) in Jes. I–XII: Eine Analyse der Beziehung zwischen Bildsprache und dem Anliegen der Verkündigung," *VT* 29 (1979): 309–24; S. Niditch, "The Composition of Isaiah 1," *Bib* 61 (1980): 509–29; M. de Roche, "Yahweh's *Rîb* against Israel: A Reassessment of the So-Called 'Prophetic Lawsuit' in the Preexilic Prophets," *JBL* 102 (1983): 563–74; J. T. Willis, "The First Pericope in the Book of Isaiah," *VT* 34 (1984): 63–77; D. R. Daniels, "Is There a 'Prophetic Lawsuit' Genre?" *ZAW* 99 (1987): 339–60; M. Dijkstra, "Lawsuit, Debate, and Wisdom Discourse in Second Isaiah," in *Studies in the Book of Isaiah: Festschrift Willem A. M. Beuken*, ed. J. van Ruiten and M. Vervenne, BETL 132 (Louvain: Leuven University Press and Peeters, 1997), 251–71.

41. R. R. Wilson, "Form-Critical Investigation of the Prophetic Literature: The Present Situation," in *One Hundred Ninth Annual Meeting, Chicago, 8–11 November, 1973*, ed. G. MacRae (Cambridge, Mass.: Society of Biblical Literature, 1973), 1:118.

42. For an introduction to and examples of this approach, see *Community, Identity, and Ideology*, ed. Carter and Meyers, and the essay by Carter in the present volume, chap. 15.

43. Wilson, *Prophecy and Society*, esp. chap. 2; idem, *Sociological Approaches;* see also M. P. Adogbo, "A Comparative Analysis of Prophecy in Biblical and African Traditions," *Journal of Theology for Southern Africa* 88 (1994): 15–20. Overholt, "The Ghost Dance of 1890"; idem, "Prophecy: The Problem of Cross-Cultural Comparison," *Semeia* 21 (1982): 55–78 (reprinted in *Anthropological Approaches to the Old Testament*, ed. B. Lang, IRT 8 [Philadelphia: Fortress; London: SPCK, 1985], 60–82); idem, *Prophecy in Cross-Cultural Perspective: A Sourcebook for Biblical Researchers*, SBLSBS 17 (Atlanta: Scholars Press, 1986); idem, *Cultural Anthropology and the Old Testament*, Guides to Biblical Literature, OT Series (Minneapolis: Augsburg Fortress, 1996).

44. E.g., G. Hölscher, *Die Propheten* (Leipzig: Hinrichs, 1914). For recent discussion of the issue see S. B. Parker, "Possession Trance and Prophecy in Pre-Exilic Israel," *VT* 28 (1978): 271–85; Wilson, *Prophecy and Society*, 3–8; Petersen, *Roles of Israel's Prophets; G.* André, "Ecstatic Prophecy in the Old Testament," in *Religious Ecstasy*, ed. N. G. Holm (Stockholm: Almqvist & Wiksell, 1982), 187–200; Uffenheimer, "Prophecy, Ecstasy, and Sympathy," 257–58; P. Michaelsen, "Ecstacy and Possession in Ancient Israel: A Review of Some Recent Contributions," *SJOT* 2 (1989): 28–54; Grabbe, *Prophets, Priests*, 108–11.

psychological mode for prophecy as being only for some societies, not universal. For Israel, the presentation of the message through stereotypical forms of prophetic speech is at least as important as the psychology of the recipient, and not all prophets were ecstatics.[45]

This important distinction was shown by Wilson to hold also in the linguistic realm. Hebrew has one verb for "prophesy" *(nbʾ)*, which occurs in two verbal stems, the *niphal* and the *hitpael*. He finds the former to designate prophetic speech, and the latter, societally characteristic prophetic behavior. The importance of this distinction can be seen in the life of Saul, whose ecstatic activity *(hitpael)* led those who saw him to ask if he also was a prophet (1 Sam. 10:11–12), even though he was technically not one, since he had no prophetic message *(niphal)*.[46]

Numerous scholars have urged caution upon practitioners of the comparative anthropology method, since the existence of evidence solely in written form presents problems. There is no direct evidence, but only secondary sources that themselves interpret the primary data.[47] There needs to be great caution in proposing that observations from societies that are greatly separated from each other in both space and time are anything more than suggestive. Practices in a contemporary, modern society could lead to investigation of the existence of similar phenomena in an earlier society, but they cannot be used to prescribe that the practices must have the same meaning in both. One must firmly establish the existence of interplay between two cultures in order to make a case for anything other than chance or cultural universals explaining similarities of practice. While potentially illuminating, such proposed parallels must be treated as suggestive, not definitive.

45. Wilson, *Prophecy and Society,* 87. Other studies on ecstasy and the prophetic experience have been done by Parker, "Possession Trance"; Rabe, "Origin of Prophecy," 125–26; R. R. Wilson, "Prophecy and Ecstasy: A Reexamination," *JBL* 79 (1978): 321–37; J. R. Porter, "The Origins of Prophecy in Israel," in *Israel's Prophetic Tradition,* ed. Coggins et al., 21–22; H. W. Wolff, "Prophet und Institution im Alten Testament," in *Charisma und Institution,* ed. T. Rendtorff (Gütersloh: Mohn, 1985), 87–101; A. D. H. Mayes, "Prophecy and Society in Israel," in *Of Prophets' Visions,* ed. McKay and Clines, 31–35.

46. Wilson, *Prophecy and Society,* 182–83; see Long, "Prophetic Authority," who also sees authority as deriving from actions, not just words.

47. W. J. Ong, *Orality and Literacy: The Technologizing of the Word* (New York and London: Methuen, 1982); J. S. Kselman, "The Social World of the Israelite Prophets: A Review Article," *RelSRev* 11.2 (1985): 120–29; W. J. Ong, "Writing Is a Technology That Restructures Thought," in *The Written Word: Literacy in Transition,* ed. G. Baumann, Wolfson College Lectures 1985 (Oxford: Clarendon, 1986); J. Goody, *The Logic of Writing and the Organization of Society* (Cambridge and New York: Cambridge University Press, 1986); Carroll, "Prophecy and Society."

Where Do the Prophets Fit in Their Historical and Geographical Time and Place?

Israelite prophets, as intermediaries between Israel's God and the people, were called upon to address contextual needs and shortcomings. As with all temporally contextual, or "occasional," literature, discovering the precise historical context of books and individual prophecies is necessary to adequately understand the message.

Brian Peckham has undertaken a recent massive attempt at historical contextualization.[48] He correlates the composition of the Pentateuch with that of the former and latter prophets as he "pursues the order and discovers the relationship of their writings, uncovers their sources . . . and articulates the cumulative and progressive contribution of the works to an ongoing, developing tradition."[49] The work proposes the interconnectedness between the prophetic, historical, and pentateuchal sources from the foundational Yahwistic epic chronologically up to the Chronicler and Malachi. Peckham provides a fascinating attempt at integration and synthesis, and will be a touchstone for future research, but his results, while ingenious, are subjective from the outset.

The past quarter century has seen a convulsion in the foundations of some of the "assured results of biblical scholarship," not least being the question of the composition of the Pentateuch.[50] Even Peckham's work mirrors this in his ordering of the putative sources not according to the "established" order of JEDP, but rather as JPED. Other proposed dates of composition and redaction are also subjective, as is expected for ancient documents with no clear internal evidence for the exact processes and dates of composition and transmission. While understandable in dealing with ancient literature, this results in a product that, while intriguing, can be considered only a suggestion rather than proof.

Other more limited studies seek to set prophetic events in their historical contexts. The plethora of new commentaries usually have this as one of their goals, as do essays on individual prophets and passages.[51]

---

48. Peckham, *History and Prophecy*. See also D. N. Freedman, *The Unity of the Hebrew Bible* (Ann Arbor: University of Michigan Press, 1991).

49. Peckham, *History and Prophecy*, vii.

50. See chap. 5 of the present volume for an overview.

51. E.g., K. N. Schoville, "A Note on the Oracles of Amos against Gaza, Tyre, and Edom," in *Studies on Prophecy*, 55–63; A. Vanel, "Ṭâbeʾél en Is. VII 6 et le roi Tubail de Tyr," in *Studies on Prophecy*, 17–24; and other contributions to the volume; D. L. Christensen, "The Acrostic of Nahum Once Again: A Prosodic Analysis of Nahum 1,1–10," *ZAW* 99 (1987): 17–30; F. J. Gonçalves, *L'expédition de Sennachérib en Palestine dans la littérature hébraïque ancienne*, Publications de l'Institut Orientaliste de Louvain 34 (Louvain-la-Neuve: Université Catholique de Louvain, Institut Orientaliste, 1986); M. A. Sweeney, *Isaiah 1–4 and the Post-Exilic Understanding of the Isaianic Tradition*, BZAW 171 (Berlin:

   Physical artifacts have recently started to come into their own as being able to throw light on prophetic texts. The background from which the prophet was speaking as well as that into which his message was sent can be potentially illuminated by the archaeology of a society. Pride of place in this archaeological area of study goes to a recent encyclopedia that presents the breadth of Near Eastern archaeology, though it does not systematically cover the prophetic material per se.[52] The most comprehensive synthetic study of this field has been undertaken by Philip King in exploring archaeology's contributions to the understanding of Amos, Hosea, and Micah, as well as of Jeremiah.[53] Other studies have looked at more limited text portions, such as the relationship of Isaiah 5:8–10 to Assyrian urban archaeology,[54] the campaign(s) of Sennacherib as it impinges on the biblical accounts,[55] the archaeology of Ezekiel 13,[56] the geography of Amos,[57] the religious views of the period of Hosea 1:2 as reflected in the Kuntillet ʿAjrud inscriptions,[58] the place of child sacrifice in Israel and its environment (Mic. 6:7),[59]

---

de Gruyter, 1988); J. R. Lundbom, *The Early Career of the Prophet Jeremiah* (Lewiston, N.Y.: Mellen Biblical Press, 1993); C. R. Seitz, "Account A and the Annals of Sennacherib: A Reassessment," *JSOT* 58 (1993): 47–57; W. McKane, "Worship of the Queen of Heaven (Jer. 44)," in *"Wer ist wie Du, HERR, unter den Göttern?" Studien zur Theologie und Religionsgeschichte für Otto Kaiser zum 70. Geburtstag,* ed. I. Kottsieper (Göttingen: Vandenhoeck & Ruprecht, 1994), 318–24; P. L. Redditt, "Nehemiah's First Mission and the Date of Zechariah 9–14," *CBQ* 56 (1994): 664–78; M. A. Sweeney, "Sargon's Threat against Jerusalem in Isaiah 10,27–32," *Bib* 75 (1994): 457–70; P. L. Redditt, "Daniel 11 and the Sociohistorical Setting of the Book of Daniel," *CBQ* 60 (1998): 463–74.

   52. E. M. Meyers, ed., *The Oxford Encyclopedia of Archaeology in the Near East,* 5 vols. (New York and Oxford: Oxford University Press, 1997).

   53. P. J. King, *Amos, Hosea, Micah: An Archaeological Commentary* (Philadelphia: Westminster, 1988); idem, *Jeremiah: An Archaeological Companion* (Louisville: Westminster/John Knox, 1993); idem, "Jeremiah's Polemic against Idols—What Archaeology Can Teach Us," *BibRev* 10.6 (1994): 22–29.

   54. F. E. Dobberahn, "Jesaja verklagt die Mörder an der menschlichen Gemeinschaft: Ein exegetischer Versuch zum 'Erkenntnistheoretischen Privileg' der Armen Lateinamerikas," *EvT* 54 (1994): 400–412.

   55. Gonçalves, *L'expédition de Sennachérib.*

   56. G. I. Davies, "An Archaeological Commentary on Ezekiel 13," in *Scripture and Other Artifacts: Essays on the Bible and Archaeology in Honor of Philip J. King,* ed. M. D. Coogan, J. C. Exum, and L. E. Stager (Louisville: Westminster/John Knox, 1994), 108–25.

   57. J. A. Burger, "Amos: A Historical-Geographical View," *JSem* 4 (1992): 130–50; E. F. Campbell, "Archeological Reflections on Amos's Targets," in *Scripture and Other Artifacts,* 130–50.

   58. W. Boshoff, "Sexual Encounters of a Different Kind: Hosea 1:2 as Foreplay to the Message of the Book of Hosea," *Religion and Theology* 1 (1994): 329–39. See the discussion by Arnold in the present volume, chap. 14.

   59. L. E. Stager, "The Rite of Child Sacrifice at Carthage: Papers of a Symposium," in *New Light on Ancient Carthage,* ed. J. G. Pedley (Ann Arbor: University of Michigan Press, 1980), 1–11.

religious iconography,[60] and the Book of Daniel.[61]

Three specific archaeological topics related to the prophets have generated special interest. The *mrzḥ* is mentioned in Jeremiah 16:5 and Amos 6:7. Based on texts from Ugarit (thirteenth century B.C.) and from Palmyra in Syria (second–fourth centuries A.D.), it appears that this is a funerary celebration in which wine and oil played a major part.[62] Suggestions of its appearance even earlier at Ebla await further confirmation.[63] A recent suggestion has seen the festivities even in texts where they are not mentioned by name, such as the debauchery of Isaiah 28:1–6.[64]

More controversial is the discovery at Tell Dan of a ninth-century Aramaic inscription that apparently includes a reference to "the house of

60. O. Keel and C. Uehlinger, *Gods, Goddesses, and Images of God in Ancient Israel*, trans. T. H. Trapp (Minneapolis: Fortress, 1998).

61. A. Merling, "Daniel y la Arqueología," *Theologika* 8.1 (1993): 2–43; P. Coxon, "Another Look at Nebuchadnezzar's Madness," in *The Book of Daniel in the Light of New Findings*, ed. A. S. van der Woude, BETL 106 (Louvain: Leuven University Press and Peeters, 1993), 211–22. Several other topics involving archaeology and the prophetic texts are discussed in *Scripture and Other Artifacts*, ed. Coogan et al.

62. A. Negev, "Nabatean Inscriptions," *IEJ* 13 (1963): 113–16; P. D. Miller Jr., "The *Mrzḥ* Text," in *The Claremont Ras Shamra Tablets*, ed. L. R. Fisher, AnOr 48 (Rome: Pontifical Biblical Institute, 1971), 37–48; M. Dahood, "Additional Notes on the *Mrzḥ* Text," in ibid., 51–54; J. Braslavi, "Jeremiah 16:5; Amos 6:7," *Beth Miqra* 48 (1971): 5–13 (in Hebrew); M. Pope, "A Divine Banquet at Ugarit," in *The Use of the Old Testament in the New and Other Essays: Studies in Honor of William Franklin Stinespring*, ed. J. M. Efird (Durham: Duke University Press, 1972), 170–203; J. Greenfield, "The *Marzēaḥ* as a Social Institution," *Acta Antiqua* 22 (1974): 451–55; T. L. Fenton, "The Claremont '*Mrzḥ*' Tablet: Its Text and Meaning," *UF* 9 (1977): 71–76; B. Halpern, "Landlord-Tenant Dispute at Ugarit?" *Maarav* 2 (1979): 121–40; B. Margalit, "The Ugaritic Feast of the Drunken Gods: Another Look at RS 24.258 (*KTU* 1.114)," *Maarav* 2 (1980): 98–105; R. E. Friedman, "The *Mrzḥ* Tablet from Ugarit," *Maarav* 2 (1980): 187–206; M. Pope, "The Cult of the Dead at Ugarit," in *Ugarit in Retrospect: Fifty Years of Ugarit and Ugaritic*, ed. G. Young (Winona Lake, Ind.: Eisenbrauns, 1981), 159–79; J. Teixidor, "Le Thiase de Belastor et de Beelshamen d'après une inscription récemment découverte à Palmyre," *CRAIBL* (1981): 306–14; M. Dietrich and O. Loretz, "Der Vertrag eines *Mrzḥ*-Klubs in Ugarit: Zum Verständnis von *KTU* 3.9," *UF* 14 (1982): 71–76; H. M. Barstad, *The Religious Polemics of Amos: Studies in the Preaching of Amos 2,7B–8; 4,1–13; 5,1–27; 6,4–7; 8,14*, VTSup 34 (Leiden: Brill, 1984); King, *Amos, Hosea, Micah*, 137–61; idem, "The *Marzeah* Amos Denounces—Using Archaeology to Interpret a Biblical Text," *BAR* 14.4 (1988): 34–44. For further bibliography and discussion, see, e.g., F. I. Andersen and D. N. Freedman, *Amos: A New Translation with Notes and Commentary*, AB 24A (New York: Doubleday, 1989), 566–68; and S. M. Paul, *Amos*, Hermeneia (Minneapolis: Fortress, 1991), 210–12.

63. G. Pettinato, *Testi Amministrativi Della Biblioteca L2769: Materiali Epigrapici di Ebla* (Naples: University of Naples, 1980); M. Dahood, "The Minor Prophets and Ebla," in *The Word of the Lord Shall Go Forth: Essays in Honor of David Noel Freedman in Celebration of His Sixtieth Birthday*, ed. C. L. Meyers and M. O'Connor (Winona Lake, Ind.: Eisenbrauns, 1983), 54.

64. B. A. Asen, "The Garlands of Ephraim: Isaiah 28.1–6 and the *Marzēaḥ*," *JSOT* 71 (1996): 73–87, which has extensive bibliography on the festival.

David" (*bytdwd*; cf. the prophecy of 2 Sam. 7:5, 7, 11, 13, 27), with some
seeing a parallel with the "tent of David" that will be restored, according
to Amos 9:11.[65] Being the earliest extrabiblical mention of the name of
David, the text is extremely important for history, and responses to its
discovery have run the gamut from positing it a forgery,[66] claiming a
misreading of the key terms,[67] or suggesting that it comes from a century or two later,[68] on the one hand, to accepting it as being authentic,
on the other.[69] In support of an earlier reading of the name David is a
suggested rereading of the Moabite Stone.[70]

Less controverted finds have been those of seals and bullae that bear
the names of figures from the Book of Jeremiah, including Gemariah,
son of Shaphan (36:10–12),[71] Jerahmeel, the king's son (36:26),[72] and
others, including Baruch, son of Neriah, the scribe of Jeremiah (32:12;
43:1–7). It is suggested that one even bears Baruch's visible fingerprint.[73]

Composition

How Did the Prophets Speak?

As preachers, the prophets endeavored to persuade their audience to
turn from their disobedience and follow God. The classical discipline of
rhetoric, the art of persuasive speech, was first articulated among the

65. P. R. Davies, "*Bytdwd* and *Swkt Dwyd:* A Comparison," *JSOT* 64 (1994): 23–24. Cf.
A. Biran and J. Naveh, "An Aramaic Stele Fragment from Tel Dan," *IEJ* 43 (1993): 81–98.

66. F. H. Cryer, "On the Recently-Discovered 'House of David' Inscription," *SJOT* 8
(1994): 3–20, esp. 14–15.

67. Ibid., 17 and n. 34; P. R. Davies, "'House of David' Built on Sand," *BAR* 20.4
(1994): 54–55; E. A. Knauf, A. de Pury, and T. Römer, "**BaytDawīd* ou **BaytDōd?*" *BN* 72
(1994): 60–69, reading *dwd* as an epithet ("beloved") of a god.

68. Cryer, "On the Recently-Discovered 'House of David' Inscription," 9, 12; N. P.
Lemche and T. L. Thompson, "Did Biran Kill David? The Bible in the Light of Archaeology," *JSOT* 64 (1994): 5, who not only date the text from the eighth century but also reinterpret *dwd* to be an epithet of Yahweh.

69. [H. Shanks], "'David' Found at Dan," *BAR* 20.2 (1994): 26–39; A. Rainey, "The
'House of David' and the House of the Deconstructionists," *BAR* 20.6 (1994): 47; D. N.
Freedman and J. C. Geoghegan, "'House of David' Is There," *BAR* 21.2 (1994): 78–79; B.
Halpern, "Erasing History: The Minimalist Assault on Ancient Israel," *BibRev* 11.6
(1995): 26–35; here Halpern sees the denial of the historicity of the inscription as a cal-
culated attempt to minimalize the ability to write any history of the period of the OT.

70. A. Lemaire, "'House of David' Restored in Moabite Inscription," *BAR* 20.3 (1994):
30–37.

71. N. Avigad, *Hebrew Bullae from the Time of Jeremiah* (Jerusalem: Israel Exploration
Society, 1986); King, *Jeremiah*, 94–95.

72. King, *Jeremiah*, 95–97.

73. H. Shanks, "Jeremiah's Scribe and Confidant Speaks from a Hoard of Clay Bullae,"
BAR 13.5 (1987): 58–68; T. Schneider, "Six Biblical Signatures," *BAR* 17.4 (1991): 26–33;
King, *Jeremiah*, 95; H. Shanks, "Fingerprint of Jeremiah's Scribe," *BAR* 22.2 (1996): 36–38.

Greeks by Aristotle.[74] Though rhetoric is not a biblical concept, Ye-
hoshua Gitay was able to use insights gleaned from classical rhetoric to
elucidate the prophets, especially Isaiah,[75] and the approach can be
fruitful for the rest of the prophetic corpus as well. It seeks to place the
message into its context by asking what the situation was that was being
addressed, how the prophets wished their audience to respond to the
message, and which persuasive techniques they used. Their words were
purposeful, in contrast to the empty eloquence of some later Sophists.[76]

Most of the prophetic texts are poetic, and numerous scholars have
explored them in studies of Hebrew poetry in general,[77] or in more limited studies of some of their poetic features such as prosody (the Hebrew metric system),[78] wordplay,[79] sound play such as alliteration or

74. Aristotle, *The "Art" of Rhetoric,* trans. H. E. Butler, LCL (Cambridge, Mass.: Harvard University Press, 1926). See Quintilian, *The Institutio Oratoria,* trans. H. E. Butler, 4
vols., LCL (Cambridge, Mass.: Harvard University Press, 1921). For a summary discussion of the discipline, see B. Witherington III, *Conflict and Community in Corinth: A
Socio-Rhetorical Commentary on 1–2 Corinthians* (Grand Rapids: Eerdmans), 39–48, 55–
61 (for bibliography).

75. Y. Gitay, *Prophecy and Persuasion: A Study of Isaiah 40–48,* Forum Theologicae
Linguisticae 14 (Bonn: Linguistica Biblica, 1981); idem, "Isaiah and His Audience,"
Prooftexts 3 (1983): 223–30; idem, "Reflections on the Study of the Prophetic Discourse,"
VT 33 (1983): 207–21; idem, *Isaiah and His Audience: The Structure and Meaning of Isaiah
1–12,* SSN 30 (Assen: Van Gorcum, 1991); idem, "Rhetorical Criticism," in *To Each Its
Own Meaning: An Introduction to Biblical Criticisms and Their Application,* ed. S. R.
Haynes and S. L. McKenzie (Louisville: Westminster/John Knox, 1993), 135–49.

76. Witherington, *Conflict and Community,* 43–65. See 1 Cor. 2:1.

77. T. Collins, *Line-Forms in Hebrew Poetry: A Grammatical Approach to the Stylistic
Study,* StPohl: Series Maior 7 (Rome: Pontifical Biblical Institute, 1978); M. O'Connor,
Hebrew Verse Structure (Winona Lake, Ind.: Eisenbrauns, 1980); P. van der Lugt, *Stro-
fische Structuren in de Bibels-Hebreeuwse Poëzie* (Kampen: Kok, 1980); J. L. Kugel, *The
Idea of Biblical Poetry* (New Haven: Yale University Press, 1981); S. A. Geller, "Theory and
Method in the Study of Biblical Poetry," *JQR* 73 (1982): 65–77; S. A. Geller, E. L. Green-
stein, and A. Berlin, *A Sense of Text: The Art of Language in the Study of Biblical Literature,*
JQRSup 1982 (Winona Lake, Ind.: Eisenbrauns, 1983); R. Alter, *The Art of Biblical Poetry*
(New York: Basic Books, 1985); A. Berlin, *The Dynamics of Biblical Parallelism* (Bloom-
ington: Indiana University Press, 1985); W. G. E. Watson, *Classical Hebrew Poetry: A
Guide to Its Techniques,* 2d ed., JSOTSup 26 (Sheffield: Sheffield Academic Press, 1986;
reprinted 1995); D. J. A. Clines, "The Parallelism of Greater Precision," in *Directions in
Biblical Hebrew Poetry,* ed. E. Follis, JSOTSup 40 (Sheffield: JSOT Press, 1987), 77–100;
J. T. Willis, "Alternation (ABA'B') Parallelism in the Old Testament Psalms and Prophetic
Literature," in ibid., 49–76.

78. D. L. Christensen, "The Acrostic of Nahum Reconsidered," *ZAW* 87 (1975): 5;
D. K. Stuart, *Studies in Early Hebrew Meter,* HSM 13 (Missoula, Mont.: Scholars Press,
1976); J. M. Vincent, *Studien zur literarischen Eigenart und zur geistigen Heimat von Jesaja, Kap 40–55,* Beiträge zur biblischen Exegese und Theologie 5 (Frankfurt am Main,
Berne, and Las Vegas: Lang, 1977); K. Kiesow, *Exodustexte im Jesajabuch: Literarkritische
und motivgeschichtliche Analysen,* OBO 24 (Freiburg, Switzerland: Universitätsverlag,
1979); J. P. Fokkelman, "Stylistic Analysis of Isaiah 40:1–11" in *Remembering All the Way,*
OTS 21 (1981): 68–90; W. R. Garr, "The Qinah: A Study of Poetic Meter, Syntax and Style,"

assonance,[80] or structure.[81] The broader field of textlinguistics (discourse analysis) has also provided insight into understanding written and oral texts. It recognizes that meaning resides in larger textual elements than simply the words and sentences that have been the domain of morphological and syntactic study, the major areas of grammatical analysis until recently. It analyzes the structure and meaning of elements on the text or story level.[82] The methodology has been fruitful in looking at aspects of prophetic structure,[83] though much room remains

---

ZAW 95 (1983): 54–75; O. Loretz, *Der Prolog Des Jesaja Buches (1,1–2,5)*, Ugaritologische und kolometrische Studien zum Jesaja-Buch 1 (Altenberg: CIS-Verlag, 1984); Christensen, "The Acrostic of Nahum Once Again"; F. I. Andersen, "The Poetic Properties of Poetic Discourse in the Book of Micah," in *Biblical Hebrew and Discourse Linguistics*, ed. R. D. Bergen (Dallas: Summer Institute of Linguistics, 1994), 520–28.

79. D. L. Christensen, "Anticipatory Paranomasia in Jonah 3:7–8 and Genesis 37:2," *RB* 90 (1983): 261–63; A. J. Petrotta, *Lex Ludens: Wordplay in the Book of Micah*, American University Studies VII/105 (New York: Lang, 1991); K. Holter, "A Note on שביה/שבי in Isa. 52,2," *ZAW* 104 (1992): 106–7; B. T. Arnold, "Wordplay and Narrative Techniques in Daniel 5 and 6," *JBL* 112 (1993): 479–85; S. Bahar, "Two Forms of the Root *Nwp* in Isaiah x 32," *VT* 43 (1993): 403–5; K. Holter, "The Wordplay on אל ('God') in Isaiah 45,20–21," *SJOT* 7 (1993): 88–98; W. A. M. Beuken, "What Does the Vision Hold: Teachers or One Teacher? Punning Repetition in Isaiah 30:20," *HeyJ* 36 (1995): 451–66.

80. J. P. van der Westhuizen, "Assonance in Biblical and Babylonian Hymns of Praise," *Semitics* 7 (1980): 81–101; L. Boadt, "Intentional Alliteration in Second Isaiah," *CBQ* 45 (1983): 353–63.

81. L. Boadt, "Isaiah 41:8–13: Notes on Poetic Structure and Style," *CBQ* 35 (1973): 6; A. R. Ceresko, "The Function of Chiasmus in Hebrew Poetry," *CBQ* 40 (1978): 1–10; J. S. Kselman, "Design and Structure in Hebrew Poetry," in *SBLSP, 1980*, ed. P. Achtemeier (Chico, Calif.: Scholars Press, 1980), 1–16; H. V. Parunak, "Oral Typesetting: Some Uses of Biblical Structure," *Bib* 62 (1981): 153–68; J. Krašovec, "Merism–Polar Expression in Biblical Hebrew," *Bib* 64 (1983): 231–39; H. V. Parunak, "Transitional Techniques in the Bible," *JBL* 102 (1983): 525–48; S. Segert, "Poetic Structures in the Hebrew Sections of the Book of Daniel," in *Solving Riddles and Untying Knots: Biblical, Epigraphic, and Semitic Studies in Honor of Jonas C. Greenfield*, ed. Z. Zevit et al. (Winona Lake, Ind.: Eisenbrauns, 1995), 261–75. This type of study is not restricted to poetry; cf. M. Rosenbaum, *Word-Order Variation in Isaiah 40–55: A Functional Perspective*, SSN 35 (Assen: Van Gorcum, 1997), noting especially his helpful bibliography, 235–56.

82. For an introduction to the field not only in biblical studies but also more widely in textual study, see P. Cotterell and M. Turner, *Linguistics and Biblical Interpretation* (Downers Grove, Ill.: InterVarsity; London: SPCK, 1989).

83. T. J. Finley and G. Payton, "A Discourse Analysis of Isaiah 7–12," *JTT* 6 (1993): 317–35; E. R. Clendenen, "Old Testament Prophecy as Hortatory Text: Examples from Malachi," *JTT* 6 (1993): 336–53; R. E. Longacre and S. J. J. Hwang, "A Textlinguistic Approach to the Biblical Hebrew Narrative of Jonah," in *Biblical Hebrew and Discourse Linguistics*, ed. Bergen, 336–58; H. V. Parunak, "Some Discourse Functions of Prophetic Quotation Formulas in Jeremiah," in ibid., 489–519; D. J. Clark, "Vision and Oracle in Zechariah 1–6," in ibid., 529–60; D. M. Carr, "Isaiah 40:1–11 in the Context of the Macrostructure of Second Isaiah," in *Discourse Analysis of Biblical Literature: What It Is and What It Offers*, ed. W. R. Bodine, SBL Semeia Studies (Atlanta: Scholars Press, 1995), 51–74; D. J. Holbrook, "Narrowing Down Haggai: Examining Style in Light of Discourse and Content," *JTT* 7 (1995): 1–12; U. Simon, *Reading Prophetic Narratives*, trans. L. J.

for further study of other prophetic texts and of increasingly larger text portions.

Syntax itself has also been an ongoing interest of scholars of Hebrew literature, not least the Prophets. New tools are being used in this analysis, including statistical and other work using the power of the computer.[84]

Going in the reverse order of text size, scholars have sought to understand the meaning of the prophetic message by utilizing lexicography, the study of lexical forms, that is, words.[85] Word use and linguistics are also used in attempts to date the composition of prophetic texts[86] and to find their geographical source through the study of dialectology.[87]

Since the prophets were preachers, the original form of most of their messages was most likely oral. The question arises whether we have any material actually written by a prophet himself. At one extreme, some deny actual writing of any prophetic material to the prophets themselves, all messages being orally delivered.[88] If they were uttered in an ecstatic state, this would necessarily be the case. Others argue that the

Schramm, Indiana Studies in Biblical Literature (Bloomington: Indiana University Press, 1997), who analyzes narratives concerning prophets from the historical books.

84. E.g., E. Talstra and A. L. H. M. van Wieringen, eds., *A Prophet on the Screen: Computerized Description of Isaianic Texts*, Applicatio 9 (Amsterdam: VU University Press, 1992).

85. Most commentaries spend much of their effort on the lexical, morphological, or syntactic levels. Pride of place would go most probably to the commentaries of F. I. Andersen and D. N. Freedman, *Hosea: A New Translation with Introduction and Commentary*, AB 24 (Garden City, N.Y.: Doubleday, 1980); Andersen and Freedman, *Amos*. Individual lexical studies also abound, e.g., T. N. D. Mettinger, "The Elimination of a *Crux?* A Syntactic and Semantic Study of Isaiah xl 18–20," in *Studies on Prophecy;* 77–83; M. A. Sweeney, "On *ûmᵉśôś* in Isaiah 8.6," in *Among the Prophets: Language, Image, and Structure in the Prophetic Writings*, ed. P. R. Davies and D. J. A. Clines, JSOTSup 144 (Sheffield: JSOT Press, 1993), 42–54; J. T. Willis, "The 'Repentance' of God in the Books of Samuel, Jeremiah, and Jonah," *HBT* 16 (1994): 156–75.

86. A. Hurvitz, *A Linguistic Study of the Relationship between the Priestly Source and the Book of Ezekiel: A New Approach to an Old Problem*, Cahiers de la Revue biblique 20 (Paris: Gabalda, 1982); M. F. Rooker, "Dating Isaiah 40–66: What Does the Linguistic Evidence Say?" *WTJ* 58 (1996): 303–12.

87. W. R. Garr, *Dialectical Geography of Syria-Palestine, 1000–586 B.C.E.* (Philadelphia: University of Pennsylvania Press, 1985); I. Young, *Diversity in Pre-Exilic Hebrew*, FAT 5 (Tübingen: Mohr, 1993).

88. J. J. Schmitt, "Prophecy, Preexilic Hebrew," *ABD*, 5:488. See further on the oral vs. literary discussion: W. Zimmerli, "Vom Prophetenwort zum Prophetenbuch," *TLZ* 104 (1979): 481–96 (translated by A. Köstenberger as "From Prophetic Word to Prophetic Book," in *Place Is Too Small*, ed. Gordon, 419–42); F. E. Deist, "The Prophets: Are We Heading for a Paradigm Shift?" in *Prophet und Prophetenbuch: Festschrift für Otto Kaiser zum 65. Geburtstag*, ed. V. Fritz, K.-F. Pohlmann, and H.-C. Schmitt, BZAW 185 (Berlin: de Gruyter, 1989), 8 (reprinted in *Place Is Too Small*, ed. Gordon, 589); Grabbe, *Prophets, Priests*, 105–7.

prophetic documents that we have are substantially from the hand of the named prophet.[89] The import of the question lies with the proximity that the present text has to the original prophetic message. What is original and what is secondary, having been supplemented or altered over a period of transmission? This area of "tradition history" is itself fraught with problems, since it often, though not necessarily, suggests that temporal proximity guarantees truth while lengthy transmission calls it into question.

What Kinds of Messages Did the Prophets Give?

Form criticism, the study of literary types or genres, continues to be an important aspect of prophetic study, as it has since the pioneering work of Hermann Gunkel.[90] German scholars such as Koch and Westermann have played major roles in this discussion of the forms of prophetic speech,[91] though critique and interaction have not been lacking.[92]

Numerous scholars have sought to find formal parallels with ancient Near Eastern texts (see above), while others look at the text itself for insight. Here there is much overlap with other sections of this review, since form-critical *Sitz im Leben* is closely tied to the role of the prophet in society.

Paul Copeland raises an interesting question: The greatest issue at stake in prophetic studies is not "What did God say through the prophets?" but "What does it mean for a prophet to claim that God had spoken to him at all?"[93] This question brings together many of the threads already noticed previously, such as definition and role. This raises the

89. E.g., Paul, *Amos*, 6.
90. For useful summaries of Gunkel's contributions, see Gordon, "Story," 12–14, and J. H. Hayes, *An Introduction to Old Testament Study* (Nashville: Abingdon, 1979), 122–54, 273–77.
91. C. Westermann, *Basic Forms of Prophetic Speech*, trans. H. C. White (Philadelphia: Westminster, 1967); idem, *Sprache und Struktur der Prophetie Deuterojesajas*, CThM 11 (Stuttgart: Calwer, 1981); idem, "Zur Erforschung und zum Verständnis der prophetischen Heilsworte," *ZAW* 98 (1986): 1–13; idem, *Prophetic Oracles of Salvation in the Old Testament*, trans. K. Crim (Louisville: Westminster/John Knox, 1991). For a brief study of Westermann, see B. T. Arnold, "Forms of Prophetic Speech in the Old Testament: A Summary of Claus Westermann's Contributions," *ATJ* 27 (1995): 30–40. See also K. Koch, *Amos: Untersucht mit den Methoden einer Strukturalen Formgeschichte*, AOAT 30 (Kevelaer: Butzon & Bercker; Neukirchen-Vluyn: Neukirchener Verlag, 1976); idem, *The Prophets*, 2 vols., trans. M. Kohl (London: SCM, 1982; Philadelphia: Fortress, 1983–84).
92. Wilson, "Form-Critical Investigation"; W. E. March, "Prophecy," in *Old Testament Form Criticism*, ed. J. H. Hayes, TUMSR 2 (San Antonio: Trinity University Press, 1974), 251–66; see G. M. Tucker, "Prophetic Speech," *Int* 32 (1978): 31–45; idem, "Prophecy and the Prophetic Literature"; M. A. Sweeney, "Formation and Form in Prophetic Literature," in *Old Testament Interpretation*, ed. Mays, Petersen, and Richards, 113–26.
93. P. E. Copeland, "A Guide to the Study of the Prophets," *Themelios* 10.1 (1984): 8.

discussion to a different level, where source and context go beyond borrowing to inspiration. The level of authority differs if one sees prophecy as simply literature on the one hand or as revelation on the other.[94] Is the prophet just insightful,[95] or is he inspired? Increasing importance has been placed on the theological aspects of the prophets' message, including the ethical aspects.[96]

An important literary form that the prophets used to express their message was metaphor. The study of metaphor has become a major area of interest for scholars. God and various of his attributes and relationships are naturally expressed in metaphorical terms, since the Wholly Other must be so described in order to make some cognitive connection with the mortal.[97] While other metaphors have also re-

94. A. Brenner, "On 'Jeremiah' and the Poetics of (Prophetic?) Pornography," in A. Brenner and F. van Dijk-Hemmes, *On Gendering Texts: Female and Male Voices in the Hebrew Bible*, Biblical Interpretation Series 1 (Leiden: Brill, 1993), 177; R. E. Clements, *Old Testament Prophecy: From Oracles to Canon* (Louisville: Westminster/John Knox, 1996), 13.

95. R. R. Deutsch, "Why Did the Hebrew Prophets Speak?" *South-East Asia Journal of Theology* 18 (1977): 26–36; Deist, "Prophets," 15 (reprinted in *Place Is Too Small*, ed. Gordon, 596); B. W. Anderson, "The Role of the Messiah," *BibRev* 11.5 (1995): 19, 48.

96. Gordon, "Story," 22; J. Barton, "Natural Law and Poetic Justice in the Old Testament," *JTS*, n.s., 30 (1979): 1–14; C. Stuhlmueller, "Deutero-Isaiah: Major Transitions in the Prophet's Theology and in Contemporary Scholarship," *CBQ* 42 (1980): 1–29; E. W. Davies, *Prophecy and Ethics: Isaiah and the Ethical Traditions of Israel*, JSOTSup 16 (Sheffield: JSOT Press, 1981); H. W. Wolff, *Confrontations with Prophets: Discovering the Old Testament's New and Contemporary Significance* (Philadelphia: Fortress, 1983); W. S. Prinsloo, *The Theology of the Book of Joel*, BZAW 163 (Berlin: de Gruyter, 1985); Westermann, "Zur Erforschung und zum Verständnis"; W. Brueggemann, *Hopeful Imagination: Prophetic Voices in Exile* (Philadelphia: Fortress, 1986); idem, *Hope within History* (Atlanta: John Knox, 1987); idem, *To Pluck Up, to Tear Down: A Commentary of the Book of Jeremiah 1–25*, ITC (Grand Rapids: Eerdmans, 1988); idem, *To Build, to Plant: A Commentary of the Book of Jeremiah 26–52*, ITC (Grand Rapids: Eerdmans, 1991); M. D. Carroll, *Contexts for Amos: Prophetic Poetics in Latin American Perspective*, JSOTSup 132 (Sheffield: JSOT Press, 1992); B. A. Levine, "An Essay on Prophetic Attitudes toward Temple and Cult in Biblical Israel," in *Minḥah le-Naḥum: Biblical and Other Studies Presented to Nahum M. Sarna in Honour of His 70th Birthday*, ed. M. Brettler and M. Fishbane, JSOTSup 154 (Sheffield: JSOT Press, 1993), 202–25; J. G. McConville, *Judgement and Promise: An Interpretation of the Book of Jeremiah* (Leicester: Apollos; Winona Lake, Ind.: Eisenbrauns, 1993); R. R. Marrs, "The Prophetic Faith: A Call to Ethics and Community," *ResQ* 36 (1994): 304–15; H. G. M. Williamson, "Isaiah and the Wise," in *Wisdom in Ancient Israel*, ed. J. Day, R. P. Gordon, and H. G. M. Williamson (Cambridge: Cambridge University Press, 1995), 133–41.

97. M. I. Gruber, "The Motherhood of God in Second Isaiah," *RB* 90 (1983): 351–59; C. E. Armerding, "Images for Today: Word from the Prophets," in *Studies in Old Testament Theology*, ed. R. L. Hubbard (Dallas, London, and Vancouver: Word, 1992), 167–86; J. D. W. Watts, "Images of Yahweh: God in the Prophets," in ibid., 135–47; J. F. A. Sawyer, "Radical Images of Yahweh in Isaiah 63," in *Among the Prophets*, ed. Davies and Clines, 72–82; K. P. Darr, "Two Unifying Female Images in the Book of Isaiah," in *Uncovering Ancient Stones: Essays in Memory of H. Neil Richardson*, ed. L. M. Hopfe (Winona Lake, Ind.: Eisenbrauns, 1994), 17–30; J. T. Willis, "'I Am Your God' and 'You Are My People' in

ceived attention,[98] marriage and sexuality have been of special interest.[99] Particular concern of late has been directed toward the brutaliz-
ing metaphors of rape and degradation, with suggestions that they
border on, or cross the border into, pornography.[100]

Hosea and Jeremiah," *ResQ* 36 (1994): 291–303; J. A. O'Brien, "Judah as Wife and Husband: Deconstructing Gender in Malachi," *JBL* 115 (1996): 241–50; B. Seifert, *Metapho-
rische Reden von Gott im Hoseabuch*, FRLANT 166 (Göttingen: Vandenhoeck & Ruprecht, 1996); S. D. Moore, "Gigantic God: Yahweh's Body," *JSOT* 70 (1996): 87–115.

98. C. Hardmeier, *Texttheorie und biblische Exegese: Zur rhetorischen Funktion der
Trauermetaphorik in der Prophetie* (Munich: Chr. Kaiser, 1978); P. A. Porter, *Metaphors and
Monsters: A Literary-Critical Study of Daniel 7 and 8*, ConBOT 20 (Lund: Gleerup, 1983);
K. Nielsen, *There Is Hope for a Tree: The Tree as Metaphor in Isaiah*, JSOTSup 65 (Sheffield:
JSOT Press, 1985); E. Follis, "The Holy City as Daughter," in *Directions in Biblical Hebrew
Poetry*, ed. Follis, 173–84; U. Worschech, "Der Assyrisch-Babylonische Löwenmensch
und der 'Menschliche' Löwe aus Daniel 7,4," in *Ad bene et fideliter seminandum;* ed. Mauer
and Magen, 322–33; M. L. Barré, "Of Lions and Birds: A Note on Isaiah 31.4–5," in *Among
the Prophets*, ed. Davies and Clines, 55–59; J. P. Heil, "Ezekiel 34 and the Narrative Strategy of the Shepherd and Sheep Metaphor in Matthew," *CBQ* 55 (1993): 37–41; G. Eidevall,
"Lions and Birds in Literature: Some Notes on Isaiah 31 and Hosea 11," *SJOT* 7 (1993):
78–87; R. Johnson, "Hosea 4–10: Pictures at an Exhibition," *SWJT* 36 (1993): 20–26; J. B.
Geyer, "Ezekiel 27 and the Cosmic Ship," in *Among the Prophets*, ed. Davies and Clines,
105–26; C. Maier, "Jerusalem als Ehebrecherin in Ezechiel 16: Zur Verwendung und
Funktion einer biblischen Metaphor," in *Feministische Hermeneutik und Erstes Testament: Analysen und Interpretationen*, ed. H. Jahnow (Stuttgart: Kohlhammer, 1994), 85–
105; P. Marinkovic, "What Does Zechariah 1–8 Tell Us about the Temple?" in *Second Temple Studies*, vol. 2, *Temple and Community in the Persian Period*, ed. T. C. Eskenazi and
K. H. Richards, JSOTSup (Sheffield: JSOT Press, 1994), 88–103; M. G. Swanepoel, "Solutions to the *Crux Interpretum* of Hosea 6:2," *OTE* 7 (1994): 39–59.

99. M. DeRoche, "Israel's 'Two Evils' in Jeremiah II 13," *VT* 31 (1981): 369–71; H. Balz-
Cochois, *Gomer: Der Höhenkult Israels im Selbstverständnis der Volksfrömmigkeit: Unter-
suchungen zu Hosea 4,1–5,7*, Europäische Hochschulschriften 23.191 (Frankfurt: Lang,
1982); D. J. Clark, "Sex-Related Imagery in the Prophets," *BT* 33 (1982): 409–13; G. Hall,
"Origin of the Marriage Metaphor," *HS* 23 (1982): 169–71; P. A. Kruger, "Israel, the Harlot
(Hos. 2.4–9)," *JNSL* 11 (1983): 107–16; H. Ringgren, "The Marriage Motif in Israelite Re-
ligion," in *Ancient Israelite Religion: Essays in Honor of Frank Moore Cross*, ed. P. D. Miller
Jr., P. D. Hanson, and S. D. McBride (Philadelphia: Fortress, 1987), 421–28; N. Stienstra,
*YHWH Is the Husband of His People: Analysis of a Biblical Metaphor with Special Reference
to Translation* (Kampen: Kok Pharos, 1993); M. A. Zipor, "'Scenes from a Marriage'—Ac-
cording to Jeremiah," *JSOT* 65 (1995): 83–91; O'Brien, "Judah as Wife and Husband";
R. C. Ortlund Jr., *Whoredom: God's Unfaithful Wife in Biblical Theology*, New Studies in
Biblical Theology (Grand Rapids: Eerdmans, 1996).

100. Clark, "Sex-Related Imagery in the Prophets"; S. McFague, *Metaphorical Theology* (Philadelphia: Fortress, 1982); G. F. Ellwood, "Rape and Judgment," *Daughters of
Sarah* 11 (1985): 9–13; R. J. Weems, "Gomer: Victim of Violence or Victim of Metaphor?"
Semeia 47 (1989): 87–102; N. Graetz, "The Haftarah Tradition and the Metaphoric Bat-
tering of Hosea's Wife," *Conservative Judaism* 45 (1992): 29–42; A. Brenner, "On Jeremiah
and the Poetic of (Prophetic?) Pornography," *European Judaism* 26.2 (1993): 9–14; F. van
Dijk-Hemmes, "The Metaphorization of Woman in Prophetic Speech: An Analysis of
Ezekiel 23," in *On Gendering Texts*, 167–76; Maier, "Jerusalem als Ehebrecherin";
Magdalene, "Ancient Near Eastern Treaty Curses"; R. J. Weems, *Battered Love: Marriage,
Sex, and Violence in the Hebrew Prophets*, OBT (Minneapolis: Fortress, 1995); A. A. Keefe,

While today's climate of "political correctness" leads some to question the validity of such metaphors since they degrade women, we must be aware that this is exactly the reaction that the author seems to be trying to convey. If we react in disgust and horror to the degradation metaphorically heaped upon women in the Prophets, the prophets themselves would have had a similar response. They were trying to raise the level of disgust in the readers to such an extent that they would ask, "How can you write this kind of pornography?" The prophet could then respond by asking: "This metaphorical expression illustrates the feeling that God has toward you, his people, when you brutalize others or prostitute yourself. Isn't God's disgust even beyond your own at the pornographic behavior in which you are actively involved?" Renita Weems does raise the important question of how scholarly work on such texts addresses practical, even pastoral, concerns raised by these texts.[101] Can academic study and human practice in real life remain distinct, and should they? (See the section below titled "Application: What Use Are the Prophets for Us Today?")

Transmission: How Did the Prophets Use Scripture, and What Were Subsequent Uses of the Prophets' Original Messages?

Redaction criticism—or the study of the process of compilation, editing, and composition from existing sources, whether written or oral—has been a flourishing field during the period under consideration. At times it is difficult to distinguish it from form criticism,[102] since prophetic messages were often a secondary application of another, original form used in other than prophetic contexts.[103] Discussions of smaller passages or entire books have appeared in commentaries and other forms.[104]

"The Female Body, the Body Politic and the Land: A Sociopolitical Reading of Hosea 1–2," in *A Feminist Companion to the Latter Prophets*, ed. Brenner, 70–100; R. P. Carroll, "Desire Under the Terebinths: On Pornographic Representation in the Prophets—A Response," in ibid., 275–307; A. Brenner, "Pornoprophetics Revisited: Some Additional Reflections," *JSOT* 70 (1996): 63–86. See P. Trible, *Texts of Terror: Literary-Feminist Readings of Biblical Narratives*, OBT (Philadelphia: Fortress, 1984).

101. Weems, *Battered Love*, 8.

102. M. A. Sweeney, *Isaiah 1–39: With an Introduction to Prophetic Literature*, FOTL 16 (Grand Rapids: Eerdmans, 1996), 13.

103. Tucker, "Prophecy and the Prophetic Literature," 338.

104. Examples are too abundant to list them all. Some are: J. Vermeylen, *Du prophète Isaïe à l'apocalyptique: Isaïe i–xxxv, miroir d'un demi-millénaire d'expérience religieuse en Israël*, 2 vols., EBib (Paris: Gabalda, 1977); B. S. Childs, "The Canonical Shape of the Prophetic Literature," *Int* 32 (1978): 46–55 (reprinted in *Place Is Too Small*, ed. Gordon, 513–22); A. Laato, "History and Ideology in the Old Testament Prophetic Books," *SJOT* 8 (1994): 267–97; J. Jeremias, "'Zwei Jahre vor dem Erdbeben' (Am 1,1)," in *Altes Testament Forschung und Wirkung: Festschrift für Henning Graf Reventlow*, ed. P. Mommer and W.

Prophets were wont to reapply previous messages, much as contemporary preachers reapply a received tradition to a contemporary situation. Aspects of the Pentateuch were a productive source of applicable tradition,[105] but other passages were also fruitful for this area of study

---

Thiel (Frankfurt am Main: Lang, 1994), 15–31; B. M. Zapff, *Schriftgelehrte Prophetie—Jes 13 und die Komposition des Jesajabuches: Ein Beitrag zur Erforschung der Redaktionsgeschichte des Jesajabuches* (Würtburg: Echter Verlag, 1995); idem, *Redaktionsgeschichtliche Studien zum Michabuch im Kontext des Dodekapropheton*, BZAW 256 (Berlin and New York: de Gruyter, 1997); C. C. Broyles and C. A. Evans, eds., *Writing and Reading the Scroll of Isaiah: Studies of an Interpretive Tradition*, VTSup 70 (Leiden: Brill, 1997).

105. Creation theology: S. Gillingham, "'Der die Morgenröte zur Finsternis Macht' Gott und Schöpfung im Amosbuch," *EvT* 53 (1993): 109–23; J. G. Janzen, "On the Moral Nature of God's Power: Yahweh and the Sea in Job and Deutero-Isaiah," *CBQ* 56 (1994): 458–78.

Eden: J. Barr, "'Thou Art the Cherub': Ezekiel 28.14 and the Post-Ezekiel Understanding of Genesis 2–3," in *Priests, Prophets, and Scribes: Essays on the Formation and Heritage of Second Temple Judaism in Honour of Joseph Blenkinsopp*, ed. E. Ulrich et al., JSOTSup 149 (Sheffield: JSOT Press, 1992), 213–23.

Tower of Babel: M. Hilton, "Babel Reversed—Daniel Chapter 5," *JSOT* 66 (1995): 99–112.

The patriarchs: C. Jeremias, "Die Erzväter in der Verkündigung der Propheten," in *Beiträge zur alttestamentlichen Theologie: Festschrift für Walther Zimmerli zum 70. Geburtstag*, ed. H. Donner, R. Hanhart, and R. Smend (Göttingen: Vandenhoeck & Ruprecht, 1977), 206–22; H. F. van Rooy, "The Names Israel, Ephraim, and Jacob in the Book of Hosea," *OTE* 5 (1993): 135–49.

The exodus: B. W. Anderson, "Exodus and Covenant in Second Isaiah and Prophetic Tradition," in *Magnalia Dei*, ed. Cross, Lemke, and Miller, 339–60; Kiesow, *Exodustexte im Jesajabuch*; Tucker, "Prophecy and the Prophetic Literature"; G. C. i Oprinell, "La Relectura de l'Exode a Ezequiel i Deuteroisaïes" [The rereading of the exodus in Ezekiel and Deutero-Isaiah], in *Tradició i traducció de la Paraula: Miscellània Guiu Camps*, ed. F. Raurell et al., Scripta et Documenta 47 (Montserrat: Associació Biblica de Catalunya, Publicacions de l'Abadia de Montserrat, 1993), 61–80; A. R. Ceresko, "The Rhetorical Strategy of the Fourth Servant Song (Isaiah 52:13–53:12): Poetry and the Exodus–New Exodus," *CBQ* 56 (1994): 42–55; C. Patton, "'I Myself Gave Them Laws That Were Not Good': Ezekiel 20 and the Exodus Traditions," *JSOT* 69 (1996): 73–90.

Covenant laws and theology: E. C. Lucas, "Covenant, Treaty and Prophecy," *Themelios* 8.1 (1982): 19–23; Clements, *Prophecy and Tradition*, 8–23; R. B. Chisholm Jr., "The 'Everlasting Covenant' and the 'City of Chaos': Intentional Ambiguity and Irony in Isaiah 24," *Criswell Theological Review* 6 (1993): 237–53; A. van der Kooij, "The Concept of Covenant *(Berît)* in the Book of Daniel," in *Book of Daniel*, ed. van der Woude, 495–501; O. H. Steck, "Der Gottesknecht als 'Bund' und 'Licht': Beobachtungen im Zweiten Jesaja," *ZTK* 90 (1993): 117–34; S. Ausin, "La Tradición de la Alianza en Oseas," in *Biblia Exegesis y Cultura: Estudios en Honor del José María Casciaro*, ed. G. Aranda, Colleción Teologica 83 (Pamplona: Eunsa, 1994), 127–46.

Moses: G. S. Ogden, "Moses and Cyrus: Literary Affinities between the Priestly Presentation of Moses in Exodus vi and the Cyrus Song of Isaiah xliv 24–xlv 13," *VT* 28 (1978): 195–203; O'Kane, "Isaiah"; Seitz, "The Prophet Moses and the Canonical Shape of Jeremiah," 3–27; Levenson, *Theology of the Program*; McKeating, "Ezekiel the 'Prophet Like Moses,'" 97–109.

Cult: S. L. Cook, "Innerbiblical Interpretation in Ezekiel 44," *JBL* 114 (1995): 193–208; A. Johnston, "A Prophetic Vision of an Alternative Community: A Reading of Isaiah 40–55," in *Uncovering Ancient Stones*, 31–40.

known as "inner-biblical exegesis," or the reuse of earlier biblical texts, including some earlier prophetic oracles.[106]

This reuse of earlier texts is one of the ways the composition of Isaiah has been explained. The debate over Isaianic composition has waxed and waned since the twelfth century, ranging from those seeing the book as completely an eighth-century B.C. composition by a single author, to those who see multiple authors from even centuries later.[107] Several scholars investigating the compositional history of the book have suggested that the constituent parts were written with knowledge of, and in the light of, previously existing oracles. In other words, Deutero-Isaiah used Isaiah of Jerusalem as a basis for his own oracles, and was not prophesying in ignorance of them, with a later redactor only uniting what were originally disparate, unrelated elements. There could thus be said to be a real "unity" in Isaianic composition, though

---

106. I. Willi-Plein, *Vorformen der Schriftexegese Innerhalb des Alten Testaments*, BZAW 123 (Berlin: de Gruyter, 1971); J. Jensen, *The Use of Tôrâ by Isaiah: His Debate with the Wisdom Tradition*, CBQMS 3 (Washington, D.C.: Catholic Biblical Association, 1973); J. Day, "A Case of Inner Scriptural Interpretation: The Dependence of Isaiah XXVI.13–XXVII.11 on Hosea XIII.4–XIV.10 (Eng. 9) and Its Relevance to Some Theories of the Redaction of the 'Isaiah Apocalypse,'" *JTS*, n.s., 31 (1980): 309–19; M. Fishbane, *Biblical Interpretation in Ancient Israel* (Oxford: Clarendon, 1985); W. Kaiser Jr., "Inner Biblical Exegesis as a Model for Bridging the 'Then' and 'Now' Gap: Hosea 12,1–6," *JETS* 28 (1985): 33–46; T. Naumann, *Hoseas Erben: Strukturen der Nachinterpretationen im Buch Hosea*, BWANT 7/11 (Stuttgart: Kohlhammer, 1991); J. T. A. G. M. van Ruiten, "The Intertextual Relationship between Isaiah 65,25 and Isaiah 11,6–9," in *The Scriptures and the Scrolls: Studies in Honour of A. S. van der Woude on the Occasion of His 65th Birthday*, ed. F. García Martínez, A. Hilhost, and A. S. Labuschagne, VTSup 49 (Leiden: Brill, 1992), 31–42; Cook, "Innerbiblical Interpretation in Ezekiel 44"; J. Lust, "Ezekiel Salutes Isaiah: Ezekiel 20,32–44," in *Studies in the Book of Isaiah*, ed. van Ruiten and Vervenne, 367–82; J. T. A. G. M. van Ruiten, "'His Master's Voice?' The Supposed Influence of the Book of Isaiah in the Book of Habakkuk," in *Studies in the Book of Isaiah*, 397–411, and other studies in ibid. by O. H. Steck, "Der neue Himmel und die neue Erde: Beobachtungen zur Rezeption von Gen 1–3 in Jes 65,16b–25," 349–65; J. C. Bastiaens, "The Language of Suffering in Job 16–19 and in the Suffering Servant Passages of Deutero-Isaiah," 421–32; and M. Vervenne, "The phraseology of 'Knowing YHWH' in the Hebrew Bible," 467–92; essays on Isaiah and its own internal intertextuality, as well as relations with Lamentations, Jeremiah, and Psalms in C. R. Seitz, *Word without End: The Old Testament as Abiding Theological Witness* (Grand Rapids: Eerdmans, 1998). An excellent commentary where this area of study is usefully highlighted is A. E. Hill, *Malachi*, AB 25D (New York: Doubleday, 1998), esp. appendix C, 401–12.

107. For a recent survey of some of the discussion, with helpful bibliography for reference to earlier writings, see H. G. M. Williamson, *The Book Called Isaiah: Deutero-Isaiah's Role in Composition and Redaction* (Oxford: Clarendon, 1994), 1–18. See also idem, "First and Last in Isaiah," in *Of Prophets' Visions*, ed. McKay and Clines, 95–108; P. A. Smith, *Rhetoric and Redaction in Trito-Isaiah: The Structure, Growth and Authorship of Isaiah 56–66*, VTSup 62 (Leiden: Brill, 1995); B. M. Zapff, *Schriftgelehrte Prophetie— Jesaja 13 und die Komposition des Jesajabuches: Ein Beitrag zur Erforschung der Redaktionsgeschichte des Jesajabuches*, FB 74 (Würzburg: Echter Verlag, 1995).

not that of a single, eighth-century prophet, as some conservatives argue.[108] Others look for structural unity, with themes, theology, or linguistic parallels tying the book together in its extant form.[109]

Discussion and exploration of an actual, extant text such as the present Book of Isaiah seems to be a useful advance from a simple atomistic approach with textual subdivision into purported sources, leaving an eviscerated text that is not attested in any documentary sources. This at least allows discussion of an objectively identifiable textual unit.

In one case at least, the units under discussion expand even beyond the boundaries of a single work. A recent area of study has been the redactional history of the "Twelve," which assumes that the Minor Prophets were a unified group during some stage of the redactional process.[110]

Text criticism seeks to go as far back into the transmission tradition as possible, but in fact occupies the watershed between oral transmission and redaction on the one hand, when there might have been some fluidity in the tradition, and its enscripturation, or more fixed written

108. R. E. Clements, "Beyond Tradition History: Deutero-Isaianic Development of First Isaiah's Themes," *JSOT* 31 (1985): 95–113; R. Albertz, "Das Deuterojesaja-Buch als Fortschreibung der Jesaja-Prophetie," in *Die hebräische Bibel und ihre zweifache Nachgeschichte: Festschrift für Rolf Rendtorff zum 65. Geburtstag,* ed. E. Blum, C. Macholz, and E. W. Stegemann (Neukirchen-Vluyn: Neukirchener Verlag, 1990), 241–56. For a recent, detailed discussion of the issue, see Williamson, *Book Called Isaiah.*

109. R. Lack, *La symbolique du livre d'Isaïe: Essai sur l'image littéraire comme élément de structuration,* AnBib 59 (Rome: Pontifical Biblical Institute, 1973); W. L. Holladay, *Isaiah: Scroll of a Prophetic Heritage* (Grand Rapids: Eerdmans, 1978), unity of theme but not authorship; J. D. W. Watts, *Isaiah 1–33,* WBC (Waco: Word, 1985), xxvii–xxxiv, who sees it as a unity from the fifth century; J. Oswalt, *The Book of Isaiah, Chapters 1–39,* NICOT (Grand Rapids: Eerdmans, 1986), 17–23; C. A. Evans, "On the Unity and Parallel Structure of Isaiah," *VT* 38 (1988): 129–47; Sweeney, *Isaiah 1–4,* 21–24; W. A. M. Beuken, "Isaiah Chapters lxv–lxvi: Trito-Isaiah and the Closure of the Book of Isaiah," in *Congress Volume: Leuven, 1989,* ed. J. A. Emerton, VTSup 43 (Leiden: Brill, 1991), 204–21; A. J. Tomasino, "Isaiah 1.1–2.4 and 63–66, and the Composition of the Isaianic Corpus," *JSOT* 57 (1993): 81–98; J. A. Motyer, *The Prophecy of Isaiah: An Introduction and Commentary* (Downers Grove, Ill., and Leicester: InterVarsity, 1993), 13–33. For critique, see D. M. Carr, "Reaching for Unity in Isaiah," *JSOT* 57 (1993): 61–80.

110. P. R. House, *The Unity of the Twelve,* JSOTSup 77 (Sheffield: JSOT Press, 1990); T. Collins, *The Mantle of Elijah: The Redaction Criticism of the Prophetical Books,* Biblical Seminar 29 (Sheffield: JSOT Press, 1993); J. D. Nogalski, *Literary Precursors to the Book of the Twelve,* BZAW 217 (Berlin: de Gruyter, 1993); idem, *Redactional Processes in the Book of the Twelve,* BZAW 218 (Berlin: de Gruyter, 1993); idem, "The Redactional Shaping of Nahum 1 for the Book of the Twelve," in *Among the Prophets,* ed. Davies and Clines, 193–202; B. A. Jones, *The Formation of the Book of the Twelve: A Study in Text and Canon,* SBLDS 149 (Atlanta: Scholars Press, 1995). See also, e.g., S. J. De Vries, *From Old Revelation to New: A Tradition-Historical and Redaction-Critical Study of Temporal Transitions in Prophetic Prediction* (Grand Rapids: Eerdmans, 1995), who looks at redactional techniques identifiable across the prophetic spectrum; and A. Schart, *Die Entstehung des Zwölfprophetenbuchs: Neubearbeitungen von Amos im Rahmen schriftenübergreifender Redaktionsprozesse,* BZAW 260 (Berlin and New York: de Gruyter, 1998).

form on the other. Jeremiah has been the subject of the most text-critical interest, due to the great differences among the various textual witnesses.[111] Other prophets have also been the focus of text-critical investigation in the more technical commentaries as well as separate articles and monographs.[112]

111. E. Tov, *The Septuagint Translation of Jeremiah and Baruch: A Discussion of an Early Revision of the LXX of Jeremiah 29–52 and Baruch 1:1–3:8*, HSM 8 (Missoula, Mont.: Scholars Press, 1976); idem, "Some Aspects of the Textual and Literary History of the Book of Jeremiah," in *Le Livre de Jérémie: Le prophète et son milieu, les oracles et leur transmission*, ed. P.-M. Bogaert, BETL 54 (Louvain: Leuven University Press and Peeters, 1981), 145–67; P.-M. Bogaert, "Les mécanismes rédactionnels en Jér. 10,1–16 (LXX et TM) et la signification des suppléments," in ibid., 222–38; S. Soderlund, *The Greek Text of Jeremiah: A Revised Hypothesis*, JSOTSup 47 (Sheffield: JSOT Press, 1985); P.-M. Bogaert, "*Urtext*, texte court et relecture: Jérémie xxxiii 14–26 TM et ses préparations," in *Congress Volume: Leuven, 1989*, 236–47; J. Lust, "Messianism and the Greek Version of Jeremiah," in *VII Congress of the International Organization for Septuagint and Cognate Studies, Leuven, 1989*, ed. C. E. Cox, SBLSCS 31 (Atlanta: Scholars Press, 1991), 87–122; H.-J. Stipp, *Jeremia im Parteinstreit: Studien zur Textentwicklung von Jer 26, 36–43 und 45 als Beitrag zur Geschichte Jeremias, seines Buches und judäischer Partein im 6. Jahrhundert*, Athenäum Monografien, Theologie, BBB 82 (Frankfurt am Main: Hain, 1992); J. Ribera, "De la traducció a la interpretació: El Targum de Jeremies (Tg Jr) i les versions primàries: La Septuaginta (LXX), la Pešiṭta (P) i la Vulgata," in *Tradició i traducció de la Paraula*, ed. Raurell, 297–304; B. Becking, "Jeremiah's Book of Consolation: A Textual Comparison: Notes on the Masoretic Text and the Old Greek Version of Jeremiah xxx–xxxi," *VT* 44 (1994): 145–69; J. Lust, "The Diverse Text Forms of Jeremiah and History Writing with Jer. 33 as a Test Case," *JNSL* 20 (1994): 31–48; H.-J. Stipp, *Das masoretische und alexandrinische Sondergut des Jeremiabuches: Textgeschichtlicher Rang, Eigenarten, Triebkräfte*, OBO 136 (Fribourg, Switzerland: Éditions universitaires; Göttingen: Vandenhoeck & Ruprecht, 1994).

112. N. L. Tidwell, "My Servant Jacob, Is. xlii 1," in *Studies on Prophecy*, 84–91; M. J. D. Servet, *Minḥat Šai de Y. S. de Norzi: Profetas Menores: Traducción y Anotación Critica*, Textos y estudios Cardenal Cisneros 40 (Madrid: Instituto de Filología del CSIC, Departamento de Filología Biblica y de Oriente Antiguo, 1987); D. Barthélemy, *Critique textuelle de l'Ancien Testament*, vol. 3, *Ezéchiel, Daniel et les 12 Prophètes*, OBO 50.3 (Fribourg, Switzerland: Éditions universitaires; Göttingen: Vandenhoeck & Ruprecht, 1992); K. J. Cathcart, "Daniel, Especially the Additions, and Chester Beatty-Cologne Papyrus 967," *PIBA* 15 (1992): 37–41; S. P. Carbone and G. Rizzi, *Il libro di Osea, Secondo Il Testo Ebraico Masoretico, Secondo la Traduzione Greca Detta Dei Settanta, Secondo la Parafrasi Aramaica del Targum* (Bologna: Edizioni dehoniane, 1992); E. Tov, *Textual Criticism of the Hebrew Bible* (Minneapolis: Fortress; Assen and Maastricht: Van Gorcum, 1992); S. P. Carbone and G. Rizzi, *Il libro di Amos: Lettura Ebraica, Greca e Aramaica* (Bologna: Edizioni dehoniane, 1993); T. Hieke, "Der Anfang des Buches Nahum I: Die Frage Des Textverlaufs in der jetzigen Gestalt: Ein antihetische Prinzip," *BN* 68 (1993): 13–17; R. Gryson and J.-M. Auwers, "L'histoire du texte Latin d'Isaïe au miroir du cantique d'Ezechias," *RTL* 24 (1993): 325–44; H.-F. Richter, "Daniel 4,7–14: Beobachtungen und Erwägungen," in *Book of Daniel*, ed. van der Woude, 244–48; D. Dimant, "The Seventy Weeks Chronology (Dan 9,24–27) in the Light of New Qumranic Texts," in ibid., 57–76; M. J. D. Servet, *Minḥat Šai de Y. S. de Norzi: Isáias: Traducción y Anotación Critica*, Textos y estudios Cardenal Cisneros 54 (Madrid: Instituto de Filología del CSIC, Departamento de Filología Biblica y de Oriente Antiguo, 1993); R. A. Taylor, *The Peshiṭta of Daniel*, Monographs of the Peshiṭta Institute 7 (Leiden: Brill, 1994); T. M. Meadowcroft, *Aramaic*

Application: What Use Are the Prophets for Us Today?

Commentaries have at times addressed the area of practical application in the course of their textual interpretation.[113] Of late this interest has also spread to the academy, with Walter Brueggemann playing an important role. His work, along with that of other writers, has applied the prophetic text across the spectrum of theological disciplines, including evangelism, pastoral theology, Christian education, and preaching.[114]

While knowledge for knowledge's sake is a valid aspect of a liberal education, practical use must also be indicated, especially in this period of more restricted financial resources for academia. Since much biblical research is undertaken under the auspices of religiously endowed institutions, relevance of that research for teaching or preaching is often expected.

Liberation theologians have applied the message of the Prophets to the socioeconomic and political spheres for years.[115] The mainline and evangelical wings of the church have also joined in the endeavor.[116]

Daniel and Greek Daniel: A Literary Comparison, JSOTSup 198 (Sheffield: Sheffield Academic Press, 1995); Jones, *Formation of the Book of the Twelve*; A. van der Kooij, "Zum Verhaltnis von Textkritik und Literarkritik: Überlegungen anhand einiger Beispiele," in *Congress Volume: Cambridge, 1995*, ed. J. A. Emerton, VTSup 66 (Leiden: Brill, 1997), 185–202.

113. Several series are primarily interested in the "then" of the text, mainly looking at understanding it in its original setting only (e.g., Hermeneia [Fortress] and International Critical Commentary [T. & T. Clark]). Several relatively recent commentary series have contemporary practical and theological application as a primary purpose. These include The Bible Speaks Today (InterVarsity), Interpretation (Westminster/John Knox), International Theological Commentary (Eerdmans/Handsel), Knox Preaching Guides (Westminster/John Knox), and Westminster Bible Companion (Westminster/John Knox). Another series that shares this goal is in preparation: The NIV Application Commentary Series (Zondervan).

114. W. Brueggemann, *Biblical Perspectives on Evangelism* (Nashville: Abingdon, 1993); idem, *The Prophetic Imagination* (Philadelphia: Fortress, 1978); idem, *The Creative Word: Canon as a Model for Biblical Education* (Philadelphia: Fortress, 1982), 40–66. In many of his writings, he addresses proclamation of the prophetic message, but see particularly idem, *Finally Comes the Poet: Daring Speech for Proclamation* (Minneapolis: Fortress, 1989). See also E. Achtemeier, *Preaching from the Old Testament* (Louisville: Westminster/John Knox, 1989); idem, *Preaching from the Minor Prophets* (Grand Rapids: Eerdmans, 1998); Seitz, *Word without End*, esp. 194–228; Weems, *Battered Love*.

115. Deist, "Prophets," 10 (reprinted in *Place Is Too Small*, ed. Gordon, 592); Carroll, *Contexts for Amos*; J. S. Croatto, "La Propuesta Querigmática del Segundo Isaías," *RevB* 56 (1994): 65–76; Dobberahn, "Jesaja Verklagt"; M. D. Carroll, "The Prophetic Text and the Literature of Dissent in Latin America: Amos, García Márquez, and Cabrera Infante Dismantle Militarism," *BibInt* 4 (1996): 76–100.

116. G. M. Tucker, "The Role of the Prophets and the Role of the Church," *Quarterly Review* 1 (1981): 5–22; Clements, *Old Testament Prophecy*; C. R. Seitz, ed., *Reading and Preaching the Book of Isaiah* (Philadelphia: Fortress, 1988), 13–22, 105–26.

Wealth and poverty, or economic problems, as addressed in the Prophets has been one of the topics of special interest, especially, although not exclusively, among Marxists such as Norman K. Gottwald.[117] This is fitting since economic oppression is important to so many of the prophets, as it is an all too real part of the lives of many today.

Feminists have also studied the Prophets from their perspective, often providing insight missed or misconstrued by other readers, such as the important roles played by women and the disadvantages that they had to face in everyday life and in their service for their God.[118]

117. B. Lang, "The Social Organization of Peasant Poverty in Biblical Israel," *JSOT* 24 (1982): 47–63; M. Silver, *Prophets and Markets: The Political Economy of Ancient Israel* (Boston: Kluwer-Nijhoff, 1983); B. J. Malina, "Interpreting the Bible with Anthropology: The Question of Rich and Poor," *Listening: Journal of Religion and Culture* 21 (1986): 148–59; M. E. Polley, "Social Justice and the Just King," in *Amos and the Davidic Empire: A Socio-Historical Approach* (Oxford: Oxford University Press, 1989), 112–38; N. K. Gottwald, "The Biblical Prophetic Critique of Political Economy: Its Ground and Import," in *God and Capitalism: A Prophetic Critique of Market Economy*, ed. J. M. Thomas and V. Visick (Madison: A-R Editions, 1991), 11–29; idem, *The Hebrew Bible in Its Social World and in Ours*, SBL Semeia Studies (Atlanta: Scholars Press, 1993), 349–64; idem, "Social Class and Ideology in Isaiah 40–55: An Eagletonian Reading," *Semeia* 59 (1992): 43–57; C. A. Newsom, "Response to Norman K. Gottwald, 'Social Class and Ideology in Isaiah 40–55,'" ibid., 73–78; J. Millbank, "'I Will Gasp and Pant': Deutero-Isaiah and the Birth of the Suffering Subject: A Response to Norman Gottwald's 'Social Class and Ideology in Isaiah 40–55,'" ibid., 59–72; M. Silver, "Prophets and Markets Revisited," in *Social Justice in the Ancient World*, ed. K. D. Irani and M. Silver (Westport, Conn.: Greenwood, 1995), 179–98; W. Schottroff, "'Unrechtmässige Fesseln auftun,' Jochstricke lösen' Jesaja 58,1–2, ein Textbeispiel zum Thema 'Bibel und Ökonomie,'" *BibInt* 5 (1997): 263–78.

118. E.g., P. Trible, *God and the Rhetoric of Sexuality*, OBT (Philadelphia: Fortress, 1978); Balz-Cochois, *Gomer*; idem, "Gomer oder die Macht der Astarte: Versuch einer feministischen Interpretation von Hos. 1–4," *EvT* 42 (1982): 37–65; Trible, *Texts of Terror*; H. S. Straumann, "Gott als Mutter in Hosea 11," *Theologische Quartalschrift* 166 (1986): 119–34; M.-T. Wacker, "Frau-Sexus-Macht: Ein feministische Relecture des Hoseabuches," in *Der Gott der Männer und die Frauen*, ed. M.-T. Wacker, Theologie zur Zeit 2 (Düsseldorf: Patmos, 1987), 101–25; M. J. W. Leith, "Verse and Reverse: The Transformation of the Woman of Israel in Hosea 1–3," in *Gender and Difference in Ancient Israel*, ed. P. L. Day (Minneapolis: Fortress, 1989), 95–108; M.-T. Wacker, "God as Mother? On the Meaning of a Biblical God-Symbol for Feminist Theology," *Concilium* 206 (1989): 103–11; K. P. Darr, "Ezekiel's Justifications of God: Teaching Troubling Texts," *JSOT* 55 (1992): 97–117; C. A. Newsom and S. H. Ringe, eds., *The Women's Bible Commentary* (Louisville: Westminster; London: SPCK, 1992); I. Pardes, *Countertraditions in the Bible: A Feminist Approach* (Cambridge, Mass.: Harvard University Press, 1992); J. C. Exum, *Fragmented Women: Feminist (Sub)Versions of Biblical Narratives*, JSOTSup 163 (Sheffield: JSOT Press, 1993); R. Törnkvist, "The Use and Abuse of Female Sexual Imagery in the Book of Hosea: A Feminist Critical Approach to Hos 1–3" (Ph.D. diss., Uppsala University, 1994); Brenner, ed., *A Feminist Companion to the Latter Prophets*; Y. Sherwood, *The Prostitute and the Prophet: Hosea's Marriage in Literary-Theoretical Perspective*, JSOTSup 212, Gender, Culture, Theory 2 (Sheffield: Sheffield Academic Press, 1996), esp. 254–322; M.-T. Wacker, *Figurationen des Weiblichen im Hosea-Buch*, Herders Biblische Studien 8 (Freiberg: Herder, 1996).

Conclusion

In summary, prophetic studies, like the proverbial bride, brings things old, new, and borrowed. Ideas and methods initiated by earlier generations of scholars have been expanded and refined, while new information, often based on newly discovered texts or artifacts, has added to our understanding of who the prophets were and what they were about. Borrowing methods from cultural anthropology and literary studies has also shone helpful light on the person and product of the prophet in ways that would not have been possible using only the traditional methods of biblical studies. While the corpus of biblical prophetic literature is fixed and well defined, methods for its study neither are nor should be so unchanging. While not all questions or approaches will produce compelling answers or useful results, any means that might advance understanding should be explored and encouraged.

11

Wisdom Literature

Bruce K. Waltke and David Diewert

All scholars take the term *wisdom literature,* when applied to the Old Testament/Hebrew Scriptures, to refer to the books of Job, Proverbs, and Ecclesiastes, together with certain psalms (e.g., Ps. 37, 49) and some books of the Apocrypha, notably Ecclesiasticus (Ben Sirach) and the Wisdom of Solomon.[1] Some scholars have applied the term to other books, but no consensus of opinion exists on these other possibilities.[2]

The introduction to wisdom literature and the sections on Proverbs and Ecclesiastes were written by Bruce K. Waltke; the section on Job by David Diewert.

1. The two best introductions to wisdom literature are D. Kidner, *An Introduction to Wisdom Literature: The Wisdom of Proverbs, Job, and Ecclesiastes* (Downers Grove, Ill., and Leicester: InterVarsity, 1985), and S. Weeks, *Early Israelite Wisdom* (Oxford: Clarendon, 1994). The best anthology on the topic is *Wisdom in Ancient Israel: Essays in Honour of J. A. Emerton,* ed. J. Day, R. P. Gordon, and H. G. M. Williamson (Cambridge: Cambridge University Press, 1995 [hereafter *WIAI*]). Three anthologies written largely within the restraints of historical criticism are: *Studies in Ancient Israelite Wisdom: Selected, with a Prolegomenon,* ed. J. L. Crenshaw, Library of Biblical Studies (New York: Ktav, 1976 [hereafter *SAIW*]); *Israelite Wisdom: Theological and Literary Essays in Honor of Samuel Terrien,* ed. J. G. Gammie et al. (New York: Scholars Press, 1978); *The Sage in Israel and the Ancient Near East,* ed. J. G. Gammie and L. G. Perdue (Winona Lake, Ind.: Eisenbrauns, 1990). A popular introduction to this literature is D. Bergant, *What Are They Saying about Wisdom Literature?* (New York: Paulist, 1984). For a history of the wisdom tradition, see D. F. Morgan, *Wisdom in the Old Testament Traditions* (Atlanta: John Knox, 1981). For a focus on individual wisdom books see J. L. Crenshaw, *Old Testament Wisdom: An Introduction* (Atlanta: John Knox, 1981); and R. E. Murphy, *The Tree of Life: An Exploration of Biblical Wisdom Literature,* ABRL (New York and London: Doubleday, 1990; 2d ed. Grand Rapids: Eerdmans, 1996).

2. For the debated influence of the wisdom tradition on other parts of the OT, see J. A. Emerton, "Wisdom," in *Tradition and Interpretation: Essays by Members of the Society for Old Testament Study,* ed. G. W. Anderson (Oxford: Clarendon, 1979), 221; R. P. Gordon, "A House Divided: Wisdom in Old Testament Narrative Traditions," in *WIAI,* 94–105; J. A.

This essay reviews the past few decades of research regarding the definition of wisdom literature and selected topics vis-à-vis the three Old Testament books.

Definition of Wisdom Literature

The precise nature and setting of the Old Testament wisdom literature is debated. According to R. N. Whybray, "J. Meinhold in 1908 published what seems to have been the first study entirely devoted to the wisdom literature of the Old Testament."[3] Wisdom literature is often said to be humanistic, international, nonhistorical, and eudaemonistic, but as James Crenshaw notes, "each term has required qualification."[4]

In addition to their distinctive vocabulary, Whybray finds that "the wisdom books are distinctive in that they are primarily concerned with man and his world, and in particular with the potentiality and limitations of the individual."[5] Walter Brueggemann takes this a step further and claims that the wisdom corpus announces the joyous news that God trusts people to steer their own lives, and Crenshaw asserts that the distinctive belief about Israelite wisdom was "in the sufficiency of human virtue to achieve well-being in this life, apart from divine assistance."[6] These two claims, however, can hardly be reconciled with the corpus itself. Proverbs 3:7 warns against being wise in one's own eyes (i.e., autonomous), and 3:6 calls for trust (*bṭḥ*) in the Lord instead. Commenting on *bṭḥ*, Alfred Jepsen says: "Most of all, man must not have confidence in himself. He must not trust in his own strength (. . . Prov 21:22), . . . or in himself, for 'he who trusts in his own mind is a fool' (Prov 28:26; [cf. 14:12; 16:25; passim])."[7] P. J. Nel

---

Soggin, "Amos and Wisdom," in *WIAI*, 119–23; A. A. Macintosh, "Hosea in the Wisdom Tradition: Dependence and Independence," in *WIAI*, 124–32; H. G. M. Williamson, "Isaiah and the Wise," in *WIAI*, 133–41; W. McKane, "Jeremiah and the Wise," in *WIAI*, 142–52; B. A. Mastin, "Wisdom and Daniel," in *WIAI*, 161–69.

3. R. N. Whybray: *The Book of Proverbs: A Survey of Modern Study*, History of Biblical Interpretation 1 (Leiden: Brill, 1995), 2; J. Meinhold, *Die Weisheit Israels in Spruch, Sage und Dichtung* (Leipzig: Quelle & Meyer, 1908).

4. J. L. Crenshaw, "The Wisdom Literature," in *The Hebrew Bible and Its Modern Interpreters*, ed. D. A. Knight and G. M. Tucker (Philadelphia: Fortress; Chico, Calif.: Scholars Press, 1985), 369.

5. R. N. Whybray, "The Social World of the Wisdom Writers," in *The World of Ancient Israel*, ed. R. E. Clements (Cambridge and New York: Cambridge University Press, 1989), 227; on vocabulary see idem, *The Intellectual Tradition in the Old Testament*, BZAW 135 (Berlin: de Gruyter, 1974), 71–155.

6. W. A. Brueggemann, *In Man We Trust* (Richmond: John Knox, 1972), 20–22, 26; Crenshaw, "Wisdom Literature," 373.

7. A. Jepsen, "בָּטַח *bāṭach*," *TDOT*, 2:91.

argued that wisdom's ethos "does not result from the goodness of man or the superior functions of human reason."[8] Because of humanity's limitations, the righteous commit their ways to the Lord for success (16:1–3). Piloting his own life under the sun, Qohelet found death better than life (Eccles. 4:2), and Job found no resolution to his questions of suffering and to the question of "why be righteous."[9] Job's angst was relieved only when the Lord answered him out of the chaotic whirlwind (Job 38:1).

The international character of wisdom, especially its connection with Egyptian instruction literature, has been established since E. A. W. Budge published what came to be known as *The Teaching of Amenemope*.[10] But Israel's wisdom uniquely lays down the fear of the Lord as the foundation for acquiring wisdom (Prov. 1:7; 9:18; Job 28:28; cf. Eccles. 12:13–14), and it is this concept, as Nel argues,[11] that represents the central religious principle in the wisdom literature. Besides, since Israel's laws, hymns, and other types of literature also show connections with the ancient Near Eastern literatures, this connection cannot be a distinctive mark of wisdom literature.

Regarding the nonhistorical nature of wisdom literature, Roland Murphy says: "The most striking characteristic of this literature is the absence of what one normally considers as typically Israelite and Jewish. There is no mention of the promises to the patriarchs, the Exodus and Moses, the covenant and Sinai, the promise to David (2 Sam. 7), and so forth."[12] This is largely so, yet Solomon, as king of Israel (Prov. 1:1), looked at humanity and his world through the lens of Israel's covenants and drew the conclusion that one could enter the world of wisdom only through the fear of the Lord (1:7). In contrast to Qohelet and Job's three friends, who spoke mostly of "God" (*'ĕlōhîm*), the title for God in his transcendence, Proverbs speaks of "the LORD" (*yhwh*), the title of Israel's immanent God who entered into covenant with them.

William McKane, Ernst Würthwein, and Walter Zimmerli think the older Israelite wisdom was utilitarian and eudaemonistic, rather than religious, but I contended already in 1979 that no distinction can be made between secular/profane and religious/pious in any ancient Near East literature.[13] In 1987 F. M. Wilson appraised critically the distinc-

---

8. P. J. Nel, *The Structure and Ethos of the Wisdom Admonitions in Proverbs*, BZAW 158 (Berlin and New York: de Gruyter, 1982), 127.

9. J. G. Janzen, *Job*, Interpretation (Atlanta: John Knox, 1985), 3.

10. E. A. W. Budge, *Facsimiles of Egyptian Hieratic Papyri in the British Museum*, 2d series (London: British Museum, 1923), plates I–XIV.

11. Nel, *Structure and Ethos*, 127.

12. Murphy, *Tree of Life*, 1.

13. W. McKane, *Prophets and Wise Men*, SBT 1/44 (Naperville, Ill.: Allenson; London: SCM, 1965); idem, *Proverbs: A New Approach*, OTL (Philadelphia: Westminster; London: SCM, 1970); E. Würthwein, *Die Weisheit Ägyptens und das Alte Testament*, Schriften der

tion between older, profane wisdom and younger, Yahwistic wisdom, and today the distinction is widely rejected.[14] Even R. N. Whybray, who formerly made this distinction, later said, "there is no awareness of the modern distinction between 'religious' and 'secular' [in Proverbs]."[15] With regard to the claim that the Book of Proverbs bases its morality on eudaemonism (i.e., a system of ethics of doing good to obtain pleasure), let it be noted that the wisdom corpus qualifies eudaemonism in the same way the rest of the Old Testament does (cf. Lev. 26 and Deut. 27–28): happiness depends on faith in God to uphold justice. Moreover, in order that the wise may not be seduced into confounding morality with pleasure, the Lord often allows them to suffer for the sake of righteousness and thereby works patience, hope, trust, and other virtues into their character before he upholds his moral order, which includes justice (see under "Theology" below).

Klaus Koch, Hartmut Gese, and H. H. Schmid have developed the notion that basic to wisdom is a search for "order," a deed-destiny nexus.[16] On the basis of these studies and the conviction that the Egyptian figure of *Ma'at* had been adapted to both the Israelite situation and the personification of Woman Wisdom in Proverbs 1:20–33 and chapter 8, Gerhard von Rad contends that God implanted wisdom (i.e., the world order of law and justice) in the creation itself, and that this primordial revelation woos people to trust this immanent revelation.[17] Daniel Estes essentially agrees but emphasizes that the

---

Philipps-Universität Marburg 6 (Marburg: Elwert, 1960); reprinted in *Wort und Existenz: Studien zum Alten Testament* (Göttingen: Vandenhoeck & Ruprecht, 1970), 197–216; translated as "Egyptian Wisdom and the Old Testament," trans. B. W. Kovacs, in *SAIW*, 113–33; W. Zimmerli, "Zur Struktur der alttestamentlichen Weisheit," *ZAW* 10 (1933): 177–204; translated as "Concerning the Structure of Old Testament Wisdom," trans. B. W. Kovacs and reprinted in *SAIW*, 175–207; B. K. Waltke, "The Book of Proverbs and Old Testament Theology," *BSac* 136 (1979): 302–17.

14. F. M. Wilson, "Sacred and Profane? The Yahwistic Redaction of Proverbs Reconsidered," in *The Listening Heart: Essays in Wisdom and the Psalms in Honour of R. E. Murphy*, ed. K. G. Hoglund et al., JSOTSup 58 (Sheffield: Sheffield Academic Press, 1987), 313–34; see Weeks, *Early Israelite Wisdom*, 57–73.

15. R. N. Whybray, *Wisdom in Proverbs: The Concept of Wisdom in Proverbs 1–9*, SBT 1/45 (Naperville, Ill.: Allenson; London: SCM, 1965), 72–104; cf. idem, *Proverbs*, NCB (Grand Rapids: Eerdmans; London: Marshall Pickering, 1994), 4.

16. K. Koch, "Gibt es ein Vergeltungsdogma im Alten Testament?" *ZTK* 52 (1955): 1–42; H. Gese, "Lehre und Wirklichkeit in der alten Weisheit," in *Um des Prinzip der Vergeltung in Religion und Recht des Alten Testaments* (Darmstadt: Wissenschaftliche Buchgesellschaft, 1972), 213–35; idem, *Essays in Biblical Theology*, trans. K. Crim (Minneapolis: Augsburg, 1981); H. H. Schmid, *Gerechtigkeit als Weltordnung: Hintergrund und Geschichte des alttestamentlichen Gerechtigkeitabgriffes*, BHT 40 (Tübingen: Mohr, 1968). For their distinctive views see Emerton, "Wisdom," 215–19.

17. G. von Rad, *Wisdom in Israel*, trans. J. D. Martin (Nashville: Abingdon; London: SCM, 1972), 191; see also 144–76.

natural world is under Yahweh's sovereignty and that life is also inscrutable.[18]

But Woman Wisdom who cries for a hearing in Proverbs 1:20–33 and chapter 8 is a personification of the father's revealed wisdom, not of wisdom in creation. Derek Kidner notes that Woman Wisdom's teaching offers precisely the same benefits to the son as the father's (cf. 6:23–24 and 7:4).[19] Moreover, her summons to the son to listen to her (8:32) matches the father's (7:24). The father's wisdom, personified as Woman Wisdom, is the Lord's revelation found in the parental sayings, not in a natural theology (cf. 2:1–6), and the conception of the *yirʾat Yahweh*, "the fear of the Lord," as Nel argues, "does not allow one to interpret wisdom as natural theology."[20] Carol Newsom explains the distribution between the call of personified wisdom to humanity and the father's: "Where the father is the authoritative voice in the family, *Hokmot* [personified wisdom] is the corresponding public voice ('in the streets,' 'in the public squares' . . .)."[21]

According to Murphy, the thesis that biblical wisdom issues from the effort to discover order is held by so many scholars that it seems to be one of the "assured results." But he himself has misgivings about this approach to Israelite wisdom.[22] E. F. Huwiler complains against the notion of a fated order: "In its extreme form, the deed-consequence syndrome removes the deity from activity in the world. According to this view, the consequence follows the deed of itself, and Yahweh, whose power is limited, is directly involved merely as a midwife or a chemical catalyst, although indirectly involved as creator, who set into motion the deed-consequence syndrome."[23] Many sayings assert the deed-destiny nexus, but they do not presuppose divine inactivity. Lennart Böstrom argues that the Israelite wisdom tradition cannot properly be described as secular.[24]

---

18. D. J. Estes, *Hear, My Son: Teaching and Learning in Proverbs 1–9,* New Studies in Biblical Theology (Grand Rapids: Eerdmans, 1997), 19–39. See also my forthcoming review of this book in *JBL.*

19. Kidner, *Introduction,* 23.

20. Nel, *Structure and Ethos,* 127.

21. C. A. Newsom, "Woman and the Discourse of Patriarchal Wisdom: A Study of Proverbs 1–9," in *Gender and Difference in Ancient Israel,* ed. P. L. Day (Minneapolis: Fortress, 1989), 146.

22. R. E. Murphy, "Wisdom—Theses and Hypotheses," in *Israelite Wisdom,* 34–35.

23. E. F. Huwiler, "Control of Reality in Israelite Wisdom" (Ph.D. diss., Duke University, 1988), 64. E. Würthwein states that in wisdom God's "power is limited to taking care that [the order] retains its validity by means of proper retribution. Hence, Yahweh becomes a calculable God," who is "entirely different" from the God of the covenant ("Egyptian Wisdom and the Old Testament," in *SAIW,* 122).

24. L. Böstrom, *The God of the Sages: The Portrayal of God in the Book of Proverbs,* ConBOT 29 (Stockholm: Almqvist & Wiksell, 1990).

According to Kidner, wisdom is distinctive for its tone, its speakers, and its appeal: "The blunt 'Thou shalt' or 'shalt not' of the Law, and the urgent 'Thus saith the Lord' of the Prophets, are joined now by the cooler comments of the teacher. . . . Where the bulk of the Old Testament calls us simply to obey and to believe, this part of it . . . summons us to think hard as well as humbly."[25] These features too need qualification.

To be sure, the tone of wisdom differs, yet the father bluntly commands the son "listen!" (1:8), "do not yield" (1:10), and so forth, and represents his sayings as *tôrâ*, "law," and "commandments," *miṣwôt* (1:3; 3:1; passim), the same terms used for the law of Moses. Moreover, his appeal is just as urgent as those of Moses and the prophets: it is a matter of life and death. Woman Wisdom "raises her voice" (2:20), an expression that denotes a fervent and emotional situation (e.g., deep human distress, Gen. 45:2; Jer. 22:20), threat (Ps. 46:7; 68:34), roaring (Amos 1:2; 3:4; Job 2:11); and the father instructs the son to call back to wisdom in the same way (Prov. 2:3).

Israel's wise men were teachers, not lawgivers and prophets, but, as Kidner would agree, they speak with as much authority. They too claim inspiration (2:6), and their counsel (*ʿēṣâ*) is a matter of a decree, not advice to be evaluated.[26] Moreover, as Christa Kayatz notes, Woman Wisdom speaks as a prophet in 1:20–33.[27]

Wisdom indeed appeals to the mind, but to know wisdom is more a matter of a loving heart (i.e., a person's center for both physical and emotional-intellectual-moral activities)[28] than of a cold intellect (cf. Prov. 1:22; 3:12; 4:6; 8:17, 36; 9:8; 12:1; 13:24; 15:9; 17:17; 19:8). More importantly, the Book of Proverbs calls for childlike faith in the Lord, who upholds the righteous order of justice he has begotten (8:22–31). As is well known, Qohelet found wickedness in the place of justice (Eccles. 3:16), and Job discerned no moral order (9:22).

In my opinion, Old Testament wisdom literature differs from other literary types by its distinctive inspiration (cf. Heb. 1:1).[29] Whereas God appeared to Moses in theophany and to the prophets in visions/auditions (cf. Num. 12:6–8), Israel's wise men and women observed God's

25. Kidner, *Introduction*, 11.

26. See B. K. Waltke, "The Authority of Proverbs: An Exposition of Proverbs 1:2–6," *Presbyterion* 13 (1987): 65–78; idem, "Lady Wisdom as Mediatrix: An Exposition of Proverbs 1:20–33," *Presbyterion* 14 (1988): 1–15.

27. C. Kayatz, *Studien zu Proverbien 1–9: Eine form- und motivgeschichtliche Untersuchung unter Einbeziehung ägyptischen Vergleichsmaterials*, WMANT 22 (Neukirchen-Vluyn: Neukirchener Verlag, 1966), 119–22.

28. B. K. Waltke, "Heart," *Evangelical Dictionary of Biblical Theology*, ed. W. A. Elwell (Grand Rapids: Baker, 1996), 331–32.

29. B. K. Waltke, "Proverbs, Theology of," *NIDOTTE*, 4:1079.

creation and coined their cogent reflections upon it. One observes the sage at work in Proverbs 24:30–34. His laboratory is the sluggard's field (vv. 30–31): "I applied my heart to what I observed and learned a lesson from what I saw" (v. 32). Whereupon he either coins or cites a proverb: "A little sleep . . . and poverty will come on you like a vagabond and scarcity like an armed man" (vv. 33–34). Qohelet begins his essay by observing the cycles of creation (Eccles. 1:3–11) and finds it all "a chasing after wind"/"a vexation of spirit," probably a deliberate double entendre, of which the sages were fond. He continued his quest for wisdom by reflecting on his experiences under the sun. Job based his religio-social reflections largely on his experienced misery, and found no resolution to his perplexity until the Lord made him see the chaos bounded by the cosmos within the creation (Job 38–41).

Their theology, however, is not natural theology. They view creation through the lens of Israel's covenant faith. Solomon and King Lemuel's mother never take that lens away. Qohelet and Job temporarily remove it but eventually replace it, and Agur confesses that apart from Moses and David, whom he quotes in Proverbs 30:5–6, he could find no wisdom (30:1–4). Nevertheless, although their inspiration differs, they claim to be inspired and to possess canonical authority (cf. Prov. 1:1; 2:1–8; 22:17–21; 25:1; 30:5–6; Eccles. 12:9–13; Job 42:1–9).

Proverbs

To give the reader a sense of the concerns in academic research on the Book of Proverbs, I have chosen to focus on its origin and background, poetics, and theology.[30]

Origin and Background

The Book of Proverbs attributes its authorship to Solomon (1:1; 10:1), "proverbs of Solomon copied by the men of Hezekiah" (25:1), Agur (30:1), and King Lemuel (31:1).[31] The ascription of chapters 1–24 to Solomon agrees with the Deuteronomist's claim that Solomon composed 3,000 proverbs (1 Kings 4:32 [5:12 MT]). But academic research during the past century has largely rejected this biblical claim and regards Solomon instead as "a figurehead to which the ascription of wisdom could be attached."[32] Crenshaw observes that "as the wealthiest

---

30. A helpful introduction to academic research in Proverbs is Whybray, *Book of Proverbs*.

31. I defend the historical credibility of these superscriptions in "Proverbs, Theology of," 1080–86.

32. R. E. Clements, *Wisdom in Theology* (Grand Rapids: Eerdmans; Carlisle: Paternoster, 1992), 19.

king in Israel's memory, Solomon must naturally have invited thoughts associating him with extraordinary wisdom," and R. E. Clements thinks the Deuteronomist made it up to create as good an image of a questionable Solomon as possible.[33] But Crenshaw confesses that "a satisfactory explanation has not surfaced for the prominence of Solomon's name."[34] André Lemaire argues that "the portrayal of Solomon's reign and of his wisdom such as appears in 1 Kings iii–xi seems generally to conform with the royal near eastern ideology of the start of the first millennium B.C."[35]

Old Testament scholars who are unwilling to accept Solomonic authorship situate the Proverbs in time and social setting by form criticism alone,[36] which entails employing the literature of the ancient Near East.

International Background

Prior to Budge's publication of *The Teaching of Amenemope*, scholars often regarded Proverbs as under some influence of Greek philosophy and as a product of a very late stage in Israel's theological development. In 1933 Johannes Fichtner laid the foundation for future research by comparing in an exemplary way the wisdom literature of Israel with that of the ancient Near East.[37] Scholars have now universally abandoned a Hellenistic background in favor of the context of the ancient Near East from the time of Israel's monarchy and earlier. I have argued that this match inferentially supports the biblical claim of Solomon's authorship.[38]

Proverb collections existed in Egypt from the Old Kingdom (2686–2160 B.C.) right through to the Late Dynastic Period and Hellenistic rule (500–300 B.C.);[39] Ebla (ca. 2400 B.C.);[40] Sumer (ca. 1700 B.C.);[41] Mesopotamia from the Kassite period (1500–1200 B.C.) and Middle

33. J. L. Crenshaw, "Proverbs," *ABD*, 5:514; R. E. Clements, "Solomon and the Origins of Wisdom in Israel," *Perspectives in Religious Studies* 15 (1988): 23–36.

34. Crenshaw, "Proverbs," 513.

35. A. Lemaire, "Wisdom in Solomonic Historiography" (trans. H. G. M. Williamson), in *WIAI*, 106–18.

36. A helpful analysis of wisdom's forms is R. E. Murphy, *Wisdom Literature: Job, Proverbs, Ruth, Canticles, Ecclesiastes, and Esther*, FOTL 13 (Grand Rapids: Eerdmans, 1981).

37. J. Fichtner, *Die altorientalische Weisheit in ihrer israelitisch-judischen Ausprägung*, BZAW 62 (Giessen: Topelmann, 1933).

38. See B. K. Waltke, "The Book of Proverbs and Ancient Wisdom Literature," *BSac* 136 (1979): 221–38.

39. See now J. D. Ray, "Egyptian Wisdom Literature," in *WIAI*, 17–29.

40. G. Pettinato, *The Archives of Ebla: An Empire Inscribed in Clay* (Garden City, N.Y.: Doubleday, 1981), 47, 238.

41. E. I. Gordon, *Sumerian Proverbs: Glimpses of Everyday Life in Ancient Mesopotamia* (New York: Greenwood, 1968), 24–152.

Assyrian times;[42] and Aramaic (704–669 B.C.).[43] In addition a few isolated proverbs or proverb-like sayings have been discovered at Mari and in the Amarna Letters (1350 B.C.).[44]

The most striking similarities exist between Proverbs and the Egyptian collections,[45] especially Amenemope, which scholars agree dates to the late Twenty-first Dynasty (ca. 1070–945 B.C., roughly contemporary with Solomon),[46] but the nature of the relationship between the two texts is disputed. Whybray presents a comprehensive review of that debate, and Paul Overland has most recently added to it by noting the structural similarity between the two texts.[47] But the precise connection of Amenemope to the so-called Thirty Sayings of the Wise is disputed. Glendon Bryce best represents a more positive critical evaluation of their relationship, and John Ruffle, A. Niccacci (with whom Whybray agrees), and Currid represent the negative.[48]

Paul Humbert years ago pointed out the analogies of the content of Proverbs with the Egyptian collections.[49] Christa Kayatz has noted the

42. W. G. Lambert, *Babylonian Wisdom Literature*, 3d ed. (Oxford: Clarendon, 1975; reprinted, Winona Lake, Ind.: Eisenbrauns, 1996), 92, 97, 222. For the Babylonian wisdom literature connected to Job and Qohelet, see idem, "Some New Babylonian Wisdom Literature," in *WIAI*, 30–42.

43. J. M. Lindenberger, "The Aramaic Proverbs of Ahiqar" (Ph.D. diss., Johns Hopkins University, 1974); idem, *The Aramaic Proverbs of Ahiqar*, JHNES (Baltimore: Johns Hopkins University Press, 1983); J. C. Greenfield, "The Wisdom of Ahiqar," in *WIAI*, 43–52.

44. See, respectively, A. Marzal, *Gleanings from the Wisdom of Mari*, StPohl 11 (Rome: Pontifical Biblical Institute, 1976); W. F. Albright, "Some Canaanite-Phoenician Sources of Hebrew Wisdom," in *Wisdom in Israel and in the Ancient Near East*, *Presented to H. H. Rowley*, ed. M. Noth and D. W. Thomas, VTSup 3 (Leiden: Brill, 1960), 1–15.

45. J. Day ("Foreign Semitic Influence on the Wisdom of Israel and Its Appropriation in the Book of Proverbs," in *WIAI*, 55–79) attempts to correct some claims for Egyptian influence on the Book of Proverbs and emphasizes that "Israel's wisdom, including the book of Proverbs, was indebted to foreign Semitic influence in addition to the Egyptian influence" (70).

46. J. D. Currid, *Ancient Egypt and the Old Testament* (Grand Rapids: Baker, 1997), 209.

47. Whybray, *Book of Proverbs*, 6–14; P. Overland, "Structure in *The Wisdom of Amenemope* and Proverbs," in *"Go to the Land I Will Show You": Studies in Honor of Dwight W. Young*, ed. J. E. Coleson and V. H. Matthews (Winona Lake, Ind.: Eisenbrauns, 1996), 275–91.

48. G. E. Bryce, *A Legacy of Wisdom: The Egyptian Contribution to the Wisdom of Israel* (Lewisburg, Pa.: Bucknell University Press; London: Associated University Presses, 1979); J. Ruffle, "The Teaching of Amenemope and Its Connection with the Book of Proverbs," *TynBul* 28 (1977): 29–68; A. Niccacci, "Proverbi 22.17–23.11," *SBFLA* 29 (1949): 42–72, summarized by R. N. Whybray, *The Composition of the Book of Proverbs*, JSOTSup 168 (Sheffield: JSOT Press, 1994), 132–47; see Whybray, "The Structure and Composition of Proverbs 22:17–24:22," in *Crossing the Boundaries: Essays in Biblical Interpretation in Honour of Michael D. Goulder*, ed. S. E. Porter et al., Biblical Interpretation 8 (Leiden: Brill, 1994), 83–96.

49. P. Humbert, *Recherches sur les sources égyptiennes de la littérature sapientiale d'Israël* (Neuchatel: Secrétariat de l'Université, 1929).

similarities in forms and motifs with reference to Proverbs 1–9, leading her to press for the preexilic date of this collection.[50] Having demonstrated that the structure of Proverbs 1–24 conforms remarkably with the structure of certain Egyptian collections precisely from the time of Solomon, Kenneth Kitchen concludes that the most probable date of chapters 1–24 "is entirely compatible with that of the named author in the title of the work, i.e., king Solomon, of *c.* 950 BC."[51] Al Wolters dated the last work (31:10–31) to the Hellenistic period because of the presence of *ṣôpiyyâ* in 31:27 (a wordplay on the Greek word *sophia*), but allows that an earlier date, before Alexander, is possible.[52] H. C. Washington documents, "During the two centuries before 332 B.C. Palestine had seen a heavy influx of Greek culture."[53] However, Claire Gottlieb thinks the pun is closer to Egyptian *sbȝyt,* "instruction."[54]

Linguistic Evidence

Many critical interpreters now think that 1:1–9:18 and chapters 30 and 31 are postexilic in origin and that the other subcollections are preexilic.[55] Washington, however, argues that these distinctions are

50. Kayatz, *Studien zu Proverbien 1–9.*

51. K. A. Kitchen, "Proverbs and Wisdom Books of the Ancient Near East: The Factual History of a Literary Form," *TynBul* 28 (1977): 69–114 (quotation on 99); Kitchen's remarkable essay has just as remarkably been overlooked or ignored by later essayists (Whybray, *Book of Proverbs,* 14, mentions Kitchen's article only in connection with his agreement with Ruffle!) and most commentators, e.g., D. Cox, *Proverbs with an Introduction to Sapiential Books,* Old Testament Message (Wilmington: Glazier, 1982); R. L. Alden, *Proverbs: A Commentary on an Ancient Book of Timeless Advice* (Grand Rapids: Baker, 1983); K. T. Aitken, *Proverbs,* DSB—OT (Philadelphia: Westminster, 1986) (to be fair, this work lacks a bibliography); O. Plöger, *Sprüche Salomos (Proverbia),* BKAT (Neukirchen-Vluyn: Neukirchener Verlag, 1984); D. A. Hubbard, *Proverbs,* Communicator's Bible (Dallas: Word, 1989); K. Farmer, *Who Knows What Is Good? A Commentary on the Books of Proverbs and Ecclesiastes,* ITC (Grand Rapids: Eerdmans; Edinburgh: Handsel, 1991); A. Meinhold, *Die Sprüche,* Zürcher Bibelkommentare (Zurich: Theologischer Verlag, 1991); Whybray, *Proverbs;* R. C. Van Leeuwen, "Proverbs," in *The New Interpreter's Bible,* vol. 5 (Nashville: Abingdon, 1997), 19–264. Notable exceptions are A. P. Ross, "Proverbs," *EBC,* vol. 5 (Grand Rapids: Zondervan, 1991), 883–1134; and D. A. Garrett, *Proverbs, Ecclesiastes, Song of Songs,* NAC (Nashville: Broadman, 1993).

52. A. Wolters, "Ṣôpiyyâ (Prov 31:27) as Hymnic Participle and Play on *Sophia,*" *JBL* 104 (1985): 577–87; idem, "Proverbs xxxi 10–31 as Heroic Hymn: A Form-Critical Analysis," *VT* 38 (1988): 457; see G. Rendsburg, "Bilingual Wordplay in the Bible," *VT* 38 (1988): 354.

53. H. C. Washington, "Wealth and Poverty in the Instruction of Amenemope and the Hebrew Proverbs: A Comparative Case Study in the Social Location and Function" (Ph.D. diss., Princeton Theological Seminary, 1992), 185–86.

54. C. Gottlieb, "The Words of the Exceedingly Wise: Proverbs 30–31," in *The Biblical Canon in Comparative Perspective,* ed. K. L. Younger Jr., W. W. Hallo, and B. F. Batto, Scripture in Context 4, ANETS 11 (Lewiston, N.Y.: Mellen, 1991), 290.

55. N. Gottwald, *The Hebrew Bible: A Socio-Literary Introduction* (Philadelphia: Fortress, 1985).

not as secure as is usually assumed. Basing his view on Claudia Camp's treatment of the question, he contends that Proverbs, though having undergone a centuries-long process of formation, much of it impossible to reconstruct, underwent "a unitary editing, transforming the diverse materials of the book into a recognizable product of the Restoration community."[56] He appeals to the book's lexical inventory to suggest a composition time after the end of the Judean monarchy, but fails to deal with Kitchen's arguments.[57] He himself confesses that "it is precarious to date biblical books on the basis of their vocabulary alone," and "none of these words singly constitutes conclusive evidence."[58]

In favor of an early date for Proverbs, W. F. Albright contended that "Proverbs teems with . . . Canaanitisms," and M. Dahood and W. A. van der Weiden made extensive use of Ugaritic (ca. 1400 B.C.) in their philological studies on Proverbs.[59]

Setting

On the questionable assumption that sages express their sociological milieu in their gnomic sayings, interpreters have searched for such evidence, but Whybray (citing Murphy) notes that the precise life setting of these sayings eludes us, calling into question the legitimacy of this approach alone for literary criticism.[60] Crenshaw is skeptical of the ability of form-critical analyses to establish the social setting of wisdom literature and, in any case, looks to a number of settings: family, court, school.[61]

Von Rad has proposed that a new scribal class in Israel produced such works as Proverbs during a so-called Solomonic Enlightenment

56. Washington, "Wealth and Poverty," 178; C. Camp, *Wisdom and the Feminine in the Book of Proverbs,* BLS 11 (Sheffield: JSOT Press, 1985), 233. He does not agree with her change of position in which she opts for a Hellenistic date for the book's final redaction in "What's So Strange about the Strange Woman?" in *The Bible and the Politics of Exegesis: Essays in Honor of Norman K. Gottwald on His Sixty-Fifth Birthday,* ed. D. Jobling et al. (Cleveland: Pilgrim, 1991), 303.

57. Kitchen, "Proverbs and Wisdom Books."

58. Washington, "Wealth and Poverty," 180, 182.

59. Albright, "Some Canaanite-Phoenician Sources," 9; M. J. Dahood, *Proverbs and Northwest Semitic Philology,* Scripta Pontificii Instituti Biblici 113 (Rome: Biblical Institute Press, 1963); W. A. van der Weiden, *Le Livre des Proverbes: Notes philologiques,* BibOr 23 (Rome: Biblical Institute Press, 1970).

60. See Whybray, "Social World," 18–29; idem, *Book of Proverbs,* 18–33; B. W. Kovacs, "Is There a Class-Ethic in Proverbs?" in *Essays in Old Testament Ethics,* ed. J. L. Crenshaw and J. T. Willis (New York: Ktav, 1974), 171–89; idem, "Sociological-Structural Constraints upon Wisdom: The Spatial and Temporal Matrix of Proverbs 15:28–22:16" (Ph.D. diss., Vanderbilt University, 1978).

61. J. L. Crenshaw, "Prolegomenon," in *SAIW,* 20.

due to Solomon's inspirational contacts with Egypt.[62] Brueggemann credits David for beginning this enlightenment.[63] Udo Skladny places three collections in the early monarchy: Proverbs 10–15; 28–29; and 16:1–22:16.[64] He interprets the last as an instruction for royal officials. Bryce reaches a similar conclusion for Proverbs 25, Raymond Van Leeuwen for chapters 25–27, and Bruce Malchow for chapters 28–29.[65] B. W. Kovacs thinks Proverbs 10–29 were the work of government officials.[66] J. K. Wiles notes that kings sponsored wisdom, and wisdom undergirded kings.[67] Weeks denies the court setting, but Michael V. Fox indirectly answers him by noting that "the sayings in question speak not only *about* kings and courtiers, but *to* and *for* them."[68]

Others prefer a folk setting to a royal setting. R. B. Y. Scott distinguishes between folk and academic sayings in Proverbs.[69] Murphy attributes the greater number of sayings to ordinary social intercourse.[70] Skladny thinks chapters 25–27 were addressed to a more agricultural sector of society.[71] Whybray argues that Solomonic collections encapsulated the traditional lore of Israelite small farmers, and subsequently were formed into larger groups for a pedagogical purpose.[72] Fontaine looks to Old Testament narrative to establish the function of proverbs in ordinary life.[73] Claus Westermann locates the bulk of chapters 10–29

---

62. G. von Rad, "The Beginnings of Historical Writing in Ancient Israel," in *The Problem of the Hexateuch and Other Essays*, trans. E. W. Trueman Dicken (New York: McGraw-Hill; Edinburgh and London: Oliver & Boyd, 1966), 166–204; so also E. W. Heaton, *Solomon's New Men: The Emergence of Ancient Israel as a National State* (New York: Pica; London: Thames and Hudson, 1974). For a critique of this hypothesis, see R. N. Whybray, "Wisdom Literature in the Reigns of David and Solomon," in *Studies in the Period of David and Solomon and Other Essays*, ed. T. Ishida (Winona Lake, Ind.: Eisenbrauns; Tokyo: Yamakawa-Shuppansha, 1982), 13–26.

63. Brueggemann, *In Man We Trust*, 64–67.

64. U. Skladny, *Die ältesten Spruchsammlungen in Israel* (Göttingen: Vandenhoeck & Ruprecht, 1962), 25–46.

65. G. E. Bryce, "Another Wisdom-'Book' in Proverbs," *JBL* 91 (1972): 145–57; R. C. Van Leeuwen, *Context and Meaning in Proverbs 25–27*, SBLDS 96 (Atlanta: Scholars Press, 1988); B. V. Malchow, "A Manual for Future Monarchs," *CBQ* 47 (1985): 238–45.

66. Kovacs, "Is There a Class-Ethic," 187.

67. J. K. Wiles, "Wisdom and Kingship in Israel," *Asia Journal of Theology* 1 (1987): 55–70.

68. Weeks, *Early Israelite Wisdom*, 1–56; M. V. Fox, "The Social Location of the Book of Proverbs," in *Texts, Temples, and Traditions: A Tribute to Menahem Haran*, ed. M. V. Fox et al. (Winona Lake, Ind.: Eisenbrauns, 1996), 227–39 (quotation on 235).

69. R. B. Y. Scott, *The Way of Wisdom in the Old Testament* (New York: Macmillan; London: Collier-Macmillan, 1971), esp. 63.

70. R. E. Murphy, "Assumptions and Problems in Old Testament Wisdom Research," *CBQ* 29 (1967): 106.

71. Skladny, *Die ältesten Spruchsammlungen*, 43.

72. Whybray, *The Composition of Proverbs*, 62.

73. C. R. Fontaine, *Traditional Sayings in the Old Testament: A Contextual Study*, BLS 5 (Sheffield: Almond, 1982), 72–138.

among the simple folk in the small agrarian village at a preliterate stage of culture.[74] Whybray, however, thinks the references to drunkenness in association with gluttony and to consorting with immoral women in Proverbs "may be an indication of an urban setting."[75]

Some recent scholarship tends to refine the folk setting to a preliterate society. Westermann, André Barucq, F. W. Golka, and Laurent Naré suggest a preliterate origin of the material in Proverbs, especially chapters 10–29, by comparing its short sayings with the aphoristic material of modern nonliterate peoples, especially in Africa.[76] Whybray thinks "this new material marks the beginning of a new era in Proverbs study comparable with that which began with the publication of *Amenemope* more than seventy years ago," but Fox cautions: "We should be wary about drawing conclusions from African parallels."[77]

Others find the origins of wisdom in law. Berend Gemser concludes that the proverbial wisdom in legal form might be very ancient.[78] J.-P. Audet and Erhard Gerstenberger think the admonitions in Proverbs and in Israel's law derived from specific codes of behavior used in Israel's patriarchal, premonarchical society (*Sippenweisheit*).[79] Joseph Blenkinsopp similarly thinks wisdom and law derived to some extent from a common origin.[80] H. W. Wolff supports the theory of *Sippenweisheit* for Amos, and J. W. Whedbee for Isaiah.[81] Wolfgang Richter speaks instead of "group ethos" (*Gruppenethos*) for the development of

74. C. Westermann, "Weisheit im Sprichwort," *Schalom: Studien zu Glaube und Geschichte Israels: Alfred Jepsen zum 70. Geburtstag*, ed. K.-H. Bernhardt, Arbeiten zur Theologie 46 (Stuttgart: Calwer, 1971), 149–61.

75. R. N. Whybray, *Wealth and Poverty in the Book of Proverbs*, JSOTSup 99 (Sheffield: JSOT Press, 1990), 90.

76. C. Westermann, *Roots of Wisdom: The Oldest Proverbs of Israel and Other Peoples*, trans. J. D. Charles (Louisville: Westminster/John Knox, 1995); A. Barucq, "Proverbes (Livre des)," *DBSup* 8 (1972), cols. 1395–476; F. W. Golka, *The Leopard's Spots: Biblical and African Wisdom in Proverbs* (Edinburgh: Clark, 1993), which incorporates his earlier essays; L. Naré, *Proverbes salomoniens et proverbes mossi: Étude comparative à partir d'une nouvelle analyse de Pr 25–29* (Frankfurt and Berne: Lang, 1986).

77. Whybray, *Book of Proverbs*, 33; Fox, "Social Location," 239.

78. B. Gemser, "The Importance of the Motive Clause in Old Testament Law," in *Congress Volume: Copenhagen, 1953*, VTSup 1 (Leiden: Brill, 1953), 50–66.

79. J.-P. Audet, "Origines comparées de la double tradition de la loi et de la sagesse dans le proche-orient ancien," *International Congress of Orientalists* 1 (1964), 352–57; E. Gerstenberger, *Wesen und Herkunft des "apodiktischen Rechts,"* WMANT 20 (Neukirchen-Vluyn: Neukirchener Verlag, 1965), 110ff.

80. J. Blenkinsopp, *Wisdom and Law in the Old Testament: The Ordering of Life in Israel and Early Judaism*, Oxford Bible Series (Oxford and New York: Oxford University Press, 1983), 9–10, 74–129.

81. H. W. Wolff, *Amos, the Prophet: The Man and His Background*, trans. F. R. McCurley, ed. J. Reumann (Philadelphia: Fortress, 1973); J. W. Whedbee, *Isaiah and Wisdom* (Nashville: Abingdon, 1971), 80–110; cf. Morgan, *Wisdom in the Old Testament Traditions*.

laws that were then taken over by the wisdom schools.[82] Nel argues, however, that the admonition form cannot establish setting, that a distinction between law and the codification of the law must be maintained in order to determine the relationship between law and wisdom, and that the identification of law and wisdom can be explained from the inherent identity in ethos and content of both.[83]

As noted above, Richter proposes a second setting for original wisdom thinking: the school. By analogy from scribal schools in Egypt, Paul Volz pictures in Israel both spiritual schools for religious formation and scribal schools for training scribes.[84] H.-J. Hermisson locates the origin of the sayings of Proverbs in schools connected with the royal court, which trained the elite for the royal bureaucracy.[85] N. Shupak defends a school setting from equivalent terms found in the writings associated with Egyptian schools, and W. Magass from metaphoric images in Proverbs.[86] Bernhard Lang, and especially Lemaire, contend for the existence of schools in ancient Israel from archaeological evidence.[87] Davies weighs in on the side of those who think schools of some sort existed in ancient Israel, but Weeks finds the evidence for schools so weak that their existence should not be presumed, and Fox, sometimes using the same data as Davies, denies that proverbs were taught in schools.[88]

Others look to a home-school setting, at least for some parts of Proverbs. Crenshaw argues for a home setting; Whybray and Fox argue against most commentators, who assume that "father" means "teacher" in wisdom literature; and Murphy says, "the home may be regarded as perhaps the original site of wisdom teaching, before and after such teaching became professionalized among the sages."[89]

In my opinion, the many references to the father, and especially those to the mother, addressing the child throughout the book (1:8;

82. W. Richter, *Recht und Ethos: Versuch einer Ortung des weisheitlichen Mahnspruches*, SANT 15 (Munich: Kösel, 1966).

83. Nel, *Structure and Ethos*, 127.

84. P. Volz, *Hiob and Weisheit*, 2d ed., Die Schriften des Alte Testaments (Göttingen: Vandenhoeck & Ruprecht, 1921), 103.

85. H.-J. Hermisson, *Studien zur israelitischen Spruchweisheit*, WMANT 28 (Neukirchen-Vluyn: Neukirchener Verlag, 1968).

86. N. Shupak, "'The Sitz im Leben' of Proverbs in the Light of a Comparison of Biblical and Egyptian Wisdom Literature," *RB* 94 (1987): 98–119; W. Magass, "Die Rezeptionsgeschichte der Proverbien," *LB* 57 (1985): 61–80.

87. B. Lang, "Schule und Unterricht im alten Israel," in *La Sagesse de l'Ancien Testament*, ed. M. Gilbert, BETL 51 (Gembloux: Duculot; Louvain: Leuven University Press, 1979), 186–201; A. Lemaire, "Sagesse et écoles," *VT* 34 (1984): 270–81.

88. G. I. Davies, "Were There Schools in Ancient Israel?" in *WIAI*, 199–211; Weeks, *Early Israelite Wisdom*, 132–56; Fox, "Social Location."

89. J. L. Crenshaw, "Education in Ancient Israel," *JBL* 104 (1985): 601–15; Whybray, *Intellectual Tradition*, 41–43; Fox, "Social Location," 230–32; Murphy, *Tree of Life*, 4.

10:1; etc.), as well as to the grandfather in 4:1–9 and to King Lemuel's mother in 31:1, suggest that Solomon intended to transmit his wisdom to Israel through the home even as Moses disseminated the law through Israel's parents (cf. Deut. 6:7–9). Fox finds a strong analogy to the ancient wisdom instructions in the medieval Jewish ethical testament: "Ethical testaments are instructions written by men in their maturity for the religious-ethical guidance of their sons and, sometimes, daughters. (These texts are, in fact, descendants of ancient Wisdom Literature, since they use Proverbs as a model.) . . . The father addresses his son (or sons) and through him speaks to a larger reading audience."[90] If so, the Israelite situation is precisely the same as that attested in the Egyptian instructional literature.

Poetics and Structure

In this survey of the history of the study, I lean heavily on Knut Heim even as he cheerfully followed the outline of the survey by Ruth Scoralick.[91]

Survey of Scholarship Denying the Existence of Structure

McKane argues "that there is, for the most part, no context in the sentence literature" (i.e., Prov. 10:1–22:16 and chaps. 25–29).[92] This conviction is part and parcel of his questionable program to rearrange the proverbs according to their historical development. According to him, the proverbs evolved from (A) those that were profane for the education of the individual, to (B) those that served the community, to (C) those that expressed "a moralism derived from Yahwistic piety."[93] For example, in his view, the word pair "righteous/wicked" belong to category C, and the word pair "wise/fool" belong to category A.

In his commentary on the Proverbs, R. B. Y. Scott recognizes some intentional arrangements (e.g., 16:1–7).[94] In a later essay on the religious and secular contents of Proverbs, he understands 10:1–22:16 as a haphazard collection of "variegated material without contextual connections."[95]

---

90. Fox, "Social Location," 232.

91. K. M. Heim, "Structure and Context in Proverbs 10:1–22:16" (Ph.D. diss., University of Liverpool, 1996), 5–53; R. Scoralick, *Einzelspruch und Sammlung*, BZAW 232 (Berlin and New York: de Gruyter, 1995).

92. McKane, *Proverbs*, 10; cf. 413–15.

93. Ibid., 11.

94. R. B. Y. Scott, *Proverbs; Ecclesiastes*, AB 18 (Garden City, N.Y.: Doubleday, 1965), 17.

95. R. B. Y. Scott, "Wise and Foolish, Righteous and Wicked," in *Studies in the Religion of Ancient Israel*, ed. J. L. Crenshaw, VTSup 23 (Leiden: Brill, 1972), 147.

Westermann has reacted against efforts to find conscious arrangements.[96] His approach is governed by the form-critical conviction that the shorter sentence literature of 10:1–22:16, in contrast to the instruction literature of 1:1–9:18, was early. Since he stresses that the primary *Sitz im Leben* of a proverb is its oral use, he denies the possibility that authors composed sayings for a written context. Although he cannot deny a relationship between some sayings in the secondary collection of the sayings,[97] his concern is with their alleged oral origin.

Proverb-Performance Context

Observing that proverbs are often contradictory (e.g., "Haste makes waste," but "He who hesitates is lost"), B. Kirshenblatt-Gimblett mentions the following factors operating in sayings according to the "proverb-performance" school of thought.

1. Proverbs express relative, not absolute, truth.
2. Life context determines a proverb's meaning and "truth."
3. A proverb that fits semantically may not be socially appropriate in terms of what the participants in the situation wish to accomplish.
4. A person tends to select a proverb on the basis of what the life situation requires.
5. Situations can be evaluated in more than one way.[98]

Carole Fontaine also prefers to speak of "proverb performance meaning" rather than "simple proverb meaning."[99] According to her, one uses proverbs in social contexts to evaluate past actions or to affect future behavior.[100] The collectors of proverbs failed to understand the need to give full contextual data about the situation in which the saying is used.[101]

Claudia Camp developed Fontaine's treatment of "performance contexts."[102] She called for "the literary de-contextualizing of proverbs"

96. C. Westermann, review of R. Van Leeuwen's *Context and Meaning in Proverbs 25–27* in *ZAW* 102 (1990): 165–67.

97. C. Westermann, *Forschungsgeschichte zur Weisheitsliteratur 1950–1990* (Stuttgart: Calwer, 1991), 35–36.

98. B. Kirshenblatt-Gimblett, "Toward a Theory of Proverb Meaning," *Proverbium* 22 (1973): 823, cited by C. R. Fontaine, *Traditional Sayings in the Old Testament*, BLS 5 (Sheffield: Almond, 1982), 50. Fontaine defines "proverb performance" as referring to a situation in which "a certain stimulus (usually human behavior) . . . has elicited the application of the proverb to the situation" (*Traditional Sayings*, 182).

99. C. Fontaine, "Proverb Performance in the Hebrew Bible," *JSOT* 32 (1985): 95.

100. Ibid., 96.

101. Ibid., 97.

102. Camp, *Wisdom and the Feminine*, 165–78.

from their "dead" collections. She also contends that the personification of wisdom as a female figure in the frame of the book recontextualized the individual proverbs into a new unity.[103]

Survey of Scholarship Affirming a Context for the Individual Sayings in Proverbs 10:1–22:16

Educational Sayings. According to K. Heim,[104] "the most detailed earlier theories about 'educational' sayings were developed in the commentaries of Heinrich Ewald and Franz Delitzsch.[105] Some of Delitzsch's suggestions were taken up by C. H. Toy and D. G. Wildeboer, the latter being used by Hermisson."[106] For the most part, however, larger contexts created by Delitzsch's suggested groupings were ignored in the interpretation of the isolated proverbs.

Paronomasia and Catchwords. Gustav Boström connects the sequential sayings in the Book of Proverbs by aural links, such as consonance, assonance, and alliteration.[107] But he is not interested in the arrangement of proverbs to create meaningfully rich contexts. S. C. Perry confirms Boström's work by a computer-based study of paronomasia in collection II (Prov. 10:1–22:16).[108] He denies that these sound plays between the successive proverbs provided a context that enriched the interpretation of individual sayings. Jutta Krispenz-Pichler identifies groupings in collections II (10:1–22:16) and V (chaps. 25–29) based on the repetition of phonemes, catchwords, and alliteration.[109] She tends to neglect other structuring devices, but she recognizes groupings based on semantic content.

Theological Reinterpretation. In his earlier works, Whybray accepted McKane's distinction between earlier secular materials and later theological sayings.[110] He argued that the latter are found at strategically important places and reinterpret their immediate context. Magne Saebø

---

103. Ibid., 209–15.

104. Heim, "Structure and Context," 16.

105. H. Ewald, *Die Dichter des Alten Bundes*, vol. 2, *Die Salomonischen Schriften*, 2d ed. (Göttingen: Vandenhoeck & Ruprecht, 1867); F. Delitzsch, *Salomonisches Spruchbuch* (Leipzig: Doerffling & Franke, 1873).

106. C. Toy, *A Critical and Exegetical Commentary on the Book of Proverbs*, 2d ed., ICC (Edinburgh: Clark, 1904), 311; D. G. Wildeboer, *Die Sprüche*, KHCAT 15 (Freiburg: Mohr, 1897), 31, 39; Hermisson, *Studien*, 176.

107. G. Boström, *Paronomasi I den äldre hebreiska Maschallitteraturen*, LUÅ 23.8 (Lund: Gleerup; Leipzig: Harrassowitz, 1928), 112–15.

108. S. C. Perry, "Structural Patterns in Proverbs 10:1–22:16" (Ph.D. diss., University of Texas, 1987).

109. J. Krispenz, *Spruchkompositionen im Buch Proverbia* (Frankfurt: Lang, 1989), 37.

110. R. N. Whybray, "Yahweh-Sayings and Their Contexts in Proverbs 10,1–22,16," in *La Sagesse de l'Ancien Testament*, ed. Gilbert, 153–65.

also came to the conclusion that Yahweh sayings provide a context for the surrounding sayings that shape their meaning theologically.[111]

Repetitions. Daniel Snell provides a comprehensive study of variant repetitions in the Book of Proverbs that often reach across its different collections.[112] But, he is not primarily interested in the contextual arrangements of sayings; indeed, he does not even entertain the notion that authors consciously employed variants to create contexts. His main interest is to determine a relative chronology of the different collections, but the results of this approach prove inconclusive. Scoralick mainly uses variant repetitions along with poetics—excluding semantics—as structural devices to find compositional arrangements in Proverbs 10–15.[113]

Semantic Significance. In 1962 Skladny set the stage for most subsequent discussion regarding the question of the arrangement of these proverbs into contexts.[114] By using analyses of form, content, and style, and by employing statistics to quantify his findings, Skladny further delineated smaller subcollections: A (chaps. 10–15), B (16:1–22:16), C (chaps. 25–27), and D (chaps. 28–29). This analysis conforms in part with the obvious editorial notices of the book's structure in 10:1; 22:17; 25:1; 30:1. Scott, McKane, and Westermann deny there is a context in the defined literary units sentence literature.[115] Hermisson carries Skladny's analysis a step further, however, by trying to discern thematic and poetic unities in collection A.[116] By using certain methods of French structuralism, Bryce shows that 25:2–27 constitutes a literary unit.[117] B. W. Kovacs finds collection B, which he begins at 15:28, as the embodiment of a consistent worldview.[118] Whybray shows that an editor deliberately chose the place of the Yahweh sayings in 10:1–22:16.[119] By using structuralism, poetics, and semantics, Van Leeuwen convincingly demonstrates that the proverbs in collection C are arranged into larger literary compositions.[120] Malchow proposes that collection D is an intricately arranged collection serving as

111. M. Saebø, "From Collections to Book," in *Proceedings of the Ninth World Congress of Jewish Studies* (Jerusalem: World Union of Jewish Studies, 1986), 99–106.

112. D. C. Snell, *Twice-Told Proverbs and the Composition of the Book of Proverbs* (Winona Lake, Ind.: Eisenbrauns, 1993).

113. Scoralick, *Einzelspruch*, 3–5, 160f., passim.

114. Skladny, *Die ältesten Spruchsammlungen*.

115. Scott, *Proverbs*, 14, 17, passim; McKane, *Proverbs*, 10, passim; Westermann, "Weisheit im Sprichwort," 73–85.

116. Hermisson, *Studien*.

117. Bryce, "Another Wisdom-'Book' in Proverbs," 145–57.

118. Kovacs, "Sociological-Structural Constraints."

119. Whybray, "Yahweh-Sayings and Their Contexts."

120. Van Leeuwen, *Context and Meaning in Proverbs 25–27*.

"A Manual for Future Monarchs."[121] By quantifying thematic, verbal, and lexical links in "Solomonic materials," Weeks paradoxically draws the conclusions that there were subunits in these collections but that they are not meaning-rich contexts.[122] I have argued for the unity of 15:30–16:15.[123] The recent commentaries by Plöger, Meinhold, Garrett, Whybray, and Van Leeuwen interpret individual proverbs within larger literary units. Meinhold and Van Leeuwen succeed best in this enterprise, though there is still much work to be done.

Numerical Coherence. A numerical system may also give the collections coherence. Paul Skehan refines the work of P. Behnke, who observed that "the proverbs of Solomon" (*mišlê šĕlōmōh*; 10:1–22:16) contain 375 single-line proverbs, a figure that is equivalent to the sum of the numerical values of the consonants of the name *šlmh*, and that the 140 verse lines (as opposed to sayings) in chapters 25–29, ascribed to Hezekiah (25:1), comport in a similar way with the numerical value of that name.[124] Skehan continues the approach by noting, among other numerical features, that the sum of the numerical value of the names in 1:1 is 930, which is remarkably close to the 934 lines of the present MT.[125] Murphy finds the network of these equivalences "too striking to be coincidental."[126]

Theology

I have already touched on some aspects of the book's theology in the discussion of wisdom's distinctives.[127] Because of the restrictions of space,

121. Malchow, "Manual for Future Monarchs," 238–45.
122. Weeks, *Early Israelite Wisdom*, 20–40.
123. B. K. Waltke, "The Dance between God and Humanity," in *Doing Theology for the People of God: Studies in Honor of J. I. Packer,* ed. D. Lewis and A. McGrath (Downers Grove, Ill.: InterVarsity, 1996), 87–104; idem, "Proverbs 10:1–16: A Coherent Collection?" in *Reading and Hearing the Word: Essays in Honor of John Stek,* ed. A. Leder (Grand Rapids: Calvin Theological Seminary and CRC Publications, 1998), 161–80; idem, "Old Testament Interpretation Issues for Big Idea Preaching: Problematic Sources, Poetics, and Preaching the Old Testament, An Exposition of Proverbs 26:1–12," in *The Big Idea of Biblical Preaching: Connecting the Bible to People,* ed. K. Willhite and S. M. Gibson (Grand Rapids: Baker, 1998), 41–52.
124. P. Behnke, "Spr. 10,1. 25,2," *ZAW* 16 (1896): 122; P. Skehan, *Studies in Ancient Israelite Poetry and Wisdom,* CBQMS 1 (Washington, D.C.: Catholic Biblical Association, 1971), 43–45. This summarizes the results of a series of earlier studies.
125. Skehan, *Studies,* 25.
126. Murphy, *Wisdom Literature,* 50.
127. The best theology is Böstrom, *God of the Sages.* D. Estes, *Hear My Son,* New Studies in Biblical Theology (Grand Rapids: Eerdmans, 1997), presents an excellent systematic statement of the pedagogical theory that underlies Prov. 1–9. See also Waltke, "Proverbs and Old Testament Theology"; Clements, *Wisdom in Theology,* which needs to be appraised critically; R. N. Whybray, *Wealth and Poverty in the Book of Proverbs,* JSOTSup 99 (Sheffield: JSOT Press, 1990); select studies in idem, *Book of Proverbs*; and R. L. Schultz,

I here merely emphasize that the "fear of the Lord" is the goal and restriction of wisdom and nuances the book's doctrine of retribution.[128]

Many academics represent Proverb's doctrine as overly simplistic and mechanistic, whether mediated by the Lord or in some other way. Clements claims: "it is asserted by the proponents of wisdom, seemingly with bland over-confidence, that wrongdoing always gets its deserts and that the wicked come to a deservedly bad end."[129] Unstated here is a correlative, common assumption that "life" in this book refers to physical life before the grave, and that "death" refers to a premature physical death. This ideal state of affairs of the so-called older, didactic wisdom, it is further argued, is contradicted by the younger reflective wisdom of Qohelet and Job. For example, von Rad says that "the whole of old wisdom has become increasingly entangled in a single false doctrine"; Williams says that Qohelet often uses "gnomic forms to contradict traditional wisdom"; and Crenshaw says: "Once the sages acknowledged exceptions, their entire scheme became problematic."[130]

But neither assumption (i.e., a simplistic, mechanistic theory of retribution or that "life" refers to physical life) comports well with the book's theology. By the "better than" proverbs (e.g., 16:8) and the many proverbs that assume the prosperity of the wicked (e.g., 10:2), Van Leeuwen documents that the book, whose epigrammatic sayings individually, by their nature, cannot express the whole truth, do not represent a tidy calculus of retribution.[131] Moreover, Graeme Goldsworthy argues that "life" is a relationship with God and that death is a disruption of that relationship; I argue on the basis of Egyptian analogy, the argument of the book, and exegesis of individual verses (e.g., 12:28; 14:32) that this life outlasts physical death in communion with God.[132] Von Rad reaches the same conclusion for Psalm 49.[133] Instructively, the

---

"Unity or Diversity in Wisdom Theology? A Canonical and Covenantal Perspective," *TynBul* 48.2 (1997): 271–306.

128. See B. K. Waltke, "Fear of the Lord," *JCBRF* 128 (1992): 12–16.

129. Clements, "Wisdom and Old Testament Theology," in *WIAI*, 279.

130. Von Rad, *Wisdom in Israel*, 233; J. G. Williams, *Those Who Ponder Proverbs: Aphoristic Thinking and Biblical Literature*, BLS 2 (Sheffield: Almond, 1981), 53; J. L. Crenshaw, "Poverty and Punishment in the Book of Proverbs," *Quarterly Review for Ministry* 9 (1989): 30–43.

131. R. C. Van Leeuwen, "Wealth and Poverty: System and Contradiction in Proverbs," *HS* 33 (1992): 25–36.

132. G. Goldsworthy, *Gospel and Wisdom: Israel Wisdom Literature in the Christian Life* (Carslisle: Paternoster, 1987); B. K. Waltke, "Does Proverbs Promise Too Much?" *AUSS* 34 (1996): 319–36. See also V. Cottini, *La vita futura nel libro dei Proverbi: Contributo alla storia dell' esegesi*, Studium Biblicum Franciscanum, Analecta 20 (Jerusalem: Franciscan Printing Press, 1984).

133. Von Rad, *Wisdom in Israel*, 204.

RSV originally sided with the LXX rendering of Proverbs 12:28: "the ways . . . [lead] to death [*ʾel-māwet*]," but the NRSV sides with the MT, which the NIV renders "along that path is immortality."[134] Similarly, I originally sided with the LXX in 14:32: "But a righteous man in his integrity [*btmw*] finds a refuge," but after more research I agree with the MT: "But a righteous person is one who seeks a refuge [in the Lord] in his death [*bmtw*]."[135] J. A. Gladson says the sayings teaching retribution embody a "dogmatism," since the future is inaccessible to verification, but Van Leeuwen contends they did not arise from a dogmatic desire to suppress reality but from the conviction that God loves righteousness and hates wickedness.[136]

Ecclesiastes

With regard to the "black sheep" of the canon, I review the research on its authorship, unity, and message.

Author and Date

The question of the book's authorship entails questions regarding its unity and message. Raymond Dillard and Tremper Longman III note: "Two voices may be heard within the Book of Ecclesiastes, Qohelet's and the unnamed wisdom teacher who introduces the book in the prologue [1:1] and evaluates Qohelet [the speaker in 1:2–9:8 apart from 7:27] in the epilogue. Qohelet is a doubter and skeptic; the unnamed speaker in the frame is orthodox and the source of the positive teaching of the book."[137] They defend their view by appeal to the similar structure in Job. Michael Eaton argued earlier, however, that it is "absurd" to think that an editor would issue a book that he fundamentally disagrees with.[138]

Who, however, is *Qohelet*, whose name means "Gatherer" (of people? of sayings? of both?)? The traditional view is that it is a nom de plume

134. See J. F. A. Sawyer, "The Role of Jewish Studies in Biblical Semantics," in *Scripta Singa Vocis: Studies about Scripts, Scriptures, Scribes, and Languages in the Near East, Presented to J. H. Hospers*, ed. H. Vanstiphout et al. (Groningen: Forsten, 1986), 204–5.

135. B. K. Waltke, "Old Testament Textual Criticism," in *Foundations for Biblical Interpretation: A Complete Library of Tools and Resources*, ed. D. S. Dockery et al. (Nashville: Broadman & Holman, 1994); idem, "Textual Criticism of the Old Testament and Its Relation to Exegesis and Theology," *NIDOTTE*, 1:51.

136. J. A. Gladson, "Retributive Paradoxes in Proverbs 10–29" (Ph.D. diss., Vanderbilt University), 237–56; Van Leeuwen, *Context and Meaning*.

137. R. B. Dillard and T. Longman III, *An Introduction to the Old Testament* (Grand Rapids: Zondervan, 1994), 253.

138. M. A. Eaton, *Ecclesiastes: An Introduction and Commentary*, TOTC 16 (Downers Grove, Ill., and Leicester: InterVarsity, 1983), 41.

for Solomon.[139] Eaton modifies this: "It is what Solomon would have said had he addressed himself to the subject of pessimism."[140] According to most scholars, the language is postexilic, between classical Hebrew and Mishnaic Hebrew. Seow assigns it to the Persian period.[141] D. C. Fredericks contends that the language could be preexilic and certainly not later than exilic, but Fox critiques his minimalist position.[142]

The usual explanation for Qohelet's representation of himself as Solomon is that it paved the way for the book's approval as Scripture. But Crenshaw notes that this explanation "overlooks the fact that a similar device failed to gain acceptance into the canon for Wisdom of Solomon and for the Odes of Solomon."[143] E. J. Young argues that Qohelet represents himself as the ideal embodiment of wisdom, and D. McCartney and C. Clayton defend Qohelet: "this is quite different than the assertion that *pseudepigrapha* are a recognized genre and therefore could occur in the Bible. Pseudepigrapha actually *claim* to be written by a particular author and hence are deliberate misinformation."[144]

Longman has argued that this anonymous book belongs to a genre labeled "royal fictional autobiography," a well-attested genre in ancient Near Eastern literatures.[145] His thesis goes a long way in explaining the book's Solomon-like appearance without being by Solomon. In his commentary, Longman describes the genre as "framed wisdom autobiography."[146]

Unity

Apart from the obvious distinction between the epilogist who wrote the frame and Qohelet whom he cites (see above), Graham Ogden says: "it would be correct to say that most modern scholars now accept that Qo-

139. W. C. Kaiser, *Ecclesiastes: Total Life* (Chicago: Moody, 1979), 25–29; R. S. Ricker and R. Pitkin, *Soulsearch: Hope for Twenty-First Century Living from Ecclesiastes*, rev. ed., Bible Commentary for Laymen (Ventura: Regal, 1985); Garrett, *Proverbs, Ecclesiastes*, 254–66.

140. Eaton, *Ecclesiastes*, 23.

141. C. L. Seow, *Ecclesiastes: A New Translation with Introduction and Commentary*, AB 18C (New York: Doubleday, 1997), 20.

142. D. C. Fredericks, *Qoheleth's Language: Reevaluating Its Nature and Date*, ANETS 3 (Lewiston, N.Y.: Mellen, 1988), 262; M. V. Fox, *Qoheleth and His Contradictions*, BLS 18, JSOTSup 71 (Sheffield: Almond, 1989), 154 n. 1a.

143. J. L. Crenshaw, *Ecclesiastes*, OTL (Philadelphia: Westminster; London: SCM, 1987), 52.

144. E. J. Young, *Introduction to the Old Testament* (Grand Rapids: Eerdmans, 1964), 348; D. McCartney and C. Clayton, *Let the Reader Understand: A Guide to Interpreting and Applying the Bible* (Wheaton: Victor, 1994), 325 n. 67.

145. T. Longman III, *Fictional Akkadian Autobiography* (Winona Lake, Ind.: Eisenbrauns, 1991), 122–28.

146. T. Longman III, *The Book of Ecclesiastes*, NICOT (Grand Rapids: Eerdmans, 1998), 17.

heleth (1:2–12:8) is the work of one sage."[147] According to J. A. Loader, the book presents a masterly arranged series of "polar structures" without one contradiction.[148] G. A. Wright argues inferentially for its unity by noting that there are 111 verses in the first half of the book, three times the numerical value of *hebel*, "vapor," which is 37, and 222 verses in the entire book or six times its numerical value.[149] He had earlier divided the book into halves on the basis of conceptual differences regarding the significance of *hebel*: in the first half a chasing after wind, and in the second, questions or denials of humanity's ability to find anything certain "under the sun."[150] Kathleen Farmer essentially agrees with his conceptual division: "Chapters 1–6 concentrate on the question of 'what is good' and chs. 7–12 explore the question of human *knowing*."[151]

Teaching

Crenshaw thinks Qohelet represents a loss of faith, and that a second epilogue (12:12–18) was added "to remove the sting from Qoheleth's skepticism."[152] Frank Zimmermann feels he was neurotic.[153] Loader thinks the patterns of polar tensions in the book led to the conclusion that all is *hebel*.[154] Similarly to Dillard and Longman, Fox finds that the epilogist distanced himself from affirming the truth of Qohelet, and that a final author, a third, allows the reader to choose between them.[155] Gerald Sheppard regards the conclusion to fear God as borrowed from Sirach 43:27 to present a second thematizing of the book, overlaying the first that all is *hebel* (1:2; 12:8).[156] Kidner allows as a second option that the book presents an agonizing debate by Qohelet between skepticism and faith, with the latter winning out.[157] His first choice, however, is that it presents a searching criticism of secularism and a positive assessment of faith. This is also the view of numerous other scholars.[158] In my

147. G. Ogden, *Qoheleth*, Readings (Sheffield: JSOT Press, 1987), 11.

148. J. Loader, *Polar Structures in the Book of Qoheleth*, BZAW 152 (Berlin and New York: de Gruyter, 1979), 133.

149. G. A. Wright, "The Riddle of the Sphinx Revisited," *CBQ* 42 (1980): 38–51.

150. G. A. Wright, "The Riddle of the Sphinx," *CBQ* 30 (1968): 313–34.

151. Farmer, *Who Knows What Is Good?* 151.

152. Crenshaw, *Ecclesiastes*.

153. F. Zimmermann, *The Inner World of Qoheleth* (New York: Ktav, 1973).

154. Loader, *Polar Structures*.

155. M. V. Fox, "Frame-Narrative and Composition in the Book of Qohelet," *HUCA* 48 (1977): 83–106.

156. G. T. Sheppard, *Wisdom as a Hermeneutical Construct: A Study in the Sapientializing of the Old Testament*, BZAW 151 (Berlin and New York: de Gruyter, 1980), 125–27.

157. Kidner, *Introduction*, 90–94.

158. R. K. Harrison, *Introduction to the Old Testament* (Grand Rapids: Eerdmans, 1969); G. S. Hendry, "Ecclesiastes," in *New Bible Commentary*, ed. D. Guthrie and J. A. Motyer, 3d ed. (Grand Rapids: Eerdmans, 1970); Ricker and Pitkin, *Soulsearch*; J. S.

opinion, that view can stand only if it is qualified not as a polemic against skepticism but as the search of an honest doubter. Georges Bernanos drew the conclusion: "In order to be prepared to hope in what does not deceive, we must first lose hope in everything that deceives."[159]

Job

I will focus on three areas in particular that have received considerable impetus in the past three decades: textual work on the Book of Job, research into its past interpretation, and contemporary literary approaches to the reading of Job. These diverse fields will, I hope, give the reader a sense of the breadth of concerns that are brought to bear on this remarkable book of the Bible.[160]

Textual and Philological Research

The Hebrew text of Job has always presented a challenge to interpreters. Its difficult syntax and the presence of numerous hapax legomena have sent commentators searching outside the Hebrew language for clues to meaning. This search has typically moved in two directions: along the path of comparative Semitic philology and along the path of the early versions.

In the case of comparative philological research on Job, significant work had been undertaken prior to the period of our focus. The early commentaries of Eduard Dhorme and of S. R. Driver and G. B. Gray devoted considerable space to philological concerns, and many brief articles appeared on the numerous problematic texts of Job.[161] In addition,

---

Wright, "The Interpretation of Ecclesiastes," in *Classical Evangelical Essays*, ed. W. Kaiser (Grand Rapids: Baker, 1973), 133–50; idem, "Ecclesiastes," *EBC*, 5:144–46; Murphy, *Ecclesiastes*; Eaton, *Ecclesiastes*, 48; idem, "Ecclesiastes," *New Bible Commentary: 21st Century Edition*, ed. D. A. Carson et al. (Leicester and Downers Grove, Ill.: InterVarsity, 1994), 609–10; Ogden, *Qoheleth*; R. N. Whybray, *Ecclesiastes*, NCB (Grand Rapids: Eerdmans; London: Marshall, Morgan & Scott, 1989); Farmer, *Who Knows What Is Good?*; Garrett, *Proverbs*.

159. Cited by J. Ellul, *Reason for Being: A Meditation on Ecclesiastes* (Grand Rapids: Eerdmans, 1990), 47.

160. Three recent anthologies of Joban studies provide a helpful way into the range of issues involved: *The Book of Job*, ed. W. A. M. Beuken, BETL 114 (Louvain: Leuven University Press and Peeters, 1994); *The Voice from the Whirlwind: Interpreting the Book of Job*, ed. L. G. Perdue and W. C. Gilpin (Nashville: Abingdon, 1992); *Sitting with Job: Selected Studies on the Book of Job*, ed. R. B. Zuck (Grand Rapids: Baker, 1992). See also N. N. Glatzer, *The Dimensions of Job: A Study and Selected Readings* (New York: Schocken, 1969).

161. E. Dhorme, *A Commentary on the Book of Job*, trans. H. Knight (London: Nelson, 1967; orig. French edition, *Le livre de Job* [Paris: Lecoffre, 1926]); S. R. Driver and G. B. Gray, *A Critical and Exegetical Commentary on the Book of Job*, ICC (Edinburgh: Clark,

theories positing an Aramaic or Arabic base were proposed, though without much acceptance.[162] Mitchell Dahood explored the significance of Ugaritic for the Hebrew text of Job in a dozen publications,[163] which led to a number of full-blown studies in this area, beginning with Anton C. M. Blommerde's *Northwest Semitic Grammar and Job*. While some studies touched on a number of selected texts, others concentrated on a block of material that posed particularly severe textual and philological problems (e.g., Job's final soliloquy, chaps. 29–31).[164] More recently, the first volume of a multivolume philological commentary on Job has appeared, focusing on Northwest Semitic.[165]

In the area of the early versions, our period has witnessed the publication of a number of significant works, from critical editions of versional texts to specific studies on these ancient translations. The Septuagint (LXX) has long been of particular interest to students of Job due to its idiosyncratic character. The Old Greek (OG) version is approximately one-sixth shorter than the Hebrew (as preserved in the MT) and at the same time contains some distinct, lengthy additions (the speech of Job's wife [2:9] and a concluding section providing background information on the characters of the story [42:17]). Thanks to the efforts of Origen, however, the portions not represented in this rather paraphrastic OG version were supplied, mainly from a translation known as "Theodotion." The result is a Greek text of Job with mixed textual character.

Prior to our period of focus, studies by Gillis Gerleman, Donald Gard, and Harry Orlinsky, among others, sought to elucidate the signif-

1921); G. A. Barton, "Some Text-Critical Notes on Job," *JBL* 42 (1923): 29–32; G. R. Driver, "Problems in Job," *AJSL* 52 (1935–36): 160–70; idem, "Problems in the Hebrew Text of Job," in *Wisdom in Israel and in the Ancient Near East*, ed. Noth and Thomas, 72–93; E. F. Sutcliffe, "Notes on Job, Textual and Exegetical," *Bib* 30 (1949): 66–90; F. Zimmerman, "Notes on Some Difficult Old Testament Passage [*sic*]," *JBL* 55 (1936): 303–8.

162. See, respectively, N. H. Tur-Sinai (H. Torczyner), *The Book of Job: A New Commentary*, rev. ed. (Jerusalem: Kiryath Sepher, 1967); A. Guillaume, *Studies in the Book of Job*, ALUOS 2 (Leiden: Brill, 1968).

163. M. Dahood, "Some Northwest Semitic Words in Job," *Bib* 38 (1957): 307–20; idem, "Northwest Semitic Philology and Job," in *The Bible in Current Catholic Thought*, ed. J. L. McKenzie, St. Mary's Theology Studies 1 (New York: Herder & Herder, 1962), 55–74; idem, "Hebrew-Ugaritic Lexicography," *Bib* 44–53 (1963–72): [10 installments]; A. C. M. Blommerde, *Northwest Semitic Grammar and Job*, BibOr 22 (Rome: Pontifical Biblical Institute, 1969).

164. See, respectively, e.g., L. L. Grabbe, *Comparative Philology and the Text of Job: A Study in Methodology*, SBLDS 34 (Missoula, Mont.: Scholars Press, 1977); A. R. Ceresko, *Job 29–31 in the Light of Northwest Semitic*, BibOr 36 (Rome: Biblical Institute Press, 1980).

165. W. L. Michel, *Job in the Light of Northwest Semitic*, vol. 1, BibOr 42 (Rome: Biblical Institute Press, 1987).

icance of the LXX for establishing the textual base of Job.[166] In the past three decades, work on the LXX has continued, though in some ways there has been a shift of emphasis and orientation. The OG version of Job is valued not only for its contribution to the textual question of the Hebrew *Vorlage* of Job, but also for its own sake, as an early reading and interpretation of the book. Explorations of the translation technique of the OG translator of Job have been carried out by Homer Heater and others, some concentrating on certain portions of the book,[167] and others exploring the relationship between the OG Job and other Jewish Hellenistic literature.[168] Of considerable significance in LXX Joban studies has been the publication of a critical edition of the Greek Job by Joseph Ziegler.[169] Ziegler's efforts to sort out the OG text and the Hexaplaric supplements have been recently fine-tuned by P. J. Gentry, who has carefully examined in a full-length study the non-OG material in the Greek Job, identifying the extent of this material, examining its translational character, and defining its textual affiliation.[170] All in all, the Greek version of Job continues to be a source of serious scholarly attention.

The past three decades have also witnessed the publication of the Aramaic Targum of Job found in cave 11 at Qumran (11QTgJob). Not only is this document the earliest example of a written targum (Aramaic translation), it was also the main material evidence of the existence of the Book of Job at Qumran. It consists of one large roll, 27 large frag-

166. G. Gerleman, *Studies in the Septuagint*, vol. 1, *The Book of Job*, LUÅ 43.2–3 (Lund: Gleerup, 1947); D. H. Gard, *The Exegetical Method of the Greek Translator of the Book of Job*, JBL Monograph Series 8 (Philadelphia: Society of Biblical Literature, 1952); H. M. Orlinsky, "Studies in the Septuagint of the Book of Job," *HUCA* 28 (1957): 53–74; 29 (1958): 229–71; 30 (1959): 153–67; 32 (1961): 239–68; 33 (1962): 119–51; 35 (1964): 57–78; 36 (1965): 37–47.

167. H. Heater, *A Septuagint Translation Technique in the Book of Job*, CBQMS 11 (Washington, D.C.: Catholic Biblical Association, 1982); C. E. Cox, "Job's Concluding Soliloquy: Chs 29–31," in *VII Congress of the International Organization for Septuagint and Cognate Studies, Leuven, 1989*, ed. C. E. Cox, SBLSCS 31 (Atlanta: Scholars Press, 1991), 325–39; idem, "The Wrath of God Has Come to Me: Job's First Speech according to the Septuagint," *SR* 16 (1987): 195–204; J. Cook, "Aspects of Wisdom in the Texts of Job (Chapter 28)—Vorlage(n) and/or Translator(s)?" *OTE* 5 (1992): 26–45; N. F. Marcos, "The Septuagint Reading of the Book of Job," in *Book of Job*, ed. Beuken, 251–66.

168. J. G. Gammie, "The Septuagint of Job: Its Poetic Style and Relationship to the Septuagint of Proverbs," *CBQ* 49 (1987): 14–31; B. Schaller, "Das Testament Hiobs und die Septuaginta-Übersetzung des Buches Hiob," *Bib* 61 (1980): 377–406.

169. J. Ziegler, ed., *Iob*, vol. 11.4 of *Septuaginta: Vetus Testamentum Graecum* (Göttingen: Vandenhoeck & Ruprecht, 1982). For a detailed review of this critical edition, see A. Pietersma, review of *Iob. Septuaginta: Vetus Testamentum Graecum*, by Joseph Ziegler, *JBL* 104 (1985): 305–11.

170. P. J. Gentry, *The Asterisked Materials in the Greek Job*, SBLSCS 38 (Atlanta: Scholars Press, 1995).

ments, and a number of smaller fragments, which together contain portions of chapters 17–42. The text ends at 42:11, and it is uncertain whether 42:12–17 were missing from its Hebrew *Vorlage*. Over against the MT, it exhibits some additions and some omissions, and at places a degree of paraphrasing, including the tendency to telescope parallel words into a single expression. On linguistic grounds, it can be dated to the second century B.C. In the years following the appearance of the editio princeps,[171] a number of studies were carried out on the Qumran targum that helped to clarify its relation to the MT and other early versions of Job.[172]

Two other versions that have received recent attention are the standard Aramaic Targum of Job and the Syriac Peshitta. David Stec edited a critical edition of the Targum of Job with a useful introduction and notes, and Mangan has added a few studies on this translation.[173] The Peshitta Institute published its fascicle of Job in 1982, and Heidi Szpek has since produced a helpful study of this Syriac translation.[174]

These early translations of Job are valuable not only because of their contribution to questions of a text-critical nature, but also because they represent early commentaries on the book. Since every translation is an interpretation, these versions preserve the insights of early readers of Job, and so belong to the long history of its interpretation.

171. J. van der Ploeg and A. van der Woude, *Le Targum de Job de la grotte XI de Qumran*, Koninklijke Nederlandse Akademie van Wetenschappen (Leiden: Brill, 1971).

172. M. Sokoloff, *The Targum to Job from Qumran Cave XI*, Bar-Ilan Studies in Near Eastern Languages and Culture (Ramat-Gan, Israel: Bar-Ilan University, 1974); H. Ringgren, "Some Observations on the Qumran Targum of Job," *ASTI* 4.11 (1977–78): 119–26; J. A. Fitzmyer, "Some Observations on the Targum of Job from Qumran Cave 11," *CBQ* 36 (1974): 503–24; J. Gray, "The Massoretic Text of the Book of Job, the Targum and the Septuagint Version in the Light of the Qumran Targum (11QtargJob)," *ZAW* 86 (1974): 331–50; B. Jongeling, "The Job Targum from Qumran Cave 11," *Folia Orientalia* 15 (1974): 181–96; S. Kaufmann, "The Job Targum from Qumran," *JAOS* 93 (1973): 317–27; F. J. Morrow, "11QTargum Job and the Masoretic Text," *RevQ* 8 (1973): 253–56.

173. D. M. Stec, *The Text of the Targum of Job: An Introduction and Critical Edition*, AGJU 20 (Leiden: Brill, 1994); C. Mangan, "Some Similarities between Targum Job and Targum Qohelet," in *The Aramaic Bible: Targums in Their Historical Context*, ed. D. R. G. Beattie and M. J. McNamara, JSOTSup 166 (Sheffield: JSOT Press, 1994), 349–53; idem, "The Interpretation of Job in the Targums," in *Book of Job*, ed. Beuken, 267–80. See also W. E. Aufrecht, "A Bibliography of Job Targumim," *Newsletter for Targumic and Cognate Studies*, Supplement 3 (1987): 1–13.

174. L. G. Rignell, *Job*, part 2.1a of *The Old Testament in Syriac according to the Peshitta Version* (Leiden: Brill, 1982); H. M. Szpek, *Translation Technique in the Peshitta to Job: A Model for Evaluating a Text with Documentation from the Peshitta to Job*, SBLDS 137 (Atlanta: Scholars Press, 1992). See also M. Weitzman, "Hebrew and Syriac Texts of the Book of Job," in *Congress Volume: Cambridge, 1995*, ed. J. A. Emerton, VTSup 66 (Leiden: Brill, 1997), 381–99.

Study of Past Interpretation

A second area of recent research on Job has been the investigation of past interpretations of the book from both the Christian and Jewish traditions. For the Christian tradition, Susan Schreiner has given particular attention to Gregory's *Moralia in Job,* a series of lectures given by Gregory in the late sixth century; to Thomas Aquinas's *Expositio super Iob ad litteram,* a commentary on Job composed in the second half of the thirteenth century; and to Calvin's 159 *Sermons on Job,* which he preached between February 1554 and March 1555.[175] Gregory, whose lectures were highly influential throughout the Middle Ages, approached the Book of Job primarily at the moral and allegorical levels of reading, stressing the importance of suffering as an opportunity for spiritual ascent. Aquinas, influenced by Maimonides, interpreted the story of Job more literally, concentrating primarily on the questions of evil and divine providence.[176] Calvin's sermons, unlike those of his predecessors, were directed to the layperson at a time of social upheaval. His literal reading of Job "demonstrated the spiritual temptation, anguish, and faith evident during those times when history appears disordered and God's rule cannot be discerned. On the basis of Job's story, Calvin directed his congregation to a God whom they could trust despite the deepest darkness and the most awful divine silences."[177] Moving closer to the present, J. Lamb has recently explored the ways in which Job was read in the eighteenth century by people such as W. Warburton, R. Lowth, R. Blackmore, and others.[178]

Studies of rabbinic and medieval Jewish interpretations of Job have also been undertaken recently. The rabbinic discussion focused mostly on the question of Job's ethnic status and his piety, while rarely touch-

---

175. S. E. Schreiner, *Where Shall Wisdom Be Found? Calvin's Exegesis of Job from Medieval and Modern Perspectives* (Chicago: University of Chicago Press, 1994); see also idem, "Why Do the Wicked Live? Job and David in Calvin's Sermons on Job," in *Voice from the Whirlwind,* ed. Perdue and Gilpin, 129–43; idem, "'Through a Mirror Dimly': Calvin's Sermons on Job," *CTJ* 21 (1986): 175–92; idem, "'Where Shall Wisdom Be Found?': Gregory's Interpretation of Job," *ABR* 39 (1988): 321–421. For treatment of a commentary on Job by Didymus the Blind (A.D. 313–398), see H. G. Reventlow, "Hiob der Mann: Ein altkirchliches Ideal bei Didymus dem Blinden," in *Text and Theology: Studies in Honour of Prof. Dr. Theol. Magne Saebø,* ed. K. A. Tangberg (Oslo: Verbum, 1994), 213–27.

176. For an English translation of Aquinas's commentary on Job, see Thomas Aquinas, *The Literal Exposition on Job: A Scriptural Commentary Concerning Providence,* trans. A. Damico, Classics in Religious Studies 7 (Atlanta: Scholars Press, 1989).

177. Schreiner, *Where Shall Wisdom Be Found?* 7.

178. J. Lamb, *The Rhetoric of Suffering: Reading the Book of Job in the Eighteenth Century* (New York: Oxford; Oxford: Clarendon, 1995).

ing on the larger issues of the book.[179] Saadiah Gaon (tenth century) and Maimonides (twelfth century) gave considerable attention to Job from a philosophical perspective.[180] The latter, in book 3 of his *Guide for the Perplexed,* maintained that the central concern of the book was divine providence. His reading of Job, in which he brought together Aristotelian metaphysics and a traditional understanding of Jewish religious tradition, had a significant influence on Thomas Aquinas as well as later Jewish interpreters. From the more philological and exegetical tradition, Moses Kimhi (twelfth century) wrote a commentary on Job in which he discussed lexical and grammatical problems, followed by a somewhat paraphrastic interpretation.[181] In another study of Jewish readings of Job, Oliver Leaman looks at the themes of evil and suffering in various Jewish philosophers from Philo to Martin Buber using Job as the place where these issues arise most poignantly.[182]

These studies in the past interpretation of Job are important since they set into historical perspective the modern attempts to read the Book of Job. Indeed, Schreiner brings her study of various past interpretations of Job to a close by looking at some modern critical/exegetical, psychoanalytical, and literary readings, maintaining that a sense of the past gives us a perspective on the present, with its own context and historical contingency.[183]

Literary Approaches to the Book of Job

A third area of recent research on Job has been the development of a number of interpretive strategies that are grounded primarily in literary theories and perspectives. Prior to the 1970s, a predominant concern in the interpretation of Job was to determine the way in which the book developed, what parts of the present composition were primary and which were secondarily added. The relationship between the prose

---

179. J. R. Baskin, "Rabbinic Interpretations of Job," in *Voice from the Whirlwind*, ed. Perdue and Gilpin, 101–10; J. Weinberg, "Job Versus Abraham: The Quest for the Perfect God-Fearer in Rabbinic Tradition," in *Book of Job*, ed. Beuken, 281–96.

180. L. E. Goodman, *The Book of Theodicy: Translation and Commentary on the Book of Job by Saadiah Ben Joseph Al-Fayyumi,* Yale Judaica Series 25 (New Haven and London: Yale University Press, 1988); Schreiner, *Where Shall Wisdom Be Found?* 55–90; M. D. Yaffe, "Providence in Medieval Aristotelianism: Moses Maimonides and Thomas Aquinas on the Book of Job," in *Voice from the Whirlwind*, ed. Perdue and Gilpin, 111–28.

181. M. Kimhi, *Commentary on the Book of Job*, ed. H. Basser and B. D. Walfish, South Florida Studies in the History of Judaism 64 (Atlanta: Scholars Press, 1992). According to the editors, some eighty commentaries on Job have survived from the Middle Ages and approximately half of these are anonymous (xi).

182. O. Leaman, *Evil and Suffering in Jewish Philosophy,* Cambridge Studies in Religious Traditions 6 (New York and Cambridge: Cambridge University Press, 1995).

183. Schreiner, *Where Shall Wisdom Be Found?* 156–90.

frame (prologue and epilogue) and the poetic core (the various speeches), arguments for and against the primary or secondary nature of the wisdom poem in chapter 28, the Elihu speeches and the second divine speech, and the problematic arrangement of the third cycle (chaps. 22–27) were all matters of serious debate. While these continue to be explored, the past three decades have witnessed a movement away from diachronic issues to focus on the present state of the text, with the application of various literary methods of analysis. This focus on the text itself—its rhetorical and poetic features, various modes of discourse, use of literary genres, and compositional coherence—has been a marked feature of the past few decades of Joban study.

Rhetorical and poetic analysis seeks to map out the structural coherence of poetic discourse. Concentrating on the elements of linguistic and thematic correspondence across small poetic units (bicola and tricola) and larger stanzas or strophes (consisting of a series of bicola or tricola), it attempts to distinguish the various compositional blocks that together constitute the poetic speeches. This formal analysis, which is heavily based on linguistic features (lexical, morphological, and syntactic), serves to demarcate the rhetorical units of speech and thus charts the basic structure and movement of the argument. Work in this area has been carried out above all by Pieter van der Lugt and Edwin Webster, and the commentaries of Habel and Clines have demonstrated considerable sensitivity to this kind of literary concern.[184] Two recent studies of more specific texts employing a similar focus on rhetorical and formal analysis have appeared as well.[185]

Poetic analysis, however, is restricted in its applicability to the speeches in Job; it is not appropriate for the prose frame. The prologue and epilogue have thus been examined on the basis of close reading and narrative theory. Here focus is given to elements of plot structure, characterization, direct speech, and narrator's point of view.[186] Others have

---

184. P. van der Lugt, *Rhetorical Criticism and the Poetry of the Book of Job*, OTS 32 (Leiden: Brill, 1995); idem, "Stanza-Structure and Word Repetition in Job 3–14," *JSOT* 40 (1988): 3–38; E. C. Webster, "Strophic Patterns in Job 3–28," *JSOT* 26 (1983): 33–60; idem, "Strophic Patterns in Job 29–42," *JSOT* 30 (1984): 95–109; N. C. Habel, *The Book of Job*, OTL (Philadelphia: Westminster; London: SCM, 1985); D. J. A. Clines, *Job 1–20*, WBC 17 (Dallas: Word, 1989).

185. J. E. Course, *Speech and Response: A Rhetorical Analysis of the Introductions to the Speeches of the Book of Job (Chaps. 4–24)*, CBQMS 25 (Washington, D.C.: Catholic Biblical Association, 1994); D. W. Cotter, *A Study of Job 4–5 in the Light of Contemporary Literary Theory*, SBLDS 124 (Atlanta: Scholars Press, 1992). The latter consists of a poetic analysis of this initial speech of Eliphaz based on the formalist approach derived from Roman Jakobson.

186. N. C. Habel, "The Narrative Art of Job: Applying the Principles of Robert Alter," *JSOT* 27 (1983): 101–11; A. Brenner, "Job the Pious? The Characterization of Job in the

applied elements of narrative theory to the book as a whole, seeing it as fundamentally a story with an extended dialogue.[187] Cheney has analyzed the narrative frame and the macro- and microstructural features of the speeches in order to assess the way in which the characterization of the participants is actualized.[188]

Narrative and poetic modes of discourse, as present in the prose frame and the speech core, distinguish these phases of the book and, in the view of many, represent two different moments in the editorial process. Either the speeches were spliced into the preexisting narrative story, or the legend of Job was added to tone down the speeches. In either case, the disjunction between the frame and the core is apparent, on both stylistic and thematic grounds. The Job of the prologue and the Job of the speeches appear to be two different characters. Recent literary readings of the book, however, have carefully explored the linkage between the prologue and the initial speeches, and have viewed the disparate Job figures as a single unified character.[189] This kind of analysis strengthens the literary integrity of the book and suggests that the frame and the core have been masterfully composed as a coherent literary work.

But what kind of composition is it? The issue of literary genre continues to be discussed, with a few new developments. Westermann maintains that Job is a dramatized lament with disputational speeches.[190] Others view Job as a dramatic tragedy or comedy.[191] Still others consider the book as a whole to be sui generis, a unique literary creation of the wisdom tradition that made use of a variety of literary forms: didactic narrative, lament, disputation, legal forms, and so

---

Narrative Framework of the Book," *JSOT* 43 (1989): 37–52; M. J. Oosthuizen, "Divine Insecurity and Joban Heroism: A Reading of the Narrative Framework of Job," *OTE* 4 (1991): 295–315; M. Weiss, *The Story of Job's Beginning* (Jerusalem: Magnes, 1983); D. J. A. Clines, "False Naivety in the Prologue to Job," *HAR* 9 (1985): 127–36; A. Cooper, "Reading and Misreading the Prologue to Job," *JSOT* 46 (1990): 67–79.

187. A. Cooper, "Narrative Theory and the Book of Job," *SR* 11 (1982): 35–44.

188. M. Cheney, *Dust, Wind, and Agony: Character, Speech, and Genre in Job,* ConBOT 36 (Stockholm: Almqvist & Wiksell, 1994).

189. R. D. Moore, "The Integrity of Job," *CBQ* 45 (1983): 17–31; R. W. E. Forrest, "The Two Faces of Job: Imagery and Integrity in the Prologue," in *Ascribe to the Lord: Biblical and Other Studies in Memory of Peter C. Craigie,* ed. L. Eslinger and G. Taylor, JSOTSup 67 (Sheffield: JSOT Press, 1988), 385–98; Y. Hoffman, "The Relation between the Prologue and the Speech-Cycles in Job: A Reconsideration," *VT* 31 (1981): 160–70; W. Vogels, "Job's Empty Pious Slogans," in *Book of Job,* ed. Beuken, 369–76.

190. C. Westermann, *The Structure of the Book of Job,* trans. C. A. Muenchow (Philadelphia: Fortress, 1981).

191. W. J. Urbrock, "Job as Drama: Tragedy or Comedy?" *CurTM* 8 (1981): 35–40; and the series of essays in R. Polzin and D. Robertson, eds., *Studies in the Book of Job, Semeia* 7 (1977).

on.[192] Cheney has argued that the present arrangement of Job formally constitutes a type of frame tale (the wisdom *tension*) that has ancient Near Eastern parallels. In this kind of literature a mythological or legendary narrative frame surrounds an extended dialogical core consisting of a disputational contest. The closing part of the frame is a judgment scene in which the winner of the dispute is announced.[193] The formal correspondence is striking, though not strictly parallel, and the generic structure does not disqualify the use of other forms in the book.

One of the literary features of Job that has been given higher profile in recent research has been the notable presence of irony, satire, and parody. Here attention is on the misuse of form, the deliberate undermining of conventional theological and moral convictions through an ironic use of form, content, and context.[194] For example, Job 7:17-18 parodies the sentiment of Psalm 8, turning a hymnic expression of praise and wonder into a protest of divine hostility. Katharine Dell has argued that the whole book is best understood as a parody that expresses skepticism (suspending of belief) toward traditional wisdom categories.[195] Bruce Zuckerman also perceives the significance of parody in the "original" core of Job, but the ironic voice of protest was silenced by the addition of contrapuntal material.[196]

Newer literary methods of reading have been applied to Job recently as well. Clines attempts a deconstructive reading of Job to show how the book undermines the philosophy it asserts, in terms of the notions of retribution and suffering.[197] David Penchansky reads Job in a sociological vein, arguing that the literary tensions in the book reflect ideological struggles within a cultural context.[198] One volume of the *Semeia*

192. L. G. Perdue, *Wisdom in Revolt: Metaphorical Theology in the Book of Job*, BLS 29, JSOTSup 112 (Sheffield: Almond, 1991). For a discussion of genre classifications for Job, see Murphy, *Wisdom Literature*, 13–45; K. J. Dell, *The Book of Job as Sceptical Literature*, BZAW 197 (Berlin and New York: de Gruyter, 1991), 57–107.

193. Cheney, *Dust, Wind, and Agony*.

194. P.-E. Dion, "Formulaic Language in the Book of Job: International Background and Ironical Distortions," *SR* 16 (1987): 187–93; Y. Hoffman, "Irony in the Book of Job," *Imm* 17 (1983–84): 7–21; J. C. Holbert, "'The Skies Will Uncover His Iniquity': Satire in the Second Speech of Zophar (Job xx)," *VT* 31 (1981): 171–79; J. G. Williams, "'You Have Not Spoken Truth of Me': Mystery and Irony in Job," *ZAW* 83 (1971): 231–55; E. M. Good, *Irony in the Old Testament* (Philadelphia: Westminster; London: SPCK, 1965); 2d ed., BLS 3 (Sheffield: Almond, 1981).

195. Dell, *Book of Job as Sceptical Literature*, 213–17.

196. B. Zuckerman, *Job the Silent: A Study in Historical Counterpoint* (New York and Oxford: Oxford University Press, 1991).

197. D. J. A. Clines, "Deconstructing the Book of Job," in *What Does Eve Do to Help? and Other Readerly Questions to the Old Testament*, JSOTSup 94 (Sheffield: JSOT Press, 1990), 106–23.

198. D. Penchansky, *The Betrayal of God: Ideological Conflict in Job*, Literary Currents in Biblical Interpretation (Louisville: Westminster/John Knox, 1990); see also C. A. New-

series was dedicated to the application of Paul Ricoeur's hermeneutical approach to Job, particularly the divine speech in chapter 38.[199] Feminist reading has been applied to Job minimally,[200] though we shall see what the future holds in this regard. A fine reading of Job "from below" is that of Gustavo Gutiérrez, who sees in Job the struggle of the poor of Latin America who, in the midst of innocent suffering, must learn to speak to and about God.[201]

In the light of the prominence of literary approaches to the Book of Job, I must mention one striking anomaly. David Wolfers, a physician who has spent the last twenty years of his life studying the Book of Job, reads Job as a historical allegory in which Job represents Judah in the late eighth–early seventh century B.C. after the invasion of Sennacherib and the Assyrians that devastated much of Judah.[202] The underlying thrust of the book is to aid the transition from Yahweh as the parochial, covenant God of Judah to Yahweh as the universal God, to whom love and devotion are still required. Wolfers is critical of the academic guild for, among other things, its faulty translations of the Hebrew text and its failure to read the book as a single piece. While it is unlikely that his views will gain wide acceptance, they provide a helpful counterpoint to the conventional lines of understanding.

Conclusion

I have not been able to touch on many, many issues here concerning Joban studies. Being a masterful literary creation, the Book of Job will continue to elicit commentary and readerly engagement on all kinds of fronts and by a variety of interpreters, from those wrestling with linguistic and textual difficulties to those who live and work with the innocent suffering poor. Job is not an easy text from any standpoint, leaving the reader challenged, if not overwhelmed, by the questions it raises and by its refusal to answer them outright. At the end of the day, every reading of the Book of Job comes up short, failing to vanquish the text in a final interpretation. We, like Job, are confronted power-

---

som, "Cultural Politics and the Reading of Job," *BibInt* 1 (1993): 119–38; D. J. A. Clines, "Why Is There a Book of Job and What Does It Do to You If You Read It?" in *Book of Job*, ed. Beuken, 1–20. In this article, Clines employs materialist and psychoanalytical criticism to suggest the social and economic circumstances implied by the text and then probes the way these affect how readers hear the text.

199. J. D. Crossan, ed., *The Book of Job and Ricoeur's Hermeneutics, Semeia* 19 (1981).

200. G. West, "Hearing Job's Wife: Towards a Feminist Reading of Job," *OTE* 4 (1991): 107–31; D. Bergant, "Might Job Have Been a Feminist?" *TBT* 28 (1990): 336–41.

201. G. Gutiérrez, *On Job: On God-Talk and the Suffering of the Innocent*, trans. M. J. O'Connell (Maryknoll, N.Y.: Orbis, 1987).

202. D. Wolfers, *Deep Things out of Darkness: The Book of Job: Essays and a New English Translation* (Grand Rapids: Eerdmans; Kampen: Kok Pharos, 1995).

fully by our own finitude, and stand back from our efforts to understand it, even reeling from its powerful and enigmatic nature. Somehow, despite all the words written about the Book of Job, the silence of limited human understanding in a perplexing universe remains. And so it should be.

$$12$$

Recent Trends in Psalms Study

David M. Howard Jr.

Psalms studies at the end of the twentieth century are very different from what they were in 1970. There has been a paradigm shift in biblical studies, whereby texts are now read *as texts,* that is, as literary entities and canonical wholes. This is manifested in Psalms studies in several ways, the most important of which is the attention to the Psalter as a *book,* as a coherent whole. It is also manifested in many literary and structural approaches. A paradigm shift has also taken place in studies of Hebrew poetry, where linguistic analysis, most especially based on syntax, now occupies an important—if not dominant—position.

As its title suggests, this essay surveys the *trends* in Psalms studies since 1970, but more particularly since the mid-1980s. Constraints of space do not allow for adequate discussion of the hundreds of books and thousands of articles produced in this period. Unfortunately, I am also unable to deal with the many works on the popular level, many of which are first-rate works produced by scholars that are important in their own right to the life of the church and the synagogue. What I highlight, however, are the prevailing trends in the scholarly discussion of the Psalms.

I begin by reviewing past overviews of Psalms studies, in order to establish a context for the period since 1970, and then consider developments in five categories: (1) the composition and message of the Psalter, (2) Hebrew poetry, (3) hermeneutics, (4) form criticism, and (5) the Psalms in the context of the ancient Near East. It is in these five areas—and especially the first three—that we find the most activity and change in Psalms studies today.

Past Overviews

For many years, the Book of Psalms occupied a marginal place in biblical studies. The major emphases in the nineteenth and early twentieth centuries were on historical-critical approaches (dominated by the search for hypothetical sources behind—and radical reconstructions of—the text), and on reconstructions of Israel's history and the history of its religion. In the first two volumes on the state of Old Testament scholarship commissioned by the Society for Old Testament Study (SOTS), there were no essays on any canonical corpus (e.g., Pentateuch, Prophets, Psalms), but rather articles on Hebrew religion, history, and psychology (*The People and the Book*), or on the literature, history, religion, theology, and archaeology of Israel (*Record and Revelation*).[1] However, the Psalms played almost no part in any of the essays in any case. Two more recent surveys that neglect the Psalms for the most part are *The Old Testament in Modern Research* and *The Bible in Modern Scholarship*.[2] Commentaries on the Psalms in this period reflect the concerns mentioned here.[3]

Beginning in the 1920s, however, with the work of Hermann Gunkel and that of his student, Sigmund Mowinckel, the focus in Psalms studies shifted dramatically, and the discipline gained influence in the larger field of biblical studies. Gunkel was a towering figure in Old Testament studies who cast his shadow on the entire century. As the father of Old Testament form criticism, he gave us the categories of psalms with which we are now so familiar, such as individual laments, communal praises (hymns), royal and wisdom psalms. His focus was on the literary forms (i.e., genres) of individual psalms, and he paid atten-

1. A. S. Peake, ed., *The People and the Book* (Oxford: Clarendon, 1925); H. W. Robinson, ed., *Record and Revelation* (Oxford: Clarendon, 1938).

2. J. P. Hyatt, ed., *The Bible in Modern Scholarship* (Nashville: Abingdon, 1965); H. F. Hahn, *The Old Testament in Modern Research*, 2d ed. (Philadelphia: Fortress, 1966; 1st ed. 1954). The original essay by Hahn dates to 1954; the 1966 reprint adds "A Survey of Recent Literature" by H. D. Hummel; both deal somewhat with Psalms under other categories (e.g., "form criticism"). In the Hyatt volume, A. S. Kapelrud's "The Role of the Cult in Old Israel" (44–56) deals only briefly with the so-called Enthronement of Yahweh psalms (52–53).

3. See G. H. A. V. Ewald, *Commentary on the Psalms*, 2 vols., trans. E. Johnson (London: Williams & Norgate, 1880); J. J. S. Perowne, *The Book of Psalms*, 7th ed., 2 vols. (Andover: Draper, 1890); T. K. Cheyne, *The Origin and Religious Contents of the Psalter in the Light of Old Testament Criticism and the History of Religions* (New York: Whittaker, 1891; idem, *The Book of Psalms*, 2 vols. (London: Kegan, Paul, Touch, 1904); J. Wellhausen, *The Book of Psalms*, trans. H. H. Furness et al., Polychrome Bible (London: Clarke, 1898); and C. A. Briggs and E. G. Briggs, *A Critical and Exegetical Commentary on the Book of Psalms*, 2 vols., ICC (Edinburgh: Clark, 1906–7).

tion to the life situations (*Sitze im Leben*) that supposedly gave rise to each form.[4]

Mowinckel's work followed Gunkel in classifications but cleared its own way in emphasizing especially the cultic background to almost all the psalms.[5] In his view, the major festival in Israel was the fall harvest and new year festival (Tabernacles), the centerpiece of which was the so-called Enthronement of Yahweh Festival, one that he reconstructed from clues he saw in the Psalms.[6] Scholarly interest in the history and content of Israel's religion was now indebted to Psalms studies in important ways, as it used the Psalms in its reconstructions.

Psalms scholarship has been shaped by the work of Gunkel and Mowinckel ever since. The essays by A. R. Johnson and J. H. Eaton in the next two SOTS volumes are almost entirely devoted to studying the forms and the cultic place and significance of the Psalms,[7] as are overviews by Ronald E. Clements, John H. Hayes, and Erhard S. Gerstenberger, all from the first half of the period covered by this essay.[8] Commentaries until very recently have reflected the same concerns to one degree or another.[9]

4. H. Gunkel, *Die Psalmen*, 4th ed., Göttinger Handkommentar zum Alten Testament (Göttingen: Vandenhoeck & Ruprecht, 1926); H. Gunkel and J. Begrich, *Introduction to the Psalms: The Genres of the Religious Lyric of Israel*, trans. J. D. Nogalski (Macon, Ga.: Mercer University Press, 1998; original German edition, 1933).

5. S. O. P. Mowinckel, *Psalmenstudien*, 6 vols. (Kristiana [Oslo], Norway: Dybwad, 1921–24); idem, *The Psalms in Israel's Worship*, trans. D. R. Ap-Thomas, 2 vols. (Nashville: Abingdon; Oxford: Blackwell, 1962; reprinted with a foreword by R. K. Gnuse and D. A. Knight; Sheffield: JSOT Press, 1992).

6. See Mowinckel, *Psalmenstudien*, vol. 2, *Das Thronbesteigungfest Jahwäs und der Ursprung der Eschatologie* (Kristiana [Oslo], Norway: Dybwad, 1922); idem, *Psalms in Israel's Worship*, 2:106–92.

7. A. R. Johnson, "The Psalms," in *The Old Testament and Modern Study: A Generation of Discovery and Research: Essays by the Members of the Society*, ed. H. H. Rowley (Oxford: Clarendon, 1951), 162–209; J. H. Eaton, "The Psalms in Israelite Worship," in *Tradition and Interpretation: Essays by Members of the Society for Old Testament Study*, ed. G. W. Anderson (Oxford: Clarendon, 1979), 238–73.

8. R. E. Clements, "Interpreting the Psalms," in his *One Hundred Years of Old Testament Interpretation* (Philadelphia: Westminster, 1976), 76–98; J. H. Hayes, "The Psalms," in his *Introduction to the Old Testament* (Nashville: Abingdon, 1979), 285–317; and E. S. Gerstenberger, "The Lyrical Literature," in *The Hebrew Bible and Its Modern Interpreters*, ed. D. A. Knight and G. M. Tucker (Philadelphia: Fortress; Chico, Calif.: Scholars Press, 1985), 409–44.

9. H. Schmidt, *Die Psalmen*, HAT 15 (Tübingen: Mohr, 1934); J. Calès, *Le livre des Psaumes*, 5th ed., 2 vols. (Paris: Beauchesne, 1936); W. O. E. Oesterley, *A Fresh Approach to the Psalms* (New York: Scribner's, 1937); idem, *The Psalms: Translated with Text-Critical and Exegetical Notes* (London: SPCK, 1939); M. Buttenwieser, *The Psalms: Chronologically Treated with a New Translation* (Chicago: University of Chicago Press, 1938); F. Nötscher, *Die Psalmen*, Echter-Bibel (Würzburg: Echter Verlag, 1947); E. A. Leslie, *The Psalms: Translated and Interpreted in the Light of Hebrew Life and Worship* (New York:

Recently, Psalms studies have focused much more on holistic analyses of the entire Psalter, the most important driving force being Gerald Wilson's work (see below). The interest in the composition and message of the Psalter as a whole, or of portions therein, has a substantial pedigree going back into the nineteenth century and beyond, but Wilson's work brought it to the forefront of Psalms studies, where it remains today. Recent surveys of work in the Psalms by J. Kenneth Kuntz, Erich Zenger, James L. Mays, David C. Mitchell, and myself all reflect this new interest,[10] and recent commentaries on Psalms by Marvin E. Tate, Frank-Lothar Hossfeld and Erich Zenger, James L. Mays, J. Clinton McCann Jr., and Klaus Seybold do so as well.[11]

The Composition and Message of the Psalter

The most important change in Psalms study since 1970 has been a shift in its dominant paradigm and a refocusing of its attention. Until very recently, the Psalter was treated almost universally as a disjointed as-

---

Abingdon, 1949); M. E. J. Kissane, *The Book of Psalms*, 2 vols. (Dublin: Richview, 1954); W. S. McCullough and W. R. Taylor, "The Book of Psalms," in *The Interpreter's Bible*, ed. G. A. Buttrick, 12 vols. (New York: Abingdon, 1952–57), 4:3–763; A. Weiser, *The Psalms*, trans. H. Hartwell, OTL (Philadelphia: Westminster, 1962); P. Drijvers, *The Psalms: Their Structure and Meaning* (New York: Herder & Herder, 1964); A. A. Anderson, *The Book of Psalms*, 2 vols., NCB (London: Oliphants, 1972; reprinted, Grand Rapids: Eerdmans, 1981); D. Kidner, *Psalms 1–72: An Introduction and Commentary on Books I and II of the Psalms*, TOTC (Downers Grove, Ill.: InterVarsity, 1973); idem, *Psalms 72–150: A Commentary on Books III–V of the Psalms*, TOTC (Downers Grove, Ill.: InterVarsity, 1975); P. C. Craigie, *Psalms 1–50*, WBC 19 (Waco: Word, 1983); H. Ringgren, *Psaltaren 1–41*, Kommentar till Gamla Testamentet (Uppsala: EFS-förlaget, 1987); H.-J. Kraus, *Psalms 1–59: A Commentary*, trans. H. C. Oswald (Minneapolis: Augsburg, 1988); idem, *Psalms 60–150: A Commentary*, trans. H. C. Oswald (Minneapolis: Augsburg, 1989); W. A. VanGemeren, "Psalms," in *EBC*, 5:1–880.

10. E. Zenger, "New Approaches to the Study of the Psalter," *PIBA* 17 (1994): 37–54; J. K. Kuntz, "Engaging the Psalms," *CR:BS* 2 (1994): 77–106; J. L. Mays, "Past, Present, and Prospect in Psalm Study," in *Old Testament Interpretation: Past, Present, and Future*, ed. J. L. Mays, D. L. Petersen, and K. H. Richards (Nashville: Abingdon, 1995), 147–56; D. C. Mitchell, *The Message of the Psalter: An Eschatological Programme in the Book of Psalms*, JSOTSup 252 (Sheffield: Sheffield Academic Press, 1997), 15–65; D. M. Howard Jr., "Editorial Activity in the Psalter: A State-of-the-Field Survey," *Word and World* 9 (1989): 274–85 (an updated version of this essay appears in *The Shape and Shaping of the Psalter*, ed. J. C. McCann, JSOTSup 159 [Sheffield: JSOT Press, 1993], 52–70); idem, *The Structure of Psalms 93–100*, Biblical and Judaic Studies from the University of California, San Diego 5 (Winona Lake, Ind.: Eisenbrauns, 1997), 1–19.

11. M. E. Tate, *Psalms 51–100*, WBC 20 (Waco: Word, 1990); F.-L. Hossfeld and E. Zenger, *Die Psalmen I: Psalms 1–50*, Neue Echter Bibel (Würzburg/Stuttgart: Echter Verlag, 1993); J. L. Mays, *Psalms*, Interpretation (Louisville: John Knox, 1994); J. C. McCann Jr., "The Book of Psalms: Introduction, Commentary, and Reflections," in *The New Interpreter's Bible*, ed. L. E. Keck et al. (Nashville: Abingdon, 1994–), 4:639–1280; and K. Seybold, *Die Psalmen*, HAT 1/15 (Tübingen: Mohr, 1996).

sortment of diverse compositions that happened to be collected loosely into what eventually became a canonical "book." The primary connections among the psalms were judged to have been liturgical, not literary or canonical. The original life setting (*Sitz im Leben*) of most psalms was judged to have been the rituals of worship and sacrifice at the temple. The psalms came together in a haphazard way, and the setting of each psalm in the Book of Psalms (*"Sitz im Text"*) was not considered. The Psalter was understood to have been the hymnbook of second-temple Judaism, and it was not read in the same way in which most other canonical books were read, that is, with a coherent structure and message.

Today, however, the prevailing interest in Psalms studies has to do with questions about the composition, editorial unity, and overall message of the Psalter as a *book* (i.e., as a literary and canonical entity that coheres with respect to structure and message) and with how individual psalms and collections fit together. Regardless of the authorship and provenience of individual psalms, or the prehistory of various collections within the Psalter, these were eventually grouped into a canonical book in the postexilic period. Studies now abound that consider the overall structure of the book, the contours of the book's disparate parts and how they fit together, or the "story line" that runs from Psalm 1 to Psalm 150. These studies diverge widely among themselves, but they can generally be categorized in two major groups: (1) those dealing with the macrostructure of the Psalter, that is, overarching patterns and themes, and (2) those dealing with its microstructure, that is, connections among smaller groupings of psalms, especially adjacent psalms. Most studies have operated on one level or the other, but in the end they are inseparable from each other. That is, what is asserted on the higher level of broad, overarching patterns and themes should be capable of verification on the lower level of specific word, thematic, and/or structural and genre links between and among individual psalms. The latter provide the building blocks for the former.

The publication of Gerald H. Wilson's 1981 Yale dissertation, *The Editing of the Hebrew Psalter*, provided the framework in which such work could unfold in a systematic fashion.[12] It was a landmark essay, a significant factor in the recent explosion of interest in the Psalter's final form. It did not appear in a vacuum, however. Wilson was a student of Brevard Childs, whose *Introduction to the Old Testament as Scripture* has helped to define the scholarly landscape since it appeared. In his treatment of the Psalms, Childs argued for understanding the book more holisti-

---

12. G. H. Wilson, *The Editing of the Hebrew Psalter*, SBLDS 76 (Chico, Calif.: Scholars Press, 1985).

cally.[13] In addition, biblical studies in general were turning toward holistic readings of individual texts and larger collections in the Bible (under the rubrics of "rhetorical criticism," "literary analysis," "structural analysis," "narrative criticism," and the like). Nevertheless, Wilson provided a programmatic treatment that has defined the discussion ever since.

In his work, Wilson lays a careful methodological foundation for examining a collection of psalms as a "book," in that he traces other examples of hymnic collections from the ancient Near East: the Sumerian Temple Hymn Collection and Catalogs of Hymnic Incipits and the Qumran Psalms manuscripts. Each of these exhibits clearly identifiable editorial techniques in the outlines of its final form, and thus provides helpful methodological controls for approaching the Psalter. Some scholars have leveled the charge against Wilson's or others' work that the Psalter's editorial coherence is merely in the eye of the beholder, with few or no controls, but these criticisms ignore the methodological framework that Wilson lays. Unfortunately, this aspect of Wilson's work has not received the attention it deserves.

Wilson then turns to the canonical Hebrew Psalter and looks for evidence of the editorial techniques he identifies in the extrabiblical collections, along with others. He finds two types of evidence: explicit and tacit (nonexplicit). For Wilson, "explicit" indicators are found in the psalm superscriptions or in the postscript to Books I–II at Psalm 72:20, while "tacit" indicators are found in editorial arrangements, such as the grouping of psalms with doxologies at the ends of Books I–IV, or the grouping of the *halĕlû-yāh* psalms (104–6, 111–17, 135, 146–50) at the ends of certain Psalter segments.[14]

The Psalter opens with an introductory Torah psalm (Psalm 1), and it comes to a close with a group of *halĕlû-yāh* psalms (Psalms 146–50). The opening psalm instructs the reader of the book to meditate on Torah, and its placement suggests that the Psalter itself is now to be regarded as Torah, as something to be studied and meditated on (just as the Torah is), and not just performed and used in cultic contexts. The concluding crescendo of praise instructs the reader that this is how life is to be lived: in praise of Yahweh.[15]

---

13. B. S. Childs, *An Introduction to the Old Testament as Scripture* (Philadelphia: Fortress, 1979), 504–25. See also his "Reflections on the Modern Study of the Psalms," in *Magnalia Dei: The Mighty Acts of God: Essays on the Bible and Archaeology in Memory of G. Ernest Wright*, ed. F. M. Cross, W. E. Lemke, and P. D. Miller Jr. (Garden City, N.Y.: Doubleday, 1976), 377–88. For reviews of previous scholarship in this area, see Howard, *Structure of Psalms 93–100*, 2–9; Mitchell, *Message of the Psalter*, 15–61.

14. Wilson, *Editing of the Hebrew Psalter*, 9–10, 182–97.

15. In his essay emphasizing the boundaries and "movement" of the Psalter ("Bounded by Obedience and Praise: The Psalms as Canon," *JSOT* 50 [1991]: 63–92), W.

Each of the five "books" within the Psalter concludes with a psalm ending with a short doxology (Psalms 41, 72, 89, 106, 145). An important indicator not only of the Psalter's structure but also of one of its themes is the occurrence of royal psalms at significant junctures (Psalms 2, 72, 89), a point noted already by Claus Westermann and Brevard Childs.[16] Wilson finds it significant that these psalms occur early in the Psalter, in Books I–III, whereas after this the focus is on psalms of Yahweh's kingship (Psalms 93–99, 145). He sees in Psalm 89 signs that the Davidic monarchy has "failed"; and therefore, in Books IV–V, royal psalms are deemphasized and Yahweh's kingship hailed (especially in Psalms 93–99), as the Psalter proclaims Yahweh's kingship above all else.

Wilson speaks in a more recent essay of a "royal covenantal frame" to the Psalter, consisting of Psalms 2, 72, 89, and 144, and a "final wisdom frame," consisting of Psalms 1, 73, 90, 107, and 145 (the first psalms of Books I, III, IV, and V, along with the final psalm of Book V proper).[17] For Wilson, the wisdom frame takes precedence over the royal covenantal frame, and thus "trust in the power of human kings and kingship is ultimately given up, and hopes rest on Yhwh, who rules forever, and who alone is able to save."[18] The Psalter, then, is ultimately a book of wisdom, containing Yahweh's instruction for the faithful and emphasizing his kingship.[19] In this scheme, Book IV (Psalms 90–106)

Brueggemann argues that Psalms 1 and 150 open and close the Psalter by emphasizing simple obedience and praise, respectively. In between, however, the very real struggles of life are indicated by the laments and even the hymns (typified by Psalms 25 and 103, respectively). He argues that a critical turning point in the Psalter is Psalm 73, which encompasses both suffering and hope. Thus the pure, unmitigated praise that is urged at the end of the Psalter (Psalm 150) is now informed by individuals' and communities' struggles and experiences of God's *ḥesed* (faithful love).

16. C. Westermann, "The Formation of the Psalter," in his *Praise and Lament in the Psalms*, trans. K. R. Crim and R. N. Soulen (Atlanta: John Knox, 1981), 250–58; Childs, *Introduction*, 515–17; Wilson, *Editing of the Hebrew Psalter*, 207–14; idem, "The Use of Royal Psalms at the 'Seams' of the Hebrew Psalter," *JSOT* 35 (1986): 85–94.

17. G. H. Wilson, "Shaping the Psalter: A Consideration of Editorial Linkage in the Book of Psalms," in *Shape and Shaping of the Psalter*, ed. McCann, 72–82, esp. 80–81.

18. G. H. Wilson, "The Qumran Psalms Scroll (11QPsª) and the Canonical Psalter: Comparison of Editorial Shaping," *CBQ* 59 (1997): 464.

19. G. H. Wilson, "The Shape of the Book of Psalms," *Int* 46 (1992): 137–38. Others who make the same point include G. T. Sheppard, *Wisdom as a Hermeneutical Construct: A Study in the Sapientializing of the Old Testament*, BZAW 151 (New York: de Gruyter, 1980), 136–44; J. P. Brennan, "Psalms 1–8: Some Hidden Harmonies," *BTB* 10 (1980): 25–29; J. Reindl, "Weisheitliche Bearbeitung von Psalmen: Ein Beitrag zum Verständnis der Sammlung des Psalters," in *Congress Volume: Vienna, 1980*, VTSup 32 (Leiden: Brill, 1981), 333–56; J. C. McCann Jr., "The Psalms as Instruction," *Int* 46 (1992): 117–28; idem, *A Theological Introduction to the Book of Psalms: The Psalms as Torah* (Nashville: Abingdon, 1993).

stands at the editorial "center" of the Psalter, with its focus on Yahweh alone as king. Wilson notes:

> As such this grouping stands as the "answer" to the problem posed in Psalm 89 as to the apparent failure of the Davidic covenant with which Books One–Three are primarily concerned. Briefly summarized, the answer given is: (1) YHWH is king; (2) He has been our "refuge" in the past, long before the monarchy existed (i.e., in the Mosaic period); (3) He will continue to be our refuge now that the monarchy is gone; (4) Blessed are they that trust in him![20]

Book V, diverse in subject matter, nevertheless sounds notes of praise of Yahweh, climaxing with an affirmation of Yahweh's kingship in Psalm 145 and a concluding crescendo of praise in Psalms 146–50.

That a major break in the Psalter is to be found after Book III is accepted by most scholars today, and it is confirmed by the evidence from Qumran, where the manuscripts containing psalms from Books I–III are predominantly in agreement with the Masoretic Text's order and arrangement, whereas in Books IV–V there are significant variations. Since these variations are most pronounced in the earliest manuscripts, this would seem to point to a stabilization of the text of Books I–III before that of Books IV–V.[21] The break after Psalm 89 is also confirmed by evidence from the psalm superscriptions. In Books I–III, psalms are grouped primarily using author and genre designations in the superscriptions, whereas in Books IV–V, the primary grouping techniques revolve around the use of superscriptions with *hôdû* and *halĕlû-yāh*.[22]

Wilson's sketches of the Psalter's contours are persuasive in the main, and they have shaped the scholarly discussion of the Psalter's composition. Almost all scholars accept his argument that Book V ends at Psalm 145 and that 146–50 comprise a concluding doxology of praise (as opposed to only Psalm 150 by itself). The same is true with his attention to the royal psalms at significant junctures, his assertion that a significant break is found after Psalm 89, his analysis of Book

---

20. Wilson, *Editing of the Hebrew Psalter*, 215.

21. G. H. Wilson, "Qumran Psalms Manuscripts and the Consecutive Arrangement of Psalms in the Hebrew Psalter," *CBQ* 45 (1983): 377–88; idem, *Editing of the Hebrew Psalter*, 93–121; idem, "Qumran Psalms Scroll," 448–64; P. W. Flint, *The Dead Sea Psalms Scrolls and the Book of Psalms*, STDJ 17 (Leiden: Brill, 1997). The nature of the Qumran Psalms Scroll as a variant copy of Scripture or as a liturgical collection is still debated. Flint's is a major and important work supporting James Sanders's and Wilson's view that it was the former, but others (including myself) hold that it was more probably the latter (see Howard, *Structure of Psalms 93–100*, 26–27 and references, to which add the comments of Mitchell, *Message of the Psalter*, 21–26).

22. Wilson, *Editing of the Hebrew Psalter*, 155–90.

IV as a "Mosaic" book harking back to exodus and wilderness themes, and more.

I have, however, registered an objection to Wilson's and others' assertions about the almost total subordination of the royal, Davidic theme to that of Yahweh's kingship. Contrary to his analysis that Psalm 2 begins Book I proper (Psalm 1 serving as the single introduction to the Psalter), a better case can be made that Psalms 1 and 2 together constitute the Psalter's introduction and that Psalm 3 is actually the beginning of Book I.[23] In this way, the themes of Yahweh's and his anointed king's sovereignty that are proclaimed in Psalm 2 also function as keynotes for the entire Psalter. That Psalm 144 is a royal, Davidic psalm, immediately alongside Psalm 145, a Kingship of Yahweh psalm, signals that, at the end of the Psalter as at the beginning, the earthly and the heavenly expressions of Yahweh's kingdom stand together as messages of hope for the Psalter's readers.[24]

A recent and impressive full-length treatment is David C. Mitchell, *The Message of the Psalter*. After a thorough review of Psalms studies interpreting the Psalter as a coherent collection,[25] he proposes his own interpretation: that the Psalter is to be interpreted eschatologically and that the Davidic kingship, far from being downplayed and viewed as "failed" in the Psalter, forms the basis for the eschatological hope in a messianic figure that is found throughout the collection. He states that "the messianic theme is central to the purpose of the collection,"[26] and that the Psalter

> was designed by its redactors as a purposefully ordered arrangement of lyrics with an eschatological message. This message . . . consists of a predicted sequence of eschatological events. These include Israel in exile, the appearing of a messianic superhero, the ingathering of Israel, the attack of the nations, the hero's suffering, the scattering of Israel in the wilderness, their ingathering and further imperilment, the appearance of a superhero from the heavens to rescue them, the establishment of his *malkut* [kingship] from Zion, the prosperity of Israel and the homage of the nations.[27]

23. For particulars, see "Wisdom and Royalist/Zion Traditions in the Psalter," in Howard, *Structure of Psalms 93–100*, 200–207. See also Mitchell, *Message of the Psalter*, 73–74.

24. A further critique of Wilson's position on this point is Mitchell's *Message of the Psalter*, which argues in extensive detail that the Psalter's message is eschatological, with the Davidic king still an integral part of the message, projected into the eschatological future; for specific comments about Wilson's view, see esp. 78–82.

25. Mitchell, *Message of the Psalter*, 15–65.

26. Ibid., 87.

27. Ibid., 15.

Mitchell faults Wilson and others for reading the Psalter historically (i.e., tying it in specifically with Israel's preexilic, exilic, and postexilic situations) rather than eschatologically, whereby the vision looks far beyond these historical periods. He combines a close reading of individual psalms, section by section through the Psalter, with plausible links of these to the development of Israel's eschatological program (esp. Psalms 2, 45, 69, 72, 82, 83, 87, 88, 89, 90, 91, 92, 95, 109, 110, the Hallel [113–18], and the Songs of Ascents [120–34], including Psalm 132) in ways already suggested by "the ancient commentators' referring to them in connection with the same or similar events."[28] Much of Mitchell's support for his thesis rests on hypothetical connections with certain events—and with the eschatological program of Zechariah 9–14—that can be debated. The overall force and logic of his argument is impressive, however, and his work will surely occupy a pivotal position in future discussions of the Psalter's composition and message.

Another important work is Matthias Millard's *Komposition des Psalters*.[29] He devotes far more attention than do Wilson or Mitchell to diachronic concerns (as is the case with several other German scholars, e.g., Reindl, Seybold, Hossfeld, Zenger), although his methodology follows that of Wilson in giving attention to genres, themes, and superscriptions. Concerning the overall outlook of the Psalter, Millard concludes that the major theme in the Psalter is Torah, with Yahweh's kingship as a central motif. In the end, David is an integrating figure as "author" of much of the book, but even more importantly in his role as one afflicted: if Israel's greatest king was so afflicted, then Yahweh's kingship is highlighted all the more. The Psalter in its final form was a postexilic collection of prayers that originated in private (family) prayer, as a prayerbook. Its purpose was to help individuals in trouble be able to address God and ultimately to lead them to communal praise of God. Millard's sensitivity to the king's afflictions is commendable, but he does not deal adequately with David as a triumphant and eschatological figure.

A final book-length treatment of the contours of the entire Psalter is Nancy L. deClaissé-Walford's *Reading from the Beginning*.[30] She is concerned with the canonical *function* of the Psalter's final shape, following the lead of James Sanders's canonical criticism. She argues that the Psalter was "adaptable for life," serving a dual purpose for the postex-

---

28. Ibid., 299.

29. M. Millard, *Die Komposition des Psalters: Ein formgeschichtlicher Ansatz,* FAT 9 (Tübingen: Mohr, 1994).

30. N. L. deClaissé-Walford, *Reading from the Beginning: The Shaping of the Hebrew Psalter* (Macon, Ga.: Mercer University Press, 1997).

ilic community: (1) as a source book for use at ceremonies and festivals and (2) as a repository of Israel's "story" (see Sanders) that, read publicly,[31] would function to constitute Israel as a nation, enabling it to survive with Yahweh as its king. Her work has many valuable suggestions about the Psalter's shape and function; it is a relatively brief work, however, and as such, it is more impressionistic and subjective than any of the three mentioned above, and its argument suffers because of it.

All four works above deal with the Psalter on a macrostructural level, paying attention to the large contours and overall theme(s) of the book. At the other end of the methodological spectrum is David M. Howard Jr., *The Structure of Psalms 93–100*, a study at the microstructural level. I accept the driving idea behind the works above, namely, that the Psalter should be read as a book with an internal coherence, but I test that hypothesis on the lowest level, by subjecting Psalms 93–100 to an exhaustive analysis of every lexeme in every possible relation with every other one. The advantage of this method is that every relation among these psalms should thereby be uncovered, but an obvious danger is that too much will be made of relations that are merely coincidental.[32] A clear development of thought, building by stages in praise of Yahweh's kingship, is visible throughout these eight psalms. A weakness in this particular work is the limited choice of psalms, in the middle of Book IV, which itself seems to be constructed in three sections—Psalms 90–94, 95–100, 101–6—that are not congruent with the section covered in this work (i.e., 93–100); thus the obvious and necessary next step is to consider Book IV in its entirety. Nevertheless, the method forms a necessary counterpart to the macrostructural works, whereby the latter's conclusions can be tested and confirmed.[33]

31. Here she parts company with Wilson, Millard, and others, who see the Psalter as a collection to be used primarily for private study.

32. I have attempted to avoid this pitfall by distinguishing among "key-word links" (which are the most significant), "thematic word links" (which show only general connections), and "incidental repetitions" (which are not significant at all) (see Howard, *Structure of Psalms 93–100*, 98–102). For two positive assessments of this method, see G. H. Wilson, "Understanding the Purposeful Arrangement of Psalms in the Psalter: Pitfalls and Promise," in *Shape and Shaping of the Psalter*, ed. McCann, 49–50; L. C. Allen, review of *The Structure of Psalms 93–100*, *JBL* (1998): 725–26. This method needs to be refined as the units under consideration grow larger. The strongest links between psalms are usually of concatenation, i.e., links between adjacent psalms, but sometimes very significant relations exist between psalms somewhat removed from each other (e.g., Psalms 95 and 100). The method does systematically take into account every lexical, thematic, and structural link among psalms.

33. See further D. M. Howard Jr., "Psalm 94 among the Kingship of YHWH Psalms," *CBQ* (forthcoming), which shows how a psalm of a very different nature fits in with the Kingship of Yahweh psalms around it, and further explains and illustrates the method.

Another study including the same corpus in its purview is Klaus Koenen, *Jahwe wird kommen, zu herrschen über die Erde*.[34] Koenen sees Psalms 90–110 as a unit, consisting of two sections—Psalms 90–101 and 102–10—each one paralleling the other.[35] Each section shows a movement from lament to announcement of future salvation (in line with the overall movement in the Psalter from lament to praise). He sees Psalms 90–110 as a *"composition,"* which he defines as a grouping of psalms in which there is an intentional ordering and a running theme, which corresponds to the structure of a lament. Koenen detects this theme by employing the keyword (or "catchword") method: overall, the collection offers good news to those suffering, and the work affirms that Yahweh will come and establish his rule (thus Koenen's title: "Yahweh will come to reign over the earth"). Koenen's is a careful work that is somewhat akin methodologically to mine. One problem with his work, however, is that it cuts across the universally accepted boundary between Books IV and V (between Psalms 106 and 107). Another is that his model of the lament is not followed exactly by the structure of his corpus; for example, whereas in the first section (Psalms 90–101) Psalm 94 corresponds to the "lament" proper and Psalms 99–100 to the "expression of trust," in the second section (Psalms 102–10) neither of these components is found at all.

Gunild Brunert's *Psalm 102 im Kontext des Vierten Psalmenbuches* treats the history, structure, and interpretation of this psalm in its first two sections, but in her third section she devotes extended attention to its place in Book IV.[36] She advances the provocative thesis that, in the final form of the Psalter, Psalms 90–100 are the words of Moses (see the title of Psalm 90), and Psalms 101–6 those of David (see the title of Psalm 101), but of the "new David," the coming king of salvation. Her work thus complements Mitchell's in instructive ways. "David's" words in Psalms 101–4 are intended to answer the questions raised about the Davidic kingship in Psalm 89. She supports her thesis by attention to verbal and thematic links between the psalms, but many are merely impressionistic and need confirmation in a more exhaustive treatment of every lexeme.

Jerome F. Creach's *Choice of Yahweh as Refuge in the Editing of the Psalter* forges a third way between works focusing on macrostructures (such as Wilson's, Mitchell's, or Millard's) and those focusing on micro-

34. K. Koenen, *Jahwe wird kommen, zu herrschen über die Erde: Ps 90–110 als Komposition*, BBB 101 (Weinheim: Beltz Athenäum, 1995).

35. See the convenient layout in ibid., 113.

36. G. Brunert, *Psalm 102 im Kontext des Vierten Psalmenbuches*, Stuttgarter biblische Beiträge 30 (Stuttgart: Katholisches Bibelwerk, 1996).

structures (such as Howard's, Koenen's, or Brunert's).[37] He takes a semantic-field (or thematic) approach, studying the associated field of one specific lexeme (in this case *ḥāsâ*, to take refuge). The concept of Yahweh as "refuge," which is found first in the programmatic Psalm 2 (v. 12), is found in a majority of psalms and it is concentrated in significant sections. Creach then uses his findings to comment on the organization of the entire work. This should be a productive third avenue for the study of the Psalter's composition and message, as other potential keywords that might have been instrumental in shaping its structure are studied.

The eight works mentioned above are the major book-length treatments of the questions about the Psalter's composition and message by individual authors since 1970—a small number for almost three decades of research. It is telling, however, that seven of the eight have publication dates of 1994 or later, indicating the rapidly expanding interest in this area of study. In addition, three recent collections of essays should be noted: *The Shape and Shaping of the Psalter, Neue Wege der Psalmenforschung,* and *Der Psalter in Judentum und Christentum.*[38] The first focuses entirely on the issue of the Psalter's composition and message, while the latter two do so in large part.

Many important scholars have not produced book-length treatments of the issues here but have nonetheless contributed significantly to the discussion and, in many cases, have helped define it. Of these, pride of place must go to Erich Zenger, whose prolific contributions range far and wide throughout the Psalter. A recent essay presents his comprehensive view of the book, which he sees as a well-ordered and well-planned collection in its final form. As he sees it, the Psalter did not originally have a liturgical or cultic *Sitz im Leben,* but it was intended to function as a "literary sanctuary" (*Heiligtum*) of sorts, where the one praying enters into Israel's liturgy by means of his prayer for the deliverance of Israel and the world and Yahweh's kingship over both Israel and the world is exalted.[39]

The net result of this recent interest in the Book of Psalms is to bring it into the same arena in which most biblical books have found themselves throughout the history of their study: one where they are treated

---

37. J. F. Creach, *The Choice of Yahweh as Refuge in the Editing of the Psalter,* JSOTSup 217 (Sheffield: Sheffield Academic Press, 1996).

38. McCann, ed., *Shape and Shaping of the Psalter*; K. Seybold and E. Zenger, eds., *Neue Wege der Psalmenforschung: Für Walter Beyerlin,* Herders biblische Studien 1 (Freiburg: Herder, 1994; 2d ed., 1995); E. Zenger, ed., *Der Psalter in Judentum und Christentum,* Herders biblische Studien 18 (Freiburg: Herder, 1998).

39. E. Zenger, "Der Psalter als Buch: Beobachtungen zu seiner Enstehung, Komposition und Funktion," in *Psalter in Judentum und Christentum,* ed. Zenger, 1–57. Entrée into Zenger's previous work may be had via the bibliography in that essay.

as unified compositions and are mined for the treasures to be found in their overall message, as well as in their component parts. This new development—a rediscovery of an earlier interest among rabbinic and Christian interpreters—can only be a salutary one.

To be sure, a few skeptical voices have been raised who argue that too much is claimed for the Psalter in reading it as a book. One objection raised is that the proposals made for the composition and message of the Psalter disagree too much among themselves for any of them to have validity. But this is an unfair charge to level against the pursuit of a complex subject that is scarcely more than a decade old. Much work remains to be done, and one should note that there is indeed significant agreement among many of the major proposals, some of which I have highlighted in this essay.

One critic, Erhard S. Gerstenberger, argues that the Psalter is *not* a book in our modern sense, but that it is nevertheless an extraordinarily rich collection that addresses the human condition in profound ways.[40] He attributes its present shape not to literary considerations but to the liturgical needs of the synagogue (as versus the second temple). In *Reading the Psalms as a Book*, R. Norman Whybray engages in a vigorous and sustained critique of efforts to read the Psalter holistically.[41] He sets out to test possible perspectives from which the Psalter might have been edited in the postexilic period and finds all of them wanting. But this work has several problems of its own that undermine the argument.[42]

I must mention the work of one more scholar who studies the Psalms' order and arrangement, but who does so from a very different perspective from those mentioned above. Michael D. Goulder has produced a series of major studies of collections within the Psalter, beginning with Book IV (Psalms 90–106), and including the Korah psalms (42–49, 84–85, 87–88), the "prayers of David" (Psalms 51–72), the Asaph psalms (50, 73–83), and Book V (Psalms 107–50), such that to date he has studied every psalm from Psalm 42 to Psalm 150.[43] The common

---

40. E. S. Gerstenberger, "Der Psalter als Buch und als Sammlung," in *Neue Wege der Psalmenforschung: Für Walter Beyerlin*, ed. K. Seybold and E. Zenger, Herders biblische Studien 1 (Freiburg: Herder, 1994), 3–13, esp. 9, 12.

41. R. N. Whybray, *Reading the Psalms as a Book*, JSOTSup 222 (Sheffield: Sheffield Academic Press, 1996).

42. See Howard, *Structure of Psalms 93–100*, 22 n. 31; and my review of Whybray, *Reading the Psalms as a Book*, in *Review of Biblical Literature* (1998), which is available online at http://www.sbl-site.org/SBL/Reviews/.

43. M. D. Goulder, "The Fourth Book of the Psalter," *JTS* 26 (1975): 269–89; idem, *The Psalms of the Sons of Korah*, vol. 1 of *Studies in the Psalter*, JSOTSup 20 (Sheffield: JSOT Press, 1982); idem, *The Prayers of David (Psalms 51–72)*, vol. 2 of *Studies in the Psalter*, JSOTSup 102 (Sheffield: Sheffield Academic Press, 1990); idem, *The Psalms of Asaph and*

thread among all of these is that Goulder takes seriously the order and arrangement of these collections, as well as the headings of the psalms. Thus, to take the example of his second book, *The Prayers of David (Psalms 51–72)*, he sees the Davidic psalms as truly Davidic, not *written* by him but composed by a court poet, probably one of David's sons, during David's lifetime. The order of Psalms 51–72 is the order in which they were written, intended to reflect specific events in David's life as they happened. Goulder does not accept the actual historicity of most of the historical superscriptions, but he does accept the idea behind them, namely, that "a psalm can be understood only in the light of the circumstances for which it was composed."[44] In this respect, he differs radically from much of Psalms scholarship, which sees the psalms as generalizing and universalizing compositions, applicable to many times and situations.[45]

Thus, in his treatments, Goulder historicizes the psalms in ways reminiscent of traditional Psalms scholars like Franz Delitzsch and Alexander Kirkpatrick, whose influence he acknowledges.[46] He is, however, squarely in the cultic and ritual camp of Mowinckel, Johnson, Engnell, and Eaton, in accepting the Festival of Tabernacles as the central festival of the Israelite religious calendar, and he has attempted to locate the various collections within that and other festivals as the actual liturgies followed during those festivals. Thus, in most groupings of psalms (e.g., 1–8, 42–49, 90–106, 107–18, 120–34, 135–50), he sees an alternation between odd- and even-numbered psalms that he attributes to their being morning and evening psalms used in a festival, and he claims to find clues to this in the wording of the psalms themselves.[47] In this he differs from Mowinckel and the others, who attempted to reconstruct the liturgies supposedly used in the festivals from clues throughout the Psalter and elsewhere, whereas Goulder sees the texts of these liturgies lying in full view before us, preserved intact in the collections of the Psalter.[48]

---

the Pentateuch, vol. 3 of *Studies in the Psalter*, JSOTSup 233 (Sheffield: Sheffield Academic Press, 1996); idem, *The Psalms of the Return (Book V, Psalms 107–150)*, vol. 4 of *Studies in the Psalter*, JSOTSup 258 (Sheffield: Sheffield Academic Press, 1998).

44. Goulder, *Prayers of David*, 25.

45. See, e.g., P. D. Miller Jr., "Trouble and Woe: Interpreting Biblical Laments," *Int* 37 (1983): 32–45.

46. Goulder, *Psalms of the Return*, 8.

47. See, e.g., Goulder's treatment of Psalms 135, 139, 141, 143, and 145—all supposedly evening psalms—in *Psalms of the Return*, 302–3, or of Psalms 90–106 in "Fourth Book of the Psalter."

48. He judges the MT to be the most faithful textual witness, and he rigorously prefers the MT to all others in almost every instance.

Goulder's scholarship is extremely broad and well informed, and his exegesis of the texts is careful and impressive. He also advances a number of provocative hypotheses about the provenience of various collections that cannot detain us here. His work differs radically from most others who pay serious attention to the order and arrangement of the Psalter in that he sees a liturgical, not a literary, rationale for this ordering. In trying to locate the specific geographical places and historical events behind verse after verse in these collections, and in attempting to correlate them with larger collections within the Pentateuch or the postexilic literature, he is often forced to make connections that are very weak, if not nonexistent.[49]

Hebrew Poetry

A second area in which there have been far-reaching changes since 1970 is in studies of Hebrew poetry. These studies naturally range beyond the Book of Psalms, but the Psalms are the largest extant corpus of Hebrew poetry. Several major monographs on poetry were produced in the short space of a few years, effecting changes in poetic studies on a par with that produced by Wilson's work discussed above. These works were aligned along two major trajectories: analyses indebted to (1) general linguistics and (2) literary studies.[50] In the discussion below, I analyze these two trajectories, along with studies of the structural relations of poetry.

Linguistic Approaches

A remarkable phenomenon developed in the late 1970s and early 1980s, with the appearance of several works that attempted to explain the workings of Hebrew poetry using linguistic methods, particularly in terms of syntax. This had not been done previously in biblical studies, so the confluence of these studies was noteworthy. These include works by Terence Collins, Stephen A. Geller, M. O'Connor, Adele Berlin, and Dennis Pardee. For the most part, these works are theoretical,

---

49. See, e.g., the critique by M. L. Barré in his review of *The Prayers of David*, *JBL* 111 (1992): 527–28; or my comments in *Structure of Psalms 93–100*, 12–14 (critique of "Fourth Book of the Psalter").

50. Recent overviews of Hebrew poetry include: Z. Zevit, "Psalms at the Poetic Precipice," *HAR* 10 (1986): 351–66; W. G. E. Watson, "Problems and Solutions in Hebrew Verse: A Survey of Recent Work," *VT* 43 (1993): 372–84; J. K. Kuntz, "Recent Perspectives on Biblical Poetry," *RelSRev* 19 (1993): 321–27; idem, "Biblical Hebrew Poetry in Recent Research, Part I," *CR:BS* 6 (1998): 31–64; idem, "Biblical Hebrew Poetry in Recent Research, Part II," *CR:BS*, forthcoming; L. Boadt, "Reflections on the Study of Hebrew Poetry Today," *Concordia Journal* 24 (1998): 156–63.

concerned to account for the driving mechanisms of Hebrew poetry and downplaying or ignoring any literary or stylistic dimensions to poetry (Berlin's is somewhat of an exception).[51] Their great advantage is that they reveal things about the workings of Hebrew poetry never before seen with such clarity, and they are rooted in the nature of language itself.

The most ambitious of these works is M. O'Connor's *Hebrew Verse Structure.* After an extended critique of what he calls the "Standard Description" of Hebrew poetry, he proposes to describe Hebrew poetry strictly in terms of syntactical patterns, and he argues that syntactical "constriction"—not meter, rhythm, or even parallelism—is the fundamental feature of Hebrew poetry. "Just as most poetic systems are shaped in part by a series of phonological requirements, i.e., by a series of *metrical* constraints, so there are poetic systems shaped in part by a series of *syntactical* requirements, i.e., by a system of syntactic constraints. Among them is Canaanite [i.e., Hebrew and Ugaritic] verse."[52]

O'Connor states that the poetic line[53] is limited in length by syntactical constraints, and he speaks of three grammatical levels: the *unit* (i.e., individual words and particles dependent on them), the *constituent* (i.e., a verb or a nominal phrase, whether adjectival or construct), and the *clause predicator* (i.e., a verbal or verbless clause).[54] There are six constraints that form the structures within which poetic lines operate, four of which are as follows: Every poetic line contains (1) no fewer than two nor more than five units, (2) no fewer than one nor more than four constituents, and (3) no more than three clause predicators. (4) Every constituent may contain no more than four units. While the possibilities for different line forms are manifold, in practice the dominant form in Hebrew poetry (close to 80 percent) is fairly simple: the poetic line con-

---

51. Another work focusing on syntax from the same time is A. M. Cooper, "Biblical Poetics: A Linguistic Approach" (Ph.D. diss., Yale University, 1976), but this was never published. (See the brief summary and critique in M. O'Connor, *Hebrew Verse Structure* [Winona Lake, Ind.: Eisenbrauns, 1980; 2d ed., 1997], 48–49, 52–53.) Cooper has since abandoned his belief that a strictly linguistic (syntactical) approach is the "key" to Hebrew poetry. His "Two Recent Works on the Structure of Biblical Hebrew Poetry," *JAOS* 110 (1990): 687–90, includes critiques of studies by Pardee (*Ugaritic and Hebrew Poetic Parallelism*) and van der Meer and de Moor (*The Structural Analysis of Biblical and Canaanite Poetry*), two works grouped under the rubric of "structural poetics" (see below). In Cooper's essay, he calls for a poetics that takes into account more than "scientific" syntactical or structural patterns, one that "concerns itself not with everything that *can* be said about a text, but with what is *worth* saying; it seeks to communicate meaning and value, not just 'facts'" ("Two Recent Works," 690, emphasis Cooper's).

52. O'Connor, *Hebrew Verse Structure*, 65.

53. O'Connor uses "line" to refer to what many other scholars refer to as "colon." There is still no generally accepted definition of a line (colon) among scholars.

54. O'Connor, *Hebrew Verse Structure*, 68, 86–87.

tains one clause and either two or three constituents (phrases) of two or three units. Knowledge of the syntactical constraints in Hebrew poetry has a practical dimension: we can more easily know how to divide up the layout of poetic texts into their true poetic lines, and thus approach a truer understanding of the mechanisms at work.

O'Connor also identifies six "tropes," that is, "a group of phenomena which occur regularly and serve as part of the verse structure."[55] These are very common and thus definitional of poetry. The six tropes are (1) repetition, (2) constituent gappings (i.e., ellipsis of words), (3) syntactical dependency, (4) coloration (i.e., the breakup of stereotyped phrases), (5) matching (i.e., what most would identify with parallelism: the coordinating of lines with identical syntactical structures),[56] and (6) mixing (i.e., two dependent and two independent lines occurring in sequence, in which the former depend on the latter). The first and fourth tropes operate on the word level, the second and fifth on the line level, and the third and sixth above the line level.[57]

O'Connor makes two major contributions of a general sort to poetic studies: (1) attention to the syntactical patterns underlying Hebrew poetry, and (2) recognition that poetic lines operate under certain constraints. Beyond these, one of his most important specific contributions is his recognition that gapping (i.e., ellipsis) is a major feature of Hebrew poetry and does not occur in prose (apart from a few, grammatically insignificant exceptions). One of the major problems with O'Connor's work is its dense and highly technical jargon, and this undoubtedly has inhibited its wider consideration in biblical studies. Yet his system "works"—at least two major works have adopted its methodology[58]—and it deserves wider exposure. The reissue of the work with an afterword by O'Connor, as well as two articles by Holladay summarizing and applying the system, should help to remedy this situation.[59] Since it operates strictly on the syntactical level, O'Connor's

55. Ibid., 87–88.

56. See also O'Connor's treatment of "Parallelism," in *The New Princeton Encyclopedia of Poetry and Poetics*, ed. A. Preminger and T. V. F. Brogan (Princeton: Princeton University Press, 1993), 877–79.

57. O'Connor, *Hebrew Verse Structure*, 132–34.

58. W. T. W. Cloete, *Versification and Syntax in Jeremiah 2–25: Syntactical Constraints in Hebrew Colometry*, SBLDS 117 (Atlanta: Scholars Press, 1989); W. L. Holladay, *Jeremiah*, 2 vols., Hermeneia (Philadelphia: Fortress, 1986–89). Cf. further the works cited in O'Connor, "The Contours of Biblical Hebrew Verse: An Afterword to Hebrew Verse Structure" (in the 1997 reissue of his book), 641–42.

59. O'Connor, "Contours of Biblical Hebrew Verse," 631–61. See also W. L. Holladay, "*Hebrew Verse Structure* Revisited (I): Which Words 'Count'?" *JBL* 118 (1999): 19–32; idem, "*Hebrew Verse Structure* Revisited (II): Conjoint Cola, and Further Suggestions," *JBL*, forthcoming.

system does not exhaust the *meaning* of a poem, and it does not deal with the artistry of poetry,[60] but it has opened new doors with its attention to the syntactical fundamentals of language.

Prior to O'Connor, Terence Collins had likewise studied Hebrew poetry syntactically in his *Line-Forms in Hebrew Poetry*.[61] Collins used the insights of generative grammar developed by Noam Chomsky in proposing a system of "Basic Sentences" and "Line-Types," which operate on the level of deep structures, and of "Line-Forms,"[62] which operate on the level of surface structures. Basic Sentences are composed of at least two of the following constituents: subject, object, verb, and modifier of the verb. General Line-Types consist of one or two Basic Sentences, in the same or different orders, while Specific Line-Types are generated when the different types of Basic Sentences are specified. The different combinations yield forty different Specific Line-Types, which can be further subdivided according to various criteria.

As just noted, the first three categories operate on the level of deep structures of language, and they are theoretical constructs that may or may not find expression in the surface structures of language (i.e., in actual sentences and lines), whereas the Line-Forms are constituted from the Specific Line-Types, depending on the ordering of constituents in each one, and operate on the level of surface structures. Thus, "the Specific Line-Type tells us what *kind* of constituents are involved in the line, whereas the Line-Form tells us *in what order* these constituents are arranged."[63]

Like O'Connor's, Collins's work is very helpful in elucidating the syntactical dimension of Hebrew poetry. He speaks more often and more self-consciously than O'Connor about different levels on which poetry operates (e.g., phonological, syntactical, semantic), and admits that his work is limited to the syntactical. He does not claim that his system is the key to unlocking every aspect of a poem (nor does O'Connor). Nevertheless, he rightly shows that one cannot fully or adequately analyze a poem without a knowledge of the syntactical patterns inherent in the deep structures and expressed in the surface structures of a poem.

---

60. These are points on which it has been criticized (see Kuntz, "Biblical Hebrew Poetry in Recent Research, Part I," 44). See also my comments below on Collins, Berlin, and various literary approaches to poetry concerning the value of studying poetry on different levels and as art.

61. T. Collins, *Line-Forms in Hebrew Poetry: A Grammatical Approach to the Stylistic Study of the Hebrew Prophets*, StPohl: Series Maior 7 (Rome: Pontifical Biblical Institute, 1978). See his convenient summary of his work in "Line-Forms in Hebrew Poetry," *JSS* 23 (1978): 228–44.

62. Collins uses the term "line" to refer to the bicolon, which O'Connor calls the "paired line."

63. Collins, "Line-Forms in Hebrew Poetry," 235.

In *Parallelism in Early Biblical Poetry*, Stephen A. Geller presents a comprehensive system of linguistic analysis that is more inclusive than O'Connor's or Collins's, in that it includes not only syntax but also semantics (i.e., meaning of words) and meter in its task.[64] He concentrates his efforts on the couplet (composed of two lines) and the levels below this. Like Collins, he deals with the deep structures of poetry; thus his emphasis on the "reconstructed sentence" allows him to show deep-structural similarities between two sentences that differ radically in their surface structures. He shows how this works with an example from 2 Samuel 22:14: "YHWH thundered from heaven; / Elyon sent forth his voice." The verbs are very different—not only in meaning, but, more importantly, in syntactical form—and yet both occupy the same syntactical "slot" and thus both are surface-level manifestations of an underlying deep structure that one can represent as follows: "[YHWH/Elyon] from-heaven [thundered/sent-forth his-voice]."[65] His attention to meter, however, is not especially helpful, in that the phenomenon is for the most part today judged not to be present in Hebrew poetry, and his focus only on the couplet and lower levels is inadequate. Nevertheless, his linking of semantics with syntax is surely an advance over earlier studies that focused on meter and semantics almost exclusively, and his point that semantics cannot be left out of the process of interpretation is well taken.

Dennis Pardee's *Ugaritic and Hebrew Poetic Parallelism* is a sustained analysis of two texts, one from the Ugaritic corpus and one from the Bible, using a comprehensive method that includes some sixteen different steps.[66] These include analysis of repetitive parallelism (where lexemes are repeated in parallel lines), semantic parallelism, grammatical parallelism (where he analyzes and uses the systems of Collins, O'Connor, and Geller), and phonetic parallelism. For our purposes here, the great strengths of Pardee's work include his extensive and sympathetic "field-testing" of these three systems—he finds useful elements in all three—and in his two essays included as appendixes (given as papers in 1981 and 1982), in which he discusses types of parallelism and further evaluates the works in question. His is not a groundbreaking theoretical work—he repeatedly asserts his status as a nonlinguist—but it is eminently valuable for what it does accomplish.

64. S. A. Geller, *Parallelism in Early Biblical Poetry*, HSM 20 (Missoula, Mont.: Scholars Press, 1979).

65. Ibid., 17.

66. D. Pardee, *Ugaritic and Hebrew Poetic Parallelism: A Trial Cut (ʿnt I and Proverbs 2)*, VTSup 39 (Leiden: Brill, 1988 [Pardee's work was completed by 1985]).

Adele Berlin's *Dynamics of Biblical Parallelism* is the most satisfying of the present group.[67] She too asserts that parallelism is a linguistic phenomenon, and she states that parallelism and "terseness" (cf. O'Connor's "constraint") are the two markers of poetic texts; when these predominate, the text is poetic.[68] Indeed, she identifies most closely—although not entirely—with O'Connor's approach to parallelism.[69] She argues persuasively that parallelism has many different aspects and operates on many different levels. It "may involve semantics, grammar, and/or other linguistic features, and it may occur on the level of the word, line, couplet, or over a greater textual span."[70] She deals in successive chapters with grammatical (i.e., morphological and syntactical), lexical and semantic, and phonological parallelism. Great strengths of her work are its clear and engaging literary style and its copious examples illustrating her points. Her observations that (1) parallelism may operate on one level (e.g., phonological) while it does not on another (e.g., lexical or syntactical), and that (2) parallelism on one level raises expectations of parallel relations on another, even when it is not formally present, are especially helpful.

Berlin thus goes beyond most of the works above by insisting that we must devote attention to both syntax and semantics (as well as to other levels). Referring to Edward Greenstein's argument that grammatical (i.e., syntactical) parallelism should define *all* parallelism, she states, "I cannot agree . . . that syntactic repetition lies at the base of parallelism and that semantic parallelism is a result of this repetition. In many cases, it may be the other way around. . . . There is no reason to give syntax priority over semantics (or vice versa); both are important aspects of parallelism."[71] Berlin's work, with its interest in *parallelism* specifically, and not *poetry* more generally, does not consider in any detail poetic levels above the paired line (couplet), certainly not poems in their entirety; as such, it is an incomplete study of poetry, but it treats parallelism in a thorough and instructive way.

67. A. Berlin, *The Dynamics of Biblical Parallelism* (Bloomington: Indiana University Press, 1985).
68. Ibid., 5. Here she is responding to J. Kugel's assertions that we cannot distinguish at all between poetry and prose (see below).
69. Ibid., 26.
70. Ibid., 25.
71. Ibid., 23. Greenstein represents one pole in studies of parallelism, in that he argues that parallelism is solely a function of grammar (i.e., syntax). See E. L. Greenstein, "How Does Parallelism Mean?" in *A Sense of Text: The Art of Language in the Study of Biblical Literature*, ed. S. A. Geller, JQRSup 1982 (Winona Lake, Ind.: Eisenbrauns, 1983), 41–70. While he admits of semantic parallelism, he does not concede that it can operate when syntactical parallelism is absent or in very different syntactical structures. See the further comments of Berlin, *Dynamics of Biblical Parallelism*, 21–25.

The foregoing survey demonstrates, then, that study of parallelism in Hebrew poetry must be rooted in syntax, for this lies at the foundation of language and how texts (including poetic texts) communicate. In the theory of signs argued by Charles W. Morris, *syntactics* is the foundation upon which other relations build; it deals with the syntactical relations of signs to one another.[72] *Semantics* presupposes syntactics, dealing with the relations of signs to the objects they denote. *Pragmatics* deals with the relation of signs to their interpreters, that is, "all the psychological, biological, and sociological phenomena which occur in the functioning of signs."[73] Syntactics is the most abstract, but it has the greatest explanatory power, that is, it can explain the workings or the mechanisms of Hebrew poetry in ways that other approaches cannot.

Nonetheless, poetic analysis—which is presumably a tool in the search for *meaning*, in the end—cannot find its abode *solely* in syntactics; it must also consider the levels of semantics, phonology, and morphology. As the literary studies below show, there is also an art to understanding poetry that is not to be found solely among the classifications and explanations of the mechanisms of Hebrew poetry. This art moves far beyond syntactics. Therefore, in the search for the meaning of a poem, syntax must be foundational, but it is not adequate by itself to elucidate meaning completely.

Literary Approaches

Consonant with the trends in the larger world of biblical studies, many works on Hebrew poetry have appeared since 1980 emphasizing literary approaches, whereby individual psalms are treated as coherent wholes and the artistic dimensions of poetry are very much the focus. Authors representing this approach include James Kugel, Robert Alter, Harold Fisch, and Luis Alonso Schökel. The great advantage of these works is their literary sensitivity in explicating the art of poetry and not just its mechanics. I also discuss in this section other works dealing with Hebrew poetic devices.

James Kugel's *Idea of Biblical Poetry* addresses the nature of parallelism.[74] His fundamental poetic unit is the paired line, or couplet, and he expresses the relationship between the two as "A is so, and what's more, B." That is, the second line of the pair will advance the thought of the

72. C. W. Morris, "Foundations of the Theory of Signs," in *International Encyclopedia of Unified Science*, ed. O. Neurath, R. Carnap, and C. Morris (Chicago: University of Chicago Press, 1938–), 1:77–137. I thank P. C. Schmitz for calling this work to my attention.

73. Ibid., 108.

74. J. L. Kugel, *The Idea of Biblical Poetry: Parallelism and Its History* (New Haven: Yale University Press, 1981). See also Kugel's remarks in "Some Thoughts on Future Research into Biblical Style: Addenda to *The Idea of Biblical Poetry*," *JSOT* 28 (1984): 107–17.

first line in a "seconding" manner of some sort. As such, he overturns the popular view of parallel lines as "synonymous."

He also argues that the distinction between prose and poetry is overdrawn. On the one hand, in many cases in Psalms, for example, the parallelistic connections between lines A and B are almost nonexistent, such as in "Blessed is the Lord / for he did not make us fall prey to their teeth" (Ps. 124:6); such a sequence is essentially indistinguishable from a prose sentence. On the other hand, we find many examples in prose texts of what we would identify as parallelism if they occurred in the Psalms, as in "God made me the cause of laughter / all who hear will laugh at me" (Gen. 21:6) or "I will surely bless you / and surely multiply your seed" (Gen. 22:17). Kugel argues that, since Hebrew has no word for "poetry," there is no such thing. But surely there are differences that can be distinguished. Hebrew has no word for "prose," either, but this does not disprove its existence. Also, in the Psalms, there are many Hebrew words for poetic compositions, such as *mizmôr, maśkîl,* or *šiggāyôn*. Nevertheless, Kugel has succeeded in reminding scholars that much poetry is "prose-like" and vice versa, and that they should think in terms of a continuum between the poles of prose and poetry, not hermetically sealed categories.

In contrast to the works above, Kugel resists any "system" for reading poetry: "there is no such thing as an 'objective' approach to biblical texts, no neutral set of literary tools that will take apart any book or passage and tell us what makes it work."[75] Kugel's great strength is his explication of the "seconding" relationship between lines A and B, demolishing the simplistic view that equates lines A and B as "synonymous." But his disdain for any foundation in a system or theory of language leaves his approach open to potentially endless subjectivity.[76]

This blurring of the lines between poetry and prose finds an echo in the work of J. C. de Moor on the Book of Ruth and William T. Koopmans on Joshua 23 and 24, who speak variously of "narrative poetry," "poetic narrative," "poetic prose," or "prosaic poetry."[77] They locate the

75. Kugel, *Idea of Biblical Poetry,* 302.

76. One distinctive of Kugel's work not found in others is his extensive and authoritative tracing of the history of the study of Hebrew poetry from the earliest rabbinic treatments to the present day, including dealing with the rabbinic and early Christian "forgetting" and obscuring of parallelism.

77. J. C. de Moor, "The Poetry of the Book of Ruth," *Or* 53 (1984): 262–83; *Or* 55 (1986): 16–46; W. T. Koopmans, "The Poetic Prose of Joshua 23," in *The Structural Analysis of Biblical and Canaanite Poetry,* ed. W. van der Meer and J. C. de Moor, JSOTSup 74 (Sheffield: Sheffield Academic Press, 1988), 83–118; idem, *Joshua 24 as Poetic Narrative,* JSOTSup 93 (Sheffield: Sheffield Academic Press, 1990), esp. 165–76. J. C. L. Gibson's use of the term "narrative poetry" differs from de Moor's and Koopmans's. He refers to poetic compositions embedded in narrative texts, such as Exodus 15 and Judges 5, and

texts in an "intermediate range"[78] between the poles of poetry and prose. Along with Kugel, these scholars remind us that the classical categories of poetry have many loose ends. It is not clear, however, how in their scheme one would be restrained from reclassifying *any* text usually judged to be prose as "poetic prose"; their work comes close to rendering any distinctions between prose and poetry meaningless.

While Kugel's work may not be "literary" in the pure sense, three works that can unquestionably be grouped together as truly literary studies are those of Alter, Alonso Schökel, and Fisch. None of these authors attempts a theoretical explanation for Hebrew poetry, but all display masterful eyes to the details and nuances of poetry as literature, as works of art. In *The Art of Biblical Poetry*,[79] Robert Alter begins with a discussion of "The Dynamics of Parallelism" that echoes Kugel's, in that he sees the second "verset" of a couplet going beyond the first in any number of ways, only one of which might be synonymity (and that only rarely). Others include complementarity, focusing, heightening, intensification, specification, consequentiality, contrast, or disjunction. Along with Kugel's observations, this work effectively demolishes the idea of complete synonymity between lines.[80] Alter's treatments of larger units ("From Line to Story") and other forms (e.g., "The Garden of Metaphor") are instructive in the appreciation of the art of poetry, and they are delights to read.

Luis Alonso Schökel's *Manual of Hebrew Poetics* is similar in that it approaches Hebrew poetry as an art form, and it is a masterpiece of sensitivity to the text and its subtleties.[81] Alonso Schökel read the Bible as literature long before this approach came into fashion in the 1980s; indeed, his work helped to usher in the approach. His discussions include parallelism, sounds and rhythms, synonymy, repetition, merismus, antithesis, polarized expression, images, and figures of speech, all discussed in concrete and readable ways that demonstrate the value of close literary reading of poetic texts.

Harold Fisch's *Poetry with a Purpose* reads the Bible's poetry and other literature with a literary eye, uncovering the rich tapestries of its

---

he calls for a grammar of narrative poetry to be written. See J. C. L. Gibson, "The Anatomy of Hebrew Narrative Poetry," in *Understanding Poets and Prophets: Essays in Honour of George Wishart Anderson*, ed. A. G. Auld, JSOTSup 152 (Sheffield: Sheffield Academic Press, 1993), 141–48.

78. Koopmans, "Joshua 23," 88.

79. R. Alter, *The Art of Biblical Poetry* (New York: Basic, 1985).

80. Essentially the same point is made by O'Connor, Geller, and Berlin from a linguistic perspective. See O'Connor, *Hebrew Verse Structure*, 50–52; Geller, *Parallelism in Early Biblical Poetry*, 41–42; and Berlin, *Dynamics of Biblical Parallelism*, 14–15, 64–65.

81. L. Alonso Schökel, *A Manual of Hebrew Poetics*, Subsidia Biblica 11 (Rome: Pontifical Biblical Institute, 1988).

art.[82] The Bible is at one and the same time *esthetic literature*, capable of being appreciated on a literary level, and also *religious literature*, which, with the claims to exclusivity contained within it, is like no other. The irony of much biblical literature is that both of these aspects of its literature are true (i.e., it is esthetic and it is religious) and that often the Bible's poems "gain their power from the devices they renounce."[83] The Bible's authors, through their use of the literary arts, urge their readers to read the Bible in ways that are not literary but theological. Fisch argues that the Bible's texts regularly subvert themselves (or perhaps we might say that they subvert the reader's normal understanding of things), in embracing and yet rejecting literary and poetic forms. Thus, to take but one example, Isaiah's treatment of beauty in 52:7 ("How beautiful are the feet . . .") shows that beauty is not at all contemplated in the usual categories of physical beauty, but rather in terms of moving feet and in the fulfillment of their mission; indeed, the beautiful feet bring a message of salvation, that the Lord reigns, a truth that leaves the usual understanding of "beauty" far behind. Thus the reader, who begins by thinking of "beauty" in its usual sense, is left with a very different conception of it.

Wilfred G. E. Watson's *Classical Hebrew Poetry* and *Traditional Techniques in Classical Hebrew Verse* are "literary" studies in the sense that they catalog in great detail numerous literary-poetic techniques in Hebrew, Ugaritic, and Akkadian, such as use of different types of parallelism (e.g., gender-matched, number, stairstep), stanzas and strophes, chiasms, sounds (assonance, alliteration, rhyme, onomatopoeia, wordplay), repetition, word pairs, and ellipsis.[84] But they are essentially catalogs for reference rather than treatments outlining any particular way of reading poetry. Watson does not propound any general theory of poetry, "largely because scholars themselves have not yet formulated such a theory."[85]

Structural Approaches

Closely bound up with the turn to literary studies of poetry are myriad structural studies. Typically, these deal synchronically with the surface structure of the Masoretic Text, and they study entire psalms as coher-

---

82. H. Fisch, *Poetry with a Purpose: Biblical Poetics and Interpretation* (Bloomington: Indiana University Press, 1988). His work is not limited to poetry, despite its title.

83. Ibid., 4 (this passage concerns two poems by George Herbert, but Fisch uses it to describe similar tensions in the Bible).

84. W. G. E. Watson, *Classical Hebrew Poetry: A Guide to Its Techniques*, 2d ed., JSOTSup 26 (Sheffield: Sheffield Academic Press, 1986); idem, *Traditional Techniques in Classical Hebrew Verse*, JSOTSup 170 (Sheffield: Sheffield Academic Press, 1994).

85. W. G. E. Watson, "Problems and Solutions in Hebrew Verse: A Survey of Recent Work," *VT* 43 (1993): 374.

ent wholes—a salutary development. They differ somewhat from the literary studies mentioned above in that the latter truly read the psalms as works of art, whereas many of these structural studies end up as catalogs of large-scale literary devices, of chiasms, *inclusios*, and the like, often spanning many verses. The structures of psalms are laid bare (although often no unanimity on a given psalm's structure is reached), with very elaborate diagrams, but too often little is said of a psalm's art or its meaning, and virtually nothing of its syntactical underpinnings. Such an approach is often called *analyse structurelle*, which studies surface structures, as opposed to *analyse structurale*, which is the deep-structural analysis of French Structuralism or semiotics.

Two leading practitioners of *analyse structurelle* are Marc Girard and Pierre Auffret, both of whom have produced a great number of structural studies. In their work, they exhaustively treat repeated patterns within individual psalms, and consider the lowest levels of the word up to the highest levels of the poem. In addition, Auffret also is attentive to such patterns between psalms and within psalm groupings. In *Les psaumes redécouverts*, Girard studies the psalms on three levels: syntagmatic (the most basic relationships, e.g., hendiadys), syntactic (e.g., parallelism), and the structural unity. He insists rightly that meaning is tied to structure, paying attention to both but also distinguishing between them.[86] Auffret has written structural analyses on almost every psalm, which are collected in a series of books.[87] While there are differences between the two,[88] overall their approach is very similar.

Another approach is that of J. C. de Moor and his students at the Kampen School of Theology in the Netherlands, exemplified in *The Structural Analysis of Biblical and Canaanite Poetry*.[89] This approach

86. M. Girard, *Les psaumes redécouverts: De la structure au sens*, 3 vols. (Quebec: Bellarmin, 1994–96).

87. See, e.g., P. Auffret, *Hymnes d'Égypte et d'Israel: Études de structures littéraires*, OBO 34 (Fribourg: Editions Universitaires Suisse, 1981); idem, *La sagesse a bâti sa maison: Études de structures littéraires dans l'Ancient Testament et specialement dans les psaumes*, OBO 49 (Fribourg: Editions Universitaires Suisse, 1982); idem, *Voyez des vos yeux: Étude structurelle de vingt psaumes dont le psaume 119*, VTSup 48 (Leiden: Brill, 1993); idem, *Merveilles à nos yeux: Étude structurelle de vingt psaumes dont celui de 1 Ch 16,8–36*, BZAW 235 (Berlin and New York: de Gruyter, 1995).

88. See P. Auffret, "L'étude structurelle des psaumes: Réponses et compléments I," *Science et esprit* 48 (1996): 45–60; idem, "L'étude structurelle des psaumes: Réponses et compléments II," *Science et esprit* 49 (1997): 39–61; idem, "L'étude structurelle des psaumes: Réponses et compléments III," *Science et esprit* 49 (1997): 149–74, where he responds to Girard's criticisms of his work.

89. Van der Meer and de Moor, eds., *Structural Analysis of Biblical and Canaanite Poetry*. The essentials of this system are explained in M. C. A. Korpel and J. C. de Moor, "Fundamentals of Ugaritic and Hebrew Poetry," *UF* 18 (1986): 173–212 (reprinted in *Structural Analysis of Biblical and Canaanite Poetry*, 1–61).

also includes analysis of poems at all levels, beginning with the foot (a word with at least one stressed syllable), and proceeding up to the colon, verse, strophe, canticle, subcanto, and canto. The levels of the strophe and above are usually held together by external parallelism, whereas internal parallelism operates at the lower levels. One weakness of this approach is that it equates form with meaning in most instances, implying (erroneously) that, when the structure of a poem is elucidated, the task of interpretation is complete.[90] A similar approach is espoused in South Africa by Willem S. Prinsloo and his students, which he calls a "text-immanent" approach.[91]

Daniel Grossberg's *Centripetal and Centrifugal Structures in Biblical Poetry* includes a study of the Psalms of Ascents (120–34) in which he analyzes these poems as a unified whole.[92] He sees elements that act centripetally to bind together the entire grouping into a tightly related, consolidated structure, but at the same time he identifies other elements that act centrifugally, working in the opposite direction. Paul R. Raabe, in *Psalms Structures*, is concerned to identify the building blocks of six psalms with refrains (42–43, 46, 49, 56, 57, 59), and he deals briefly with four more (39, 67, 80, 99).[93] They consist of strophes, which are combined into stanzas. The refrains (verses repeated at regular intervals) link stanzas together into larger wholes called "sections."

Hermeneutics

One of the most striking features of biblical studies today is its vast diversity. The Bible is studied from a seemingly endless list of perspectives, using a multiplicity of critical approaches. No longer is the historical-critical method, the history-of-religions approach, or form criticism the dominant paradigm of interpretation in any area of biblical studies. For example, Stephen Haynes and Steven McKenzie's *To Each Its Own*

90. See the similar comments by Cooper, "Two Recent Works on the Structure of Biblical Hebrew Poetry," *JAOS* 110 (1990): 689–90. Cooper categorizes this work as a purely "linguistic" work, but, given its lack of theoretical discussion, I judge that it is a "literary" work focusing almost entirely on form and structure.

91. This approach is a text-based and text-oriented framework for interpretation, dealing with morphological, syntactical, stylistic, and semantic components of poetry. See, e.g., W. S. Prinsloo, "Psalm 116: Disconnected Text or Symmetrical Whole?" *Bib* 74 (1993): 71–82; idem, "Psalm 149: Praise Yahweh with Tambourine and Two-Edged Sword," *ZAW* 109 (1997): 395–407; G. T. M. Prinsloo, "Analysing Old Testament Poetry: An Experiment in Methodology with Reference to Psalm 126," *OTE* 5 (1992): 225–51.

92. D. Grossberg, *Centripetal and Centrifugal Structures in Biblical Poetry*, SBLMS 39 (Atlanta: Scholars Press, 1989). His study of the Psalms of Ascents is on pp. 15–54.

93. P. R. Raabe, *Psalms Structures: A Study of Psalms with Refrains*, JSOTSup 104 (Sheffield: JSOT Press, 1990).

Meaning, a standard introduction to the scholarly disciplines, lists no less than thirteen critical approaches in biblical studies today, and entire dictionaries devoted solely to interpretation have appeared.[94] Today, Psalms studies can be found using almost every one of these methods.

Several recent works self-consciously use different methods on one psalm. For example, in *The Psalms and Their Readers*, Donald K. Berry applies different critical methodologies—textual, structural (poetic), form-critical, rhetorical-critical (literary), reader-oriented—to Psalm 18, showing the value of each one.[95] His special interest is to show how reader-oriented study can help to recontextualize the psalm in the twentieth century. William H. Bellinger Jr. takes a similar approach in *A Hermeneutic of Curiosity and Readings of Psalm 61*, using form, canonical, rhetorical, and reader-response criticisms, ending with a theological analysis.[96] His "hermeneutic of curiosity" is one in which the text invites us to ask questions and to explore, and thus we should read it using all available methods. The text becomes a window into its world of origin, its own shape and message, and its readers in relation to it, and, among them, the critical approaches must cover all three of these elements. Jutta Schröten, in *Entstehung, Komposition und Wirkungsgeschichte des 118. Psalms*, reviews the range of critical approaches to Psalm 118 throughout the history of interpretation, and then offers two parallel readings, from synchronic (poetics and form criticism) and diachronic (source and redaction criticism) perspectives.[97] In *Mijn God, mijn God, waarom hebt Gij mij verlaten?* ("My God, my God, why have you forsaken me?"), scholars in separate disciplines employ nine different approaches in the study of Psalm 22: exegetical, poetic (structural), textual (LXX), psychological, pastoral, systematic theology, church history, and its use in Jewish commentary (the psalm of Esther) and the New Testament (Mark 15).[98]

94. S. R. Haynes and S. L. McKenzie, eds., *To Each Its Own Meaning: An Introduction to Biblical Criticisms and Their Application* (Louisville: Westminster/John Knox, 1993). Cf. J. Barton, *Reading the Old Testament: Method in Biblical Study*, rev. ed. (Louisville: Westminster/John Knox, 1996), who lays out the range of critical approaches; and the following two dictionaries of interpretation: R. J. Coggins and J. L. Houlden, eds., *A Dictionary of Biblical Interpretation* (Philadelphia: Trinity Press International; London: SCM, 1990); J. H. Hayes, ed., *Dictionary of Biblical Interpretation*, 2 vols. (Nashville: Abingdon, 1999).

95. D. K. Berry, *The Psalms and Their Readers: Interpretive Strategies for Psalm 18*, JSOTSup 153 (Sheffield: Sheffield Academic Press, 1993).

96. W. H. Bellinger Jr., *A Hermeneutic of Curiosity and Readings of Psalm 61*, Studies in Old Testament Interpretation 1 (Macon, Ga.: Mercer University Press, 1995). See also idem, "Psalm xxvi: A Test of Method," *VT* 43 (1993): 452–61.

97. J. Schröten, *Entstehung, Komposition und Wirkungsgeschichte des 118. Psalms*, BBB 95 (Weinheim: Beltz Athenäum, 1995).

98. M. Poorthuis, ed., *Mijn God, mijn God, waarom hebt Gij mij verlaten? Een interdisciplinaire bundel over psalm 22* (Baarn: Ten Have, 1997).

Herbert J. Levine's *Sing unto God a New Song* is a more theoretical approach, not focusing on one psalm, but he too argues for using several disciplines in order to uncover their power, showing how the Psalms can be used even in the modern day, in both religious and secular cultures.[99] He uses history, anthropology, linguistic philosophy, phenomenology of religion, literary discourse, "biblical interpretation," and post-Holocaust interpretation.

Several works have focused on the history of interpretation of psalms. For example, in a fascinating study entitled *Psalms of the Way and the Kingdom*, John H. Eaton engages two groups of psalms—the three "Torah" psalms (1, 19, 119) and three "Kingship of Yahweh" psalms (93, 97, 99)—using ten commentators from the 1890s through 1960s (Delitzsch, Baethgen, Duhm, Briggs, Kittel, Gunkel, Bentzen, Mowinckel, Kraus, Dahood) as his conversation partners in working his way through each psalm.[100] In addition, he enlists three more recent interpreters for each group (Westermann, Gerstenberger, and Spieckermann for the Torah psalms, and Lipinski, Gray, and Jeremias for the Kingship of Yahweh psalms). Lars Olov Eriksson's *"Come, Children, Listen to Me!"* deals with Psalm 34 and consists of two major parts: (1) the distinctives of this psalm in its Old Testament context and (2) its use in the New Testament and in the early Greek fathers. He also points to the need for study of rabbinical and patristic writings.[101] Uriel Simon discusses four rabbinic approaches to the Psalms in the tenth through twelfth centuries A.D. in *Four Approaches to the Book of Psalms*.[102] Saadiah Gaon treated the Book of Psalms as a second Pentateuch, revealed to David. The Karaites Salmon ben Yeruḥam and Yefet ben ʿAli saw the Psalms as perfect prophetic prayers for all ages. Moses Ibn Giqatilah disagreed, seeing the Psalms as *non*prophetic prayers and poems. Abraham Ibn Ezra emphasized the Psalms' sacred character as prophetic prayers and divine songs. Adele Berlin also treats medieval Jewish exegesis in *Biblical Poetry through Medieval Jewish Eyes*.[103]

Many modern critical approaches, common today in the academy, are also used in Psalms studies. For example, *feminist criticism* is rep-

99. H. J. Levine, *Sing unto God a New Song: A Contemporary Reading of the Psalms*, Indiana Studies in Biblical Literature (Indianapolis: Indiana University Press, 1995).

100. J. H. Eaton, *Psalms of the Way and the Kingdom: A Conference with the Commentators*, JSOTSup 199 (Sheffield: Sheffield Academic Press, 1995).

101. L. O. Eriksson, *"Come, Children, Listen to Me!" Psalm 34 in the Hebrew Bible and in Early Christian Writings*, ConBOT 32 (Stockholm: Almqvist & Wiksell, 1991).

102. U. Simon, *Four Approaches to the Book of Psalms: From Saadiyah Gaon to Abraham Ibn Ezra*, trans. L. J. Schramm (Albany: State University of New York Press, 1991).

103. A. Berlin, *Biblical Poetry through Medieval Jewish Eyes* (Bloomington: Indiana University Press, 1991).

resented by Ulrike Bail's *Gegen das Schweigen klagen*.[104] She sees Psalms 6 and 55 as the laments of a woman who has been raped, and links them with the story of Tamar in 2 Samuel 13. Support comes from the shared terms and imagery in the narrative story (and also Judges 19) and the two psalms (cf., e.g., the "feminine" imagery of the besieged city in 55:9–11 [55:10–12 MT]). Marchiene Vroon Rienstra's *Swallow's Nest* is very different, as it is a devotional guide for daily reading, but it emphasizes and celebrates the "feminine" aspects of God, using feminine pronouns for God and offering suggestions as to settings each psalm might fit in a contemporary woman's life.[105]

Sociological and *liberationist* approaches are represented by several authors. In J. David Pleins's *The Psalms: Songs of Tragedy, Hope, and Justice*, he speaks of "a poetry of justice."[106] He lays out the manifold form-critical genres with attention to sociopolitical issues of justice, mercy, and hope, provides his own fresh translations for many psalms, and consistently brings the Psalms to bear on the modern situation. Stephen Breck Reid deals with similar issues of marginalization of the poor and the outsider (the "other," represented in the Psalms by the enemies) in *Listening In: A Multicultural Reading of the Psalms*.[107] He employs insights from the Two-Thirds World in understanding the Psalms' appeal to those outside the gate, and he too shows how the Psalms speak to the contemporary world.

Walter Brueggemann's is a prominent voice employing sociological insights in biblical studies, including attention to the poor and oppressed, and his Psalms studies are permeated with these.[108] One stimulating example is *Israel's Praise*. In this book, he argues that the praise of God is fundamental to the life of faith and that praise must be rooted firmly in the here and now, in the experiences of life. Furthermore, the "world" that believers inhabit is formed or shaped, in a very real way, by the contents and attitudes of the praise they express. If this praise is shallow, empty, unthinking, then their "world" will reflect that;

104. U. Bail, *Gegen das Schweigen klagen: Eine intertextuelle Studie zu den Klagepsalmen Ps 6 und Ps 55 und die Erzählung von der Vergewaltigung Tamars* (Gütersloh: Chr. Kaiser, 1998).

105. M. V. Rienstra, *Swallow's Nest: A Feminine Reading of the Psalms* (Grand Rapids: Eerdmans, 1992).

106. J. D. Pleins, *The Psalms: Songs of Tragedy, Hope, and Justice* (Maryknoll, N.Y.: Orbis, 1993).

107. S. B. Reid, *Listening In: A Multicultural Reading of the Psalms* (Nashville: Abingdon, 1997).

108. W. Brueggemann, *Israel's Praise: Doxology against Idolatry and Ideology* (Philadelphia: Fortress, 1988); idem, *Abiding Astonishment: Psalms, Modernity, and the Making of History*, Literary Currents in Biblical Interpretation (Louisville: Westminster/John Knox, 1991); idem, *The Psalms and the Life of Faith*, ed. P. D. Miller (Minneapolis: Fortress, 1995).

whereas if their praise is based on their genuine experience of God and his faithfulness in their lives, including their experiences of pain and discomfort, then this "God" they worship is indeed the true God. In *Abiding Astonishment*, Brueggemann speaks again of "world-making," dealing with several "historical psalms" (78, 105, 106, 136). He addresses the questions of (1) how these psalms that recite history with a supernatural dimension fit into the modern world of history writing (where the supernatural is excluded) and (2) how they, written by and for "insiders," can be used in an inclusive, rather than exclusive, manner. *The Psalms and the Life of Faith* is a collection of fourteen of his essays from 1974 to 1993, including his seminal essay on "Psalms and the Life of Faith,"[109] and several from similar (sociological) perspectives.

Many other critical approaches are represented in numerous essays, including *rhetorical criticism* (i.e., close literary and structural readings), *deconstruction, speech-act theory, discourse analysis, ecological* readings, and what might be called *"physiological"* readings.[110]

109. See W. Brueggemann, "Psalms and the Life of Faith: A Suggested Typology of Function," *JSOT* 17 (1980): 3–32 (reprinted in idem, *Psalms and the Life of Faith*, 3–32).

110. For introductions to these interpretive methods, see Hayes, ed., *Dictionary of Biblical Interpretation*. Examples of rhetorical criticism: L. C. Allen, "The Value of Rhetorical Criticism in Psalm 69," *JBL* 105 (1986): 577–98; J. K. Kuntz, "King Triumphant: A Rhetorical Study of Psalms 20 and 21," *HAR* 10 (1986): 157–76; L. D. Crow, "The Rhetoric of Psalm 44," *ZAW* 104 (1992): 394–401. See also the discussion above of "Structural Approaches," which in many cases are similar methodologically.

Deconstruction: D. P. McCarthy, "A Not-So-Bad Derridean Approach to Psalm 23," *Proceedings, Eastern Great Lakes and Midwest Biblical Society* 8 (1988): 177–92; D. Jobling, "Deconstruction and the Political Analysis of Biblical Texts: A Jamesonian Reading of Psalm 72," *Semeia* 59 (1992): 95–127; D. J. A. Clines, "A World Established on Water (Psalm 24): Reader-Response, Deconstruction, and Bespoke Interpretation," in *The New Literary Criticism and the Hebrew Bible*, ed. J. C. Exum and D. J. A. Clines, JSOTSup 143 (Sheffield: Sheffield Academic Press, 1993), 79–90.

Speech-act theory: H. Irsigler, "Psalm-Rede als Handlungs-, Wirk- und Aussageproze: Sprechaktanalyse und Psalmeninterpretation am Beispiel von Psalm 13," in *Neue Wege der Psalmenforschung*, ed. K. Seybold and E. Zenger (Freiburg: Herder, 1994), 63–104.

Discourse analysis: E. R. Wendland, "Genre Criticism and the Psalms: What Discourse Typology Can Tell Us about the Text (with Special Reference to Psalm 31)," in *Biblical Hebrew and Discourse Linguistics*, ed. R. D. Bergen (Winona Lake, Ind.: Eisenbrauns, 1994), 374–414.

Ecological readings: B. J. Raja, "Eco-Spirituality in the Psalms," *Vidyajyoti* 53 (1989): 637–50; E. Zenger, "'Du kannst das Angesicht der Erde erneuern' (Ps 104,30): Das Schöpferlob des 104. Psalms als Ruf zur ökologischen Umkehr," *Bibel und Liturgie* 64 (1991): 75–86; K. V. Mathew, "Ecological Perspectives in the Book of Psalms," *Bible Bhashyam* 19 (1993): 159–68; J. Limburg, "Down-to-Earth Theology: Psalm 104 and the Environment," *Currents in Theology and Mission* 21 (1994): 340–46; M. A. Bullmore, "The Four Most Important Biblical Passages for a Christian Environmentalism," *TJ* 19 (1998): 139–62 (includes Ps. 104).

"Physiological" readings: G. A. Rendsburg and S. L. Rendsburg, "Physiological and Philological Notes to Psalm 137," *JQR* 83 (1993): 385–99 (who argue that in vv. 5–6, which

Such is the vast new diversity in Psalms studies that even traditional, christological approaches have received new and stimulating treatments, such as Bruce K. Waltke's "Canonical Process Approach to the Psalms" and Georg Braulik's "Christologisches Verständnis der Psalmen—schon im Alten Testament?"[111] Waltke argues for different stages of reading the Psalms, following the process of canonical formation (individual psalm, collections, Psalter, OT, Christian canon), and argues that in the final analysis the entire Psalter should be read christologically.[112] Braulik likewise sees a messianic (re)interpretation of individual psalms as these were incorporated into large collections.[113]

William L. Holladay's *Psalms through Three Thousand Years* is a work that resists categorization, but I include it here because of Holladay's call for a christological interpretation of the Psalms.[114] It traces the history of the psalms through their origin and development in the biblical period, and then through the history of Jewish and Christian interpretation from Qumran to the modern day. His work is very sophisticated and is not only cognizant of modern critical scholarship but also sensitive to religious and nonreligious traditions that would not revere the Psalms in the ways in which Christians do. Nevertheless, in his final chapter—entitled "Through Jesus Christ Our Lord"—Holladay calls for Christians to read the Psalms christologically.

Form Criticism

The middle half of the twentieth century was dominated by form-critical and cultic S*itz im Leben* studies, following the programs laid out by Gunkel and Mowinckel mentioned above. Since 1970, although the

---

speak of the psalmist's right hand withering and his tongue cleaving to the roof of his mouth, the psalmist is describing a cerebrovascular accident, or stroke, in the left side of the brain); S. Levin, "Let My Right Hand Wither," *Judaism* 45 (1996): 282–86 (who argues that vv. 5–6 describe cerebral palsy).

111. B. K. Waltke, "A Canonical Process Approach to the Psalms," in *Tradition and Testament,* ed. J. S. Feinberg and P. D. Feinberg (Chicago: Moody, 1981), 3–18; G. Braulik, "Christologisches Verständnis der Psalmen—schon im Alten Testament?" in *Christologie der Liturgie: Der Gottesdienst der Kirche—Christusbekenntnis und Sinaibund,* ed. K. Richter and B. Kranemann, Quaestiones disputatae 159 (Freiburg: Herder, 1995), 57–86.

112. A full development and defense of Waltke's idea is J. E. Shepherd, "The Book of Psalms as the Book of Christ: The Application of the Christo-Canonical Method to the Book of Psalms" (Ph.D. diss., Westminster Theological Seminary, 1995).

113. A thorough review of the patristic treatments (mid-second to mid-sixth centuries A.D.) of Psalm 45 is to be found in E. Grünbeck, *Christologische Schriftargumentation und Bildersprache,* Supplements to Vigiliae Christianae 26 (Leiden: Brill, 1994).

114. W. L. Holladay, *The Psalms through Three Thousand Years: Prayerbook of a Cloud of Witnesses* (Minneapolis: Fortress, 1993).

most creative energies have been devoted elsewhere and such studies are no longer dominant, they have by no means ceased.

Pride of place must be given to the recent translation of Hermann Gunkel's *Introduction to the Psalms*.[115] Sixty-five years after publication in German, the results of Gunkel's form-critical analyses are now accessible to English readers; they can discover for themselves Gunkel's categories of individual and communal laments, praise hymns, thanksgiving psalms, royal psalms, and the minor categories, including his assignment of specific situations in life corresponding to these (for Gunkel, these were mostly the cult, i.e., in public ritual situations associated with the temple). His interest in a single *Sitz im Leben* behind each psalm type is no longer sustainable today. But his form-critical categories continue to frame the discussion to this day, even though they have been revised and augmented somewhat.

Another major work made available in English is Claus Westermann's *Praise and Lament in the Psalms*.[116] This includes his seminal work, *The Praise of God in the Psalms* (1965), and several other essays. Westermann's most distinctive insight is that Hebrew had no separate word for "to thank"—the word normally used in contexts where this is expected is "to bless"—and that thus the word translated "thanksgiving" (*tôdâ*) should be understood as another word for "praise." He thus argues that the distinction between psalms of praise and psalms of thanksgiving is misguided; he calls the first type "psalms of descriptive praise," where the praises of God describe his attributes in general, universal terms, and those of the second type "psalms of narrative (or 'declarative') praise," where God's praises are recited (declared) in the form of specifics of what God has done for the nation or the individual. Westermann overstates the case somewhat, because certainly there are some meaningful distinctions between thanksgiving and praise. Nevertheless, his is a most helpful distinction, by revealing that all of the psalms are ultimately to be considered "praises" (a point he makes with reference even to the laments, which move toward praise in their concluding vows to praise).

Another work with refinements to Gunkel's is Erhard S. Gerstenberger's *Psalms, Part I*, a form-critical study of the first sixty psalms.[117] He follows Gunkel's classifications, but his distinctive contribution is his attention to social settings of the psalms, including a focus on "in-group and out-group" dynamics. He argues that many psalms arose in

---

115. H. Gunkel and J. Begrich, *Introduction to the Psalms: The Genres of the Religious Lyric of Israel*, trans. J. D. Nogalski (Macon, Ga.: Mercer University Press, 1998).

116. C. Westermann, *Praise and Lament in the Psalms*, trans. K. R. Crim and R. N. Soulen (Atlanta: John Knox, 1981).

117. E. S. Gerstenberger, *Psalms, Part I: With an Introduction to Cultic Poetry*, FOTL 14 (Grand Rapids: Eerdmans, 1988).

the context of "the small, organic group of family, neighborhood, or community" (the "out-groups"), not in "the central temple or famous wisdom academies" (the "in-groups").[118] As such, the origin *and* function of many psalms was not liturgical or connected with the cult at all.

An important enterprise that can be classed as "form-critical" is Walter Brueggemann's "Psalms and the Life of Faith."[119] In this essay Brueggemann suggests a new way of categorizing psalms by function. In his scheme (suggested by the work of Paul Ricoeur) "psalms of orientation" are those characterized by the absence of tension, in which the world is ordered and goodness prevails, such as psalms of creation, wisdom, retribution, and blessing. The second type is "psalms of disorientation," made up of laments. The third type is "psalms of reorientation," composed of thanksgivings and hymns of praise. In these Brueggemann detects a greater sense of excitement than in the "ordered" psalms of orientation, and in these there is evidence of the psalmists' having gone through disorientation and now having progressed to a new place of orientation, which is much more secure and mature than the original orientation. In this scheme, then, hymns and thanksgivings (Westermann's psalms of descriptive and declarative praise), while they differ formally from each other, are similar in function, in that they belong to the new orientation, informed by trouble and God's gracious intervention.[120] While Brueggemann's new categories do not do away with the standard form-critical ones, his model is very useful and has had a significant influence in Psalms studies since 1980.

As a form-critical category, the psalms of lament have attracted the most scholarly interest over the years, and form-critical investigations since 1970 continue this trend. Studies have focused on specific elements of the laments and on their overall function.

For example, William H. Bellinger Jr., in *Psalmody and Prophecy,* deals with prophetic elements in psalms of lament, particularly on the "certainty of a hearing" portion of these, which he links (following Begrich) with the oracle of salvation: as the promise of deliverance is delivered to the individual praying the psalm, this individual then responds with words indicating the faith that he or she will be (or has been) heard.[121] Bellinger challenges the notion of the "cultic prophet,"

118. Ibid., 33.

119. He has pursued the central idea of this essay in later writings and synthesized it for a popular audience in *The Message of the Psalms* (Minneapolis: Augsburg, 1984).

120. In later writings Brueggemann places some hymns (e.g., Psalm 150) in the category of "psalms of orientation," because they are "static," with no evidence, in his view, of the life-transforming experiences found in the psalms of reorientation. See, e.g., *Israel's Praise*, 92–93.

121. W. H. Bellinger Jr., *Psalmody and Prophecy*, JSOTSup 27 (Sheffield: JSOT Press, 1984).

arguing that the oracle of salvation could easily have been uttered by a priest as well. By contrast, in *Seeing and Hearing God in the Psalms,* Raymond Jacques Tournay argues that authentic cultic prophets did exist; they were the postexilic Levitical singers.[122] He focuses on theophanic evocations and cultic oracles to show that there is an important prophetic dimension to the Psalms, which the Levitical singers composed in order to bring hope to bear on the postexilic community. He ties this prophetic hope in with the messianic hope, and argues that the church can recover some of this hope by focusing on this prophetic dimension. His argument depends heavily on the postexilic origin of many of the psalms, however, a point that cannot be verified conclusively in most cases.

In *The Conflict of Faith and Experience in the Psalms,* Craig C. Broyles distinguishes between psalms of plea, in which God is praised and asked to intervene on the psalmist's behalf, and psalms of complaint, in which the psalmist challenges God, who is seen either as an aloof bystander or an active antagonist.[123] The complaints are not complaints per se, but rather intend to summon God to be faithful to his promises and act on the psalmists' behalf.

Two works have studied the community laments in the context of the ancient Near East. Paul W. Ferris Jr.'s *Genre of Communal Lament in the Bible and the Ancient Near East* studies nineteen psalms plus the Book of Lamentations, along with the communal forms of the Mesopotamian city laments, *balags,* and *eršemmas.* His work is "an attempt to develop a unified comparative description of the Hebrew communal lament in light of the phenomenon of public lament in neighboring cultures."[124] His theory of genre is more advanced than traditional form criticism, and stresses that the constituent parts of a given genre do not need to be completely uniform and are not necessarily dependent on only one *Sitz im Leben.* Ferris concludes there is no connection of dependency between the Israelite and Mesopotamian laments, but rather that they both go back to a common cultural inheritance. Walter C. Bouzard Jr., on the other hand, disagrees in *We Have Heard with Our Ears, O God.* He investigates the possible Mesopotamian sources behind the community laments, and concludes that the evidence "points to the strong possibility of a specifically literary connection between the two collections," although he admits that the specific evidence for borrowing is

---

122. R. J. Tournay, *Seeing and Hearing God in the Psalms: The Prophetic Liturgy of the Second Temple in Jerusalem,* JSOTSup 118 (Sheffield: Sheffield Academic Press, 1991).

123. C. C. Broyles, *The Conflict of Faith and Experience in the Psalms,* JSOTSup 52 (Sheffield: JSOT Press, 1989).

124. P. W. Ferris Jr., *The Genre of Communal Lament in the Bible and the Ancient Near East,* SBLDS 127 (Atlanta: Scholars Press, 1992), 13.

only circumstantial.[125] Bouzard questions Westermann's structural elements, the "expression of confidence" and especially the "certainty of a hearing," since they are not present at all in the Israelite laments he examines—Psalms 44, 60, 74, 79, 80, 83, 89.[126]

In Anneli Aejmelaeus's *Traditional Prayer in the Psalms*, she proposes to call Westermann's form-critical genre of complaint psalms (Gunkel's individual laments) "prayer psalms of the individual," because of the prominent place of imperative prayer to God in these.[127] In the tradition of classical form critics, she posits an evolutionary development of "traditional" prayers (i.e., prayers using conventional language that reach back into Israel's preexilic history) from simple (preexilic) to complex (postexilic) forms. The main problem with her approach is this evolutionary hypothesis, which has been abandoned by most biblical scholars; nevertheless, her treatment of the form and function of imperative prayer is useful.

Two works focus on the individual in the psalms. The first, Steven J. L. Croft's *Identity of the Individual in the Psalms*, engages the often-asked question about who the individual was.[128] He argues that the speaker in the "I" psalms (ninety-six psalms) is either the king, a private person, or a minister of the cult, whether a cultic prophet, wisdom teacher, or temple singer. Martin Ravndal Hauge, in *Between Sheol and Temple*, does not address the question of the identity of the individual, but rather seizes upon three fundamental motifs in the psalms—"temple," "the way," and "Sheol"—to describe the emotional and mental location of the individual's religious experience.[129]

Mowinckel's hypothesis of an Enthronement of Yahweh Festival is kept alive in J. H. Eaton's *Kingship and the Psalms*.[130] Eaton accepts Mowinckel's reconstruction of this supposed festival and its connection with the Festival of Tabernacles,[131] along with A. R. Johnson's argument that the Israelite king was closely involved in this. He thus ex-

125. W. C. Bouzard Jr., *We Have Heard with Our Ears, O God: Sources of the Communal Laments in the Psalms,* SBLDS 159 (Atlanta: Scholars Press, 1997), 201.

126. Ibid., 109–13, 204–5.

127. A. Aejmelaeus, *The Traditional Prayer in the Psalms,* BZAW 167 (Berlin: de Gruyter, 1986).

128. S. J. L. Croft, *The Identity of the Individual in the Psalms,* JSOTSup 44 (Sheffield: JSOT Press, 1987).

129. M. R. Hauge, *Between Sheol and Temple: Motif Structure and Function in the I-Psalms,* JSOTSup 178 (Sheffield: Sheffield Academic Press, 1995).

130. J. H. Eaton, *Kingship and the Psalms,* 2d ed., Biblical Seminar 3 (Sheffield: JSOT Press, 1986).

131. As does J. Jeremias in *Das Königtum Gottes in den Psalmen: Israels Begegnung mit dem kanaanäischen Mythos in den Jahwe-König-Psalmen,* FRLANT 141 (Göttingen: Vandenhoeck & Ruprecht, 1987), although he does not go to the lengths that Mowinckel did in reconstructing the festival.

pands the category of royal psalm to include close to half of the psalms: the individual laments are actually prayers of the king in most cases. This expansion has been disputed by many, but the canonical form of the Psalter supports his view, in that to David the king are attributed seventy-three psalms.[132]

The Psalms in the Context of the Ancient Near East

In the early part of the twentieth century, interest in ancient Near Eastern connections for the Psalms focused primarily on parallels with Mesopotamian hymns, prayers, and laments. Gunkel looked to these in his identification of the basic psalm forms, as did Mowinckel in reconstructing his hypothetical Festival of the Enthronement of Yahweh. Such interest still continues in several form-critical studies (see above).

In the middle of the century, however, interest shifted to parallels with Ugaritic literature, which consisted of texts written in a West Semitic language closely related to Hebrew and including many poetic compositions. The zenith of Ugaritic influence on Psalms study came with Mitchell J. Dahood's Psalms commentary, in which he radically rewrote many of the psalms on the basis of supposed Ugaritic parallels.[133] His influence has been negligible in the past two decades, however, principally because of the excesses in so many of his proposals.

Today, the primary interest in Ugaritic among Psalms scholars lies in study of the poetic features common to both, paramount among which are word pairs. Often called "fixed word pairs," the term "parallel word pairs" is more appropriate, and it refers to words occurring relatively frequently in parallel lines belonging to the same grammatical class (e.g., noun, verb, participle). Obvious examples are *snow* and *rain*, *left* and *right*, *sun* and *moon*, *father* and *mother*. Many variations occur, including repetition of the same verb in a different form (masculine vs. feminine, singular vs. plural, *qatal* vs. *yiqtol*, etc.), augmentation of the same word (e.g., *desert* and *holy desert*, *wreaths* and *gold wreaths*), or the metaphorical pairing of words (e.g., *honey* and *oil*).[134] Dahood studied these extensively,[135] but the standard study today is Yitzhak Avishur,

---

132. Cf. Waltke, "Canonical Process Approach to the Psalms," 3–18.

133. M. J. Dahood, *Psalms*, 3 vols., AB 16–17A (Garden City, N.Y.: Doubleday, 1966–70).

134. See the brief introductions in Berlin, *Dynamics of Biblical Parallelism*, 65–72; Watson, *Classical Hebrew Poetry*, 128–44.

135. M. J. Dahood, "Ugaritic-Hebrew Parallel Pairs," in *Ras Shamra Parallels*, ed. L. Fisher and S. Rummel, AnOr 49–51 (Rome: Pontifical Biblical Institute, 1972, 1975, 1981), 1:71–382; 2:1–39; 3:1–206; Dahood listed more than a thousand parallel pairs in these articles. See also P. Yoder, "A-B Pairs and Oral Composition in Hebrew Poetry," *VT* 21 (1971): 470–89.

Stylistic Studies of Word-Pairs in Biblical and Ancient Semitic Literatures.[136] Avishur catalogs the different types of word pairs and plots their occurrence in the Bible and extrabiblical languages (Ugaritic, Phoenician, Aramaic, and Akkadian). He also corrects many of Dahood's excesses, noting, for example, that perhaps 70 percent of Dahood's examples cannot be considered "common word-pairs." He concludes that there are less than two hundred common word-pairs, some of which Dahood did not identify.[137]

In another work, *Studies in Hebrew and Ugaritic Psalms*, Avishur takes up the problem of the relationship between Ugaritic and Hebrew psalms, and he concludes that there is no strong connection between Israelite tradition and Ugaritic-Canaanite tradition, but rather that the similarities can be accounted for by common formal, thematic, linguistic, and stylistic elements.[138] Opposed to this, in *Yahweh's Combat with the Sea*, Carola Kloos argues on the basis of Psalm 29 and the Song of the Sea (Exod. 15) that Baalism did indeed form the basis for an important strand of Old Testament religion, that Yahweh functioned as an "Israelite Baal" in his conflict with the sea (Yam).[139]

Interest in the ancient Near East has not been limited to literary or form-critical studies. A valuable study of ancient Near Eastern iconography as it relates to the Psalms is Othmar Keel's *Symbolism of the Biblical World.*[140] It organizes its material around ancient Near Eastern conceptions of the cosmos, destructive forces (death, enemies), the temple, conceptions of God (in the temple, in creation, in history), the king, and humans before God, and includes comments—and usually illustrations: there are 556 in the book—for 146 of the 150 psalms.

Conclusion

The most remarkable features of Psalms studies since 1970 are (1) the paradigm shift in interpreting the Psalter, which is now read more and more as a unified collection; (2) the paradigm shift in interpreting Hebrew poetry, which is now read more and more syntactically; (3) and the exponential growth in the number of different approaches to indi-

136. Y. Avishur, *Stylistic Studies of Word-Pairs in Biblical and Ancient Semitic Literatures*, AOAT 210 (Kevelaer: Butzon & Bercker; Neukirchen-Vluyn: Neukirchener, 1984).
137. Ibid., 40.
138. Y. Avishur, *Studies in Hebrew and Ugaritic Psalms* (Jerusalem: Magnes, 1994).
139. C. Kloos, *Yahweh's Combat with the Sea: A Canaanite Tradition in the Religion of Ancient Israel* (Leiden: Brill, 1986).
140. O. Keel, *The Symbolism of the Biblical World: Ancient Near Eastern Iconography and the Book of Psalms*, trans. T. J. Hallett (New York: Seabury, 1978). Cf. also Ringgren, *Psaltaren 1–41*, which devotes a great deal of attention to ancient Near Eastern parallels and iconography.

vidual psalms and psalm types. Each of these has its great advantages, which have been touched on above.

Each has potential pitfalls as well. In the first area, the greatest dangers are those of subjectivity and overgeneralization. This approach must develop proper methodological controls and also be able to articulate the results of its investigations with clarity and with sufficient specificity as to be meaningful. Research in this area must proceed along at least four fronts.

1. *Macrostructures:* Most of the research to date is devoted to this level, and it needs to continue. But it alone cannot definitively answer all of the questions about the Psalter's composition and message.
2. *Microstructures:* More attention needs to be devoted to the intricate networks of lexical and other connections between and among individual psalms and psalm groupings, including the redactional dynamics where preexisting collections begin and end.
3. *Semantic Fields:* The semantic-field approach employed by Jerome Creach promises to yield useful results and should be employed with various key lexemes.
4. *Parallels:* Further research on other biblical collections (e.g., Proverbs, Isaiah, Jeremiah, the Twelve), as well as extrabiblical ones (e.g., Mesopotamian, Egyptian, Qumran) should offer further insights and controls.

In the area of Hebrew poetry, the attention to syntax must be wedded to semantics and poetics in the pursuit of meaning, as I have argued above. Attention to syntax, by itself, will yield an understanding of the workings of Hebrew poetry, but it cannot yield a complete picture of the *meaning* of poetic lines, let alone entire poems.

In the area of different approaches, the danger is that overcompartmentalization of the discipline of Psalms study will result in few or no checks and balances on interpretive approaches. This is true of biblical studies at large: increasing specialization in every discipline can lead to scholars of one viewpoint talking with only those who agree with them and no one else, and the salutary effects of critical review are sometimes missing. The exponential growth in approaches to the study of the Psalms reflects the postmodern times in which we live at the end of the twentieth century: any and all approaches to a text—and any and all conclusions about a text—are deemed to be equally valid. However, the search for authorial meaning and intent, despite the difficulties associated with recovering these, should not be abandoned in the ever-expanding embrace of new approaches, and each should be subjected to critical review, not only in terms of conclusions reached but also in terms of the validity and usefulness of the approaches themselves.

Psalms studies are vibrant and flourishing in 1999, compared to their status in the academy a century ago. They have taken their place in the mainstream of biblical studies and have grown exponentially.[141] For the most part, they have reflected the larger trends visible elsewhere in biblical studies since 1970. And, at the turn of the millennium, when many people are looking for eschatological signs, the message of eschatological hope in the Psalter is as fresh and as relevant as ever.[142]

141. The virtual explosion in the number of books and articles on Psalms, as well as approaches to them, parallels the numerical growth of the professional societies since 1970. In the Society of Biblical Literature, membership more than doubled in the period under consideration, from 2820 in 1970 to 7121 in 1998. In the Evangelical Theological Society, membership more than tripled, from 802 in 1970 to 2539 in 1998. (These figures are courtesy of Andrew D. Scrimgeour and Gregory L. Glover of the SBL and James A. Borland of the ETS.)

142. I thank Chris Franke, Mark D. Futato, William L. Holladay, Patrick D. Miller Jr., Michael Patrick O'Connor, Philip C. Schmitz, and Erich Zenger for offering helpful suggestions on portions of the manuscript, and William L. Holladay and J. Kenneth Kuntz for placing forthcoming manuscripts of their own at my disposal. A few portions of this essay are adapted from my review of Psalms studies in *The Structure of Psalms 93–100* (Winona Lake, Ind.: Eisenbrauns, 1997), 1–19, and are used by permission.

13

Recent Studies in Old Testament Apocalyptic

John N. Oswalt

Renewed Interest in Apocalyptic

If one of the marks of apocalyptic is the periodization of history,[1] then modern historians are surely the true descendants of the apocalyptists. For what is more characteristic of modern history writing than its attempt to isolate periods and ages? This same instinct can be seen at work in studies of the topic under consideration here. It cannot be doubted that during recent years we have experienced a resurgence of interest in apocalyptic and in its significance in the emergence of Judaism and Christianity. That being so, we want to know precisely when this resurgence began. Equally important, we wish to know what sparked this resurgence.

Klaus Koch has no reticence in dating the beginning of this renewed interest in a precise fashion. It began, he says, with Ernst Käsemann's address in 1959 in which he announced that "apocalyptic is the mother of Christian theology."[2] Such a pronouncement came undoubtedly as a shock to German scholars nurtured on a Bultmannian denial of any

---

Portions of this material first appeared in *JETS* 24 (1981): 289–302; they have been revised for inclusion here.

1. D. E. Gowan, *Bridge between the Testaments*, 2d ed., PTMS 14 (Pittsburgh: Pickwick, 1980), 449.

2. E. Käsemann, "The Beginnings of Christian Theology" (trans. J. W. Leitch), *JTC* 6 (1969): 40; K. Koch, *The Rediscovery of Apocalyptic*, trans. M. Kohl, SBT 2/22 (Naperville, Ill.: Allenson; London: SCM, 1972), 14; cf. also E. F. Tupper, "The Revival of Apocalyptic in Biblical and Theological Studies," *RevExp* 72 (1975): 279.

connection between a Christian eschatology and a Jewish apocalyptic. Nor could such a statement be lightly dismissed, coming as it did on the heels of Wolfhart Pannenberg's lecture in which he enunciated his now-famous philosophy of history, which saw the apocalyptic understanding as an essential link in the development of genuinely historical understanding.[3]

Without doubting the importance of Käsemann and Pannenberg, especially for German-speaking scholars, one can still raise a question as to whether the "present age" dawned quite as precipitately as Koch suggests. As he recognizes, H. H. Rowley had already in 1944 offered a mediating view from Bultmann's that had found wide acceptance in the English-speaking world.[4] In 1952 a similar position was expressed by S. B. Frost.[5] In 1957 G. E. Ladd also posed the connection.[6] Nor was this recognition of the significance of apocalyptic confined to English speakers. Otto Plöger's investigation of the relationship of prophecy to apocalyptic had already appeared in 1959, and von Rad's comments about the rootage of apocalyptic in wisdom, while primarily negative, still constitute more attention than given in, say, Eichrodt.[7]

Thus Käsemann and Pannenberg did not inaugurate a movement. Rather, they were part of one. To be sure, their formulations probably crystallized the thoughts of many others and gave the movement new impetus, but the movement was already there. But if the scholars' pronouncements did not create the movement, what did? D. S. Russell has suggested that it is the nature of the events of our time that accounts for the interest of both scholars and laypeople in the end times.[8] Faced with events that make "life as usual" impossible, yet believing there must be more than merely interior meaning to existence, men and women have been forced to turn to a philosophy of history that will incorporate and transcend those events.[9] Along with this sociological factor, there may

---

3. W. Pannenberg, "Redemptive Event and History," in *Basic Questions in Theology: Collected Essays*, trans. G. H. Kehm, 2 vols. (Philadelphia: Fortress; London: SCM, 1970–71), 1:15–80.

4. Koch, *Rediscovery*, 51–53; H. H. Rowley, *The Relevance of Apocalyptic* (New York: Association Press; London: Lutterworth, 1944; 3d ed. 1963).

5. S. B. Frost, *Old Testament Apocalyptic: Its Origins and Growth* (London: Epworth, 1952).

6. G. E. Ladd, "Why Not Prophecy-Apocalyptic?" *JBL* 76 (1957): 192–200.

7. O. Plöger, *Theocracy and Eschatology*, trans. S. Rudman (Richmond: John Knox; Oxford: Basil Blackwell, 1968); G. von Rad, *Old Testament Theology*, trans. D. M. G. Stalker, 2 vols. (New York: Harper & Row; Edinburgh: Oliver & Boyd, 1962–65), 2:301–15.

8. D. S. Russell, *Apocalyptic: Ancient and Modern* (Philadelphia: Fortress; London: SCM, 1978), 5. Cf. also Koch, *Rediscovery*, 51, for a comment on the timing of the appearance of Rowley's book.

9. So, for instance, Augustine's *City of God*.

be an intellectual one. J. J. Collins has pointed out that the Wellhausenian view of Israel's history, which held sway over Old Testament studies for the first half of the twentieth century, sharply denigrated the value of apocalyptic, seeing it as a denial of "true" Old Testament faith. Collins implies that the loosening of Wellhausen's hold on Old Testament thought left space for a reconsideration of the significance of apocalyptic.[10] It is in this sense that Koch's assertion concerning the importance of Käsemann's address is at least exaggerated. Käsemann and Pannenberg gave visibility and point to the larger movement of which they were a part, but they did not create it.[11]

Defining Apocalyptic

Given the renewed interest in apocalyptic in recent years, two foci of scholarly attention have emerged: definition and derivation. What actually constitutes apocalyptic? Where did it come from? The problem of definition has been and remains central, because the literary material that has been labeled "apocalyptic" shows a bewildering variety in content, style, and focus.[12] Furthermore, the historical information concerning the Jewish people during the period when this literature was produced (ca. 300 B.C. to A.D. 200) is so scanty that it provides few tools for categorizing the literature by sources or sociological factors. It is not known who used the literature, or how widespread its influence was. But, even more seriously, it has been difficult to say what are the precise characteristics of apocalyptic literature. There have been several attempts to produce definitive lists of these characteristics.[13] When the lists are complete, however, no one of the pieces that has been labeled "apocalyptic" by one or another meets all the criteria. Thus, as Margaret Barker points out, Daniel is frequently used as a starting point from which to characterize apocalyptic, yet Daniel lacks many of the

10. J. J. Collins, *The Apocalyptic Imagination: An Introduction to the Jewish Matrix of Christianity* (New York: Crossroad, 1984), 1, 12–13.

11. Thus they certainly were not responsible for the phenomenal interest in Hal Lindsay's books. For a pointed critique of Lindsay, see P. D. Hanson, *Old Testament Apocalyptic* (Nashville: Abingdon, 1987), 53–58.

12. While there are some differences of opinion, apocalyptic literature is generally held to include the canonical books of Daniel and Revelation, the noncanonical books of 1–3 Enoch, 2–3 Baruch, Jubilees, 4 Ezra, the Apocalypse of Abraham, the Testimony of Levi, the Testimony of Abraham, the Apocalypse of Zephaniah, the Sibylline Oracles, and portions of several of the Qumran scrolls. All of the Pseudepigrapha are conveniently available in J. H. Charlesworth, *The Old Testament Pseudepigrapha*, 2 vols. (Garden City, N.Y.: Doubleday; London: Darton, Longman & Todd, 1983–85).

13. Examples of such lists may be found in Koch, *Rediscovery*, 24–30; and in D. S. Russell, *The Method and Message of Jewish Apocalyptic*, OTL (Philadelphia: Westminster, 1964), 104–39.

characteristics of apocalyptic that appear on any final list.[14] Collins and others argue that the fault here lies in oversimplification of very complex material.[15] Some have even gone so far as to suggest that the term *apocalyptic* should be dropped altogether since it has come to include so much that it is meaningless.[16]

A helpful approach to the problem of definition has emerged from the discussion. This is the recommendation that we distinguish among literary genre, social ideology, and literary ideas and motifs. Thus, some argue, we should talk about apocalypses, apocalypticism, and apocalyptic eschatology, while avoiding the use of *apocalyptic* as a noun altogether. But even here the diversity of the material is such that there is room for disagreement. For example, F. García Martínez argues that the limitation of "apocalyptic" to a literary genre (the net effect of the above move) is excessively reductionistic.[17]

García Martínez's objections notwithstanding, such a set of distinctions as proposed above seems a helpful approach to the problem. Out of this approach, the following definition has emerged from the work of a Society of Biblical Literature seminar devoted to the study of apocalyptic and chaired by Collins:

> a genre of revelatory literature with a narrative framework, in which a revelation is mediated by an otherworldly being to a human recipient, disclosing a transcendent reality which is both temporal, insofar as it envisages eschatological salvation, and spatial insofar as it involves another, supernatural world.[18]

This definition has the virtue of being broad enough to include all the various literatures that have been designated apocalyptic, and yet specific enough to be useful.[19] For instance, even though classic Israelite

---

14. M. Barker, "Slippery Words III. Apocalyptic," *ExpTim* 89 (1977–78): 325. See P. R. Davies, "Eschatology in the Book of Daniel," *JSOT* 17 (1980): 33–53, for a similar point of view. He wonders whether it is even helpful to call Daniel an apocalyptic book.

15. D. S. Russell seems to attempt to take account of this criticism in his latest book (*Divine Disclosure: An Introduction to Jewish Apocalyptic* [Minneapolis: Fortress; London: SCM, 1992]), in which he highlights the diversities among the materials to a greater degree than in some of his former books.

16. See the discussion of definition in J. Carmignac, "Description du phenomene de l'Apocalyptique dans l'Ancien Testament," in *Apocalypticism in the Mediterranean World and the Near East*, ed. D. Hellholm (Tübingen: Mohr, 1983), 163–66.

17. F. García Martínez, "Encore l'Apocalyptique," *JSJ* 17 (1987): 230.

18. Collins, *Apocalyptic Imagination*, 4, citing idem, "Introduction: Towards the Morphology of a Genre," *Semeia* 14 (1979): 9.

19. In contrast, compare a definition such as that of U. H. J. Kortner: "Apocalyptic is speculation that—preferably in allegorical form—interprets the course of events and reveals the end of the world" ("Weltzeit, Weltangst und Weltende," *TZ* 45 [1989]: 32–52).

prophecy would include the concepts of revelation, and to some extent, eschatological salvation, the mediation by an otherworldly being is conspicuously absent. At the same time, it is possible that some subdefinitions will become necessary in order to distinguish between various expressions of the genre. Thus, are there characteristics that define the books of Daniel and Revelation over against the other apocalyptic writings and that explain why these were designated canonical by the Jewish and Christian communities in contrast to any of the others? There has already emerged one such distinction between so-called historical apocalypses and otherworldly journeys,[20] but it appears other, even more precise distinctions may be useful.

At least two objections to this definition have been raised. One is voiced by Christopher Rowland, who argues cogently that the expectation of a new age of redemption is not uniquely found in apocalypses but was characteristic of much of Judaism during late pre-Christian times. Therefore, he maintains that there is no distinctive apocalyptic eschatology, and that this feature should not appear in a definition of the genre apocalypse.[21] But Robert Webb seems to be correct when he observes that just because eschatological concerns are not unique to apocalypse does not mean that they are not one of the genre's defining characteristics.[22] To be sure, if such concerns were presented as the only or even the main characteristic in the definition, Rowland's objection might carry more weight. But if they are presented as one of the characteristics, which they certainly are, a good definition should not exclude them.

Another concern has been raised by David Hellholm, who points out that the definition contains no indication of the function of the genre. Thus he and others have proposed the following addition: "intended for a group in crisis with the purpose of exhortation and/or consolation by means of divine authority."[23] Even though it has been widely accepted that this was the function of apocalyptic writings, however, no concrete evidence supports this assumption. Lester Grabbe, for one, maintains that these writings were the product not of marginalized communities in crisis but simply of visionary groups analogous to modern millenarian groups.[24] In the absence of clear evidence, and given the presence

20. Collins, *Apocalyptic Imagination*, 6.

21. C. Rowland, *The Open Heaven: A Study of Apocalyptic in Judaism and Early Christianity* (New York: Crossroad; London: SPCK, 1982), 29–37, 71.

22. R. Webb, "'Apocalyptic': Observations on a Slippery Term," *JNES* 49 (1990): 124.

23. D. Hellholm, "The Problem of Apocalyptic Genre and the Apocalypse of John," *Semeia* 36 (1986): 27.

24. L. L. Grabbe, "The Social Setting of Early Jewish Apocalypticism," *Journal for the Study of Pseudepigrapha* 4 (1989): 27–47.

of dissenting voices like Grabbe's, it does not seem wise to make the addition Hellholm recommends.

The Origin of Apocalyptic

Along with the attempt to reach a more workable definition, there has been great interest in the derivation of apocalypticism in recent years. Earlier studies attempted to define the precise relationship between prophetic and apocalyptic eschatology. Was apocalyptic an unfortunate byroad away from the prophets?[25] Was it a linear but unfortunate descendant?[26] Was it an appropriate and necessary development of the prophetic vision?[27] Intrinsic to all of this is the uncertainty as to what actually distinguishes prophetic eschatology from apocalyptic eschatology. Hanson suggests that the critical point lies in whether the vision of the future can be integrated with the events of ordinary life or whether that vision requires a more or less complete break with ordinary history.[28] Yet his ability to find such distinctions in biblical literature depends on a rather tenuous reinterpretation and restructuring of that literature. Barker suggests that the feature which led normative Judaism to accept Daniel and to reject the apocalyptic writers was the absence of apocalyptic eschatology in Daniel. While she is not explicit on the point, she apparently means by "apocalyptic eschatology" the apocalyptic writers' denial of God's activity in ordinary history.[29] On that basis there is no apocalyptic in the Old Testament, and the question might even be raised about the New Testament book whose name "The Apocalypse" has given a label to the whole enterprise!

Prophecy and Apocalyptic

From about 1960 until about 1980 the trend was to see the apocalyptic understanding as a more-or-less direct descendant of prophecy. The only serious attempt to root apocalyptic elsewhere was made by von Rad in his positing of wisdom as the originating source. Yet the complete lack of any future orientation in wisdom literature tended to make this suggestion questionable from the outset. Indeed, as Peter von der Osten-Sacken argues, it may be that both apocalypticism and the late

25. Von Rad, *Old Testament Theology,* 2:303–5. Cf. also idem, *Wisdom in Israel,* trans. J. D. Martin (Nashville: Abingdon; London: SCM, 1972), especially the excursus on "The Divine Determination of Times," 263–83.

26. R. P. Carroll, "Second Isaiah and the Failure of Prophecy," *ST* 32 (1978): 125.

27. Pannenberg, "Redemptive Event," 23.

28. P. D. Hanson, "Apocalypticism," *IDBSup,* 32.

29. Barker, "Slippery Words III. Apocalyptic"; Davies, "Eschatology in the Book of Daniel," 33–53.

forms of wisdom are dependent on the prophets' vision of God as both Lord of history and Creator of nature.[30] At any rate, von Rad's position was not taken very seriously until the too-facile connection with prophecy began to be called into question after 1980 (see below).

While Jürgen Moltmann does not make a major issue of proving that apocalypticism, and particularly its eschatology, came from the prophets, nonetheless his *Theology of Hope* does much to define such a derivation and make it credible. It may well be that his arguments are the more convincing because he is not attempting to prove a case on that point. He does insist that the entire Old Testament was eschatological in that it looked to the fulfillment of greater and greater promises.[31] If that point is correct, as I think it is, then the apocalyptist's basic orientation, although on a different level than the prophet's, is still of the same order. Furthermore, when Moltmann describes later (eschatological) prophecy as marked by a refusal to lose hope in God in the face of his judgments, with instead a projection of that hope out to the ultimate bounds of existence,[32] he again shows that apocalyptic is not doing something completely different from prophecy. Indeed, "in apocalyptic the whole cosmos becomes interpreted in the light of truth learned from God's revelation in Israel's history."[33] In the end, Moltmann's conviction that apocalyptic is a legitimate extension of prophecy brings him to the point of insisting that their vision is correct: all of history is under God's "no"; the only hope is in a future of God that will be radically discontinuous with present reality.[34]

Moltmann's connection of prophecy and apocalyptic is, however, somewhat too easy. Even if one accepts that the two ways of looking at the world have the same starting point and share a similar concern, there are still significant discontinuities between them.[35] In the early 1970s, three different kinds of synthetic study appeared, each of which underlined this same point. Koch surveys the literature and concludes, among other things, that "the era of the easy theory of the prophetic connection will one day come to an end."[36] Leon Morris summarizes the main features of apocalyptic, and in so doing, he too notes the dis-

---

30. P. von der Osten-Sacken, *Die Apokalyptik in ihrem Verhältnis zu Prophetie und Weisheit*, Theologische Existenz heute 157 (Munich: Chr. Kaiser, 1969), 60.

31. J. Moltmann, *Theology of Hope*, trans. J. W. Leitch (New York: Harper & Row; London: SCM, 1967), 124, 126.

32. Ibid., 132.

33. Ibid., 137.

34. Ibid., 229; cf. also Koch, *Rediscovery*, 108; Tupper, "Revival of Apocalyptic," 300.

35. As already maintained by Rowley, *Relevance* (1963), 15. Cf. also Russell, *Method and Message*, 91.

36. Koch, *Rediscovery*, 130.

tinctions from prophecy at point after point.[37] The most comprehensive of the three studies is that of Walter Schmithals.[38] In his chapter on the relationship of Old Testament and apocalyptic, he systematically notes points of agreement and then moves on to indicate what are to him fundamental differences. Among the commonalities are: the same understanding of existence—historical; the same concept of God—Lord of history; the same view of humanity—historical possibility; the same conceptualization of time—linear progression toward a goal.[39]

These are fundamental similarities, but they are also exceedingly general, as becomes obvious when Schmithals begins to list the distinctions. First of all is the apocalyptic writers' own sense of discontinuity with the past. They are bearers of a completely new revelation that has not even been thought of in the Old Testament witnesses.[40] Coupled with this is the radical pessimism about this aeon. There is no sense in which this creation will be cleansed and redeemed (contra Rom. 8:19–23). Since there is nothing good about this age, there is no historical responsibility and no salvation in history. Historical activity is thus replaced by historical knowledge concerning the meaning and outcome of historical events.[41] Schmithals sums up his findings succinctly:

> Apocalyptic thinks historically in principle, . . . but it despairs of history itself. . . . In the apocalypticist's conviction that he stands at the end of history there is expressed therefore the hopeful, joyous assurance that history is coming to its end—an attitude utterly impossible for the Old Testament.[42]

Schmithals's statement raises concern that he has said too much. First, he makes it appear that the Old Testament knows nothing of any salvation beyond historical salvation. Second, he implies (and later makes explicit) that apocalyptic is a decline, a retreat from the insights of prophecy.[43] Both of these points of view are open to serious modification.

In the first place, Schmithals can limit the Old Testament to salvation within history only by denying that postexilic prophecy is consistent with the Old Testament.[44] One can only marvel at such a tour de

37. L. Morris, *Apocalyptic* (Grand Rapids: Eerdmans; London: Inter-Varsity, 1972), 31, 34, 42, 60, 63, etc.

38. W. Schmithals, *The Apocalyptic Movement: Introduction and Interpretation*, trans. J. E. Steely (Nashville: Abingdon, 1975).

39. Ibid., 73–77.

40. Ibid., 70.

41. Ibid., 80–82.

42. Ibid., 88.

43. Ibid., 132.

44. Ibid., 79, 80.

force. Unfortunately it is not possible merely to dismiss data that undercut one's conclusions. By what right does Schmithals exclude parts of the canonical Old Testament from the Old Testament? Indeed, some features in the Old Testament writings exhibit more of a transition than Schmithals seems willing to recognize. Georg Fohrer mentions several of these transitional features in his analysis of Isaiah 40–55: a distinction between the old and new ages, the belief in the imminent change from the old to the new, the desire to escape history, and the belief that salvation will become eternal with the dawn of this new age.[45] Without automatically agreeing with the details of the phrasing, one can accept the broad outlines of Fohrer's observations. To suggest that genuine Old Testament thought knows nothing of a salvation that extends beyond ordinary history is insupportable.

This raises the further question: Is Old Testament prophetic teaching so thoroughly wedded to a salvation within history that any thought of salvation extending beyond history must be seen as a decline leading to eventual death? Schmithals is by no means alone in such an assertion. Von Rad believes that prophecy died with Ezra, whereas Cross sees its demise along with kingship in Zerubbabel.[46] R. P. Carroll sees the end as being implicit in, of all places, "II Isaiah," whom others have called the greatest of the prophets. Nevertheless, Carroll argues that it contains "grandiose predictions" couched in "empty rhetoric which fail miserably."[47]

Once more it appears that the descriptions are too small for the phenomena. Was prophecy really limited to a restrictive, narrow view of salvation and existence? Have not scholars overemphasized the historical aspect of Hebrew religion? Undoubtedly, the Old Testament's recognition of the significance of this world as the arena of God's self-revelation is of great importance. To say, however, that this is all the prophets recognized and that any extension beyond our history is a departure from the faith looks suspiciously dependent on a modern view of reality with its bifurcation between history and meaning. In this respect, Moltmann's interpretation of the nature of the prophetic movement seems much more true to the totality of the data. On the one hand, by what right are Haggai, Zechariah, and Malachi labeled less "prophetic" than Amos or Hosea? On the other hand, note the vi-

---

45. G. Fohrer, *Introduction to the Old Testament,* trans. D. Green (Nashville: Abingdon, 1968; London: SPCK, 1970), 383.

46. Von Rad, *Old Testament Theology,* 2:297; F. M. Cross, "New Directions in the Study of Apocalyptic," *JTC* 6 (1969): 157–65.

47. Carroll, "Second Isaiah," 126. From the intensity of the language used, one cannot help but feel that Carroll derives pleasure from debunking what virtually all other critics have called a masterpiece.

sionary language of Habakkuk 3 or Joel 3 or Jeremiah 31 or Ezekiel 36–38. Shall these be called "grandiose predictions" and "empty rhetoric"? No simple isolation of the historical from the extrahistorical can be made. The prophets knew a God who, although revealed in the cosmos, yet transcended the cosmos. Thus, although God's salvation was demonstrated and explained in terms of human historical experience, it became increasingly clear that that experience was finally inadequate to reveal the whole scope of God's salvific intent. This is not an escape from history, nor a denial of the lessons learned from it. Rather, eschatological prophecy is a projection of those lessons, an extension of them, onto a broader plane.[48] Thus Malachi is not a denial of historical responsibility; rather it argues that salvation within history is but part of God's ultimate plan (e.g., 2:17–3:7).[49] Thus, if we disagree with Moltmann in his seeming to say that prophetic eschatology leads straight into apocalyptic eschatology, we must disagree even more forcefully with Schmithals when he seems to say that apocalyptic eschatology, while spawned by prophetic eschatology, represents at the end a completely different understanding of salvation.

Myth and Apocalyptic

For those who have explored the mechanisms leading from prophetic eschatology to apocalyptic eschatology, the contributions of Cross have been especially important.[50] He has argued that it was eschatological prophecy's reintroduction of myth into the mainstream of Hebrew thought that prepared the way for the apocalyptic vision.[51] According to this thesis, the exilic and postexilic prophets, faced with the failure of salvation in history, appropriated the various myths of creation and of the Divine Warrior that had been latent in Israel but

48. So H. D. Preuss, *Jahweglaube und Zukunftserwartung*, BWANT 87 (Stuttgart: Kohlhammer, 1968), esp. 205–14.

49. For other studies showing developmental connections between the theologies of the prophets and apocalypticism, see L. C. Allen, "Some Prophetic Antecedents of Apocalyptic Eschatology and Their Hermeneutic Value," *Ex Auditu* 6 (1990): 15–28; R. J. Bauckham, "The Rise of Apocalyptic," *Themelios* 3 (1978): 10–23; R. E. Clements, "The Interpretation of Prophecy and the Origin of Apocalyptic," *Baptist Quarterly* (1989 supplement): 28–34; K. Koch, "Is Daniel among the Prophets?" *Int* 39 (1985): 117–30; B. Otzen, "Himmelrejser og himmelvisioner i jodisk Apokalyptik," *Dansk teologisk tidsskrift* 58 (1995): 16–26; J. C. VanderKam, "Recent Studies in Apocalyptic," *Word and World* 4 (1984): 70–77; B. Vawter, "Apocalyptic: Its Relation to Prophecy," *CBQ* 22 (1960): 33–46.

50. In addition to Cross, "New Directions," see also his "Divine Warrior in Israel's Early Cult," in *Biblical Motifs: Origins and Transformations*, ed. A. Altmann (Cambridge, Mass.: Harvard University Press, 1966), 11–30; idem, "The Song of the Sea and Canaanite Myth," *JTC* 5 (1968): 1–25.

51. Cross, "New Directions," 165 n. 23.

somewhat suppressed. They did this, he argues, in order to transfer their hope from the disappointing historical plane to the cosmic plane, where it was not subject to disproof.[52] Whether this suggestion is supportable will be treated below. Nonetheless, its impact through Cross's students has been notable, at least in the United States. The best-known of these is Paul Hanson, with his book *The Dawn of Apocalyptic*.[53] There Hanson proposes that the origins of apocalyptic are to be found in the immediate postexilic community as represented by Third Isaiah, Haggai, and Zechariah. The causes of these origins are to be found in Second Isaiah's eschatological vision, which utilized mythical motifs in such a way that a group of visionary followers grew up who were opposed to the rebuilding of the temple that Ezekiel's followers were carrying out. As the realists became more powerful, the visionaries retreated more into an apocalyptic hope. As seen in Ezra and the Chronicler, however, the realists' triumph was eventually complete and the visionary group died out. Nevertheless, its particular vision was preserved in the books mentioned above so that it resurfaced on a national scale in the dark days of the Seleucids and the Hasmoneans.

Another student of Cross, W. R. Millar, brings the same outlook to the study of Isaiah 24–27 and arrives at much the same results, although he does not make as much of the supposed sociological conflict as does Hanson. He concludes that the chapters stem from the period immediately following the exile and represent a new openness to mythic themes in response to the crises of the times.[54] Thus, in the United States at least, the most influential opinion came to be that the apocalyptic vision grew directly out of prophetic eschatology.

> As historical and social conditions made it increasingly difficult to identify contemporary individuals and structures with divine agents and end-time realities, as the elect increasingly were deprived of power within social and religious institutions, and as the vision of ancient myth began to offer world-weary individuals a means of resolving the tension between brilliant hopes and bleak realities, the perspective of prophetic eschatology yielded to that of apocalyptic eschatology.[55]

52. So, e.g., in *Canaanite Myth and Hebrew Epic* (Cambridge, Mass: Harvard University Press, 1973), 344–46; cf. also R. P. Carroll, *When Prophecy Failed: Cognitive Dissonance in the Prophetic Traditions of the Old Testament* (New York: Seabury; London: SCM, 1979), 215–18.

53. P. D. Hanson, *The Dawn of Apocalyptic* (Philadelphia: Fortress, 1975).

54. W. R. Millar, *Isaiah 24–27 and the Origin of Apocalyptic*, HSM 11 (Missoula, Mont.: Scholars Press, 1976).

55. Hanson, "Apocalypticism," 30.

But as valuable as these insights are in demonstrating that the eschatological and apocalyptic visions are not incompatible, the way in which the connection is established bristles with difficulties. Among these are: an overemphasis on the later prophets' use of mythical sources; an unwarranted application of the Cosmic Warrior motif; overconfidence in typologies of development, both literary and sociological, resulting in rearrangement of the text with little or no consideration of possible alternative arrangements or explanations; and heavy dependence on hypothetical reconstructions of Israelite society and history.

Hanson and Millar are by no means alone in asserting that the later prophets depended on mythical motifs to expand the concept of God from the too-narrow association with mundane history it had received at the hand of the preexilic prophets.[56] For these authors, however, this assertion becomes a linchpin in their argument that the antihistorical bias of the apocalyptists has its origins in the prophets. But this linchpin is very fragile. Unmistakable references to the ancient Near Eastern myths are few and far between, and none of them appears in anything but a radically altered form. The way in which they are altered is to bring them out of the cosmic, mythic dimension. For instance, Leviathan in Job is no cosmic monster at all, but a figure from within creation that God easily brought under control.[57] To be sure, this is not God acting in human history. But neither is it saying, as the creation myths do, that meaning is found in struggles taking place outside the created order, predetermining what takes place within that order. Even more to the point are Isaiah 27:1 and 51:9–10, where the prophet makes plain that the meaning of the conflict with the serpent is to be found within Israel's history, in the crossing of the Red Sea, and in the coming deliverance from Babylon.[58] There is thus ample reason to assume that these accounts are being used in a literary way and not in any sense as an affirmation of their value as a way of thinking. In particular, the appropriation of mythical thinking is incomprehensible in a prophet like Isaiah, who attacks idolatry with such vehemence.

Furthermore, it is not clear that these scattered allusions to myth are a postexilic phenomenon. At least some studies in the poetry of Job suggest that this book shows features consistent with Israel's earliest po-

---

56. Cf. S. Mowinckel, *He That Cometh*, trans. G. W. Anderson (New York: Abingdon, 1954; Oxford: Blackwell, 1956), 52–95; S. B. Frost, "Eschatology and Myth," *VT* 2 (1952): 70–80; Carroll, *When Prophecy Failed*, 124.

57. Cross, "New Directions," 162.

58. Cf. Ps. 74:12–14 for this same point of view. For a more lengthy discussion of this idea, see my "Myth of the Dragon and Old Testament Faith," *EvQ* 49 (1977): 163–72.

etry, not its latest.[59] The late dating of Isaiah 24–27 has distinctly circular features about it. It is dated according to the appearance of certain "late" elements in it, and then these elements are proved late by their appearance in the "Isaianic apocalypse." R. J. Coggins's comment on this point is especially apropos:

> The supra-historical element appears to me to be present in every section of the book of Isaiah and though we may be more aware of it in some sections than in others, I am very doubtful whether a kind of table can be drawn up to show that the historical sense gradually faded and some other presentation of reality took its place. 2:2–5 and 4:2–6 provide sufficient illustration of this from the first part of the book.[60]

I must also say, despite the massive body of scholarly opinion to the contrary, that it is still true that the supposed postexilic date of Isaiah 40–66 is only hypothetical. Thus the reference to Rahab in Isaiah 51:9, like the reference to Leviathan in 27:1, is not necessarily postexilic. Both may come from a period well before the exile. Indeed, none of the specific allusions to myths comes from any of the three undoubtedly postexilic authors: Haggai, Zechariah, and Malachi. All the examples of this "reappropriation of myth" come from passages whose date is open to serious question.

To sum up this point, the evidence, far from supporting a broadscale return to the thought patterns of myth among postexilic prophets, shows that throughout Israel's history, but especially from the monarchy onward, there were scattered allusions in their literature to what were the dominant literary works of the day. In none of these is there a flight from this world of time and space into a world or timeless reality. Rather, the linguistic forms of myth are used to underscore the same point that all the canonical literature makes: it is in this world where God is to be known—no other.

Some may say, however, that it is not so much these few specific allusions that demonstrate the use of myth as it is the more general appropriation of certain motifs and genres. An example of this is the Cosmic Warrior motif. Cross holds that the later prophets utilize this vehicle to represent God's ultimate conquest of evil.[61] According to Millar the presence of this motif can be recognized by the appearance of the structural elements that have derived from the Canaanite Baal and Anat cycle: threat, war, victory, feast.[62] The extreme generality of

---

59. D. A. Robertson, *Linguistic Evidence in Dating Early Hebrew Poetry,* SBLDS 3 (Missoula, Mont.: Scholars Press, 1972), 155.
60. R. J. Coggins, "The Problem of Isaiah 24–27," *ExpTim* 90 (1978–79): 332.
61. Cross, "Divine Warrior," 30.
62. Millar, *Isaiah 24–27,* 71.

such a structure is obvious. Clearly the presence of these four elements in an account can say little about the genre of a piece or even of its intent. Furthermore, the central truth of the Baal and Anat cycle is that the struggle is played out among deities on a cosmic stage. But Yahweh's struggles, if it is right to call them that, are with recalcitrant humans on an explicitly spatiotemporal stage. Nevertheless, both Hanson and Millar, following Cross, find the Cosmic Warrior motif present in the Old Testament and with increasing prominence in prophetic eschatology.[63] But an examination of the materials they cite raises grave doubts about the applicability of the idea, not to mention questions about its being present at all where they profess to find it.[64]

No one would contest that Yahweh is depicted as a warrior at various places in the Old Testament. But that is just the point. There is no greater incidence of this image in the later prophets than in the earlier. To assert that every representation of him as a warrior indicates a borrowing of the Canaanite motif, especially when his warfare is of another nature (over ethical breaches) and on another plane (the spatiotemporal), is to overreach the evidence.

Hanson cites a number of psalms in which the Cosmic Warrior motif appears.[65] Yet, when they are examined, the elements of the motif are difficult to find. An example is Psalm 9. Here the psalmist asserts that although he has been surrounded by enemies, God has, *from his throne*, issued a righteous judgment against them. There is no threat to God, no march to battle, no struggle with cosmic forces, no triumphal return, and no feast of celebration. Nor is Psalm 9 atypical. Indeed, the one striking feature of most of these psalms is their statement that God has not left his throne.

Millar's use of the motif is equally questionable. He argues that it is central to Isaiah 24–27 and furthermore finds there traces of a ritual procession in which the Divine Warrior's victory was reenacted.[66] While this aspect was not new, having been part of the royal cult, its application to the broad sweep of history by the prophet opened the door for apocalyptic to enter. Yet when Millar looks for the specific elements of the motif, which as already noted are exceedingly general, he cannot find them at several points, and where he professes to find them, they

---

63. Hanson, *Dawn*, 98; Millar, *Isaiah 24–27*, 71ff.

64. Note that while Carroll broadly agrees with Hanson and Cross on the prophetic use of myth, he has grave misgivings about some of the particular usages ("Twilight of Prophecy or Dawn of Apocalyptic," *JSOT* 14 [1978]: 18) as does M. Delcor in his review of Hanson's *Dawn* (*Bib* 57 [1976]: 578).

65. Hanson, *Dawn*, 305–8; Ps. 2, 9, 24, 29, 46, 47, 48, 65, 68, 76, 77, 89, 97, 98, 104, 106, 110.

66. Millar, *Isaiah 24–27*, 82–90; following Cross, "Divine Warrior," 24–27.

are obscure at best. So in his six main segments, the elements of threat and feast are missing in four. In the two where they supposedly appear, they are either insignificant or questionable.[67] For instance, it is difficult to see anything of feast in 27:2–6, which speaks merely of the rejuvenated land. It is also difficult to see how one tricolon of a verse, 27:1c, qualifies as a major thematic element, that of victory, as Millar is forced to apply it.

As stated above, there is no doubt that Yahweh is depicted as a warrior throughout the Old Testament. Nor is there any question that his victory over sin and evil is given the broadest dimensions, particularly in the prophets. I do not see much evidence, however, that Baal's warriorship heavily influenced the Hebrew conception, nor that "late" prophecy, through an increased use of the motif, created an openness for the ahistorical stance of apocalyptic.[68]

Millar and Hanson base much of their claim to have discovered the process by which apocalyptic grew out of late prophecy on a methodology that Hanson calls "contextual-typological." Through the application of a particular style of prosodic analysis and of an evolutionary pattern of social conflict, they profess to be able to put the various portions of the postexilic prophets into their original order. That proposed original order is quite different from both the canonical order and from the various proposals of other scholars. This in itself provokes some questions about the reliability of the proposed method.

The method of prosodic analysis they utilize is the syllable-count approach proposed by Cross and Freedman.[69] Using this method, the authors claim to be able to distinguish documents from as little as thirty years apart on the basis of their prosody.[70] Thus they could completely restructure the text upon their discovery of a "more baroque" style in a sentence or part of a sentence, when that baroque quality might be nothing more than the increase of one or two syllables in a colon.[71] Several reviewers, especially Europeans, express special reserve about this aspect of these studies.[72] Coggins's comment is typical: "In view of our extremely

---

67. Millar, *Isaiah 24–27*, 70, 71.

68. Hanson (*Dawn*, 185) regards Isa. 66:15–16 as containing mythical war language, but such language also appears in Ps. 104, which many relate to Ikhnaton's sun hymn of the fourteenth century B.C. Thus, the use of such language is not necessarily a mark of apocalyptic.

69. For a handy introduction to this system, see D. Stuart, *Studies in Early Hebrew Meter*, HSM 13 (Missoula, Mont.: Scholars Press, 1976). For the contribution of Cross and Freedman, see Stuart, *Studies*, 8–9 and notes.

70. Hanson, *Dawn*, 60.

71. Ibid., 118.

72. So I. Willi-Plein, *VT* 29 (1979): 123; R. Tournay, *RB* 83 (1976): 151, 152; P. R. Ackroyd, *Int* 30 (1976): 413.

limited knowledge of Hebrew language and literature, it [the method] seems to reconstruct a development on gravely inadequate bases. . . . They must not be given more weight than they will bear.[73] Indeed, this entire approach to prosody is now greeted with considerable skepticism.[74]

It is particularly characteristic of Hanson that he brings certain sociological assumptions to bear upon the text. At least one reviewer was unable to refrain from pointing out that the two groups he posits (the priestly realists and the anti-institutional visionaries) have remarkable analogs in the groupings of the 1960s, when Hanson's research was done.[75] Furthermore, it is not at all certain that Max Weber's and Karl Mannheim's programmatic views on class struggle can be imported into the Near East of 2,500 years ago.[76] That Isaiah 56–66 must be completely restructured not only from the canon but from the views of other scholars in order to support the hypothesis suggests the serious possibility that history has been forced onto a procrustean bed of sociological theory.

The polemic in Isaiah 56–66 is no more indicative of a struggle between the "establishment" and the dispossessed than is that in other parts of Scripture, including Isaiah 1–39. Carroll goes so far as to suggest that "mudslinging" was essential to the creation of the biblical traditions.[77] Without going so far as that, one may still recognize that long before the supposed visionary followers of Second Isaiah appeared on the scene, serious charges flew back and forth between prophet and priest, prophet and prophet, prophet and king (Isa. 1 and 7; Hos. 4; Jer. 7 and 28). Nor were these charges addressed merely to sinful individuals. They also included groups and classes (Amos 5 and 6; Isa. 3). Thus the presence of an intense polemic in the latter chapters of Isaiah does not require the hypothesis of a group of the dispossessed to explain it.[78]

But even if the rather large concession were made that some such conflict as Hanson hypothesizes did exist in postexilic Judah, how far toward explaining the rise of apocalypticism would such a hypothesis take us? Not far enough. Even those writers sympathetic to the ideas of Cross and his students find the claims to have established a direct connection between prophecy and apocalyptic to be exaggerated.[79] Rowland puts it this way:

73. Coggins, "Problem of Isaiah," 332.
74. See especially the comments of M. O'Connor, *Hebrew Verse Structure* (Winona Lake, Ind.: Eisenbrauns, 1981), 138, 150.
75. Carroll, "Twilight," 26–27.
76. Hanson, *Dawn,* 21.
77. Carroll, "Twilight," 19.
78. I. Willi-Plein, review of Hanson, *Dawn,* in *VT* 29 (1979): 124–25.
79. J. G. Gammie, review of Hanson, *Dawn,* in *JBL* 95 (1976): 654; W. Roth, "Between Tradition and Expectation: The Origin and Role of Biblical Apocalyptic," *Explor* 4 (1978): 10.

Nevertheless, it would be wrong to suppose that, by recovering the resurgence of certain myths in the eschatology of the visionary group which produced some of the oracles in Third Isaiah, one has necessarily uncovered the essential ingredient in apocalyptic, or even, for that matter, in apocalyptic eschatology.[80]

He goes on to point out that what he considers to be the essential feature of apocalypses, the disclosure of divine secrets in a clearly defined form, is not found in Third Isaiah. Beyond that, he is uncertain that a movement oriented toward redemption by God in some supernatural sphere is really the key to apocalyptic at all.[81]

In brief, this particular effort to explain how the move was made from prophecy to apocalypse, like many others, falls short in the end. That there was a connection seems clear, but precisely what that connection was remains frustrated by a twofold irony: the complexity of the apocalypses themselves,[82] and the paucity of information concerning their origins and originators. As both Gammie and Rowland point out, there are too many additional features in apocalyptic for which the Cross school's hypotheses cannot account.[83] Or as Carroll puts it, "late prophecy contributed a stance that was a necessary condition, but not a sufficient condition, for the development of a full-grown apocalyptic consciousness."[84] In the years between 425 and 175 B.C., over which Hanson glosses all too easily,[85] some critical influences apparently entered the mix, influences that moved the apocalypses of the second century outside the limits of Old Testament faith.

The Apocalyptic Mindset

This recognition that the attempts to find a straight-line connection between prophecy and apocalypticism have failed has spawned a new approach to the problem of derivation since 1980. This new approach has assumed that there is no single dominant ancestor, but that a complex of factors must be sought. Furthermore, it is taken as a given that the evidence of those factors must be sought in the apocalypses themselves. Rowland's *Open Heaven* was the first of the major efforts along these

80. Rowland, *Open Heaven*, 196.
81. Ibid., 197.
82. So Russell, *Divine Disclosure*, 12, has argued that apocalypticism is more of an attitude manifested in various ways than a tightly controlled set of themes or forms.
83. Rowland, *Open Heaven*, 196–97. Gammie, *JBL* 95 (1976): 654, cites H.-P. Müller's *Ursprunge und Strukturen alttestamentlicher Eschatologie*, BZAW 109 (Berlin: Töpelmann, 1969), as a good discussion of elements omitted by Hanson. Schmithals (*Apocalyptic Movement*, 138) had the same criticism of Plöger.
84. Carroll, "Twilight," 31.
85. Hanson, "Apocalyptic," 33.

lines. It was followed shortly by Collins's *Apocalyptic Imagination*. While expressing appreciation for Hanson's study, both make clear that it is necessary to go well beyond his conclusions.

One factor that led in this direction was the discovery of apocalyptic features in several books in the Qumran library. This led to the conclusion that the apocalyptic mentality may have been more a part of the general Jewish outlook than scholars had previously supposed. One of these features is the evidence of *merkavah* material. Visions in which the speaker is taken up to heaven in a chariot (*merkavah*) have been known previously from the rabbinic period, but the evidence from Qumran points to the existence of the material even in pre-Christian Judaism. As early as 1980, Ithamar Gruenwald argued that neither wisdom nor prophecy could account for apocalyptic, and suggested that Jewish mysticism would be a more fertile field of investigation.[86] Although most of the evidence of this mysticism is later than the apocalyptic literature, and may therefore derive from it, the essential similarity with some of the earliest apocalypses such as 1 Enoch suggests that the same mystical motivations may prevail throughout. Likewise, Rowland argues that if anything connects prophecy and apocalypse it is the preoccupation with revelation received by direct divine inspiration.[87] He too notes the continuity with rabbinic mysticism, but takes it to be more a result of the apocalypses than a contributor to them.[88] Nonetheless, both Gruenwald and Rowland articulate the conviction that apocalypticism must be understood more in the light of the Jewish experience of the Seleucid and Hasmonean periods than through a direct connection with the Old Testament canon. This conviction has been pursued further by more recent writers such as Collins, Stephen Cook, and Grabbe.[89] They have all argued in one way or another that apocalypticism is the result of a combination of factors: the eschatological concerns and divine inspiration of classical prophecy, the mantic wisdom of the seer,[90] the passion to know the true meanings of Scripture (coupled with the idea that every figure of speech has a hidden, mysterious meaning),[91] the desire for cer-

---

86. I. Gruenwald, *Apocalyptic and Merkavah Mysticism*, AGJU 14 (Leiden: Brill, 1980), 29.

87. Rowland, *Open Heaven*, 246.

88. Ibid., 348.

89. Collins, *Apocalyptic Imagination*; Cook, *Prophecy and Apocalypticism: The Postexilic Social Setting* (Minneapolis: Fortress, 1995); Grabbe, *Priests, Prophets, Diviners, and Sages: A Socio-Historical Study of Religious Specialists in Ancient Israel* (Valley Forge, Pa.: Trinity Press International, 1995).

90. Rowland in particular sees in a positive light von Rad's suggestion that the wisdom traditions were a significant factor (*Open Heaven*, 202–8).

91. It is a mistake, I believe, to label such use of imagery as mythological thinking, as Collins (*Apocalyptic Imagination*, 15–16) does. Mythology involves much more than the

tainty in uncertain times.[92] It is suggested that all of these and more in differing combinations in different settings came together to produce the unique features of apocalypticism.

In addition, Collins has argued that more attention needs to be paid to the diverse cultural setting in which early Judaism found itself. Thus he calls attention to the potential influence of the Babylonian, Persian, Egyptian, and Hellenistic cultures upon the thinking of the people of Judea. More than perhaps at any other time in its history, Judea found itself the object of a tug-of-war between these conflicting groups and their ideas. Particularly with Judea's own religious views in flux because of the disappearance of the Hebrew kingdom, there is every reason to believe that all these cultures could have had a significant effect on Jewish thought. If it is correct that the imagery and some of the thought patterns of the apocalypses show similarity with that found in the ancient myths, it seems much more likely that the avenue of entry was through this interaction than through any of the prophets.

While both Collins and Rowland agree that multiple influences shaped apocalyptic thinking, both conclude that among the influences, the Persian one may have been the most significant.[93] Neither is able to flesh out his thinking much because of the scantiness of the evidence already mentioned. Some of the apparent analogs are: the periodization of history, eschatological woes, resurrection, and supernatural forces of good and evil.[94] Once again, as pointed out above in regard to supposed parallels with Canaanite myth, these connections seem remarkably general, especially when they are hedged about with questions concerning the date and composition of much of the Persian material.

As agreement has emerged that no one cultural/literary setting accounts for the rise of apocalyptic thinking, so it has also emerged that no single social setting accounts for it either. As noted above, it is no longer believed that this kind of thinking is typical of marginalized subgroups.[95] Again, developing thought about Qumran has played a part here. More and more scholars are convinced that the Qumran library is not the work of a single isolated sect but represents something of a

---

idea that there are invisible realities that have a determinative impact on the visible world. For further discussion, see my "A Myth Is a Myth Is a Myth: Toward a Working Definition," in *A Spectrum of Thought: Essays in Honor of Dennis Kinlaw*, ed. M. L. Peterson (Wilmore, Ky.: Asbury, 1982), 135–45.

92. See also Russell, *Divine Disclosure*, 64.

93. Collins, *Apocalyptic Imagination*, 25; Rowland, *Open Heaven*, 209, in apparent agreement with Plöger.

94. Collins, *Apocalyptic Imagination*, 25.

95. See Grabbe, "Social Setting"; cf. Rowland, *Open Heaven*, 212.

literary cross section of Jewish thinking in the late pre-Christian era.[96] Thus the evidence of apocalypticism there is not the result of an isolated subgroup but represents one strand in the thinking of the community as a whole. Nevertheless, attempts to relate the literature to what we know of the historical events of the period continue to be frustrated by the fragmentary nature of the material available.

Canonicity and Apocalyptic

If it is true that prophecy is not the direct antecedent of apocalyptic, what shall we say about the appearance of the books of Daniel and Revelation in the Hebrew and Christian canons? Why do these two appear and not others? Indeed, why does Daniel appear at all, if apocalypticism is not the true descendant of prophecy?[97] Earlier writers such as Rowley argued that Daniel was the transition between prophetic eschatology and truly apocalyptic eschatology.[98] More recently the discovery of portions of 1 Enoch at Qumran dated late in the third century b.c. has called Rowley's argument into question and thus also the scholarly consensus that the final form of Daniel must date after 169 b.c. This evidence is especially interesting since 1 Enoch shows less of an eschatological coloration than many of the apocalypses, and certainly less than Daniel. If anything, these findings make the inclusion of Daniel in the canon even more difficult to understand. On the other hand, if one could grant that Daniel is not pseudonymous,[99] then Rowley's arguments are not called into question by the Qumran findings. If Daniel is the precursor to the other apocalypses, this could well explain why it lacks many of the features they include.[100] In this sense, it may be that Daniel pushed the limits of visionary revelation as found in the prophets to their farthest extreme consistent with the Old Testament view of history. Beyond that the community may not have felt it was possible to go. This same explanation might apply if the 169 b.c. date for Daniel were accepted, but it seems much more difficult to understand why the community should have recognized this example of apocalypse as authoritative while rejecting the others. The late date for Daniel also makes it difficult to explain how one gets from Zechariah to 1 Enoch.

96. N. Golb, *Who Wrote the Dead Sea Scrolls? The Search for the Secret of Qumran* (New York: Scribner, 1995), 382–83; L. H. Schiffman, *Reclaiming the Dead Sea Scrolls* (New York: Doubleday, 1995), 33–35.

97. What Revelation is doing in the NT may be left to the NT scholars.

98. Rowley, *Relevance*, 37ff.

99. Were the others excluded because of their obvious pseudonymity?

100. See the comments of Barker ("Slippery Words III. Apocalyptic") and Davies ("Eschatology in the Book of Daniel") referred to above.

For even if one grants that the visions of Zechariah have an apocalyptic flavor, they are still far from being an example of apocalyptic literature. Thus it appears that no straight line can be drawn between Zechariah and 1 Enoch.[101] There is a breach not only in time but in thought. The books of Daniel and Revelation seem to be adaptations of apocalyptic thought in that both are firmly rooted in the call to faithful living now in the light of what is to come. Perhaps this feature causes them to be included in the Jewish and Christian canons while other examples of the genre are excluded.

Conclusion

As is evident, study of apocalyptic during the last three decades has wrestled with the question of the relationship between prophecy and apocalyptic. In general, the conclusion has been that while there is an undoubted connection, apocalyptic thought is more of a mutation than a logical development. This conclusion seems to be supported by the fact that apocalyptic, in its narrow sense, holds that God's work in current history is hidden in inscrutable predetermination, while it retains the conviction that human events have no meaning apart from the ultimate purposes of God. Furthermore, if apocalyptic is the logical development of prophecy, one would expect the earlier stage to fall by the wayside. In fact, this does not happen; for the New Testament, while clearly availing itself of the expanded imagery and thought forms of apocalyptic, equally clearly retains a point of view fully consonant with Old Testament prophecy: God is at work in a creation essentially good, intending to transform that creation through the faithful response of persons who will own his kingship in their day-to-day behavior. To be sure, God will bring his work to a final consummation at the end of time, but it will be a consummation of his work in history, and not a rejection of history.[102] This consonance between the Old and New Testament points of view suggests that the apocalyptic understanding did

101. So Carroll, "Twilight," 30; Willi-Plein, *VT* 29 (1979): 126–27.

102. Russell notes how little of the NT, relatively speaking, betrays an apocalyptic outlook (*Divine Disclosure*, 130–31). Whatever the apocalyptic expectations of the community may have been, its literature, formulated within the first and second Christian generations, shows that the community retained, along with those expectations, an expectation that transformation of persons and institutions in this world was a real possibility through the power of the Holy Spirit imparted by the risen Jesus Christ. Holding that the mark of apocalypse is visionary experience resulting in direct revelation, Rowland (*Open Heaven*, 356, etc.) argues that much of the NT betrays an outlook completely compatible with the Jewish outlook of the same time. See also Collins, *Apocalyptic Imagination*, 207ff., for the argument that the Christian doctrine of Christ's resurrection, which permeates the NT, is fundamentally apocalyptic in nature.

not replace the prophetic one but rather existed beside it, enriching and expanding it, but never supplanting it. If prophecy argued for the reality of this world and for the responsibility of humans to live responsibly in it in response to the grace of the God who is the Lord of history, the canonical apocalyptic vision argued that we could continue to live responsibly even when the short-term outcomes did not seem to support that decision. We could do so secure in the knowledge that although history is real, it is not all there is to reality. Beyond all that we know, God is real, and he will achieve his purposes. Thus the apocalyptic understanding does not replace the prophetic one but complements it.

14

Religion in Ancient Israel

Bill T. Arnold

Developments in the study of Israelite religion over the past three decades reflect the changes that occurred on the face of Old Testament studies more generally. The turbulent 1960s witnessed significant paradigm shifts in many areas of theological studies, and these shifts are reflected in biblical scholarship as well. The intense interest in a specifically biblical theology approach waned during that decade and the demise of the biblical theology movement may be traced to numerous internal and external pressures.[1] But in point of fact, the biblical theology movement never ceased as a productive movement; it spawned several important works on topics traditionally classified as biblical theology all through the 1970s and 1980s to the present.[2] Rather, the change occurred in the prestige that biblical theology had among the other disciplines. It ceased to wield the kind of authority and persuasive power it had enjoyed since the end of World War II.[3] Concurrent with the demise of biblical theology, if it should even be called such, was a renewed interest in the history of religions, and specifically for our purposes here, a renewed interest in the history of ancient Israelite religion.

I express my appreciation to Daniel E. Fleming, Theodore J. Lewis, and Brent A. Strawn for reading and making helpful suggestions on the manuscript.
  1. B. S. Childs, *Biblical Theology in Crisis* (Philadelphia: Westminster, 1970), 61–87.
  2. For a survey of the contributions during this period, see R. W. L. Moberly's essay in the present volume, chap. 16.
  3. J. Barr, "The Theological Case against Biblical Theology," in *Canon, Theology, and Old Testament Interpretation: Essays in Honor of Brevard S. Childs*, ed. G. M. Tucker, D. L. Petersen, and R. R. Wilson (Philadelphia: Fortress, 1988), 3–5. The process was much slower in Germany (see R. Albertz, *A History of Israelite Religion in the Old Testament Period*, vol. 1, *From the Beginnings to the End of the Monarchy*, trans. J. Bowden, OTL [Louisville: Westminster/John Knox; London: SCM, 1994], 1–12).

I offer here a survey of significant contributions on the history of Israelite religion during this period, followed by brief discussions of selected major topics. Finally, I make suggestions for future work on the
history of ancient Israel's religion.

Trends and Methodologies of the Past Three Decades

Several developments in European and North American scholarship
converged during the 1960s to set the stage for the current recrudes-
cence of interest in the history of Israelite religion. The paradigm shift
is marked by new epigraphic and archaeological evidence from the ancient Near East, combined with renewed calls to reexamine older evidence available from earlier excavations. Important monographs by
Klaus Koch, Rolf Rendtorff, and Claus Westermann appeared in Germany calling for a renewed investigation of these comparative materials and offering methodological suggestions for the work. During the
1960s, other scholars offered surveys of the history of Israel's religion,
though no clear consensus emerged (among these were T. C. Vriezen,
Helmer Ringgren, Georg Fohrer, and Werner H. Schmidt).[4] Just before
the dawn of the period under investigation here, William F. Albright offered his last book-length contribution on this subject in an important
survey of Canaanite and other comparative materials.[5]

Though a new period of investigation was burgeoning, the methodologies used during the past three decades have been mostly unchanged
from those of previous generations of scholars. Many continue to utilize the comparative method for setting Israel against its ancient Near
Eastern backdrop. I shall emphasize especially the sweeping studies of
Frank Moore Cross and Mark S. Smith in which the texts from Ugarit
are of paramount importance, and several more specialized studies on
topics such as the cult of the dead. Others have pursued the history of
Israelite religion along the lines of a traditio-historical approach to the
biblical texts, combined in the case of Rainer Albertz with innovative
sociological observations.[6] But in large measure, the discipline has
hardly advanced beyond the lines of the older differentiation between

4. For a summary of developments in the 1960s, see P. D. Miller, "Israelite Religion,"
in *The Hebrew Bible and Its Modern Interpreters,* ed. D. A. Knight and G. M. Tucker (Philadelphia: Fortress; Chico, Calif.: Scholars Press, 1985), 206–8.

5. *Yahweh and the Gods of Canaan: An Historical Analysis of Two Conflicting Faiths*
(Garden City, N.Y.: Doubleday; London: Athlone, 1968).

6. In some cases, scholars have taken a more distinctly social-science approach (N. K.
Gottwald, *The Tribes of Yahweh: A Sociology of the Religion of Liberated Israel, 1250–1050*
B.C.E. [Maryknoll, N.Y.: Orbis, 1979; London: SCM, 1980]), or a feminist approach (T.
Frymer-Kensky, *In the Wake of the Goddesses: Women, Culture, and the Biblical Transfor-
mation of Pagan Myth* [New York: Free Press, 1992]).

the American archaeological school (Albright, Bright, etc.) and the German traditio-historical approach (Alt, Noth).

Standing as a benchmark near the beginning of this period is the significant volume by Cross, which advances our understanding of Israelite religion unlike any other work since Albrecht Alt.[7] Cross did not intend to present a systematic reconstruction of Israelite religion, but rather produced preliminary studies addressing unsolved problems in the description of Israel's religious development.[8] At the beginning of his work, Cross articulated several barriers that he believed obstructed progress toward a new synthesis of Israel's religion. These were, first, the overwhelming nature of the burgeoning archaeological evidence, the sheer mass of which had thrown the field into chaos. The second barrier was the obstinate survival of remnants of the "idealistic synthesis initiated by Wilhelm Vatke and given classic statement by Julius Wellhausen." Cross is often in agreement with Wellhausen's penetrating insights on the text, while wanting to disassociate himself from the German doyen's basic assumptions and overall approach. The third barrier Cross identified was the tendency of scholars "to overlook or suppress continuities between the early religion of Israel and the Canaanite (or Northwest Semitic) culture from which it emerged." Cross rejected the radical uniqueness of Israel stressed by earlier biblical theologians, and presented the definitive statement of the influence of Canaanite cultic tradition on early Israelite religion.[9]

Central to Cross's approach is his distinction between the Canaanite cosmogonic myth and the Israelite epic cycle, which was associated with covenant rites in early Israel. This epic cycle was created under the impact of historical experiences, but was shaped by the shared mythic patterns and language of Canaan. Thus the Hebrew epic had both a historical (horizontal) stance and a mythopoeic (vertical) dimension. Cross opts for "epic" rather than "historical" because the epic narrative relates the interaction of both the people and the deity through time. In this sense, the term *historical* is not an illegitimate designation for the Hebrew epic. The confusion arises because "historical" narrative usually refers more narrowly to human actors.[10]

7. F. M. Cross, *Canaanite Myth and Hebrew Epic: Essays in the History of the Religion of Israel* (Cambridge, Mass.: Harvard University Press, 1973); and see A. Alt's classic work *Der Gott der Väter*, BWANT 3.12 (Stuttgart: Kohlhammer, 1929); reprinted in *Kleine Schriften zur Geschichte des Volkes Israel*, vol. 1 (Munich: Beck, 1953), 1–78; and in translation as "The God of the Fathers," in *Essays on Old Testament History and Religion*, trans. R. A. Wilson (Garden City, N.Y.: Doubleday, 1968), 3–86.

8. Cross, *Canaanite Myth*, vii.

9. Ibid., vii–viii. See also idem, "Alphabets and Pots: Reflections on Typological Method in the Dating of Human Artifacts," *Maarav* 3.2 (1982): 130–31.

10. Cross, *Canaanite Myth*, viii.

Furthermore, Israel's choice of epic (over a mythic) genre is significant both for its illustration of Israel's continuity with Canaanite culture and for its uniqueness. For, as Cross reminds us, the epic genre was also well attested in Canaanite religious literature, though it was of marginal interest. According to Cross, the implications are clear: "Israel's choice of the epic form to express religious reality, and the elevation of this form to centrality in their cultic drama, illustrates both the linkage of the religion of Israel to its Canaanite past and the appearance of novelty in Israel's peculiar religious concern with the 'historical.'"[11]

After a penetrating and judicious survey of the ancient Near Eastern epigraphic evidence and the relevant biblical texts pertaining to Canaanite and early Israelite religion, Cross agrees generally with Alt's earlier assessment of patriarchal religion as a type of personal clan religion. He argues, however, that the patriarchs worshiped the high god of Canaan (i.e., El), as opposed to Alt's view that the patriarchs worshiped various anonymous deities to whom names such as El Shaddai, El Elyon, El Olam, and so on were given after the settlement in Canaan. Cross emphasized the continuity between Canaanite El and Israelite Yahweh, concluding that "Yahweh" was originally a cultic name of El. Many of the traits and features of El appear as functions of Yahweh in the earliest traditions of Israel, though Yahwism "split off from El in the radical differentiation" of the cult of early Israel.[12] Further, Yahwism absorbed and transformed many of the Canaanite mythic elements relating to Baal until the ninth century B.C., at which time "a less wholesome syncretism" emerged. Yahwism began to give way to the popular cult of Baal, and the prophetic movement, begun with Elijah, may be defined as a battle against this syncretism.[13] Thus Yahweh was primarily a Canaanite El figure, though many of the features that distinguished him from El were adapted from Baal mythic

11. Ibid., ix. See also idem, "Epic Traditions of Early Israel: Epic Narrative and the Reconstruction of Early Israelite Institutions," in *The Poet and the Historian: Essays in Literary and Historical Criticism*, ed. R. E. Friedman, HSS 26 (Chico, Calif.: Scholars Press, 1983), 13–19; see also J. J. M. Roberts, "Myth versus History," *CBQ* 38 (1976): 1–13. On Israelite historiography as a historicizing of older poetic epic, a confluence of poetic epic and historical chronicle, see D. Damrosch, *The Narrative Covenant: Transformations of Genre in the Growth of Biblical Literature* (San Francisco: Harper & Row, 1987); and for speculation on the transformation from myth to epic, see B. F. Batto, *Slaying the Dragon: Mythmaking in the Biblical Tradition* (Louisville: Westminster/John Knox, 1992), 41–72.

12. Cross, *Canaanite Myth*, 71. On the basis of terms describing the gods and their world in Ugaritic literature that are also used to describe Yahweh in the OT, M. C. A. Korpel concluded that Israel's religion is the result of a schism within the religion of Canaan (*A Rift in the Clouds: Ugaritic and Hebrew Descriptions of the Divine* [Münster: Ugarit-Verlag, 1990], 621–35).

13. Cross, *Canaanite Myth*, 190–94.

images. This association with Baal elements resulted in the subsequent syncretism that became the object of prophetic scorn. Cross's reconstruction of the religion of Israel has earned acceptance among many Old Testament scholars. The enduring significance of his contributions may be illustrated by the important *Festschriften* his students and friends have published, which contain many articles devoted to this subject.[14]

The impressive work of Mark S. Smith also takes up the comparative Canaanite material, though with several different results.[15] He surveys the data gleaned from the Canaanite (Ugaritic) religious literature in light of the consensus among biblical scholars that the gods of Ugarit (El, Asherah, Baal, Anat, and the solar deity) were Canaanite, not Israelite, deities. Scholars following Albright had assumed that early Israel was essentially monolatrous (worshiping only Yahweh, although not denying the existence of other deities). This consensus considered Canaanite influences on ancient Israel to be syncretistic and outside "normative" Israelite religion, and scholars often used the distinction between "popular religion" and "official religion" to explain away such influences.[16] Smith contends, however, that the new epigraphic and archaeological evidence since Albright calls this consensus into question. He argues that Israelite culture was largely Canaanite in nature: "Baal and Asherah were part of Israel's Canaanite heritage, and the process of the emergence of Israelite monolatry was an issue of Israel's breaking with its own Canaanite past and not simply one of avoiding Canaanite neighbors."[17] Smith avers that religious pluralism in ancient Israel led to conflict about the nature of correct Yahwistic practice, and this conflict in turn "produced the differentiation of Israelite religion from its Canaanite heritage during the second half of the monarchy."[18] Thus he rejects the consensus view (of Albright, Cross, and others) of a syncre-

---

14. B. Halpern and J. D. Levenson, eds., *Traditions in Transformation: Turning Points in Biblical Faith* (Winona Lake, Ind.: Eisenbrauns, 1981); P. D. Miller Jr., P. D. Hanson, and S. D. McBride, eds., *Ancient Israelite Religion: Essays in Honor of Frank Moore Cross* (Philadelphia: Fortress, 1987).

15. M. S. Smith, *The Early History of God: Yahweh and the Other Deities in Ancient Israel* (San Francisco: Harper & Row, 1990); idem, "Yahweh and Other Deities in Ancient Israel: Observations on Old Problems and Recent Trends," in *Ein Gott allein? JHWH-Verehrung und biblischer Monotheismus im Kontext der israelitischen und altorientalischen Religionsgeschichte*, ed. W. Dietrich and M. A. Klopfenstein, OBO 139 (Göttingen: Vandenhoeck & Ruprecht; Freibourg, Switzerland: Universitätsverlag, 1994), 197–234. For a different perspective on the impact of the discoveries at Ugarit, see O. Loretz, *Ugarit und die Bibel: Kanaanäische Götter und Religion im Alten Testament* (Darmstadt: Wissenschaftliche Buchgesellschaft, 1990).

16. Smith, *Early History*, xix–xx.

17. Ibid., xxiii.

18. Ibid., xxxi.

tistic tendency in Israel, beginning especially in the ninth century. Rather than syncretism, Smith refers to a "differentiation" of Israelite cult from its Canaanite heritage, a differentiation apparently beginning in the ninth century.[19]

Smith contends that the consensus opinion has crumbled because of significant changes in scholarly perspective due to epigraphic and archaeological advances made in the years since Albright's *Yahweh and the Gods of Canaan* (1968). He outlines four changes as follows: First, Israel's cultural identity was Canaanite, as evidenced by a large stock of shared religious terminology.[20] Second, the understanding of Israel as a Canaanite culture has meant a reevaluation of the nature of the Yahwistic cult. Baal and Asherah were part of Israel's Canaanite heritage. There was no religious syncretism of a native Israelite cult with pagan Canaanite practices during the ninth century as the Bible portrays, and as the older scholarly consensus assumed. Third, greater significance has been credited to the monarchy for its role in the development of Yahwism. The monarchy fostered the convergence of other deities and their cultic features in exalting Yahweh as the national god during the first half of its existence (down to ca. 722 B.C.). During the second half of the monarchy (ca. 722 to 587), religious programs (especially those of Hezekiah and Josiah) led to the differentiation of Israelite religion from its Canaanite roots, and led to the eventual emergence of monotheism during the exile. Fourth, recent interest in ancient goddesses and their roles in the Israelite cult has led to greater scholarly scrutiny of the roles of such deities in Israelite religion.[21]

Many scholars working on the history of Israelite religion may be surprised to learn that these changes are *required* by "major epigraphic and archaeological discoveries" since 1968. There is no doubt that scholarly perspective has changed over the past few decades. But it is a non sequitur to say the changes are required by new epigraphic evidence since Albright,[22] and it is certainly an overstatement to claim that "the data illuminating the religion of Israel have changed substantially in the last twenty years."[23] Most of the changes Smith outlines are due more to a shifting scholarly climate and new interpretations of older data in light of this new climate than to new discoveries.[24] This may be described as a general new wave of scholarly minimalism or

19. Ibid., xxiv.
20. Ibid., 2.
21. Ibid., xxii–xxvii.
22. Ibid., xxi.
23. Ibid., xxii.
24. That is not to deny that there have been a few important epigraphic discoveries since 1970, as discussed below.

neo-nihilism. The second change Smith mentions (the Canaanite nature of early Yahwism) grows logically from the first (the Canaanite-Israelite continuum), and the first is tied to developments happening in the larger study of Israel's history, which are sometimes quite minimalistic and still very much open to question.[25] The third of Smith's "changes in scholarly perspective" (i.e., the role of the monarchy in Israel's religion) is a matter of reinterpreting the biblical record. This part of his presentation simply applies his assumptions in points one and two (Israel was Canaanite, and her cult was initially polytheistic) to the biblical story line. Israel during the judges period knew three, possibly four, deities (El, Asherah, Yahweh, and possibly Baal).[26] These deities or features of their cults converged into a national Yahwism during the first half of the monarchy, and monolatry emerged during the second half of the monarchy by the process of differentiation. The fourth change (greater interest in ancient goddesses) is a matter of vacillating scholarly interests. Smith admits "the relative paucity of primary material bearing on goddesses in ancient Israel"[27] but refers to recent interest and greater scrutiny of the ancient sources for information on their role in Israel's religion. Most of these changes have more to do with shifting scholarly opinion and new interpretations of older data than with new archaeological evidence that requires such constructions (notwithstanding the "Yahweh and his asherah/Asherah" inscriptions; see discussion of Kuntillet ʿAjrud and Khirbet el-Qôm below).

In addition to these comparative approaches, other scholars have taken up the study of theophoric personal names from Palestine as the starting point for investigating ancient Israelite religion. The important work of Jeffrey Tigay surveys the evidence of divine elements in proper names in Hebrew epigraphic documents.[28] His work illustrates the overwhelming preponderance of Yahwistic names (i.e., names that have Yahweh as their theophoric element) in ancient Israel and the relative paucity of non-Yahwistic names. On the basis of this evidence, Tigay argues that Israel was monotheistic (or at least monolatrous) during the monarchy, and that Baal was worshiped briefly and Asherah not at all in Israel. The problems of historical and religious reconstructions based on personal names are well known, and Tigay has come under

25. See the essays by K. Lawson Younger Jr. (chap. 7) and Gary N. Knoppers (chap. 8) in the present volume.
26. Smith, *Early History*, 22. This is based largely on a faulty understanding of Gen. 49:25e (see the review of T. J. Lewis in *JITC* 18 [1990–91]: 158–59).
27. *Early History*, xxvi.
28. J. H. Tigay, *You Shall Have No Other Gods: Israelite Religion in the Light of Hebrew Inscriptions*, HSS 31 (Atlanta: Scholars Press, 1986).

criticism in some quarters.[29] Nonetheless, his volume is suggestive, and the evidence from such names probably reflects what we may call "normative" religion in ancient Israel.

In addition to Tigay's seminal study of epigraphic documents, others have studied personal names in the biblical text in light of their significance for Israel's religion. Using a less rigorous methodology, Johannes de Moor has calculated theophoric personal names in the biblical text as his starting point, and concludes that Yahwism must have started long before David, and that El and Yahweh were equally popular designations of God long before David's time.[30] De Moor's investigation of theophoric toponyms, on the other hand, reveals almost exclusively the names of Canaanite deities. This divergence between the personal names and toponyms argues against the supposition that Israelite religion was continuous with that of Canaan. The presence of only one personal name containing the name of a goddess (*bn ʿnt*, son of Anat) suggests that even in the premonarchical period, Yahweh did not have an official consort.[31]

An additional innovative use of comparative materials may be found in the work of Othmar Keel and Christoph Uehlinger.[32] In an impressive collection of epigraphic and inscriptional remains from the Middle Bronze, Late Bronze, and Iron ages, Keel and Uehlinger base their observations regarding the forms and manifestations of ancient Palestin-

---

29. J. A. Emerton, "New Light on Israelite Religion: The Implications from Kuntillet ʿAjrûd," *ZAW* 94 (1982): 16 n. 10; S. Olyan, *Asherah and the Cult of Yahweh in Israel,* SBLMS 34 (Atlanta: Scholars Press, 1988), 35–36; but see the positive review by T. J. Lewis in *Maarav,* forthcoming.

30. J. C. de Moor, *The Rise of Yahwism: The Roots of Israelite Monotheism* (Louvain: Leuven University Press, 1990), 10–34. This study omits the onomastic evidence of the Chronicler, which would have raised the share of Yahwistic names significantly. De Moor felt this evidence reflected the time of the Chronicler and was not genuinely representative of the period before David (32). J. D. Fowler has studied both biblical and epigraphic onomastica (*Theophoric Personal Names in Ancient Hebrew: A Comparative Study,* JSOT-Sup 49 [Sheffield: JSOT Press, 1988]). Though her work contains a number of flaws, most of her basic conclusions concerning the distinctiveness of Israel and the dominance of exclusivistic Yahwism in the religion of ancient Israel are valid. Other important works to consult: S. C. Layton, *Archaic Features of Canaanite Personal Names in the Hebrew Bible,* HSM 47 (Atlanta: Scholars Press, 1990); R. Zadok, *The Pre-Hellenistic Israelite Anthroponymy and Prosopography,* OLA 28 (Louvain: Peeters, 1988); N. Avigad, "The Contribution of Hebrew Seals to an Understanding of Israelite Religion and Society," in *Ancient Israelite Religion,* ed. Miller et al., 195–208; and again J. Tigay, "Israelite Religion: The Onomastic and Epigraphic Evidence," in ibid., 157–94.

31. De Moor, *Rise of Yahwism,* 40–41. One limitation of this line of investigation is that goddesses do not appear frequently in the personal names of Syria and Mesopotamia, certainly not in proportion to their general religious significance. I owe this word of caution to Daniel E. Fleming, personal communication, April 11, 1996.

32. *Gods, Goddesses, and Images of God in Ancient Israel,* trans. T. H. Trapp (Minneapolis: Fortress, 1998).

ian deities on artifacts from Palestine itself. Such a unique approach allows the authors to outline the development from a period in which standing stones, sacred trees, and sexually defined cults were prominent (Middle Bronze IIB) to a time when these features (usually associated with "Canaanite fertility" religion) were marginalized and the storm god became viewed more as a warrior deity under Egyptian influence (Late Bronze). The Iron Age brought a progression from the time when deities were depicted in military images (Iron I), to a time when anthropomorphic depictions of the deity were in general found outside Israel and Judah. Iron II also witnessed the rise of solar elements on seals and ivories, often associated with Israelite Yahwism. In general, Keel and Uehlinger do not believe that the iconographic evidence supports the current emphasis on an extended period of polytheism in preexilic Israel. Their work provides one of the most important and unique contributions from the period under review to the study of Israelite religion and its Canaanite antecedents.

Rainer Albertz has attempted to go beyond the chronological distinctions that regularly control histories of Israelite religion, that is, premonarchic religion, monarchic religion, and exilic and postexilic religion. In addition to these, he holds in tension two "foci of identity": the family and the people, which bring together two different strata of Israelite religion. The main stratum of "official religion" functioned in regard to the wider group, and the substratum of "personal piety" related to the individual in the smaller group of the family.[33] To this he has now added a third level, the local level, or the village community, which functioned sociologically between the level of the family and that of the people or state. Thus he refers to an "internal religious pluralism" for this socially conditioned stratification within the religion of Israel. All of this is in addition to the standard sociological observations concerning Israel's religion, such as reform groups like the prophets or Deuteronomists.[34]

Albertz argues that the faith commonly referred to as "patriarchal religion" reflected in the traditions of Genesis 12–50 is the faith of the smaller social group (the personal piety of the typical family) during the judges and early monarchic periods of Israel's history.[35] He also recon-

33. R. Albertz, *Persönliche Frömmigkeit und offizielle Religion: Religionsinterner Pluralismus in Israel und Babylon*, CThM A/9 (Stuttgart: Calwer, 1979). For more on sociological approaches, see E. S. Gerstenberger, "The Religion and Institutions of Ancient Israel: Toward a Contextual Theology of the Scriptures," in *Old Testament Interpretation: Past, Present, and Future: Essays in Honor of Gene M. Tucker*, ed. J. L. Mays, D. L. Petersen, and K. H. Richards (Nashville: Abingdon, 1995), 261–76.

34. R. Albertz, *A History of Israelite Religion in the Old Testament Period*, trans. J. Bowden, 2 vols., OTL (Louisville: Westminster/John Knox; London: SCM, 1994).

35. Ibid., 1:28–29.

structs the faith of a "liberated larger group," which had been an economically assimilated but socially declassed group of foreign conscripts to
forced labor in Egyptian society under the Ramesides.[36] Israel's Yahweh
religion arose in the liberation process of this group. Yahwism had originated in Midian and been given to Moses by Jethro/Reuel (perhaps related to the Shasu of Edom). Sinai traditions were later added to this Yahwism. Various Midianite tribes (and now the exodus group) participated
in a Yahweh cult at a mountain sanctuary in the frontier area between
Edom and Midian.[37] This Yahweh was a storm god not unlike Baal/
Hadad of Syria-Palestine. In his discussion of the religion of the "pre-
state alliance of larger groups," Albertz concludes that the exodus group
arrived and contributed the essential unifying element for the tribes
emerging in the central hills of Palestine. The unifying element was Yahwism, which fused with Canaanite El religion and provided the God of Israel, the God who defended the oppressed and resisted domination.[38]

Developments on Central Issues

Many various topics have received attention during the past three decades, and in most instances these were the same issues that previous
scholars investigated. This is especially true of the origins of Yahwism
and the history of monotheism. Other topics have presented relatively
new areas of research, such as the cult of the dead, which prior to this
period was not believed to have existed in ancient Israel and received
little attention among modern scholars. Many of these topics are interconnected and are discussed briefly here in an attempt to summarize
the advances made in each area of research.[39]

The Origins of Yahwism

As I have said, there is a sense in which scholarship has made few advances beyond the older dichotomy between the American archaeological school and the German traditio-historical school. Thus most schol-

---

36. Ibid., 1:45.

37. Ibid., 1:54–55.

38. Ibid., 1:76–79. I explore below the implications of Albertz's approach, but space
does not permit me to elaborate further on his views of the monarchy as the singular development that transformed Yahweh from a god of liberation into a god of state oppression, or the application of his sociological approach to the exilic and postexilic periods—
all of which are important contributions to the field of Israelite religion.

39. A survey of this nature cannot treat every issue of importance, and the following
discussion should be accepted as selective. For summaries of developments in the study
of prophecy, wisdom, and apocalyptic, see the appropriate chapters elsewhere in the
present volume.

ars sought the origins of Yahweh in either the Canaanite religious perceptions exemplified most in the Ugaritic material (Albright and his students) or in an awe-inspiring, numinous encounter of an "exodus group" with a volcanically active mountain in southern Palestine (Noth and his students).

Cross has assiduously resisted the volcano explanation in favor of the view that Yahweh originated as a genuine innovation of the earliest Israelites, a "radical differentiation" of Yahwism from its Canaanite roots. The name Yahweh was a shortened form of a primitive Hebrew cultic name for El, which became a divine name: *ʾēl zū yahwī ṣabaʾōt,* "El, who creates the heavenly armies." Earliest Yahwism originated in the worship of tutelary clan deities identified with the high god El of Amorite and Canaanite religion, modified by images and practices from the mythology of Baal. The fire, light, smoke, cloud, thunder, and quaking features of Yahweh's theophanies are, in Cross's view, no cause to "send for seismologists" but poetic descriptions of the theophany of the storm god, or of the attack of the Divine Warrior. Cross concludes that Israel's early descriptions of Yahweh's theophany derived from traditional Canaanite language originating in the northern storms of Lebanon, Cassius, or Amanus rather than Sinai or the southern mountains.[40]

Others have argued for a southern origin for Yahwism on the basis of Egyptian epigraphic evidence and the witness of the biblical traditions. Two Egyptian topographical lists from the Late Bronze Age preserve a place-name that should be understood as "Yahweh in the Shasu land," or "the Shasu land of Yahweh."[41] These references may indicate a pre-Israelite form of Yahwism practiced among tribal nomads ("the Shasu") who roamed about east of the Egyptian Delta, south and southeast of Palestine. Some scholars have associated the earliest Hebrews with these Edomite Shasu Bedouin, who were transhumant pastoralists and revered a deity by the same name as the Israelite God, Yahweh. Donald B. Redford argues that Yahwism originated among these Shasu nomads, who later became a major component in the amalgam that constituted Israel.[42]

---

40. *Canaanite Myth*, 60–75; and for his views on seismological explanations, 167–69. In his treatment of the Divine Warrior motif, however, Cross also acknowledges the march of Yahweh from the southern mountains in the oldest poetry of the OT, e.g., Judg. 5:4–5; Deut. 33:2–3; Ps. 68:18; and Hab. 3:3–6 (100–103).

41. Texts from Amenophis III and Rameses II attest *šꜣsw yhw*, where *yhw* is either a geographical or ethnic designation in *šꜣsw* land. See R. Giveon, *Les bédouins Shosou des documents égyptiens* (Leiden: Brill, 1971), docs. 6a (26–28) and 16a (74–77).

42. Redford also assumes that the first extrabiblical reference to Israel (Merenptah's Stela, ca. 1208 B.C.) describes a group with the character of a Shasu enclave on the hills of Ephraim (D. B. Redford, *Egypt, Canaan, and Israel in Ancient Times* [Princeton: Princeton University Press, 1992], 273–75).

The biblical evidence for the southern origins of Yahwism is well known and led long ago to the so-called Kenite hypothesis.[43] This theory assumes that Yahweh was a specifically Midianite or Kenite God (Kenites being a subgroup of the Midianites). Moses allegedly learned of the cult of Yahweh from his father-in-law Jethro, a Midianite priest.[44] Based then on these biblical and epigraphical data, Albertz can conclude: "So the god Yahweh is older than Israel; he was a southern Palestinian mountain god before he became the god of liberation for the Moses group."[45] In his sociological reconstruction of Israelite religion, Albertz argues that this liberated exodus group contributed Yahwism as the unifying element to the pre-state alliance of larger groups. Likewise, Niels Peter Lemche believes that Yahweh was originally located in the Sinai Peninsula and was brought to Palestine near the end of the Late Bronze Age. Concerning the question of how this Yahwism was transported to Palestine, however, Lemche demurs. He is convinced the late biblical sources elevated Moses to the level of the one who introduced Yahwism into national Israel, while in reality he is a figure quite beyond our reach. Since Moses was probably created by the late tradents, we cannot settle the question.[46]

Though the biblical references to Yahweh's association with a southern mountain are indisputable, the Kenite hypothesis is not without its problems. The Israelites and Edomites/Midianites were closely related and may have enjoyed alliances and cooperative relations at various periods in their history. But we possess evidence that the Kenites were ordinary polytheists, and it is possible that the Midianites learned the cult of Yahweh from the Israelites (as indeed Exod. 18:11 implies).[47] Greater questions attend the scant Egyptian epigraphic evidence. It remains to be seen whether the Shasu Bedouin were in any way connected or associated with the tribes of Israel, either as an eventual component of later Israel or as originators of Yahwism. Indeed, the enigmatic lists may have nothing to do with Yahwism, since the name *yhw* may actually refer to a people, a seminomadic group plaguing Egypt from the fourteenth century onward, in which case we have no reference here to a divine name at all.[48] Whether the place-name *š³sw*

---

43. For a summary, see J. A. Dearman, *Religion and Culture in Ancient Israel* (Peabody, Mass.: Hendrickson, 1992), 22–23.

44. This has been taken up again most recently by Albertz, *History of Israelite Religion*, 1:51–52.

45. Ibid., 1:52.

46. N. P. Lemche, *Ancient Israel: A New History of Israelite Society* (Sheffield: JSOT Press, 1988), 252–56.

47. De Moor, *Rise of Yahwism*, 224.

48. Ibid., 111–12.

yhw was even located in Edom at all is still controverted. One scholar has placed this site in the Beqaᶜ-Orontes region of Syria, much farther to the north.[49]

So did Yahweh originate as a Midianite/Kenite storm god in the south, or as a differentiation from Yahweh-El Canaanite religion as attested in the north, especially at Ugarit? Numerous biblical traditions reflect the southern connections (Albertz), but the most ancient texts also bear witness to an early Yahweh-El union, which suggests northern origins (Cross).[50] As Cross has emphasized, it is an extraordinary fact that El "is rarely if ever used in the Old Testament as the proper name of a non-Israelite, Canaanite deity in the full consciousness of a distinction between ʾĒl and Yahweh, god of Israel."[51] The influence of the El cult on earliest Yahwism seems undeniable, and Cross's argument for a radical theological differentiation in early Israel is convincing. But herein is the problem: we lack any specific extrabiblical references to Yahweh in the north, and we are uncertain of Canaanite El worship as far south as Sinai, or even southern and southeastern Palestine.[52]

The initial claim of Giovanni Pettinato that Yahweh appears as a divine name at Ebla created a stir.[53] But this has been discredited by the realization that the element *-yà*, which is written with the sign NI, is most likely an abbreviation of NI.NI = *ì-lí*, "my god," and stands for the personal guardian deity.[54] Likewise, there has been much speculation about the *yw* in the Ugaritic Baal Cycle.[55] De Moor has argued unconvincingly that this identification of Yahweh is philologically defensible, and has offered the unlikely suggestion that Ilimilku has identified Yahweh as a god of chaos and anarchy who would eventually, like Yammu, be conquered by Baal, the champion of prosperity. Thus, in de Moor's view, the Ugaritic text is a deliberate caricature of Yahweh as the god

49. M. C. Astour, "Yahweh in Egyptian Topographic Lists," in *Festschrift Elmar Edel: 12 März 1979,* ed. M. Görg and E. Pusch, Ägypten und Altes Testament 1 (Bamberg: Görg, 1979), 17–34.

50. Though Cross also traced Divine Warrior motifs to southern regions (*Canaanite Myth,* 100–103).

51. Ibid., 44.

52. It is possible to integrate the Kuntillet ᶜAjrud and Teman materials in one's discussion of southern traditions (see T. Hiebert, *God of My Victory: The Ancient Hymn in Habakkuk 3,* HSM 38 [Atlanta: Scholars Press, 1986], 85–92).

53. G. Pettinato, "Il calendario di Ebla al tempo del re Ibbi-Sipiš sulla base di TM.75.G.427," *AfO* 25 (1974–77): 1–36.

54. H.-P. Müller, "Der Jahwename und seine Deutung Ex 3,14 im Licht der Textpublikationen aus Ebla," *Bib* 62 (1981): 305–7; idem, "Gab es in Ebla einen Gottesnamen Ja?" *ZA* 70 (1980): 70–92.

55. *KTU* 1.1.IV.14.

of fearsome 'apiru warriors.[56] However, this parallel use of *yw* with the sea god Yammu has been challenged on the basis of phonetics, and probably has nothing to do with Yahweh.[57]

Since we lack explicit extrabiblical references to Yahweh (besides inscriptional Hebrew materials), and we cannot be sure of the prevalence of Canaanite El worship in the south, the origins of Yahwism continue to be wrapped in obscurity. Opinions continue to gravitate to either a northern Ugaritic/Canaanite connection or the older southern Midianite/Kenite association. But a rapprochement between these two is possible in the future. De Moor believes that the aggressively propagated cult of Amun-Re resulted in a "crisis of polytheism" across the ancient Near East, and influenced the cult of El and Yahweh in southern Palestine toward the end of the second millennium.[58] T. N. D. Mettinger has recently argued that the aniconic Amun cult may have played a role "in the formation of Israelite aniconism."[59] Though much of de Moor's reconstruction is open to question (Yahweh-El in Bashan in the Late Bronze Age and the identification of Moses as Beya, a Canaanite who became a high official in the Nineteenth Dynasty), he is certainly correct about the common Amorite cultural milieu linking Ugarit and early Israel, and he has made us realize that a Yahweh-El connection in the south is possible. Only more information in the future will be able to shed light on this problem.[60]

56. De Moor, *Rise of Yahwism*, 113–18; taken up again by de Moor in "Ugarit and Israelite Origins," in *Congress Volume: Paris, 1992*, ed. J. A. Emerton, VTSup 61 (Leiden: Brill, 1995), 219–23.

57. D. N. Freedman and M. P. O'Connor, "YHWH," *TDOT*, 5:510; and see Müller, "Jahwename," 325–27.

58. De Moor, *Rise of Yahwism*, 42–100. He has also recently argued unconvincingly that Ugarit's well-known relations with several cities in the south and the apparent origins of the proto-Ugaritic ruling class in Edomite territory of Transjordan (as argued by Dietrich and Loretz) suggest a possibility of a direct link between Ugarit and the proto-Israelites at the end of the Late Bronze Age. These connections would have included religious traditions and may have stemmed from a common Amorite cultural continuum ("Ugarit and Israelite Origins," 205–38, esp. 236–38).

59. T. N. D. Mettinger, *No Graven Image? Israelite Aniconism in Its Ancient Near Eastern Context*, ConBOT 42 (Stockholm: Almqvist & Wiksell, 1995), 56; and see the review of T. J. Lewis, "Divine Images and Aniconism in Ancient Israel," *JAOS* 118 (1998): 36–53.

60. Cross had already emphasized that the Ugaritic Baal Cycle reflects a literary heritage common to the Canaanites "and to those who shared their culture from the border of Egypt to the Amanus in the Middle and Late Bronze Age" (*Canaanite Myth*, 113). See now Mark Smith's speculations concerning possible reverberations of the West Semitic conflict myth across the ancient Near East, including Mari, Egypt, and the Mesopotamian heartland: M. S. Smith, ed., *The Ugaritic Baal Cycle*, vol. 1, *Introduction with Text, Translation, and Commentary of KTU 1.1–1.2*, VTSup 55 (Leiden and New York: Brill, 1994), 107–14.

The History of Israelite Monotheism

The most immediate difficulty in discussing the history of monotheism is precision in terminology. On the one hand, the terms *polytheism* and *monotheism* are clear enough. Scholars are relatively consistent in the use of "monotheism" for a religion that believes in the existence of only one god, and "polytheism" for one that believes in and worships a variety of deities. On the other hand, descriptors such as *henotheism* and *monolatry* are used with less clarity. The former variously denotes a rudimentary monotheism, a momentary veneration of only one deity during a crisis, or a more persistent worship of one god without denying the existence of others. The use of this term developed out of an evolutionary explanation to describe "practical monotheism" as a stage between polytheism and true monotheism. "Monolatry" appears to have the same general meanings as "henotheism." Though the two terms have a different origin, their current usage among Old Testament scholars appears to be interchangeable.[61]

The best model for this discussion has been proposed by David L. Petersen.[62] He uses three catchwords to synopsize the various general theories regarding the history of monotheism: *evolution, revolution,* and *devolution*. As Petersen avers, the concept that monotheism developed out of a prior polytheistic religious milieu (i.e., the evolutionary approach) has dominated Old Testament studies in general, and developments over the past three decades have continued that dominance.

There are several variations on the evolutionary approach to the history of Israelite monotheism. Morton Smith portrays an essentially polytheistic Israel until the emergence of a "Yahweh-alone" movement in the ninth century and afterward, which eventually gave rise to an expression of Yahweh as the only God during the postexilic period.[63] Bernhard Lang builds on Smith's sociological approach, though with much more emphasis on political factors in the movement from polytheism to monotheism.[64] Lang is able to isolate five phases in which the

---

61. D. L. Petersen, "Israel and Monotheism: The Unfinished Agenda," in *Canon, Theology, and Old Testament Interpretation,* ed. Tucker et al., 97–98. Baruch Halpern can assert that Israel's "monolatrous henotheism" was essentially monotheism, calling the religion of monarchic Israel "unselfconscious monotheism" ("'Brisker Pipes Than Poetry': The Development of Israelite Monotheism," in *Judaic Perspectives on Ancient Israel,* ed. J. Neusner, B. A. Levine, and E. S. Frerichs [Philadelphia: Fortress, 1987], 88).

62. Petersen, "Israel and Monotheism," 92–107.

63. M. Smith, *Palestinian Parties and Politics That Shaped the Old Testament* (New York: Columbia University Press; London: SCM, 1971), 15–31.

64. B. Lang, *Monotheism and the Prophetic Minority: An Essay in Biblical History and Sociology,* SWBAS 1 (Sheffield: Almond, 1983), 13–56. From a distinctly different sociological approach, one could compare Norman Gottwald's "mono-Yahwism," which

"Yahweh-aloneists" progress from opposition to Israelite polytheism to "the breakthrough to monotheism" after the fall of Jerusalem in 586 B.C. In Lang's view, the political crisis stimulated the "Yahweh-alone" ideology already present in what he calls "proto-Judaism," resulting in the idea of monotheism. "Monotheism . . . is the answer to political emergency, in which no solution is to be expected from diplomatic maneuvering or foreign military help."[65]

In a more general fashion, Albertz describes an intrinsic exclusiveness in early Yahwism due to the combination of the social and religious factors from which it emerged: the political liberation and extended wilderness experience of the exodus group, which forged "a close personal relationship" with Yahweh.[66] This innate exclusiveness yielded naturally to a claim by later prophetic opposition groups to the sole worship of Yahweh from the middle period of the monarchy onward, thus paving the way for monotheism in the exile. Similarly, for Lemche, monotheistic Yahwism was a religion of the elite during and after the exile.[67]

Mark Smith has argued that the appearance of monotheism in Israel was both evolutionary and revolutionary.[68] On close examination, however, his reconstruction is a simple evolutionary model. He begins his reconstruction in the period of the judges when, he believes, Israel was polytheistic. Its cult included features of worship to El, Asherah, Yahweh, and perhaps Baal. Approximately 1100 B.C., a process of convergence began in Israel, by which Smith means the "incorporation of divine attributes into Yahweh."[69] The monarchy played a significant role in the emergence of monolatrous religion in Smith's view. During the first half of the monarchy (ca. 1000–800), Yahweh became a national, male deity closely associated with the Davidic dynasty. The emphasis on a covenantal relationship with the deity, innovative centralization of national worship, the appearance of the "Yahweh-only party" in the ninth century (cf. Morton Smith), and the role of writing in Israelite society all contributed to the process of convergence. During this period the monarchy encouraged the religious imagery of other deities within

---

served as a corollary to a new, egalitarian form of social organization (*Tribes of Yahweh*, 16, 616, and 693). Gottwald's views have been severely criticized on several fronts, not the least of which is the sociological evidence that a considerable degree of hierarchical complexity is present wherever societies affirm monotheism. See G. E. Swanson, *The Birth of the Gods: The Origin of Primitive Beliefs* (Ann Arbor: University of Michigan Press, 1960); and Petersen, "Israel and Monotheism," 100.

65. Lang, *Monotheism*, 54.
66. Albertz, *History of Israelite Religion*, 1:62.
67. Lemche, *Ancient Israel*, 209–23.
68. Smith, *Early History*, especially the introduction (xix–xxxiv), and chap. 6 (145–60).
69. Ibid., 147.

the cult of Yahweh.[70] The second half of the monarchy (ca. 800–587) witnessed a process of "differentiation" in the religion of Israel, by which Smith means the "eliminating from the cult of Yahweh features associated with Baal or other deities."[71] Certain features were dropped from the cult, such as devotion to the cult of Baal and specific practices associated with the dead, resulting in a distinct change from the previous period. This process of differentiation was due largely to prophetic and legal criticisms of the monarchy's support of religious imagery of other deities within Yahwism. Their criticism gained wider influence in Israelite society because of a growing literacy and the influence of writing.[72] This differentiation, which Smith refers to as a "revolution,"[73] gradually resulted in monolatrous faith in preexilic Israel and unambiguous expressions of monotheism in the exile.

Among other questions raised by Smith's construction, I should mention at least two here. First, he has failed to explain fully "normative Yahwism" as opposed to "popular religion." Many scholars have rightly abandoned defining any rigid distinction between ancient Israel's popular religion and so-called official religion. There can be no doubt, however, that certain Canaanite concepts were rejected by what we may call, for lack of better term, "normative" Yahwism. As the biblical text attests, many of the features of Canaanite religion were present in ancient Israel and were soundly opposed by normative Yahwism. Second, and more specifically, Smith fails to give adequate attention to the absence of sex and death associated with depictions of Yahweh.[74] This absence is profound and deep-seated, and marks an early distinction between Israelite Yahwism and other religious expressions in the ancient Near East.

Karel van der Toorn credits the appearance of genuine monotheism in Israel (not a momentary henotheistic impulse) to a "theology of exaltation," which was in fact present throughout the ancient Near East.[75] Each community strove to promote its deity to the highest rank, and exaltation theologies achieved this goal. Thus the Baal Cycle elevated Baal among the gods of Ugarit, the Mesha Stela attempts to show that Chemosh has no equal, the *Enuma Elish* puts Marduk at the center of

70. Ibid., 147–50.
71. Ibid., 150.
72. Ibid., 150–52.
73. Ibid., 156.
74. As pointed out by Lewis, the absence of these features in Yahwism formed the cornerstone of the important earlier work by Yehezkel Kaufmann and constituted a major aspect of the differentiation process (review of Smith in *JITC* 18 [1990–91]: 162).
75. K. van der Toorn, "Theology, Priests, and Worship in Canaan and Ancient Israel," in *Civilizations of the Ancient Near East*, ed. J. M. Sasson, 4 vols. (New York: Scribner, 1995), 3:2056–57.

the Babylonian pantheon, and likewise, the exodus narrative teaches the incomparability of Yahweh over the deities of Egypt. In each case, the theology of exaltation leads to a monotheism that is politically motivated. Ancient monotheism is portrayed not as an intellectual and theological answer to polytheism but as a polemic "against the pretenses of political rivals."

H. W. F. Saggs has proposed an intriguing evolutionary theory that has not received great attention among Old Testament scholars.[76] In comparing Israelite religion with Mesopotamian, he reasons that they were really alike in basic principle, though quite different in details and points of emphasis. The differences arose because of the great antiquity and diversity of Mesopotamian culture in conjunction with its intrinsic conservatism. In Mesopotamian religion, "the new did not lead to rejection of the old; rather, the old continued to exist alongside the new."[77] Saggs argues that, though there was no static difference of basic principle between Mesopotamian and Israelite religion, there was a dynamic difference in the way in which religious concepts developed. Thus, on the one hand, in Mesopotamia the rise of a new city-state to preeminence meant the rise of a new deity in the pantheon, but not the exclusion of lesser, previously important deities. All were included in an ever-growing list of deities. The Israelites, on the other hand, had come into Palestine relatively recently and had no cultural moorings. They had less reverence for tradition and could more readily reject the old in acceptance of the new. Saggs argues that, like early Sumerian religion with its numerous independent city-state deities, a presettlement Israelite group began with one god. Other Israelite groups each had their respective deities, the patriarchal numina. But instead of the accretive principle of early Mesopotamian religion, Yahwism exercised selectivity and rejection. He concludes: "What began as monolatry in both Sumerian city-states and Israel developed on one side into polytheism and on the other into monotheism."[78] While Saggs presents a fascinating possibility, his reconstruction fails to account for the uniqueness of this intolerance in early Israel. Why did Israel's new cultural circumstances result in exclusive monotheism, while other West Semites, who were recent emigrants into Syria-Palestine and under similar circumstances, continued along the paths of polytheism?[79]

76. H. W. F. Saggs, *The Encounter with the Divine in Mesopotamia and Israel* (London: Athlone, 1978), 182–88.

77. Ibid., 184.

78. Ibid., 186.

79. It is also doubtful that the Sumerian city-states may be called "monolatrous" in any sense of the word. See T. Jacobsen, *The Treasures of Darkness: A History of Mesopotamian Religion* (New Haven: Yale University Press, 1976), 25–27, and passim.

Old Testament studies during the period under review here have been dominated by evolutionary explanations for Israelite monotheism. Yet there has not been enough attention given to the onomastic and iconographic evidence assembled by Tigay, Keel and Uehlinger, and others,[80] which speaks against the theory of an extended period of polytheism in preexilic Israel (à la Morton Smith, Bernhard Lang, Mark Smith, etc.). Furthermore, such explanations fail to account for the revolutionary nature of monotheistic religions in general. They appear to arise in each case out of previously existing polytheistic surroundings, not in a natural evolutionary process, but rather as a revolution, and often as the work of a religious reformer.[81]

Few Old Testament scholars have followed this line of inquiry. Most recently, de Moor's *Rise of Yahwism* is worthy of consideration. He begins with an observation on the remarkable divergence between the personal names in the Bible and the toponyms, which, he says, speaks against the supposition that the religion of the early Israelites was in no way distinct from that of their neighbors.[82] He argues on the basis of the onomastic evidence for the rise of Yahwism from the spiritual climate of the Late Bronze Age. Similar to van der Toorn's "theology of exaltation," de Moor speaks of "a crisis of polytheism" all over the ancient Near East as a result of the monotheistic revolution of Akhenaten. An Egyptian countermovement promulgated the doctrine that all gods were in reality nothing but manifestations of one god, Amun-Re. This reduction of the polytheistic principle had reverberated throughout Syria-Palestine and Mesopotamia. In Egypt and Mesopotamia, polytheism adjusted through the concentration on one god who was thought to manifest himself in all other deities: Amun-Re and Marduk, respectively. But in Canaan the struggle between El and Baal rendered any such concentration impossible. Though people of Ugarit remained true polytheists, it was not without tension.[83] And southern Palestine, de Moor argues, had felt the influence of the Egyptian Amun-Re movement earlier and more profoundly than Ugarit. In the earliest biblical traditions, de Moor believes that Yahweh-El had already attained a status similar to that of Amun-Re in Egypt or Marduk in Mesopotamia at the end of the Late Bronze Age. The existence of other deities is not denied, though they are considered insignificant.[84] De Moor's reconstruction

---

80. Tigay, *No Other Gods;* Keel and Uehlinger, *Gods, Goddesses, and Images of God.*

81. R. Pettazzone, "The Formation of Monotheism," in *Reader in Comparative Religion: An Anthropological Approach,* ed. W. Lessa and E. Vogt (New York: Harper & Row, 1965), 34–39; P. D. Miller, "The Absence of the Goddess in Israelite Religion," *HAR* 10 (1986): 244.

82. De Moor, *Rise of Yahwism,* 41.

83. Ibid., 97–100.

84. Ibid., 226.

may be a "revolutionary" approach, though in contrast to Mark Smith, Lemche, and others, he places the revolution early in Israel's history.

In addition to evolution and revolution, Petersen speaks of another view that has argued for the existence of primitive monotheism (*Urmonotheismus*), or the idea that humankind began with the concept of one god, but in later weakness adopted a number of deities. From an ancient and positively valued religious conception (monotheism), there developed a less sophisticated and ignoble one, polytheism.[85] Few indeed are the Old Testament scholars who have argued for such an ideological dissolution, though the primeval history traditions of Genesis may be interpreted to portray such a process. On the other hand, those who maintain an early revolutionary experience for Israel (de Moor, and certainly Albright; see below) would no doubt see a similar devolution occurring from that point onward in Israelite religion. One may place such scholars in this category who, though they may not argue for a common *Urmonotheismus* for humankind, nevertheless believe that Israel was monotheistic (or at least monolatrous) at the dawn of its appearance in Palestine and that its subsequent religious conceptions tended toward syncretism.[86]

The American Albright school was dominated by the view of an unadulterated form of Yahwism in early Israel, which was vitiated by contacts with Canaanite religion (apparent in the works of G. Ernest Wright, George Mendenhall, John Bright, and others). Though the collapse of this consensus is one of the major developments in the study of Israelite religion over the past three decades, the monotheistic revolution in Egypt and Mesopotamia at the close of the Bronze Age makes monotheism (or at least monolatry) entirely plausible at the time of Moses and even of Abraham, as argued recently by Alan R. Millard.[87] In the face of wide diversity of opinion among scholars arguing for some form of evolutionary process, it remains curious that the biblical traditions consistently portray a process of devolution; curious, that is, that the Israelite tradents should preserve their history with so much veracity, coupled with such an unflattering portrayal. Perhaps van der Toorn's "theology of exaltation" is on the right course, though no doubt less politically motivated than he states and occurring earlier in Israel than he presumes. Many of the processes he observes in ancient Near Eastern theology were certainly occurring at the same time Mosaic religion was formed.

85. Petersen, "Israel and Monotheism," 93.

86. I also have in mind here Cross's portrayal of Yahwism's differentiation from El during the proto-Israelite league and its subsequent "less wholesome syncretism" under the influence of Baalism (*Canaanite Myth*, 71 and 190).

87. A. R. Millard, "Abraham, Akhenaten, Moses, and Monotheism," in *He Swore an Oath: Biblical Themes from Genesis 12–50*, ed. R. S. Hess, G. J. Wenham, and P. E. Satterthwaite (Cambridge: Tyndale House, 1993), 119–29.

The themes struck by Albright on Israelite monotheism (and followed by many of his students) seem unthinkable in today's scholarly climate. Albright referred to the "most exalted emotional experiences known to man" in reference to religious conversion and mystical union with God.[88] Perhaps the next generation of scholars should hear again his contention that Israel was monotheistic, though its creed was implicit because it lacked the analytic logic necessary to formulate it.[89]

The Kuntillet ʿAjrud and Khirbet el-Qôm Inscriptions

Of the new epigraphic evidence coming from the period under investigation, by far the most important for the study of Israelite religion is that from Khirbet el-Qôm and Kuntillet ʿAjrud. The former yielded a tomb inscription, which is the second-longest funerary inscription yet discovered from the Israelite period.[90] Important inscriptions from the ruins of Kuntillet ʿAjrud, dated to the eighth century B.C., have provoked an enormous body of secondary literature during the past three decades.[91] Of particular importance to this discussion are the various blessings pronounced in the name of "Yahweh of Samaria and his asherah/Asherah"[92] and "Yahweh of Teman," which has led to reexamination of the complex nature of preexilic Israelite religion.

88. *Archaeology and the Religion of Israel*, 5th ed. (reprinted, Garden City, N.Y.: Doubleday, 1969), 22; see John Dougherty's explanation of the unique appearance of Israel's monotheism as due to "transcendent causes" or "mystical experience [which] obviously lie outside the control of archaeology" ("The Origins of Hebrew Religion: A Study in Method," *CBQ* 17 [1955]: 138–56, esp. 154–56).

89. Albright, *Archaeology and the Religion of Israel*, 170–71.

90. After the royal steward's tomb inscription (J. S. Holladay Jr., "Kom, Khirbet el-," *ABD*, 4:98). See the editio princeps in W. G. Dever, "Iron Age Epigraphic Material from the Area of Khirbet el-Kôm," *HUCA* 40–41 (1970): 139–204; also idem, "Asherah, Consort of Yahweh? New Evidence from Kuntillet Ajrud," *BASOR* 255 (1984): 21–37; Z. Zevit, "The Khirbet el-Qôm Inscription Mentioning a Goddess," *BASOR* 255 (1984): 39–47; J. M. Hadley, "The Khirbet el-Qom Inscription," *VT* 37 (1987): 50–62; M. O'Connor, "The Poetic Inscription from Khirbet el-Qôm," *VT* 37 (1987): 224–30; B. Margalit, "Some Observations on the Inscription and Drawing from Khirbet el-Qôm," *VT* 39 (1989): 371–78; W. H. Shea, "The Khirbet el-Qom Tomb Inscription Again," *VT* 40 (1990): 110–16.

91. For an introduction to the texts and their interpretation, see R. S. Hess, "Yahweh and His Asherah? Epigraphic Evidence for Religious Pluralism in Old Testament Times," in *One God, One Lord in a World of Religious Pluralism*, ed. A. D. Clarke and B. W. Winter (Cambridge: Tyndale House, 1991), 11–23; various articles in *Ancient Israelite Religion*, ed. Miller et al; and Keel and Uehlinger, *Gods, Goddesses, and Images of God*, 210–48.

92. The final two letters of the word *wlʾšrth*, "and by his a/Asherah," have been much disputed. Z. Zevit has argued the whole word is a "quaint, yet authentically Hebrew" name, with a feminine ending, "Asherata" ("Khirbet el-Qôm Inscription," 46). But the form would be doubly marked as feminine, and the suggestion is not likely, though it is possible (see S. Olyan, *Asherah and the Cult of Yahweh in Israel*, SBLMS 34 [Atlanta: Scholars Press, 1988], 25).

Most of the discussion on these inscriptions has to do with the precise interpretation of the noun *asherah/Asherah* and its broader implications for understanding monarchic religion. This is not the venue for a thorough review of the epigraphic and philological complexities of the problem (nor is such a review necessary in light of the literature available). But the various views may be summarized as follows. The term refers either to the goddess Asherah, or to a symbol of the goddess (such as her sacred tree), or to a symbol of Yahweh designated as an "asherah." Whatever our understanding of the expression, the implications are provocative, and have led several scholars to conclude that the goddess Asherah played some role in Israelite popular religion.[93] Some have concluded on the basis of this evidence that the Kuntillet ʿAjrud site is "a half-pagan Israelite temple, where both Baal and Asherah could be worshipped alongside Yahweh" far from the watchful eye of the Jerusalem religious establishment.[94] P. K. McCarter has suggested the "asherah" here is the personification of a cult object as a goddess, specifically a hypostatic form of Yahweh, and therefore not syncretistic in the strictest sense.[95]

Although the new epigraphic evidence *may* indicate heterodox tendencies in preexilic Israelite religion, several caveats should be mentioned in connection with its interpretation. First, Dever and others have assumed a close association between the drawings on one of the Kuntillet ʿAjrud inscriptions and the inscription itself; such an assumption frequently affects the outcome of one's analysis.[96] But several considerations call into question whether the lyre player is related to the inscription mentioning the "asherah," and the drawings may have been from a different hand and from a different time altogether than the inscription.[97]

93. Olyan argues that the asherah was acceptable in both northern and southern kingdoms as a general feature of Israelite religion. Asherah was a native Israelite Yahwistic cult object instead of a Jezebel import, since Baal was not associated with Asherah as consort in Canaanite religion. Asherah became Yahweh's consort by virtue of the identification of Yahweh and El, and the later Deuteronomistic tradition was the only sector of Israelite society opposed to the goddess Asherah (Olyan, *Asherah*, 37).

94. W. G. Dever, *Recent Archaeological Discoveries and Biblical Research* (Seattle: University of Washington Press, 1990), 148.

95. P. K. McCarter Jr., "Aspects of the Religion of the Israelite Monarchy: Biblical and Epigraphic Data," in *Ancient Israelite Religion*, ed. Miller et al., 147–49.

96. Pithos A portrays a female lyre player, which Dever takes as the goddess Asherah, even though he admits the linguistic problems of taking "asherah" in the nearby text as a divine name (Dever, "Asherah, Consort of Yahweh?"). For criticism of this view, see J. M. Hadley, "Yahweh and 'His Asherah': Archaeological and Textual Evidence for the Cult of the Goddess," in *Ein Gott allein?* ed. Dietrich and Klopfenstein, 247.

97. P. Beck, "The Drawings from Horvat Teiman (Kuntillet ʿAjrud)," *Tel Aviv* 9 (1982): 4, 43–47; and Keel and Uehlinger, *Gods, Goddesses, and Images of God*, 240–41.

Second, when analyzing the Kuntillet ʿAjrud inscriptions in particular, one should remember that we are dealing here with graffiti. As Richard Hess has warned, these inscriptions "may represent the musings of a semiliterate person as easily as they could represent the work of a trained scribe."[98] It is unwarranted, therefore, to extrapolate from this evidence a view of widespread heterodoxy in ancient Israelite society.

Third, the location of Kuntillet ʿAjrud should not be dismissed as insignificant when interpreting these inscriptions. Its geographical locale (approximately forty miles south/southwest of Kadesh-barnea) made it a convenient juncture of three caravan routes through the northern Sinai, serving apparently as a military outpost and temporary lodging place for desert caravaners and other travelers. This is certainly the type of site where one might expect to find religious syncretism and admixtures due to foreign influences. The site probably does not inform us about the extent of the Judean kingdom during the eighth century, nor does it illustrate "the dimensions of the official Judean religion," as Ahlström asserted.[99]

Fourth, the attention given to these inscriptions has overshadowed the significance of other archaeological and epigraphical evidence from the Judean heartland, which supports the view of a widely Yahwistic society. Yahweh is by far the most frequently used divine name in Hebrew preexilic inscriptions, and preexilic Israelite onomastic evidence confirms the biblical portrait of the primacy of Yahweh as the sole deity of Israel.[100] Almost all of these data are from sites near Israelite population centers (Lachish, Arad, Megiddo, Samaria, Khirbet Beit Lei, etc.), rather than from peripheral sites such as Kuntillet ʿAjrud.[101] The reference to Yahweh in the Mesha Inscription also speaks of the predominant nature of Israelite religion toward the end of the ninth century B.C. (line 18 refers to "the [ves]sels of Yahweh"). In sum, with regard to the Kuntillet ʿAjrud inscriptions in particular, one should not accept aberrations of classical Yahwism from the fringes of Israelite culture as normative expressions of preexilic religion.

---

98. Hess, "Yahweh and His Asherah?" 23.

99. G. W. Ahlström, *Royal Administration and National Religion in Ancient Palestine*, SHANE 1 (Leiden: Brill, 1982), 43. Ahlström goes on to aver: "It can be concluded that this find corrects the picture of the religious history of Judah as advocated by the later biblical writers. Their censorship has been broken" (43).

100. Yahwistic names make up 94 percent, and names that are plausibly pagan were only 6 percent (Tigay, *No Other Gods*, 15). But many of the plausibly pagan names were Baal names in the Samaria Ostraca, which would not be unexpected in light of the biblical evidence.

101. Only the Khirbet el-Qôm inscription is from the heartland of Israelite settlement, a point emphasized by Tigay ("Israelite Religion," 176).

Cult of the Dead

The past decade or so has been a remarkable period of scholarly pro-
ductivity on ancestor worship and cults of the dead in an attempt to
set the biblical evidence in its ancient Near Eastern context.[102]
Whereas previous scholarship tended to deny the presence of ancestral worship in ancient Israel, it is now generally agreed that normative Yahwism battled against the practice of necromancy and other
death rituals, such as self-laceration and offerings to deceased ancestors.[103] As with such practices in comparable cultures, it is assumed
that Israelite cults of the dead sought to appease the dead or to secure
favors from them.

Ancestor worship in Egypt and Mesopotamia is well attested and was
thought to be an effective way to gain the favor of the dead, who it was
believed could either bestow blessings or act malevolently on behalf of
the living. But the most important comparative material has only come
to light in the last few decades in the newly available material from
Ugarit.[104] The most important of these is a tablet discovered at Ras
Shamra in 1973 and made available to the scholarly community in
1975. Since then it has generated a considerable literature.[105] This text
describes a liturgy of a mortuary ritual invoking the deceased royal ancestors to assist in bestowing blessings upon the living king (Ammurapi
III, the last known king of Ugarit).[106] The liturgy is likely the funeral ritual for Ammurapi's immediate predecessor, Niqmaddu III. The ritual
summons both the *rp᾽m* (related to Heb. *rĕpā᾽îm*), the long-dead ancestors, and the *mlkm* (the recently dead rulers) to participate in the ritual.
As with cults of the dead elsewhere in the ancient Near East, this liturgy

102. In addition to the large number of articles, I can cite here only a few of the most
important monographs: T. J. Lewis, *Cults of the Dead in Ancient Israel and Ugarit*, HSM
39 (Atlanta: Scholars Press, 1989); B. B. Schmidt, *Israel's Beneficent Dead: Ancestor Cult
and Necromancy in Ancient Israelite Religion and Tradition*, FAT 11 (Tübingen: Mohr,
1994; reprinted, Winona Lake, Ind.: Eisenbrauns, 1996); K. Spronk, *Beatific Afterlife in
Ancient Israel and in the Ancient Near East*, AOAT 219 (Kevelaer: Butzon & Bercker; Neukirchen-Vluyn: Neukirchener Verlag, 1986); and somewhat earlier N. J. Tromp, *Primitive
Conceptions of Death and the Nether World in the Old Testament*, BibOr 21 (Rome: Pontifical Biblical Institute, 1969).

103. Particularly Lewis, *Cults of the Dead*. See especially his helpful distinction between the "Yahwism which became normative" and "popular religion" (1–2).

104. Though it should be cautioned that funerary practices and beliefs concerning afterlife may have been sui generis for Ugarit compared to the rest of Canaan, as a reassessment of Ugaritic tombs suggests (W. T. Pitard, "The 'Libation Installations' of the Tombs
at Ugarit," *BA* 57.1 [1994]: 20–37).

105. *KTU*, 1.161. See W. T. Pitard, "RS 34.126: Notes on the Text," *Maarav* 4.1 (1987):
75 n. 2; and now Schmidt, *Israel's Beneficent Dead*, 101 n. 275.

106. Contra Schmidt, who argues instead that we have here a coronation ritual that
incorporates mourning rites on behalf of Niqmaddu (*Israel's Beneficent Dead*, 100–120).

was intended to provide the deceased with essential services and to secure blessings for the living, and in this case the ritual itself presumably helped to legitimate the succession.[107] This text, along with others from Ugarit, has illuminated a vibrant cult of ancestor worship at Ugarit, comparable to that in Mesopotamia and Egypt.[108]

A reassessment of the biblical evidence in light of these new data reflects a cultural continuity between Israel and its neighbors. Lewis contends that Israelite Yahwism borrowed many Canaanite motifs while rejecting others. He believes that early Yahwism is difficult to distinguish from Canaanite religion. As Yahwism progressed, a normative expression of Israelite religion emerged, which is reflected in the prophetic and the Deuteronomistic literature. The Yahwism that became normative consistently condemned ancestor worship and death rituals. But a strong case can be made based on the texts that ancestor worship and necromancy continued in certain forms of popular religion. That vestiges of such rituals persisted in the texts at all (and in some cases, descriptions comparable to those practices at Ugarit; see 1 Sam. 28) probably reflects their veracity, since one may assume that prophetic and Deuteronomistic editors would have sought to expunge them from the records. Thus the biblical text portrays an ongoing battle throughout Israel's history between normative Yahwism and practitioners of death rituals in the popular religion.[109]

Topics and Suggestions for the Future

Arising from the work done over the past three decades, several topics demand attention in future research.

The Canaanite Continuum

The modus operandi for most scholars currently working on ancient Israel involves the assumption that earliest Israel was Canaanite in culture, language, and religion. The continuity versus discontinuity ques-

---

107. B. A. Levine and J.-M. de Tarragon, "Dead Kings and Rephaim: The Patrons of the Ugaritic Dynasty," *JAOS* 104.4 (1984): 649–59.

108. The new information has also led to a reappraisal of the function of the Semitic institution known as the *marzēaḥ*, which has been taken as a feast for and with the departed ancestors. But earlier studies may have gone beyond the evidence, since all that can be said with certainty is that the *marzēaḥ* was an organization known for its drinking festivals, which in some cases came secondarily to be associated with funerary feasts. On all the pertinent Akkadian and Ugaritic texts, see Lewis, *Cults of the Dead*, 80–94; idem, "Banqueting Hall/House," *ABD*, 1:581–82; and Schmidt, *Israel's Beneficent Dead*, 22–23, 62–66, 246–49.

109. See Lewis (*Cults of the Dead*, 171–81) for this reconstruction.

tion must begin and end, ultimately, with Israel's perceptions of deity. All other related issues, such as Israel's view of history,[110] Yahweh's relationship to the cycle of nature,[111] or his sexuality and relationship to Canaanite fertility rites,[112] must begin with the basic paradigm of Israel's unique monotheism. This is necessary particularly in light of Israel's many self-claims to distinctiveness, self-claims that are prominent in the text of the Old Testament itself and that are clearly centered in its special relationship to its God.[113] Peter Machinist has recently called us to look not for a list of individual "pure traits" to prove the distinctiveness of a given culture but for "configurations of traits" that illustrate how that culture magnified certain ancient Near Eastern features while obliterating others.[114]

Cross and others have demonstrated the high degree of religious continuity between Canaan and Israel, and the Israelite tendency toward syncretism. Research during the closing decades of the twentieth century has offered a corrective to the earlier convictions of scholars in the biblical theology movement who stressed the radical uniqueness of Israel (particularly G. Ernest Wright and Yehezkel Kaufmann). But our growing understanding of the continuity has overshadowed some of the valid observations made by previous scholarship. There can be no question that Israel shared much with its Canaanite forebears, such as its understanding of the kind creator God (El), and of Yahweh as God of the storm, provider of rain and fertility, and God of war (Baal), not to mention the common agricultural-religious festivals and temple pattern. But during this corrective period, the pendulum has swung too far to the opposite extreme. As with the pendulum, which spends more time in the middle, so the truth lies somewhere between these extremes.

---

110. B. Albrektson, *History and the Gods: An Essay on the Idea of Historical Events as Divine Manifestations in the Ancient Near East and in Israel,* ConBOT 1 (Lund: Gleerup, 1967); B. T. Arnold, "The Weidner Chronicle and the Idea of History in Israel and Mesopotamia," in *Faith, Tradition, and History: Old Testament Historiography in Its Near Eastern Context,* ed. A. R. Millard, J. K. Hoffmeier, and D. W. Baker (Winona Lake, Ind.: Eisenbrauns, 1994), 129–48.

111. G. Fohrer, *History of Israelite Religion,* trans. D. E. Green (Nashville: Abingdon, 1972), 101–6.

112. T. C. Vriezen, *The Religion of Ancient Israel,* trans. H. Hoskins (Philadelphia: Westminster, 1967), 73.

113. P. Machinist, "The Question of Distinctiveness in Ancient Israel: An Essay," in *Ah, Assyria . . . : Studies in Assyrian History and Ancient Near Eastern Historiography Presented to Hayim Tadmor,* ed. M. Cogan and I. Ephʾal (Jerusalem: Magnes, 1991), 196–212.

114. Ibid., 200. Lewis has recently argued that Israel's unique cultural configuration included among others: monotheism, aniconism, the extension of divine-human treaties into a pervasive "covenant theology," and the absence of sex and death associated with depictions of Yahweh (Lewis, "Divine Images and Aniconism," 53).

Attention to Ancient Near Eastern Sources

The period under consideration here has witnessed the discovery of Ebla, Emar, and several smaller finds, all having a bearing on Old Testament research. The texts from Emar may be particularly illuminating for the study of ancient Israelite history and religion, since the Late Bronze Age site on the Middle Euphrates was pulled and pushed by both city-state cultures and tribally organized societies, and thus presents a close sociocultural match for ancient Israel.[115] Emar texts and recently published texts from Mari have already provided the first known cognate to the Hebrew word for "prophet" (*nābî*).[116] Moreover, Emar's ritual texts broaden our understanding of Syrian religion in a way that may eventually transcend the value of the Ugaritic texts for biblical studies, not only because they reveal a mixed urban and small-town Syrian community, but also because Emar was distinctly West Semitic but not Canaanite, and therefore portrays a more nuanced picture of Syrian culture and religion.[117] In addition to new finds, scholars working on the history of Israelite religion have benefited from a reevaluation of previously published material from the ancient Orient, especially Ugarit and Mari.

We have every indication that further work on the comparative materials will bear rich fruit on investigations of Israelite religion. Surely the way to progress in the endeavor is to continue to pursue comparative ancient Near Eastern religions, not simply in an effort to find parallels, but in order to illuminate the unique convergence of features that constituted ancient Israel's religion. The warnings of Benno Landsberger can help us avoid the dangers of parallelomania on the one hand, and on the other hand, the call of Westermann and Hallo can and must provide the parameters for a genuinely productive comparative approach.[118] Any future constructions of ancient Israel's religion that

---

115. D. E. Fleming, "More Help from Syria: Introducing Emar to Biblical Study," *BA* 58.3 (1995): 139–47.

116. D. E. Fleming, "*Nabû* and *Munabbiatu:* Two New Syrian Religious Personnel," *JAOS* 113.2 (1993): 175–83; idem, "The Etymological Origins of the Hebrew *nābî*: The One Who Invokes God," *CBQ* 55 (1993): 217–24.

117. D. E. Fleming, *The Installation of Baal's High Priestess at Emar: A Window on Ancient Syrian Religion,* HSS 42 (Atlanta: Scholars Press, 1992), 1.

118. B. Landsberger, *The Conceptual Autonomy of the Babylonian World,* trans. T. Jacobsen et al., Monographs on the Ancient Near East 1.4 (Malibu: Undena, 1976), originally published as "Die Eigenbegrifflichkeit der babylonischen Welt," *Islamica* 2 (1926): 355–72; C. Westermann, "Das Verhältnis des Jahweglaubens zu den ausser-israelitischen Religionen," in *Forschung am Alten Testament,* TBü 24 (Munich: Chr. Kaiser, 1964), 189–218; idem, "Sinn und Grenze religionsgeschichtliche Parallelen," in *Forschung am Alten Testament,* vol. 2, TBü 55 (Munich: Chr. Kaiser, 1974), 84–95; W. W. Hallo, "Biblical History in Its Near Eastern Setting: The Contextual Approach," in *Scripture in Context:*

deserve our attention must consider the ancient Near Eastern milieu from which it emerged. The benefits of such comparisons go beyond simply showing how Israel was similar to Mesopotamian, Egyptian, or Syro-Palestinian religion. The importance of this approach is to demonstrate how Israel shared with, borrowed from, *and* reacted against its cultural contemporaries. This total picture will continue to illumine and frame our understanding of Israel's God and the cultic expressions of its relationship with him.

Clarification of the Relationship to Old Testament Theology

The problem of how to define the precise relationship between the history of Israelite religion and the discipline of Old Testament theology continues to plague both endeavors. The question has occupied biblical theologians since the time of J. P. Gabler,[119] and is evident in the monumental work of Gerhard von Rad, who began his *Old Testament Theology* with a 100-page study of the early history of Israelite faith.[120] But his approach creates a tension in his work, since it is unclear exactly how this introduction is related to his theological exposition. Erhard Gerstenberger's recent attempt to hold the disciplines together by means of leaping to a pluralistic divine reality is untenable. He wants to abandon all claims of absolute, timeless truth, valid through the ages, and accept individual theological configurations of different groups as "road signs to the Absolute."[121]

Now that the history of religion has been revived, the problem has become more acute, since now the two disciplines must forge a symbiosis. Some have called for a radical bifurcation, a parting of the ways.[122] But one suspects that these scholars assume a level of objectivity for the

---

Essays on the Comparative Method, ed. C. D. Evans, W. W. Hallo, and J. B. White, PTMS 34 (Pittsburgh: Pickwick, 1980), 1–26; see also S. Talmon, "The 'Comparative Method' in Biblical Interpretation—Principles and Problems," *Congress Volume: Göttingen, 1977*, VTSup 29 (Leiden: Brill, 1978), 320–56.

119. J. P. Gabler, "An Oration on the Proper Distinction between Biblical and Dogmatic Theology and the Specific Objectives of Each," in *The Flowering of Old Testament Theology: A Reader in Twentieth-Century Old Testament Theology, 1930–1990*, ed. B. C. Ollenburger, E. A. Martens, and G. F. Hasel, SBTS 1 (Winona Lake, Ind.: Eisenbrauns, 1992), 489–502.

120. "A History of Jahwism and of the Sacral Institutions in Israel in Outline," in *Old Testament Theology*, trans. D. M. G. Stalker, 2 vols. (New York: Harper & Row, 1962–65), 1:3–102. See also R. W. L. Moberly's discussion of this problem in chap. 16 of the present volume and the summary in Albertz, *History of Israelite Religion*, 1:2–12.

121. Gerstenberger, "Religion and Institutions of Ancient Israel," 274.

122. Of the many examples, see recently W. G. Dever, "'Will the Real Israel Please Stand Up?': Archaeology and Israelite Historiography: Part I," *BASOR* 297 (1995): 61–80, esp. 73–74.

historian that is unattainable in reality (as opposed to the subjectivity of the theologian, which they see as undesirable and unavoidable). The problems are complex, and I do not presume to offer a solution here. But I do offer a few observations that may provide a framework for work in the future. The much discussed question whether Old Testament theology ought to be purely descriptive or whether it ought in some way to make statements of faith need not cripple progress in either discipline. In a debate of the 1920s, Otto Eissfeldt argued for a sharp distinction between the history of Israelite religion and Old Testament theology. But Walther Eichrodt emphasized the *theological* character of historical investigation, choosing rather to expose the "subjective moment" as the epistemological problem of historical research.[123] Eichrodt critiqued historicism's mistake: the assumption that we can move from historical-empirical means to norms or universally valid propositions. Similarly, positivism errs in assuming that a particular discipline can renounce all philosophical grounding, and indeed *must* do so if it is to be "objective." Instead, Eichrodt encouraged scholars to embrace their guiding conceptions with methodological self-consciousness, and "not to set to work in the cheery optimism of absolute objectivity."[124]

Neither discipline, then, can be thoroughly descriptive. The history of Israelite religion will be primarily a historical endeavor, engaged in analysis of texts in light of archaeological, iconographical, and epigraphical materials from ancient Israel and surrounding cultures. It is possible, at least to some extent, to pursue this line of investigation independent of faith-based theological interests. Yet the historian of Israel's religion who believes himself or herself to be independently descriptive is misguided, and Eichrodt's warnings about "historicism" and "positivism" are apropos. To be independent of faith-based interests is not to be free of all metaphysical or theoretical presuppositions! On the other hand, the Old Testament theologian is engaged in analysis of the text as well, not so much in the light of archaeology, iconography, and epigraphy but in the light of other texts. And like the historian, the theologian can never be entirely descriptive. In my estimation, the difference is that the biblical theologian should not be independent of historical research, as the historian may endeavor to be independent of the

---

123. See now the translations of their articles by B. C. Ollenburger in *Flowering of Old Testament Theology,* ed. Ollenburger, Martens, and Hasel: O. Eissfeldt, "The History of Israelite-Jewish Religion and Old Testament Theology," 20–29; and W. Eichrodt, "Does Old Testament Theology Still Have Independent Significance within Old Testament Scholarship?" 30–39.

124. Eichrodt, "Does Old Testament Theology Still Have Independent Significance?" 34.

theological. The theologian must work with the data and explorations of the more non-theological discipline. But the warning of Eichrodt is pertinent for both. The purely objective and unbiased scholar, free from all beguiling preconceptions, is a figment of our scientific age and an unrealistic goal for modern scholars.

A major difference between these disciplines, then, is that Old Testament theology is largely canonical in its approach, which marks it as distinct from the history of Israel's religion. The former is concerned not with discontinuity in the text, but with exegeting the meaning of that discontinuity and applying it to the larger canonical context.[125] Biblical theology, in the main, accepts the received canon of the church and often plays a role in confessional communities and may thus have direct impact on the modern church. The history of religion also should have an impact, but secondarily so, as prolegomenon to and partner in the exegetical analysis of the text.

125. Sailhamer has recently argued for (and illustrated) a diachronic, confessional, and canonical approach to the text: J. H. Sailhamer, *Introduction to Old Testament Theology: A Canonical Approach* (Grand Rapids: Zondervan, 1995).

15

Opening Windows onto Biblical Worlds
Applying the Social Sciences to Hebrew Scripture

Charles E. Carter

Since the rise of critical scholarship in the period of the Enlightenment, scholars have approached the biblical texts from a humanities perspective.[1] Typical of all scholarship, whatever its theological presuppositions, have been analyses of the historical, linguistic, religious, and literary contexts of ancient Israel. What was often missing, however, was an analysis of Israelite culture in its social contexts, an assessment of its beliefs, social structures, and institutions from the perspective of the social sciences. Despite a few forays of anthropologists and sociologists into biblical studies, social science approaches remained peripheral to biblical studies until the last three decades. Yet, Scripture itself contains several "proto-sociological" observations, clues to the social significance of rituals or institutions. When the writer of the Holiness Code equates Yahweh's command for ritual purity with the proscription for ethnic purity, he is touching on the social significance for religious and social boundaries (Lev. 20:22–26).[2] Likewise, the Deuteronomic histo-

---

1. See N. K. Gottwald's evaluation in "Domain Assumptions and Societal Models in the Study of Pre-Monarchic Israel," in *Congress Volume: Edinburgh, 1974*, VTSup 28 (Leiden: Brill, 1975), 89–100; idem, *The Tribes of Yahweh: A Sociology of the Religion of Liberated Israel, 1250–1050 B.C.E.* (Maryknoll, N.Y.: Orbis, 1979), 5–22; idem, "Sociology of Ancient Israel," *ABD*, 6:79–89; and idem, "Reconstructing the Social History of Early Israel," *EI* 24 (1993): 77*–82*.
2. See C. E. Carter, "Purity and Distinction in Leviticus 20:22–26" (paper presented at the annual meeting of the Society of Biblical Literature, Washington, D.C., November 1993), available online at http://www.BiblicalResource.com/papers/Leviticus. See M. Douglas, *Purity and Danger: An Analysis of the Concepts of Pollution and Taboo* (London: Routledge & Kegan Paul, 1966). See also D. Smith-Christopher, "The Mixed Marriage

rian comments on the shifting role and function of prophets in his par-
enthetic statement that prophets were formerly called "seers" and "men
of God" (1 Sam. 9:8–9). Provisional observations of this type are also
found in classical texts, with some scholars identifying Herodotus and
others Plato or Aristotle as the first "sociologist";[3] early rabbinic texts
often explore the social function of customs from ancient Israel's and
their own cultures.[4] Even so, however, these sociological observations
tended to be peripheral, subjugated to the overarching religious or theological interpretation of Israelite and Jewish texts.

In the rest of this chapter, I provide a brief historical account of the
emergence of the social sciences and their subsequent application to
biblical cultures and then assess the contributions of this emerging
field of study to knowledge of the biblical world. I conclude with an
analysis of the points of concern evangelicals may raise regarding its
application to Scripture and a discussion of the appropriate methods
for using the social sciences to study the warp and woof of Israelite life.

The Emergence of the Social Sciences

With its perspectives rooted in the priority of human reason over revelation and the empirical analysis of experience, the Enlightenment is
generally seen as having provided the impetus for the social and behavioral sciences to develop.[5] Philosophical treatises by Hobbes, Locke,
Mill, and other Enlightenment thinkers proposed that human societies
possessed certain common elements and that all societies exist on a

---

Crisis in Ezra 9–10 and Nehemiah 13: A Study of the Sociology of the Post-Exilic Judaean
Community," in *Second Temple Studies*, vol. 2, *Temple and Community in the Persian Pe-
riod*, ed. T. C. Eskenazi and K. H. Richards, JSOTSup 175 (Sheffield: Sheffield Academic
Press, 1994), 242–65.

3. D. C. Benjamin and V. H. Matthews, "Social Sciences and Biblical Studies," *Semeia*
68 (1994): 14; see also G. Lenski and J. Lenski, *Human Societies: An Introduction to Mac-
rosociology*, 5th ed. (New York: McGraw-Hill, 1987), 24.

4. See the helpful study of R. R. Wilson, *Sociology and the Old Testament* (Philadelphia: Fortress, 1979), 10.

5. The social and behavioral sciences refer to anthropology, sociology, political science, archaeology, economics, psychology, and the study of the behavioral aspects of cultural anthropology, social psychology, and biology. The term used for all of these studies
before the 1950s was the *social sciences;* after 1950, the *behavioral sciences* came to be
preferred, though the terms are still often used synonymously. For a more complete discussion of the rise and context of the social sciences, see my article, "A Discipline in Transition: The Contributions of the Social Sciences to the Study of the Hebrew Bible," in
Community, Identity, and Ideology: Social Science Approaches to the Hebrew Bible, ed.
C. E. Carter and C. L. Meyers (Winona Lake, Ind.: Eisenbrauns, 1996), 3–39. For an exhaustive treatment of the role of the Enlightenment in the emergence of the social sciences, see also M. Harris, *The Rise of Anthropological Theory: A History of Theories of Culture* (New York: Columbia University Press, 1968).

continuum of social complexity. These ideas formed the foundation for both sociology and anthropology, viewing societies from a common, humanist perspective and providing a basis for the comparative analysis of human culture and its institutions.

Many of the seminal scholars within the social sciences—from Tönnies and Spencer to W. Robertson Smith, Durkheim, and Weber—developed these ideas into the two related disciplines of anthropology and sociology.[6] Several distinct lines of social analysis have emerged in the last century. These are typically categorized as the conflict tradition, the structural-functional approach, the idealist perspective, and the materialist perspective. The *conflict model* of analysis examines the way that societies and social entities respond to the influences of internal or external social, economic, military, and political pressures. It explores the strategies of these sometimes competing groups as they respond to each other's concerns, their attempts to assert their own influence and to legitimate their interests. It is concerned with the way in which societies achieve balance in the face of the flux that often results from the interrelationship of groups with competing interests. When societies fail to achieve balance they may instead weaken and ultimately implode.[7]

In contrast to the conflict tradition, the *structural-functional approach* emphasizes the basic unity that exists within societies. While it does not deny the existence of conflict and competing ideologies within a particular society, it suggests that even in the face of these tensions, balance is achieved by consensus rather than being imposed. The structural-functional approach emerged as an alternative to the naively evolutionary and deterministic perspective that was introduced by Spencer and that dominated the social sciences for nearly a century. It grew out of the French structuralist school that traces itself to Durkheim, and has been the most prominent method of inquiry in European and American sociology since the 1950s. As its name implies, it commonly examines the structure and function of both institutions and ideologies within societies as well as the complex relationships and interrelationships that result from their interaction.[8]

6. Articles by M. Weber, A. Causse, and W. R. Smith appear in *Community, Identity, and Ideology*, 40–118. For an in-depth analysis of the growth of the social sciences and their use in the study of the Hebrew Bible, see A. D. H. Mayes, *The Old Testament in Sociological Perspective* (London: Pickering, 1989).

7. For a discussion of the conflict model, see B. Malina, "The Social Sciences and Biblical Interpretation," *Int* 37 (1982): 229–42, esp. 233–35; and Mayes, *Old Testament in Sociological Perspective*, 18–27 and 36–77.

8. On the structural-functional approach, see Malina, "Social Sciences and Biblical Interpretation," 233–35; Lenski and Lenski, *Human Societies*, 25–26; Mayes, *Old Testament in Sociological Perspective*, 27–35 and 78–117; and Harris, *Rise of Anthropological Theory*, 468–74 and 514–28.

The *materialist* perspective (often referred to as cultural materialism) is frequently associated with the theory of Marx and is typically contrasted with the *idealist* orientation.[9] Both approaches agree on the power of social, religious, and political ideologies. They differ, however, on the origin of these ideologies, the factors that make them effective, and their role in cultural change. The materialist viewpoint posits that the physical realities of a culture give rise to the ideologies whereas the idealist perspective emphasizes the impact of ideologies on particular social structures. A good example of these approaches concerns the emergence and significance of the Israelite dietary laws. Marvin Harris, writing from a materialist orientation, maintains that the pork taboo resulted from the economic and environmental constraints of Syria-Palestine. Pigs, he suggests, compete with humans for natural resources such as water, food, and shade. The costs—both economic and in terms of human capital—were too great for both pigs and humans to flourish concurrently in this environment with its limited resources. Thus pork taboo emerged in order to protect human culture and ensure its survival.

Mary Douglas, writing from an idealist perspective, claims that the dietary restrictions come instead from a more comprehensive concept of order and purity. In her view, many of the Priestly writings establish categories of "normalcy"; any animal or practice that violates that normal order is considered out of place and therefore unclean.[10] While it is true that much, if not most, sociological theory is idealist in nature,[11] what is often overlooked is that some of the early anthropological and sociological theorists recognized the effect of material realities in the development of social structures, cultural practices, and ideology. Thus W. Robertson Smith called attention to the materialist origin and significance of rituals; and L. Wallis and A. Causse independently argued that the prophetic emphasis on social justice was rooted in class divisions, in the material effects of oppression.[12]

9. The term *cultural materialism* was introduced by M. Harris and subsequently adapted by biblical scholars and Syro-Palestinian archaeologists. See Harris's work, *Cultural Materialism: The Struggle for a Science of Culture* (New York: Vintage, 1980).

10. See the selections by Harris (135–51) and Douglas (119–34) on this topic in *Community, Identity, and Ideology*.

11. G. Herion, "The Impact of Modern and Social Science Assumptions on the Reconstruction of Israelite History," *JSOT* 34 (1986): 3–33; reprinted in *Community, Identity, and Ideology*, 230–57.

12. W. R. Smith, *Lectures on the Religion of the Semites: First Series: The Fundamental Institutions* (Edinburgh: Black, 1889), 437ff. See the discussion in my "Discipline in Transition," 13–15; and T. O. Beidelman, *W. Robertson Smith and the Sociological Study of Religion* (Chicago: University of Chicago Press, 1975), 56–57. See L. Wallis, "Sociological Significance of the Bible," *American Journal of Sociology* 12 (1907): 532–52; and A. Causse, *Les "pauvres" d'Israël: Prophètes, psalmistes, messianistes* (Strasbourg: Librairie Istra, 1922).

Sociology and the Hebrew Bible: A Brief Overview

The most influential work of the twentieth century on the social setting of ancient Israel is without question Max Weber's *Ancient Judaism*.[13] A cursory look at his analysis of ancient Israel demonstrates its impact even on the most recent social science studies of the Hebrew Bible. His understanding of the covenant and its centrality to ancient Israel's social and religious formation, his analysis of the social structure of Israel—based on the *bêt ʾāb*, *mišpāḥâ*, and *šebeṭ*—his assessment of Yahweh as a war deity, his analysis of the role of law and the social context of the Levites, his description of the judges as charismatic leaders, his analysis of the origin and growth of the prophetic tradition, and his treatment of the origins of sectarian Judaism continue to be discussed, even when newer data require that his ideas be revised. Weber's studies embody the conflict tradition within sociology; biblical scholars whose work follows this general tradition include G. Mendenhall's peasant revolt model of Israelite origins and B. Lang's *Monotheism and the Prophetic Minority*.[14]

Antonin Causse analyzed Israelite society through the lens of the French sociological school and its most prominent thinkers, Émile Durkheim and Lucien Lévy-Bruhl.[15] He consciously applied to ancient Israel Durkheim's notion of "group mentality" and Lévy-Bruhl's notion of the development of human consciousness from a primitive, collective phase to a logical, individualistic phase.[16] Causse's analyses of Israel were published initially in a series of articles in the *Revue d'histoire et de philosophie religeuses*, but then revised and collected into several

13. Published initially as a series of essays in the journal *Archiv für Sozialwissenschaft und Sozialforschung* (1917–1919), the work was edited by his wife and published posthumously as *Das antike Judentum* in 1921. See H. H. Gerth and D. Martindale, eds. and trans., "Preface," in *Ancient Judaism* (Glencoe, Ill.: Free Press, 1952), ix.

14. G. Mendenhall, "The Hebrew Conquest of Palestine," *BA* 25 (1962): 66–87; reprinted in *Community, Identity, and Ideology*, ed. Carter and Meyers, 152–69. B. Lang, *Monotheism and the Prophetic Minority: An Essay in Biblical History and Sociology*, SWBAS 1 (Sheffield: Almond, 1983).

15. For a complete discussion of Causse's thought and significance, see S. T. Kimbrough Jr., "A Non-Weberian Sociological Approach to Israelite Religion," *JNES* 31 (1972): 197–202; idem, *Israelite Religion in Sociological Perspective: The Work of Antonin Causse*, Studies in Oriental Religions 4 (Wiesbaden: Harrassowitz, 1978); Mayes, *Old Testament in Sociological Perspective*, 78–87.

16. Causse's reliance on Lévy-Bruhl's categories is generally seen as his greatest weakness. "His adherence to the categories of pre-logical and logical thinking, which allowed him to state a development from a primitive collectivism binding together worshippers and their God into a ritual community, to an individual rationalism, went beyond what Durkheim considered the proper task of sociology. Moreover, it reflected an understanding of the nature of human thinking which was quickly shown to be inappropriate, at least for ancient Israel" (Mayes, *Old Testament in Sociological Perspective*, 87).

books.[17] Although his work is not as widely known as Weber's, it is no less insightful; and though many of the scholars who have commented on his work have considered it "Weberian" in outlook and perspective,[18] his writings instead exemplify the structural-functional approach to sociology.

In Causse's analysis, a communal, primitive stage is characteristic of the tribal period, with its emphasis on kinship and family bonds, and relates to Durkheim's concept of "organic solidarity." As Israelite society became more complex not only did these social bonds lose significance, but the class distinction and social stratification of the monarchy weakened the earlier social unity. Urban centers increased in power and importance, usurping the role of villages and their ruling structures. Causse held that during this phase, and under the impetus of the prophetic movement, a shift began toward a more individualistic mentality. The influence of the earlier corporate solidarity could still be seen in the moralizing tone of the Deuteronomic History and the judgment oracles of the eighth-century B.C. prophets. With Ezekiel and the exilic prophets, however, a new notion emerges: the responsibility of the individual for his or her own actions. This shift toward individualism is completed with the emergence of sectarian Judaism in the late fifth and early fourth centuries B.C.[19]

The sociological perspective came to the fore once again in the work of George Mendenhall and Norman K. Gottwald. Though they approach ancient Israel very differently in the details of their scholarship, both raise significant methodological questions, both challenge the assumptions that had previously dominated biblical scholarship, and both agree that biblical Israel can be understood fully only when one analyzes its social setting. Mendenhall's initial contribution concerns the question of Israel's emergence in Palestine and the role of Yahwism

17. See his *Les "pauvres" d'Israël;* idem, *Les dispersés d'Israël: Les origines de la diaspora et son rôle dans la formation du Judaïsme* (Paris: Alcan, 1929); and his most important work, *Du groupe ethnique à la communauté religieuse: Le problème sociologique de la religion d'Israël* (Paris: Alcan, 1937).

18. According to Kimbrough, no less a scholar than W. F. Albright considered Weber to have been the source of Causse's biblical sociology ("Non-Weberian Sociological Approach," 199, 202).

19. Causse's "From an Ethnic Group to a Religious Community: The Sociological Problem of Judaism," is reproduced in *Community, Identity, and Ideology,* 95–118; see also Mayes, *Old Testament in Sociological Perspective,* 85–86. The number of scholars who have followed Causse and applied an even more rigorous structural-functional approach to the Hebrew Bible is impressive. To Causse, one can add N. K. Gottwald's groundbreaking work, *The Tribes of Yahweh;* R. R. Wilson's *Prophecy and Society in Ancient Israel* (Philadelphia: Fortress, 1980); and F. Frick's *The Formation of the State in Ancient Israel: A Survey of Models and Theories,* SWBAS 4 (Decatur, Ga.: Almond, 1985).

as a cultural tradition that gave the newly formed Israel its social and religious coherence. He questions the validity of using a nineteenth-century model of Bedouin culture as a model for Israelite society; he shows that the notion of the tribe had been poorly defined in previous research, which had not approached tribal structure from a social science perspective; he suggests that Israel's emergence was a complex social process that originated from Canaanite unrest, as demonstrated in the Amarna Letters, and converged as the *ʿapiru* joined with the band of slaves who had escaped Egyptian oppression under Moses' leadership. In his view, both the Moses group and the Canaanite peasants along with the *ʿapiru* shared a common identity when they adopted Yahwism as a religious tradition and rejected enslavement and oppression. But Mendenhall's contribution goes far beyond his programmatic "peasant revolt model" of Israelite origins. He develops Weber's concept of the covenantal community as the basis for Israelite unity and studies the social and religious context of law.

Gottwald accepts the basic outline of Mendenhall's peasant revolt model, but approaches earliest Israel from a materialist rather than an idealist perspective. Gottwald's groundbreaking study on "Domain Assumptions and Societal Models" also critiques the basic working assumptions of biblical scholars, as well as what he refers to as the "humanist" approach rooted in linguistics, theology, and literary and historical studies. He identifies three assumptions that have formed the basis of theories on Israel's emergence: that social change results primarily from population displacement, originates from the desert regions, and is idiosyncratic or arbitrary. He suggests instead that social change is a normal, internal process, that the desert cultures had a minimal influence on this change, and that such change is multifaceted and complex. Gottwald's critique anticipated a major change in both biblical archaeology and anthropology. In questioning these ruling assumptions and replacing them with ones that define social change in more broadly based and nuanced ways, he places a greater emphasis on indigenous developments and views Israelite culture and cultural change from a more systemic and holistic viewpoint.

Mendenhall and Gottwald have been both roundly criticized and widely praised for their pioneering work. Both, for example, have been criticized for lacking sophistication on the one hand, and for being too comprehensive on the other.[20] Gottwald's *Tribes of Yahweh* has been al-

---

20. Both criticisms can be found in N. P. Lemche's "On the Use of 'Systems Theory,' 'Macro Theories,' and 'Evolutionistic Thinking,'" *SJOT* 2 (1990): 73–88, and in his longer work, *Early Israel and Historical Studies on the Israelite Society before the Monarchy* (Leiden: Brill, 1985).

ternately dismissed as "the worst of arm-chair sociology"[21] and compared to Julius Wellhausen's *Prolegomena to the History of Ancient Israel* and W. F. Albright's *From the Stone Age to Christianity* in its
potential impact on the field of biblical studies.[22] If there is a major
weakness in Gottwald's early work, one particularly demonstrated in
Tribes, it is his personal commitment to a Marxist dialectic. The cultural materialist perspective at times seems to be forced upon Israelite
tradition, causing him to draw conclusions that the data do not necessarily warrant. For example, while it is true that "only as the full *mate-
riality* of ancient Israel is more securely grasped will we be able to make
proper sense of its *spirituality*,"[23] Gottwald is clearly off the mark when
he interprets Israelite literacy as a social tool designed to celebrate its
difference from the Canaanite context from which it emerged.[24] Instead, writing is a tool intended to encourage social order and to control
access to goods and resources; as such, it promotes social control rather
than independence. Similarly, Gottwald may be correct in observing
that a critical element of premonarchic Israel is its egalitarian (and he
would add, "anti-statist") ideology. But he may be criticized for being
inconsistent in applying his materialist model to biblical Israel. It is
more likely that any egalitarianism that may have existed in tribal Israel
was due to the social realities from which Israel emerged. The earliest
settlements in the hill country are characterized by crude pottery and
architectural traditions and a subsistence economy with little, if any,
surplus. Societies with these features tend to be egalitarian by nature,
since stratification tends to occur only when a substantial surplus is
produced.[25] A commitment to egalitarianism, and possible legitimiza-
tion of it in Yahwistic religion, would probably have been secondary
and socially influenced.

Toward a Sociology of Biblical Israel

As the interest in applying the social sciences to the biblical world has
increased over the last thirty years, several distinct areas of interest
have emerged. Since many different scholars apply different models

21. A. Rainey's acerbic review of *Tribes* in *JAOS* 107 (1987): 541–43.
22. W. Brueggemann, "*The Tribes of Yahweh:* An Essay Review," *JAAR* 48 (1980):
441–51.
23. Gottwald, *Tribes*, xxv.
24. Ibid., 409.
25. G. Lenski, *Power and Privilege* (New York: McGraw-Hill, 1966), discusses the influence of economic surplus on social stratification. In particular note chap. 3, "The Dynamics of Distributive Systems," and chap. 4, "The Structure of Distributive Systems,"
43–93.

and approaches to the biblical data and to these interests, it may be helpful to frame the following discussion in terms of a few fundamental questions and then to present some of the basic answers they have received. These central questions include, but are not limited to, the following: What social forces led to the emergence of Israel in Palestine's central hill country and what was the shape of Israelite society during this time period? What led to the emergence of a monarchy from a loosely federated group of tribes? How should one define the role and function of Israelite prophecy? To what degree is it possible to recover the role and place of women within Israelite society—both its sanctioned and suppressed forms? What is the social function of the biblical traditions and to what degree do they reflect the real versus the ideal Israel? To what degree do changes in the social fabric after the exile affect the concept of a "divinely chosen" community called "Israel" and how do those changes affect emergent Judaism? Perhaps most fundamentally, what social models are appropriate analogs for biblical Israel, and how should these models be applied?

The Origins of Israel and Development of the Monarchy

Since the initial question that Mendenhall and Gottwald addressed was Israel's emergence, it is no surprise that this question has evoked the most discussion in the recent social science analysis of biblical cultures. What is surprising, however, is that even now no consensus has been reached. Albright's "conquest model," which closely parallels the biblical traditions of the Book of Judges, has been largely abandoned in the scholarly world. The peaceful infiltration and the peasant revolt theories remain the most widely held theories that account for the Israelite settlement. Both seek to combine archaeological, biblical, and extra-biblical textual data to achieve a comprehensive picture of nascent Israel, but both have radically different points of departure. The peaceful infiltration theory, most recently revised by Israel Finkelstein,[26] maintains that the Israelites entered the central hills from Transjordan, abandoning a seminomadic lifestyle in favor of a sedentary existence. The model remains heavily influenced by analogs from Bedouin and other seminomadic cultures. The peasant revolt theory suggests that the earliest Israelites were in effect disillusioned Canaanites, who either rebelled against or withdrew from a stratified, oppressive Canaanite city-state system that is reflected in the Amarna Letters and in the archaeological record of Syria-Palestine. Essentially, these Canaanites

26. *The Archaeology of the Israelite Settlement* (Jerusalem: Israel Exploration Society, 1988).

"retribalized"—that is, they left a more developed social setting of the city-state for a more open tribal system.

Several refinements of the basic peasant revolt model have been proposed. Attempting to merge both Mendenhall's and Gottwald's theories, Marvin Chaney has reexamined the Amarna correspondence as a social indicator and seeks to harmonize archaeological data and the unrest documented in the Amarna Letters with the traditions of Joshua and Judges. What emerges from his study is a more comprehensive portrait of both biblical and social worlds. Gerhard Lenski, a sociologist who critiques Gottwald's work, suggests that Gottwald's reconstruction of Israelite society fails to answer a more basic question.[27] Lenski maintains that while peasant unrest and even revolts are common in agrarian and semifeudal societies, they are seldom successful. Given this typical failure of peasant revolts, he suggests that more fundamental questions for biblical sociologists are: Why did this revolt succeed? and Why did a monarchy replace the more egalitarian tribal social organization so quickly? Lenski contends that a social model that more directly answers both questions is the "frontier model." In this model, a republican organization—which tribal Israel loosely embodies—is typically replaced by a more centralized monarchic structure, as is the case in Israel.[28]

Several scholars have analyzed the nature of Israelite society in the premonarchic period and the forces that led toward the monarchy. Abraham Malamat applied Max Weber's notion of the ideal type and the various stages of social development to the "judges." According to Weber, societies typically progress from ad hoc to institutional forms of leadership. Weber referred to this process as the "routinization" of authority, and suggested that such authority begins in a "charismatic" phase in which leaders arise in times of social duress; these leaders function for a limited time and for a specific purpose. Often, however, the position of the charismatic leader becomes "routinized" as the position that was originally spontaneous and centered around the leader becomes part of the social fabric. Weber refers to this as the "rational" phase of leadership. Malamat identifies Israel's "judges" as charismatic leaders and suggests that the Philistine threat produced the necessary impetus for the charismatic phase to end and the monarchy, a routinized, rational institution, to emerge.

27. Review of Gottwald's *Tribes of Yahweh* in *RelSRev* 53 (1980): 275–78.
28. Gottwald answers Lenski's observations in "Two Models for the Origins of Ancient Israel: Social Revolution or Frontier Development," in *The Quest for the Kingdom of God: Studies in Honor of George E. Mendenhall*, ed. H. B. Huffmon et al. (Winona Lake, Ind.: Eisenbrauns, 1983), 5–24. I have developed the frontier model further in an unpublished manuscript, "The Emerging Frontier in the Highlands of Canaan: New Models for an Old Problem," available online at http://www.BiblicalResource.com/papers/Frontier.

In the years following Malamat's study, several scholars have applied a different model to the social setting of the "tribal period" and the development of the monarchy. The studies of Frank Frick, James Flanagan, Israel Finkelstein, and Robert Coote and Keith Whitelam have contributed to the emergence of a new consensus. All identify this period as a chiefdom, a type of society that frequently precedes a monarchy or centralized form of government in social development.[29] Several elements unify these studies. They all are rooted in anthropological and/or macrosociological theory, they all make significant use of archaeological data, and they all agree that such external data provide a more accurate portrait of such a dramatic change than does the Philistine threat model that relies rather uncritically on the biblical narratives in Judges and 1 Samuel. This marks a significant departure from previous scholarship. It recognizes that the perspective of the biblical writers was not sociological but theological/ideological and maintains that in order fully to understand the social development of ancient Israel one can profit from applying models of social development from the social sciences to the biblical data. This perspective, and this use of models from other cultures, unites virtually all social science criticism of the Hebrew Scriptures.

Each of these studies concentrates on different elements of chiefdoms. Flanagan directly applies to ancient Israel the theory of social evolution initially developed by Elman Service. He suggests that Israel evolved from a tribal or segmented society, to a chiefdom, and finally to a monarchy. He identifies the rule of Saul, and then of David, as chiefdoms. In a subsequent study, he analyzes the forces that led to a full-fledged monarchy, employing the notion of a hologram and its multifaceted image to suggest that any social analysis of Israelite society must be multilayered and account for multiple factors in order to present a coherent picture of Israelite society.[30]

Frick's study is more archaeological in nature. He demonstrates the weaknesses in the former consensus view that slaked-lime cisterns, ter-

29. R. Coote and K. Whitelam, "The Emergence of Israel: Social Transformation and State Formation Following the Decline in Late Bronze Age Trade," *Semeia* 37 (1986): 109–47; I. Finkelstein, "The Emergence of the Monarchy in Israel: The Environmental and Socio-Economic Aspects," *JSOT* 44 (1989): 43–74; J. Flanagan, "Chiefs in Israel," *JSOT* 20 (1981): 47–73; Frick, *Formation of the State*; and A. Malamat, "Charismatic Leadership in the Book of Judges," in *Magnalia Dei: The Mighty Acts of God: Essays on the Bible and Archaeology in Memory of G. Ernest Wright*, ed. F. M. Cross, W. E. Lemke, and P. D. Miller Jr. (Garden City, N.Y.: Doubleday, 1976), 293–310. With the exception of Frick's work on state formation, these articles are reprinted in *Community, Identity, and Ideology*.

30. J. Flanagan, *David's Social Drama: A Hologram of Ancient Israel*, SWBAS 2 (Sheffield: Almond, 1988).

race agriculture, and iron tools were the prime technological forces that allowed Israelite settlement in the hill country of Palestine. Instead, he suggests, these technologies were not developed by the Israelites to enable settlement, but rather were technological adaptations that allowed a surplus to be produced in an agriculturally marginal area in response to the pressures of population growth. In most societies, as a surplus is produced social complexity concomitantly increases. In the case of Israel, the increase in agricultural production both allowed a chiefdom to emerge and made controlling its territory more desirable to other political entities such as the Philistines. Frick finds evidence for the social differentiation that typifies chiefdoms in the site of Tel Masos. Excavations in the northeastern sector of the tell (Area A) revealed a belt of ten houses with similar size, plan, and artifacts. Apart from other data, this might suggest that the social structure of the settlement was egalitarian. In Area H, located in the southern part of the site, however, a large building was discovered that was twice the size of those in Area A. It contained pottery that was more sophisticated in both form and decoration, evidence of imported wares, and luxury items, such as an ivory lion's head. Thus both the size of the building and its contents suggest that its inhabitants were of a different social rank than those of the buildings in Area A, that the family was that of the local area's chieftain.[31]

Coote and Whitelam identify the various social pressures that existed at the end of the Late Bronze Age and the beginning of the Iron Age as factors that allowed first the emergence of Israel and then its transition from chiefdom to monarchy. They suggest that the perspective of the French theorist Ferdnand Braudel of *la longue durée* best explains Israelite political and sociological evolution. Rather than view the tribal and monarchic periods as two opposite poles or even two distinct developments, they concentrate on the *processes* behind the various social changes that occurred in Syria-Palestine and view them as developments on a continuum. Among the factors influencing the emergence of Israel and the formation of the monarchy are the collapse of Egyptian hegemony and trade at the end of the Late Bronze Age, agricultural intensification in the Early Iron Age, social stratification, and population pressures.

Israel Finkelstein also addresses the emergence of Israel and transition toward a monarchy from the perspective of *la longue durée*. While his studies are conversant with important social science theories, he does not always apply social models consistently or in a methodologi-

---

31. In particular, see the section "Tel Masos, Agriculture, and the Archaeology of Chiefdoms," in *Formation of the State*, 159–69.

cally sound manner.[32] Nonetheless, his sensitivity to the environmental features of the land of Israel, his understanding of the demographic patterns from the mid-thirteenth through the tenth centuries, and his ability to interpret these data in a comprehensive manner make his studies essential reading for a careful study of earliest Israel.[33] Finkelstein advocates a neo-Altian, peaceful infiltration model to explain the settlement of Israel in the central highlands of Canaan and suggests that the settlement process was one of sedentarization of nomads.[34] He argues that the four-room house, once identified with a specifically Israelite material culture, follows the pattern of the nomadic tents, and that archaeological features such as storage pits that are independent of architectural remains for early settlements such as Isbet Sarta also represent a nomadic lifestyle and the first phases of sedentarization. Like Frick, Flanagan, and Coote and Whitelam, he views much of the premonarchic period as a chiefdom, and uses site distribution and population estimates to suggest an increased social and economic structure that led to the establishment and increasing complexity of kingship and petty statehood.

Prophecy and the Prophetic Tradition

Biblical scholars of all theological persuasions have identified the prophetic tradition as one of the enduring contributions of Israelite religion to subsequent human civilization. Much scholarship has concentrated on the prophetic office, the prophetic message, and the literary and moral force of prophetic literature. But the social sciences have also been applied to the prophetic tradition from the earliest efforts of W. Robertson Smith to the more recent work of Robert R. Wilson. Several lines of interest have been particularly fruitful. Max Weber viewed the prophetic tradition as emerging from the early Israelite notion of YHWH as a war deity and from the perspective of covenant.[35] While

32. I have analyzed Finkelstein's sometimes insightful, sometimes uncritical use of social modeling in "A Social and Demographic Study of Post-Exilic Judah" (Ph.D. diss., Duke University, 1991), see in particular chaps. 3, 5, and 6.

33. See in particular *Archaeology of the Israelite Settlement* and "Emergence of the Monarchy in Israel."

34. By describing Finkelstein's study as "neo-Altian," I am drawing attention to two things. On the one hand, his work follows the basic outline of Israelite emergence first proposed by A. Alt (see "Die Landnahme der Israeliten in Palästina," in A. Alt, *Kleine Schriften zur Geschichte des Volkes Israel*, 3 vols. [Munich: Beck, 1953–59], 1:89–125; in English as "The Settlement of the Israelites in Palestine," in A. Alt, *Essays on Old Testament History and Religion*, trans. R. A. Wilson [Oxford: Blackwell, 1966], 135–69). On the other hand, his work brings to bear new data from archaeological studies not available to Alt but that augment the peaceful infiltration model.

35. Weber, *Ancient Judaism*, 90–117.

certainly not all scholars have adopted his conceptual framework of the war deity, virtually all scholars speak of the covenantal, and therefore sociological, nature of prophecy. Further, Weber was one of the first scholars to speak of what he called the "social psychology of the prophets" and to seek to uncover their social context.[36] Writing from a different perspective, both Louis Wallis and Antonin Causse saw the prophetic call for social justice as rooted in the growing stratification and class struggles that accompanied the development of Israelite society after the period of the judges.[37] Gottwald stresses this notion of the influence of an increased level of material and economic differentiation on the prophetic ideal in his most recent social reconstructions.[38]

Recently, social science approaches to prophecy have used cross-cultural parallels to concentrate on such issues as social location and context, prophetic authority, and the rise of the apocalyptic tradition. Robert R. Wilson's *Prophecy and Society in Ancient Israel* identifies the Israelite prophets as intermediaries and finds social parallels for Israelite prophecy in shamanism and spirit possession of contemporary tribal societies. He analyzes spirit possession that is considered "positive" and "negative" by their social groups and is particularly interested in the social context of prophets and the level of cultural support that is necessary for prophetic survival. He identifies two distinct prophetic traditions, the Ephraimite tradition of such figures as Samuel, Elijah and Elisha, Hosea and Jeremiah, and the Judean tradition of Nathan, Isaiah of Jerusalem, and Amos. While these traditions have distinct theological perspectives, they are similar in that individual prophets function either as central intermediaries—those who have direct access to and the approval of the ruling establishment—or peripheral intermediaries—those whose access is limited and who frequently lead protest movements against the establishment.

Thomas Overholt and Burke Long focus more on prophetic authority and, like Wilson, introduce ethnographic parallels for biblical prophecy. Overholt concentrates on Native American shamans as a source for prophetic models, using the Ghost Dance movement of the late nineteenth century and the Seneca holy man Handsome Lake.[39]

---

36. Ibid., 267–96.

37. Causse, *Les "pauvres" d'Israël;* Wallis, "Sociological Significance of the Bible."

38. This is particularly evident in his "Sociology of Ancient Israel," *ABD*, 6:84. Gottwald's "Hypothesis about Social Class" delineates the notion of increasing class differentiation but does not include the prophetic protest against the upper classes.

39. T. Overholt, "The Ghost Dance of 1890 and the Nature of the Prophetic Process," *Ethnohistory* 21 (1974): 37–63; idem, "Prophecy: The Problem of Cross-Cultural Comparison," *Semeia* 21 (1982): 55–78; B. O. Long, "Prophetic Authority as Social Reality," in *Canon and Authority,* ed. G. W. Coats and B. O. Long (Philadelphia: Fortress, 1977), 3–20.

He builds on Long's suggestion that prophetic authority resides not only in the spoken word but also in the community to which the prophet speaks. He develops a dynamic idea of authority, suggesting that prophecy was not simply a function of the message from YHWH but also was affected by the audience to whom he or she spoke. Comparing Handsome Lake with Jeremiah, he maintains that the prophet would typically receive feedback from the hearers, which would in turn help the prophet to refocus the message. As members of the community accept the revised message, they in turn validate the prophet's authority.

Bernhard Lang views the prophetic movement with its monotheistic ideal as a minority religious tradition.[40] Lang's study identifies the salient points in the development of monotheism within ancient Israelite religious tradition, and like Wallis, Causse, and Gottwald, places the prophetic minority tradition within a social context of peasant poverty. Prophets, like Amos with his concern for social justice, often stood in a position of social critics.

Paul Hanson and Steven Cook present opposing accounts of the rise of apocalyptic tradition. Both see the crisis of exile and return as providing a major impetus for apocalyptic literature to emerge from the prophetic movement. Hanson applies the conflict tradition of the social sciences to the period and the literature of Haggai, First and Second Zechariah, Joel, and Third Isaiah. In his view, a critical tension existed between the hierocratic party represented by the Jerusalem priestly establishment and the disenfranchised visionaries.[41] Cook suggests instead that apocalyptic tradition need not arise from marginalized groups. He notes that prophets with priestly origins or influences, such as Ezekiel, First Zechariah, and Joel, operated from an apocalyptic perspective with its hope for a radical inbreaking of God's kingdom. By rooting his position in the study of millenarian groups in many different historical and social settings, Cook shows not only that priestly groups can and do demonstrate eschatological fervor but that they also frequently hold central positions of power and leadership.[42] Thus he contends that it was not internecine conflict but a priestly, millennial context that best explains apocalyptic literature, the apocalyptic worldview, and an apocalyptic community.

40. Lang, *Monotheism and the Prophetic Minority*.

41. P. Hanson, *The Dawn of Apocalyptic: The Historical and Sociological Roots of Jewish Apocalyptic Eschatology*, rev. ed. (Philadelphia: Fortress, 1979), 70–79, 258–70; idem, ed., *Visionaries and Their Apocalypses*, IRT 2 (Philadelphia: Fortress; London: SPCK, 1983), 37–60.

42. S. L. Cook, *Prophecy and Apocalypticism: The Postexilic Social Setting* (Minneapolis: Augsburg Fortress, 1995), 19–84.

Gender in Cult and Culture

One of the most important areas of the social setting of ancient Israel to be recovered is the role and place of women within Israelite culture in general and in Israelite religion in particular. While a significant portion of this recovery has come through feminist scholarship, often literary and linguistic studies of the Hebrew text and comparative analyses of ancient Near Eastern documents,[43] the social sciences—particularly archaeology, sociology, and anthropology—have shed considerable light on these issues as well. Thus the most important works on women in ancient Israel have been both cross-cultural and interdisciplinary in nature; most have built in some way on early works of both Rosemary Radford Ruether and Phyllis Trible.[44] The result of the more recent studies is on the one hand a clearer understanding of male/female roles and authority and on the other hand an indication of the degree to which women enjoyed positions of status. What is clear is that where traditional, male-dominated areas of society are restrictive, women often find positions of power and influence outside the accepted social frameworks. Thus women exercised significant authority within the wisdom tradition and functioned as prophets and official cultic functionaries, as did Miriam, Deborah, and Huldah.[45] As Phyllis Bird points out, male-dominated biblical scholarship often devalued other important roles of women as cult functionaries, such as their role as professional mourners, singers, and celebrants. In this respect, Bird has furthered the discussion of women's place in ancient Israel by making scholars more aware of the ways in which interpretive bias has further skewed the record of the Hebrew Bible; for males dominated not only

43. See, e.g., *Women's Earliest Records from Ancient Egypt to Western Asia*, ed. B. S. Lesko, BJS 166 (Atlanta: Scholars Press, 1989); for a detailed bibliography of works applying feminist perspectives to the study of Scripture, see M. I. Gruber, *Women in the Biblical World: A Study Guide*, vol. 1, *Women in the World of Hebrew Scripture*, ATLA Bibliography Series 38 (Philadelphia: ATLA; Lanham, Md.: Scarecrow, 1995).

44. Ruether, *Religion and Sexism: Images of Women in the Jewish and Christian Traditions* (New York: Simon & Schuster, 1974); Trible, *God and the Rhetoric of Sexuality*, OBT (Philadelphia: Fortress, 1978); idem, *Texts of Terror: Literary Feminist Readings of Biblical Narratives*, OBT (Philadelphia: Fortress, 1984).

45. C. Camp, "The Wise Women of 2 Samuel: A Role Model for Women in Early Israel," *CBQ* 43 (1981): 14–29; idem, *Wisdom and the Feminine in the Book of Proverbs*, BLS 11 (Decatur, Ga.: Almond, 1985); P. Trible, "Huldah's Holy Writ: On Women and Biblical Authority," *Touchstone* 3 (1985): 6–13; J. Ochshorn, *The Female Experience and the Nature of the Divine* (Bloomington: Indiana University Press, 1981), 182; and C. E. Carter, "Huldah as Prophet and Legal Authority: A Linguistic and Social-Science Approach" (paper presented at the annual meeting of the Society of Biblical Literature [Social Sciences and the Interpretation of Hebrew Scripture section], San Francisco, Calif., November 1997), available online at http://www.BiblicalResource.com/papers/Huldah.

ancient culture but until recently also modern scholarship. Two layers of interpretation, then, must be shed in order better to understand the cultural landscape of ancient Israel: that of the Hebrew Bible itself and that of its modern interpreters.[46] Further, modern scholarship has tended to look exclusively at sanctioned institutional avenues of power and influence, such as the priesthood, rather than those that were suppressed, and the public roles rather than those that were private. By opening the study of women's roles within the cultus to the private sphere and the suppressed traditions, we can better understand the significance of women's power and influence.

Carol Meyers's work has concentrated more on the place of women within the family and village economy of ancient Israel.[47] She also distinguishes between private and public spheres of influence, suggesting that while women were often excluded from positions of public power, they often wielded considerable influence—if not power—in the domestic sphere. Women's roles within the family were focused on production—not just childbearing and child rearing, but also tending flocks and herds and producing foodstuffs, clothing, and household goods. Meyers evaluates these roles within a broader construct of agrarian societies. She demonstrates that within such societies, gender roles are often clearly defined, but women are more highly considered than in other cultural contexts due to their vital contribution to family, village, and clan survival.

Tikva Frymer-Kensky brings a more global approach to the cultic sphere within ancient Israel. Her study, *In the Wake of the Goddesses: Women, Culture, and the Biblical Transformation of Pagan Myth*, examines the forces that led to the exclusion of women from the priesthood in ancient Israel. She notes that in Mesopotamian tradition women performed official priestly functions and that goddesses were an important part of the Sumerian, Akkadian, and Babylonian pantheons in the ear-

---

46. Bird, "The Place of Women in the Israelite Cultus," in *Ancient Israelite Religion: Essays in Honor of Frank Moore Cross*, ed. P. D. Miller Jr., P. D. Hanson, and S. D. McBride (Philadelphia: Fortress, 1987), 397–419. See also idem, "Women's Religion in Ancient Israel," in *Women's Records*, 283–98.

47. Meyers's most comprehensive work on women in Israel is *Discovering Eve: Ancient Israelite Women in Context* (New York: Oxford University Press, 1988). See also idem, "Gender Roles and Genesis 3:16 Revisited," in *The Word of the Lord Shall Go Forth: Essays in Honor of David Noel Freedman in Celebration of His Sixtieth Birthday*, ed. C. L. Meyers and M. O'Connor (Winona Lake, Ind.: Eisenbrauns, 1983), 337–54; idem, "Procreation, Production and Protection: Male-Female Balance in Early Israel," *JAAR* 51 (1983): 569–73; reprinted in *Community, Identity, and Ideology*, ed. Carter and Meyers, 489–514; idem, "Gender Imagery in the Song of Songs," *HAR* 10 (1987): 209–23; and idem, "An Ethnoarchaeological Analysis of Hannah's Sacrifice," in *Pomegranates and Golden Bells: Studies in Biblical, Jewish, and Near Eastern Ritual, Law, and Literature in Honor of Jacob Milgrom*, ed. D. P. Wright, D. N. Freedman, and A. Hurvitz (Winona Lake, Ind.: Eisenbrauns, 1995), 77–91.

liest written texts until the middle of the second millennium B.C.[48] Frymer-Kensky observes that while women were allowed prominent social and religious functions until this time, their public role began to decline so that by the first millennium women were "practically invisible" in the texts from Mesopotamia. The Mesopotamian world "by the end of the second millennium was a male's world, above and below; and the ancient goddesses have all but disappeared."[49]

According to Frymer-Kensky, as the Israelites moved gradually toward monotheism, the functions and characteristics of both male and female deities within the ancient Near Eastern pantheons were subsumed within Yahwistic religion. But the Israelite social and religious traditions were, at their heart, more egalitarian than those of Israel's neighbors. Thus, while Israel did not fully comprehend or even establish an entirely gender-neutral tradition, monotheism allows a more holistic attitude toward gender and sexuality. This would change in both Judaism and Christianity as they were influenced by a Hellenistic culture that was often misogynist in its orientation. Frymer-Kensky's work is appealing in that it examines carefully the Mesopotamian traditions and their developments, the social worlds that produced them, and the differences that emerged with Israelite monotheistic impulses. It is perhaps too facile, however, in attributing the negative attitudes toward women primarily to the influences of Hellenism.

Exile and Identity

The Persian period, once neglected in favor of periods considered more important, has enjoyed a recent surge of interest.[50] Although most scholars are highly skeptical of the accounts of Ezra and much of the Nehemiah tradition, there is a growing sense that the Persian period is the turning point of biblical history. Virtually all scholars place much of the editing and transmission—some would argue, even the origin—of much of the Hebrew Bible in the Persian period.[51] These renewed assessments

48. The same may be observed for the other major cultures and mythic traditions of the ancient Near East, including Syria, Egypt, Anatolia, and Palestine.

49. T. Frymer-Kensky, *In the Wake of the Goddesses: Women, Culture, and the Biblical Transformation of Pagan Myth* (New York: Free Press; Toronto: Maxwell Macmillan Canada, 1992), 79–80.

50. For a discussion of recent developments in the study of this period, see my "Province of Yehud in the Persian Period: Soundings in Population and Demography," in *Second Temple Studies*, 2:106–45; and my *Emergence of Yehud in the Persian Period: A Social and Demographic Study* (Sheffield: Sheffield Academic Press, forthcoming).

51. P. R. Davies, *In Search of "Ancient Israel,"* JSOTSup 148 (Sheffield: JSOT Press, 1992); idem, "The Society of Biblical Israel," in *Second Temple Studies*, 2:22–33; G. Garbini also argues for a Persian period date for most of the writing and editing of the Hebrew Bible in "Hebrew Literature in the Persian Period," in *Second Temple Studies*, 2:180–88.

of the importance of the period make the social setting and ideological developments within the postexilic community of great significance.

Several scholars have applied the conflict tradition to the social community of Yehud between 538 and 332. This tradition is at the heart of Hanson's understanding of the tension between the hierocrats of the temple establishment and the visionaries of Isaiah 56–66. It is also fundamental to Joel P. Weinberg's influential *Bürger-Tempel-Gemeinde* (citizen-temple community) model for the postexilic community, though clearly his work employs a cultural materialist viewpoint as well.[52] Weinberg suggests that the province of Yehud was structured around a temple economy, a structure found throughout Mesopotamia in various periods of its history. He identifies Yehud as a rare type of citizen-temple community in which the temple itself did not hold any land, but suggests that the temple functionaries gradually came to rule not only the temple but also civic affairs. One of the weaknesses of his model is the uncritical manner in which he takes the biblical numbers of deportees in Jeremiah and 2 Kings, and returnees in Ezra 2 = Nehemiah 7. This leads him to suggest a province with a population in excess of 200,000 persons in the fifth century B.C., a figure that the demographic evidence does not support. As his model seems to depend in part on a substantial population for the province, it is surprising how widely accepted his model has become. Yet his model does address one of the major questions of the period, that of the identity of the *gôlâ* community. Weinberg believes that the conflict that is alluded to in some of the prophetic books and in Ezra–Nehemiah comes from the tension that arose when the returnees (the members of the *gôlâ* community) attempted to assume power over those who had remained in Palestine during the exile. The effect of this idea is that the official history (Ezra, Nehemiah, the Chronicler) can be trusted only to present the perspectives of the members of the exilic community who returned to Yehud from Babylon from 538 through the middle to end of the fifth century.

Daniel Smith has contributed much to our understanding of the sociology of the exile and the importance of identity.[53] Smith relates the sociology and psychology of the exilic community to other societies that have been dispossessed, conquered, or marginalized. He identifies four major types of responses: structural adaptation, in which the ruling structure of the social group changes in response to a new reality; a

---

52. Weinberg's most important essays are collected in *The Citizen-Temple Community*, trans. D. L. Smith-Christopher, JSOTSup 151 (Sheffield: JSOT Press, 1992).

53. D. L. Smith, *The Religion of the Landless: The Social Context of the Babylonian Exile* (Bloomington, Ind.: Meyer-Stone, 1989). See also idem, "The Politics of Ezra: Sociological Indicators of Postexilic Judean Society," in *Second Temple Studies*, vol. 1, *Persian Period*, ed. P. R. Davies, JSOTSup 117 (Sheffield: Sheffield Academic Press, 1991), 73–97.

split in leadership, in which traditional leaders and new vie for influence as the larger group attempts to adapt and survive; the development of new rituals that redefine the boundaries between the community and its rulers; and the development of folk heroes and a literature of resistance. These strategies of survival functioned to keep the social and religious structures of the *gôlâ* community intact. Their strong identity and belief that they represented the "true Israel" in turn led to a protracted struggle for power between their leaders and those of the indigenous community of Judeans who had remained in the land.

As mentioned above, what makes Weinberg's proposal of the citizen-temple community problematic is his lack of reliable data concerning site distribution and population for the province during the Persian period. My own research suggests that the total population of the province ranged between a low of about 13,000 and a high of 21,000 from 538–332 B.C., a population of less than 10 percent of Weinberg's proposal. It is not currently clear whether this difference in population invalidates his model, but these data do raise significant questions concerning the nature of the political and social structure of the province. If the province was as small as the most recent archaeological reconstructions suggest, the need to construct meaningful boundaries between Judeans (the "true seed of Israel") and various "outsiders" is more intelligible.

Economic Perspectives: Subsistence Strategies and Mode of Production

Several of the previous aspects of Israel's social setting are directly related to its economic context—the prophetic call for justice, the role of women in production, the emergence of Israel, and the monarchy, for example. The various socioeconomic contexts that developed in antiquity can be approached from two distinct, but sometimes complementary, perspectives: that of subsistence strategy and that of mode of production. *Subsistence strategy* is a more general term that refers to the methods and technologies that cultures, groups, and societies use to adapt to and survive within their environment.[54] It applies a taxonomy

---

54. This is developed in Lenski and Lenski, *Human Societies*, 78–93. Lenski and Lenski propose a basic time line for societal development as follows: The hunter-gatherer strategy dominated from the earliest hominid culture until approximately 7000 B.C.; horticultural societies were dominant from 7000 to 4000 B.C.; agrarian societies emerged in approximately 4000 B.C. and extended until roughly A.D. 1800; the Industrial Age lasted from the late nineteenth century until the present. If one adds, as I do, the information age, it would begin in about the 1980s with the advent of the personal computer and will continue well into the twenty-first century. On the latter, see M. G. Dolence and D. M. Norris, *Transforming Higher Education: A Vision for Learning in the 21st Century* (Ann Arbor, Mich.: Society for College and University Planning, 1995).

to societies from the simplest hunter-gatherer cultures to the most complex industrial societies, and defines four basic types and three environmentally specialized types. These include hunter-gatherer, horticultural, agrarian, and industrial; of these, horticultural and agrarian are typically subdivided into their simple and complex forms according to technological developments. So, for example, use of a hoe rather than a wooden digging stick distinguishes a complex horticultural society from its simple counterpart; agrarian societies develop where a plow replaces a hoe; and a complex agrarian society constructs tools and weapons from iron rather than the copper or bronze tools used in a simple agrarian society. Fishing, maritime, and herding societies are environmentally specialized types that develop to allow survival in ecologically marginal areas (such as herding societies), or areas in which specific environmental factors make a particular strategy more attractive (fishing and maritime cultures). Cultures that use two or more strategies to survive within their environment are considered hybrid societies. Given this taxonomy, one would identify early Israel as a hybrid culture, one that applied both herding and agrarian subsistence strategies to the various environmental niches of Syria-Palestine. Although Israel cannot be compared to its larger neighbors in terms of its social complexity, the development of iron tools and weapons suggests that it evolved from a simple to an advanced agrarian culture.[55]

Scholars analyzing ancient Israel's economic context from the perspective of the *mode of production* would argue that a society's place in the taxonomy of cultures tells only part of the story. While it is important to understand the various subsistence strategies and technologies, they would argue that these factors alone cannot account for the complex interrelationships that exist within the society. Mode of production is a concept that Marx and Engels applied to the industrial setting of late-nineteenth-century Europe. They proposed that cultures could be divided among three or four types based on the relationship between the political and economic sectors of society. Marx called this relationship the political economy, and highlighted the relationship between the "material forces of production" and the "social relations of production."[56] Marx divided societies into four phases through which human cultures have progressed: an egalitarian, classless society, a slave-based

---

55. For a useful analysis of Israel's subsistence strategies and its response to its environment, see D. Hopkins, *The Highlands of Canaan: Agricultural Life in the Early Iron Age*, SWBAS 3 (Decatur, Ga.: Almond, 1985); idem, "Life on the Land: The Subsistence Struggles of Early Israel," *BA* 50 (1987): 471–88.

56. Gottwald, "A Hypothesis about Social Class," 144–53; idem, "Sociology of Ancient Israel," 82–83.

social order, a feudal society, and the capitalist society that has typified Western culture since the industrial age. Some scholars have argued that a fifth phase be added, the Asiatic Mode of Production, or AMP. This type of social order exists when the cultural elite controls a centralized state, when there is a self-sufficient village economy, and when there is little or no private land ownership. On the evolutionary scale, this mode of production would best fit between the classless and the slave-based society. Marx predicted an eventual return to a classless society when the underprivileged masses revolt against their bourgeois oppressors, a theory that led to the establishment of communist states in the former Soviet Union, the People's Republic of China, and other similar cultural experiments.

According to Gottwald, when one applies the perspectives of political economy and mode of production to Iron Age Israel, the following features stand out. During most of the premonarchic phase, during its transition from a tribal society to a chiefdom, Israel functioned as an egalitarian society. The material cultural evidence from the few excavated villages demonstrates a rustic, subsistence-level culture, with little class differentiation.[57] As a chiefdom and then monarchy emerge, there is greater economic specialization and a transition to an Asiatic, or tributary, mode of production. This involves the elite siphoning off surplus from the peasantry, which in turn causes an increasing economic gap between the upper and lower classes. During the monarchic period, the surplus—extracted through taxation and debt slavery— went to the growing bureaucracy in order to finance the needs of the emergent state. With the fall of the northern and later the southern kingdoms, this internal tributary mode of production shifted to an external, or foreign, tributary mode, with the resources extracted from the peasantry going both to indigenous elite and foreign overlords. It is only in the Roman period that a modified slave-based mode of production emerges.

Evangelical Scholarship and Social Science Criticism

At the same time that social science criticism has become more accepted in mainstream scholarship, evangelical scholars have generally been slow in adopting this new method of biblical study; until recently few evangelical works applied anthropological or sociological perspectives to the Hebrew Scriptures and the cultures that produced

---

57. Several village excavations suggest this. See Finkelstein's *'Izbet Sarta: An Early Iron Age Site near Rosh Ha'ayin, Israel* (Oxford: British Archaeological Reports, 1986); idem, *Archaeology of the Israelite Settlement*.

them.[58] Instead, some prominent evangelical scholars consider social science interpretation of Scripture to be peripheral, mere "fluff" subject to the whims of the practitioner.

I attribute this type of dismissive attitude to a number of specific concerns, including: (1) a theological commitment to the uniqueness of Israel coupled with a desire to avoid cultural and religious relativism; (2) a hesitation to apply cross-cultural parallels to the biblical world and an attempt to avoid reading modern worldviews onto ancient Israel; and (3) a concern that social science criticism will take away from the more legitimate aspects of biblical interpretation. As these concerns are closely interrelated and therefore somewhat difficult to separate, I discuss them briefly together, giving examples of each where possible.

1. *A theological commitment to the uniqueness of biblical Israel coupled with a desire to avoid cultural and religious relativism.* Perhaps the greatest concern evangelicals have regarding social science criticism stems from the tendency of the social sciences to view human culture on a continuum. This cross-cultural approach stands in stark contrast to the commitment of the biblical authors—and of evangelical scholars—to the uniqueness of Israel.[59] Throughout the biblical narratives—whether of the call and covenant with Abraham, the exodus event, the emergence of Israel in Canaan, or the prophetic ideals—the Israelite authors define themselves and their commitment to Yahweh as completely distinct from the faith of their neighbors in other gods and goddesses. While the biblical writers certainly considered their words God's word to Israel, some evangelicals have added the theological concepts of plenary inspiration and the inerrancy of Scripture. These theological perspectives are not necessarily in conflict with sociological or anthropological theory, though some scholars who apply the social sciences to Scripture do so as a rejection of any theological commitment. The social scientist would speak of Israel's belief in its uniqueness, but would examine other cultural traditions to see whether they shared this concept. If other cultures can be shown to have a concept of a special call from their gods or goddesses, then the social scientist would see Israel's uniqueness as a cultural concept rather than a theological truth. The evangelical scholar would begin with the theological presupposition of the universal truth of the biblical traditions, whereas the social

58. This section raises concerns that are more evident within the American evangelical community, which most commentators would agree is considerably more conservative than the British evangelical tradition. The latter community is generally more open in its use of critical scholarship and the application of some of the newer critical methods than American evangelicals are.

59. This is a departure from literary studies within evangelical scholarship, which readily looks for parallels to Israelite literature within its ancient Near Eastern context.

scientist would begin with an examination of Israel's beliefs as religious ideology. Thus, for example, rather than looking solely at the provisions of the Decalogue as divinely given law, the sociologist or anthropologist might examine the Decalogue primarily from a social and communal perspective. This emphasis ought not to be problematic for evangelicals in and of itself; indeed, one's understanding of the ancient force of the command—and therefore its modern application—could be enhanced by a social science study of covenant and law.

It is important to note that it is not only evangelical or conservative scholars who defend the distinctiveness of Israel or who would place specific controls on the use of the social sciences in biblical studies. Roland de Vaux sought to delineate the difference between Israelite and other ancient Near Eastern sacrificial traditions by showing that while Canaanite and Mesopotamian sacrifices were intended to provide food for the deities, the Israelite priesthood was oriented toward a more "ethical" understanding of sacrifice. Yahweh, who was spirit, needed no sustenance (Ps. 50:12–14). As Gary Anderson has shown, however, the notion of sacrifice as food for YHWH, while perhaps diminished for ideological reasons in the Hebrew Bible, is still evident in both legal and poetic traditions and is present in texts that span biblical genres and historical periods alike.[60]

2. *A hesitation to apply cross-cultural parallels to the biblical world and an attempt to avoid reading modern worldviews onto ancient Israel.* Recent studies of the nature of earliest Israel and of the focal point of its ideology suggest that early Israel was a more complex society than the biblical narratives indicate. If one follows the biblical story line for the transition from tribal league to monarchy, the Philistine threat stands out as the prime mover for the rise of Saul and the Davidic monarchy. As noted above, the social sciences propose a multilevel cause for Israel's emergence and political development, one rooted in the collapse of Late Bronze Age social structures, a declining economy, a volatile political atmosphere, and a rise of available surplus and, with it, of specialization. This perspective of *la longue durée*, tracing Israel's evolution from a tribal league, to a chiefdom, to a petty kingship does not in itself necessarily conflict with biblical narratives, but it does require supplementing the biblical traditions with social science models. Once again, the critical issues are the priority and perspective of the social science data regarding the biblical traditions, and the degree to which parallels from other societies can be appropriately applied to the biblical narratives. Here additional concerns emerge: Is it legitimate to supplement

---

60. G. Anderson, *Sacrifices and Offerings in Ancient Israel: Studies in Their Social and Political Importance,* HSM 41 (Atlanta: Scholars Press, 1987), 14–16.

biblical narratives with modern social science models? Does doing so necessarily undermine one's commitment to Scripture as God's Word?

Similar questions arise when one seeks to place Israelite religion within its ancient Near Eastern context. Evangelicals have long rejected the history of religions school *(Religionsgeschichtliche Schule)*. This perspective suggests that Israelite religion is best understood as a form of Syro-Palestinian cultus, with strong influence from the Mesopotamian, Syrian, Ugaritic, and to a lesser extent, Egyptian cultures. Once again, the issue that is brought into sharp focus is the evangelical belief in the uniqueness of Israelite religion as *revealed* religion and truth and the social science analysis of religion as a human phenomenon. This tension makes it particularly difficult for many evangelical scholars to accept the use of sociological parallels when analyzing Israelite religious practices, although the use of literary parallels from ancient Near Eastern cultures is a common practice. Few evangelical scholars would hesitate to use the Mari texts to compare Mesopotamian and Israelite prophetic practices,[61] texts from Emar to shed light on the priesthood,[62] Ugaritic language and texts as parallels to Biblical Hebrew or Israelite poetic traditions,[63] or suzerainty-vassal treaties to help define Israel's relationship with Yahweh.[64] While evangelical scholars may draw different conclusions from their mainstream scholarly counterparts, they employ a similar critical methodology in applying these parallel texts to the biblical record.

Those same scholars might be less comfortable applying practices of Native American holy men as parallels to Jeremiah's prophetic ministry and the nature of prophetic authority within a community. One may indeed ask whether it is appropriate to compare biblical prophecy with "spirit possession" or shamanism. The issue of Israel's

61. The definitive article on the Mari prophecy texts was written by W. L. Moran, "New Evidence from Mari on the History of Prophecy," *Bib* 50 (1969): 15–56. See also H. Huffmon, "Prophecy in the Mari Letters," *BA* 31 (1968): 101–24.

62. The recent study of D. Fleming, *The Installation of Baal's High Priestess at Emar*, HSS 42 (Atlanta: Scholars Press, 1992), makes an important contribution in this regard.

63. D. Stuart, *Studies in Early Hebrew Meter*, HSM 13 (Missoula, Mont.: Scholars Press, 1976); M. D. Coogan, ed., *Stories from Ancient Canaan* (Philadelphia: Westminster, 1978); P. C. Craigie, *Ugarit and the Old Testament* (Grand Rapids: Eerdmans, 1983); idem, *Psalms 1–50*, WBC 19 (Waco: Word, 1983). See also the voluminous works of Mitchell J. Dahood, whose usages of Ugaritic as a basis for understanding Hebrew literature are well known even if not universally accepted. See in particular his commentaries on the Book of Psalms (3 vols., AB 16, 17, and 17A [Garden City, N.Y.: Doubleday, 1965–70]) and his *Ugaritic-Hebrew Philology: Marginal Notes on Recent Publications*, BibOr 17 (Rome: Pontifical Biblical Institute, 1965).

64. See M. Kline, *Treaty of the Great King: The Covenant Structure of Deuteronomy: Studies and Commentary* (Grand Rapids: Eerdmans, 1963); idem, *The Structure of Biblical Authority* (Grand Rapids: Eerdmans, 1972).

uniqueness would again be the sticking point for some scholars. If Israelite prophecy is unique, and the place of the prophet in the community is different from ancient Near Eastern analogs, then Israel's uniqueness is preserved. But if the role and status of the prophet are shown to have legitimate social parallels with spiritual leaders from other tribal cultures, then the commonness of spiritual power is emphasized, ostensibly at the expense of Israel's distinctiveness. Again, I believe that aspects of the social parallels drawn by Overholt and Wilson (mentioned above) add to, rather than take away from, one's view of prophecy. Such parallels reinforce the power of the prophet in his or her community, and in particular provide a clearer understanding of the struggles that peripheral prophets such as Elijah and Jeremiah faced in proclaiming the word of YHWH to their fellow Israelites and Judeans.

3. *A concern that social science criticism may diminish the more legitimate aspects of biblical interpretation.* For the evangelical community, the ultimate aim of all of the methods of critical scholarship—from archaeological excavation to historical and literary studies—is the interpretation of Scripture for the community of faith. For this reason, establishing the text, understanding the literary, linguistic, and historical contexts of Scripture, and then applying certain hermeneutical principles to Scripture to allow its current application(s) are considered fundamental tasks for the interpreter. Biblical exegesis—establishing the original meaning of the text—and hermeneutics—proposing a contemporary meaning of that text—are together a *theological* work. Scripture is not simply a historical document that informs us of the beliefs and story of an ancient culture. It is instead a *living* document that can transform individuals, churches, and even cultures when it is heeded and practiced. This belief allows us to speak with conviction about current issues, such as social justice, religious orthodoxy, the virtue of love, gender equality, and environmental ethics.

The concern that the social sciences in fact take away from rather than add to the interpretive task is amplified when some mainstream critical scholars advocate social science criticism as an *alternative* to theologically oriented biblical scholarship. Robert Oden's *The Bible without Theology*[65] and Philip Davies's *In Search of "Ancient Israel"* advocate such a position. Both suggest, though in different ways, that biblical scholarship has too long been subject to theological agendas that, they claim, render such scholarship biased by nature. Further, they suggest that in order for critical scholarship to be truly objective, it must

---

65. R. A. Oden Jr., *The Bible without Theology: The Theological Tradition and Alternatives to It*, NVBS (San Francisco: Harper & Row, 1987).

extract itself from any theological commitment. In many respects, this marks but the most recent volley in the long-standing tension between theologically oriented studies and a supposedly more "neutral" religious studies approach to Scripture. This tension has led to an increasingly theologically independent discipline within colleges and universities as compared to that of seminaries, and this continues to be a point of discussion within academe. What makes this different, however, and more threatening to evangelicals, is the clear repudiation of the theological method as an authentic, objective enterprise and the replacement of theology with the social science ideology. I would argue, however, that the social sciences are by no means anti-theological in and of themselves; nor need they be peripheral in the theologically oriented interpretive task. Indeed, they can underpin and enhance both the understanding of the original social and historical context of a text *and* its current proclamation. Understanding the nature of social and class differentiation allows us better to grasp the severity of Amos's critique of oppression and oppressors in eighth-century Israel and thereby to proclaim responsibility to be a voice for the voiceless in twentieth- and twenty-first-century culture. Understanding patriarchy and the significance of the place of women—such as Deborah and Huldah—who rose to power despite the limitations imposed on them by a patriarchal system allows us to empower women to assume positions of leadership in the church today.

It is in that spirit that some evangelical scholars have made initial forays into social science criticism. One of the first evangelicals to do so was Gordon Wenham in his commentaries on Leviticus and Numbers.[66] He turns primarily to anthropology to shed light on issues such as sacrifice, purity, and ritual practices. He quotes extensively and approvingly from Mary Douglas's study *Purity and Danger* throughout his commentary on Leviticus, using her concepts of ritual and victual purity as stemming from the need to establish social boundaries and order. Similarly, he cites anthropological sources on tribal societies as showing that Israelite sacrificial rituals were not mere magic but were instead part of a meaningful symbolic world. What is impressive about his work is that it is sensitive to the complex methodological issues that surround the appropriate use of anthropological analogs for the study of Scripture.[67]

---

66. G. J. Wenham, *The Book of Leviticus*, NICOT (Grand Rapids: Eerdmans, 1979); idem, *Numbers: An Introduction and Commentary*, TOTC (Downers Grove, Ill.: InterVarsity, 1981); idem, *Numbers*, Old Testament Guides (Sheffield: Sheffield Academic Press, 1997).

67. See, e.g., Wenham, *Numbers*, TOTC, 32–39, 146–47.

Two other recent works deserve mention, both of which provide social science backgrounds for the worldviews of the biblical writers. The
more ambitious of the two is a collaboration between Victor Matthews
and Don Benjamin, *Social World of Ancient Israel, 1250–587 B.C.E.*[68] In
it, Matthews and Benjamin attempt to demonstrate for the reader the
ways in which a social science perspective can augment other, more
traditional forms of interpretation. Matthews and Benjamin have collected an impressive amount of anthropological and sociological material in the research for their work. The application of these sources is
often uneven, however, with assumptions from the social sciences applied to the biblical text somewhat uncritically. The volume is a useful
introduction to social science criticism and its benefits, but falls short
of being a true social history of either the tribal or monarchic periods
of Israelite and Judean history. It is inferior even to some of the groundbreaking works that approached biblical studies from a social science
methodology; it lacks the breadth and critical perspective of works by
Gottwald, Wilson, or Frick. To be fair to Matthews and Benjamin, however, this may be in part a function of its intended audience, which is
not that of biblical scholars but of an educated laity or even of under-
graduate students.

A second volume is a collaborative effort by Victor Matthews and
John Walton, *The IVP Bible Background Commentary: Genesis–Deuteronomy*.[69] As its title implies, it is concerned with general backgrounds
to the texts of the Torah and the cultural traditions it represents. The
work, like *Social World of Ancient Israel*, is aimed at lay readers rather
than the community of scholars. Further, it is not strictly interested in
sociological or anthropological settings of the biblical texts but has a
wider scope, one that includes literary, legal, and religious backgrounds. As such, it does make a contribution to biblical scholarship,
since one of its overall goals is an improved, if not more accurate, interpretation of Scripture. Matthews and Walton therefore present the
evangelical audience with an instructive, if brief, commentary on the
biblical world and culture behind the Torah.

The Future of Social Science Criticism

I have argued above that the critiques from those who would reject the
use of the social sciences in interpreting the Hebrew Bible are not convincing. Instead, they sometimes reflect a type of scholarly hubris or
siege mentality that both liberal and conservative scholars show when

68. Peabody, Mass.: Hendrickson, 1993.
69. Downers Grove, Ill.: InterVarsity, 1997.

new methodologies are introduced to biblical studies.[70] This response is different, however, from those who suggest specific controls that would make the use of the social sciences more productive. Gary Herion cautions biblical scholars not to be too quick to read modern parallels onto ancient Israel so as not to be either deterministic or positivistic in the reading of ancient Israelite society. He is further concerned that a cultural relativism that reflects modern interpretations of reality not be read back on ancient Israel, a culture that was far more rigid and exclusivistic—at least in its official presentation that we have received in the Hebrew traditions—than is our own. What makes Herion's cautions more helpful, however, is that he seeks a middle ground, one that views the social sciences as a genuine source of data for biblical interpretation. Thus his criticisms of the early work of both Gottwald and Wilson are tempered with suggestions for the profitable applications of social science criticism to biblical studies. To this end, he suggests that biblical scholars first come to a more complete understanding of sociopolitical functions of religions in other cultures *before* seeking to apply the sociopolitical model to a biblical culture to which it may not be appropriate. In urging this, he seeks an approach that is more intentionally interdisciplinary in its analysis of biblical cultures. Herion also encourages scholars to be aware of their implicit "modern tempocentrism and urban ethnocentrism" and therefore of their "need to acquire a more sympathetic awareness of the simple, 'folk' or primitive" societies. Such sensitivity would allow them to approach Israelite society with a "conceptual 'continuum' of societal typologies." Finally, he encourages scholars to make greater use of legitimate ethnographic materials for their analyses of biblical cultures and to be more rigorous in their analysis of social science models.[71]

Inasmuch as it was the influence of Norman Gottwald that, more than any other scholar, put the recent use of the social sciences on a more systematic and methodologically sound footing,[72] it is fitting to

70. The comments of B. Halpern exemplify both attitudes: "social-scientific (methods) . . . call on models extrinsic not just to the text, but to the culture as a whole. They apply universal, unhistorical schematics, like those of the natural sciences, yet deal, like the human sciences, in variables (e.g., forms of society) whose components, whose atoms, are never isolated. Such tools cannot usher in a revolution in historical certainty. Their promise, like that of the positivist program of the nineteenth century, is an eschatological one" (*The First Historians: The Hebrew Bible and History* [New York: Harper & Row, 1988], 5).

71. Herion, "Impact," 22–25 (reprint, 250–54); for another discussion of determinism and positivism in social science studies of biblical cultures see Malina, "Social Sciences and Biblical Interpretation."

72. This concern for methodology is evident in his foundational article, "Domain Assumptions and Societal Models," and is developed further throughout *The Tribes of Yahweh*.

conclude our discussion with his most recent musings on methodology. In what Gottwald describes as a more mature presentation of the issues involved in reconstructing a history or social science analysis of biblical Israel, he identifies four characteristics such interpretations should share. In being sensitive to these four elements, scholars will demonstrate a greater awareness of the complexity of social processes. In some early studies of Israelite culture, monolithic or simplistic models were imposed on the data, which led to a study in which the complex is described in terms of the simple. This has led to the charges discussed above that the social science studies of Israel are positivistic and deterministic, and that such studies are "eclectic" rather than comprehensive.[73] In order to ensure a more comprehensive understanding of Israelite culture, Gottwald suggests that scholars relate four distinct elements in a series of grids to form a cultural overlay.[74] The *physical grid* examines the skills and technologies necessary to deal with the features of the natural geography and environment in which the culture is located. The *cultural grid* analyzes the self-understanding that emerges within a society through its use of language, symbols, mores, and customs. The social *organizational/political grid* is concerned with the various social structures that develop within a society, including the manner in which power is used to establish order or to promote the interests of the sometimes competing groups that exist. The *religious grid* concentrates on identifying the rituals, beliefs, and practices of a culture's popular, official, and suppressed traditions. None of these aspects of culture existed in a vacuum, and therefore when one does not examine them within the overall social context, one introduces the possibility of distortion. Gottwald therefore contends that a whole range of sources should be consulted, including social science models, textual data, and artifactual data in order to create an anthropological "triangulation." This, he maintains, will allow scholars to reconstruct the social setting of ancient Israel—or any culture from antiquity—with the greatest possible clarity and depth.

The social sciences have already added much to the study of Hebrew Scripture. Without a solid understanding of tribal cultures, of kinship patterns, of protest movements, of insider-outsider status in social groups, and without the social parallels that modern ethnographic studies provide, our understanding of biblical cultures would be impov-

---

73. J. W. Rogerson offers an extensive critique along these lines in "The Use of Sociology in Old Testament Studies," in *Congress Volume: Salamanca, 1983*, ed. J. A. Emerton, VTSup 36 (Leiden: Brill, 1985), 245–56.

74. Gottwald lays out his new methodology in "Reconstructing the Social History of Early Israel."

erished. To be sure, the field, particularly as a discipline within biblical scholarship, needs to continue to mature and become more rigorous in its methodology. But it is clear that the social science study of the First Testament is no longer an ancillary and optional mode of interpretation but has become a critical element of biblical exegesis. As the discipline grows, we can look forward to a more comprehensive understanding of both the biblical cultures and the literature they produced.

16

Theology of the Old Testament

R. W. L. Moberly

Recent Old Testament theology presents a somewhat uncertain face to the onlooker. There *may* be a smile; there is certainly plenty of literature and lively debate. But the smile is at least enigmatic.

General Survey of Recent Literature

The initial problem is perhaps that it is unclear precisely what to look for. If one is looking for volumes entitled "Theology of the Old Testament" (or something similar), there is a curious situation. That is, there are a good number of recent books, but they are almost entirely from scholars more concerned to make the discipline accessible than to develop fresh insights. For example, Walther Zimmerli's *Old Testament Theology in Outline* reads rather like a committal to print of lectures to his students, while Claus Westermann's *Elements of Old Testament Theology* clearly has the nonspecialist in view—and, as such, is an admirable introductory guide to a characteristically German way of presenting the theological content of the Old Testament.[1] Ronald E. Clements, in his *Old Testament Theology: A Fresh Approach*, readably thinks through some of the basic theological implications of the Old Testament.[2] John Goldingay lucidly relates recent debate to a fresh theological structuring of the content of the Old Testament in his *Theological Diversity and*

---

1. W. Zimmerli, *Old Testament Theology in* Outline, trans. D. E. Green (Edinburgh: Clark; Atlanta: John Knox, 1978); C. Westermann, *Elements of Old Testament Theology*, trans. D. W. Stott (Atlanta: John Knox, 1982).
2. R. E. Clements, *Old Testament Theology: A Fresh Approach* (Basingstoke: Marshall, Morgan & Scott; Atlanta: John Knox, 1978).

the Authority of the Old Testament.[3] Not least because Goldingay discusses obvious problems that scholars sometimes neglect to discuss—What about "contradictions"? Can we affirm some viewpoints and criticize others?—his is a good way into the subject for the student and nonspecialist.[4]

In terms of weightier volumes, Horst Dietrich Preuss has recently published a two-volume *Old Testament Theology*.[5] Although this contains useful material, organized around the theme of election, it does not really offer any conceptual advances over the two major landmarks of the modern discipline, Walther Eichrodt's *Theology of the Old Testament* and Gerhard von Rad's *Old Testament Theology*,[6] and may rather represent something of a step backward. Since he makes no real use of insights that have unsettled and enlivened recent Old Testament study, Preuss may be a guide more to where Old Testament theology has been than to where it is and will be. Indeed, if one wants a work utilizing older categories, good theological insights can be found in Hans Urs von Balthasar's *Theology: The Old Covenant*.[7] Von Balthasar is one of the most distinguished Roman Catholic theologians of the twentieth century; but he was not a biblical specialist, and his work has been almost entirely neglected by Old Testament scholars.[8]

Two of the leading American contributors toward a fresh rethinking of theological interpretation of the Old Testament have produced major

3. J. Goldingay, *Theological Diversity and the Authority of the Old Testament* (Grand Rapids: Eerdmans, 1987).

4. Various other short books relate Old Testament theology to contemporary faith, for example, from a Roman Catholic perspective, N. Lohfink, *Great Themes from the Old Testament* (Chicago: Franciscan Herald; Edinburgh: Clark, 1982); or, from an evangelical Protestant perspective, W. J. Dumbrell, *Covenant and Creation: An Old Testament Covenantal Theology* (Exeter: Paternoster; Flemington Markets, N.S.W.: Lancer, 1984; published in the U.S. as *Covenant and Creation: A Theology of the Old Testament Covenants* [Nashville: Nelson, 1984; reprinted, Grand Rapids: Baker, 1993]); and, at an elementary level, W. Dyrness, *Themes in Old Testament Theology* (Exeter: Paternoster; Downers Grove, Ill.: InterVarsity, 1979).

5. H. D. Preuss, *Theologie des Alten Testaments*, 2 vols. (Stuttgart: Kohlhammer, 1991–92); English edition: *Old Testament Theology*, trans. L. G. Perdue, 2 vols. (Edinburgh: Clark; Louisville: Westminster/John Knox, 1995–96).

6. W. Eichrodt, *Theology of the Old Testament*, trans. J. A. Baker, 2 vols., OTL (London: SCM; Philadelphia: Westminster, 1961–67); G. von Rad, *Old Testament Theology*, trans. D. M. G. Stalker, 2 vols. (Edinburgh: Oliver & Boyd; New York: Harper, 1962–65).

7. H. U. von Balthasar, *The Glory of the Lord: A Theological Aesthetics*, vol. 6, *Theology: The Old Covenant*, trans. B. McNeil and E. Leiva-Merikakis, ed. J. Riches (Edinburgh: Clark; San Francisco: Ignatius, 1991). It is the sixth volume in a seven-volume magnum opus on the nature of theological aesthetics. Although part of von Balthasar's larger theological thesis, the OT volume can be understood and profitably read in its own right.

8. One looks in vain for any reference to von Balthasar even in the OT theology survey volumes listed below.

works.[9] Brevard Childs's *Old Testament Theology in a Canonical Context* is, however, surprisingly thin and, in terms of approach, stands in something of an unresolved tension with his more substantial *Biblical Theology of the Old and New Testaments*.[10] Walter Brueggemann's recent *Theology of the Old Testament* moves in a different direction from that of Childs and, in some ways, from his own previous work.[11] Both Childs and Brueggemann are discussed more fully later.

Much of the most interesting work in Old Testament theology has appeared in contexts other than explicit *Theologies*. First, there has been a renewed interest in Old Testament theology within the context of biblical theology.[12] The monograph series Overtures to Biblical Theology contains, for example, Walter Brueggemann, *The Land;* Phyllis Trible, *Texts of Terror;* Terence Fretheim, *The Suffering of God;* Rolf Rendtorff, *Canon and Theology;* and my own *The Old Testament of the Old Testament*.[13] Four recent periodicals, *Biblical Theology Bulletin, Horizons in Biblical Theology, Ex Auditu,* and *Jahrbuch für biblische Theologie,* all focus both on hermeneutics and on exegesis, and in their various ways

9. Mention should also be made of R. P. Knierim, *The Task of Old Testament Theology* (Grand Rapids: Eerdmans, 1995), which contains thought-provoking and sophisticated reflections on both method and content.

10. B. S. Childs, *Old Testament Theology in a Canonical Context* (London: SCM; Philadelphia: Fortress, 1985); idem, *Biblical Theology of the Old and New Testaments: Theological Reflection on the Christian Bible* (London: SCM; Minneapolis: Fortress, 1992). Concerning unresolved tensions in Childs's work, see under "The Work of Brevard Childs" in the present essay.

11. W. Brueggemann, *Theology of the Old Testament: Testimony, Dispute, Advocacy* (Minneapolis: Fortress, 1997).

12. The term *biblical theology* is, unfortunately, too rarely defined. OT scholars tend to use it as a synonym for "Old Testament theology" (see the quotations by Trible and Collins under "Rethinking the Nature of the Subject via Its Terminology" in the present essay), while NT scholars tend to use it as a synonym for "New Testament theology." The Christian canon as a whole presents fundamental theological issues in christological form, which are usually posed in terms of the relationship between the testaments, an issue regularly ignored or marginalized in separate Old and New Testament theologies. On this, see D. L. Baker, *Two Testaments, One Bible: A Study of the Theological Relationship between the Old and New Testaments* (Leicester: Apollos; Downers Grove, Ill.: InterVarsity, 1976; 2d ed. 1991); H. G. Reventlow, *Problems of Biblical Theology in the Twentieth Century,* trans. J. Bowden (London: SCM; Philadelphia: Fortress, 1986); M. Oeming, *Gesamtbiblische Theologien der Gegenwart* (Stuttgart: Kohlhammer, 1985; 2d ed. 1987); also my *The Old Testament of the Old Testament: Patriarchal Narratives and Mosaic Yahwism,* OBT (Minneapolis: Fortress, 1992), chaps. 4 and 5.

13. Brueggemann, *The Land: Place as Gift, Promise, and Challenge in Biblical Faith* (Philadelphia: Fortress, 1977); Trible, *Texts of Terror: Literary-Feminist Readings of Biblical Narratives* (Philadelphia: Fortress, 1984); Fretheim, *The Suffering of God: An Old Testament Perspective* (Philadelphia: Fortress, 1984); Rendtorff, *Canon and Theology: Overtures to an Old Testament Theology,* trans. and ed. M. Kohl (Minneapolis: Fortress, 1993).

well represent the contemporary differences in approach between the United States and Germany.

Second, there has been a spate of monographs and articles. It is difficult to select, and only three categories will be briefly noted, all characterized by the writers' explicit concern with the bearing of the Old Testament on Christian faith (and none is included in standard discussions of OT theology; see below). First, although ethics can be treated separately from theology, the biblical text always links the two, and so do recent attempts to interpret Old Testament ethics, such as Christopher J. H. Wright, *Living as the People of God* and *God's People in God's Land;* Bruce C. Birch, *Let Justice Roll Down;* and Waldemar Janzen, *Old Testament Ethics.*[14] Second, a renewed interest in prayer is evident in Henning Graf Reventlow, *Gebet im Alten Testament;* Patrick D. Miller, *They Cried to the Lord;* and Samuel Balentine, *Prayer in the Hebrew Bible.*[15] While studies of the Psalter have always been plentiful, studies of prayer as such are few. Third, two works relate to the general area of spirituality. Robert Davidson's *The Courage to Doubt* is almost a miniature Old Testament theology arranged around the theme of Israel's questioning of God.[16] Questioning is integral to the Old Testament presentation of the nature of faith (most obviously in the psalms of lament, to the study of which Brueggemann has made many contributions),[17] and is a recurrent issue in the life of faith today. Davidson's thoughtful treatment combines academic with pastoral wisdom, as does Deryck Sheriffs in his *The Friendship of the LORD*, a work that in explicit and sophisticated ways relates the study of the Old Testament as an ancient Near Eastern text to questions of how one should walk with God today.[18]

14. C. J. H. Wright, *Living as the People of God: The Relevance of Old Testament Ethics* (Leicester: InterVarsity, 1983); in the U.S. published as *An Eye for an Eye: The Place of Old Testament Ethics Today* (Downers Grove, Ill.: InterVarsity, 1983); idem, *God's People in God's Land: Family, Land, and Property in the Old Testament* (Exeter: Paternoster; Grand Rapids: Eerdmans, 1990); B. C. Birch, *Let Justice Roll Down: The Old Testament, Ethics, and Christian Life* (Louisville: Westminster/John Knox, 1991); W. Janzen, *Old Testament Ethics: A Paradigmatic Approach* (Louisville: Westminster/John Knox, 1994).

15. H. G. Reventlow, *Gebet im alten Testament* (Stuttgart: Kohlhammer, 1986); P. D. Miller, *They Cried to the Lord: The Form and Theology of Biblical Prayer* (Minneapolis: Fortress, 1994); S. Balentine, *Prayer in the Hebrew Bible: The Drama of Divine-Human Dialogue,* OBT (Minneapolis: Fortress, 1993).

16. R. Davidson, *The Courage to Doubt: Exploring an Old Testament Theme* (London: SCM; Philadelphia: Trinity Press International, 1983).

17. E.g., W. Brueggemann, *The Message of the Psalms* (Minneapolis: Augsburg, 1984). See now his volume of collected essays on the Psalms, *The Psalms and the Life of Faith,* ed. P. D. Miller (Minneapolis: Augsburg Fortress, 1995), esp. chaps. 1–5; see further below.

18. D. Sheriffs, *The Friendship of the LORD: An Old Testament Spirituality* (Carlisle: Paternoster, 1996).

A third locus for Old Testament theological contributions is commentaries. In particular, three important commentary series are aimed at ministers and teachers. The contributors to the Interpretation series and the *Expositor's Bible Commentary* read almost like a Who's Who of American Old Testament theologians from general Protestant and specifically evangelical perspectives, while the International Theological Commentary has a more international range of contributors.[19]

A Survey of Surveys of Recent Literature

It would be easy to devote this whole essay simply to enumerating recent literature and to discussing recurring issues of debate. This is unnecessary, however, for guides to (all but the most recent) scholarly literature already exist, and those seeking an overview of debate are well served by them. First and foremost, there is *The Flowering of Old Testament Theology: A Reader in Twentieth-Century Old Testament Theology, 1930–1990*.[20] In addition to overview essays by the editors, we are given excerpts from the works of all the major scholars who have contributed to Old Testament theology in that period together with a bibliography of writings by and about each scholar and a brief theological synopsis of each.

Apart from quibbling over editorial decisions, I would raise one question of principle about this volume. On the one hand, there is nothing on Martin Buber and Abraham Heschel, two leading Jewish thinkers who, perhaps precisely because they were not primarily biblical scholars and yet had thought deeply about the biblical material, regularly contain insights not found elsewhere, and, whatever their defects, are never less than thought-provoking.[21] On the other hand, Karl Barth is conspicuous by his absence. It is not just because of his influence on Old Testament specialists, especially von Rad and Childs, that Barth is

19. Interpretation, a Bible Commentary for Teaching and Preaching, ed. J. L. Mays, P. D. Miller, P. J. Achtemeier (Atlanta and Louisville: John Knox, 1982–); *Expositor's Bible Commentary*, ed. F. E. Gaebelein (Grand Rapids: Zondervan, 1979–92); International Theological Commentary, ed. F. C. Holmgren and G. A. F. Knight (Grand Rapids: Eerdmans; Edinburgh: Handsel, 1983–).

20. Ed. B. C. Ollenburger, E. A. Martens, and G. F. Hasel, SBTS 1 (Winona Lake, Ind.: Eisenbrauns, 1992).

21. For example, M. Buber, *Two Types of Faith*, trans. N. P. Goldhawk (London: Routledge & Paul; New York: Macmillan, 1951); A. J. Heschel, *The Prophets*, 2 vols. (New York: Harper & Row; Burning Bush, Jewish Publication Society, 1962). Heschel's classic work *The Sabbath: Its Meaning for Modern Man* (1951; reprinted, New York: Noonday, 1990) draws out much of the inner logic of the biblical material precisely by contextualizing it within Jewish thought and practice.

important.[22] For Barth himself could produce outstanding theological interpretation of the Old Testament. For example, his handling of 1 Kings 13, surely one of the most perplexing stories in the whole Old Testament, is seminal; alternatively, his interpretation of Genesis 1–3 is full of suggestion, probing theological issues that most commentators neglect (if only Barth were not so long-winded!).[23] The (seemingly paradoxical) point is that it may be a mistake to limit Old Testament theology to Old Testament scholars. Since (to anticipate our later discussion) the very nature of what Old Testament theology is and should be is a central issue in recent debate, it may be that to restrict what counts as Old Testament theology to Old Testament specialists, who represent an institutional embodiment of precisely those assumptions that need reexamination, may be to some extent effectively to beg the question. Nonetheless, despite this caveat (which applies equally to the works in the next few paragraphs), *The Flowering of Old Testament Theology* must surely be a primary resource for every student of the subject.

Second, there is the dissertation of Frederick Prussner, revised and updated by John H. Hayes, *Old Testament Theology: Its History and Development*.[24] This does not bring the story up to the present, as does *The Flowering of Old Testament Theology*, apart from its final twenty-five pages on "Continuing and Contemporary Issues in Old Testament Theology" (which already looks somewhat dated). Yet its publication is eloquent testimony to the search for self-understanding that has characterized recent Old Testament theology; here the history of the discipline is traced behind its conventional starting point in the 1787 lecture of Gabler[25] back to the Reformation and post-Reformation scholasticism, Pietism, and rationalism. As with all significant human concerns, it is doubtful how far one will be able to make real progress in the future without a grasp of the historical roots of the present. Since, however, it is the interpretation of the historical development that is of crucial significance, one must remember that this history can be understood in more than one way. Childs in particular offers an important construal

22. For von Rad see R. Rendtorff, "'Where Were You When I Laid the Foundation of the Earth?' Creation and Salvation History," in his *Canon and Theology: Overtures to an Old Testament Theology*, trans. and ed. M. Kohl, OBT (Minneapolis: Fortress, 1993), 92–113. For Childs, see C. S. Scalise, "Canonical Hermeneutics: Childs and Barth," *Scottish Journal of Theology* 47 (1994): 61–88.

23. On 1 Kings 13 see *Church Dogmatics*, vol. 2.2, trans. G. W. Bromiley et al. (Edinburgh: Clark, 1957), 393–409; on Gen. 1–3 see ibid., vol. 3.1, trans. J. W. Edwards et al. (Edinburgh: Clark, 1958), 94–329.

24. J. H. Hayes and F. C. Prussner, *Old Testament Theology: Its History and Development* (London: SCM; Atlanta: John Knox, 1985).

25. The text of Gabler's address is conveniently given in *Flowering of Old Testament Theology*, ed. Ollenburger, Martens, and Hasel, 489–502.

that differs from that of many other scholars, a construal that is part of his reconceptualization of the discipline as a whole.[26]

Third, there are various monographs devoted to surveying the field of Old Testament theology. These provide discussion of the issues and more or less comprehensive bibliographies. Four may be noted.[27] First, Gerhard Hasel's *Old Testament Theology: Basic Issues in the Current Debate*, which has several times been revised and updated, offers wide coverage and is deservedly a well-known resource.[28] Second, Henning Graf Reventlow, *Problems of Old Testament Theology in the Twentieth Century*, has a format that makes it not particularly readable, but it is useful and contains material that does not simply overlap with Hasel, though it is less up-to-date.[29] Third, Leo Perdue, *The Collapse of History: Reconstructing Old Testament Theology*, is comparable to Hasel and Reventlow, but focuses on wider theological trends and the way they are represented in selected Old Testament scholars, whose positions receive substantial exposition.[30]

Finally, there is the newly published major and magisterial work of James Barr, *The Concept of Biblical Theology: An Old Testament Perspective*,[31] which eclipses in scope that of the three books just mentioned and is particularly strong on recent German contributions. Barr freshly and pungently reconsiders well-worn issues, and his book has an obvious claim to be *the* survey of the field. Yet even so, the book is less definitive than it might be. It is somewhat prolix and repetitive. It assumes that conventional approaches are basically satisfactory and gives little sense of why some scholars have recently tried to reconceptualize the discipline. In particular, the concerns motivating Childs and Brueggemann are unrecognizable; in each case Barr sees some of the trees but not the forest. And Barr's own sense of what constitutes theology is open to question (see below).

---

26. Childs, *Old Testament Theology*, chap. 1. This needs to be read in conjunction with Childs's fuller discussions elsewhere, esp. his *Introduction to the Old Testament as Scripture* (London: SCM; Philadelphia: Fortress, 1979), part 1; *The New Testament as Canon: An Introduction* (London: SCM; Philadelphia: Fortress, 1984), part 1; *Biblical Theology of the Old and New Testaments*, 3–94. See further below.

27. There are others. For example, J. Hogenhaven, *Problems and Prospects of Old Testament Theology*, Biblical Seminar 6 (Sheffield: JSOT Press, 1987), is a curious book. An initial analysis of problems has real value; yet the positive proposals for a way forward simply and obviously repeat the very problems he has just pointed out.

28. G. Hasel, *Old Testament Theology: Basic Issues in the Current Debate* (Grand Rapids: Eerdmans, 1972; subsequent editions 1975, 1982, 1991).

29. H. G. Reventlow, *Problems of Old Testament Theology in the Twentieth Century*, trans. J. Bowden (London: SCM; Philadelphia: Fortress, 1985).

30. L. Perdue, *The Collapse of History: Reconstructing Old Testament Theology*, OBT (Minneapolis: Fortress, 1994).

31. London: SCM, 1999.

Two comments may be made about these overview monographs. First, they are best used by those who have already done some work in Old Testament theology. They are not for beginners, for whom a few pages of von Rad or Childs themselves are far more likely to be of interest and value than any number of pages discussing possible problems with von Rad's or Childs's approaches.[32] If one wants a brief introductory overview in order to get one's bearings, it is better to go for an article rather than a book. From among the many such articles, Robert L. Hubbard Jr., "Doing Old Testament Theology Today," lucidly sets out a standard account, while John J. Collins, "Is a Critical Biblical Theology Possible?" sharply describes precisely the assumptions with which Old Testament theology must wrestle—and beyond which, in my judgment, it must move.[33] Second, the monographs are all "talks about talks," discussions of discussions of the biblical text (like this present volume!). There is no exegesis or persuasive and memorable interpretation of the biblical text. Yet without such firsthand engagement with the primary text, discussions can rapidly lose their bearings and significance, especially for the nonspecialist.

Rethinking the Nature of the Subject via Its Terminology

So far, so good. The trouble is that one might think that in all this talk about "Old Testament theology" there is a basic agreement as to what one is talking about. This, however, is hardly the case. As Phyllis Trible has put it, "Biblical theologians, though coming from a circumscribed community, have never agreed on the definition, method, organization, subject matter, point of view, or purpose of their enterprise."[34] That does not leave much out! Even more seriously, the very place of Old Testament theology as, arguably, the goal toward which other Old Testament disciplines should aim and converge is in question. In the words of John J. Collins:

32. There are, of course, selections from von Rad and Childs in *Flowering of Old Testament Theology*, ed. Ollenburger, Martens, and Hasel. Alternatively, or in addition to them, I would suggest von Rad on Jeremiah (*Old Testament Theology*, 2:191–219) and Childs on "How God Is Known" (*Old Testament Theology*, 28–42).

33. R. L. Hubbard Jr., "Doing Old Testament Theology Today," in *Studies in Old Testament Theology*, ed. R. L. Hubbard Jr., R. K. Johnston, and R. P. Meye (Dallas: Word, 1992), 31–46; J. J. Collins, "Is a Critical Biblical Theology Possible?" in *The Hebrew Bible and Its Interpreters*, ed. W. H. Propp, B. Halpern, and D. N. Freedman (Winona Lake, Ind.: Eisenbrauns, 1990), 1–17.

34. P. Trible, "Five Loaves and Two Fishes: Feminist Hermeneutics and Biblical Theology," *TS* 50 (1989): 279–95; reprinted in *Flowering of Old Testament Theology*, ed. Ollenburger, Martens, and Hasel (quotation is from p. 451); also reprinted in *The Promise and Practice of Biblical Theology*, ed. J. Reumann (Minneapolis: Augsburg Fortress, 1991), 51–70.

Biblical theology is a subject in decline. The evidence of this decline is not so much the permanent state of crisis in which it seems to have settled, or the lack of a new consensus to replace the great works of Eichrodt or von Rad. Rather the decline is evident in the fact that an increasing number of scholars no longer regard theology as the ultimate focus of biblical studies, or even as a necessary dimension of those studies at all. The cutting edges of contemporary biblical scholarship are in literary criticism on the one hand and sociological criticism on the other. Not only is theology no longer queen of the sciences in general, its place even among the biblical sciences is in doubt.[35]

The underlying problems may perhaps be approached through reflection on the very words "Old Testament theology." "Old Testament" is a value-laden term, while "theology" is ambiguous. On the one hand, attention has increasingly been given to the fact that "Old Testament" is explicitly a Christian name for the Hebrew Scriptures. In particular, "Old" is a correlative of "New"; that is, there is no "Old Testament" without a "New Testament." Until recently this was rarely deemed worthy of comment, because of a lingering cultural presupposition that the Christian name was *the* name. Greater awareness of contemporary religious and cultural plurality has shown that the Christian presupposition at the very least needs justification. One of the striking features of recent biblical scholarship has been the contribution from Jewish scholars. From a Jewish perspective,[36] the Hebrew Scriptures are not "Old Testament" (except out of conformity to traditional Western usage or deference to Christian sensibilities), but rather are Tanakh, Miqra', or simply "Bible."[37] It is increasingly common to argue that because "Old Testament" is a specifically Christian name for the biblical text, it is therefore an affront to Jewish sensibilities and ought, in a multicultural context, to be dropped.[38]

35. Collins, "Is a Critical Biblical Theology Possible?" 1.

36. This does not apply, of course, to those Jews who have a Christian faith, for whom, whatever continuing significance they may give to their Jewish religious and cultural roots, it is ultimately Jesus as the Christ, more than Torah, that is the determinative key to God and humanity.

37. Tanakh is an acronym of the three constituent parts, Torah, Nebi'im, Ketubim. Miqra' is that which is read out in public worship (from Hebrew *qārā'*, "to call out, to read"). When Jewish scholars write a book with a title that includes the word *biblical,* they understand that word in accordance with their own tradition; that is, the content is restricted to the Hebrew Scriptures without consideration of the Christian NT. See, e.g., R. Alter, *The Art of Biblical Narrative* (London: Allen & Unwin; New York: Basic Books, 1981); M. Sternberg, *The Poetics of Biblical Narrative,* ILBS (Bloomington: Indiana University Press, 1985); S. Bar-Efrat, *Narrative Art in the Bible,* trans. D. Shefer-Vanson, JSOTSup 70 (Sheffield: Almond, 1989); H. C. Brichto, *Toward a Grammar of Biblical Poetics* (New York: Oxford University Press, 1992).

38. See, e.g., P. van Buren, "On Reading Someone Else's Mail," in *Die Hebräische Bibel und ihre zweifache Nachgeschichte: Festschrift für Rolf Rendtorff zum 65. Geburtstag,* ed.

I have addressed these issues in *The Old Testament of the Old Testament*. There I argue that the problem of a Christian approach to the Hebrew Scriptures as Old Testament is closely paralleled by a similar problem within the heart of Torah. When God reveals Himself[39] to Moses as YHWH at the burning bush, this constitutes a new beginning in relation to the patriarchal knowledge of God in Genesis 12–50 comparable to the new beginning in Christ in relation to the Old Testament. The problem that the Old Testament poses to Christians—How do we use it when we know the one God differently, and Jesus relativizes Torah?—is the problem that the patriarchal traditions posed to the writers of the Pentateuch, for the patriarchal context is pre-Torah, and the patriarchs do not observe Torah; how then should those who obey Torah understand and use the patriarchal stories? The hermeneutical assumptions of promise and fulfillment and typology, which Christians have used to appropriate the Old Testament, were used by Mosaic Yahwistic writers of the Pentateuch to appropriate the patriarchal traditions. It follows from this that the language of "Old/New Testament" is christological and embodies basic Christian assumptions about a Christian relationship to Hebrew Scripture (the one God, truly revealed to Israel, known definitively in Christ). Moreover, the fact that a similar phenomenon can be found in the heart of Torah opens the way to understanding the notion of "Old Testament" in a way that may perhaps be more readily accessible to Jews.[40]

E. Blum, C. Macholz, and E. W. Stegemann (Neukirchen-Vluyn: Neukirchener Verlag, 1990), 595–606. A replacement for "Old Testament" is less obvious. "Hebrew Bible" is widely favored, despite the obvious problems it poses for the small portions in Aramaic, and, more seriously, for the Septuagint (study of which is hardly well classified under "Hebrew Bible"). Moreover, the term *Bible* is still ultimately a word whose significance depends on recognition of a Jewish or Christian canon (i.e., a selective procedure made on a religious basis) and whose meaning varies according to Jewish or Christian context. For a significant recent discussion, see C. R. Seitz, "Old Testament or Hebrew Bible? Some Theological Considerations," in his *Word without End: The Old Testament as Abiding Theological Witness* (Grand Rapids: Eerdmans, 1998), 61–74.

39. At a time when the propriety of applying masculine pronouns to God is under intense scrutiny, I use a capitalized form to make the point that (quite apart from not confusing grammatical gender with biological gender) masculine terms have a different significance when applied to God from their conventional usage with reference to human beings. That such a capitalized form is also an ancient reverential usage is a bonus.

40. There are many implicit wider issues about how best to affirm Christian faith in a culture in which, as in the early Christian centuries, Christian beliefs about God and humanity are in a minority. It should at least be clear that, although Christians must be open to learn from those of other outlooks, there is nothing to be gained from sacrificing identity and integrity on the altar of cultural pluralism (which may be a guise for an imperialistic cultural homogeneity).

The Meanings of "Theology"

The term *theology* is ambiguous and all too rarely defined. Often "Old Testament theology" is simply set over against "history of Israelite religion." The difference between the two is rarely entirely clear (and on most library shelves they are intermingled). There are, I suggest (to oversimplify somewhat a complex issue), two basic distinguishing features.

First, the issue is whether one can make the affirmation of faith that the God of whom the biblical text speaks is the one God whom Christians know and worship today through Jesus Christ. That is, there is a question of *religious truth* at stake. The belief that what the Old Testament says may be, in some sense (with however many qualifications one may add), true with regard to God and humanity constitutes a basic division between those who do, and those who do not, practice Old Testament theology (as distinct from histories of Israelite religion). If the question of truth is bracketed out or denied, then any kind of account of the religious content of these ancient Israelite texts, no matter how much it focuses on beliefs portrayed as normative within the text, is not in principle different in kind from an account of the religious beliefs of, say, ancient Egypt, Babylon, Greece, Persia, or Arabia. All may be accounts of belief systems of no continuing normative significance (i.e., truth content) for the interpreter; or whose continuing significance is an arbitrary matter of individual choice. Conversely, some explicitly developmental accounts of Israelite religion may have high "theological" content precisely because writers believe in the continuing truth of that witness to reality whose early historical embodiments they describe.

To be sure, most writers of Old Testament theology have assumed the enduring truth, in some sense, of what the Old Testament says. But often they have simply assumed it, without arguing it. If doubts about the possibility of doing Old Testament theology are to be met, the grounds for the Christian assumption must be spelled out and be shown to be coherent and integrated with the handling of the biblical text. (Both here and elsewhere in this essay, similar concerns obviously apply, mutatis mutandis, for Jewish scholars.)

Second, the all-important and supremely difficult question is that of establishing criteria by which biblical truth may be meaningfully claimed and discussed. How may one understand, weigh, and respond appropriately to claims about the nature of reality, about God and humanity, life and death? The Christian faith has many such criteria, but they are too little used or understood in the context of biblical scholarship. Too often the criteria are thought to be solely the creeds and dogmas of Christian theology—which, in part, they are—and that these are to be excluded from Old Testament (and New Testament) study as anachronistic and debilitating (one needs only a moderate level of historical understanding to recognize that the writer of Gen. 1 would not have had the Trinity in mind).

One basic difficulty has to do with the nature of God Himself. God is not a person or object in the world like any person or object with which we may be familiar. How then may we *know* Him? If someone speaks about God, how can we know that they know what they are talking about? In the development of modern culture, in which scientific knowledge and method became the norm of knowledge and epistemology, fateful moves were made. On the one hand, since God could not be studied scientifically, the focus shifted to the human dimension that could be so studied—human language, thoughts, and feelings about God could all be analyzed and classified. On the other hand, the category of knowledge was reserved for that which was scientifically established, and religious claims were demoted in status. Belief became an inferior alternative to knowledge, reserved for things whose status was more or less doubtful. These factors, among many others, have tended to leave would-be biblical theologians in somewhat of a limbo—wanting to talk about God, yet in practice analyzing human beliefs in God, beliefs whose status is often unclear, not least because of a separation of biblical interpretation both from the realities of Christian living and from a broader context of dogmatic, systematic, and philosophical theology.

Challenges to continuing (and often insufficiently thought through) Christian assumptions about the biblical text are recurrent in recent debate. John J. Collins, for example, maintains the importance of a strictly descriptive approach to the biblical text (as in a typical agenda of the nineteenth century) and at the same time removes the question of truth from the biblical agenda (for the ready evaluations of liberal Protestantism, which initially accompanied the historical agenda, can no longer be taken for granted, and he has no alternative that can be justified within his descriptive agenda):

> The biblical texts must also be recognized as proposals about metaphysical truth, as attempts to explain the workings of reality. . . . The question here is whether any of these biblical accounts can now be accorded any explanatory value; whether any of the biblical world views can be said to be true as well as useful. The problem is that we lack any acceptable yardstick by which to assess metaphysical truth. . . . It is not within the competence of biblical theologians as such to adjudicate the relative adequacy of metaphysical systems. Their task is to clarify what claims are being made, the basis on which they are made, and the various functions they serve.[41]

41. Collins, "Is a Critical Biblical Theology Possible?" 14.

Alternatively, one fashionable aspect of some literary studies is to focus on the text as ideological artifact in such a way as to bracket out questions about the truth of the God depicted therein. This is usually, however, accompanied by the reconstrual of the text within the terms of a contemporary ideology; that is, the interpretation of the text is seen necessarily to relate to a framework of meaning beyond itself, but this framework is not that of Christian (or Jewish) theology.[42] For example, David Clines writes:

> There seem to me to be three kinds of data we could use in constructing a picture of God in the Pentateuch. The first is what the character God says about himself. . . . [This] might seem to some readers a very reliable type of information; for here it might appear that it is God himself who is talking about himself. But we need to realize that when the narrative says—"The LORD . . . proclaimed, 'the LORD, the LORD, a God gracious and merciful, slow to anger and abounding in steadfast love and faithfulness'" (Exod. 34:6)—this self-description does not consist of the words of God himself (what language does *he* speak?) but of the words of the narrator (in Hebrew). These are no more than words put in the mouth of the character God by the narrator, and, behind the narrator, by the author. Such sentences of self-description contribute to our overall picture of the character God, of course, but the words in the mouth of God have no privileged status compared with words spoken directly by the narrator in describing God's motives and actions.[43]

The questionable assertion, of course, is that what the text says is *no more than* words put in the mouth of the character God. In literary terms, the words *are* that. But whether they are also *more than* that is precisely the fundamental question at stake about the nature of reality, which can be resolved positively only by relating the biblical text to a context larger than itself in which the truth claims are critically affirmed (i.e., the continued living of Jewish or Christian faith).[44]

---

42. Theological concerns are not necessarily lacking. D. Patrick has written a curious book, *The Rendering of God in the Old Testament*, OBT (Philadelphia: Fortress, 1981), in which he portrays God as a "character" in Scripture but argues: "I believe that the God rendered in Scripture has the capacity to convince us of his reality. To entertain this God as an imaginary character, one must finally recognize that he actually exists" (14; cf. xxiii, chaps. 8 and 9). Imaginative power is indeed a significant element if the biblical portrayal of God is to become a transforming reality for people. But Patrick's argument as it stands, a strange kind of reworking of the ontological argument for the existence of God, is simply absurd.

43. D. J. A. Clines, "God in the Pentateuch: Reading against the Grain," in *Interested Parties: The Ideology of Writers and Readers of the Hebrew Bible*, JSOTSup 205 (Sheffield: Sheffield Academic Press, 1995), 187–211 (quotation from p. 187). This is a revision of his earlier "Images of Yahweh: God in the Pentateuch," in *Studies in Old Testament Theology*, ed. Hubbard, Johnston, and Meye, 79–98.

44. Clines himself recognizes that his way of putting things invites an obvious response—"No doubt there is a serious question here, namely what the relationship is

Such questions about the reality of that to which the Bible witnesses are of course particularly difficult with regard to the Old Testament. On the one hand, the primary focus for Christian faith in God is Jesus Christ, and this naturally raises questions about the nature and value of the pre-Christian faith of Israel and the centrality of Torah in the Old Testament as it now stands. On the other hand, the Old Testament ascribes words and deeds to God that Christians have always found difficult to accept as true of the God in whom they believe.[45] But this simply means that the question of criteria for assessing the truth of what the Old Testament says about God is all the more important to engage fully and explicitly.

Possible Ways Ahead

The Work of Brevard Childs

What then may be the way ahead for Old Testament theology? In asking this question I do not seek to describe the present and likely future activity of those within the guild of Old Testament scholars.[46] Rather, I wish to bring to bear some explicit concerns of contemporary Christian faith, and to do this via the work of two eminent scholars who, in one way or other, exemplify such concerns.[47]

---

between the God who is a character in a book and the 'real God'"—but has no more to say about the question than that "we cannot begin to address it until we have systematically made a distinction between the two. How else could we approach the issue of their relationship?" ("God in the Pentateuch," 191 = "Images of Yahweh," 82). His rhetorical question obscures both the tendentious nature of his systematic distinction and the fact that there are many criteria within Christian theology for weighing and assessing what the Bible says about God. His recent writing elsewhere suggests that a materialist ideological criticism provides a norm by which the Bible may be assessed (and, unsurprisingly, regularly found wanting): "Biblical Interpretation in an International Perspective," *BibInt* 1 (1993): 67–87, esp. 84–86.

45. This applies especially to God's command to put to death all the inhabitants of Canaan (Deut. 7; Josh. 1–11), and the command *always* to blot out Amalek (Exod. 17:8–16; Deut. 25:17–19; 1 Sam. 15:1–3). On the former, see my "Toward an Interpretation of the Shema," in *Theological Exegesis: Essays in Honor of Brevard S. Childs*, ed. C. Seitz and K. Greene-McCreight (Grand Rapids: Eerdmans, 1999), 124–44.

46. For a brief account on these lines, see B. Childs, "Old Testament Theology," in *Old Testament Interpretation: Past, Present, and Future: Essays in Honor of Gene M. Tucker*, ed. J. L. Mays, D. L. Petersen, and K. H. Richards (Nashville: Abingdon, 1995), 293–301.

47. A focus on Childs and Brueggemann means that, for better or worse, the contributions of other scholars must be passed over. From a Jewish perspective, some of the most stimulating work in recent years has come from J. D. Levenson. Although Levenson's approach is that of a historian of religion, his concern to integrate such work with a context of historical and continuing Jewish faith gives a genuinely theological dimension to what he does (in significant ways analogous to the Christian approach of Childs). See especially his *Creation and the Persistence of Evil: The Jewish Drama of Divine Omnip-*

First and foremost, a key contribution to the debate has been made by Brevard Childs.[48] For Childs's primary concern is precisely to address the question of how these ancient Hebrew texts can responsibly be understood and appropriated as Christian Scripture, as texts *received* (in their canonical form) and lived with by Christians down through the ages. To do this he has sought fundamentally to rethink a common approach to the text in which scholars primarily apply the common criteria of ancient historical method and then, if they are so inclined, add some "theological" icing to the cake thus baked. For to assume that Christians can use the text as Scripture only by initially bracketing out their Christian perspectives and then subsequently bringing them to bear is what makes the whole task of theological appropriation impossible from the outset; for then, by definition, the Christian perspective is marginal, not foundational and integral, to the whole enterprise. What Childs has argued for is nothing less than reconceptualizing the discipline of biblical study as a whole by reuniting it to the wider context of Christian faith and theology from which, at least in theory,[49] it has been separated in the name of a critical historical awareness that has sought to understand the text in its own right and with its own authentic voice by freeing it from the shackles of anachronistic ecclesiastical dogma.[50] Simultaneously Childs has consistently argued that one

---

otence (San Francisco: Harper & Row, 1988), which offers a challenging reformulation of a doctrine of creation, and *The Death and Resurrection of the Beloved Son: The Transformation of Child Sacrifice in Judaism and Christianity* (New Haven: Yale University Press, 1993), which offers, in effect, a theology of election. Also, the robust recent essays on theology, hermeneutics, and exegesis by Christopher Seitz (*Word without End*) make it likely that Seitz will be an increasingly significant contributor to the debate in coming years.

48. See n. 26.

49. Levenson has recently argued for the enduring influence of Christian assumptions upon the study of the Hebrew Scriptures, even when Christian scholars were in principle renouncing them. Unquestioned assumptions are often best seen by those who do not share them. It should be noted, however, that Levenson is not at all hostile to relating the Bible to faith, for this is his own concern in his Jewish context. His critique rather is directed at the failure to be properly self-critical about the way in which biblical study is in fact done. See "The Hebrew Bible, the Old Testament, and Historical Criticism" (1–32) and "Why Jews Are Not Interested in Biblical Theology" (33–61) in *The Hebrew Bible, the Old Testament, and Historical Criticism* (Louisville: Westminster/John Knox, 1993).

50. The slogans of eighteenth- and nineteenth-century debates are still repeated today: "The historical-critical study of the Bible . . . allows the biblical literature to be read in the context of the time of its production rather than in accordance with the dictates of later dogmatic systems of belief. . . . The critical approach to the Bible has released its great literary and aesthetic qualities from the ecclesiastical captivity of the book. The Hebrew Bible has been freed from the christological manacles imposed on it in Christian circles" (R. P. Carroll, *Wolf in the Sheepfold: The Bible as a Problem for Christianity* [London: SPCK, 1991]; in the U.S. as *The Bible as a Problem for Christianity* [Philadelphia: Trinity Press International, 1991], 21–22, 24).

must incorporate the many genuine insights of historically oriented criticism and not seek to negate them as many who have sought to hold the Bible and Christian theology together have sometimes tended to do. Crucial to the task of rethinking the relationship between text and theology is attention to the received, canonical shape of the biblical material, on the grounds that the shaping the biblical texts have received is integral to a process whereby the enduring significance, and possible continuing appropriations, of the text has been made accessible to those who come after its original addressees or recipients. To ignore the received shaping of the texts, and to prefer instead some kind of reconstruction of something more "original" behind the text (the person of a prophet, the course of religious history), exacerbates rather than solves questions of responsible use and application by continuing communities of faith.

Problems with Childs's work abound. Childs has not always expressed himself as clearly as he might, his use of key terms like *canon* has sometimes been imprecise, some of his arguments are stronger than others, and sometimes he has realized that his own earlier proposals have been inadequate (though if one is trying fundamentally to rethink several centuries of debate and an established consensus, one can hardly be expected to get everything right the first time). Moreover, a comparison between his *Old Testament Theology* and his *Biblical Theology of the Old and New Testaments* suggests significant uncertainties about aspects of method still within Childs's own mind, not least with regard to the relationship between tradition history and the received text.[51] Much of this is well documented in the literature discussing Childs's work. Too often, however, Childs's critics have discussed particular trees and missed the forest, focusing on questions about the final form of the text at the expense of the relationship between received text and Christian faith and theology.[52] Even a full exposition and critique of Childs such as Mark Brett's *Biblical Criticism in Crisis?* does not succeed in penetrating to the heart of Childs's concerns.[53] For to sug-

---

51. See the comments in F. Watson's significant essay, "Old Testament Theology as a Christian Theological Enterprise," in *Text and Truth: Redefining Biblical Theology* (Edinburgh: Clark; Grand Rapids: Eerdmans, 1997), esp. 209–19.

52. This particularly applies to J. Barton, *Reading the Old Testament: Method in Biblical Study* (London: Darton, Longman & Todd; Philadelphia: Westminster, 1984; 2d ed., Louisville: Westminster/John Knox, 1996), chaps. 6 and 7; and J. Barr, *Holy Scripture: Canon, Authority, Criticism* (Oxford: Clarendon; Philadelphia: Westminster, 1983); and the situation is not improved in Barr's recent *Concept of Biblical Theology*.

53. M. Brett, *Biblical Criticism in Crisis? The Impact of the Canonical Approach on Old Testament Studies* (Cambridge: Cambridge University Press, 1991). See also now P. R. Noble, *The Canonical Approach: A Critical Reconstruction of the Hermeneutics of Brevard S. Childs*, Biblical Interpretation Series 16 (Leiden and New York: Brill, 1995), which has many good insights into Childs's approach.

gest that ultimately Childs's approach is one among many, to be used alongside others,[54] is to miss his point—"Old Testament theology" can remain a meaningful concept only if the fundamental placement of the biblical text within Christian faith and theology is made explicit and maintained. Otherwise there is neither an "Old Testament" (but only Tanakh or ancient Israelite texts) nor a "theology" in the sense of understanding a living reality today rooted in God's self-revelation in Israel and in Christ (but only accounts of ancient religious thought of ultimately rather arbitrary interest and significance today). If the status of the biblical text as Christian Scripture be retained, then sociocritical, feminist, narratological, and other approaches to the text may be of significance for contemporary appropriation of the text. If the link be lost, then the biblical text becomes a text "like any other," and it becomes difficult to see why it should continue to receive privileged status in terms of time and resources devoted to it and expectations of special contemporary significance in the results of any study.

Childs's approach is thus basic to the very nature and definition of the discipline in a way that most other contemporary approaches are not. This is not to say that Childs, as such, is right. It is to say that unless the issues of Bible and theology that Childs highlights are resolved, at least to the extent of being seen to be interdependent within a coherent conceptual framework of Christian faith and to be concerned with the truth about God and humanity, then Old Testament theology (and New Testament theology) has no future ahead of it other than steady diminution—diminution not to nothing but to a small niche within ancient Near Eastern religion and culture and a somewhat larger niche within Western literary and cultural studies. But either way, it would be solely evidence of past beliefs (i.e., theology as religious history) divorced from knowledge of God as a present reality.

One possible attempt to blur the sharpness of this alternative would be to appeal to the category of a "classic"—a work of high literary quality and enduring imaginative appeal that contains valuable insights into the human situation.[55] The Old Testament is at least this, and for many people it functions in this way—a way that may be a prelude to an acceptance of the text in the more demanding category of Scripture. But there are at least two problems here.[56] First, there would be little future or demand for "theology" of such a text, for, other than as religious history,

---

54. Brett, *Biblical Criticism in Crisis?* 156–67.

55. See, e.g., D. Tracy, *The Analogical Imagination* (New York: Crossroad, 1981); K. Stendahl, "The Bible as a Classic and the Bible as Holy Scripture," *JBL* 103 (1984): 3–10; W. C. Smith, *What Is Scripture?* (London: SCM; Minneapolis: Fortress, 1993), 182–95.

56. Childs himself dismisses the concept of a classic rather brusquely without exploring its possible strengths and weaknesses (*Biblical Theology*, 72–73).

such an exercise makes no sense apart from a living religious community concerned to understand the truth about God and humanity today in the light of the biblical text as a unique witness to that truth. The Bible as cultural classic would attract a different kind of study—perhaps of the kind that Robert Alter elegantly practices,[57] but more likely focusing increasingly on the interpretation and use of the Bible within Western culture. Second, the pluralism of contemporary culture makes the notion of a classic itself problematic, for the notion depends on precisely the kind of consensus recognition and sense of the enduring value of the past for present self-understanding and identity that is being eroded. If it is not possible to sustain the Old Testament as a witness to a living faith rooted in the past, the Hebrew Bible as a cultural artifact (and an all too hierarchical, sexist, and heteronomous artifact) may not fare much better.

To accept Childs's proposals, at least in outline, as a possible basis for the future of Old Testament theology is not to deny that there are problems with his proposals. In my judgment the most serious weaknesses are twofold. First, in his recent works Childs has so concentrated on analyzing and engaging with the scholarly debates that he has failed to produce convincing and memorable exegesis and interpretation of the biblical text. Until the Christian framework is seen to be fruitful in its results, there is a danger that it will remain either unpersuasive or unduly abstract. In his *Biblical Theology* Childs speaks of "those who confess Christ struggling to understand the nature and will of the One who has already been revealed as Lord. The true expositor of the Christian scriptures is the one who awaits in anticipation toward becoming the interpreted rather than the interpreter." Childs also speaks of "the ability of biblical language to resonate in a new and creative fashion when read from the vantage point of a fuller understanding of Christian truth."[58] This is a fine statement of the interpretive task. But when Childs takes as an exegetical case study Genesis 22, one of the most memorable and influential of all biblical stories, the result, while not without interest, hardly exemplifies his own principles. This is perhaps ironic when it is set alongside the interpretation of von Rad, whose christological and cross-oriented interpretation of Abraham as "on a road out into Godforsakenness, a road on which Abraham does not know that God is only testing him," is, while not without its own problems, surely a clear demonstration of the principles that Childs advocates.[59]

57. Especially Alter's *Art of Biblical Narrative.*
58. Childs, *Biblical Theology,* 86, 87.
59. G. von Rad, *Genesis,* trans. J. H. Marks, 2d ed., OTL (London: SCM; Philadelphia: Westminster, 1972), 244. I have analyzed von Rad and also attempted my own preliminary exemplification of a Christian approach to Genesis 22 in my "Christ as the Key to Scripture: Genesis 22 Reconsidered," in *He Swore an Oath: Biblical Themes from Genesis*

Second, Childs is weak in offering criteria for assessing the truth of what the Bible says. The concern should be not to establish the truth of God in Christ by criteria other than this truth itself, a process that Childs would rightly reject as improper, for (at the risk of oversimplifying complex issues) ultimate reality ceases to be ultimate if there are truths beyond itself by which it is established. Rather, the need is to discern the evaluative procedures already present within the biblical canon and to draw out their potential wider significance for contemporary theology. Childs does this primarily for the status of the canonical text in relation to its possible prehistory, but has little to say about how the canonical text should function with regard to the dynamics of faith today, for example with regard to distinguishing between more and less valid claims with regard to knowing God, or to establishing appropriate use of language about God. Childs affirms the whole of Scripture as the norm for knowledge of God, but leaves unclear how the norm should function.

This lack may be in part because Childs reacts against the idea of a "canon within the canon." To decry a "canon within the canon" should not, however, be allowed to obscure the fact that interpretive decisions must be made, that some parts of Scripture are more important than others, and that God's self-revelation in Christ transforms the continuing significance of His previous self-revelation to Israel. Too often, however, it must be said that interpreters do utilize a questionable form of a "canon within the canon" that can be used to play down, or even denigrate, those portions of Scripture that do not obviously agree with a prescribed norm (itself often narrowly conceived).[60]

A clear example of the kind of thing Childs is worried about can be seen in several recent works of Old Testament theology that have been influenced by Norman Gottwald's *Tribes of Yahweh*.[61] In this work Gottwald takes as normative the earliest period of Israel's history (as reconstructed by himself) in which Israel is an "egalitarian" and therefore "free" society formed in opposition to "hierarchical" and therefore "oppressive" Canaanite society.[62] Egalitarianism is good because it means freedom, and hierarchy is bad because it means oppression (these

---

12–50, ed. R. S. Hess, G. J. Wenham, and P. E. Satterthwaite (Carlisle: Paternoster; Grand Rapids: Baker, 1994), 143–73; and more fully in my *The Bible, Theology, and Faith: A Study of Abraham and Jesus* (Cambridge: Cambridge University Press, forthcoming).

60. At worst, of course, interpretation can degenerate to the self-serving principle that one attends only to those parts of Scripture that conform to one's existing presuppositions and preferences.

61. N. K. Gottwald, *The Tribes of Yahweh: A Sociology of the Religion of Liberated Israel, 1250–1050 B.C.E.* (Maryknoll, N.Y.: Orbis, 1979; London: SCM, 1980).

62. Ibid., e.g., 464–65, 692.

terms being extensively elaborated through a materialist analysis and neo-Marxian rhetoric). Thus Gottwald takes a dim view of the Davidic-Solomonic monarchy (while recognizing it as a military necessity to counter the Philistines) because it is intrinsically hierarchical.[63] As the Old Testament links David and Zion traditions, so doubts about David extend equally to Zion.

Bruce C. Birch, while avowedly pursuing a "canonical" approach that "protects against the selection of only portions of the biblical text as authoritative,"[64] comes out with a consistently negative assessment of Solomon and the Jerusalem temple.

> Israel under Solomon ceases to live as an alternative community in the world (although some kept this tradition alive), and instead adopts a model of royal ideology and management borrowed from surrounding Canaanite culture. . . . Under Solomon the covenant politics of justice are replaced by the politics of power. . . . It is the Jerusalem temple that most epitomizes Solomon's attack on the covenant religion of Yahweh . . . The domestication of the radically free God of covenant is also accomplished through the creation of a nationalized religion where the interests of God are considered inseparable from the interests of the king. . . . The temptation is always to believe that the patterns of community put forward by the world can be indulged in to some degree without compromising the covenant.[65]

How then we should understand the dedication of the temple in 1 Kings 8, which is clearly presented by the Old Testament as one of the high points of Israel's history, we are not told.

It is evident from Birch's language that his motivating concern is to find in the Old Testament an "alternative community" that can serve as a model for the Christian church; and similar concerns seem to motivate Gottwald also. Since, however, the Old Testament's generally positive (though not uncritical) presentation of the kingship of the house of David and of the Jerusalem temple does not fit Birch's notion of an "alternative community," supposedly derived from the Sinai covenant traditions, he does not adjust his notion of the possible forms that desirable community might take but rather reinterprets and downgrades the biblical material that disagrees with his notion. Birch's lack of any self-critical reflection on the internal tensions, indeed contradictions, within his approach to the biblical text is remarkable. One can see more clearly why Childs's stress on the normative nature of the canon as a

---

63. Ibid., 415, 417.
64. Birch, *Let Justice Roll Down*, 45.
65. Ibid., 221–22, 223, 225, 226, 228.

whole may serve as a safeguard against a too easy co-opting of the biblical text to serve the fashions of the day.

The Work of Walter Brueggemann

Walter Brueggemann has been one of the most prolific contributors to Old Testament theology in recent years, and his consistent concern has been to relate the biblical text to Christian life today. How many other leading Old Testament scholars would produce a title like *Interpretation and Obedience: From Faithful Reading to Faithful Living?*[66] His breadth of reading is remarkable, and he draws on, and makes accessible, insights from sociology, psychology, literary theory, and the wider post-modern debate. Three recent volumes of collected essays clearly show his characteristic approach and concerns: *Old Testament Theology, A Social Reading of the Old Testament,* and *The Psalms and the Life of Faith.*[67] To these may now be added a full-scale *Theology of the Old Testament.*[68] Interestingly, this latest work veers away from some of the perspectives set out in two preliminary essays, "A Shape for Old Testament Theology, I: Structure Legitimation," and "A Shape for Old Testament Theology, II: Embrace of Pain."[69] One receives the impression that Brueggemann, like Childs, may in certain respects be less resolved in his own mind than either his admirers or his detractors tend to allow.

In the essays Brueggemann argues that there is a constructive (necessary, indissoluble, and life-enhancing) tension between "structure legitimation" and "the embrace of pain." The former concerns a publicly structured and institutionally embodied understanding of morality, rationality, and coherence in life and faith. The latter represents the actual, experienced pain and conflict of life for many, a pain frequently caused by the public structures of morality and order, a pain that therefore critiques and opposes such public structures. Brueggemann sees the former as a "common theology" of the ancient world, based on creation and concerned for order, while the latter is Israel's distinctive pro-

66. W. Brueggemann, *Interpretation and Obedience: From Faithful Reading to Faithful Living* (Minneapolis: Fortress, 1991).

67. W. Brueggemann, *Old Testament Theology: Essays on Structure, Theme, and Text,* ed. P. D. Miller (Minneapolis: Fortress, 1992); idem, *A Social Reading of the Old Testament: Prophetic Approaches to Israel's Communal Life,* ed. P. D. Miller (Minneapolis: Fortress, 1994); idem, *The Psalms and the Life of Faith,* ed. P. D. Miller (Minneapolis: Fortress, 1995).

68. W. Brueggemann, *Theology of the Old Testament: Testimony, Dispute, Advocacy* (Minneapolis: Fortress, 1997).

69. The essays originally appeared in *CBQ* 47 (1985): 28–46, 395–415; reprinted in Brueggemann, *Old Testament Theology,* 1–21, 22–44. Pages 31, 395–402, and 407–15 are excerpted in *Flowering of Old Testament Theology,* ed. Ollenburger, Martens, and Hasel, 409–26.

phetic witness, concerned for justice. He also makes the move of aligning the David/Zion/creation/wisdom traditions with the former, and the Mosaic/prophetic/Job/lament-psalm traditions with the latter.

Much of the attraction of Brueggemann's writing lies in a powerful pastoral concern, with much of which any Christian can hardly disagree: "What we make of pain is perhaps the most telling factor for the question of life and the nature of faith. It has to do with the personal embrace of suffering as possibly meaningful in our lives. It also has to do with social valuing of the pained and the pain-bearers—the poor, the useless, the sick, and the other marginal ones."[70] Yet there is an obvious difficulty. On the one hand, Brueggemann says programmatically that the two primary traditions must be held in tension, that both are valid and necessary: "The main dynamic of the Old Testament is the tension between the celebration of that legitimation and a sustained critique of it";[71] "the practice of pain-embrace *must always be in tension* with the legitimation of structure, never in place of it. It is this tension that is the stuff of biblical faith and it is the stuff of human experience; however, simply to choose the embrace of pain instead of legitimation of structure as a rubric for theology is romanticism."[72]

On the other hand, in these essays Brueggemann in practice tends to handle the relationship not as an intrinsic tension of two legitimate polarities but as one of enduring problem (structure legitimation) and ever-renewed solution (embrace of pain). Crucial here is an explicit hermeneutic of suspicion, informed by Marx's classic critique of religion as ideology, refined by the Frankfurt School of postwar Germany. In Marx's classic formulation, ideology (with which theology is readily identified) is an outlook that promotes the interests of the powerful in society by obscuring the nature of their power and so perpetuating it; this perpetuation of power is at the expense of the powerless, who are duped by the ideology into acquiescence in their powerlessness instead of doing something to change the situation.

> Every theological claim about moral rationality is readily linked to a political claim of sovereignty and a political practice of totalitarianism. Such linkage need not be so. There is no necessity to it, but it regularly is so. Creation theology readily becomes imperial propaganda and ideology. Then, when the order of life is celebrated, it is the political order with which we agree. Indeed, it becomes the legitimated order from which we benefit and that we maintain in our own interest, if at all possible. The political order may be derived from, reflect, and seek to serve the cosmic

70. Brueggemann, "Shape I," in *Old Testament Theology*, 19.
71. Ibid., 17.
72. Brueggemann, "Shape II," in ibid., 26.

order, but derivation is so easily, readily, and frequently inverted that the cosmic order becomes a legitimation for the political order, and so there is a convenient match (often regarded as an ontological match) between God's order and our order. What starts as a statement about *transcendence* becomes simply *self-justification*, self-justification made characteristically by those who preside over the current order and who benefit from keeping it so.[73]

Of course, once one has felt the force of a Marxian critique, it can never be lightly dismissed; nor should it be, for it presents, in secularized form, much that is characteristic of Hebrew prophecy (which is not entirely surprising, given Marx's Jewish background). Yet it is vital that an appropriately (self-)critical hermeneutic of suspicion should not become indiscriminating and facilely brand all concern for structural, and sometimes hierarchical, order as intrinsically oppressive of the poor and marginalized. The biblical and historical Christian construal of institutional order as mandated by God, with power as a means of *service*, needs always to be kept in view.

In his recent *Theology* Brueggemann retains a dialectical structure to the theology, but differs from the previous essays in at least two ways.[74] First, the basic structure of the work is provided by the dialectic between Israel's "core testimony," that is, its positive and foundational affirmations about the nature of God, and its "countertestimony," that is, its affirmations of puzzling and difficult aspects of the divine nature. Second, the suspicions about Davidic and Zion traditions play a relatively minor role within the whole, and there is more consistent and explicit concern that such suspicions should not be allowed to reduce language about God to mere human ideology and self-interest.

Thus, for example, in a discussion of Psalm 96:10, "Say among the nations, 'The Lord is king!'" Brueggemann first says: "The locus of this assertion is the Jerusalem temple, which means that the Yahwistic claim is shadowed by the interest of the Davidic-Solomonic establishment. That is, the Yahwistic claim, surely theological in intent, is never completely free of socioeconomic-political-military interest." Yet in the next paragraph he continues: "Recognition of the ideological element in the assertion of Ps. 96:10 in itself does not dispose of nor delegitimate the theological claim that is here made. Simply because we recognize such an interest does not mean that the claim of Yahweh's sovereignty is reduced to and equated with Israelite interest, for this is, nonetheless,

---

73. Brueggemann, "Shape I," 16–17.

74. The following remarks are amplified in my book review in *Ashland Theological Journal* 30 (1998): 100–104.

a God who is committed to justice and holiness that are not cotermi-
nous with Israel's political interest."[75]

There are, however, other areas where Brueggemann's *Theology* is
likely to prove controversial. First and foremost is the question of the
status of Israel's testimony to God as Brueggemann expounds it. He
makes much (rightly) of the significance of language and rhetoric, and
warns against too-easy transposition of Israel's language about God
("testimony") into other forms. On the one hand he makes the move, familiar already from von Rad (though still controversial), of severing
such testimony from historical-critical reconstructions of Israel's history and religion. On the other hand, and rather more surprisingly, he
severs such testimony from any ontological claims about the reality of
God. He is entirely explicit about this: "I insist that it is characteristic
of the Old Testament, and characteristically Jewish, that God is given
to us (and exists as God 'exists') only by the dangerous practice of rhetoric. . . . *I shall insist, as consistently as I can, that the God of Old Testament theology as such lives in, with, and under the rhetorical enterprise
of this text, and nowhere else and in no other way.*"[76] The only qualification to this which he allows is that "any faithful utterance about Yahweh must at the same time be an utterance about Yahweh's partner,"
that is, that language about Israel's God necessarily implies and entails
"characteristic social practice that generates, constitutes, and mediates
Yahweh in the midst of life," social practice that is supremely the practice of "justice as the core focus of Yahweh's life in the world and Israel's life with Yahweh."[77]

Brueggemann has undoubtedly put his finger on something both
central to the biblical material and regularly absent from modern biblical scholarship: valid language about God cannot be separated from
human engagement in particularly demanding forms of living. Nonetheless, the way he does this creates grave unease. For he consistently
sets up classic and ecclesial Christian theology as a rigid, constricted,
and constricting straitjacket from which Old Testament theology
must be liberated (in a way reminiscent of eighteenth- and nineteenth-century rhetoric), rather than as a context of disciplines that
precisely enable language about God to be true rather than idolatrous,
faithful rather than manipulative, and to be rightly related to human
living.[78] Underlying this, one senses Brueggemann's deep dismay at

75. Brueggemann, *Theology of the Old Testament*, 493.
76. Ibid., 66 (italics original).
77. Ibid., 409, 574, 735.
78. He mentions "classic theology" only so as to dismiss it brusquely, e.g., ibid., 82,
230, 332, 559, 563. Yet the great theologians are not such men of straw as Brueggemann
seems to imply.

battles for the Bible and for control of seminaries that have marked recent Christian history in the United States, battles in which, in his judgment, appeals to orthodoxy have been used to preempt genuine engagement with the biblical text or with other people and in which power struggles have displaced justice.[79] But even if Brueggemann were entirely right about such recent events (a matter that I am not in a position to evaluate), it remains a gross travesty to tar all classic and ecclesial Christian theology with the brush of its abuse. One must always insist that abuse does not remove right use, and that the answer to poor use of Christian theology must be good use, not its caricature and abandonment.

The problems that Brueggemann's approach may lead to can be clearly seen in his brief and casual treatment of the issue of true and false prophecy, which should be an issue of prime importance, for here the biblical writers themselves focus on the key question as to how claims to the (invisible) reality of God can be appropriately given visible public recognition. Brueggemann says that "prophetic mediation makes a claim of authority that is impossible to verify. That is, all of these claims and uses are reports of a quite personal, subjective experience. No objective evidence can be given that one has been in the divine council. . . . Scholars are agreed that there are no objective criteria for such an issue."[80] Where decisions have been made by the canonizing process as to which prophets should be recognized as "true," this is simply the result of an "ideological struggle."[81] It is dismaying that at the crucial moment, where what is needed is the classic language and disciplines of moral and spiritual discernment (the primary and perennial form of theological hermeneutics), Brueggemann lapses into the language of pure positivism, with its clean, clear dichotomies of "objective" (public, accessible, and discussable) and "subjective" (private, inaccessible, and incapable of discussion), where encounter with God is entirely relegated to the latter (and thus apparently evacuated of all genuine significance). In other words, whatever Brueggemann's insistence upon the nonreducible nature of Israel's testimony to God and its relationship to human practices of justice, his account in fact, because of an inability sufficiently to articulate basic issues of theology, tends to sever the artery between humanity and the reality of God that is foundational to the Old Testament. On this view, biblical testimony to God is in danger of becoming an elaborate code for the practice of justice and of ceasing to be simultaneously the kind of revelation of, and en-

79. Ibid., 106.
80. Ibid., 631.
81. Ibid.

gagement with, an ultimate gracious and just Reality with whom Jews and Christians, in differing ways, have always believed their faiths have had to do.[82]

Conclusion

It is disappointing that Childs and Brueggemann, who both have much to offer, seem to have no real dialogue with each other and tend to present their approaches as mutually exclusive alternatives. Childs, in his *Old Testament Theology in a Canonical Context*, never discusses or even mentions Brueggemann (except in bibliographies), and in his *Biblical Theology of the Old and New Testaments* brusquely and startlingly dismisses Brueggemann in less than a page as one who "is sincerely striving to be a confessing theologian of the Christian church and would be horrified at being classified [as Childs classifies him] as a most eloquent defender of the Enlightenment."[83] Sadly, Brueggemann in his turn gives as good as he gets and dismisses Childs as "massively reductionist," and caricatures Childs's appeal to recontextualize the Bible within the "Rule of Faith" as "an unqualified embrace of the Tridentine inclination to subject the text and its possible interpretation to the control of church categories."[84] It is a matter of great dismay that eminent scholars who argue for, and display, learned openness to the biblical text can become so opaque when they read each other's writings. In my judgment Childs's work is the more profound and far-reaching and will have the most enduring significance for the discipline, but Brueggemann's engagement of the text with contemporary life represents an indispensable element within the theological task. Although one cannot simply combine the two, one can learn from both.

In sum, Old Testament theology has a potentially rich future ahead of it, if it can relearn the disciplines of being truly theological. This will be demanding because the scholar will need to be conversant not only with the classic disciplines of Old Testament study but also with the nature of Christian theology in its historical and contemporary forms and

---

82. For other evaluations of the strengths and weaknesses of Brueggemann's proposals, see N. K. Gottwald, "Rhetorical, Historical, and Ontological Counterpoints in Doing Old Testament Theology" (11–23); and T. E. Fretheim, "Some Reflections on Brueggemann's God" (24–37), in *God in the Fray: A Tribute to Walter Brueggemann*, ed. T. Linafelt and T. K. Beal (Minneapolis: Fortress, 1998). This collection of essays is intended as a companion volume to Brueggemann's *Theology of the Old Testament*.

83. Childs, *Biblical Theology*, 73.

84. Brueggemann, *Theology of the Old Testament*, 92. Compare the astonishing depiction of Childs as seduced by a neo-Hellenistic lust for ontology (p. 714).

be able to integrate them convincingly. But if an Old Testament theology does not make clear that the witness of the Old Testament entails a transformative engagement with God that is as demanding as it is gracious, as corporate as it is individual, as strange as it is familiar, and that receives its deepest realization in the life, death, and resurrection of Jesus, it will be failing in its task.

Subject Index

Author Index

490

Scripture Index

Old Testament

New Testament